RICHARD MATHESON'S

I AM LEGEND™

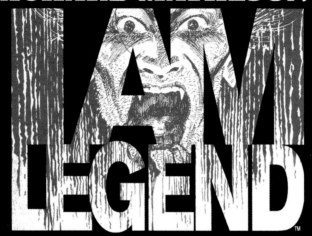

RICHARD MATHESON'S

I AM LEGEND

adapted by **STEVE NILES** and **ELMAN BROWN**

IDW Publishing
San Diego
www.idwpublishing.com

Richard Matheson's
I AM LEGEND™

Adaptation by
Steve Niles

Illustrated by
Elman Brown

Book design by
Robbie Robbins and Cindy Chapman

IDW Publishing is
Ted Adams, President
Robbie Robbins, EVP/Sr. Graphic Artist
Chris Ryall, Publisher/Editor-in-Chief
Clifford Meth, EVP of Strategies/Editorial
Alan Payne, VP of Sales
Neil Uyetake, Art Director
Justin Eisinger, Editor
Tom Waltz, Editor
Andrew Steven Harris, Editor
Chris Mowry, Graphic Artist
Amauri Osorio, Graphic Artist
Matthew Ruzicka, CPA, Controller
Alonzo Simon, Shipping Manager
Kris Oprisko, Editor/Foreign Lic. Rep.

ISBN: 978-1-933239-21-7

10 09 08 07   7 6 5 4 3

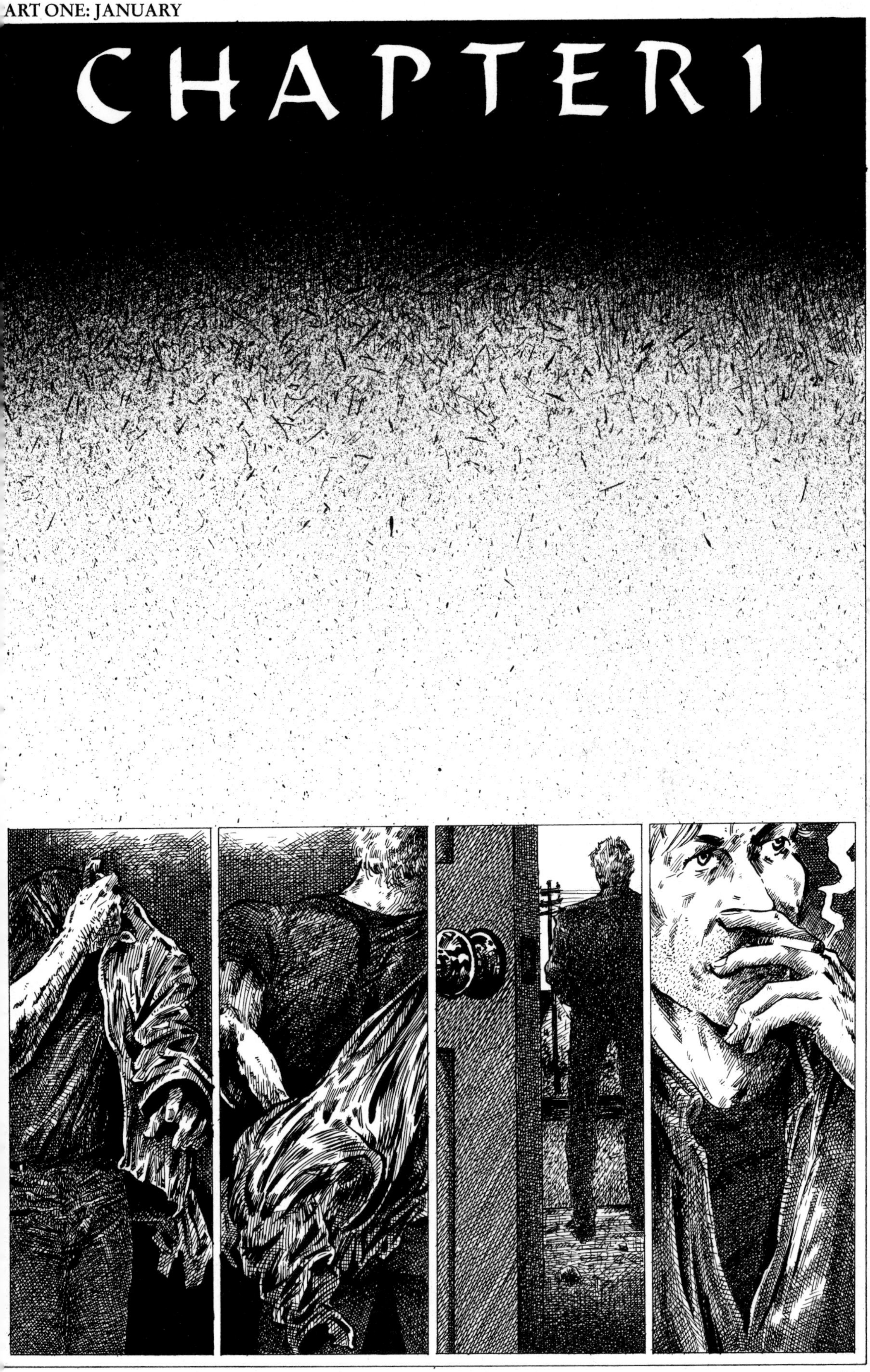
CHAPTER I

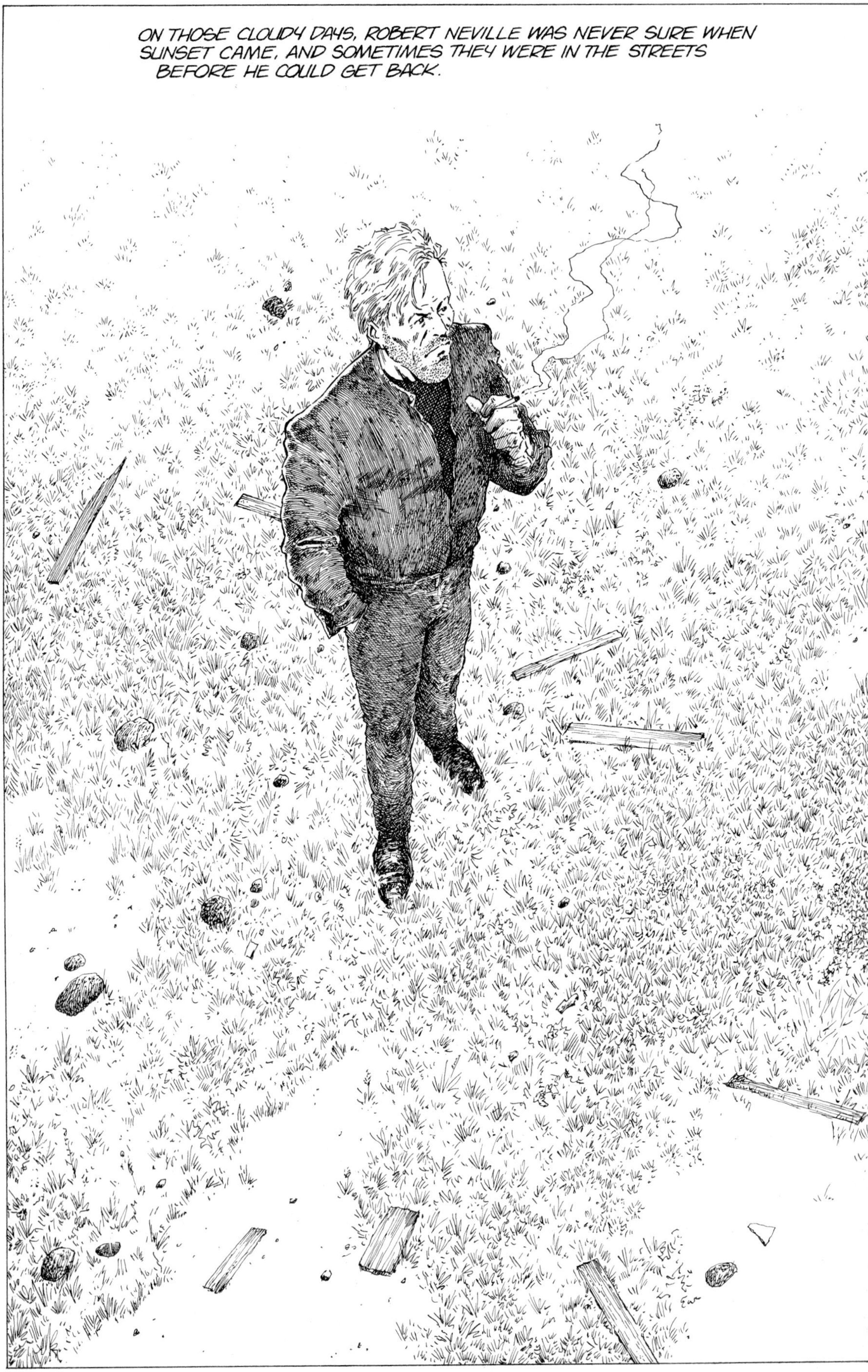
ON THOSE CLOUDY DAYS, ROBERT NEVILLE WAS NEVER SURE WHEN SUNSET CAME, AND SOMETIMES THEY WERE IN THE STREETS BEFORE HE COULD GET BACK.

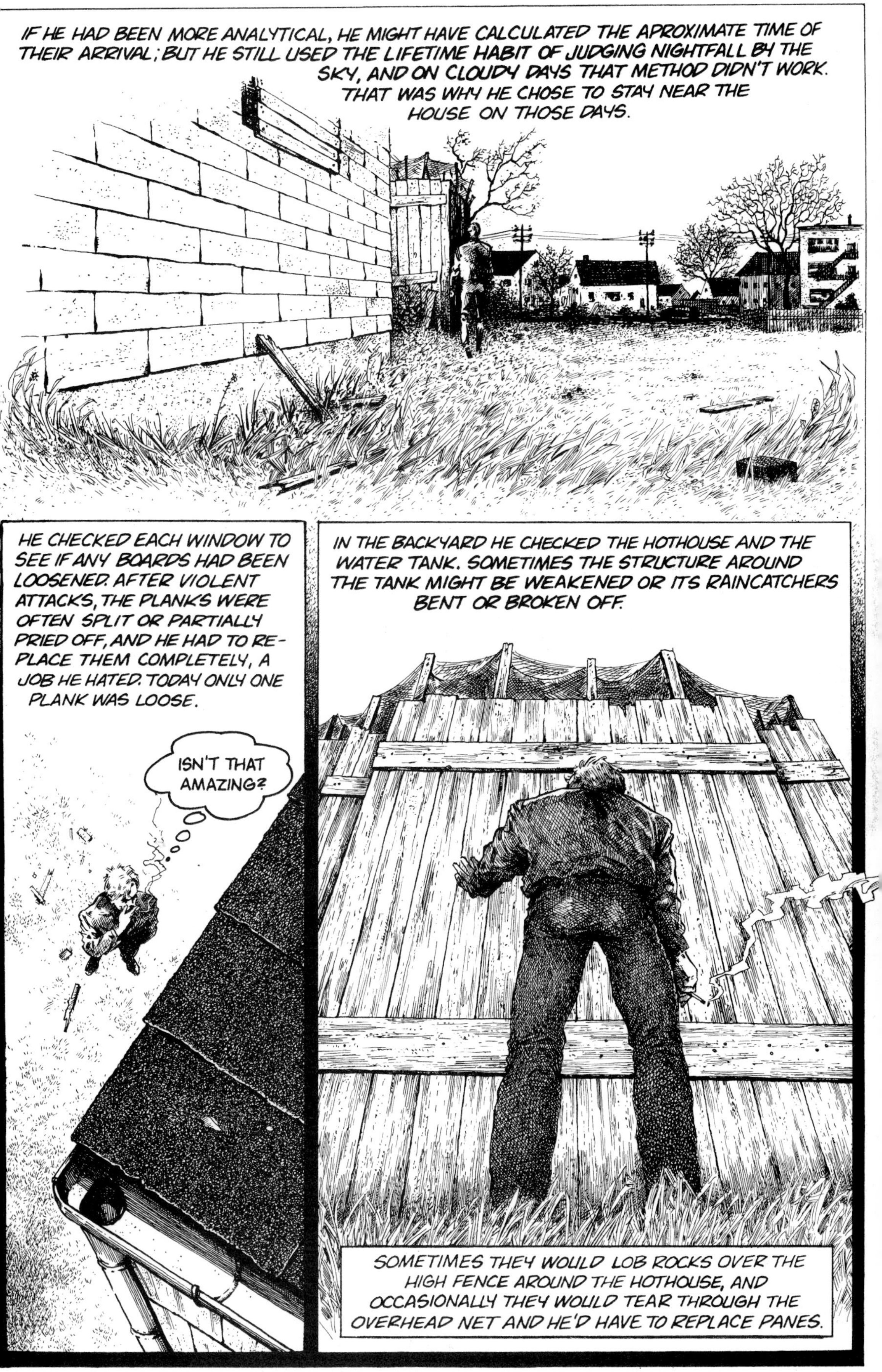
IF HE HAD BEEN MORE ANALYTICAL, HE MIGHT HAVE CALCULATED THE APROXIMATE TIME OF THEIR ARRIVAL; BUT HE STILL USED THE LIFETIME HABIT OF JUDGING NIGHTFALL BY THE SKY, AND ON CLOUDY DAYS THAT METHOD DIDN'T WORK. THAT WAS WHY HE CHOSE TO STAY NEAR THE HOUSE ON THOSE DAYS.
HE CHECKED EACH WINDOW TO SEE IF ANY BOARDS HAD BEEN LOOSENED. AFTER VIOLENT ATTACKS, THE PLANKS WERE OFTEN SPLIT OR PARTIALLY PRIED OFF, AND HE HAD TO REPLACE THEM COMPLETELY, A JOB HE HATED. TODAY ONLY ONE PLANK WAS LOOSE.
ISN'T THAT AMAZING?
IN THE BACKYARD HE CHECKED THE HOTHOUSE AND THE WATER TANK. SOMETIMES THE STRUCTURE AROUND THE TANK MIGHT BE WEAKENED OR ITS RAINCATCHERS BENT OR BROKEN OFF.
SOMETIMES THEY WOULD LOB ROCKS OVER THE HIGH FENCE AROUND THE HOTHOUSE, AND OCCASIONALLY THEY WOULD TEAR THROUGH THE OVERHEAD NET AND HE'D HAVE TO REPLACE PANES.

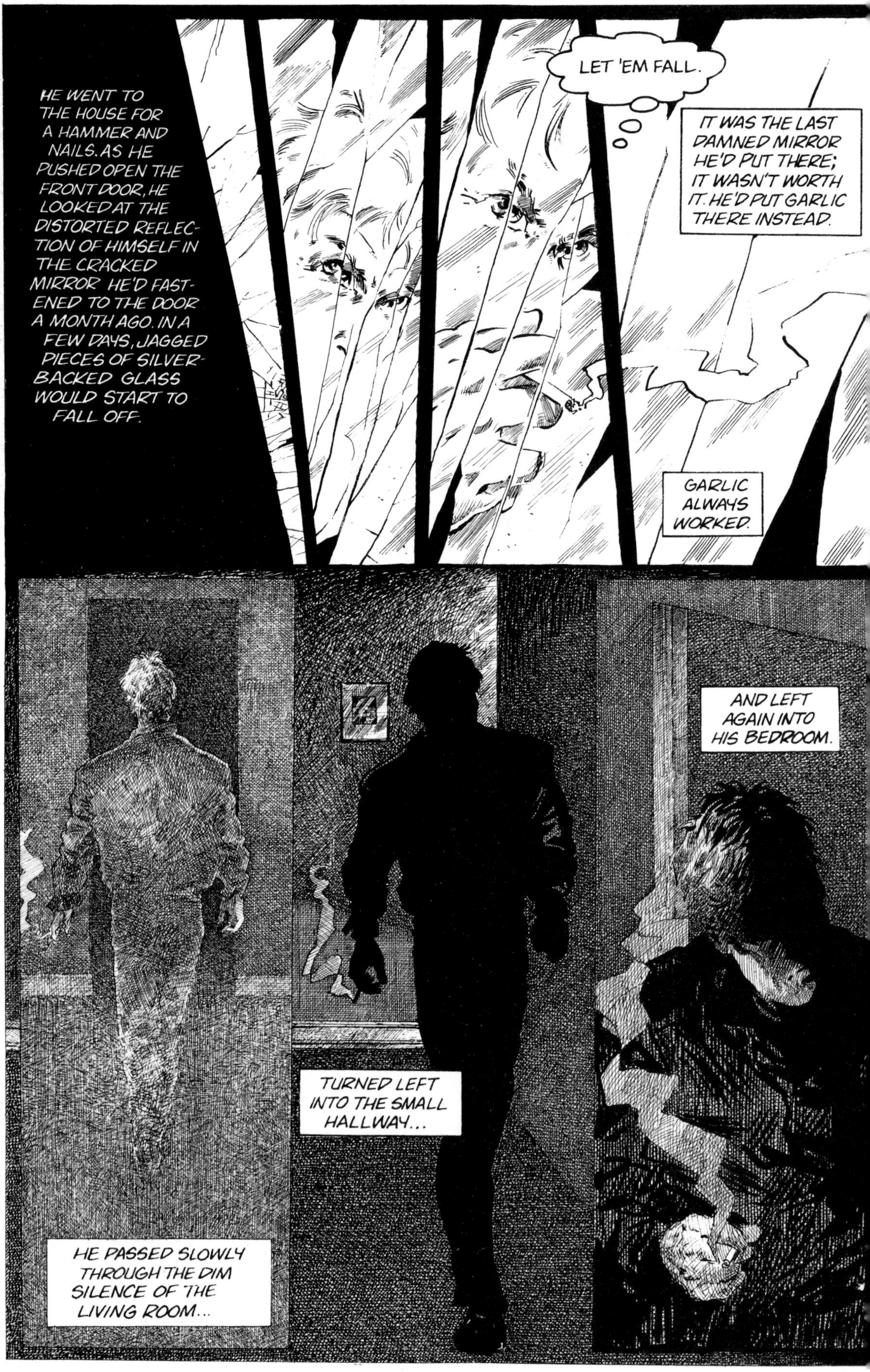
HE WENT TO THE HOUSE FOR A HAMMER AND NAILS. AS HE PUSHED OPEN THE FRONT DOOR, HE LOOKED AT THE DISTORTED REFLECTION OF HIMSELF IN THE CRACKED MIRROR HE'D FASTENED TO THE DOOR A MONTH AGO. IN A FEW DAYS, JAGGED PIECES OF SILVER-BACKED GLASS WOULD START TO FALL OFF.
LET 'EM FALL.
IT WAS THE LAST DAMNED MIRROR HE'D PUT THERE; IT WASN'T WORTH IT. HE'D PUT GARLIC THERE INSTEAD.
GARLIC ALWAYS WORKED.
HE PASSED SLOWLY THROUGH THE DIM SILENCE OF THE LIVING ROOM...
TURNED LEFT INTO THE SMALL HALLWAY...
AND LEFT AGAIN INTO HIS BEDROOM.

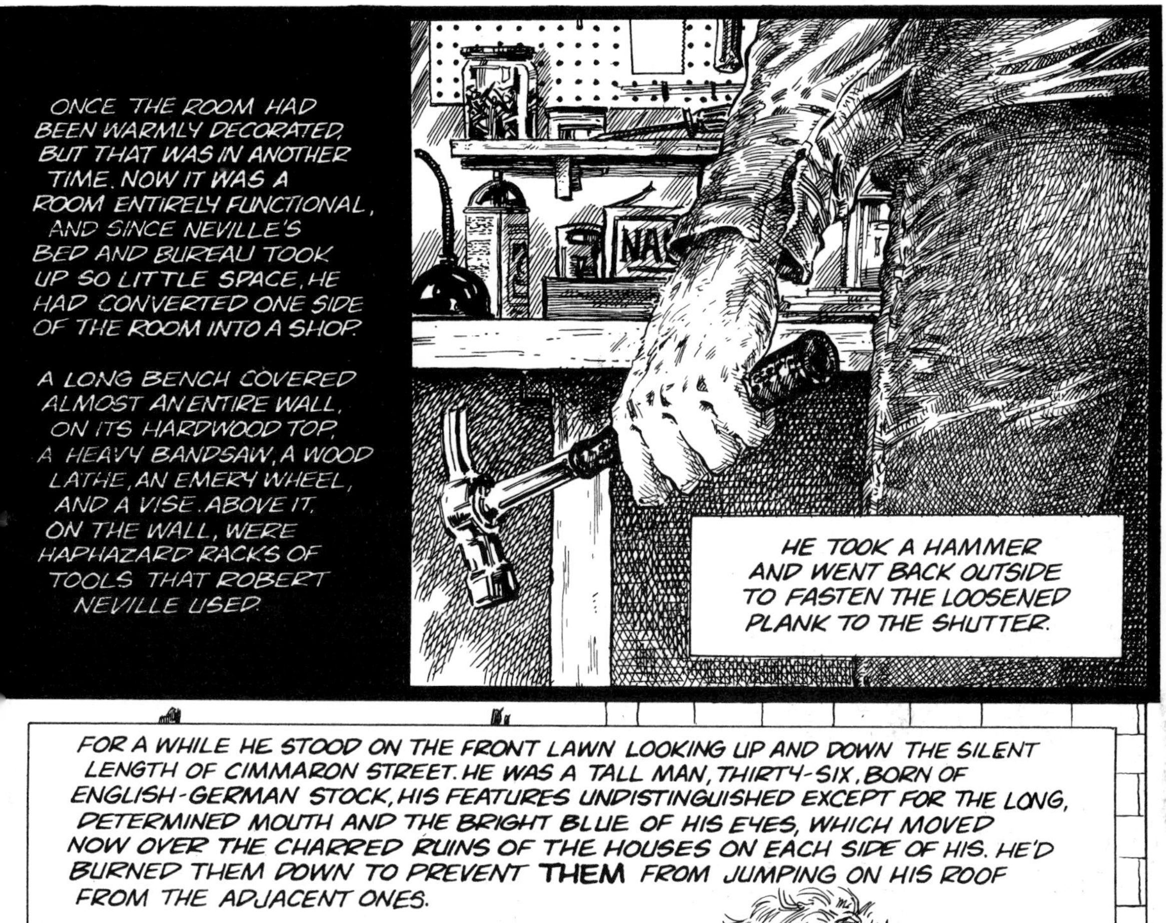

ONCE THE ROOM HAD BEEN WARMLY DECORATED, BUT THAT WAS IN ANOTHER TIME. NOW IT WAS A ROOM ENTIRELY FUNCTIONAL, AND SINCE NEVILLE'S BED AND BUREAU TOOK UP SO LITTLE SPACE, HE HAD CONVERTED ONE SIDE OF THE ROOM INTO A SHOP.

A LONG BENCH COVERED ALMOST AN ENTIRE WALL, ON ITS HARDWOOD TOP, A HEAVY BANDSAW, A WOOD LATHE, AN EMERY WHEEL, AND A VISE. ABOVE IT, ON THE WALL, WERE HAPHAZARD RACKS OF TOOLS THAT ROBERT NEVILLE USED.

HE TOOK A HAMMER AND WENT BACK OUTSIDE TO FASTEN THE LOOSENED PLANK TO THE SHUTTER.

FOR A WHILE HE STOOD ON THE FRONT LAWN LOOKING UP AND DOWN THE SILENT LENGTH OF CIMMARON STREET. HE WAS A TALL MAN, THIRTY-SIX, BORN OF ENGLISH-GERMAN STOCK, HIS FEATURES UNDISTINGUISHED EXCEPT FOR THE LONG, DETERMINED MOUTH AND THE BRIGHT BLUE OF HIS EYES, WHICH MOVED NOW OVER THE CHARRED RUINS OF THE HOUSES ON EACH SIDE OF HIS. HE'D BURNED THEM DOWN TO PREVENT **THEM** FROM JUMPING ON HIS ROOF FROM THE ADJACENT ONES.

HE FASTENED THE PLANK AND WENT BACK INTO THE HOUSE.

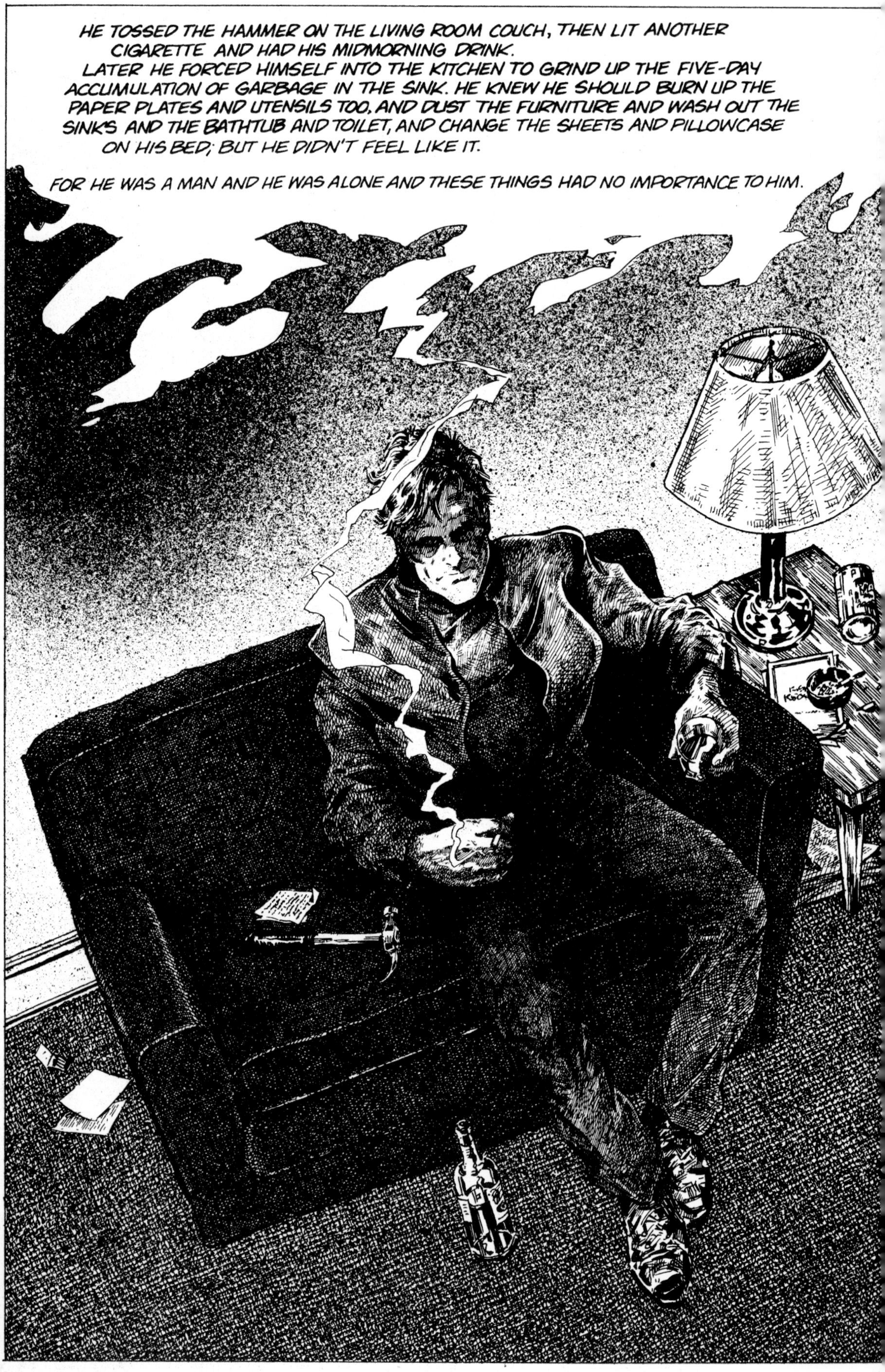
HE TOSSED THE HAMMER ON THE LIVING ROOM COUCH, THEN LIT ANOTHER CIGARETTE AND HAD HIS MIDMORNING DRINK.
LATER HE FORCED HIMSELF INTO THE KITCHEN TO GRIND UP THE FIVE-DAY ACCUMULATION OF GARBAGE IN THE SINK. HE KNEW HE SHOULD BURN UP THE PAPER PLATES AND UTENSILS TOO, AND DUST THE FURNITURE AND WASH OUT THE SINKS AND THE BATHTUB AND TOILET, AND CHANGE THE SHEETS AND PILLOWCASE ON HIS BED; BUT HE DIDN'T FEEL LIKE IT.
FOR HE WAS A MAN AND HE WAS ALONE AND THESE THINGS HAD NO IMPORTANCE TO HIM.

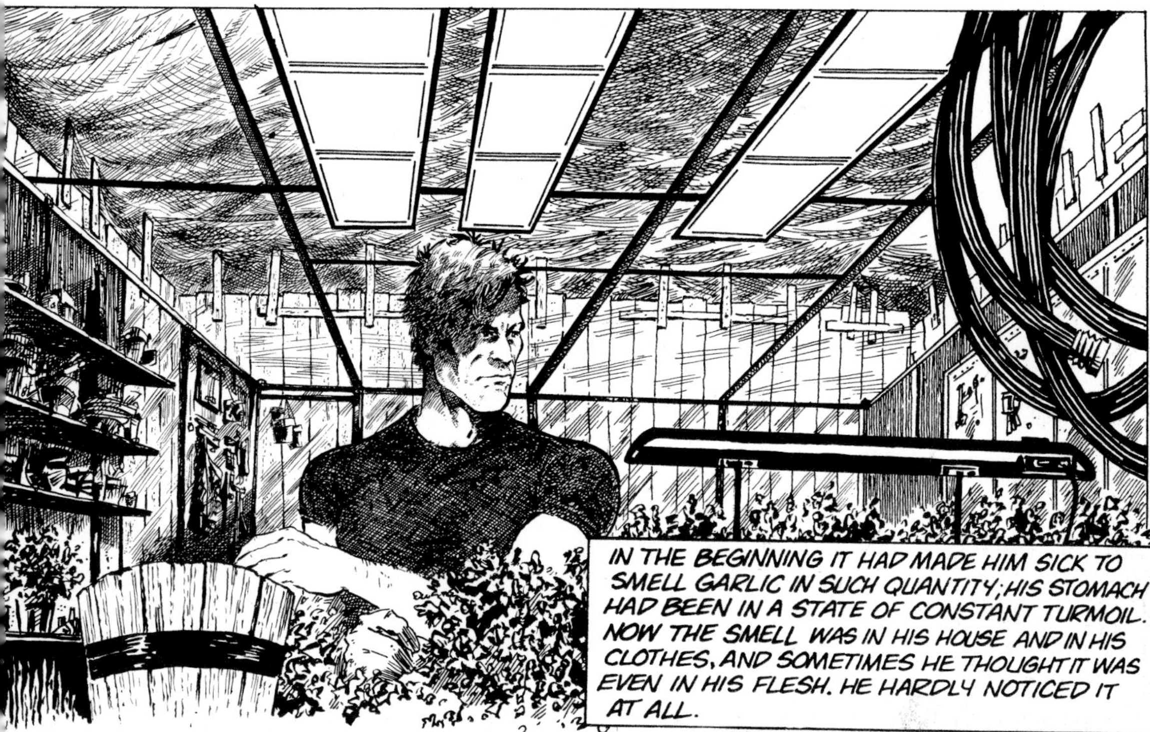
IN THE BEGINNING IT HAD MADE HIM SICK TO SMELL GARLIC IN SUCH QUANTITY; HIS STOMACH HAD BEEN IN A STATE OF CONSTANT TURMOIL. NOW THE SMELL WAS IN HIS HOUSE AND IN HIS CLOTHES, AND SOMETIMES HE THOUGHT IT WAS EVEN IN HIS FLESH. HE HARDLY NOTICED IT AT ALL.

WHEN HE HAD ENOUGH BULBS, HE WENT BACK TO THE HOUSE AND DUMPED THEM ON THE DRAIN-BOARD OF THE SINK. AS HE FLICKED THE WALL SWITCH, THE LIGHT FLICKERED, THEN FLARED INTO NORMAL BRILLIANCE. A DISGUSTED HISS PASSED HIS CLENCHED TEETH. THE GENERATOR WAS AT IT AGAIN. HE'D HAVE TO GET OUT THAT DAMNED MANUAL AGAIN AND CHECK THE WIRING. AND IF IT WERE TOO MUCH TROUBLE TO REPAIR, HE'D HAVE TO INSTALL A NEW GENERATOR.

ANGRILY, HE JERKED A HIGH-LEGGED STOOL TO THE SINK, GOT A KNIFE, AND SAT DOWN WITH AN EXHAUSTED GRUNT.

FIRST HE SEPARATED THE BULBS INTO SMALL SICKLE-SHAPED CLOVES, THEN HE CUT EACH PINK, LEATHERY CLOVE IN HALF, EXPOSING THE FLESHY CENTER BUDS. THE AIR THICKENED WITH THE MUSKY, PUNGENT ODOR. WHEN IT GOT TOO OPPRESSIVE, HE SNAPPED ON THE AIR-CONDITIONING AND SUCTION DREW AWAY THE WORST OF IT.

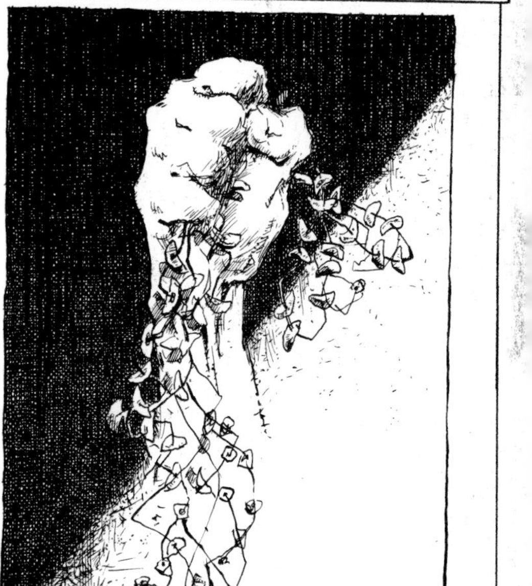

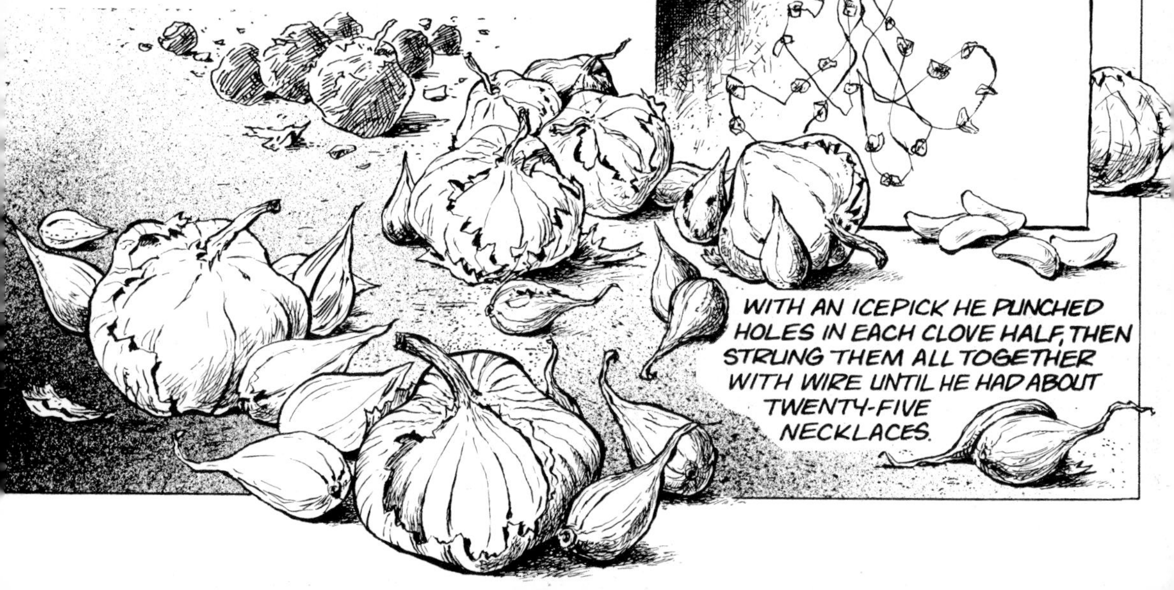
WITH AN ICEPICK HE PUNCHED HOLES IN EACH CLOVE HALF, THEN STRUNG THEM ALL TOGETHER WITH WIRE UNTIL HE HAD ABOUT TWENTY-FIVE NECKLACES.

IN THE BEGINNING HE HAD HUNG THESE NECKLACES OVER THE WINDOWS. BUT FROM THE DISTANCE THEY'D THROWN ROCKS UNTIL HE'D BEEN FORCED TO COVER THE BROKEN PANES WITH PLYWOOD SCRAPS. FINALLY, ONE DAY HE'D TORN OFF THE PLYWOOD AND NAILED UP EVEN ROWS OF PLANKS INSTEAD. IT HAD MADE THE HOUSE A GLOOMY SEPULCHER, BUT IT WAS BETTER THAN HAVING ROCKS COME FLYING INTO HIS ROOMS IN A SHOWER OF SPLINTERED GLASS. AND ONCE HE HAD INSTALLED THE THREE AIR-CONDITIONING UNITS, IT WASN'T TOO BAD. A MAN COULD GET USED TO ANYTHING IF HE HAD TO.

WHEN HE FINISHED STRINGING THE GARLIC CLOVES, HE WENT OUTSIDE AND NAILED THEM OVER THE WINDOW BOARDING, TAKING DOWN THE OLD STRINGS, WHICH HAD LOST MOST OF THEIR POTENT SMELL.

HE HAD TO GO THROUGH THIS PROCESS TWICE A WEEK. UNTIL HE FOUND SOMETHING BETTER, IT WAS HIS FIRST LINE OF DEFENSE.

DEFENSE? HE THOUGHT. FOR **WHAT**?

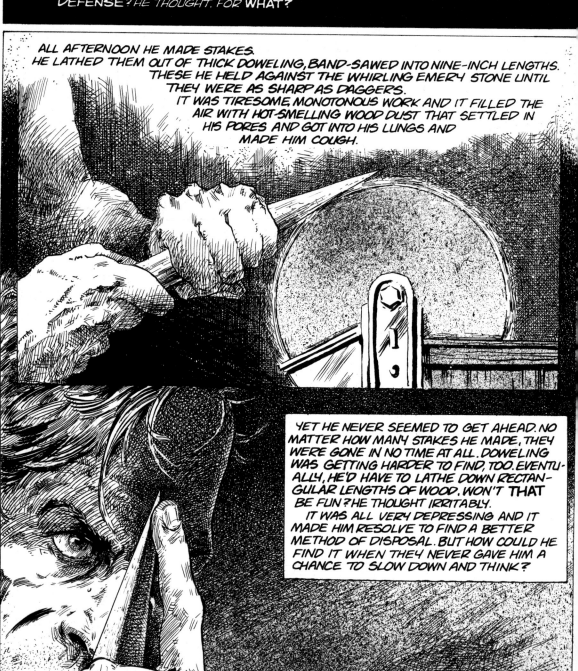

ALL AFTERNOON HE MADE STAKES.
HE LATHED THEM OUT OF THICK DOWELING, BAND-SAWED INTO NINE-INCH LENGTHS. THESE HE HELD AGAINST THE WHIRLING EMERY STONE UNTIL THEY WERE AS SHARP AS DAGGERS.
IT WAS TIRESOME, MONOTONOUS WORK AND IT FILLED THE AIR WITH HOT-SMELLING WOOD DUST THAT SETTLED IN HIS PORES AND GOT INTO HIS LUNGS AND MADE HIM COUGH.

YET HE NEVER SEEMED TO GET AHEAD. NO MATTER HOW MANY STAKES HE MADE, THEY WERE GONE IN NO TIME AT ALL. DOWELING WAS GETTING HARDER TO FIND, TOO. EVENTUALLY, HE'D HAVE TO LATHE DOWN RECTANGULAR LENGTHS OF WOOD. WON'T THAT BE FUN? HE THOUGHT IRRITABLY.
IT WAS ALL VERY DEPRESSING AND IT MADE HIM RESOLVE TO FIND A BETTER METHOD OF DISPOSAL. BUT HOW COULD HE FIND IT WHEN THEY NEVER GAVE HIM A CHANCE TO SLOW DOWN AND THINK?

AS HE LATHED, HE LISTENED TO RECORDS — BEETHOVEN'S THIRD, SEVENTH, AND NINTH SYMPHONIES. HE WAS GLAD HE'D LEARNED EARLY IN LIFE, FROM HIS MOTHER, TO APPRECIATE THIS KIND OF MUSIC. IT HELPED FILL THE TERRIBLE VOID OF HOURS. FROM FOUR O'CLOCK ON, HIS GAZE KEPT SHIFTING TO THE CLOCK ON THE WALL.

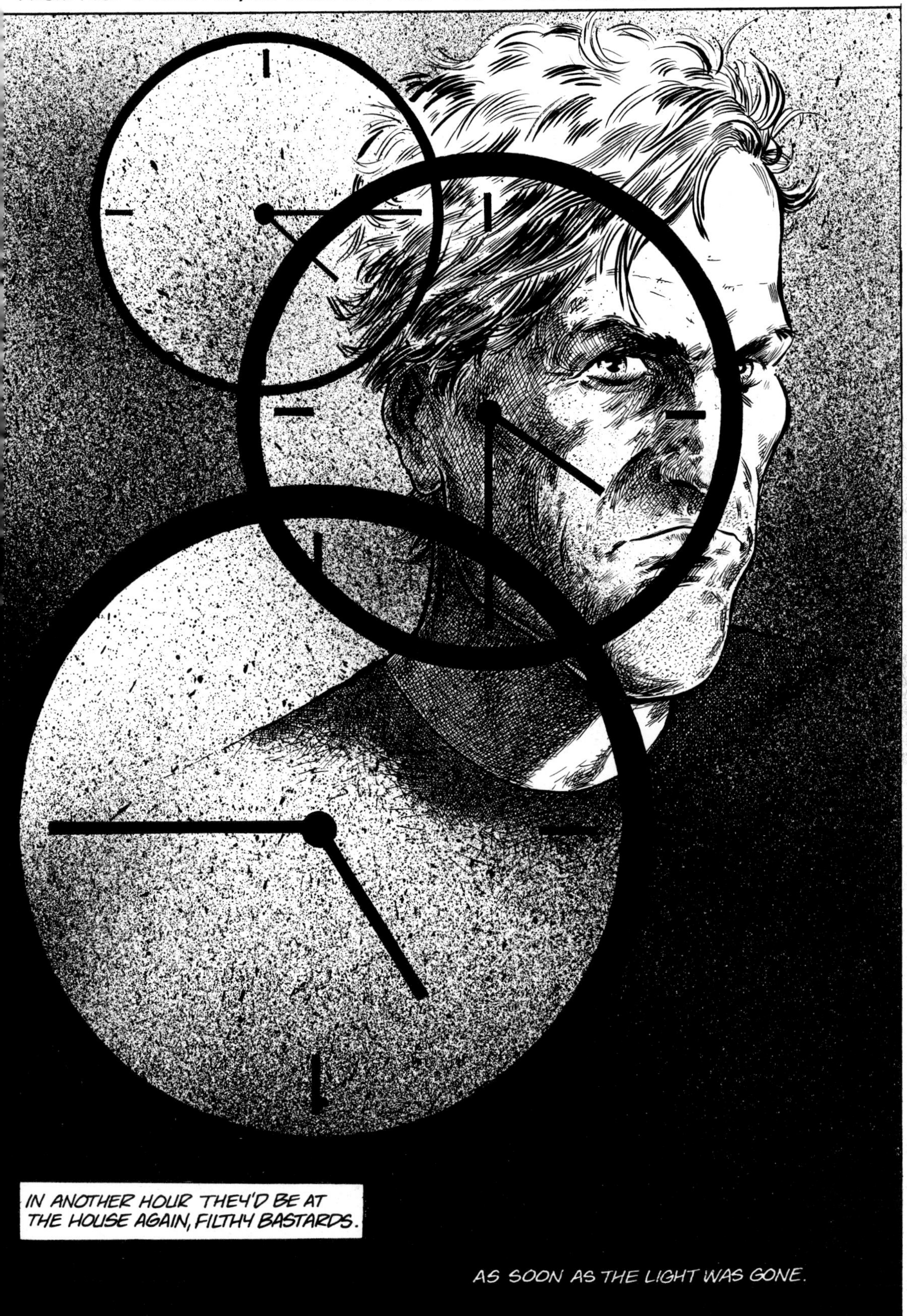
IN ANOTHER HOUR THEY'D BE AT THE HOUSE AGAIN, FILTHY BASTARDS.
AS SOON AS THE LIGHT WAS GONE.

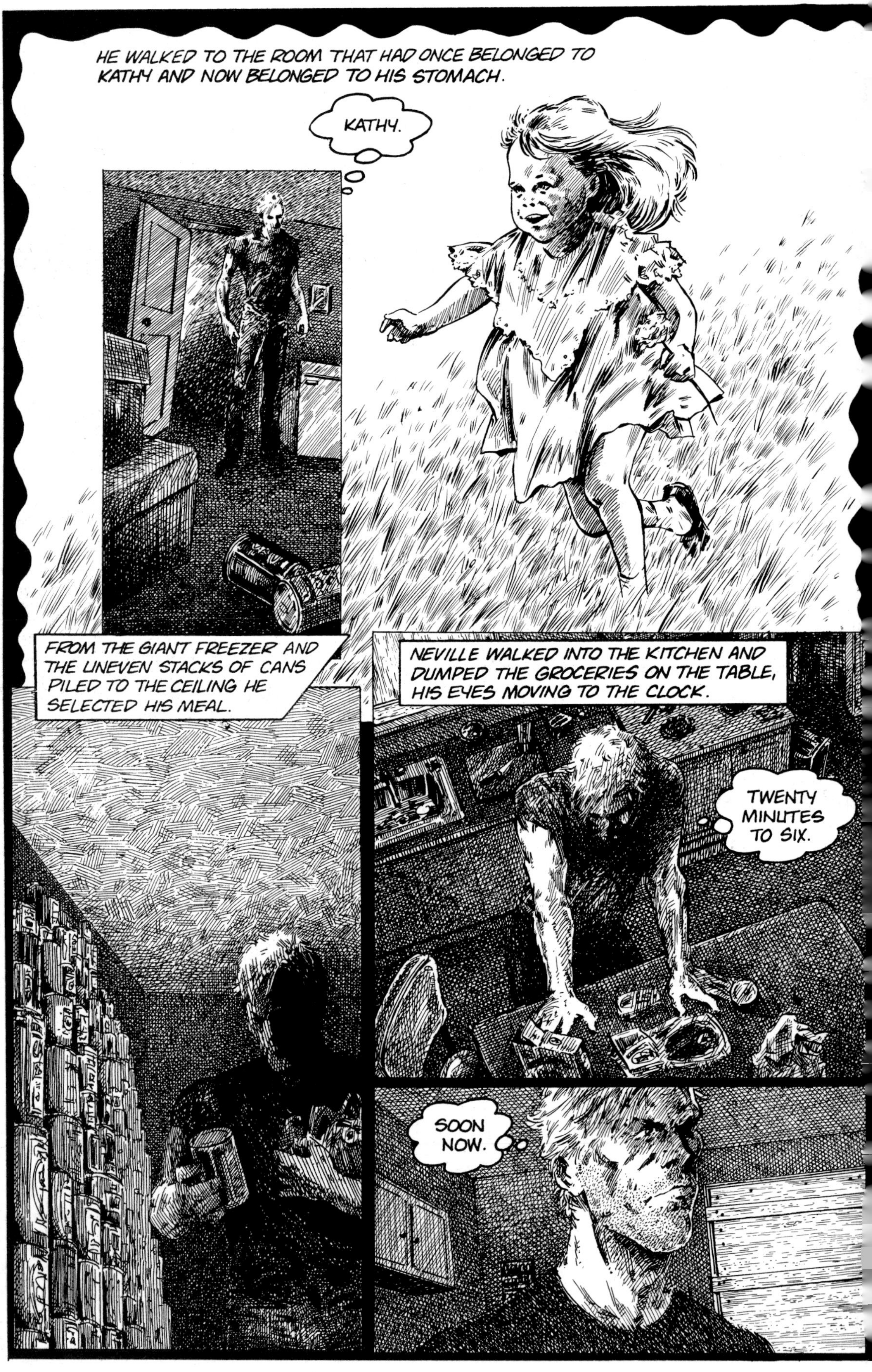
HE WALKED TO THE ROOM THAT HAD ONCE BELONGED TO KATHY AND NOW BELONGED TO HIS STOMACH.
KATHY.
FROM THE GIANT FREEZER AND THE UNEVEN STACKS OF CANS PILED TO THE CEILING HE SELECTED HIS MEAL.
NEVILLE WALKED INTO THE KITCHEN AND DUMPED THE GROCERIES ON THE TABLE, HIS EYES MOVING TO THE CLOCK.
TWENTY MINUTES TO SIX.
SOON NOW.

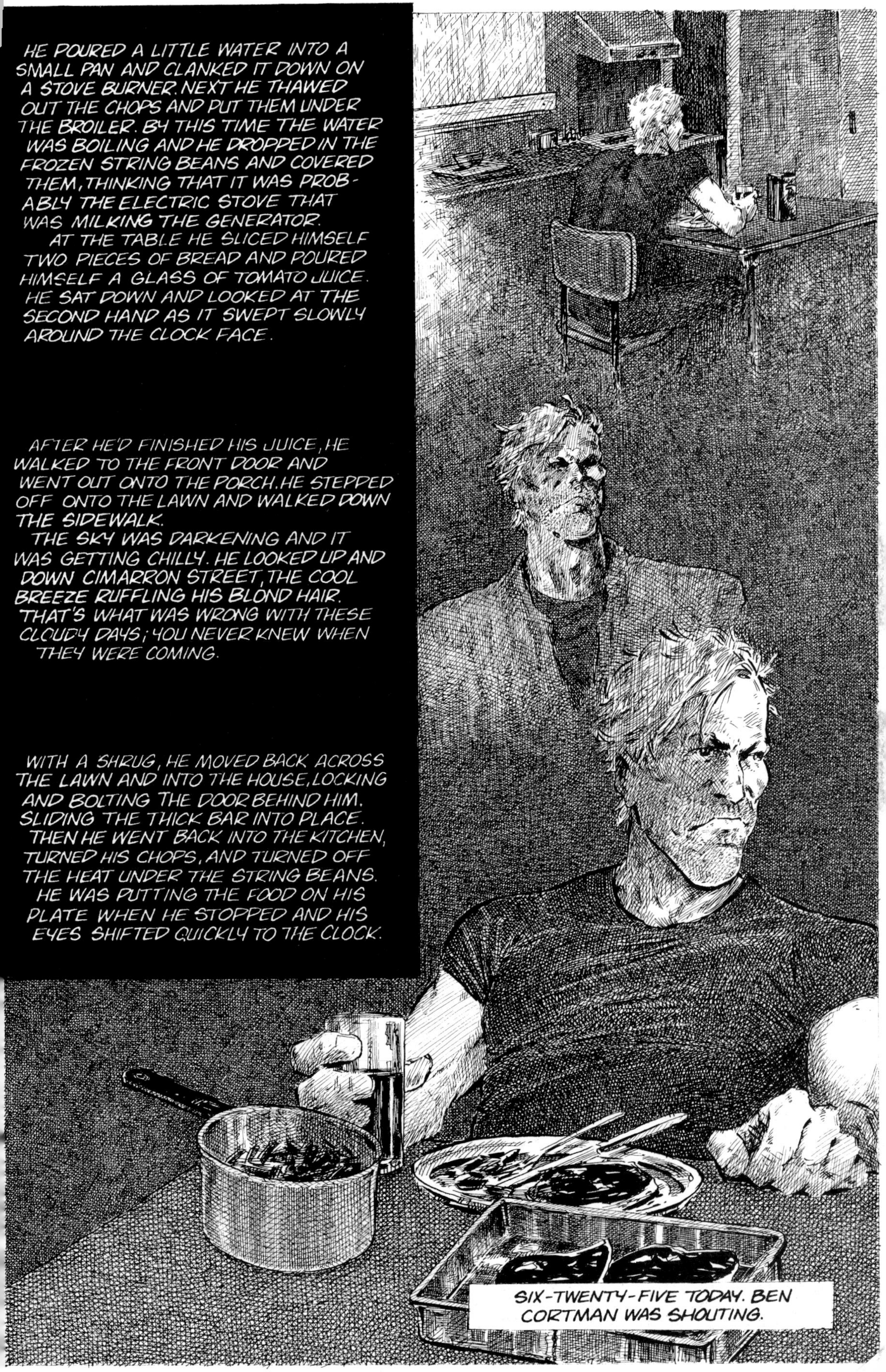
HE POURED A LITTLE WATER INTO A SMALL PAN AND CLANKED IT DOWN ON A STOVE BURNER. NEXT HE THAWED OUT THE CHOPS AND PUT THEM UNDER THE BROILER. BY THIS TIME THE WATER WAS BOILING AND HE DROPPED IN THE FROZEN STRING BEANS AND COVERED THEM, THINKING THAT IT WAS PROBABLY THE ELECTRIC STOVE THAT WAS MILKING THE GENERATOR.
AT THE TABLE HE SLICED HIMSELF TWO PIECES OF BREAD AND POURED HIMSELF A GLASS OF TOMATO JUICE. HE SAT DOWN AND LOOKED AT THE SECOND HAND AS IT SWEPT SLOWLY AROUND THE CLOCK FACE.
AFTER HE'D FINISHED HIS JUICE, HE WALKED TO THE FRONT DOOR AND WENT OUT ONTO THE PORCH. HE STEPPED OFF ONTO THE LAWN AND WALKED DOWN THE SIDEWALK.
THE SKY WAS DARKENING AND IT WAS GETTING CHILLY. HE LOOKED UP AND DOWN CIMARRON STREET, THE COOL BREEZE RUFFLING HIS BLOND HAIR. THAT'S WHAT WAS WRONG WITH THESE CLOUDY DAYS; YOU NEVER KNEW WHEN THEY WERE COMING.
WITH A SHRUG, HE MOVED BACK ACROSS THE LAWN AND INTO THE HOUSE, LOCKING AND BOLTING THE DOOR BEHIND HIM. SLIDING THE THICK BAR INTO PLACE.
THEN HE WENT BACK INTO THE KITCHEN, TURNED HIS CHOPS, AND TURNED OFF THE HEAT UNDER THE STRING BEANS.
HE WAS PUTTING THE FOOD ON HIS PLATE WHEN HE STOPPED AND HIS EYES SHIFTED QUICKLY TO THE CLOCK.
SIX-TWENTY-FIVE TODAY. BEN CORTMAN WAS SHOUTING.

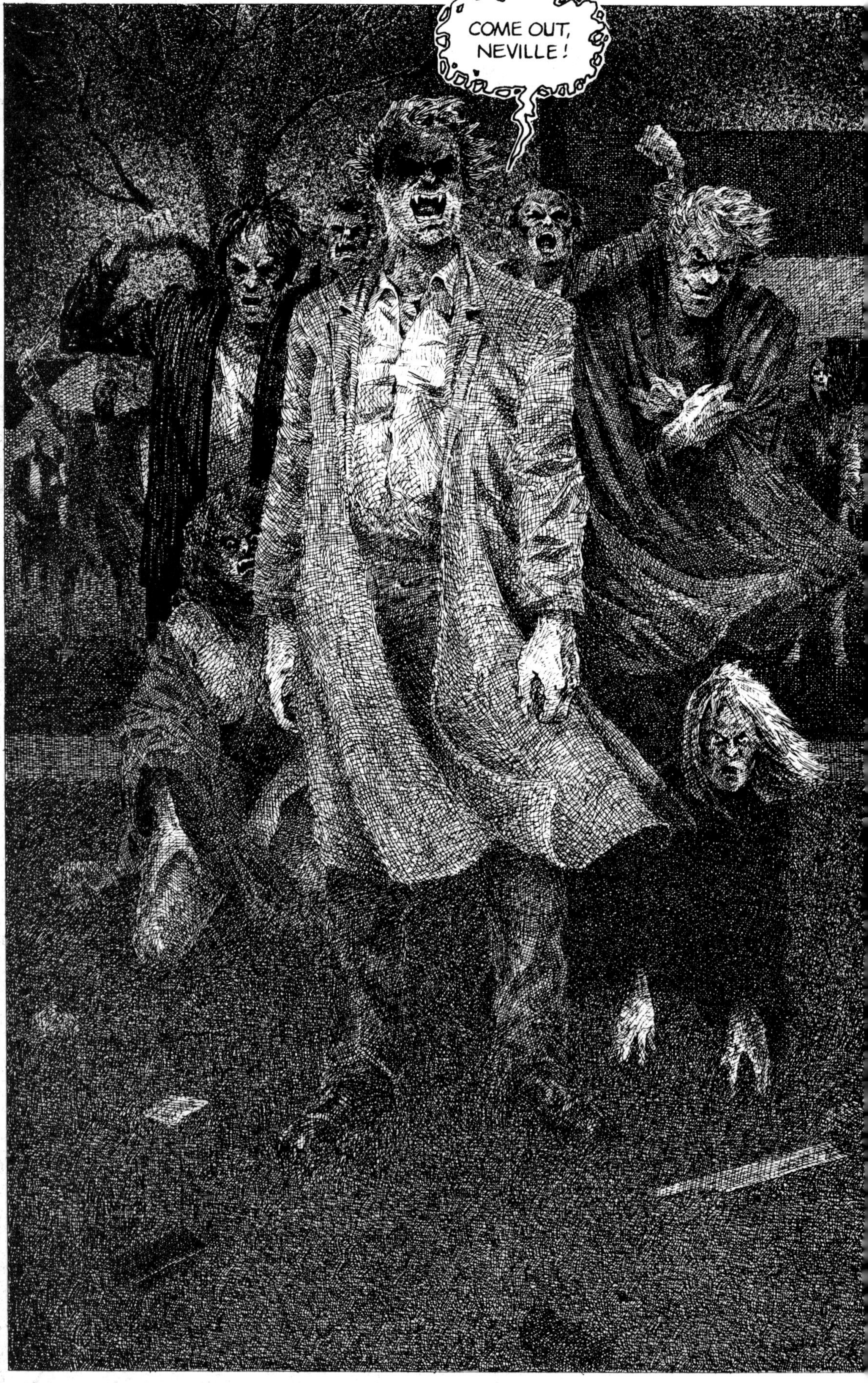
COME OUT, NEVILLE!

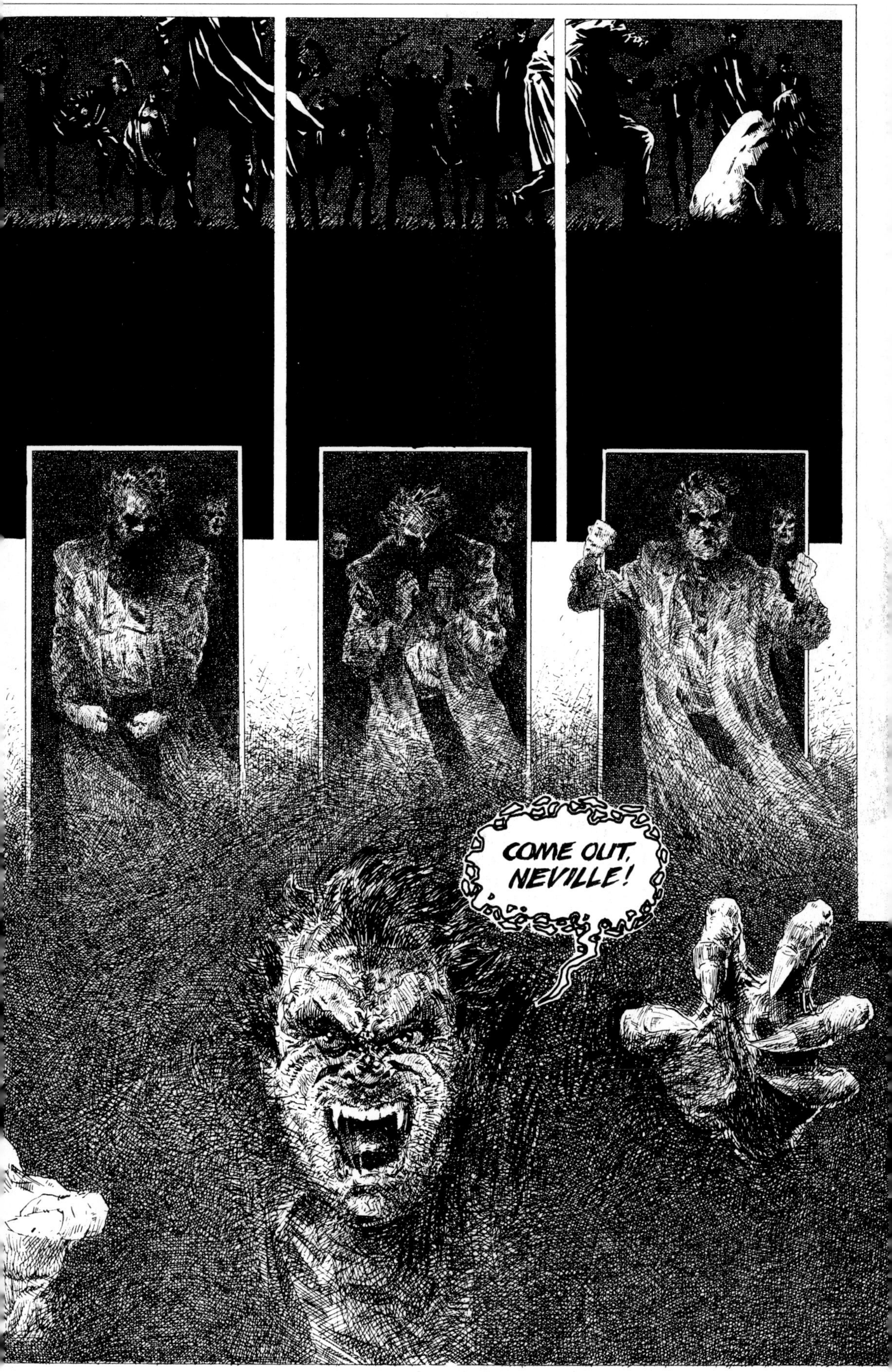
COME OUT, NEVILLE!

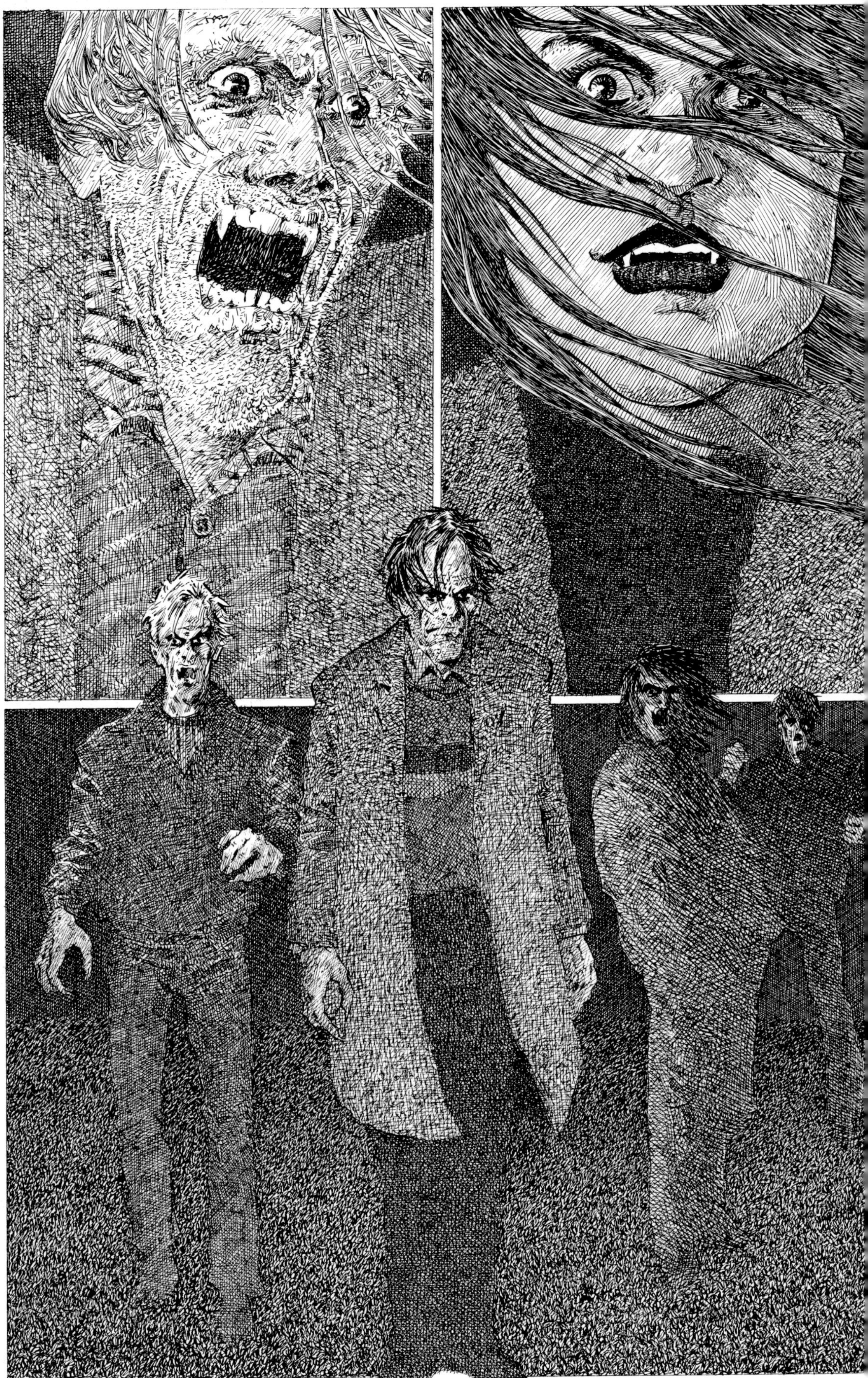

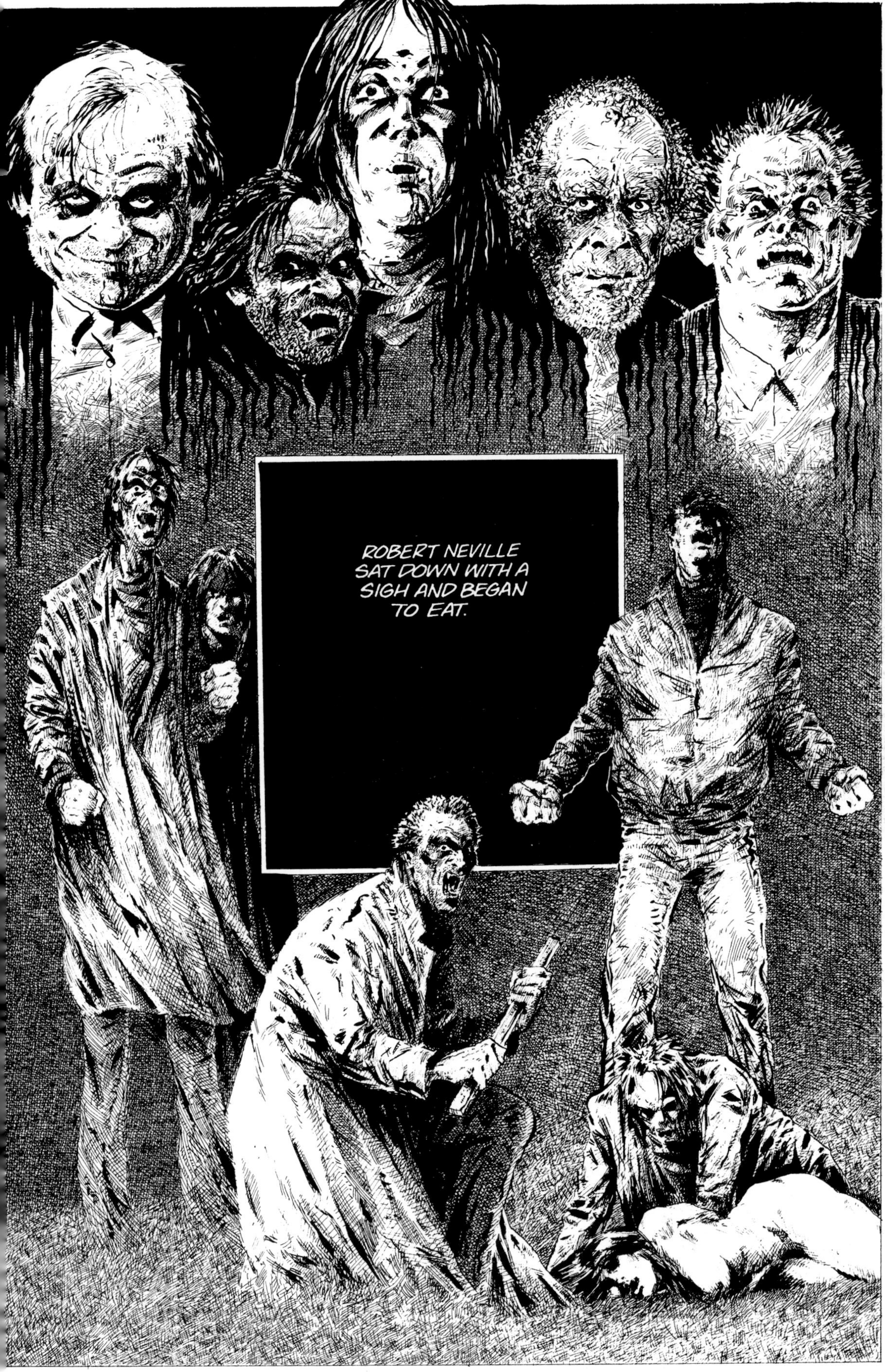
ROBERT NEVILLE SAT DOWN WITH A SIGH AND BEGAN TO EAT.

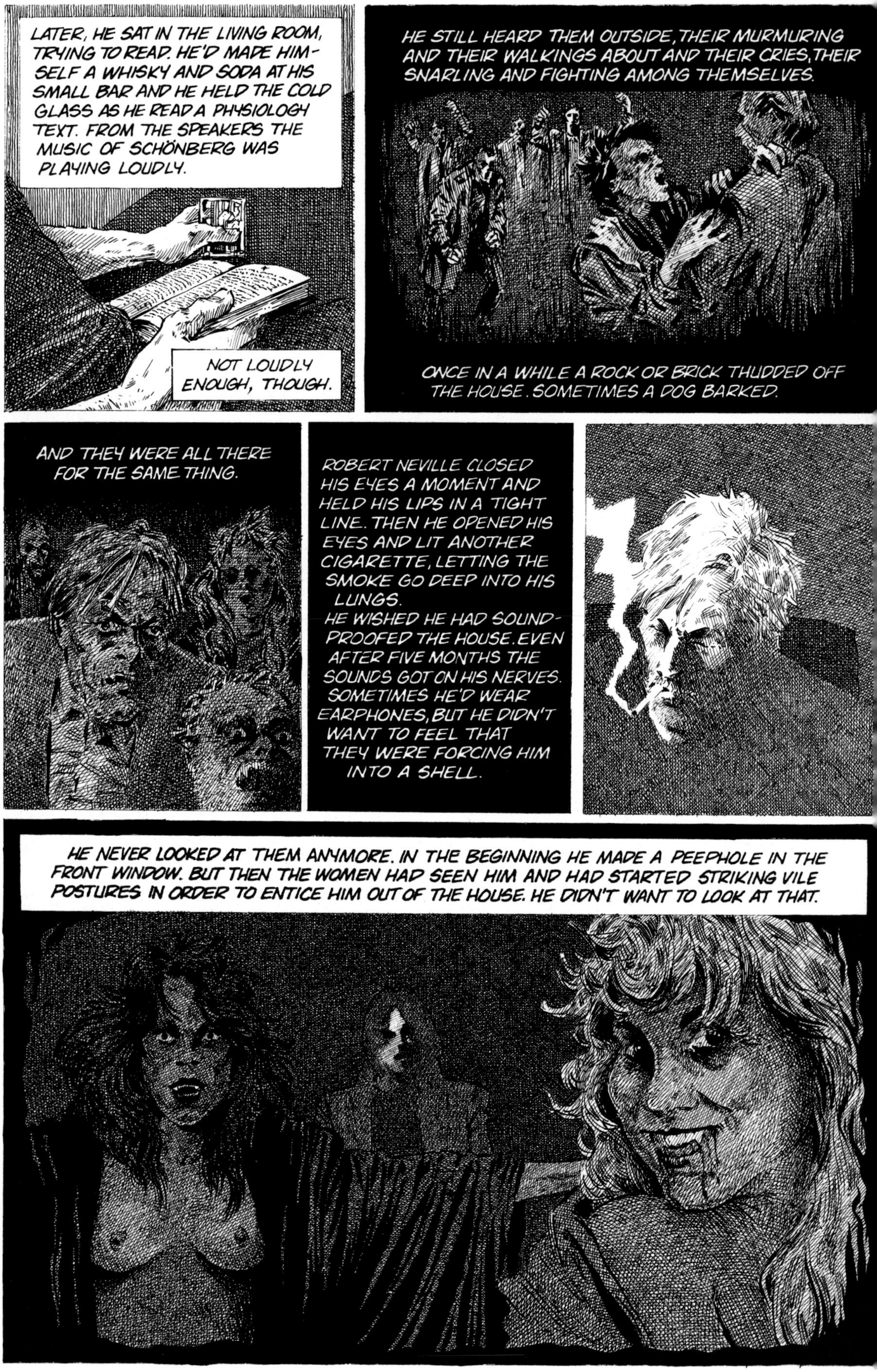
LATER, HE SAT IN THE LIVING ROOM, TRYING TO READ. HE'D MADE HIMSELF A WHISKY AND SODA AT HIS SMALL BAR AND HE HELD THE COLD GLASS AS HE READ A PHYSIOLOGY TEXT. FROM THE SPEAKERS THE MUSIC OF SCHÖNBERG WAS PLAYING LOUDLY.
NOT LOUDLY ENOUGH, THOUGH.
HE STILL HEARD THEM OUTSIDE, THEIR MURMURING AND THEIR WALKINGS ABOUT AND THEIR CRIES, THEIR SNARLING AND FIGHTING AMONG THEMSELVES.
ONCE IN A WHILE A ROCK OR BRICK THUDDED OFF THE HOUSE. SOMETIMES A DOG BARKED.
AND THEY WERE ALL THERE FOR THE SAME THING.
ROBERT NEVILLE CLOSED HIS EYES A MOMENT AND HELD HIS LIPS IN A TIGHT LINE. THEN HE OPENED HIS EYES AND LIT ANOTHER CIGARETTE, LETTING THE SMOKE GO DEEP INTO HIS LUNGS.
HE WISHED HE HAD SOUNDPROOFED THE HOUSE. EVEN AFTER FIVE MONTHS THE SOUNDS GOT ON HIS NERVES. SOMETIMES HE'D WEAR EARPHONES, BUT HE DIDN'T WANT TO FEEL THAT THEY WERE FORCING HIM INTO A SHELL.
HE NEVER LOOKED AT THEM ANYMORE. IN THE BEGINNING HE MADE A PEEPHOLE IN THE FRONT WINDOW. BUT THEN THE WOMEN HAD SEEN HIM AND HAD STARTED STRIKING VILE POSTURES IN ORDER TO ENTICE HIM OUT OF THE HOUSE. HE DIDN'T WANT TO LOOK AT THAT.

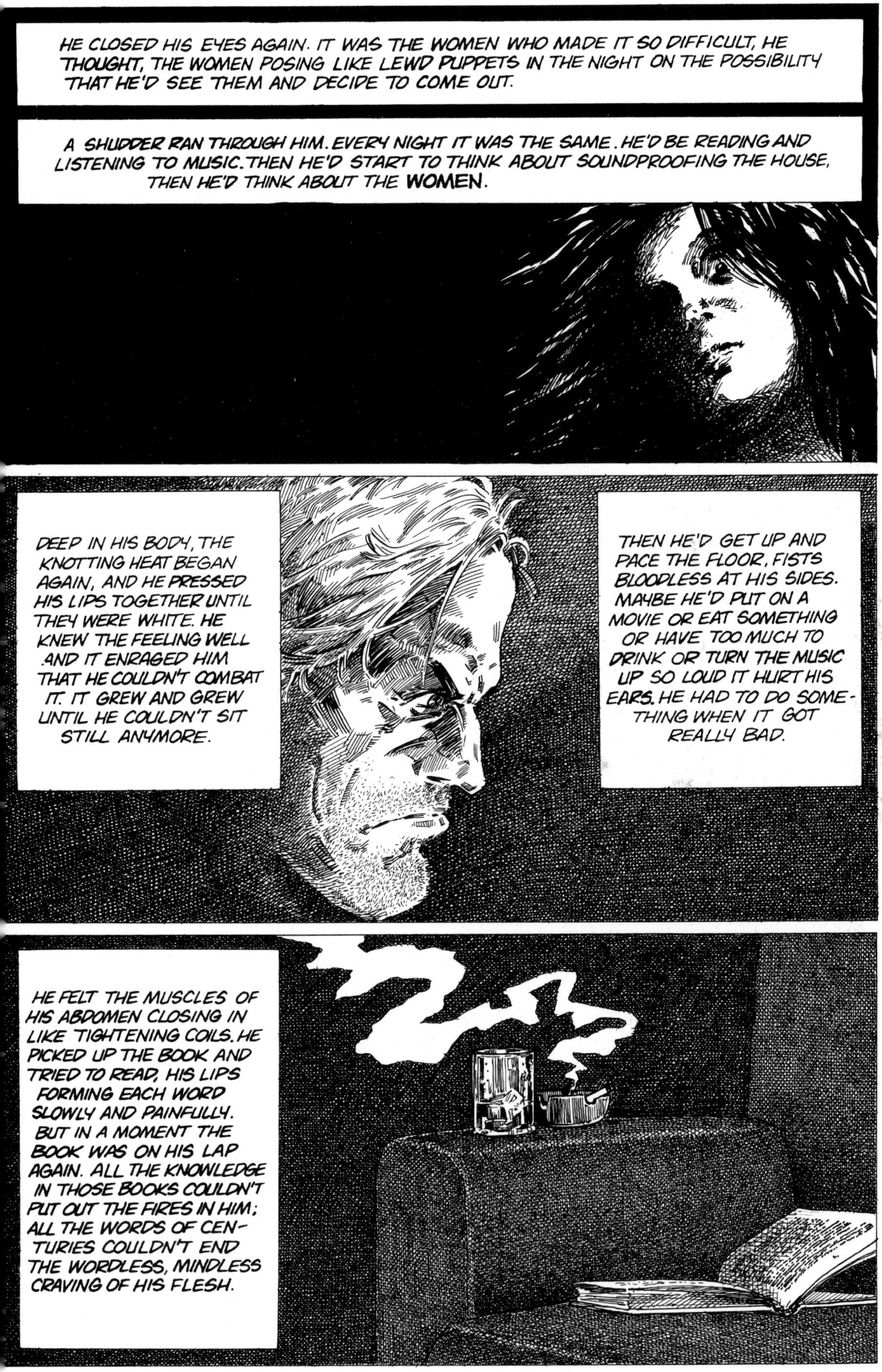
HE CLOSED HIS EYES AGAIN. IT WAS THE WOMEN WHO MADE IT SO DIFFICULT, HE THOUGHT, THE WOMEN POSING LIKE LEWD PUPPETS IN THE NIGHT ON THE POSSIBILITY THAT HE'D SEE THEM AND DECIDE TO COME OUT.
A SHUDDER RAN THROUGH HIM. EVERY NIGHT IT WAS THE SAME. HE'D BE READING AND LISTENING TO MUSIC. THEN HE'D START TO THINK ABOUT SOUNDPROOFING THE HOUSE, THEN HE'D THINK ABOUT THE WOMEN.
DEEP IN HIS BODY, THE KNOTTING HEAT BEGAN AGAIN, AND HE PRESSED HIS LIPS TOGETHER UNTIL THEY WERE WHITE. HE KNEW THE FEELING WELL AND IT ENRAGED HIM THAT HE COULDN'T COMBAT IT. IT GREW AND GREW UNTIL HE COULDN'T SIT STILL ANYMORE.
THEN HE'D GET UP AND PACE THE FLOOR, FISTS BLOODLESS AT HIS SIDES. MAYBE HE'D PUT ON A MOVIE OR EAT SOMETHING OR HAVE TOO MUCH TO DRINK OR TURN THE MUSIC UP SO LOUD IT HURT HIS EARS. HE HAD TO DO SOMETHING WHEN IT GOT REALLY BAD.
HE FELT THE MUSCLES OF HIS ABDOMEN CLOSING IN LIKE TIGHTENING COILS. HE PICKED UP THE BOOK AND TRIED TO READ, HIS LIPS FORMING EACH WORD SLOWLY AND PAINFULLY. BUT IN A MOMENT THE BOOK WAS ON HIS LAP AGAIN. ALL THE KNOWLEDGE IN THOSE BOOKS COULDN'T PUT OUT THE FIRES IN HIM; ALL THE WORDS OF CENTURIES COULDN'T END THE WORDLESS, MINDLESS CRAVING OF HIS FLESH.

THE REALIZATION MADE HIM SICK. IT WAS AN INSULT TO A MAN.

...BUT THERE WAS NO OUTLET FOR IT. THEY'D FORCED CELIBACY ON HIM.

YOU HAVE A **MIND**, DON'T YOU? WELL, **USE** IT!

ALL RIGHT, IT'S A NATURAL DRIVE.

HE TURNED THE MUSIC STILL LOUDER. THEN FORCED HIMSELF TO READ A WHOLE PAGE WITHOUT PAUSE.

HE READ ABOUT BLOOD CELLS BEING FORCED THROUGH MEMBRANES, ABOUT PALE LYMPH CARRYING THE WASTES THROUGH TUBES BLOCKED BY LYMPH NODES, ABOUT LYMPHOCYTES AND PHAGOCYTIC CELLS.

"...to empty, in the left shoulder region, near the thorax, into a large vein of the blood circulating system."

WHY DON'T THEY LEAVE ME ALONE? DO THEY THINK THEY CAN **ALL** HAVE ME? ARE THEY SO STUPID THEY **THINK** THAT?

WHY DO THEY KEEP COMING EVERY NIGHT? AFTER FIVE MONTHS, YOU'D THINK THEY'D GIVE UP AND TRY ELSEWHERE.

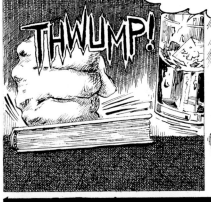

THWUMP!

ABOVE THE NOISE OF STONES RATTLING DOWN ACROSS THE ROOF AND LANDING WITH THUDS IN THE SHRUBBERY, HE HEARD BEN CORTMAN SHOUT AS HE ALWAYS SHOUTED...

COME OUT, NEVILLE!

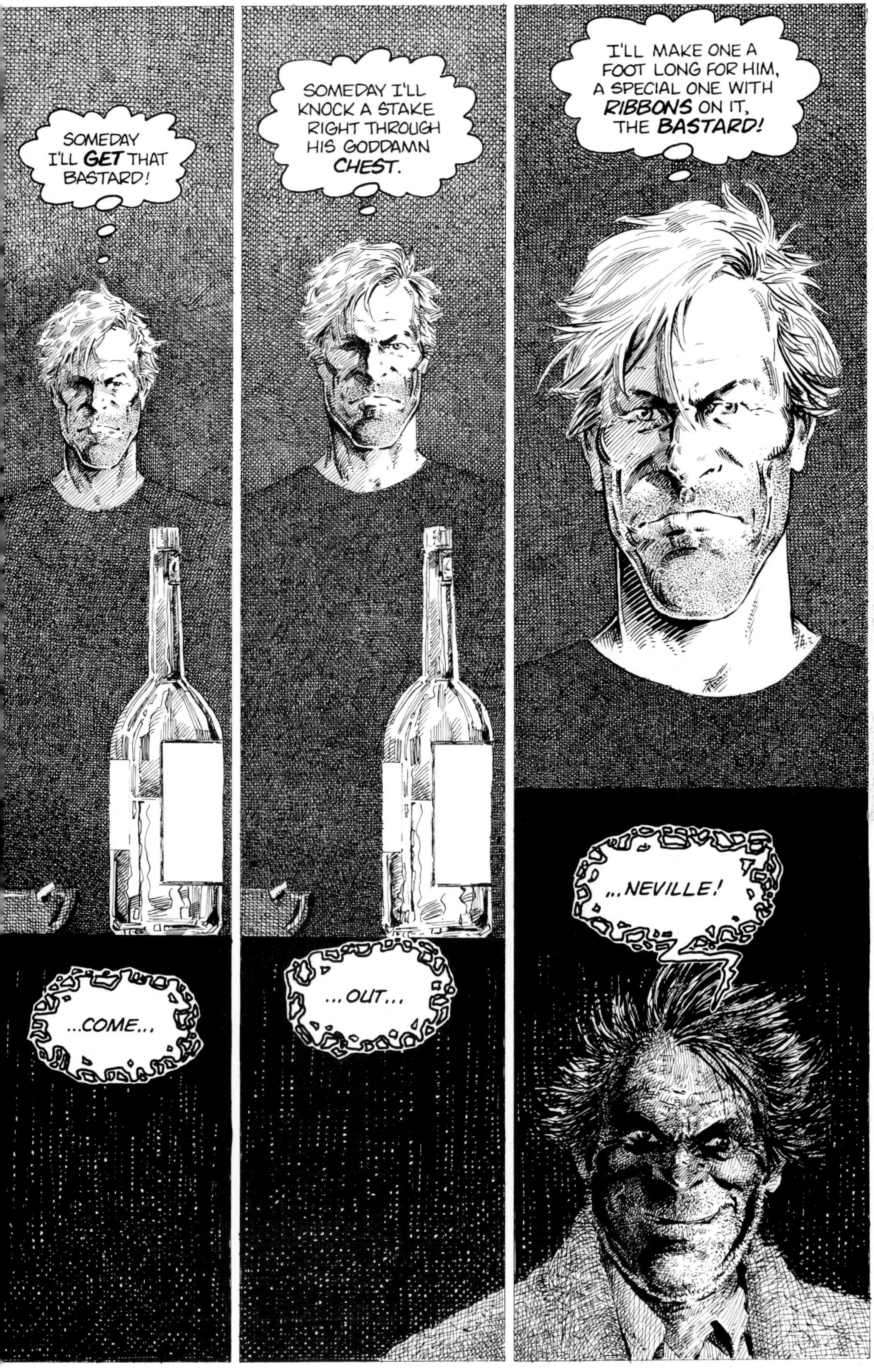
SOMEDAY I'LL GET THAT BASTARD!
...COME...
SOMEDAY I'LL KNOCK A STAKE RIGHT THROUGH HIS GODDAMN CHEST.
...OUT...
I'LL MAKE ONE A FOOT LONG FOR HIM, A SPECIAL ONE WITH RIBBONS ON IT, THE BASTARD!
...NEVILLE!

TOMORROW.

TOMORROW HE'D SOUNDPROOF THE HOUSE.

HE COULDN'T STAND THINKING ABOUT THOSE WOMEN. IF HE DIDN'T HEAR THEM, MAYBE HE WOULDN'T THINK ABOUT THEM.

"THE YEAR OF THE PLAGUE," BY ROGER LEIE, FILLED HIS EARS.

NOW HE COULD HEAR THEM MORE CLEARLY OUTSIDE. HE REACHED FOR THE FIRST NEW RECORD HE COULD GET AND PUT IT ON THE TURNTABLE AND TWISTED THE VOLUME UP TO ITS HIGHEST POINT.

THE MUSIC ENDED.

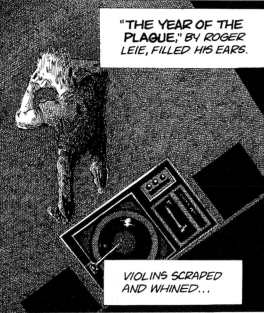

VIOLINS SCRAPED AND WHINED...

...TYMPANI THUDDED LIKE THE BEATS OF A DYING HEART...

...FLUTES PLAYED WEIRD ATONAL MELODIES.

WITH A STIFFENING RAGE, HE WRENCHED UP THE RECORD AND SNAPPED IT OVER HIS KNEE. HE'D MEANT TO BREAK IT LONG AGO.

HE WALKED ON RIGID LEGS TO THE KITCHEN AND FLUNG THE PIECES INTO THE TRASH BOX.

LEAVE ME ALONE.

LEAVE ME ALONE.

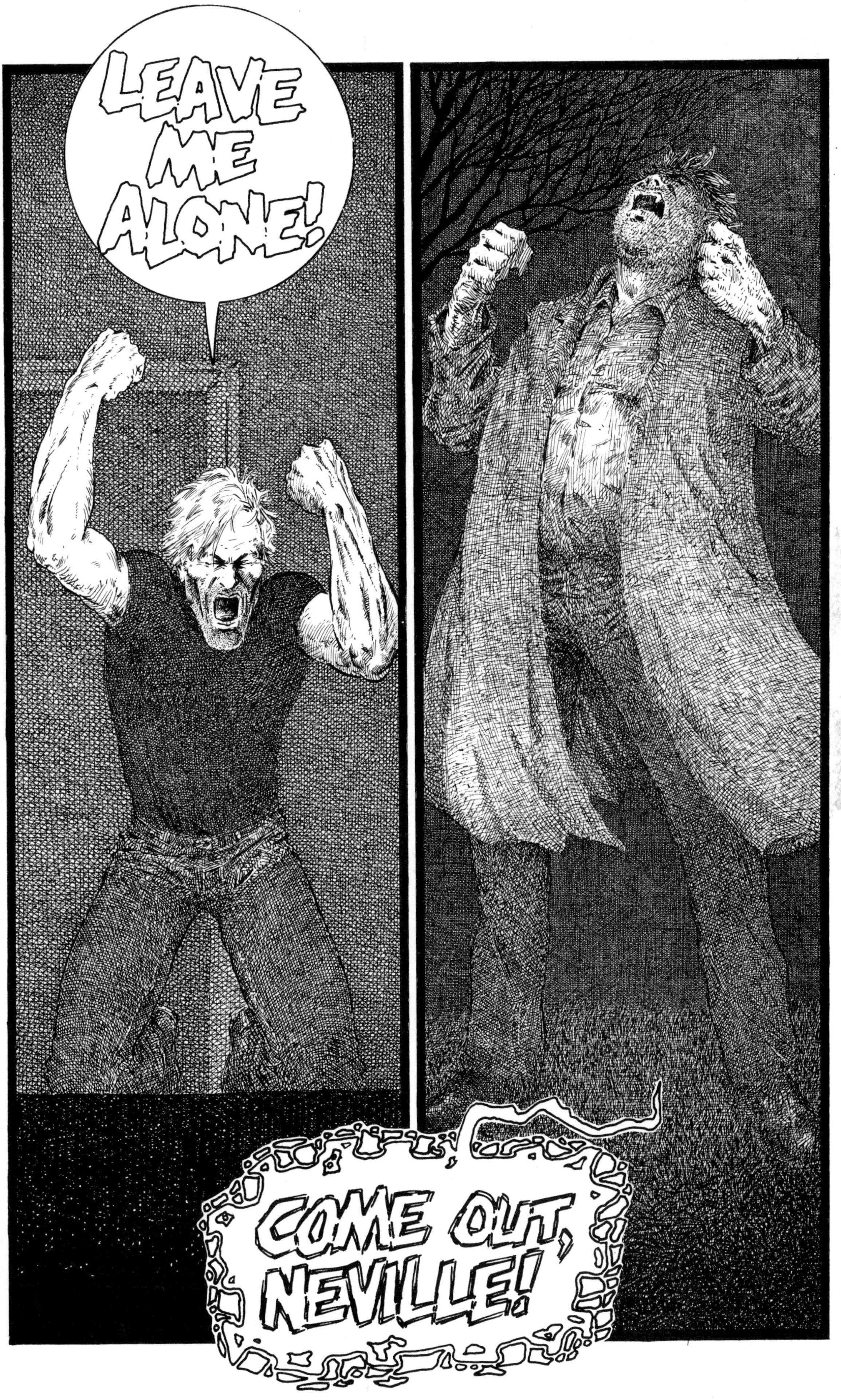
LEAVE ME ALONE!
COME OUT, NEVILLE!

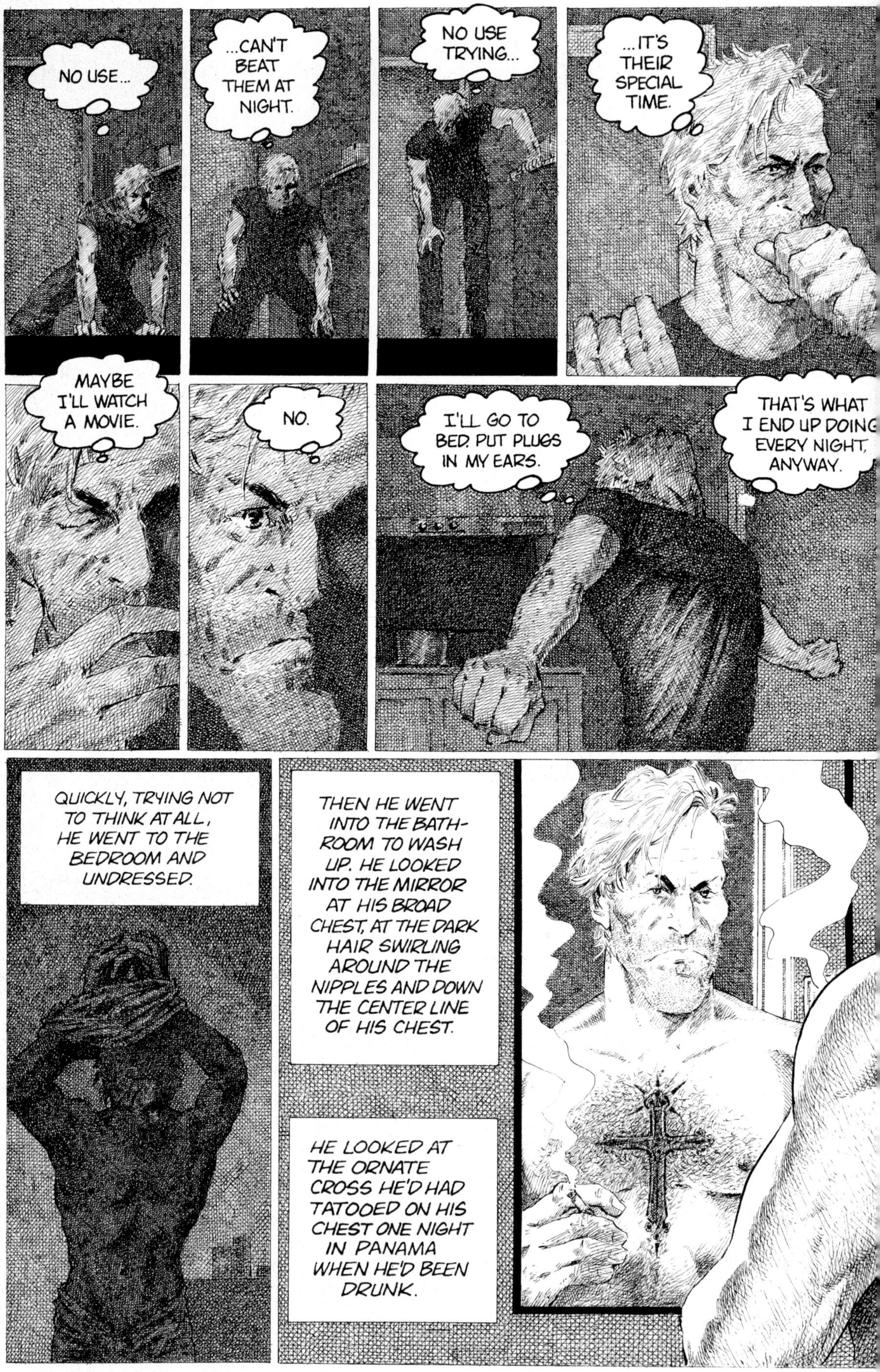
NO USE...
...CAN'T BEAT THEM AT NIGHT.
NO USE TRYING...
...IT'S THEIR SPECIAL TIME.
MAYBE I'LL WATCH A MOVIE.
NO.
I'LL GO TO BED. PUT PLUGS IN MY EARS.
THAT'S WHAT I END UP DOING EVERY NIGHT, ANYWAY.
QUICKLY, TRYING NOT TO THINK AT ALL, HE WENT TO THE BEDROOM AND UNDRESSED.
THEN HE WENT INTO THE BATH-ROOM TO WASH UP. HE LOOKED INTO THE MIRROR AT HIS BROAD CHEST, AT THE DARK HAIR SWIRLING AROUND THE NIPPLES AND DOWN THE CENTER LINE OF HIS CHEST.
HE LOOKED AT THE ORNATE CROSS HE'D HAD TATOOED ON HIS CHEST ONE NIGHT IN PANAMA WHEN HE'D BEEN DRUNK.

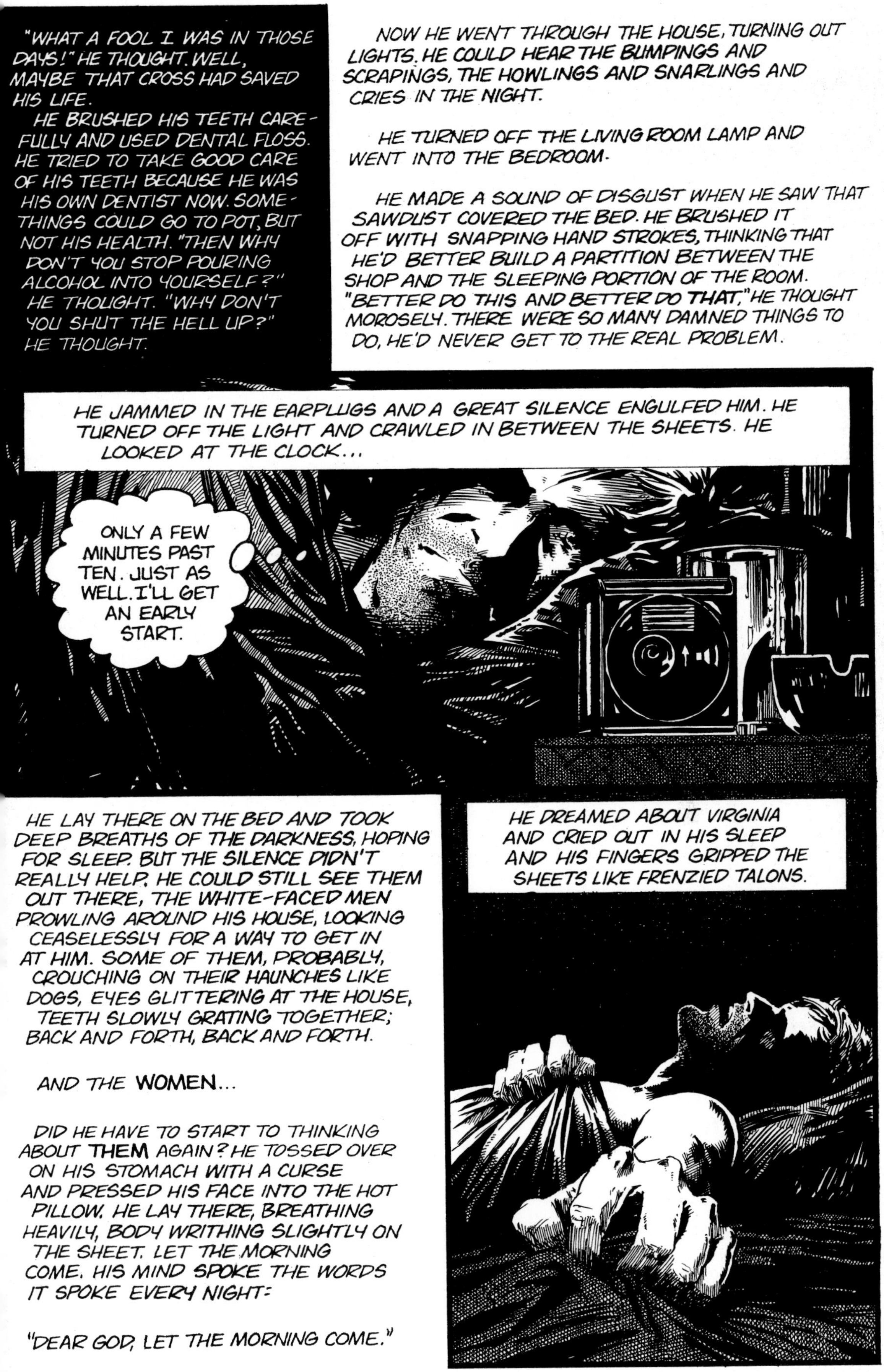
"WHAT A FOOL I WAS IN THOSE DAYS!" HE THOUGHT. WELL, MAYBE THAT CROSS HAD SAVED HIS LIFE.
HE BRUSHED HIS TEETH CAREFULLY AND USED DENTAL FLOSS. HE TRIED TO TAKE GOOD CARE OF HIS TEETH BECAUSE HE WAS HIS OWN DENTIST NOW. SOMETHINGS COULD GO TO POT, BUT NOT HIS HEALTH. "THEN WHY DON'T YOU STOP POURING ALCOHOL INTO YOURSELF?" HE THOUGHT. "WHY DON'T YOU SHUT THE HELL UP?" HE THOUGHT.
NOW HE WENT THROUGH THE HOUSE, TURNING OUT LIGHTS. HE COULD HEAR THE BUMPINGS AND SCRAPINGS, THE HOWLINGS AND SNARLINGS AND CRIES IN THE NIGHT.
HE TURNED OFF THE LIVING ROOM LAMP AND WENT INTO THE BEDROOM.
HE MADE A SOUND OF DISGUST WHEN HE SAW THAT SAWDUST COVERED THE BED. HE BRUSHED IT OFF WITH SNAPPING HAND STROKES, THINKING THAT HE'D BETTER BUILD A PARTITION BETWEEN THE SHOP AND THE SLEEPING PORTION OF THE ROOM. "BETTER DO THIS AND BETTER DO THAT," HE THOUGHT MOROSELY. THERE WERE SO MANY DAMNED THINGS TO DO, HE'D NEVER GET TO THE REAL PROBLEM.
HE JAMMED IN THE EARPLUGS AND A GREAT SILENCE ENGULFED HIM. HE TURNED OFF THE LIGHT AND CRAWLED IN BETWEEN THE SHEETS. HE LOOKED AT THE CLOCK...
ONLY A FEW MINUTES PAST TEN. JUST AS WELL. I'LL GET AN EARLY START.
HE LAY THERE ON THE BED AND TOOK DEEP BREATHS OF THE DARKNESS, HOPING FOR SLEEP. BUT THE SILENCE DIDN'T REALLY HELP. HE COULD STILL SEE THEM OUT THERE, THE WHITE-FACED MEN PROWLING AROUND HIS HOUSE, LOOKING CEASELESSLY FOR A WAY TO GET IN AT HIM. SOME OF THEM, PROBABLY, CROUCHING ON THEIR HAUNCHES LIKE DOGS, EYES GLITTERING AT THE HOUSE, TEETH SLOWLY GRATING TOGETHER; BACK AND FORTH, BACK AND FORTH.
AND THE WOMEN...
DID HE HAVE TO START TO THINKING ABOUT THEM AGAIN? HE TOSSED OVER ON HIS STOMACH WITH A CURSE AND PRESSED HIS FACE INTO THE HOT PILLOW. HE LAY THERE, BREATHING HEAVILY, BODY WRITHING SLIGHTLY ON THE SHEET. LET THE MORNING COME. HIS MIND SPOKE THE WORDS IT SPOKE EVERY NIGHT:
"DEAR GOD, LET THE MORNING COME."
HE DREAMED ABOUT VIRGINIA AND CRIED OUT IN HIS SLEEP AND HIS FINGERS GRIPPED THE SHEETS LIKE FRENZIED TALONS.

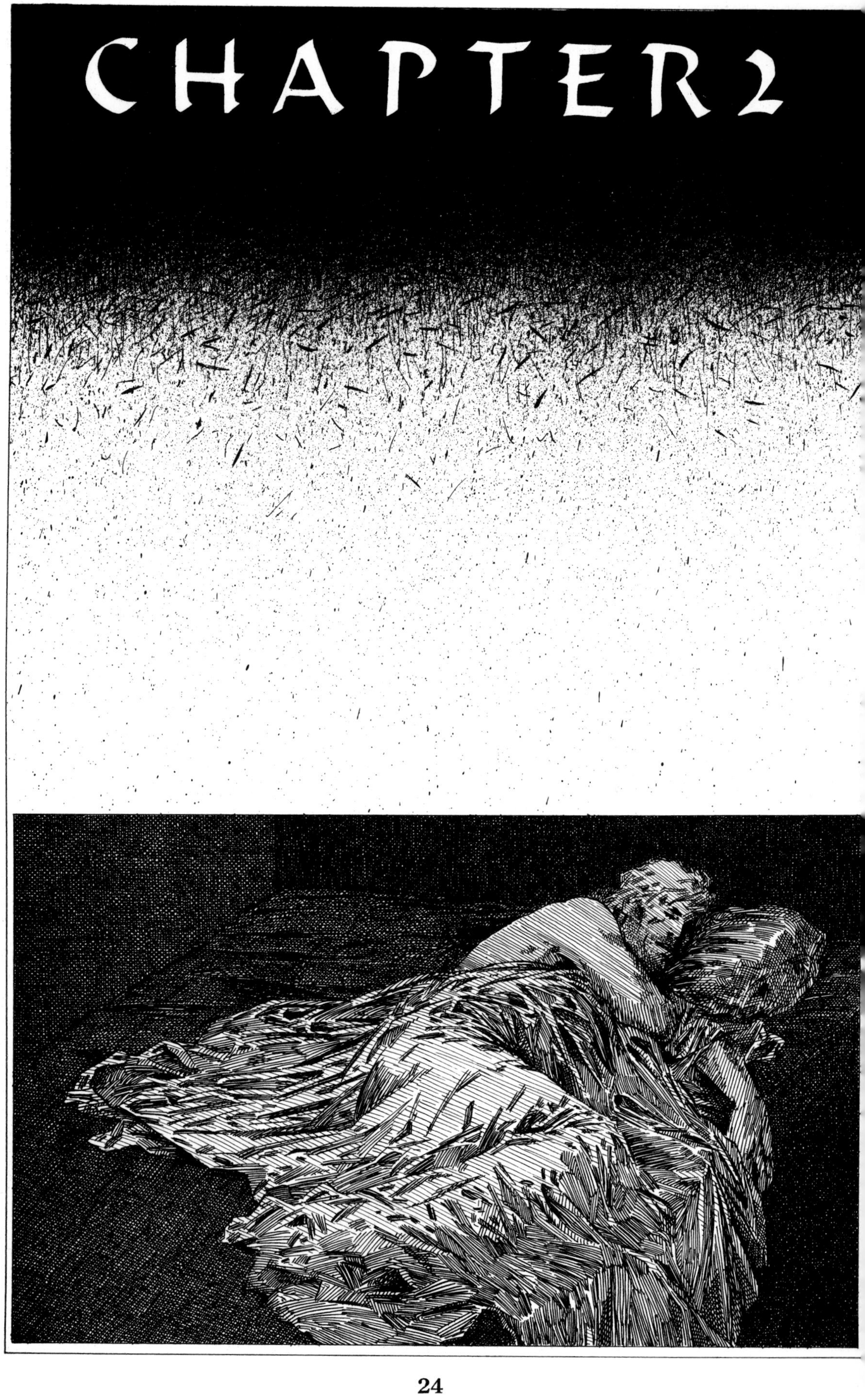
CHAPTER 2

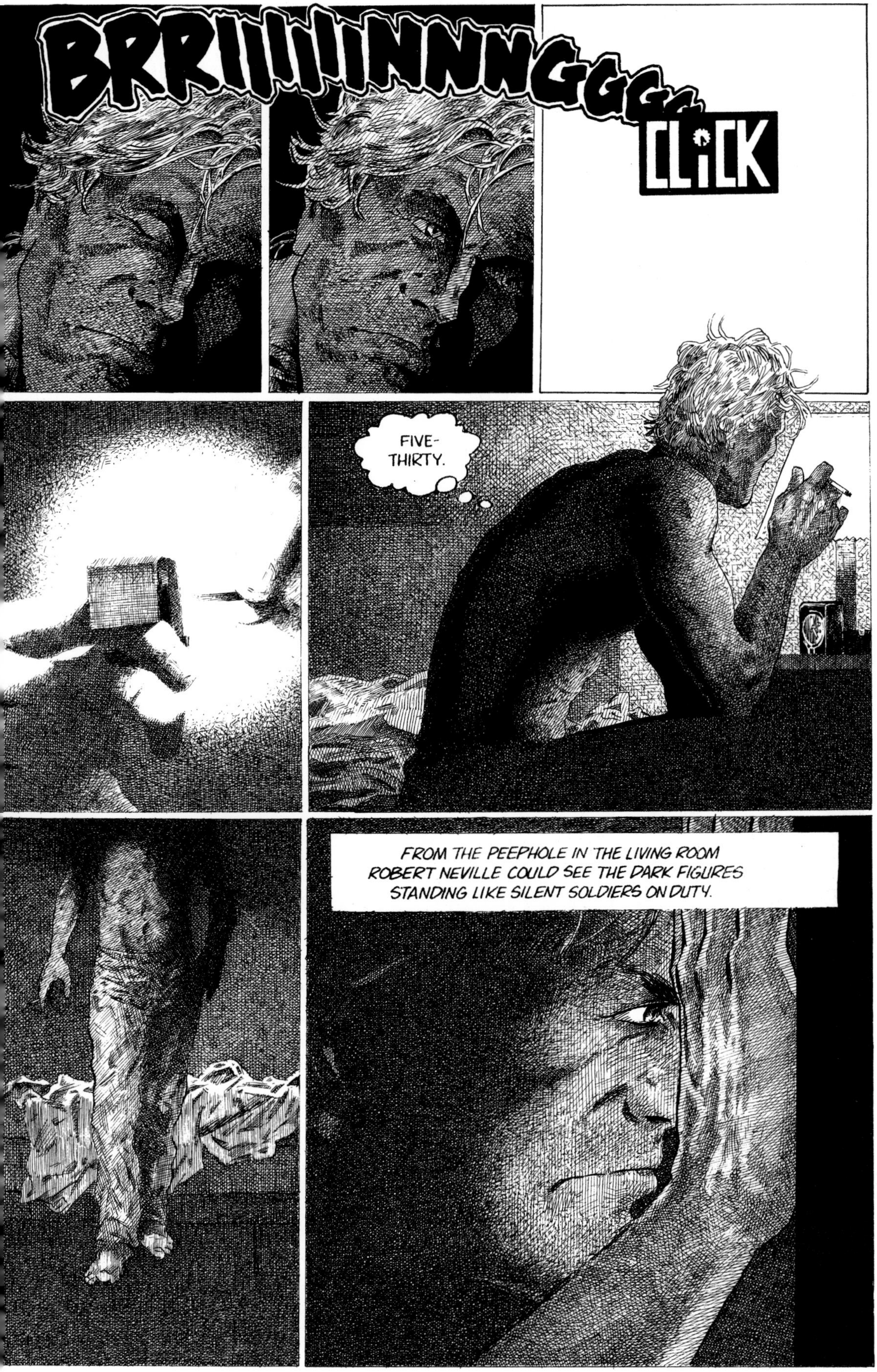
BRRIIIIIINNNNGGGG
CLICK
FIVE-THIRTY.
FROM THE PEEPHOLE IN THE LIVING ROOM ROBERT NEVILLE COULD SEE THE DARK FIGURES STANDING LIKE SILENT SOLDIERS ON DUTY.

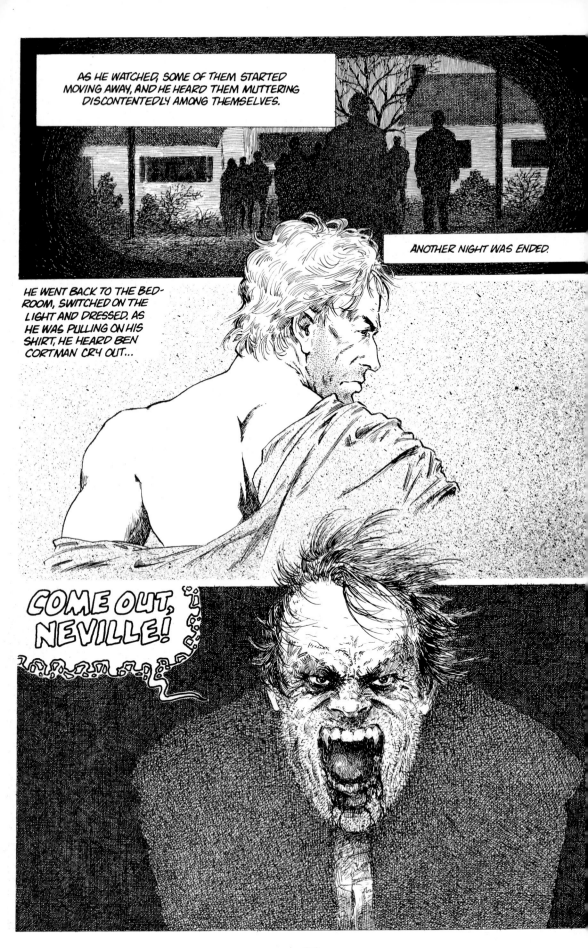

AS HE WATCHED, SOME OF THEM STARTED MOVING AWAY, AND HE HEARD THEM MUTTERING DISCONTENTEDLY AMONG THEMSELVES.

ANOTHER NIGHT WAS ENDED.

HE WENT BACK TO THE BED-ROOM, SWITCHED ON THE LIGHT AND DRESSED. AS HE WAS PULLING ON HIS SHIRT, HE HEARD BEN CORTMAN CRY OUT...

COME OUT, NEVILLE!

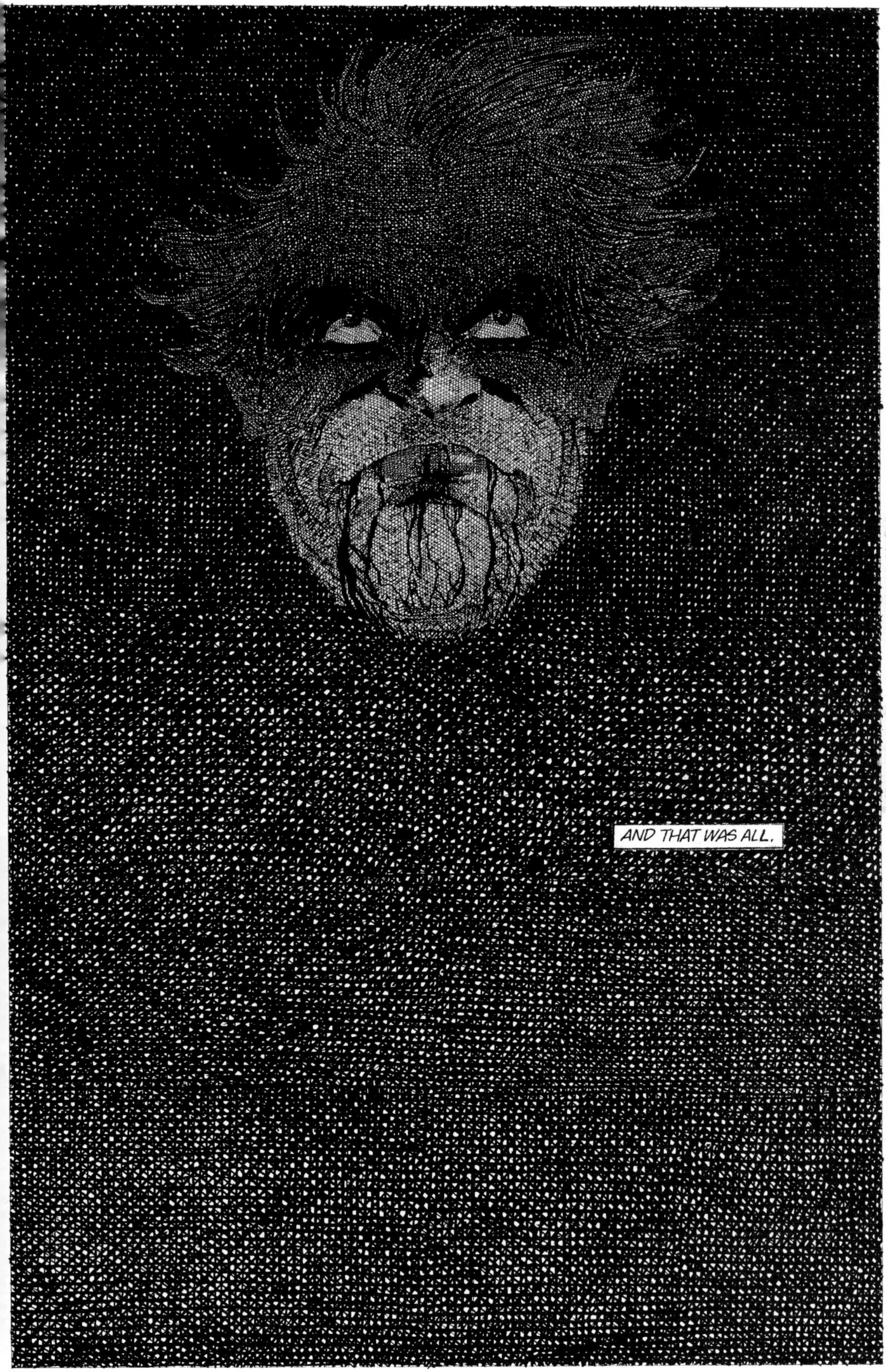
AND THAT WAS ALL.

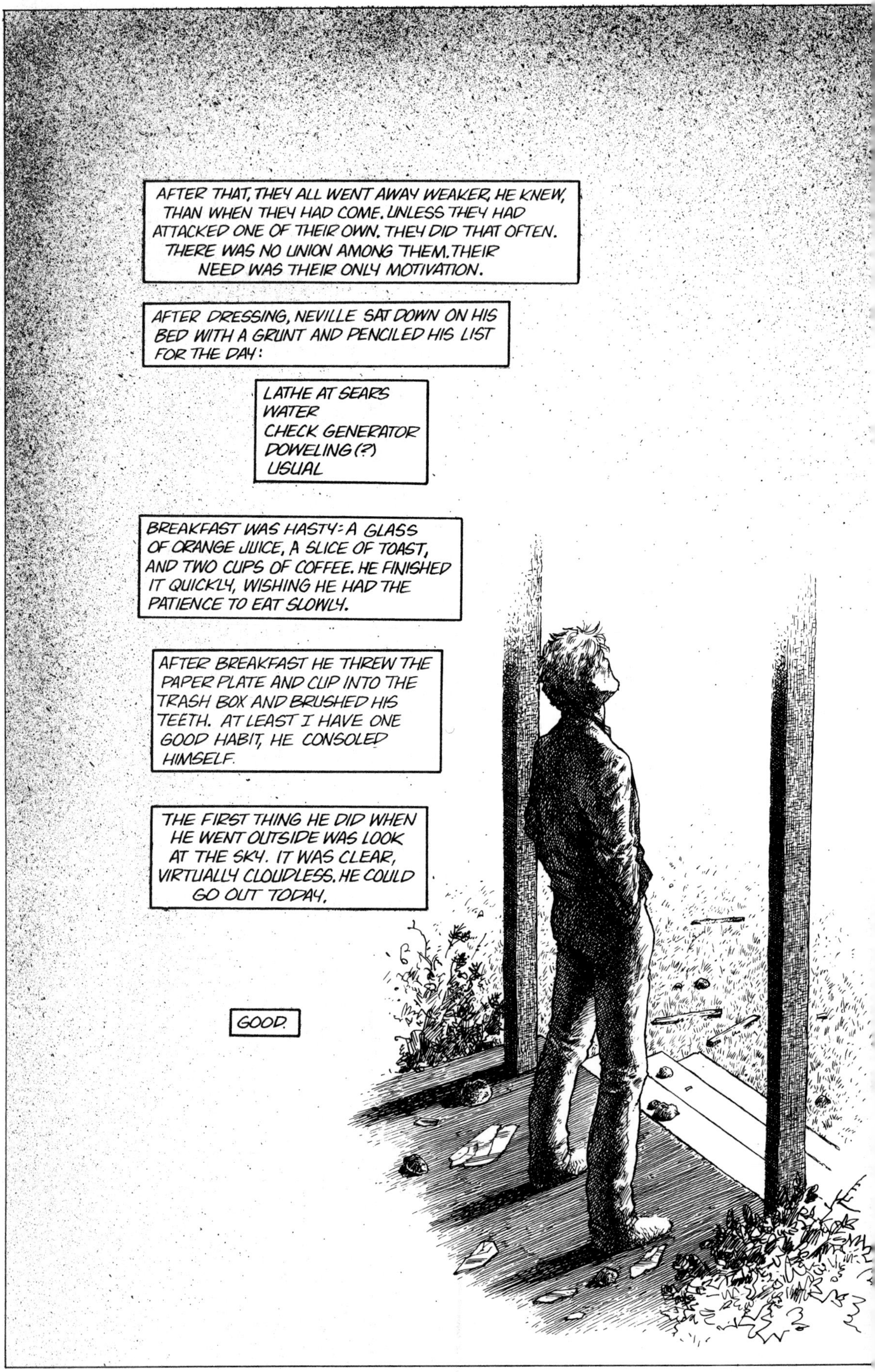
AFTER THAT, THEY ALL WENT AWAY WEAKER, HE KNEW, THAN WHEN THEY HAD COME. UNLESS THEY HAD ATTACKED ONE OF THEIR OWN. THEY DID THAT OFTEN. THERE WAS NO UNION AMONG THEM. THEIR NEED WAS THEIR ONLY MOTIVATION.
AFTER DRESSING, NEVILLE SAT DOWN ON HIS BED WITH A GRUNT AND PENCILED HIS LIST FOR THE DAY:
LATHE AT SEARS
WATER
CHECK GENERATOR
DOWELING (?)
USUAL
BREAKFAST WAS HASTY: A GLASS OF ORANGE JUICE, A SLICE OF TOAST, AND TWO CUPS OF COFFEE. HE FINISHED IT QUICKLY, WISHING HE HAD THE PATIENCE TO EAT SLOWLY.
AFTER BREAKFAST HE THREW THE PAPER PLATE AND CUP INTO THE TRASH BOX AND BRUSHED HIS TEETH. AT LEAST I HAVE ONE GOOD HABIT, HE CONSOLED HIMSELF.
THE FIRST THING HE DID WHEN HE WENT OUTSIDE WAS LOOK AT THE SKY. IT WAS CLEAR, VIRTUALLY CLOUDLESS. HE COULD GO OUT TODAY.
GOOD.

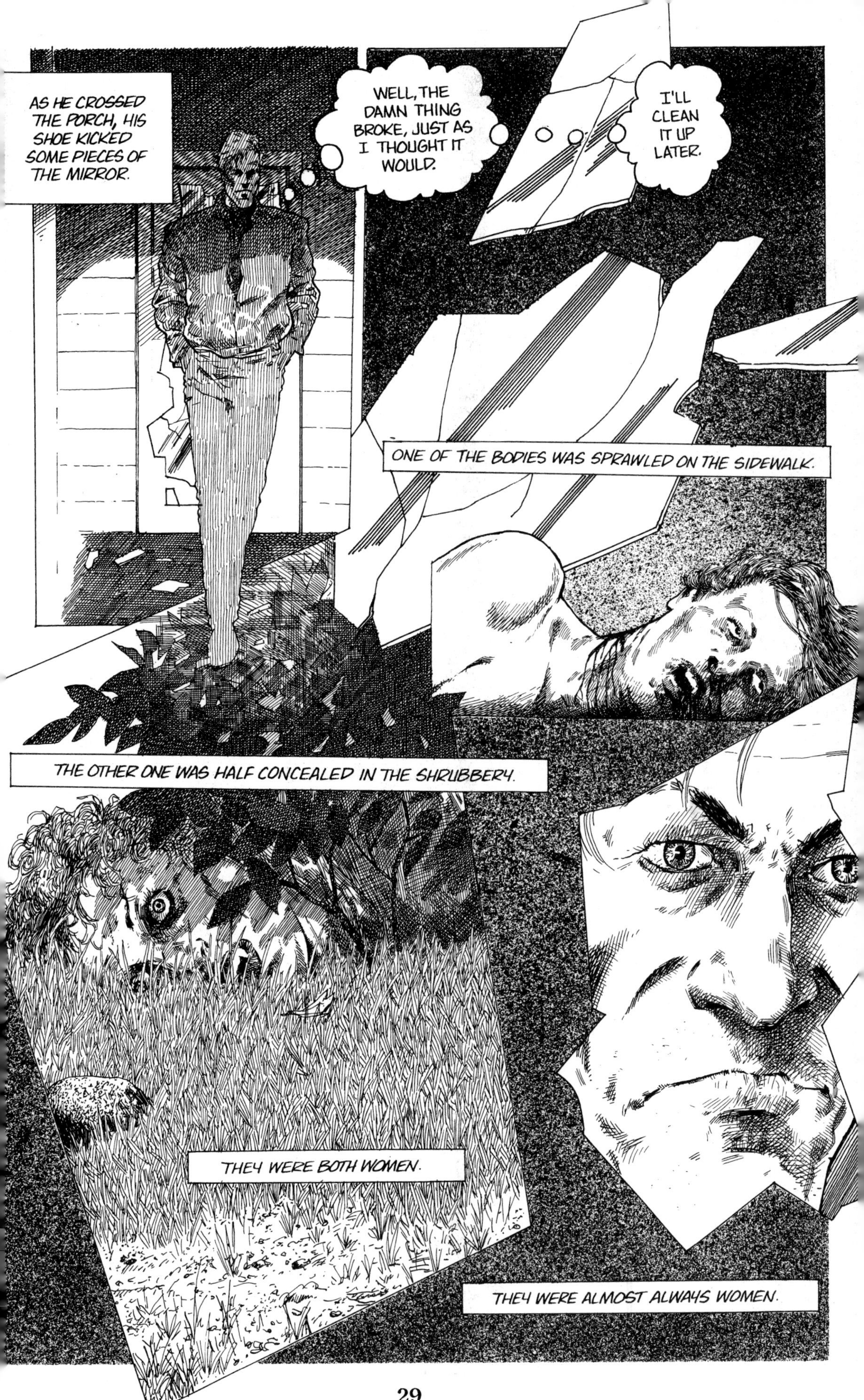
AS HE CROSSED THE PORCH, HIS SHOE KICKED SOME PIECES OF THE MIRROR.
WELL, THE DAMN THING BROKE, JUST AS I THOUGHT IT WOULD.
I'LL CLEAN IT UP LATER.
ONE OF THE BODIES WAS SPRAWLED ON THE SIDEWALK.
THE OTHER ONE WAS HALF CONCEALED IN THE SHRUBBERY.
THEY WERE BOTH WOMEN.
THEY WERE ALMOST ALWAYS WOMEN.

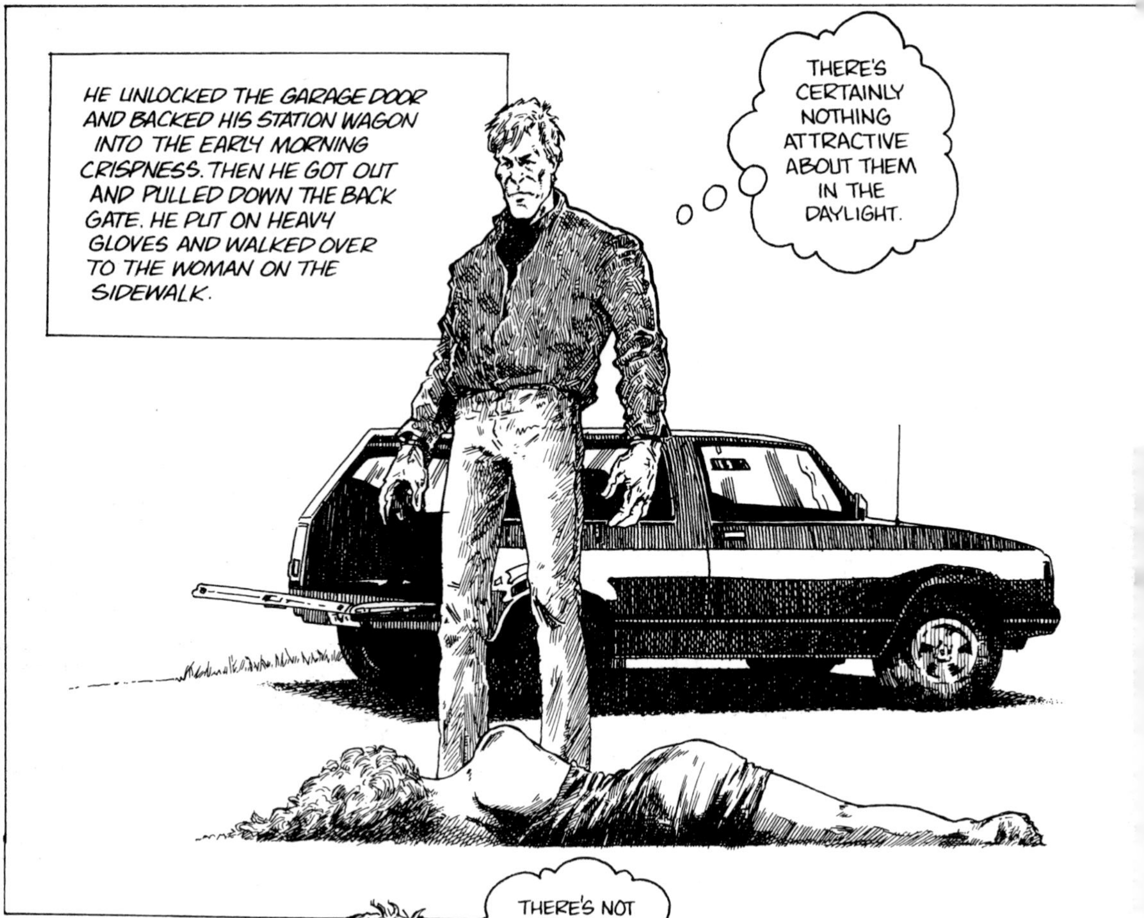
HE UNLOCKED THE GARAGE DOOR AND BACKED HIS STATION WAGON INTO THE EARLY MORNING CRISPNESS. THEN HE GOT OUT AND PULLED DOWN THE BACK GATE. HE PUT ON HEAVY GLOVES AND WALKED OVER TO THE WOMAN ON THE SIDEWALK.
THERE'S CERTAINLY NOTHING ATTRACTIVE ABOUT THEM IN THE DAYLIGHT.

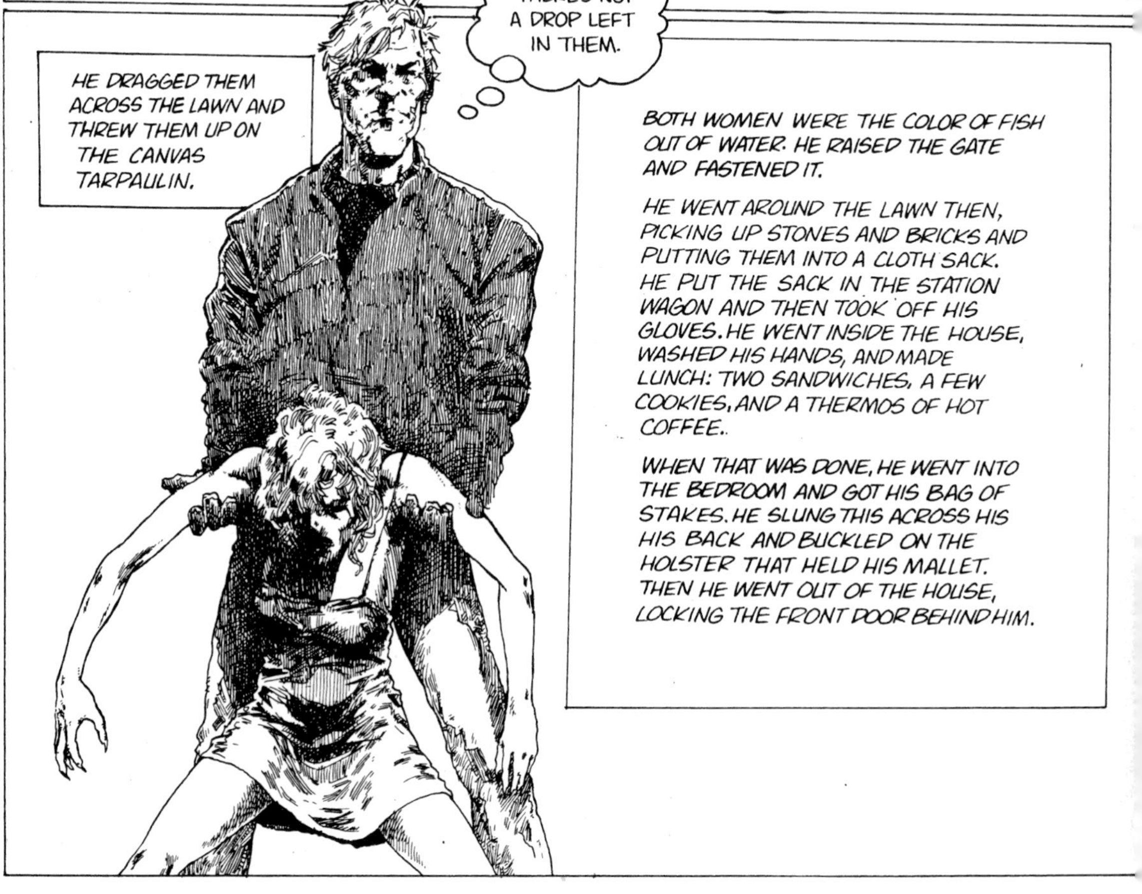
HE DRAGGED THEM ACROSS THE LAWN AND THREW THEM UP ON THE CANVAS TARPAULIN.
THERE'S NOT A DROP LEFT IN THEM.
BOTH WOMEN WERE THE COLOR OF FISH OUT OF WATER. HE RAISED THE GATE AND FASTENED IT.
HE WENT AROUND THE LAWN THEN, PICKING UP STONES AND BRICKS AND PUTTING THEM INTO A CLOTH SACK. HE PUT THE SACK IN THE STATION WAGON AND THEN TOOK OFF HIS GLOVES. HE WENT INSIDE THE HOUSE, WASHED HIS HANDS, AND MADE LUNCH: TWO SANDWICHES, A FEW COOKIES, AND A THERMOS OF HOT COFFEE..
WHEN THAT WAS DONE, HE WENT INTO THE BEDROOM AND GOT HIS BAG OF STAKES. HE SLUNG THIS ACROSS HIS HIS BACK AND BUCKLED ON THE HOLSTER THAT HELD HIS MALLET. THEN HE WENT OUT OF THE HOUSE, LOCKING THE FRONT DOOR BEHIND HIM.

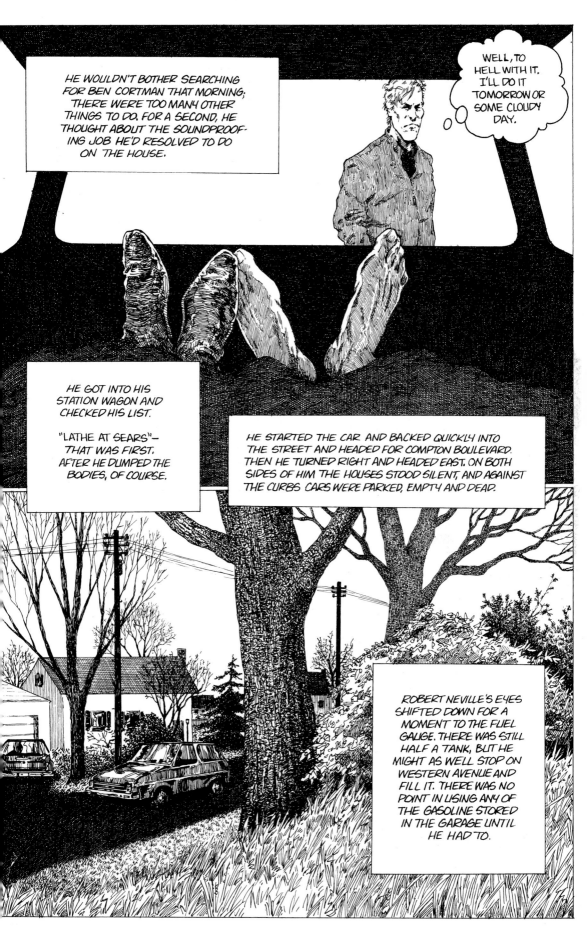

HE WOULDN'T BOTHER SEARCHING FOR BEN CORTMAN THAT MORNING; THERE WERE TOO MANY OTHER THINGS TO DO. FOR A SECOND, HE THOUGHT ABOUT THE SOUNDPROOF-ING JOB HE'D RESOLVED TO DO ON THE HOUSE.

WELL, TO HELL WITH IT. I'LL DO IT TOMORROW OR SOME CLOUDY DAY.

HE GOT INTO HIS STATION WAGON AND CHECKED HIS LIST.

"LATHE AT SEARS"— THAT WAS FIRST. AFTER HE DUMPED THE BODIES, OF COURSE.

HE STARTED THE CAR AND BACKED QUICKLY INTO THE STREET AND HEADED FOR COMPTON BOULEVARD. THEN HE TURNED RIGHT AND HEADED EAST. ON BOTH SIDES OF HIM THE HOUSES STOOD SILENT, AND AGAINST THE CURBS CARS WERE PARKED, EMPTY AND DEAD.

ROBERT NEVILLE'S EYES SHIFTED DOWN FOR A MOMENT TO THE FUEL GAUGE. THERE WAS STILL HALF A TANK, BUT HE MIGHT AS WELL STOP ON WESTERN AVENUE AND FILL IT. THERE WAS NO POINT IN USING ANY OF THE GASOLINE STORED IN THE GARAGE UNTIL HE HAD TO.

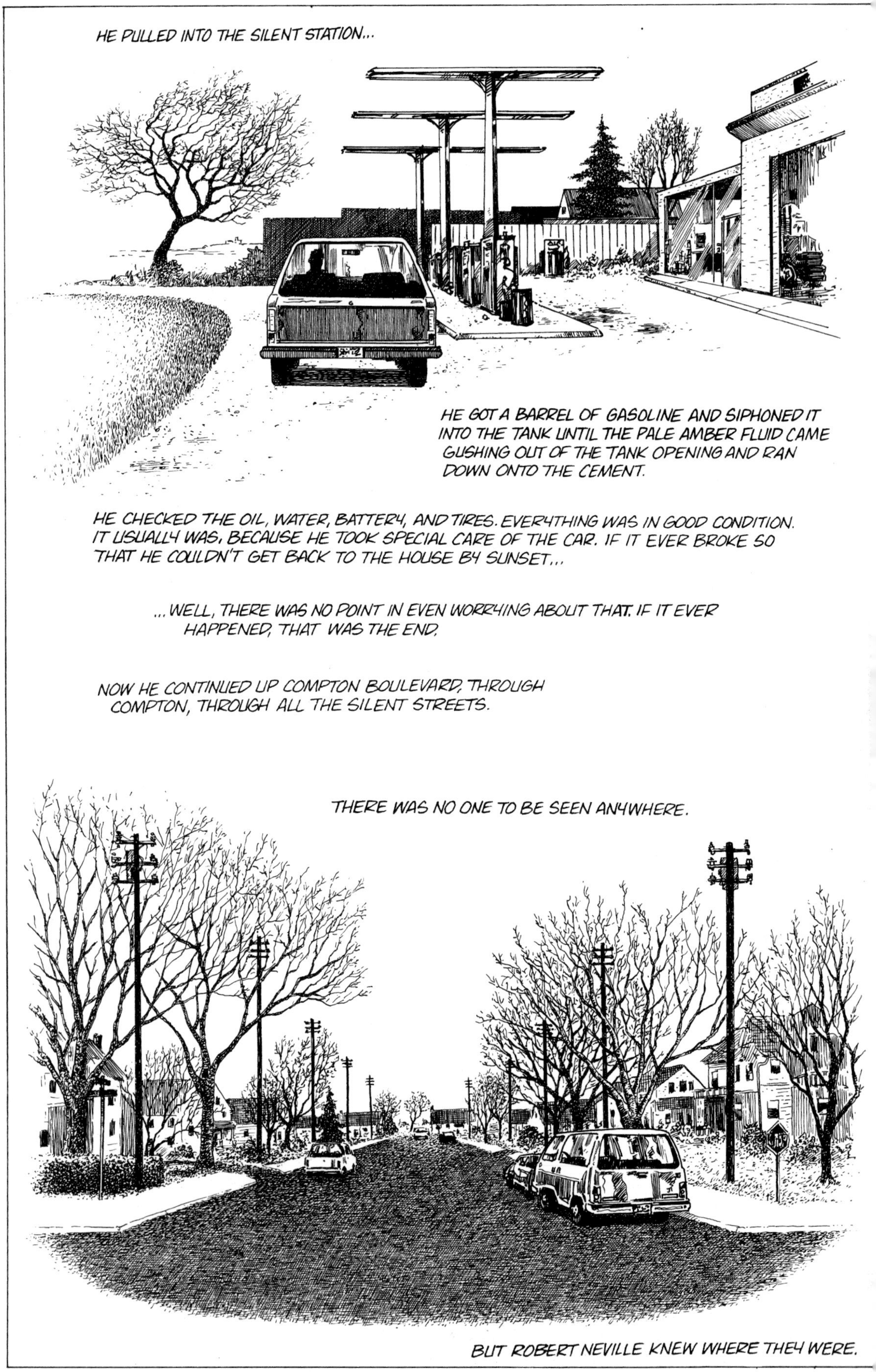
HE PULLED INTO THE SILENT STATION...
HE GOT A BARREL OF GASOLINE AND SIPHONED IT INTO THE TANK UNTIL THE PALE AMBER FLUID CAME GUSHING OUT OF THE TANK OPENING AND RAN DOWN ONTO THE CEMENT.
HE CHECKED THE OIL, WATER, BATTERY, AND TIRES. EVERYTHING WAS IN GOOD CONDITION. IT USUALLY WAS, BECAUSE HE TOOK SPECIAL CARE OF THE CAR. IF IT EVER BROKE SO THAT HE COULDN'T GET BACK TO THE HOUSE BY SUNSET...
...WELL, THERE WAS NO POINT IN EVEN WORRYING ABOUT THAT. IF IT EVER HAPPENED, THAT WAS THE END.
NOW HE CONTINUED UP COMPTON BOULEVARD, THROUGH COMPTON, THROUGH ALL THE SILENT STREETS.
THERE WAS NO ONE TO BE SEEN ANYWHERE.
BUT ROBERT NEVILLE KNEW WHERE THEY WERE.

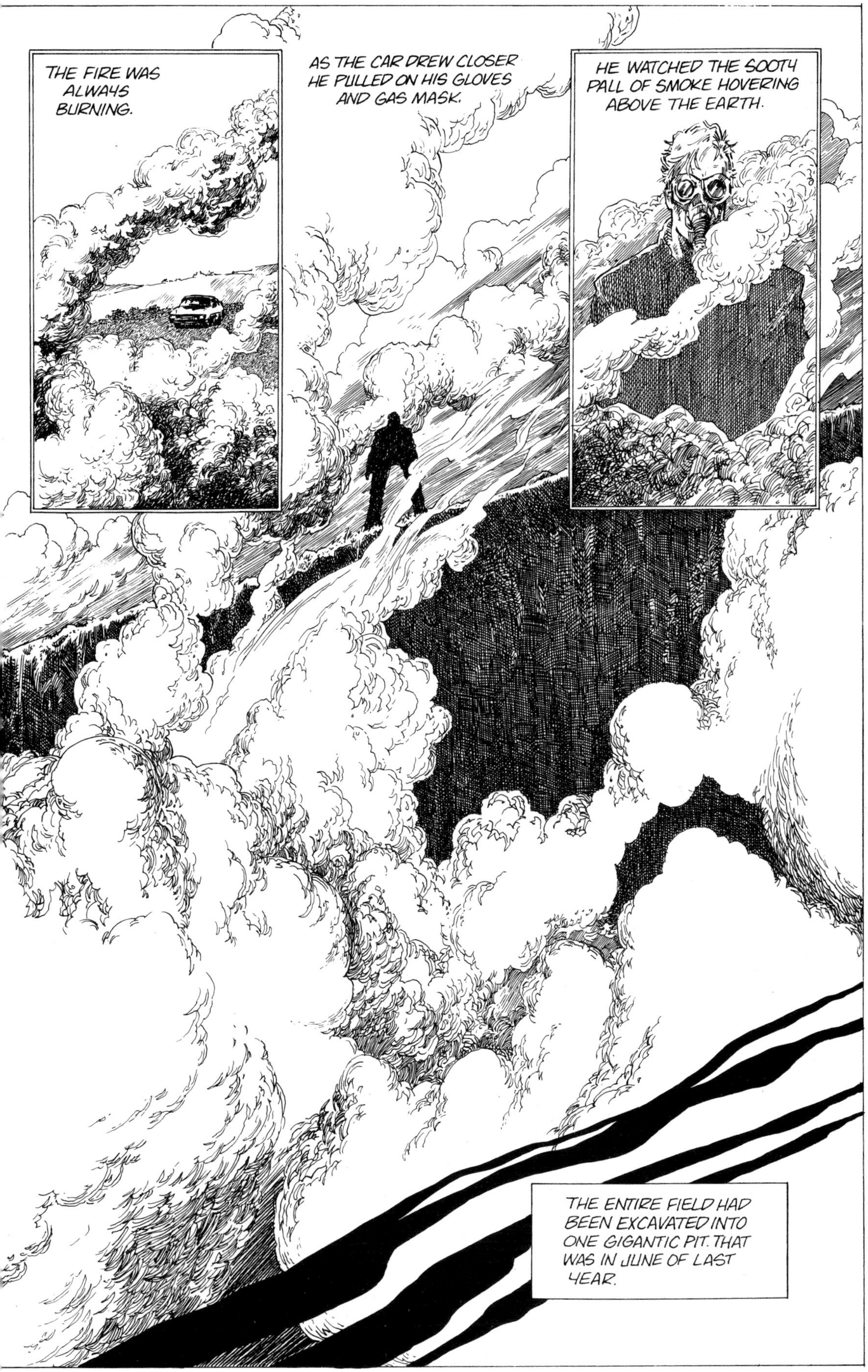
THE FIRE WAS ALWAYS BURNING.
AS THE CAR DREW CLOSER HE PULLED ON HIS GLOVES AND GAS MASK.
HE WATCHED THE SOOTY PALL OF SMOKE HOVERING ABOVE THE EARTH.
THE ENTIRE FIELD HAD BEEN EXCAVATED INTO ONE GIGANTIC PIT. THAT WAS IN JUNE OF LAST YEAR.

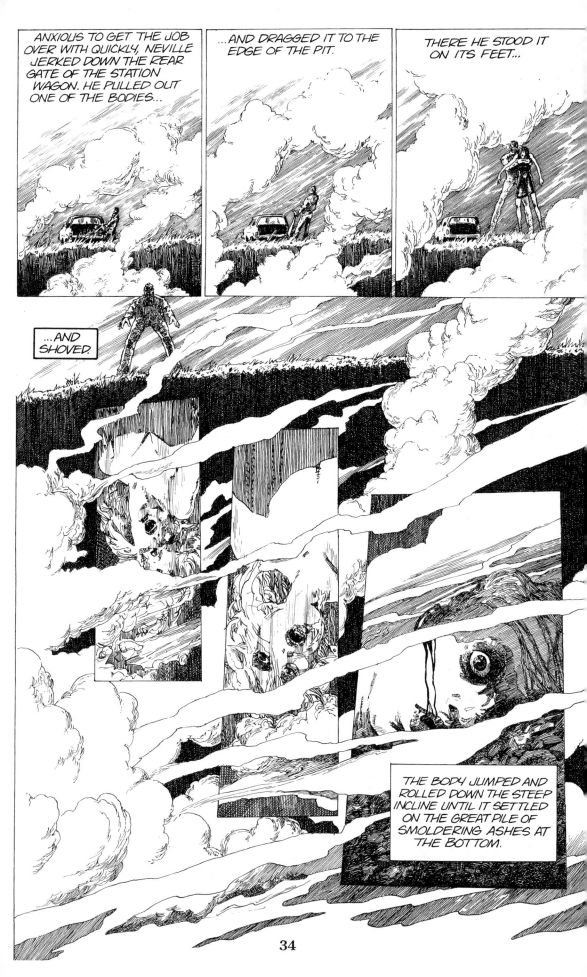

ANXIOUS TO GET THE JOB OVER WITH QUICKLY, NEVILLE JERKED DOWN THE REAR GATE OF THE STATION WAGON. HE PULLED OUT ONE OF THE BODIES...

...AND DRAGGED IT TO THE EDGE OF THE PIT.

THERE HE STOOD IT ON ITS FEET...

...AND SHOVED.

THE BODY JUMPED AND ROLLED DOWN THE STEEP INCLINE UNTIL IT SETTLED ON THE GREAT PILE OF SMOLDERING ASHES AT THE BOTTOM.

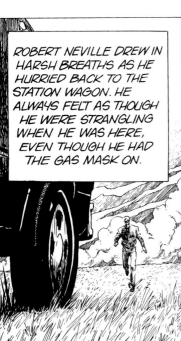

ROBERT NEVILLE DREW IN HARSH BREATHS AS HE HURRIED BACK TO THE STATION WAGON. HE ALWAYS FELT AS THOUGH HE WERE STRANGLING WHEN HE WAS HERE, EVEN THOUGH HE HAD THE GAS MASK ON.

NOW HE DRAGGED THE SECOND BODY TO THE BRINK OF THE PIT AND PUSHED IT OVER.

THEN, AFTER TOSSING THE SACK OF ROCKS DOWN, HE HURRIED BACK TO THE CAR AND SPED AWAY.

AFTER HE'D DRIVEN A HALF MILE, HE SKINNED OFF THE MASK AND GLOVES AND TOSSED THEM INTO THE BACK. HIS MOUTH OPENED AND HE DREW IN DEEP LUNGFULS OF FRESH AIR. HE TOOK THE FLASK FROM THE GLOVE COMPARTMENT AND TOOK A LONG DRINK OF BURNING WHISKY; THEN HE LIT A CIGARETTE AND INHALED DEEPLY.

SOMETIMES HE HAD TO GO TO THE BURNING PIT EVERY DAY FOR WEEKS AT A TIME, AND IT ALWAYS MADE HIM SICK.

SOMEWHERE DOWN THERE WAS KATHY.

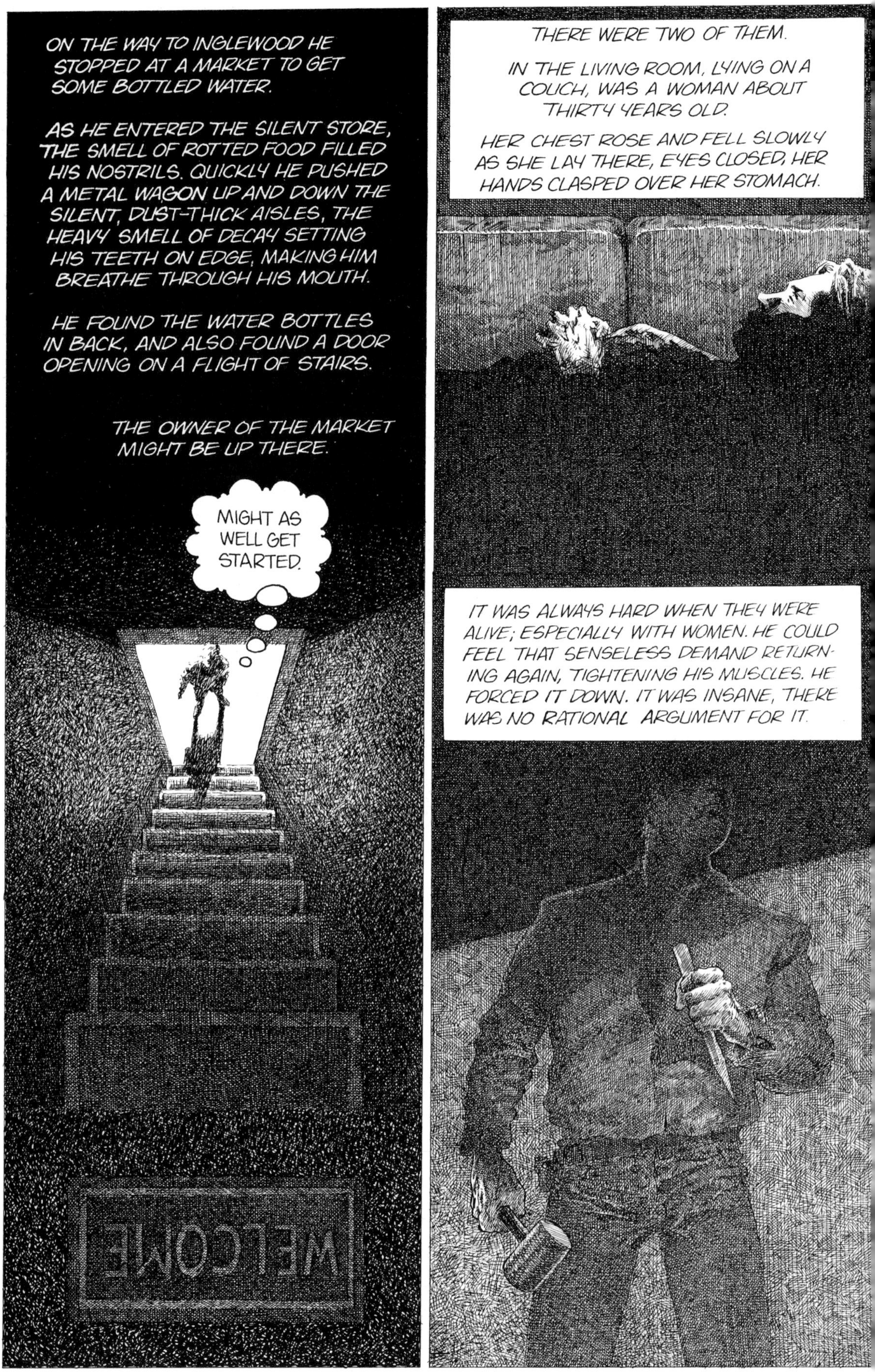
ON THE WAY TO INGLEWOOD HE STOPPED AT A MARKET TO GET SOME BOTTLED WATER.
AS HE ENTERED THE SILENT STORE, THE SMELL OF ROTTED FOOD FILLED HIS NOSTRILS. QUICKLY HE PUSHED A METAL WAGON UP AND DOWN THE SILENT, DUST-THICK AISLES, THE HEAVY SMELL OF DECAY SETTING HIS TEETH ON EDGE, MAKING HIM BREATHE THROUGH HIS MOUTH.
HE FOUND THE WATER BOTTLES IN BACK, AND ALSO FOUND A DOOR OPENING ON A FLIGHT OF STAIRS.
THE OWNER OF THE MARKET MIGHT BE UP THERE.
MIGHT AS WELL GET STARTED.
THERE WERE TWO OF THEM.
IN THE LIVING ROOM, LYING ON A COUCH, WAS A WOMAN ABOUT THIRTY YEARS OLD.
HER CHEST ROSE AND FELL SLOWLY AS SHE LAY THERE, EYES CLOSED, HER HANDS CLASPED OVER HER STOMACH.
IT WAS ALWAYS HARD WHEN THEY WERE ALIVE; ESPECIALLY WITH WOMEN. HE COULD FEEL THAT SENSELESS DEMAND RETURNING AGAIN, TIGHTENING HIS MUSCLES. HE FORCED IT DOWN. IT WAS INSANE, THERE WAS NO RATIONAL ARGUMENT FOR IT.

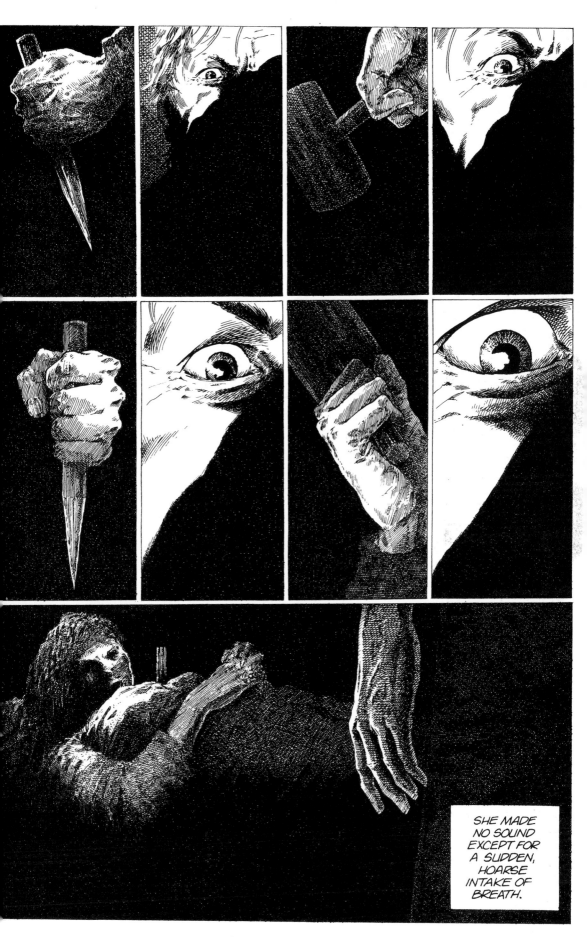

SHE MADE NO SOUND EXCEPT FOR A SUDDEN, HOARSE INTAKE OF BREATH.

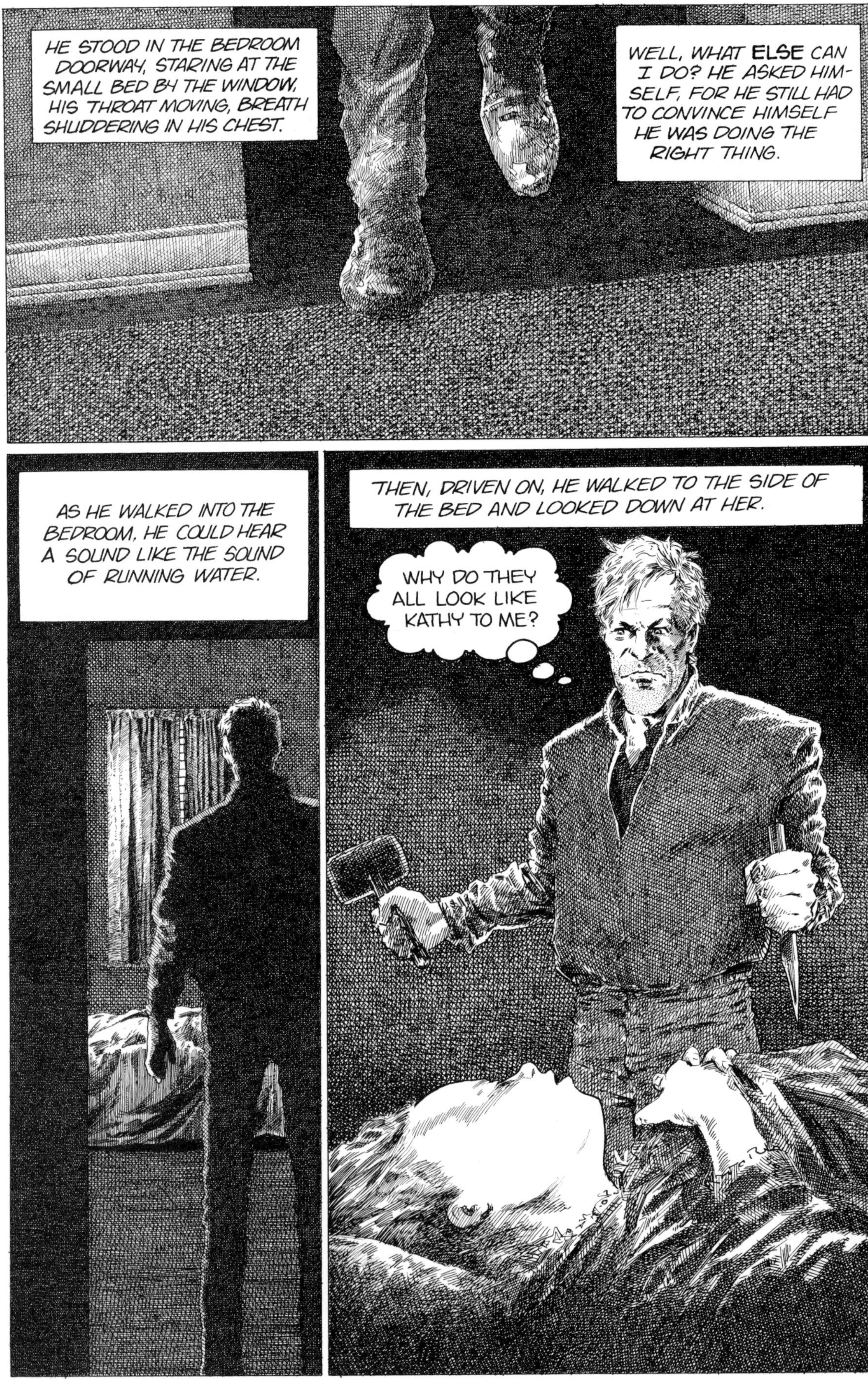
HE STOOD IN THE BEDROOM DOORWAY, STARING AT THE SMALL BED BY THE WINDOW, HIS THROAT MOVING, BREATH SHUDDERING IN HIS CHEST.
WELL, WHAT ELSE CAN I DO? HE ASKED HIMSELF, FOR HE STILL HAD TO CONVINCE HIMSELF HE WAS DOING THE RIGHT THING.
AS HE WALKED INTO THE BEDROOM, HE COULD HEAR A SOUND LIKE THE SOUND OF RUNNING WATER.
THEN, DRIVEN ON, HE WALKED TO THE SIDE OF THE BED AND LOOKED DOWN AT HER.
WHY DO THEY ALL LOOK LIKE KATHY TO ME?

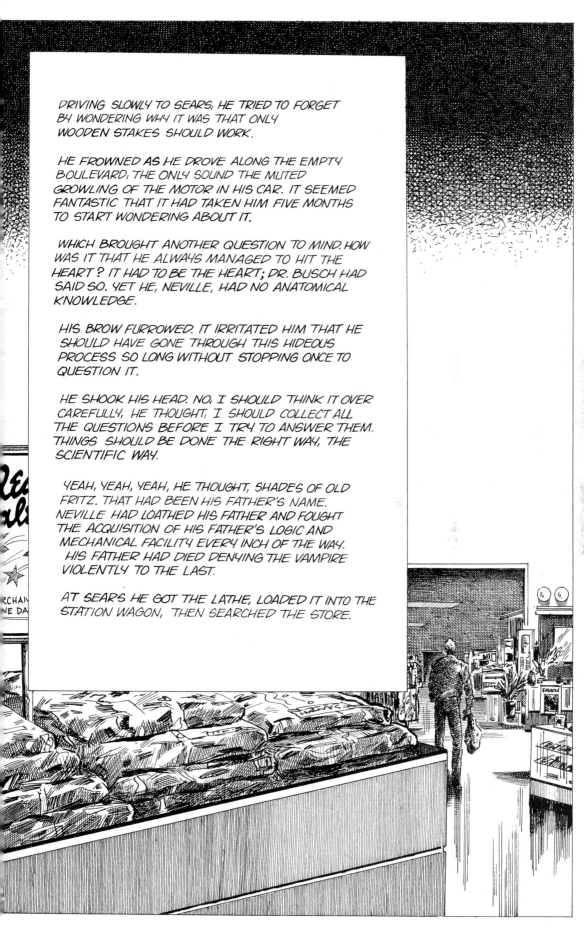

DRIVING SLOWLY TO SEARS, HE TRIED TO FORGET BY WONDERING WHY IT WAS THAT ONLY WOODEN STAKES SHOULD WORK.

HE FROWNED AS HE DROVE ALONG THE EMPTY BOULEVARD, THE ONLY SOUND THE MUTED GROWLING OF THE MOTOR IN HIS CAR. IT SEEMED FANTASTIC THAT IT HAD TAKEN HIM FIVE MONTHS TO START WONDERING ABOUT IT.

WHICH BROUGHT ANOTHER QUESTION TO MIND. HOW WAS IT THAT HE ALWAYS MANAGED TO HIT THE HEART? IT HAD TO BE THE HEART; DR. BUSCH HAD SAID SO. YET HE, NEVILLE, HAD NO ANATOMICAL KNOWLEDGE.

HIS BROW FURROWED. IT IRRITATED HIM THAT HE SHOULD HAVE GONE THROUGH THIS HIDEOUS PROCESS SO LONG WITHOUT STOPPING ONCE TO QUESTION IT.

HE SHOOK HIS HEAD. NO, I SHOULD THINK IT OVER CAREFULLY, HE THOUGHT, I SHOULD COLLECT ALL THE QUESTIONS BEFORE I TRY TO ANSWER THEM. THINGS SHOULD BE DONE THE RIGHT WAY, THE SCIENTIFIC WAY.

YEAH, YEAH, YEAH, HE THOUGHT, SHADES OF OLD FRITZ. THAT HAD BEEN HIS FATHER'S NAME. NEVILLE HAD LOATHED HIS FATHER AND FOUGHT THE ACQUISITION OF HIS FATHER'S LOGIC AND MECHANICAL FACILITY EVERY INCH OF THE WAY. HIS FATHER HAD DIED DENYING THE VAMPIRE VIOLENTLY TO THE LAST.

AT SEARS HE GOT THE LATHE, LOADED IT INTO THE STATION WAGON, THEN SEARCHED THE STORE.

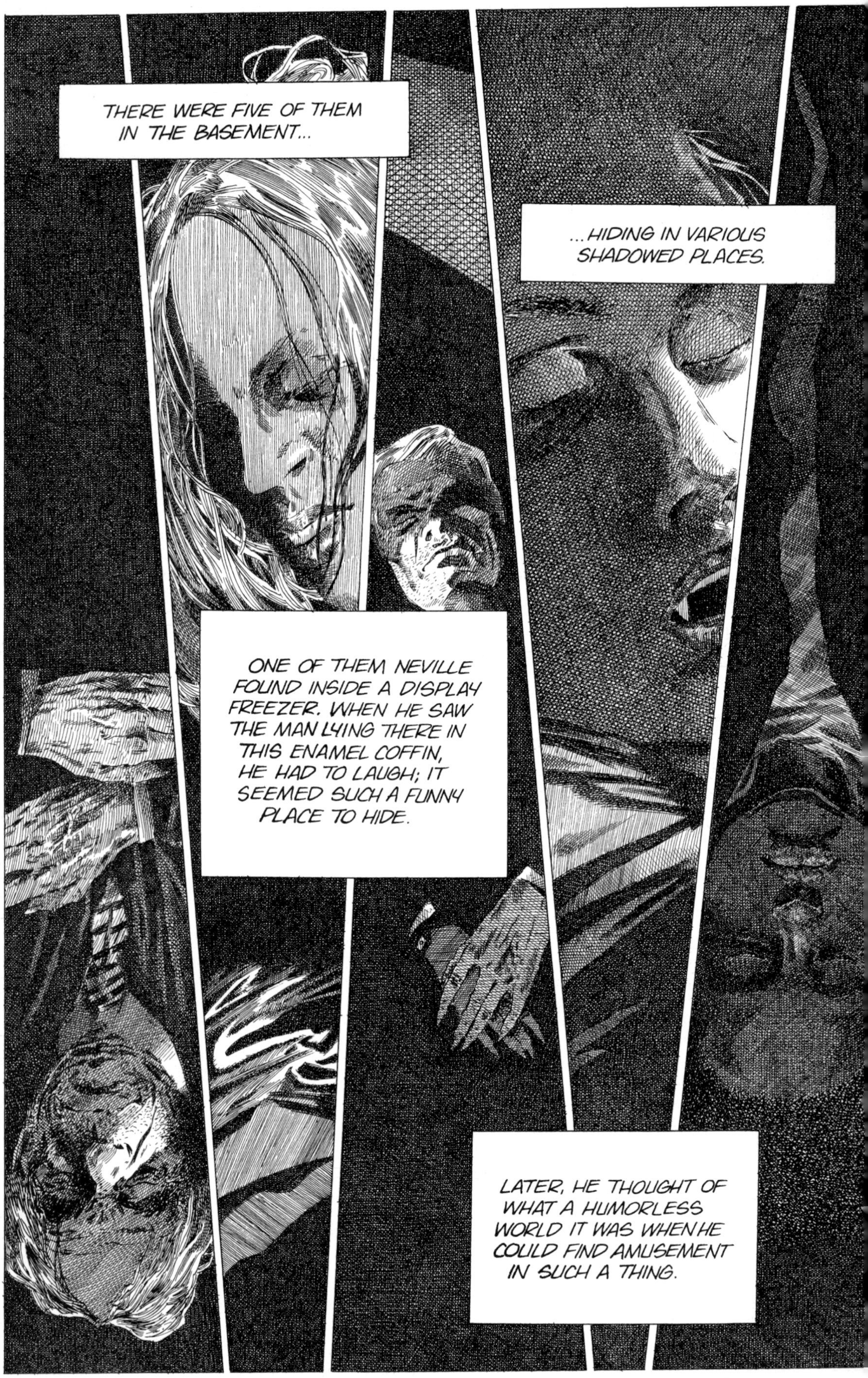

THERE WERE FIVE OF THEM IN THE BASEMENT...
...HIDING IN VARIOUS SHADOWED PLACES.
ONE OF THEM NEVILLE FOUND INSIDE A DISPLAY FREEZER. WHEN HE SAW THE MAN LYING THERE IN THIS ENAMEL COFFIN, HE HAD TO LAUGH; IT SEEMED SUCH A FUNNY PLACE TO HIDE.
LATER, HE THOUGHT OF WHAT A HUMORLESS WORLD IT WAS WHEN HE COULD FIND AMUSEMENT IN SUCH A THING.

ABOUT TWO O'CLOCK HE PARKED AND ATE HIS LUNCH.
EVERYTHING SEEMED TO TASTE OF GARLIC.

AND THAT SET HIM WONDERING ABOUT THE EFFECT
GARLIC HAD ON THEM. IT MUST HAVE BEEN
THE SMELL THAT CHASED THEM OFF, BUT WHY?

THEY WERE STRANGE, THE FACTS ABOUT THEM:
THEIR STAYING INSIDE BY DAY, THEIR AVOIDANCE
OF GARLIC, THEIR DEATH BY STAKE, THEIR REPUTED
FEAR OF CROSSES, THEIR SUPPOSED DREAD OF
MIRRORS.

TAKE THAT LAST, NOW. ACCORDING TO LEGEND, THEY
WERE INVISIBLE IN MIRRORS, BUT HE KNEW THAT
WAS UNTRUE. AS UNTRUE AS THE BELIEF THAT THEY
TRANSFORMED THEMSELVES INTO BATS. THAT WAS A
SUPERSTITION THAT LOGIC PLUS OBSERVATION HAD
EASILY DISPOSED OF. IT WAS EQUALLY FOOLISH TO
BELIEVE THAT THEY COULD TRANSFORM THEMSELVES
INTO WOLVES. WITHOUT A DOUBT THERE WERE
VAMPIRE DOGS; HE HAD SEEN AND HEARD THEM
OUTSIDE HIS HOUSE AT NIGHT. BUT THEY WERE
ONLY DOGS.

ROBERT NEVILLE COMPRESSED HIS LIPS SUDDENLY.
FORGET IT, HE TOLD HIMSELF; YOU'RE NOT READY
YET. THE TIME WOULD COME WHEN HE'D TAKE A CRACK
AT IT, DETAIL FOR DETAIL, BUT THE TIME WASN'T NOW.
THERE WERE ENOUGH THINGS TO WORRY ABOUT NOW.

AFTER LUNCH, HE WENT FROM HOUSE TO HOUSE
AND USED UP ALL HIS STAKES. HE HAD
FORTY-SEVEN STAKES.

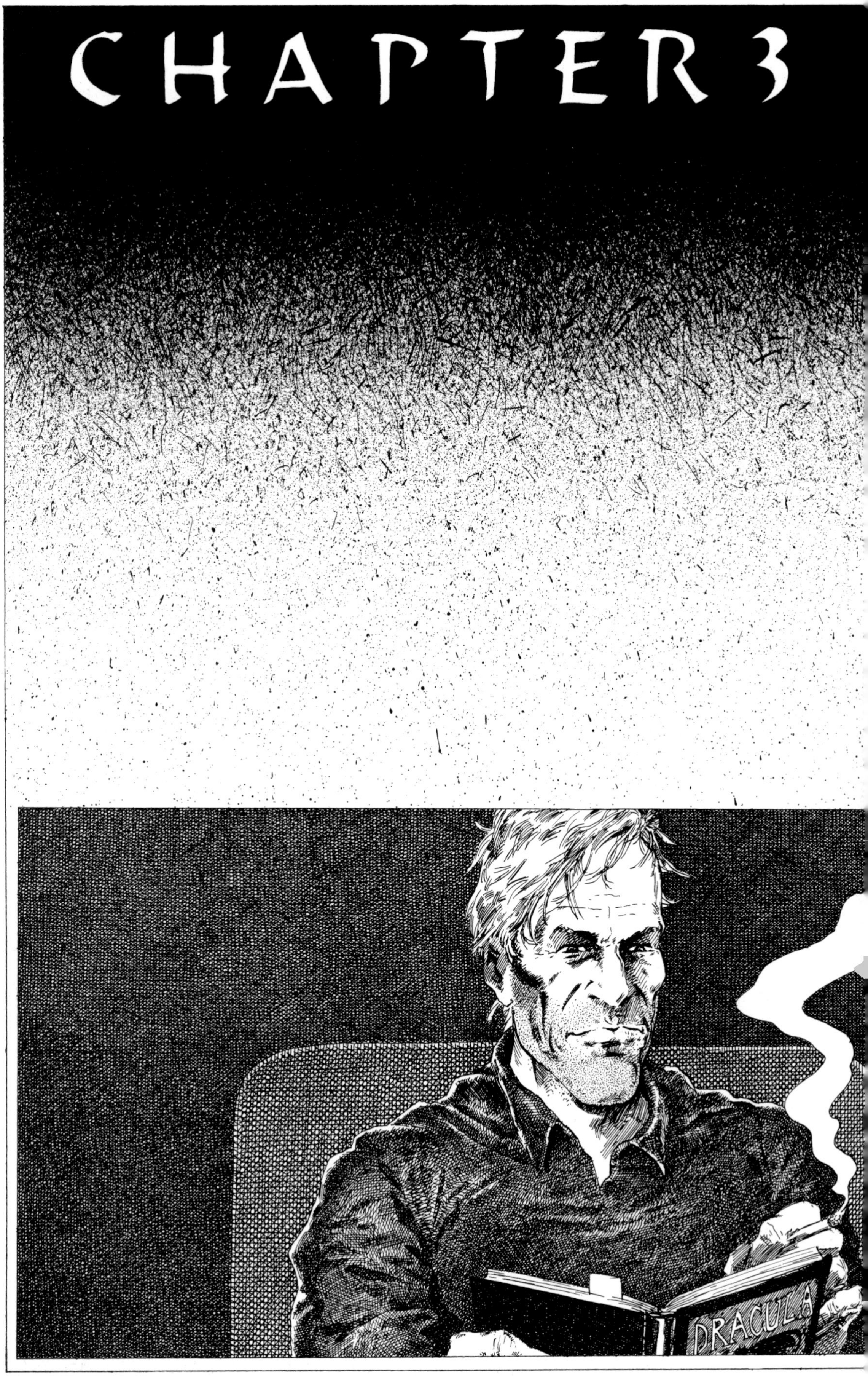
CHAPTER 3
DRACULA

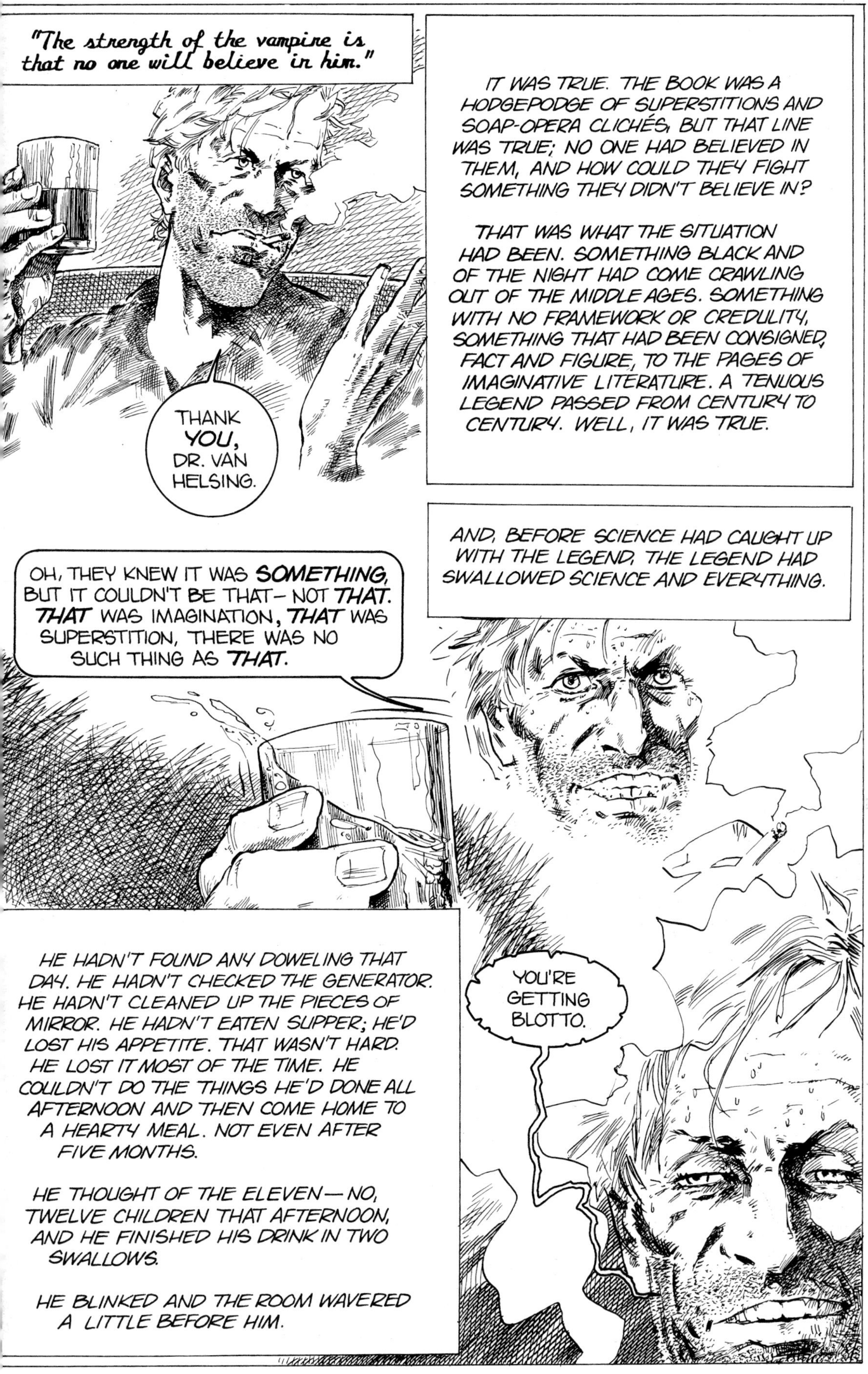
"The strength of the vampire is that no one will believe in him."
IT WAS TRUE. THE BOOK WAS A HODGEPODGE OF SUPERSTITIONS AND SOAP-OPERA CLICHÉS, BUT THAT LINE WAS TRUE; NO ONE HAD BELIEVED IN THEM, AND HOW COULD THEY FIGHT SOMETHING THEY DIDN'T BELIEVE IN?
THAT WAS WHAT THE SITUATION HAD BEEN. SOMETHING BLACK AND OF THE NIGHT HAD COME CRAWLING OUT OF THE MIDDLE AGES. SOMETHING WITH NO FRAMEWORK OR CREDULITY, SOMETHING THAT HAD BEEN CONSIGNED, FACT AND FIGURE, TO THE PAGES OF IMAGINATIVE LITERATURE. A TENUOUS LEGEND PASSED FROM CENTURY TO CENTURY. WELL, IT WAS TRUE.
THANK YOU, DR. VAN HELSING.
AND, BEFORE SCIENCE HAD CAUGHT UP WITH THE LEGEND, THE LEGEND HAD SWALLOWED SCIENCE AND EVERYTHING.
OH, THEY KNEW IT WAS SOMETHING, BUT IT COULDN'T BE THAT— NOT THAT. THAT WAS IMAGINATION, THAT WAS SUPERSTITION, THERE WAS NO SUCH THING AS THAT.
HE HADN'T FOUND ANY DOWELING THAT DAY. HE HADN'T CHECKED THE GENERATOR. HE HADN'T CLEANED UP THE PIECES OF MIRROR. HE HADN'T EATEN SUPPER; HE'D LOST HIS APPETITE. THAT WASN'T HARD. HE LOST IT MOST OF THE TIME. HE COULDN'T DO THE THINGS HE'D DONE ALL AFTERNOON AND THEN COME HOME TO A HEARTY MEAL. NOT EVEN AFTER FIVE MONTHS.
HE THOUGHT OF THE ELEVEN— NO, TWELVE CHILDREN THAT AFTERNOON, AND HE FINISHED HIS DRINK IN TWO SWALLOWS.
HE BLINKED AND THE ROOM WAVERED A LITTLE BEFORE HIM.
YOU'RE GETTING BLOTTO.

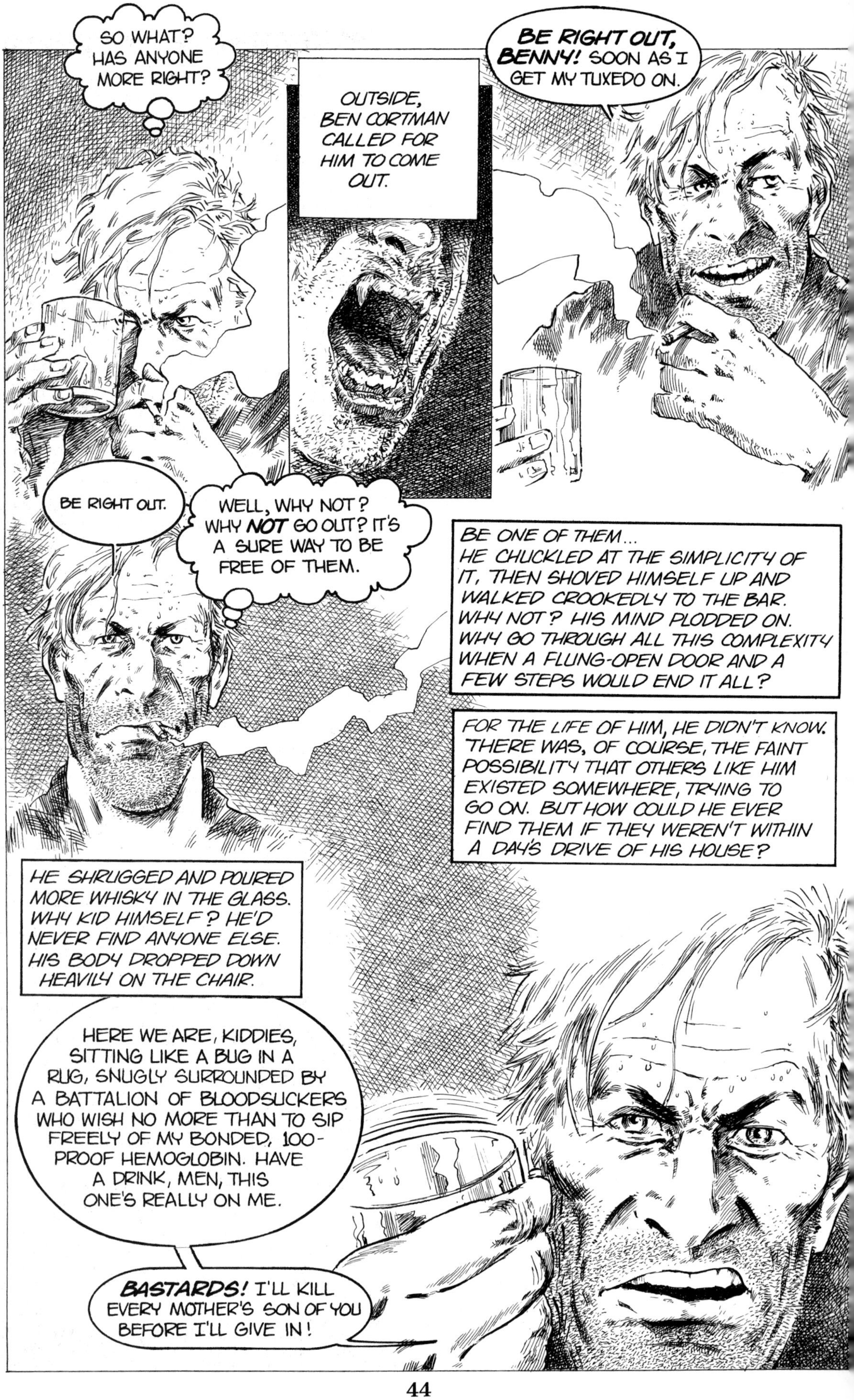
SO WHAT? HAS ANYONE MORE RIGHT?
OUTSIDE, BEN CORTMAN CALLED FOR HIM TO COME OUT.
BE RIGHT OUT, BENNY! SOON AS I GET MY TUXEDO ON.
BE RIGHT OUT.
WELL, WHY NOT? WHY NOT GO OUT? IT'S A SURE WAY TO BE FREE OF THEM.
BE ONE OF THEM... HE CHUCKLED AT THE SIMPLICITY OF IT, THEN SHOVED HIMSELF UP AND WALKED CROOKEDLY TO THE BAR. WHY NOT? HIS MIND PLODDED ON. WHY GO THROUGH ALL THIS COMPLEXITY WHEN A FLUNG-OPEN DOOR AND A FEW STEPS WOULD END IT ALL?
FOR THE LIFE OF HIM, HE DIDN'T KNOW. THERE WAS, OF COURSE, THE FAINT POSSIBILITY THAT OTHERS LIKE HIM EXISTED SOMEWHERE, TRYING TO GO ON. BUT HOW COULD HE EVER FIND THEM IF THEY WEREN'T WITHIN A DAY'S DRIVE OF HIS HOUSE?
HE SHRUGGED AND POURED MORE WHISKY IN THE GLASS. WHY KID HIMSELF? HE'D NEVER FIND ANYONE ELSE. HIS BODY DROPPED DOWN HEAVILY ON THE CHAIR.
HERE WE ARE, KIDDIES, SITTING LIKE A BUG IN A RUG, SNUGLY SURROUNDED BY A BATTALION OF BLOODSUCKERS WHO WISH NO MORE THAN TO SIP FREELY OF MY BONDED, 100-PROOF HEMOGLOBIN. HAVE A DRINK, MEN, THIS ONE'S REALLY ON ME.
BASTARDS! I'LL KILL EVERY MOTHER'S SON OF YOU BEFORE I'LL GIVE IN!

HIS RIGHT HAND CLOSED LIKE A CLAMP AND THE GLASS SHATTERED IN HIS GRIP.

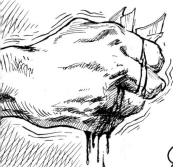

HE LOOKED DOWN, DULL-EYED, AT THE FRAGMENTS ON THE FLOOR, AT THE JAGGED PIECE OF GLASS STILL IN HIS HAND, AT THE WHISKY-DILUTED BLOOD DRIPPING OFF HIS PALM.

WOULDN'T THEY LIKE TO GET SOME OF IT, THOUGH?

HE STARTED UP WITH A FURIOUS LURCH AND ALMOST OPENED THE DOOR SO HE COULD WAVE THE HAND IN THEIR FACES AND HEAR THEM HOWL.

WISE UP, BUDDY. GO BANDAGE YOUR GODDAMN HAND.

HE STUMBLED INTO THE BATHROOM, WASHED HIS HAND AND BANDAGED IT CLUMSILY.

BACK IN THE LIVING ROOM, NEVILLE PLAYED BRAHMS; LIT A CIGARETTE AND POURED MORE WHISKY. GRADUALLY, THE ROOM SHIFTED ON ITS GYROSCOPIC CENTER AND WOVE AND UNDULATED ABOUT HIS CHAIR. A PLEASANT HAZE, FUZZY AT THE EDGES, TOOK OVER SIGHT. HE LOOKED AT THE GLASS, AT THE RECORD PLAYER. HE LET HIS HEAD FLOP FROM SIDE TO SIDE.

OUTSIDE, THEY PROWLED AND MUTTERED AND WAITED.

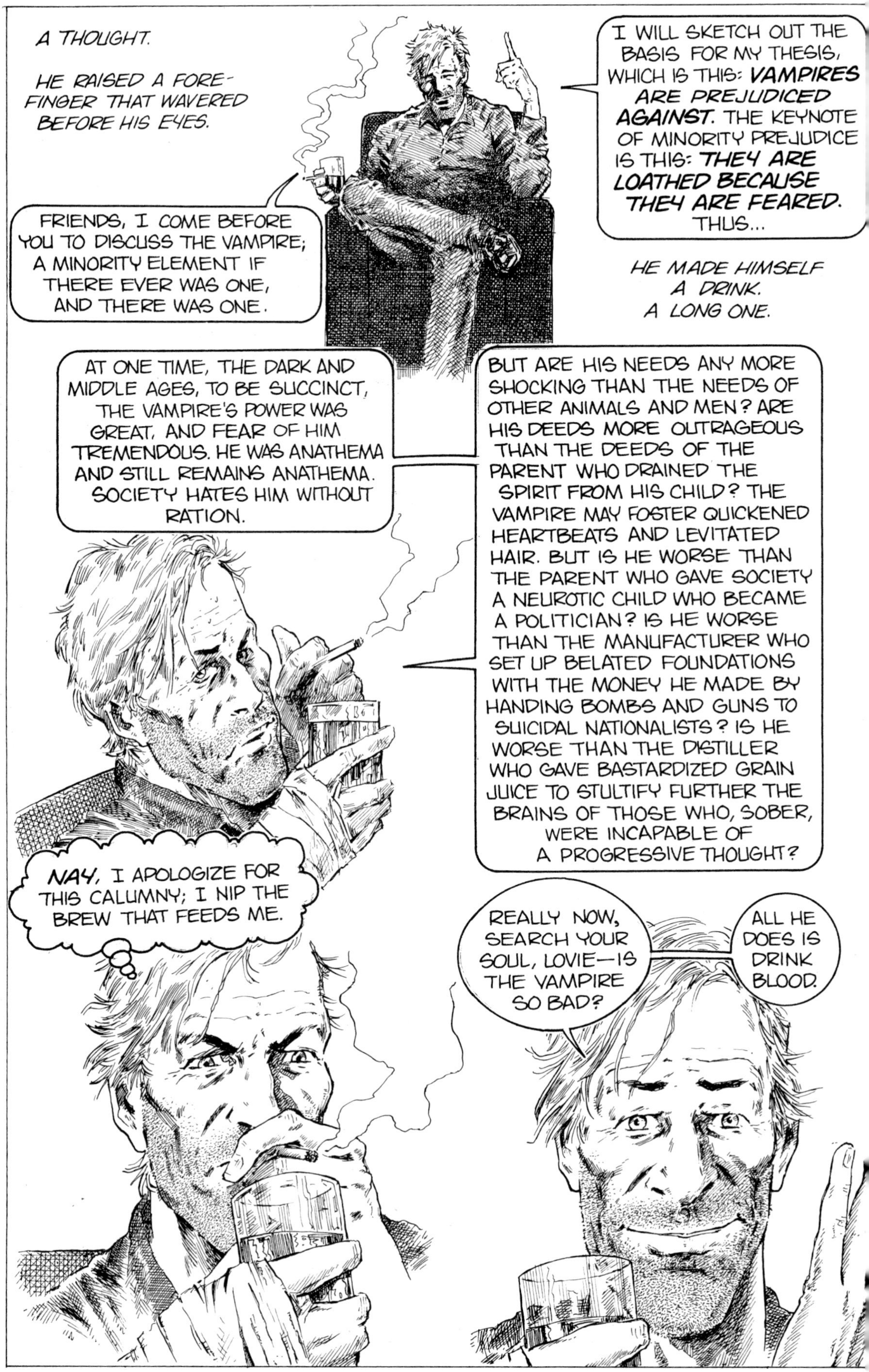

A THOUGHT.
HE RAISED A FOREFINGER THAT WAVERED BEFORE HIS EYES.
FRIENDS, I COME BEFORE YOU TO DISCUSS THE VAMPIRE; A MINORITY ELEMENT IF THERE EVER WAS ONE, AND THERE WAS ONE.
I WILL SKETCH OUT THE BASIS FOR MY THESIS, WHICH IS THIS: VAMPIRES ARE PREJUDICED AGAINST. THE KEYNOTE OF MINORITY PREJUDICE IS THIS: THEY ARE LOATHED BECAUSE THEY ARE FEARED. THUS...
HE MADE HIMSELF A DRINK. A LONG ONE.
AT ONE TIME, THE DARK AND MIDDLE AGES, TO BE SUCCINCT, THE VAMPIRE'S POWER WAS GREAT, AND FEAR OF HIM TREMENDOUS. HE WAS ANATHEMA AND STILL REMAINS ANATHEMA. SOCIETY HATES HIM WITHOUT RATION.
BUT ARE HIS NEEDS ANY MORE SHOCKING THAN THE NEEDS OF OTHER ANIMALS AND MEN? ARE HIS DEEDS MORE OUTRAGEOUS THAN THE DEEDS OF THE PARENT WHO DRAINED THE SPIRIT FROM HIS CHILD? THE VAMPIRE MAY FOSTER QUICKENED HEARTBEATS AND LEVITATED HAIR. BUT IS HE WORSE THAN THE PARENT WHO GAVE SOCIETY A NEUROTIC CHILD WHO BECAME A POLITICIAN? IS HE WORSE THAN THE MANUFACTURER WHO SET UP BELATED FOUNDATIONS WITH THE MONEY HE MADE BY HANDING BOMBS AND GUNS TO SUICIDAL NATIONALISTS? IS HE WORSE THAN THE DISTILLER WHO GAVE BASTARDIZED GRAIN JUICE TO STULTIFY FURTHER THE BRAINS OF THOSE WHO, SOBER, WERE INCAPABLE OF A PROGRESSIVE THOUGHT?
NAY, I APOLOGIZE FOR THIS CALUMNY; I NIP THE BREW THAT FEEDS ME.
REALLY NOW, SEARCH YOUR SOUL, LOVIE—IS THE VAMPIRE SO BAD?
ALL HE DOES IS DRINK BLOOD.

WHY, THEN, THIS UNKIND PREJUDICE, THIS THOUGHTLESS BIAS? WHY CANNOT THE VAMPIRE LIVE WHERE HE CHOOSES? WHY MUST HE SEEK OUT HIDING PLACES WHERE NONE CAN FIND HIM OUT? WHY DO YOU WISH HIM DESTROYED? AH, SEE, YOU HAVE TURNED THE POOR GUILELESS INNOCENT INTO A HAUNTED ANIMAL. HE HAS NO MEANS OF SUPPORT, NO MEASURES FOR PROPER EDUCATION, HE HAS NOT THE VOTING FRANCHISE. NO WONDER HE IS COMPELLED TO SEEK OUT A PREDATORY NOCTURNAL EXISTENCE.

SURE, SURE, BUT WOULD YOU LET YOUR *SISTER* MARRY ONE?

YOU GOT ME THERE, BUDDY, YOU GOT ME THERE.

THE MUSIC ENDED. THE NEEDLE SCRATCHED BACK AND FORTH IN THE BLACK GROOVES. THE SOUNDS OUTSIDE WERE STARTING TO NIBBLE AT HIS EARDRUMS.

COME OUT, NEVILLE!

COME OUT, NEVILLE!

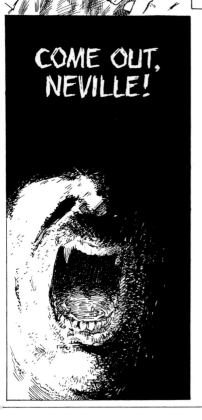

COME OUT, NEVILLE!

GODDAMN THEM, WHAT ARE THEY WAITING FOR? DO THEY THINK I'M GOING TO COME OUT AND HAND MYSELF OVER?

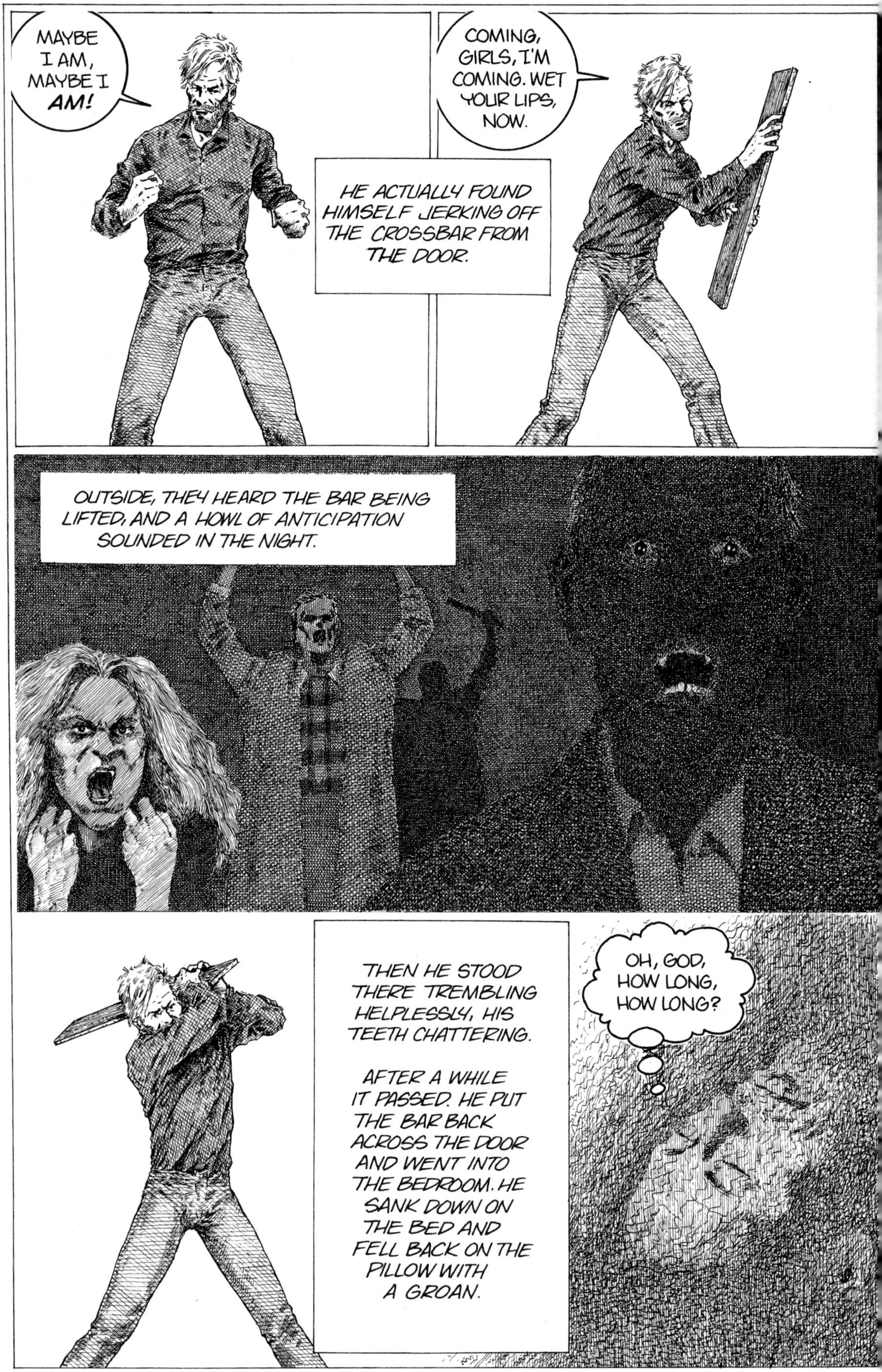
MAYBE I AM, MAYBE I AM!
COMING, GIRLS, I'M COMING. WET YOUR LIPS, NOW.
HE ACTUALLY FOUND HIMSELF JERKING OFF THE CROSSBAR FROM THE DOOR.
OUTSIDE, THEY HEARD THE BAR BEING LIFTED, AND A HOWL OF ANTICIPATION SOUNDED IN THE NIGHT.
THEN HE STOOD THERE TREMBLING HELPLESSLY, HIS TEETH CHATTERING.
AFTER A WHILE IT PASSED. HE PUT THE BAR BACK ACROSS THE DOOR AND WENT INTO THE BEDROOM. HE SANK DOWN ON THE BED AND FELL BACK ON THE PILLOW WITH A GROAN.
OH, GOD, HOW LONG, HOW LONG?

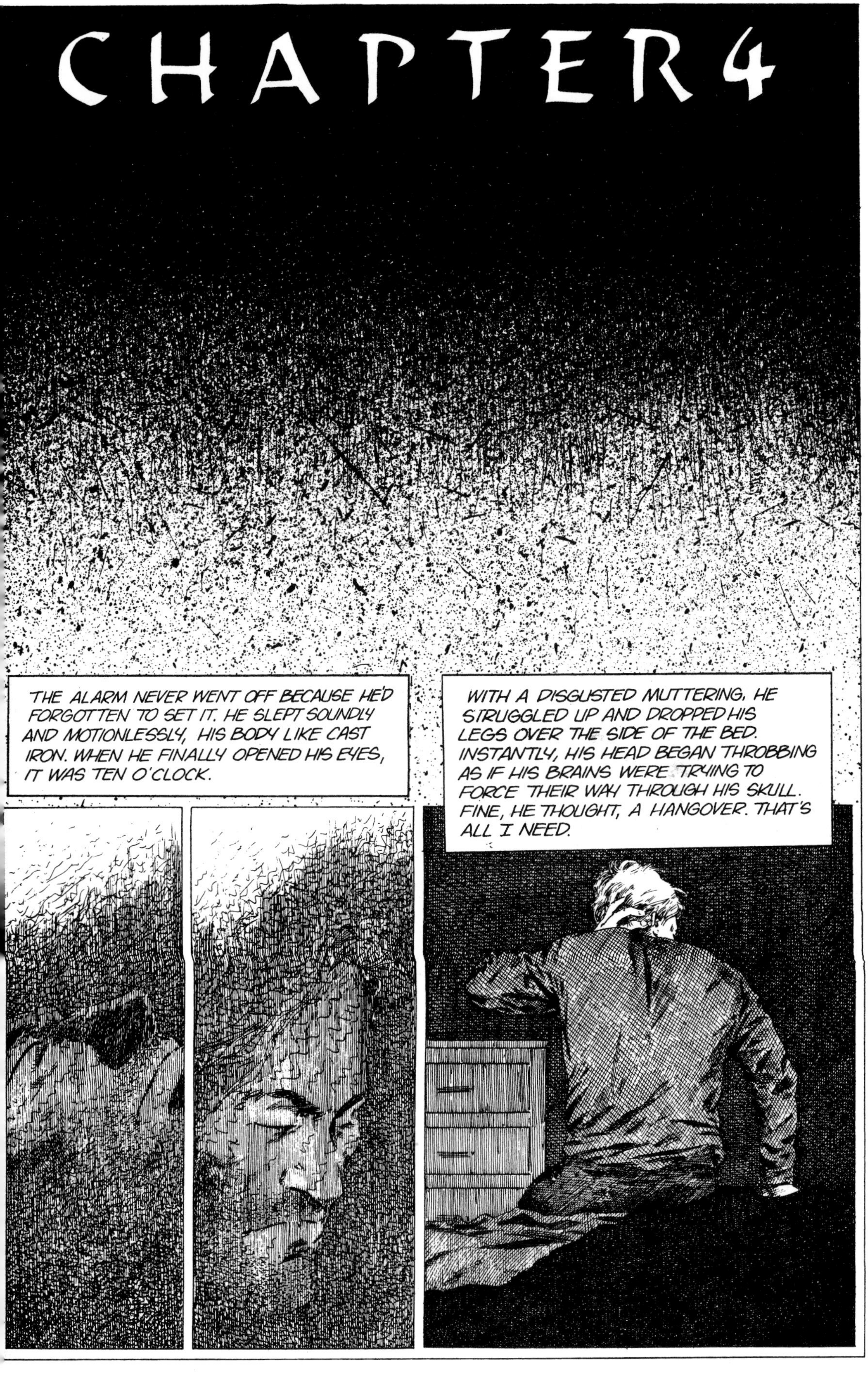
CHAPTER 4
THE ALARM NEVER WENT OFF BECAUSE HE'D FORGOTTEN TO SET IT. HE SLEPT SOUNDLY AND MOTIONLESSLY, HIS BODY LIKE CAST IRON. WHEN HE FINALLY OPENED HIS EYES, IT WAS TEN O'CLOCK.
WITH A DISGUSTED MUTTERING, HE STRUGGLED UP AND DROPPED HIS LEGS OVER THE SIDE OF THE BED. INSTANTLY, HIS HEAD BEGAN THROBBING AS IF HIS BRAINS WERE TRYING TO FORCE THEIR WAY THROUGH HIS SKULL. FINE, HE THOUGHT, A HANGOVER. THAT'S ALL I NEED.

HE PUSHED HIMSELF UP WITH A GROAN AND STUMBLED INTO THE BATHROOM, THREW WATER IN HIS FACE AND SPLASHED SOME OVER HIS HEAD. NO GOOD, HIS MIND COMPLAINED, NO GOOD. I STILL FEEL LIKE HELL. IN THE MIRROR HIS FACE WAS GAUNT, AND VERY MUCH LIKE THE FACE OF A MAN IN HIS FORTIES.

HE WALKED SLOWLY INTO THE LIVING ROOM AND OPENED THE FRONT DOOR. A CURSE FELL THICKLY FROM HIS LIPS AT THE SIGHT OF THE WOMAN CRUMPLED ACROSS THE SIDEWALK. HE STARTED TO TIGHTEN ANGRILY, BUT IT MADE HIS HEAD THROB TOO MUCH AND HE HAD TO LET IT GO. I'M SICK, HE THOUGHT.

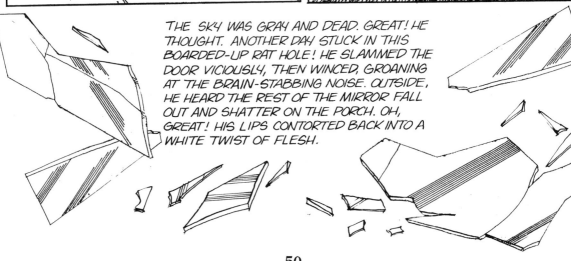

THE SKY WAS GRAY AND DEAD. GREAT! HE THOUGHT. ANOTHER DAY STUCK IN THIS BOARDED-UP RAT HOLE! HE SLAMMED THE DOOR VICIOUSLY, THEN WINCED, GROANING AT THE BRAIN-STABBING NOISE. OUTSIDE, HE HEARD THE REST OF THE MIRROR FALL OUT AND SHATTER ON THE PORCH. OH, GREAT! HIS LIPS CONTORTED BACK INTO A WHITE TWIST OF FLESH.

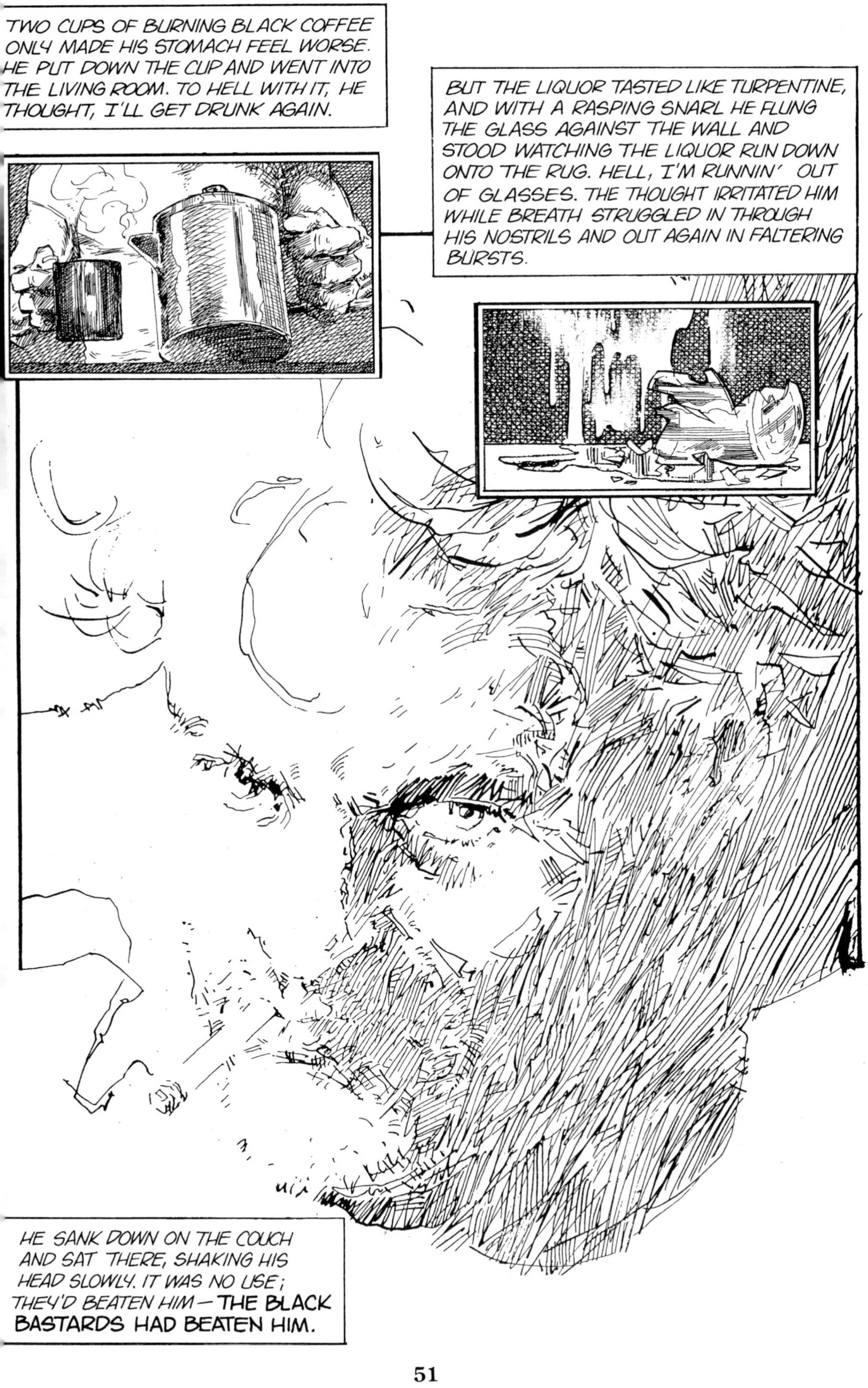
TWO CUPS OF BURNING BLACK COFFEE ONLY MADE HIS STOMACH FEEL WORSE. HE PUT DOWN THE CUP AND WENT INTO THE LIVING ROOM. TO HELL WITH IT, HE THOUGHT, I'LL GET DRUNK AGAIN.
BUT THE LIQUOR TASTED LIKE TURPENTINE, AND WITH A RASPING SNARL HE FLUNG THE GLASS AGAINST THE WALL AND STOOD WATCHING THE LIQUOR RUN DOWN ONTO THE RUG. HELL, I'M RUNNIN' OUT OF GLASSES. THE THOUGHT IRRITATED HIM WHILE BREATH STRUGGLED IN THROUGH HIS NOSTRILS AND OUT AGAIN IN FALTERING BURSTS.
HE SANK DOWN ON THE COUCH AND SAT THERE, SHAKING HIS HEAD SLOWLY. IT WAS NO USE; THEY'D BEATEN HIM—THE BLACK BASTARDS HAD BEATEN HIM.

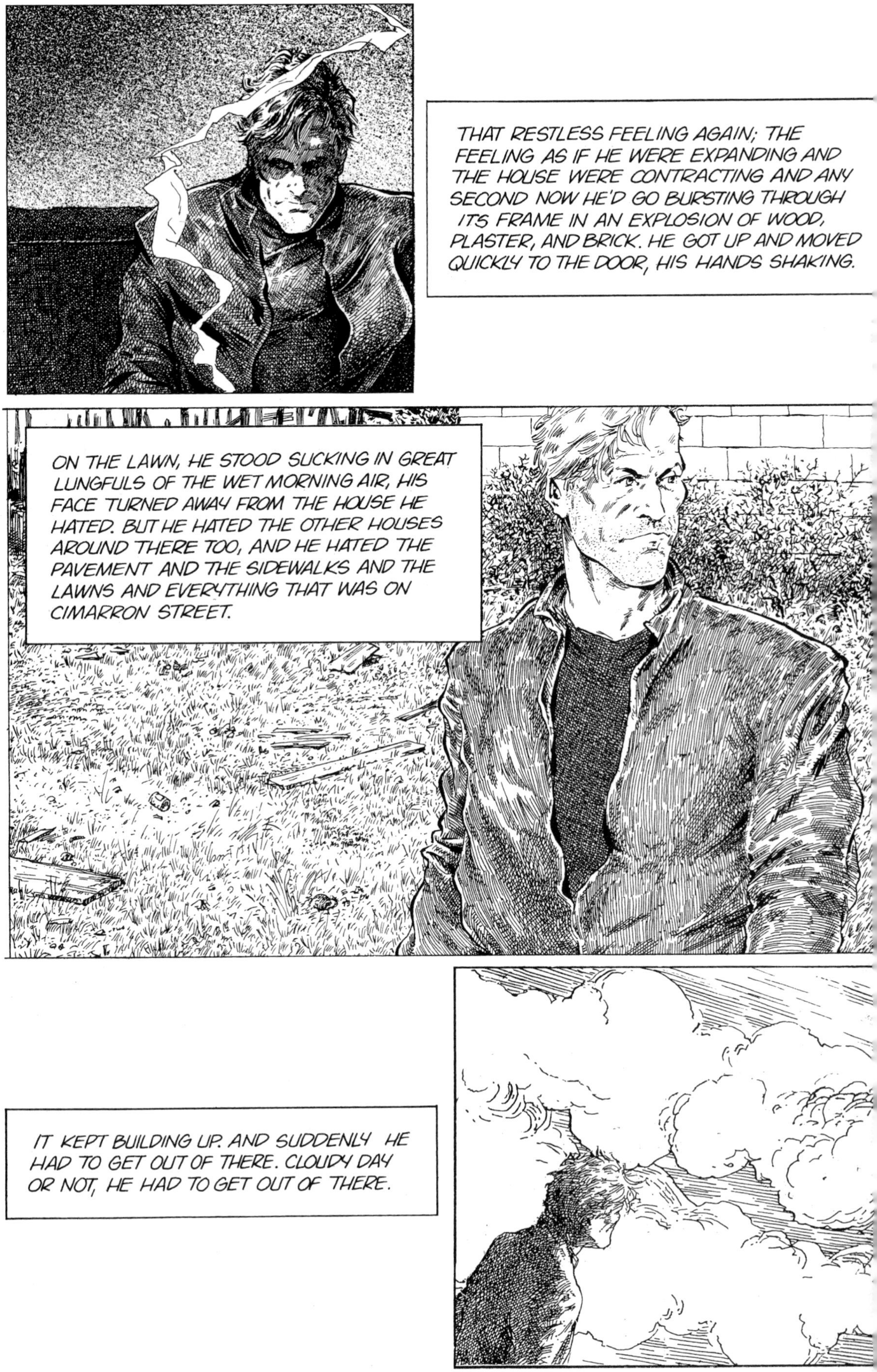
THAT RESTLESS FEELING AGAIN; THE FEELING AS IF HE WERE EXPANDING AND THE HOUSE WERE CONTRACTING AND ANY SECOND NOW HE'D GO BURSTING THROUGH ITS FRAME IN AN EXPLOSION OF WOOD, PLASTER, AND BRICK. HE GOT UP AND MOVED QUICKLY TO THE DOOR, HIS HANDS SHAKING.
ON THE LAWN, HE STOOD SUCKING IN GREAT LUNGFULS OF THE WET MORNING AIR, HIS FACE TURNED AWAY FROM THE HOUSE HE HATED. BUT HE HATED THE OTHER HOUSES AROUND THERE TOO, AND HE HATED THE PAVEMENT AND THE SIDEWALKS AND THE LAWNS AND EVERYTHING THAT WAS ON CIMARRON STREET.
IT KEPT BUILDING UP. AND SUDDENLY HE HAD TO GET OUT OF THERE. CLOUDY DAY OR NOT, HE HAD TO GET OUT OF THERE.

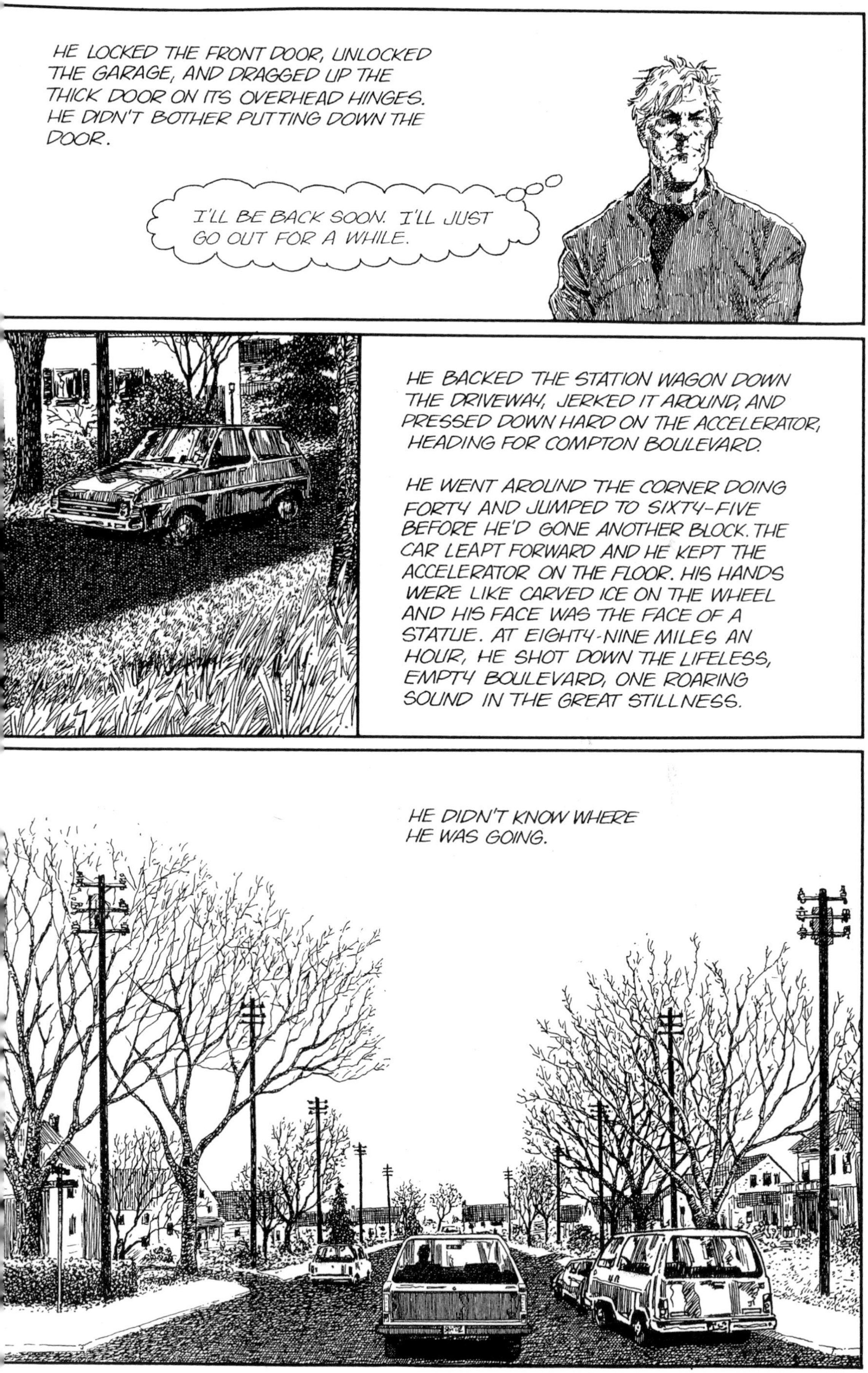
HE LOCKED THE FRONT DOOR, UNLOCKED THE GARAGE, AND DRAGGED UP THE THICK DOOR ON ITS OVERHEAD HINGES. HE DIDN'T BOTHER PUTTING DOWN THE DOOR.
I'LL BE BACK SOON. I'LL JUST GO OUT FOR A WHILE.
HE BACKED THE STATION WAGON DOWN THE DRIVEWAY, JERKED IT AROUND, AND PRESSED DOWN HARD ON THE ACCELERATOR, HEADING FOR COMPTON BOULEVARD.
HE WENT AROUND THE CORNER DOING FORTY AND JUMPED TO SIXTY-FIVE BEFORE HE'D GONE ANOTHER BLOCK. THE CAR LEAPT FORWARD AND HE KEPT THE ACCELERATOR ON THE FLOOR. HIS HANDS WERE LIKE CARVED ICE ON THE WHEEL AND HIS FACE WAS THE FACE OF A STATUE. AT EIGHTY-NINE MILES AN HOUR, HE SHOT DOWN THE LIFELESS, EMPTY BOULEVARD, ONE ROARING SOUND IN THE GREAT STILLNESS.
HE DIDN'T KNOW WHERE HE WAS GOING.

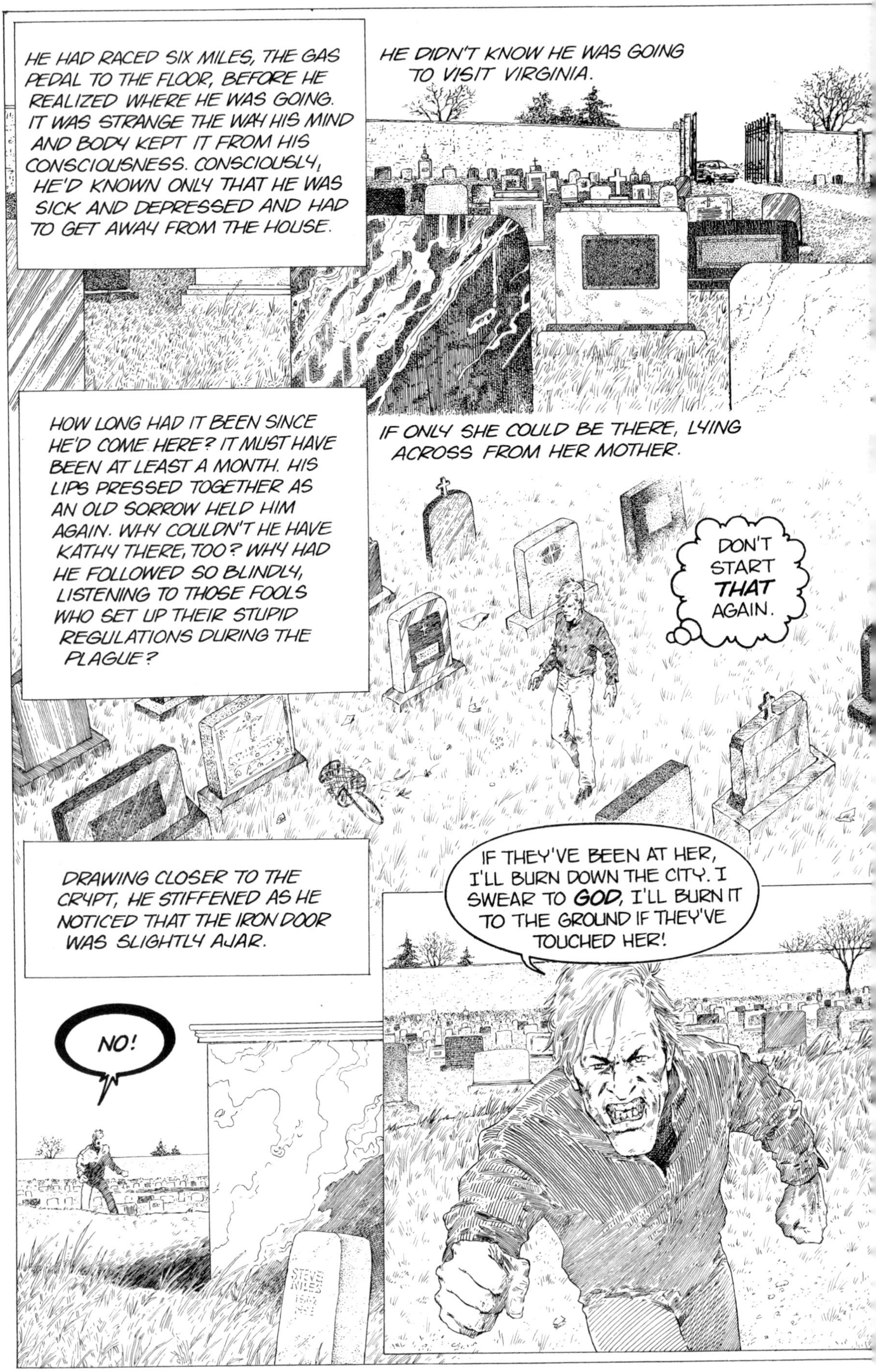

HE HAD RACED SIX MILES, THE GAS PEDAL TO THE FLOOR, BEFORE HE REALIZED WHERE HE WAS GOING. IT WAS STRANGE THE WAY HIS MIND AND BODY KEPT IT FROM HIS CONSCIOUSNESS. CONSCIOUSLY, HE'D KNOWN ONLY THAT HE WAS SICK AND DEPRESSED AND HAD TO GET AWAY FROM THE HOUSE.
HE DIDN'T KNOW HE WAS GOING TO VISIT VIRGINIA.
HOW LONG HAD IT BEEN SINCE HE'D COME HERE? IT MUST HAVE BEEN AT LEAST A MONTH. HIS LIPS PRESSED TOGETHER AS AN OLD SORROW HELD HIM AGAIN. WHY COULDN'T HE HAVE KATHY THERE, TOO? WHY HAD HE FOLLOWED SO BLINDLY, LISTENING TO THOSE FOOLS WHO SET UP THEIR STUPID REGULATIONS DURING THE PLAGUE?
IF ONLY SHE COULD BE THERE, LYING ACROSS FROM HER MOTHER.
DON'T START **THAT** AGAIN.
DRAWING CLOSER TO THE CRYPT, HE STIFFENED AS HE NOTICED THAT THE IRON DOOR WAS SLIGHTLY AJAR.
NO!
IF THEY'VE BEEN AT HER, I'LL BURN DOWN THE CITY. I SWEAR TO **GOD**, I'LL BURN IT TO THE GROUND IF THEY'VE TOUCHED HER!

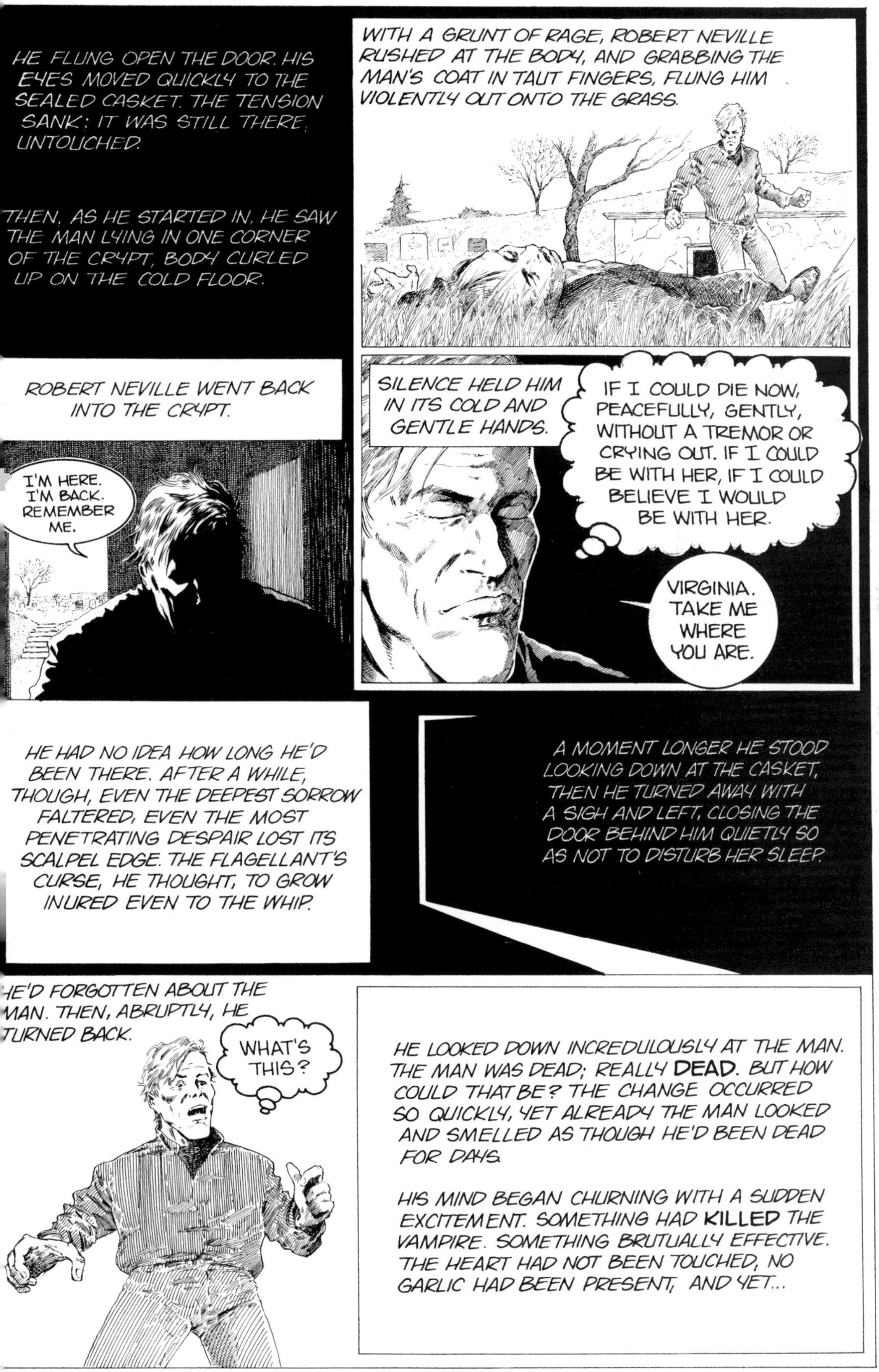
HE FLUNG OPEN THE DOOR. HIS EYES MOVED QUICKLY TO THE SEALED CASKET. THE TENSION SANK: IT WAS STILL THERE, UNTOUCHED.
THEN, AS HE STARTED IN, HE SAW THE MAN LYING IN ONE CORNER OF THE CRYPT, BODY CURLED UP ON THE COLD FLOOR.
WITH A GRUNT OF RAGE, ROBERT NEVILLE RUSHED AT THE BODY, AND GRABBING THE MAN'S COAT IN TAUT FINGERS, FLUNG HIM VIOLENTLY OUT ONTO THE GRASS.
ROBERT NEVILLE WENT BACK INTO THE CRYPT.
I'M HERE. I'M BACK. REMEMBER ME.
SILENCE HELD HIM IN ITS COLD AND GENTLE HANDS.
IF I COULD DIE NOW, PEACEFULLY, GENTLY, WITHOUT A TREMOR OR CRYING OUT. IF I COULD BE WITH HER, IF I COULD BELIEVE I WOULD BE WITH HER.
VIRGINIA. TAKE ME WHERE YOU ARE.
HE HAD NO IDEA HOW LONG HE'D BEEN THERE. AFTER A WHILE, THOUGH, EVEN THE DEEPEST SORROW FALTERED, EVEN THE MOST PENETRATING DESPAIR LOST ITS SCALPEL EDGE. THE FLAGELLANT'S CURSE, HE THOUGHT, TO GROW INURED EVEN TO THE WHIP.
A MOMENT LONGER HE STOOD LOOKING DOWN AT THE CASKET, THEN HE TURNED AWAY WITH A SIGH AND LEFT, CLOSING THE DOOR BEHIND HIM QUIETLY SO AS NOT TO DISTURB HER SLEEP.
HE'D FORGOTTEN ABOUT THE MAN. THEN, ABRUPTLY, HE TURNED BACK.
WHAT'S THIS?
HE LOOKED DOWN INCREDULOUSLY AT THE MAN. THE MAN WAS DEAD; REALLY DEAD. BUT HOW COULD THAT BE? THE CHANGE OCCURRED SO QUICKLY, YET ALREADY THE MAN LOOKED AND SMELLED AS THOUGH HE'D BEEN DEAD FOR DAYS.
HIS MIND BEGAN CHURNING WITH A SUDDEN EXCITEMENT. SOMETHING HAD KILLED THE VAMPIRE. SOMETHING BRUTUALLY EFFECTIVE. THE HEART HAD NOT BEEN TOUCHED, NO GARLIC HAD BEEN PRESENT, AND YET...

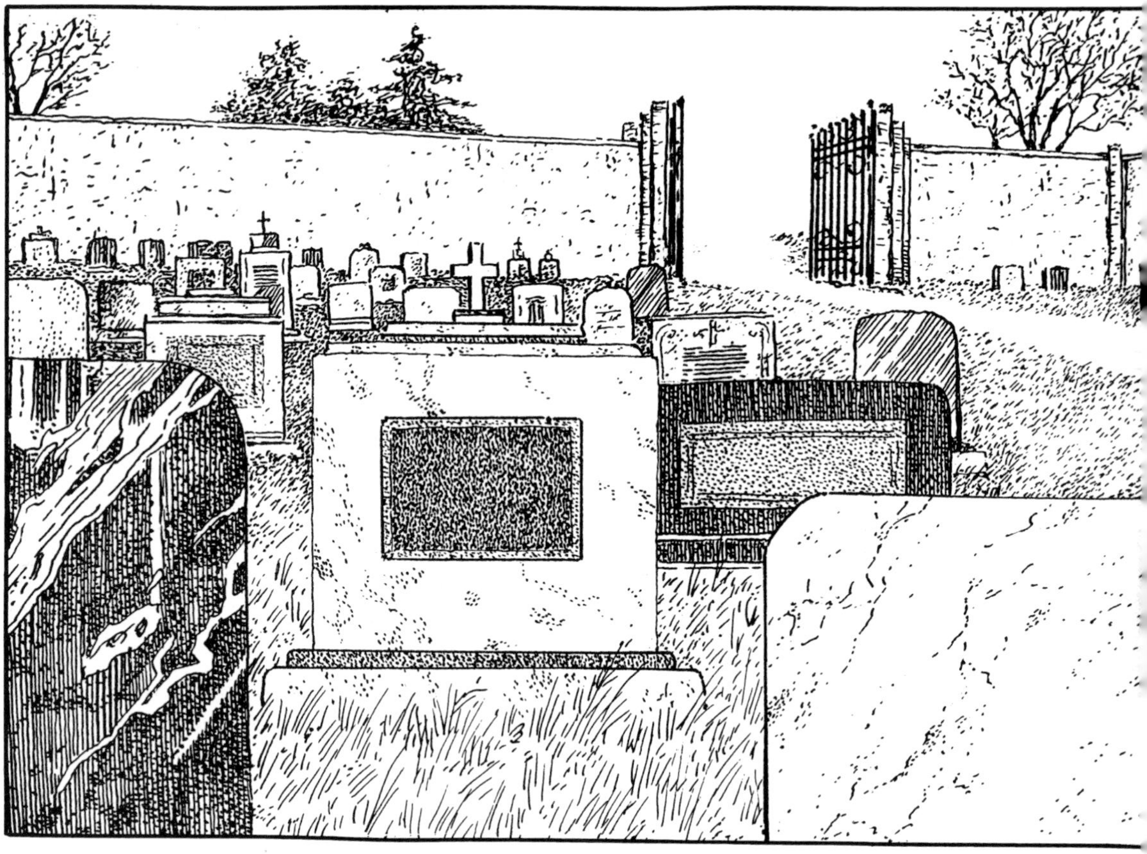

IT CAME, SEEMINGLY, WITHOUT EFFORT. OF COURSE — **THE DAYLIGHT!**

A BOLT OF SELF-ACCUSATION STRUCK HIM. TO KNOW FOR FIVE MONTHS THAT THEY REMAINED INDOORS BY DAY AND NEVER **ONCE** TO MAKE THE CONNECTION! HE CLOSED HIS EYES, APPALLED BY HIS OWN STUPIDITY.

THE RAYS OF THE **SUN**: THE INFRARED AND ULTRAVIOLET. IT HAD TO BE THEM. BUT **WHY**? DAMN IT, WHY DIDN'T HE KNOW ANYTHING ABOUT THE EFFECTS OF SUNLIGHT ON THE HUMAN SYSTEM?

ANOTHER THOUGHT: THAT MAN HAD BEEN ONE OF THE **TRUE VAMPIRES**: THE LIVING DEAD. WOULD SUNLIGHT HAVE THE SAME EFFECT ON ON THOSE WHO WERE STILL ALIVE?

THE FIRST EXCITEMENT HE'D FELT IN MONTHS MADE HIM BREAK INTO A RUN FOR THE STATION WAGON.

AS THE DOOR SLAMMED SHUT BESIDE HIM, HE WONDERED IF HE SHOULD HAVE TAKEN AWAY THE DEAD MAN. WOULD THE BODY ATTRACT OTHERS, WOULD THEY INVADE THE CRYPT? NO, THEY WOULDN'T GO NEAR THE CASKET ANYWAY; HE'D SEALED IT WITH GARLIC. BESIDES, THE MAN'S BLOOD WAS DEAD NOW, IT—— ?!

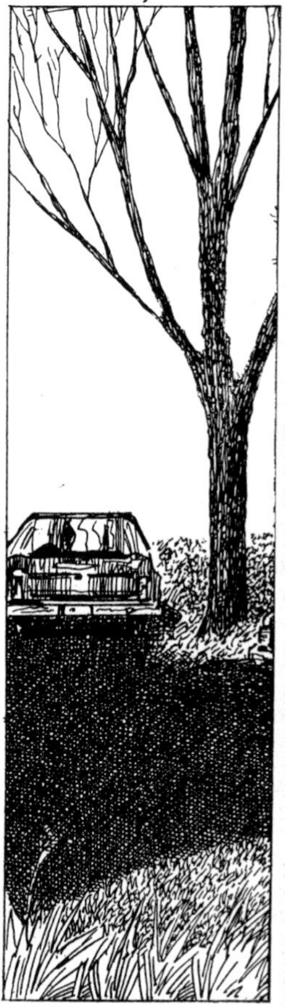

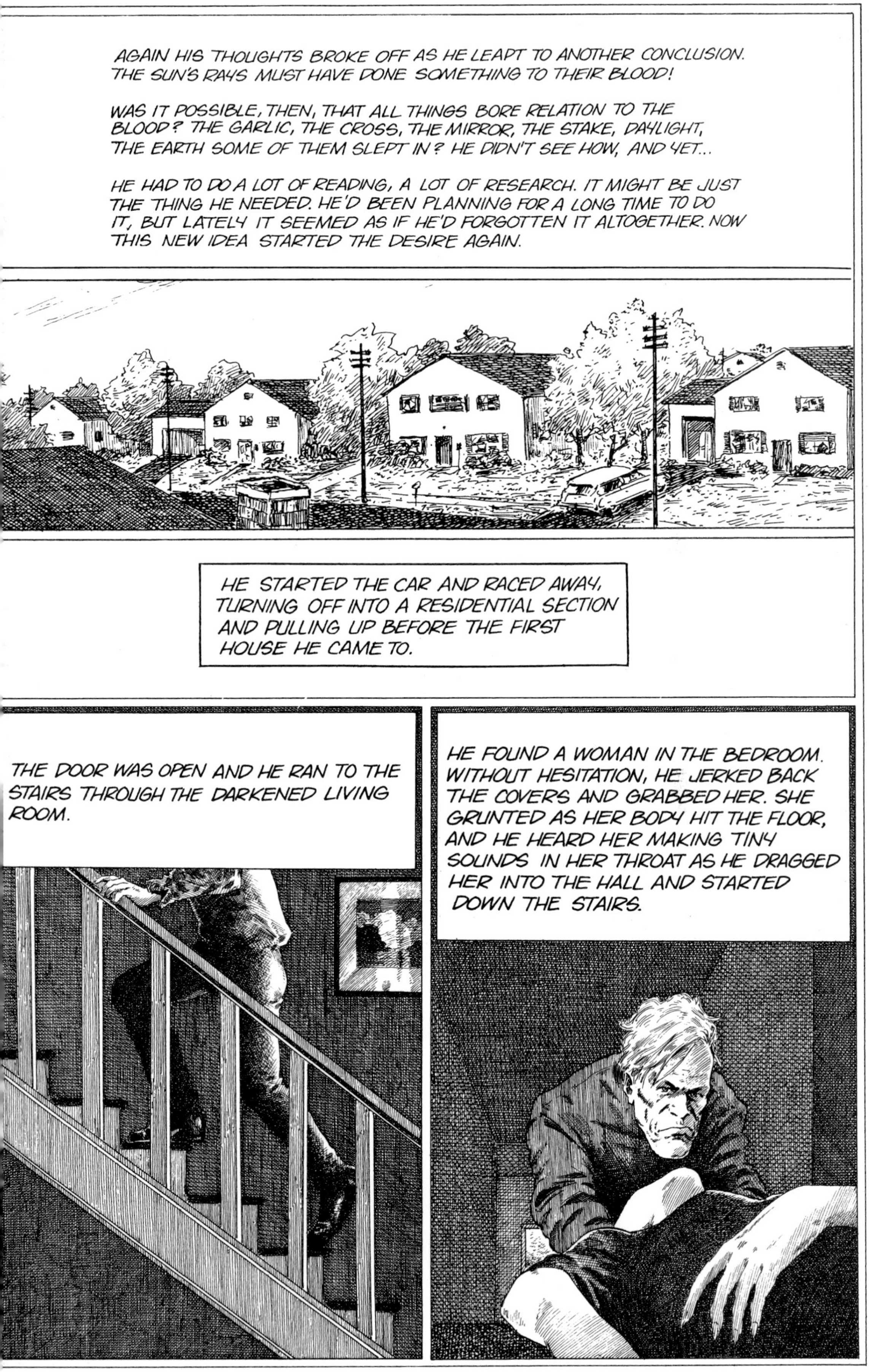
AGAIN HIS THOUGHTS BROKE OFF AS HE LEAPT TO ANOTHER CONCLUSION. THE SUN'S RAYS MUST HAVE DONE SOMETHING TO THEIR BLOOD!
WAS IT POSSIBLE, THEN, THAT ALL THINGS BORE RELATION TO THE BLOOD? THE GARLIC, THE CROSS, THE MIRROR, THE STAKE, DAYLIGHT, THE EARTH SOME OF THEM SLEPT IN? HE DIDN'T SEE HOW, AND YET...
HE HAD TO DO A LOT OF READING, A LOT OF RESEARCH. IT MIGHT BE JUST THE THING HE NEEDED. HE'D BEEN PLANNING FOR A LONG TIME TO DO IT, BUT LATELY IT SEEMED AS IF HE'D FORGOTTEN IT ALTOGETHER. NOW THIS NEW IDEA STARTED THE DESIRE AGAIN.
HE STARTED THE CAR AND RACED AWAY, TURNING OFF INTO A RESIDENTIAL SECTION AND PULLING UP BEFORE THE FIRST HOUSE HE CAME TO.
THE DOOR WAS OPEN AND HE RAN TO THE STAIRS THROUGH THE DARKENED LIVING ROOM.
HE FOUND A WOMAN IN THE BEDROOM. WITHOUT HESITATION, HE JERKED BACK THE COVERS AND GRABBED HER. SHE GRUNTED AS HER BODY HIT THE FLOOR, AND HE HEARD HER MAKING TINY SOUNDS IN HER THROAT AS HE DRAGGED HER INTO THE HALL AND STARTED DOWN THE STAIRS.

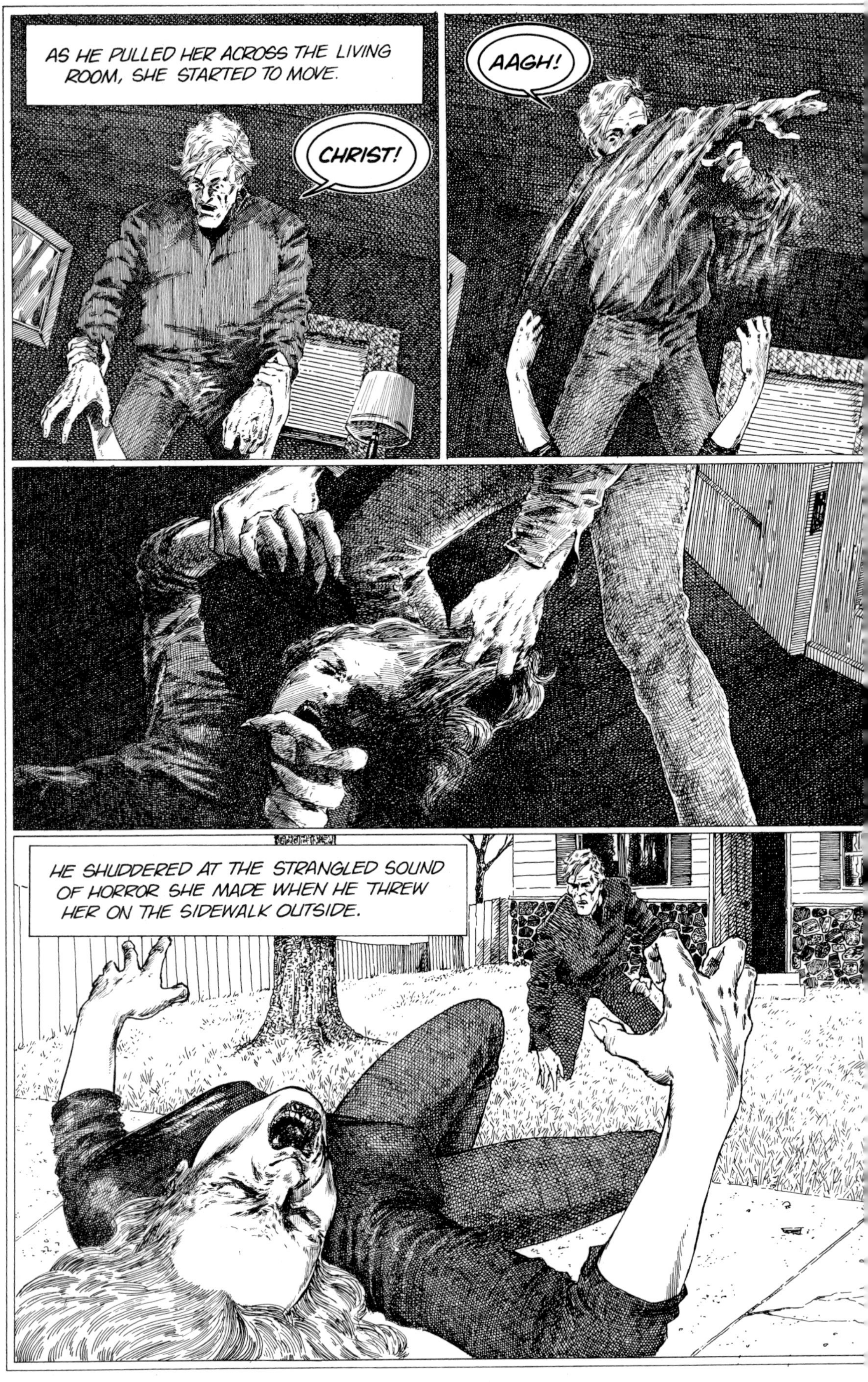
AS HE PULLED HER ACROSS THE LIVING ROOM, SHE STARTED TO MOVE.
CHRIST!
AAGH!
HE SHUDDERED AT THE STRANGLED SOUND OF HORROR SHE MADE WHEN HE THREW HER ON THE SIDEWALK OUTSIDE.

SHE LAY TWISTING HELPLESSLY, HANDS OPENING AND CLOSING, LIPS DRAWN BACK. ROBERT NEVILLE WATCHED TENSELY. HIS THROAT MOVED. IT WOULDN'T LAST, THIS FEELING OF CALLOUS BRUTALITY.

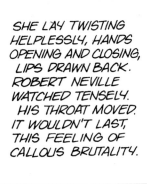

ALL RIGHT, ALL RIGHT, SHE'S SUFFERING, BUT SHE'S ONE OF *THEM* AND SHE'D KILL ME GLADLY IF SHE GOT THE CHANCE. YOU'VE GOT TO LOOK AT IT THAT WAY, IT'S THE ONLY WAY.

IN A FEW MINUTES SHE STOPPED MOVING, STOPPED MUTTERING, AND HER HANDS UNCURLED SLOWLY LIKE WHITE BLOSSOMS ON THE CEMENT. ROBERT NEVILLE CROUCHED DOWN AND FELT FOR HER HEARTBEAT. THERE WAS NONE. ALREADY HER FLESH WAS GROWING COLD.

IT'S TRUE, THEN. I DON'T NEED STAKES. AFTER ALL THIS TIME, I'VE FINALLY FOUND A BETTER METHOD. BUT HOW CAN I BE SURE SHE'S REALLY DEAD? HOW CAN I BE SURE UNTIL SUNSET?

THE THOUGHT FILLED HIM WITH A NEW, MORE RESTLESS ANGER. WHY DID EACH QUESTION **BLIGHT** THE ANSWERS BEFORE IT?

HE THOUGHT ABOUT IT AS HE SAT DRINKING A CAN OF TOMATO JUICE HE'D GOTTEN FROM THE MARKET BEHIND WHICH HE WAS NOW PARKED.

HOW WAS HE GOING TO BE SURE? HE COULDN'T VERY WELL STAY WITH HER UNTIL SUNSET CAME.

TAKE HER **HOME** WITH YOU, FOOL. A SHUDDER OF IRRITATION. HE WAS MISSING ALL THE OBVIOUS ANSWERS TODAY. NOW HE'D HAVE TO GO ALL THE WAY BACK AND FIND HER, AND HE WASN'T EVEN SURE WHERE THE HOUSE WAS.

HE STARTED THE MOTOR AND PULLED AWAY FROM THE PARKING LOT, GLANCING DOWN AT HIS WATCH.

THREE O'CLOCK. PLENTY OF TIME TO GET BACK BEFORE THEY COME OUT.

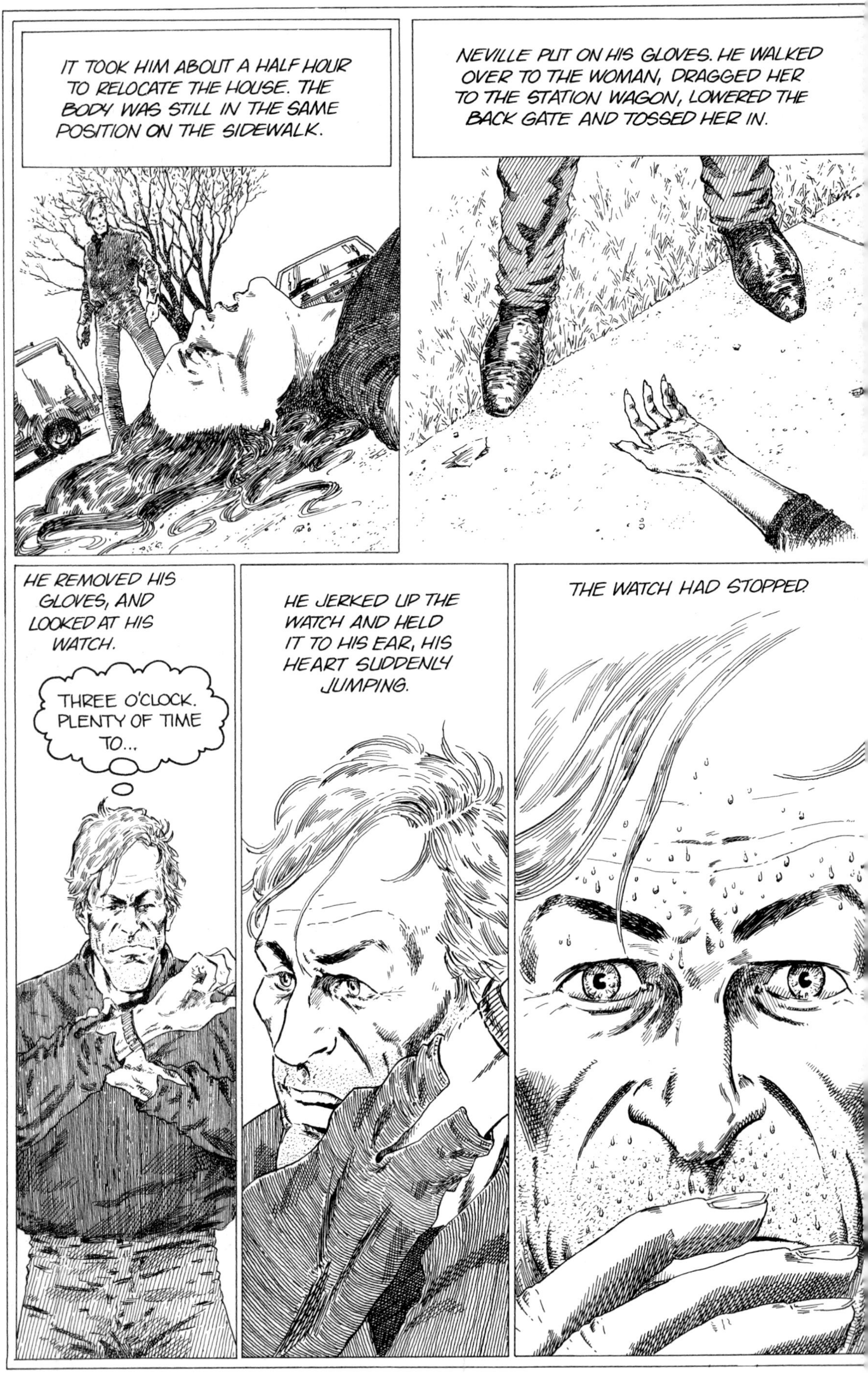
IT TOOK HIM ABOUT A HALF HOUR TO RELOCATE THE HOUSE. THE BODY WAS STILL IN THE SAME POSITION ON THE SIDEWALK.
NEVILLE PUT ON HIS GLOVES. HE WALKED OVER TO THE WOMAN, DRAGGED HER TO THE STATION WAGON, LOWERED THE BACK GATE AND TOSSED HER IN.
HE REMOVED HIS GLOVES, AND LOOKED AT HIS WATCH.
THREE O'CLOCK. PLENTY OF TIME TO...
HE JERKED UP THE WATCH AND HELD IT TO HIS EAR, HIS HEART SUDDENLY JUMPING.
THE WATCH HAD STOPPED.

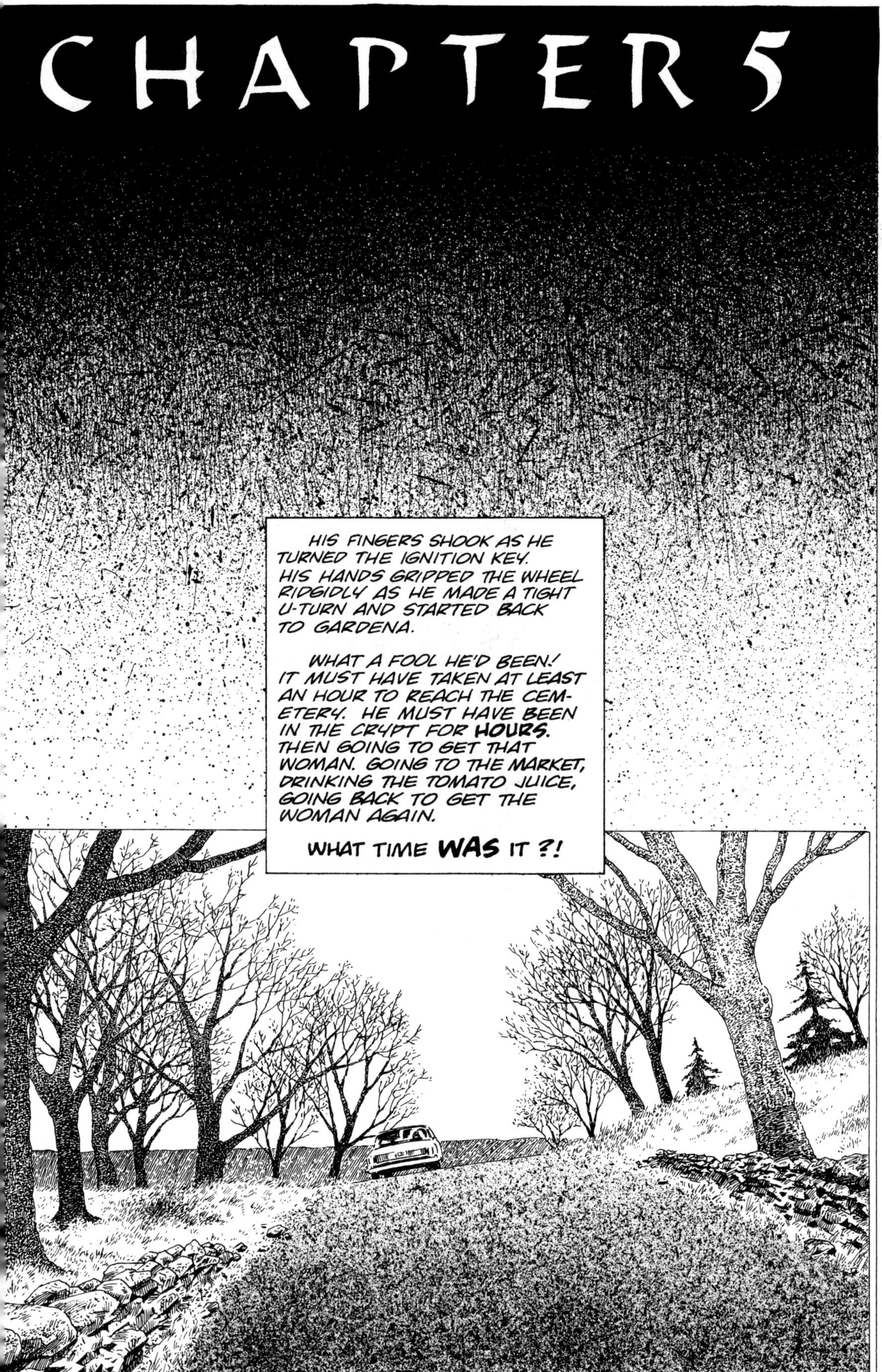
CHAPTER 5
HIS FINGERS SHOOK AS HE TURNED THE IGNITION KEY. HIS HANDS GRIPPED THE WHEEL RIDGIDLY AS HE MADE A TIGHT U-TURN AND STARTED BACK TO GARDENA.
WHAT A FOOL HE'D BEEN! IT MUST HAVE TAKEN AT LEAST AN HOUR TO REACH THE CEMETERY. HE MUST HAVE BEEN IN THE CRYPT FOR HOURS. THEN GOING TO GET THAT WOMAN. GOING TO THE MARKET, DRINKING THE TOMATO JUICE, GOING BACK TO GET THE WOMAN AGAIN.
WHAT TIME WAS IT ?!

FOOL! COLD FEAR POURED THROUGH HIS VEINS AT THE THOUGHT OF THEM ALL WAITING FOR HIM AT HIS HOUSE. OH, MY GOD, AND HE'D LEFT THE GARAGE DOOR OPEN! THE GASOLINE, THE EQUIPMENT-- **THE GENERATOR!**

A GROAN CUT ITSELF OFF IN HIS THROAT AS HE JAMMED THE GAS PEDAL TO THE FLOOR AND THE SMALL STATION WAGON LEAPED AHEAD, THE SPEEDOMETER NEEDLE FLUTTERING, THEN MOVING STEADILY PAST THE SIXTY-FIVE MARK, THE SEVENTY, THE SEVENTY-FIVE. WHAT IF THEY WERE ALREADY WAITING FOR HIM? HOW COULD HE POSSIBLY GET IN THE HOUSE?

HE FORCED HIMSELF TO BE CALM. HE MUSTN'T GO TO PIECES NOW; HE HAD TO KEEP HIMSELF IN CHECK. HE'D GET IN. DON'T WORRY, YOU'LL GET INSIDE, HE TOLD HIMSELF. BUT HE DIDN'T SEE HOW.

ONE HAND RAN NERVOUSLY THROUGH HIS HAIR. THIS IS FINE, FINE, COMMENTED HIS MIND. YOU GO TO ALL THAT TROUBLE TO PRESERVE YOUR EXISTENCE, AND THEN ONE DAY YOU JUST DON'T COME BACK IN TIME. **SHUT UP!** HIS MIND SNAPPED BACK AT ITSELF. BUT HE COULD HAVE KILLED HIMSELF FOR FORGETTING TO WIND HIS WATCH THE NIGHT BEFORE. DON'T BOTHER KILLING YOURSELF, HIS MIND REFLECTED, THEY'LL BE GLAD TO DO IT FOR YOU. SUDDENLY, HE REALIZED HE WAS ALMOST WEAK FROM HUNGER. THE SMALL AMOUNT OF CANNED MEAT HE'D EATEN WITH THE TOMATO JUICE HAD DONE NOTHING TO ALLEVIATE HIS HUNGER.

THE SILENT STREETS FLEW PAST AND HE KEPT LOOKING FROM SIDE TO SIDE TO SEE IF ANY OF THEM WERE APPEARING IN THE DOORWAYS. IT SEEMED AS IF IT WERE ALREADY GETTING DARK, BUT THAT COULD HAVE BEEN IMAGINATION. IT COULDN'T BE **THAT** LATE-- **IT COULDN'T BE.**

HE'D JUST GONE HURTLING PAST THE CORNER OF WESTERN AND COMPTON WHEN HE SAW THE MAN COME RUNNING OUT OF A BUILDING AND SHOUT AT HIM. HIS HEART WAS CONTRACTED IN AN ICY HAND AS THE MAN'S CRY FLUTTERED IN THE AIR BEHIND THE CAR.

HE COULDN'T GET ANY MORE SPEED OUT OF THE STATION WAGON. AND NOW HIS MIND BEGAN TORTURING HIM WITH VISIONS OF ONE OF THE TIRES GOING, THE STATION WAGON VEERING, LEAPING THE CURB AND CRASHING INTO A HOUSE. HIS LIPS STARTED TO SHAKE AND HE JAMMED THEM TOGETHER TO STOP THEM. HIS HANDS ON THE WHEEL FELT NUMB.

HE HAD TO SLOW DOWN AT THE CORNER OF CIMARRON. OUT OF THE CORNER OF AN EYE, HE SAW A MAN COME RUSHING OUT OF A HOUSE AND START CHASING THE CAR.

THEN, AS HE TURNED THE CORNER WITH A SCREECH OF CLINGING TIRES, HE COULDN'T HOLD BACK THE GASP.

THEY WERE ALL IN FRONT OF HIS HOUSE-- **WAITING.**

A SOUND OF HELPLESS TERROR FILLED H'S THROAT. HE DIDN'T WANT TO [D]E. HE MIGHT HAVE THOUGHT [AB]OUT IT, EVEN CONTEM[PL]ATED IT. BUT HE DIDN'T [W]ANT TO DIE. NOT LIKE THIS.

[ ]NOW HE SAW THEM ALL [TU]RN THEIR WHITE FACES AT [TH]E SOUND OF THE MOTOR. [S]OME MORE OF THEM RUNNING [OU]T OF THE OPEN GARAGE [A]ND HIS TEETH GROUND [TO]GETHER IN IMPOTENT FURY. [W]HAT A STUPID, BRAINLESS [W]AY TO DIE!

NOW HE SAW THEM START RUNNING STRAIGHT TOWARD THE [S]TATION WAGON, A LINE OF THEM ACROSS THE STREET. AND SUDDENLY, [H]E KNEW HE COULDN'T STOP. HE PRESSED DOWN ON THE ACCELER-[A]TOR, AND IN A MOMENT, THE CAR WENT PLOWING THROUGH THEM, [K]NOCKING THREE OF THEM ASIDE LIKE TENPINS. HE FELT THE CAR [FR]AME JOLT AS IT STRUCK THE BODIES. THEIR SCREAMING WHITE FACES [W]ENT FLASHING BY HIS WINDOW, THEIR CRIES CHILLING HIS BLOOD.

NEVILLE!

HE SAW IN THE REARVIEW [M]IRROR THAT THEY WERE [A]LL PURSUING HIM. A PLAN [C]AUGHT HOLD IN HIS MIND. [I]MPULSIVELY, HE SLOWED [D]OWN, EVEN BRAKING, [F]ALLING TO THIRTY, THEN [T]WENTY MILES AN HOUR.

HE LOOKED BACK AND [S]AW THEM GAINING, SAW [T]HE FACES APPROACHING, [T]HEIR DARK EYES FAS-[T]ENED TO THE CAR, [T]O HIM.

SUDDENLY, HE TWITCHED [W]ITH SHOCK AS A [S]NARL SOUNDED NEARBY, [A]ND JERKING HIS HEAD [A]ROUND, HE SAW THE [C]RAZED FACE OF BEN [C]ORTMAN BESIDE [T]HE CAR.

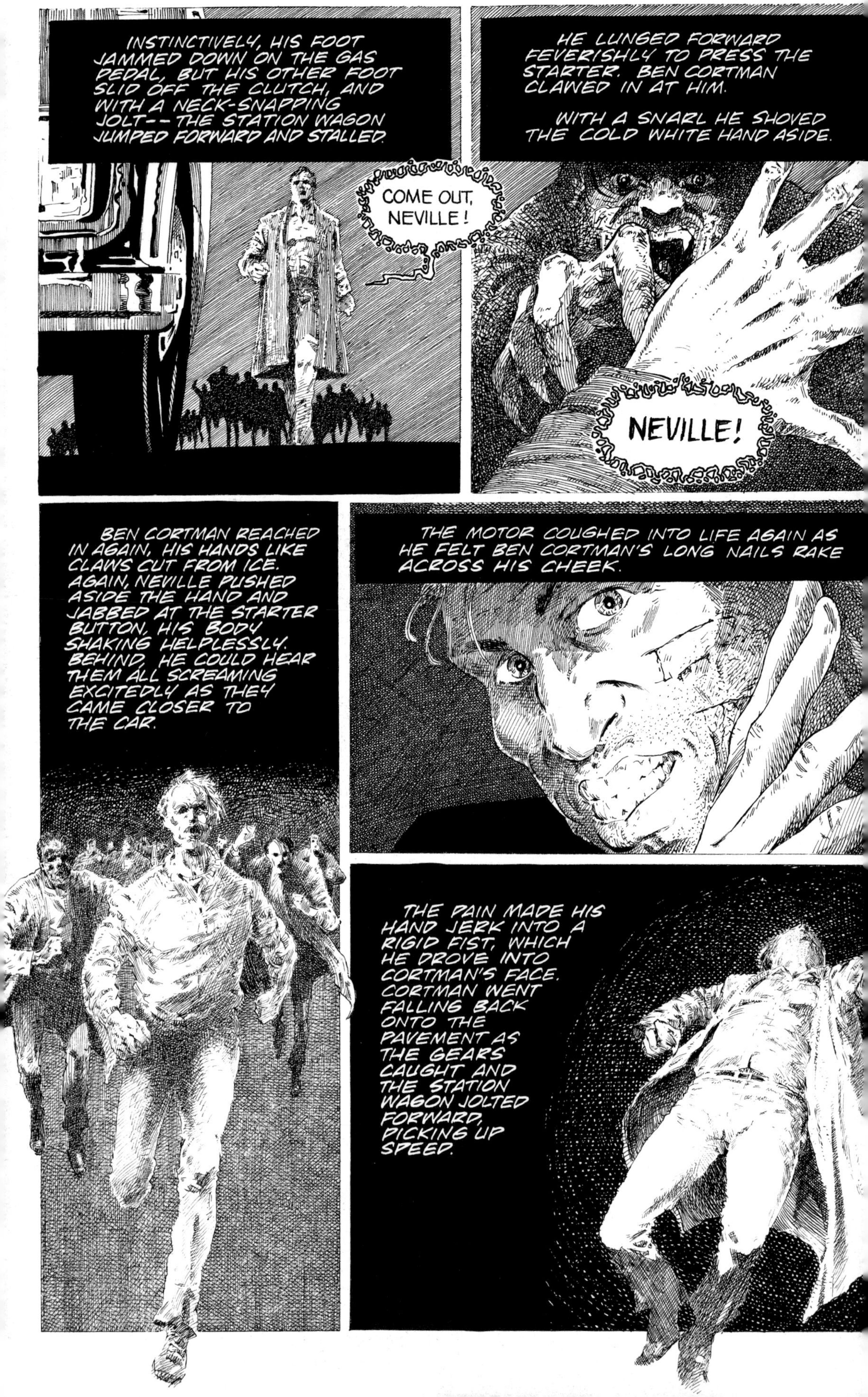
INSTINCTIVELY, HIS FOOT JAMMED DOWN ON THE GAS PEDAL, BUT HIS OTHER FOOT SLID OFF THE CLUTCH, AND WITH A NECK-SNAPPING JOLT-- THE STATION WAGON JUMPED FORWARD AND STALLED.
COME OUT, NEVILLE!
HE LUNGED FORWARD FEVERISHLY TO PRESS THE STARTER. BEN CORTMAN CLAWED IN AT HIM.
WITH A SNARL HE SHOVED THE COLD WHITE HAND ASIDE.
NEVILLE!
BEN CORTMAN REACHED IN AGAIN, HIS HANDS LIKE CLAWS CUT FROM ICE. AGAIN, NEVILLE PUSHED ASIDE THE HAND AND JABBED AT THE STARTER BUTTON, HIS BODY SHAKING HELPLESSLY. BEHIND, HE COULD HEAR THEM ALL SCREAMING EXCITEDLY AS THEY CAME CLOSER TO THE CAR.
THE MOTOR COUGHED INTO LIFE AGAIN AS HE FELT BEN CORTMAN'S LONG NAILS RAKE ACROSS HIS CHEEK.
THE PAIN MADE HIS HAND JERK INTO A RIGID FIST, WHICH HE DROVE INTO CORTMAN'S FACE. CORTMAN WENT FALLING BACK ONTO THE PAVEMENT AS THE GEARS CAUGHT AND THE STATION WAGON JOLTED FORWARD, PICKING UP SPEED.

ONE OF THE OTHERS CAUGHT UP AND LEAPED AT THE REAR OF THE CAR. FOR A MINUTE HE HELD ON, AND ROBERT NEVILLE COULD SEE HIS ASHEN FACE GLARING INSANELY THROUGH THE BACK WINDOW. THEN HE JERKED THE CAR OVER TOWARD THE CURB, SWERVED SHARPLY, AND SHOOK THE MAN OFF.

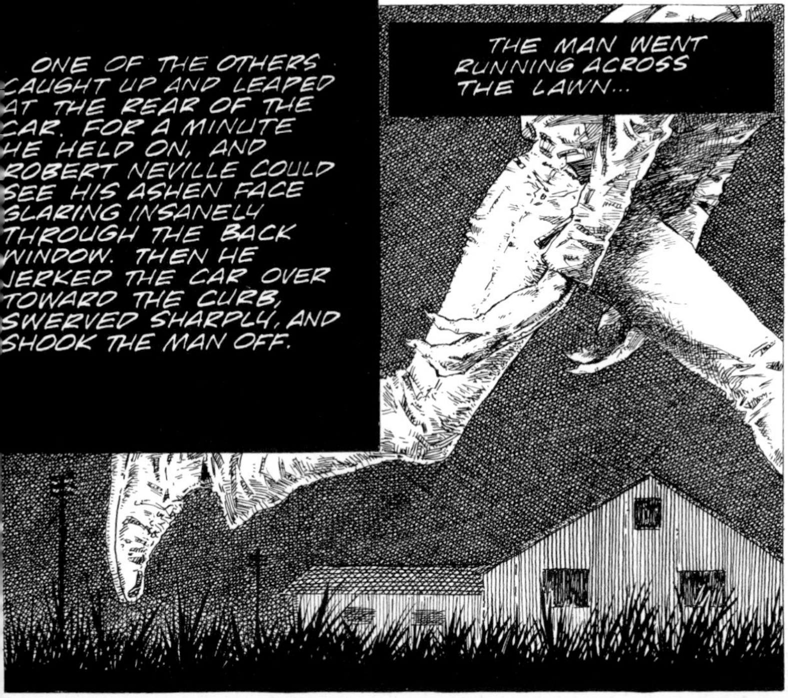
THE MAN WENT RUNNING ACROSS THE LAWN...

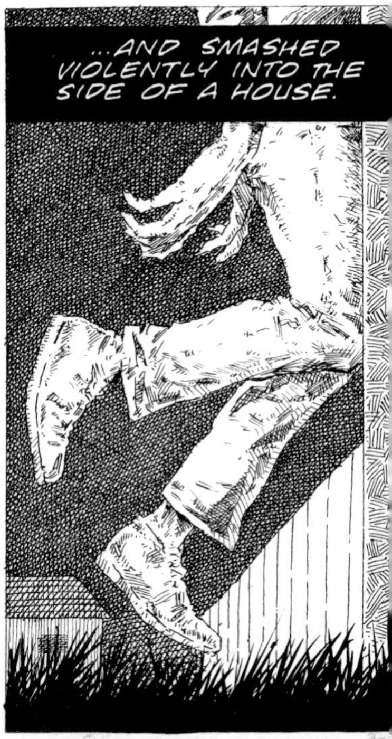
...AND SMASHED VIOLENTLY INTO THE SIDE OF A HOUSE.

ROBERT NEVILLE'S HEART WAS POUNDING SO HEAVILY NOW IT SEEMED AS IF IT WOULD DRIVE THROUGH HIS CHEST WALLS. BREATH SHUDDERED IN HIM AND HIS FLESH FELT NUMB AND COLD. HE COULD FEEL THE TRICKLE OF BLOOD ON HIS CHEEK, BUT NO PAIN. HASTILY, HE WIPED IT OFF WITH ONE SHAKING HAND.

NOW HE SPUN THE STATION WAGON AROUND THE CORNER, TURNING RIGHT. HE KEPT LOOKING AT THE REARVIEW MIRROR, THEN LOOKING AHEAD. HE WENT THE SHORT BLOCK TO HAAS STREET AND TURNED RIGHT AGAIN. WHAT IF THEY CUT THROUGH THE YARDS AND BLOCKED HIS WAY?

HE SLOWED DOWN A LITTLE UNTIL THEY CAME SWARMING AROUND THE CORNER LIKE A PACK OF WOLVES. THEN HE PRESSED DOWN ON THE ACCELERATOR. HE'D HAVE TO TAKE A CHANCE THAT THEY WERE ALL FOLLOWING HIM. WOULD SOME OF THEM GUESS WHAT HE WAS TRYING?

HE SHOVED DOWN THE GAS PEDAL ALL THE WAY AND THE STATION WAGON JUMPED FORWARD, RACING UP THE BLOCK. HE WHEELED IT AROUND THE CORNER AT FIFTY MILES AN HOUR, GUNNED UP THE SHORT BLOCK TO CIMMARON, AND TURNED RIGHT AGAIN.

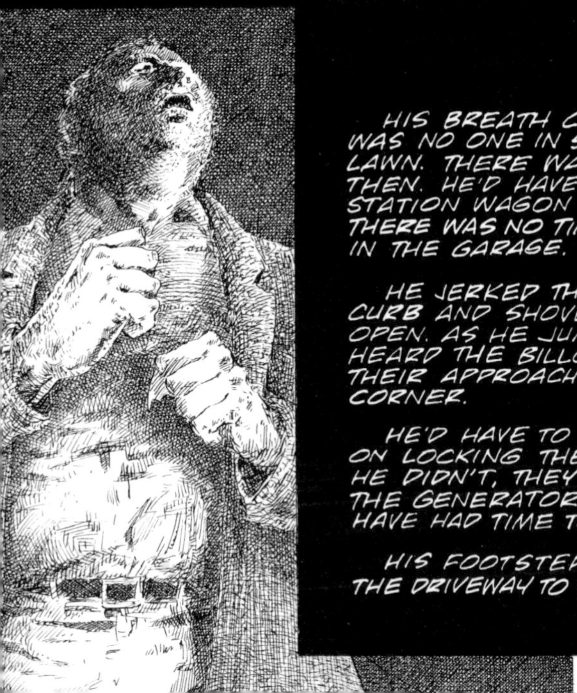

HIS BREATH CAUGHT. THERE WAS NO ONE IN SIGHT ON HIS LAWN. THERE WAS STILL A CHANCE, THEN. HE'D HAVE TO LET THE STATION WAGON GO, THOUGH; THERE WAS NO TIME TO PUT IT IN THE GARAGE.

HE JERKED THE CAR TO THE CURB AND SHOVED THE DOOR OPEN. AS HE JUMPED OUT HE HEARD THE BILLOWING CRY OF THEIR APPROACH AROUND THE CORNER.

HE'D HAVE TO TAKE A CHANCE ON LOCKING THE GARAGE. IF HE DIDN'T, THEY MIGHT DESTROY THE GENERATOR; THEY COULDN'T HAVE HAD TIME TO DO IT ALREADY.

HIS FOOTSTEPS POUNDED UP THE DRIVEWAY TO THE GARAGE.

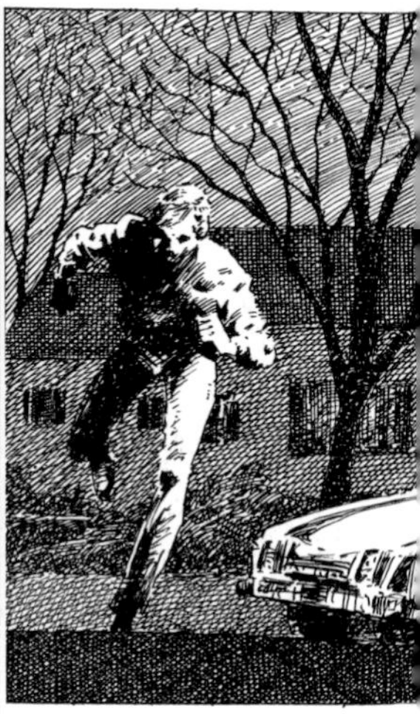

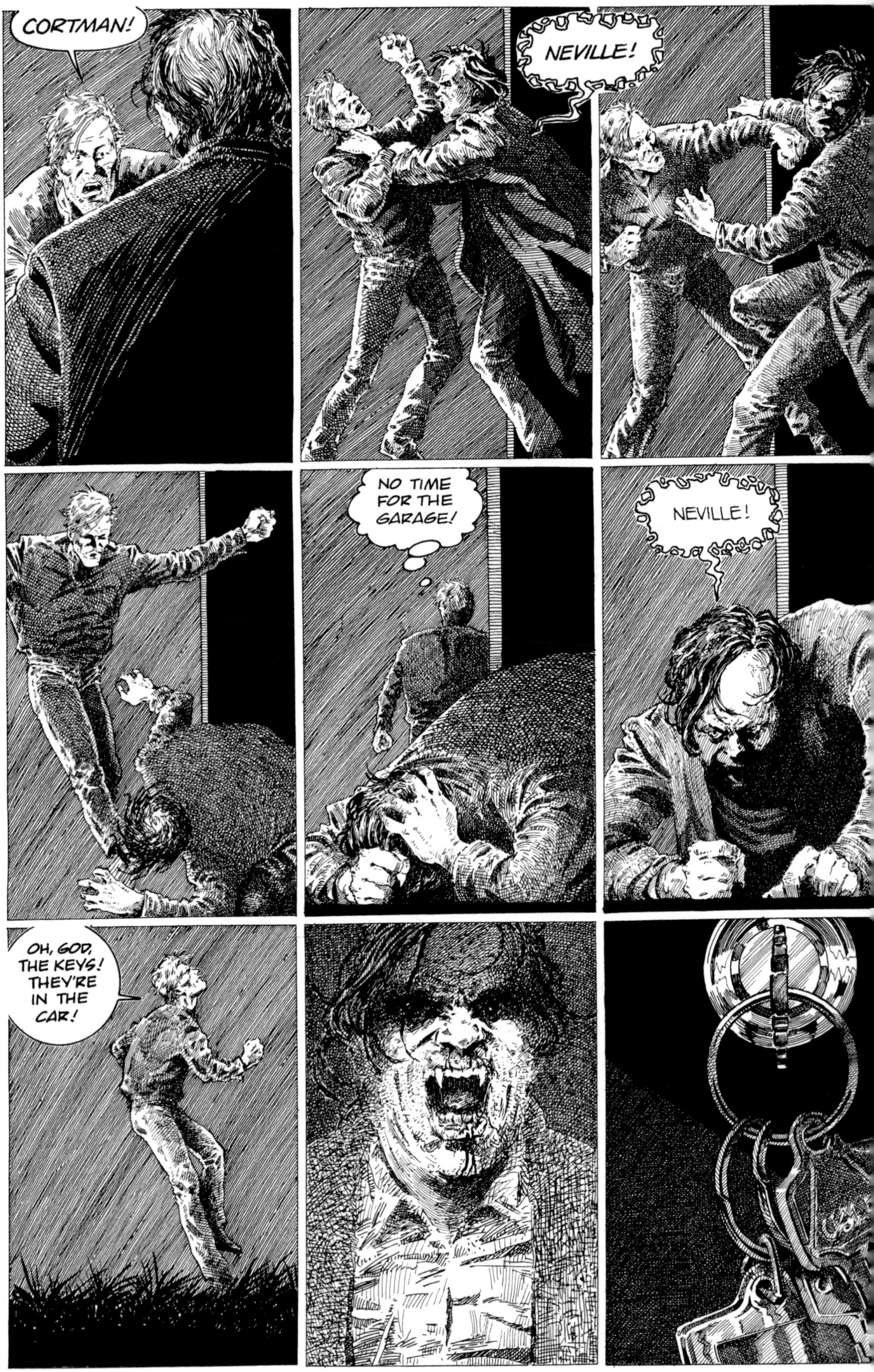
CORTMAN!
NEVILLE!
NO TIME FOR THE GARAGE!
NEVILLE!
OH, GOD, THE KEYS! THEY'RE IN THE CAR!

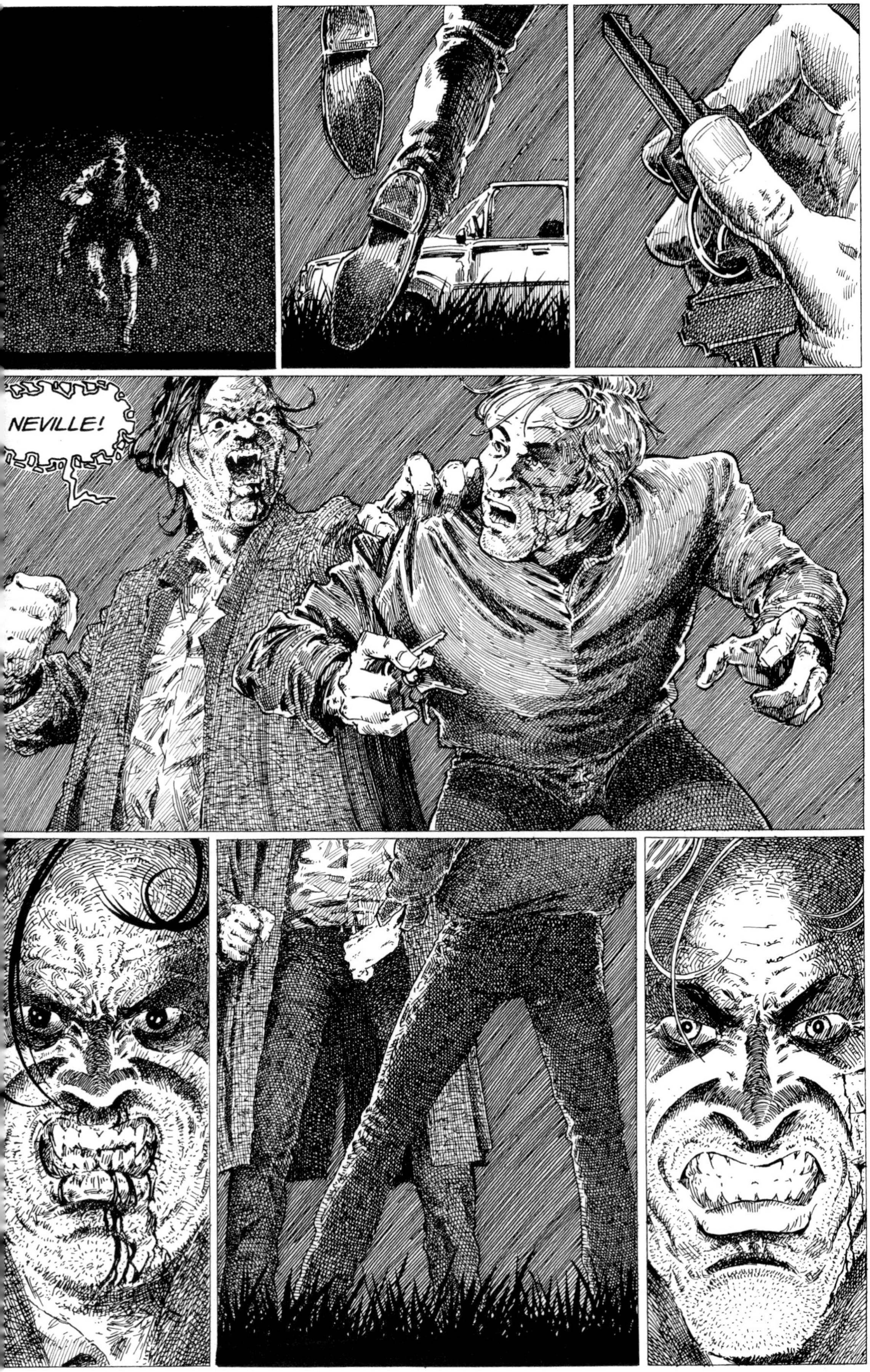
NEVILLE!

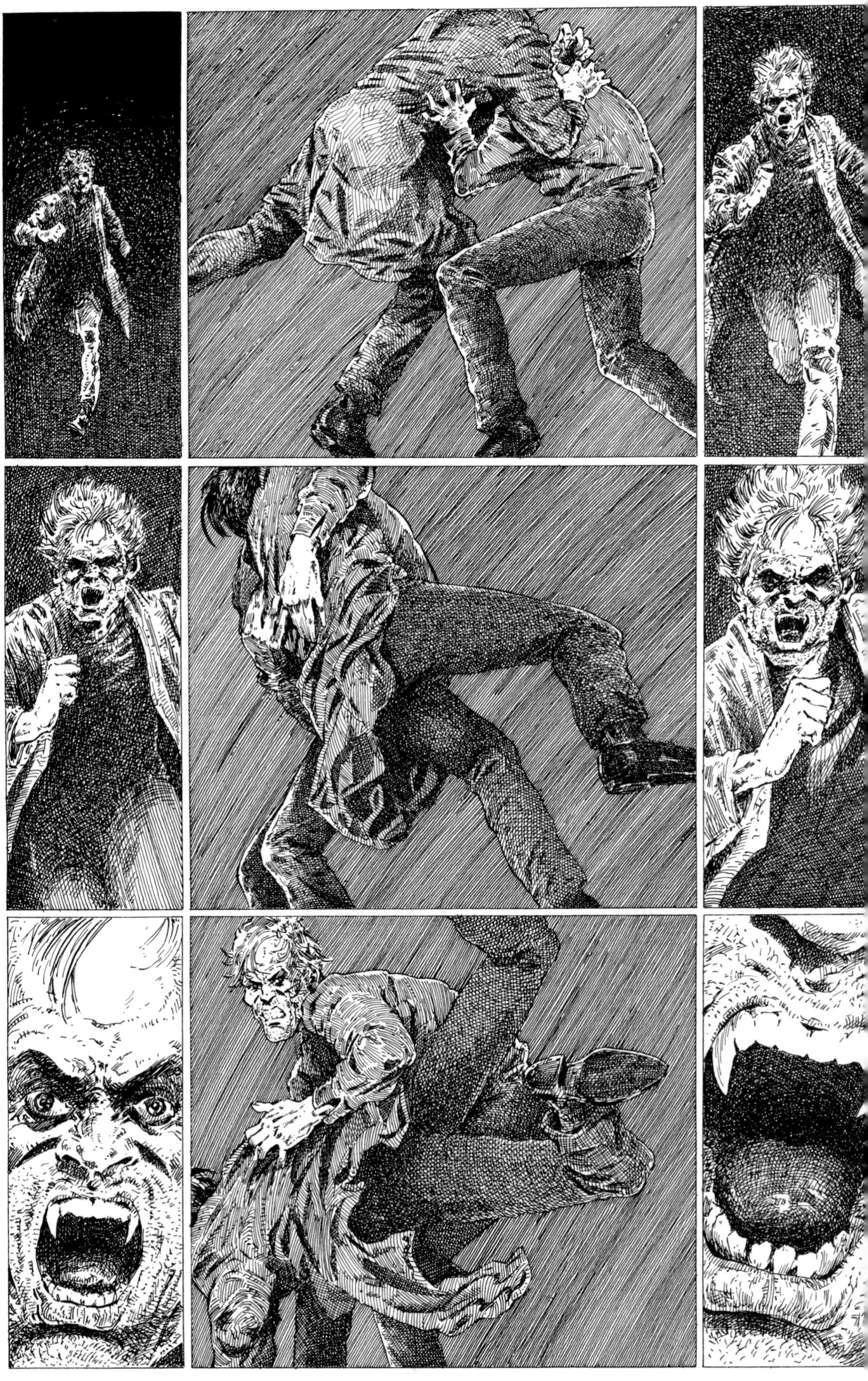

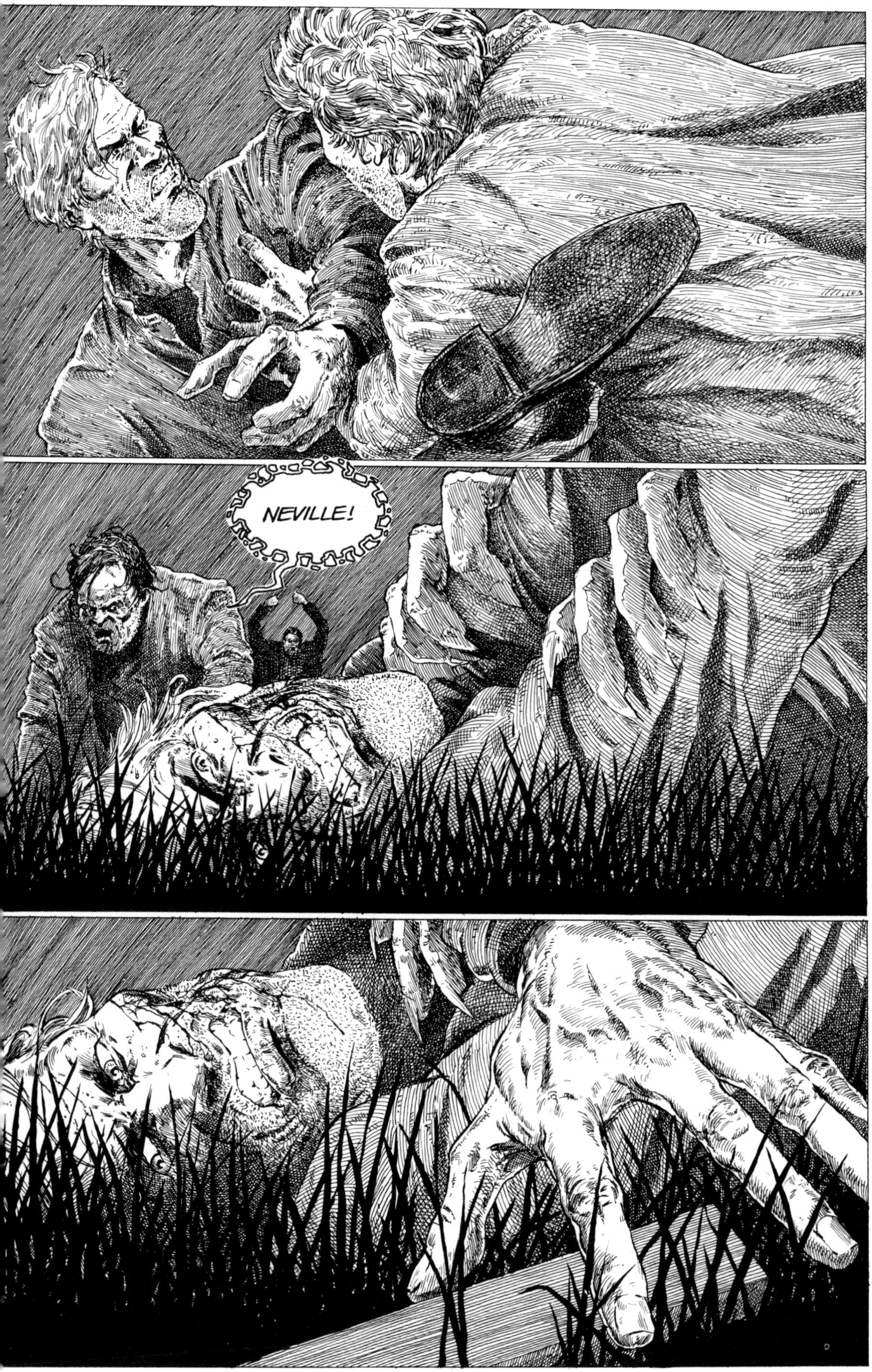
NEVILLE!

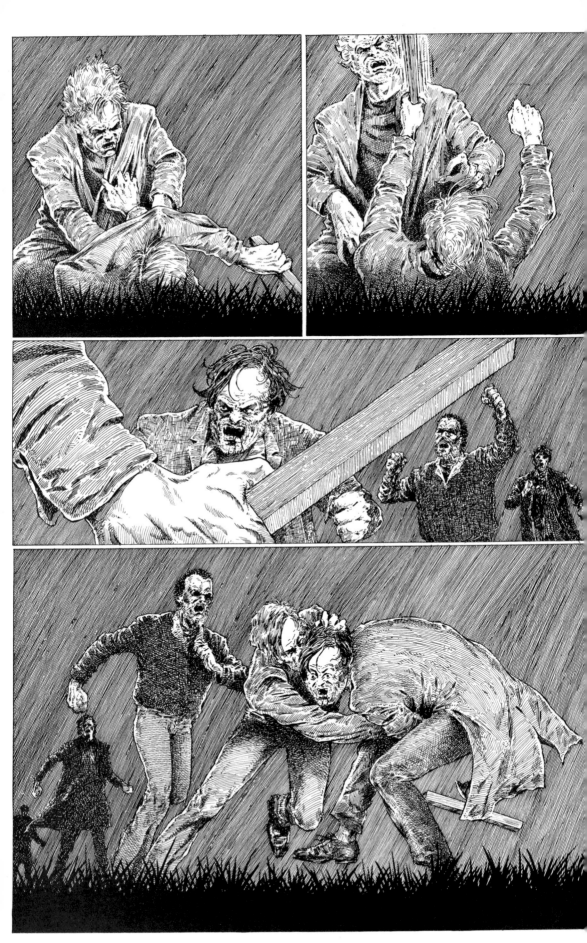

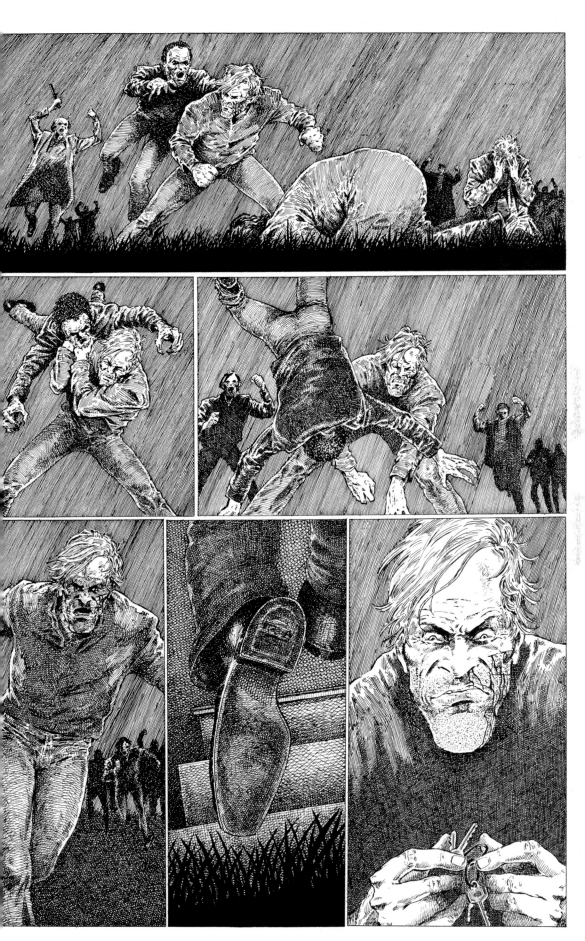

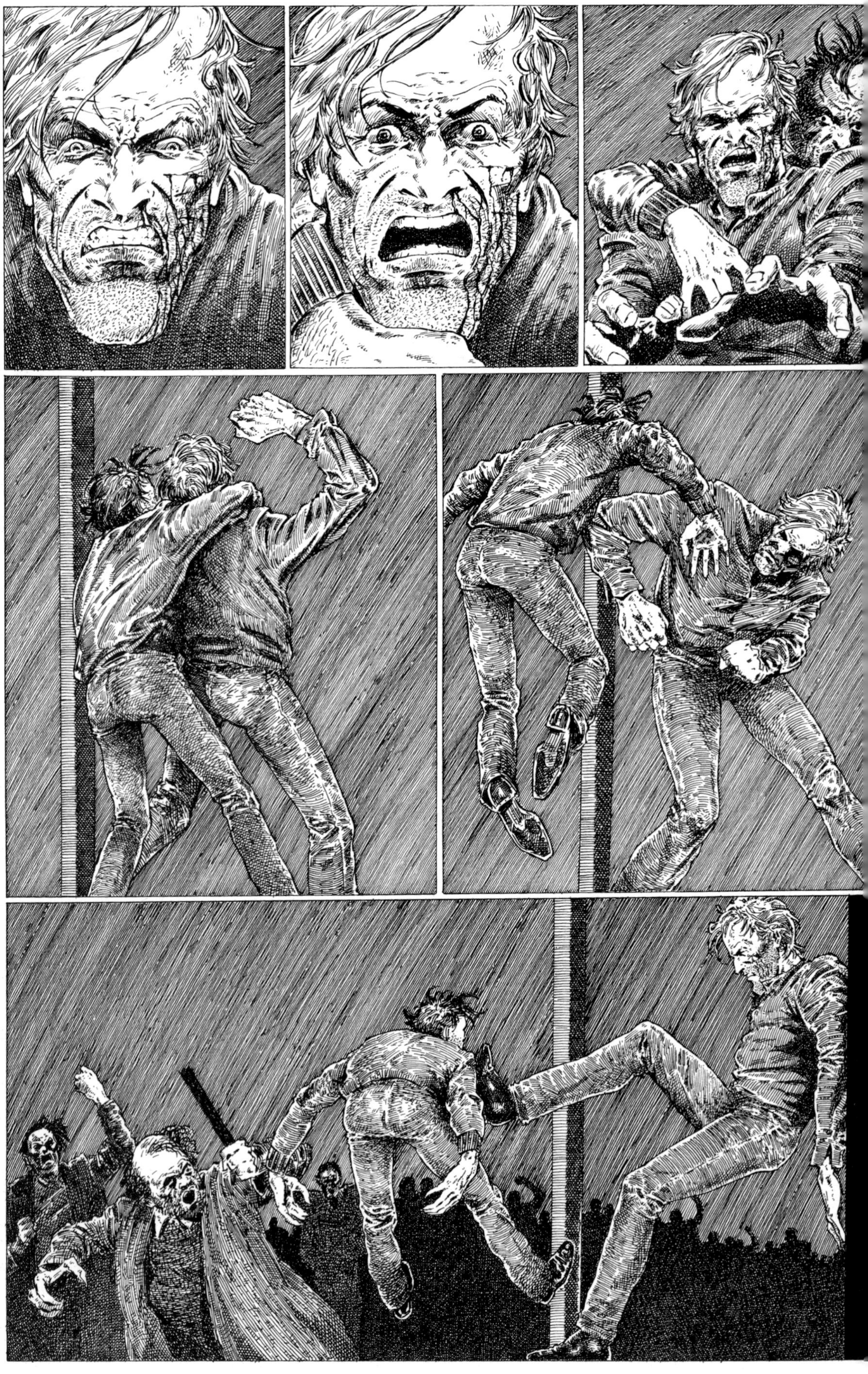

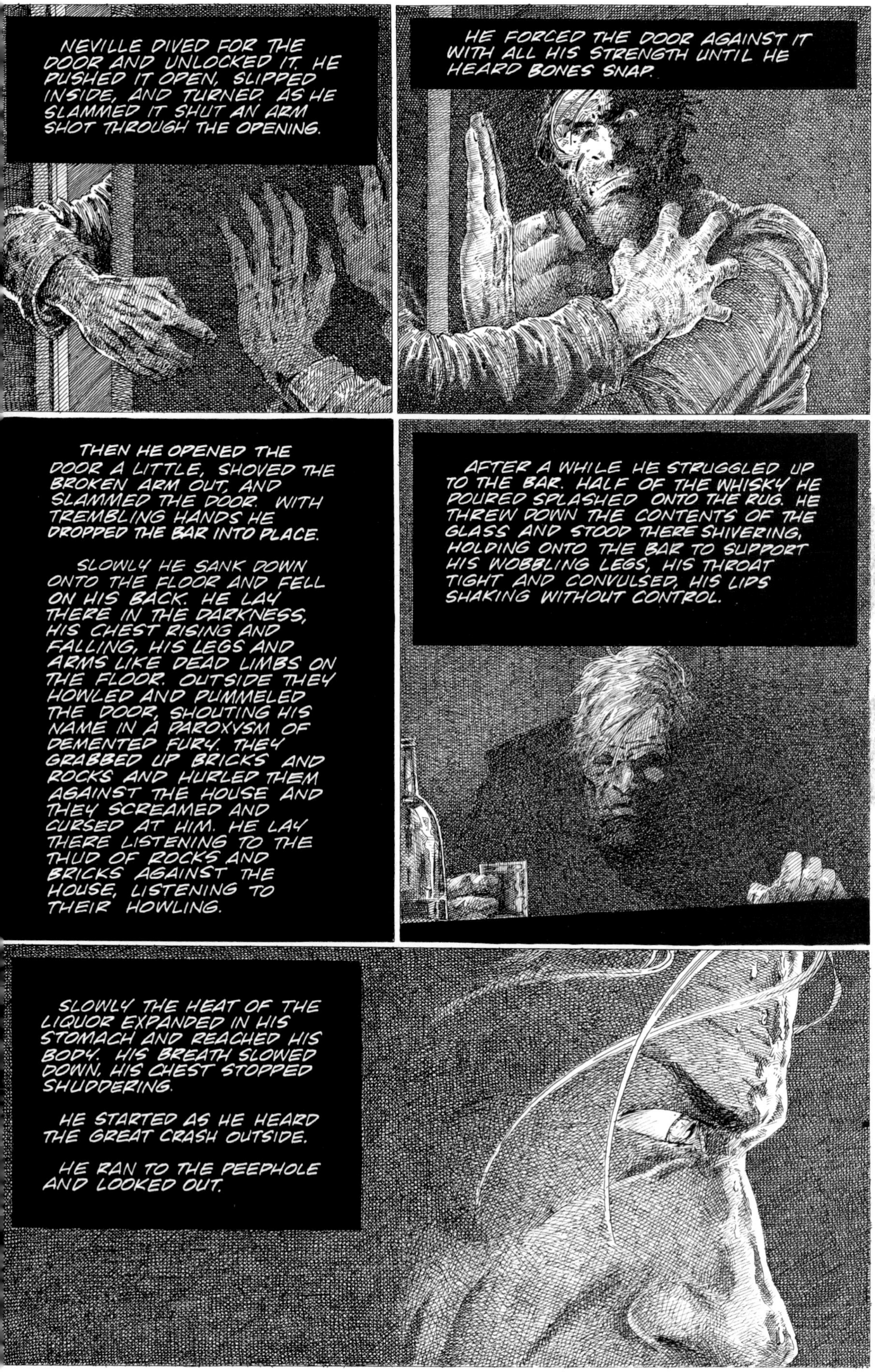

NEVILLE DIVED FOR THE
DOOR AND UNLOCKED IT. HE
PUSHED IT OPEN, SLIPPED
INSIDE, AND TURNED. AS HE
SLAMMED IT SHUT AN ARM
SHOT THROUGH THE OPENING.

HE FORCED THE DOOR AGAINST IT
WITH ALL HIS STRENGTH UNTIL HE
HEARD BONES SNAP.

THEN HE OPENED THE
DOOR A LITTLE, SHOVED THE
BROKEN ARM OUT, AND
SLAMMED THE DOOR. WITH
TREMBLING HANDS HE
DROPPED THE BAR INTO PLACE.

SLOWLY HE SANK DOWN
ONTO THE FLOOR AND FELL
ON HIS BACK. HE LAY
THERE IN THE DARKNESS,
HIS CHEST RISING AND
FALLING, HIS LEGS AND
ARMS LIKE DEAD LIMBS ON
THE FLOOR. OUTSIDE THEY
HOWLED AND PUMMELED
THE DOOR, SHOUTING HIS
NAME IN A PAROXYSM OF
DEMENTED FURY. THEY
GRABBED UP BRICKS AND
ROCKS AND HURLED THEM
AGAINST THE HOUSE AND
THEY SCREAMED AND
CURSED AT HIM. HE LAY
THERE LISTENING TO THE
THUD OF ROCKS AND
BRICKS AGAINST THE
HOUSE, LISTENING TO
THEIR HOWLING.

AFTER A WHILE HE STRUGGLED UP
TO THE BAR. HALF OF THE WHISKY HE
POURED SPLASHED ONTO THE RUG. HE
THREW DOWN THE CONTENTS OF THE
GLASS AND STOOD THERE SHIVERING,
HOLDING ONTO THE BAR TO SUPPORT
HIS WOBBLING LEGS, HIS THROAT
TIGHT AND CONVULSED, HIS LIPS
SHAKING WITHOUT CONTROL.

SLOWLY THE HEAT OF THE
LIQUOR EXPANDED IN HIS
STOMACH AND REACHED HIS
BODY. HIS BREATH SLOWED
DOWN, HIS CHEST STOPPED
SHUDDERING.

HE STARTED AS HE HEARD
THE GREAT CRASH OUTSIDE.

HE RAN TO THE PEEPHOLE
AND LOOKED OUT.

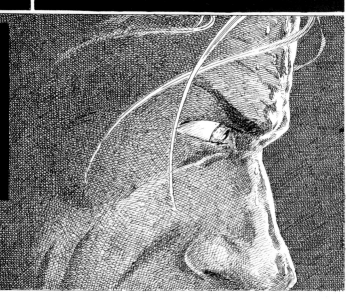

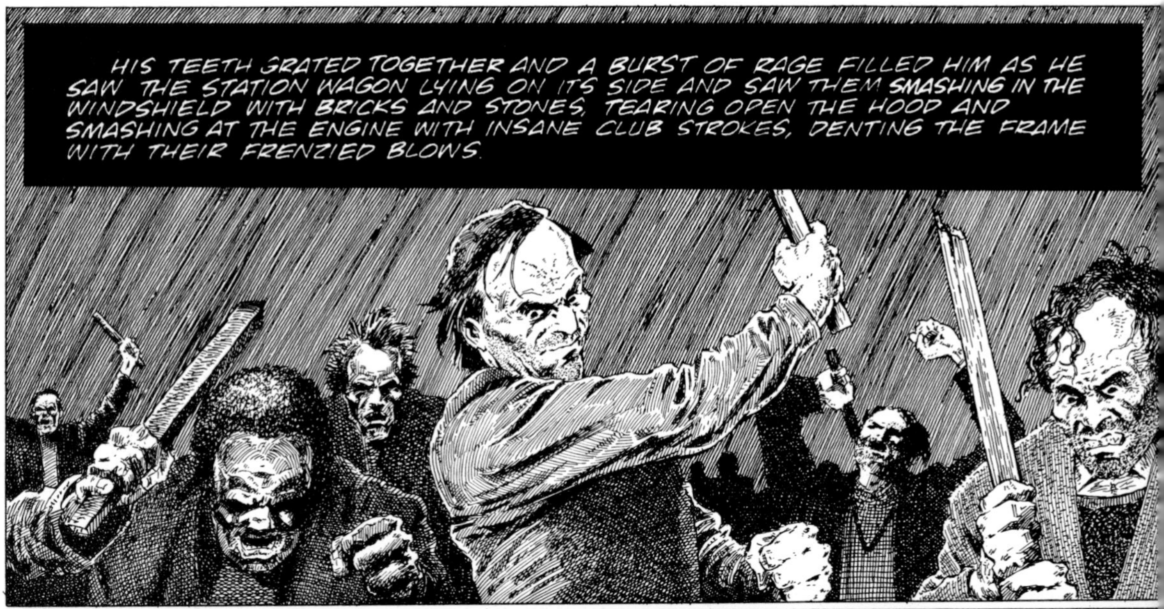
HIS TEETH GRATED TOGETHER AND A BURST OF RAGE FILLED HIM AS HE SAW THE STATION WAGON LYING ON IT'S SIDE AND SAW THEM SMASHING IN THE WINDSHIELD WITH BRICKS AND STONES, TEARING OPEN THE HOOD AND SMASHING AT THE ENGINE WITH INSANE CLUB STROKES, DENTING THE FRAME WITH THEIR FRENZIED BLOWS.

AS HE WATCHED, FURY POURED THROUGH HIM LIKE A CURRENT OF HOT ACID AND HALF-FORMED CURSES SOUNDED IN HIS THROAT WHILE HIS HANDS CLAMPED INTO GREAT WHITE FISTS AT HIS SIDES.

TURNING SUDDENLY, HE MOVED TO THE LAMP AND TRIED TO LIGHT IT. IT DIDN'T WORK. WITH A SNARL HE TURNED AND RAN INTO THE KITCHEN. THE REFRIGERATOR WAS OUT. HE RAN FROM ONE DARK ROOM TO ANOTHER. THE FREEZER WAS OFF; ALL THE FOOD WOULD SPOIL. HIS HOUSE WAS A DEAD HOUSE.

FURY EXPLODED IN HIM. **ENOUGH!**

HIS RAGE-PALSIED HANDS RIPPED OUT CLOTHES FROM THE BUREAU DRAWER UNTIL THEY CLOSED ON THE LOADED PISTOLS.

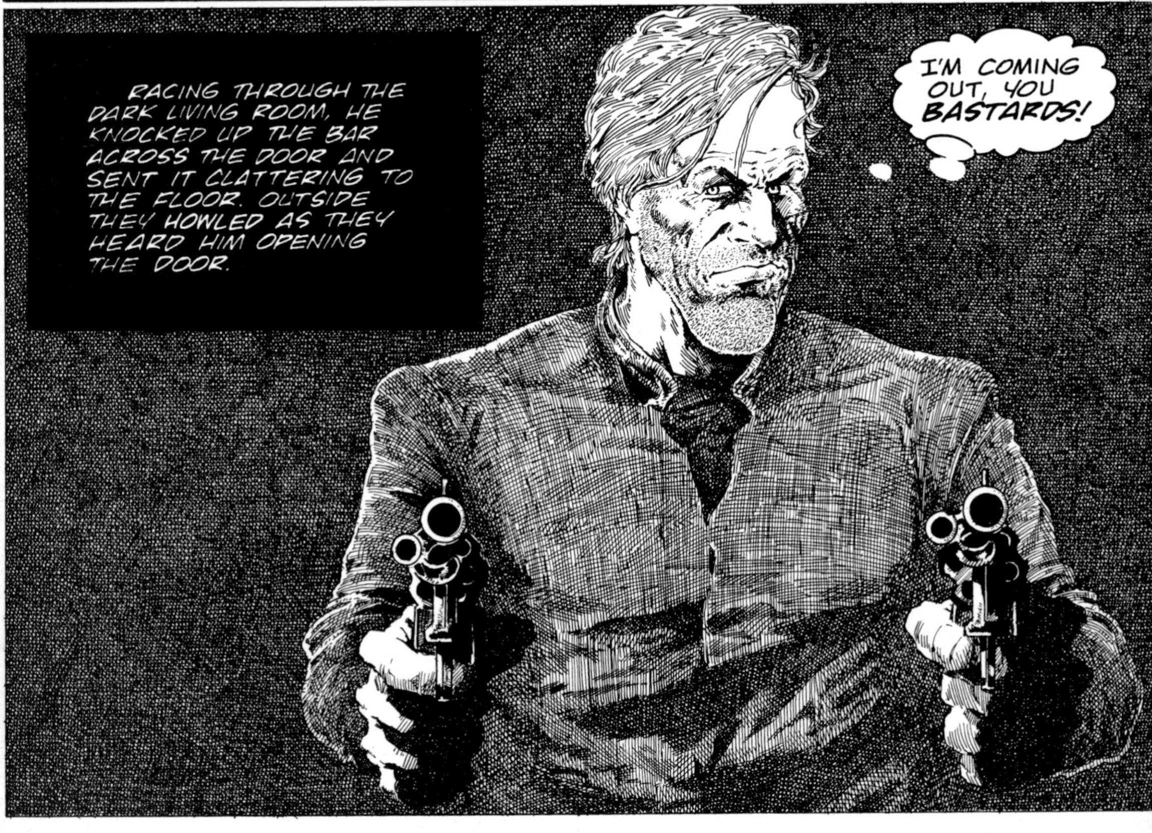
RACING THROUGH THE DARK LIVING ROOM, HE KNOCKED UP THE BAR ACROSS THE DOOR AND SENT IT CLATTERING TO THE FLOOR. OUTSIDE THEY HOWLED AS THEY HEARD HIM OPENING THE DOOR.
I'M COMING OUT, YOU BASTARDS!

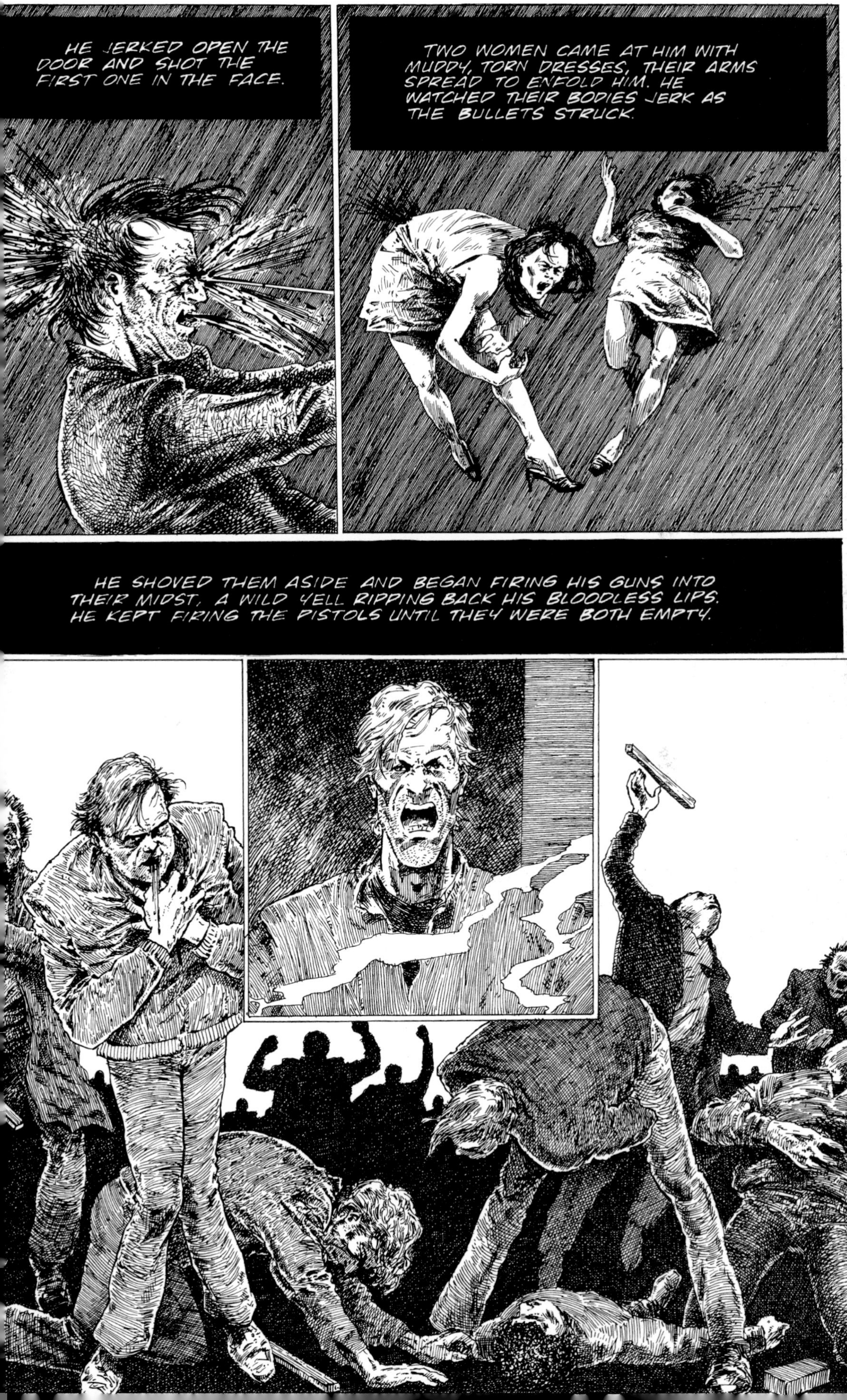
HE JERKED OPEN THE DOOR AND SHOT THE FIRST ONE IN THE FACE.
TWO WOMEN CAME AT HIM WITH MUDDY, TORN DRESSES, THEIR ARMS SPREAD TO ENFOLD HIM. HE WATCHED THEIR BODIES JERK AS THE BULLETS STRUCK.
HE SHOVED THEM ASIDE AND BEGAN FIRING HIS GUNS INTO THEIR MIDST, A WILD YELL RIPPING BACK HIS BLOODLESS LIPS. HE KEPT FIRING THE PISTOLS UNTIL THEY WERE BOTH EMPTY.

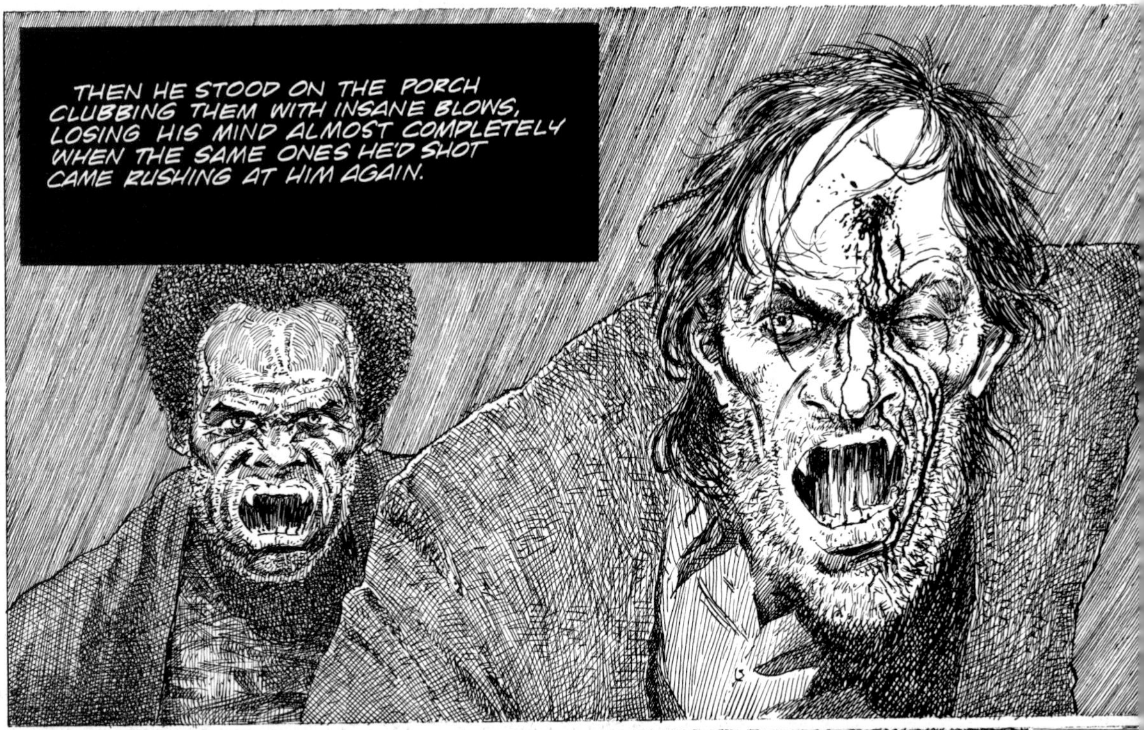
THEN HE STOOD ON THE PORCH CLUBBING THEM WITH INSANE BLOWS, LOSING HIS MIND ALMOST COMPLETELY WHEN THE SAME ONES HE'D SHOT CAME RUSHING AT HIM AGAIN.

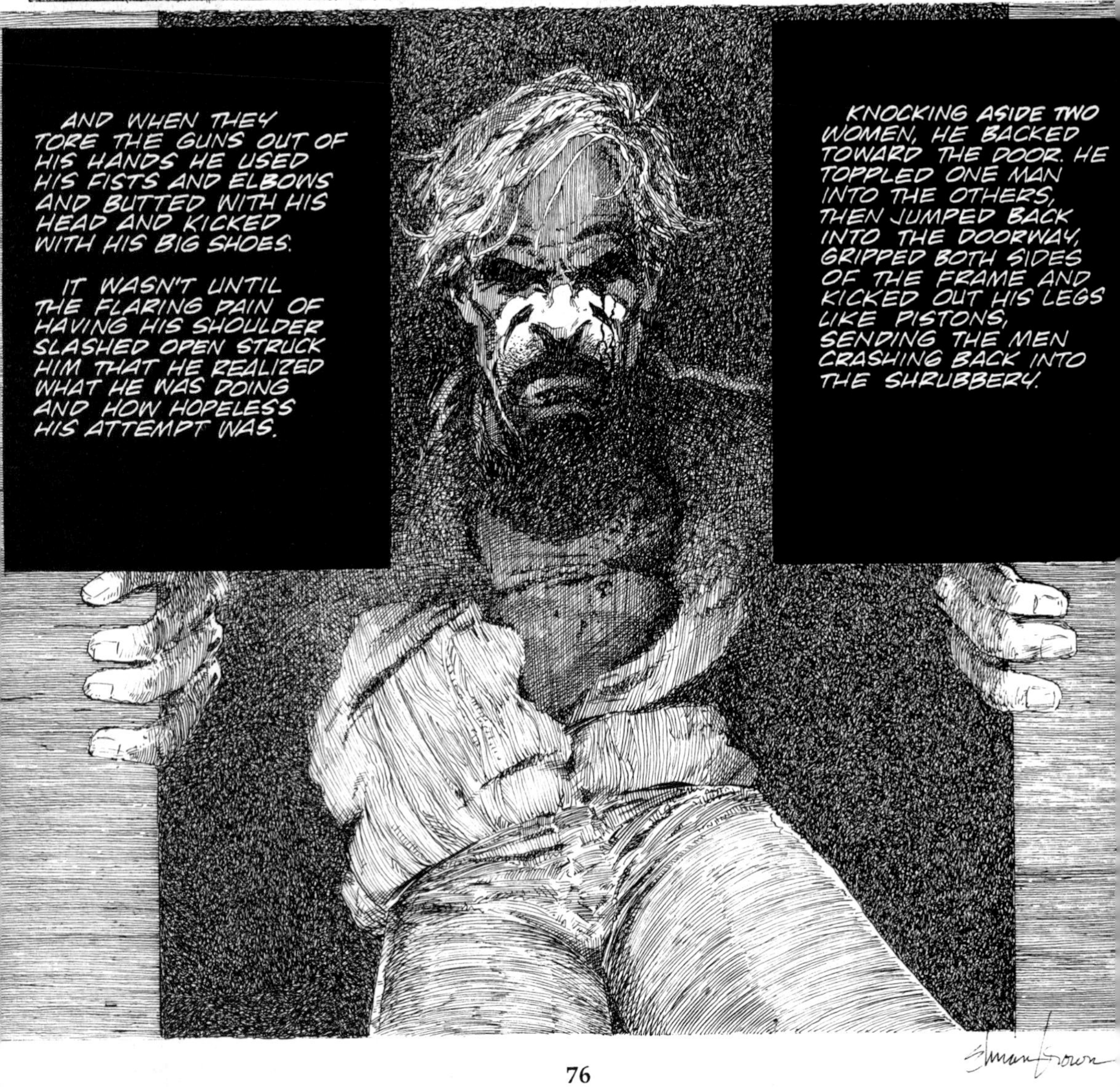
AND WHEN THEY TORE THE GUNS OUT OF HIS HANDS HE USED HIS FISTS AND ELBOWS AND BUTTED WITH HIS HEAD AND KICKED WITH HIS BIG SHOES.
IT WASN'T UNTIL THE FLARING PAIN OF HAVING HIS SHOULDER SLASHED OPEN STRUCK HIM THAT HE REALIZED WHAT HE WAS DOING AND HOW HOPELESS HIS ATTEMPT WAS.
KNOCKING ASIDE TWO WOMEN, HE BACKED TOWARD THE DOOR. HE TOPPLED ONE MAN INTO THE OTHERS, THEN JUMPED BACK INTO THE DOORWAY, GRIPPED BOTH SIDES OF THE FRAME AND KICKED OUT HIS LEGS LIKE PISTONS, SENDING THE MEN CRASHING BACK INTO THE SHRUBBERY.

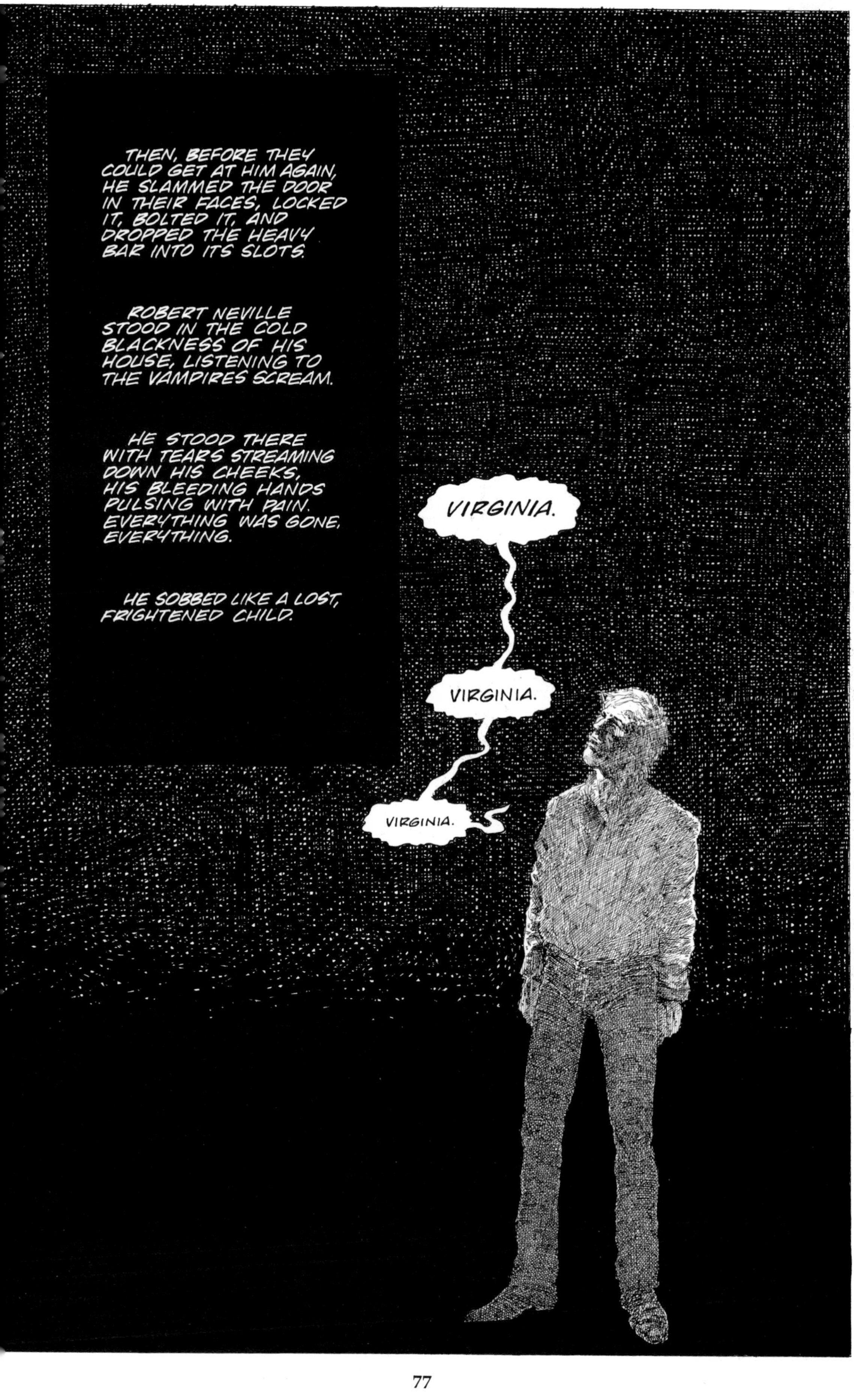

THEN, BEFORE THEY COULD GET AT HIM AGAIN, HE SLAMMED THE DOOR IN THEIR FACES, LOCKED IT, BOLTED IT, AND DROPPED THE HEAVY BAR INTO ITS SLOTS.
ROBERT NEVILLE STOOD IN THE COLD BLACKNESS OF HIS HOUSE, LISTENING TO THE VAMPIRES SCREAM.
HE STOOD THERE WITH TEARS STREAMING DOWN HIS CHEEKS, HIS BLEEDING HANDS PULSING WITH PAIN. EVERYTHING WAS GONE. EVERYTHING.
HE SOBBED LIKE A LOST, FRIGHTENED CHILD.
VIRGINIA.
VIRGINIA.
VIRGINIA.

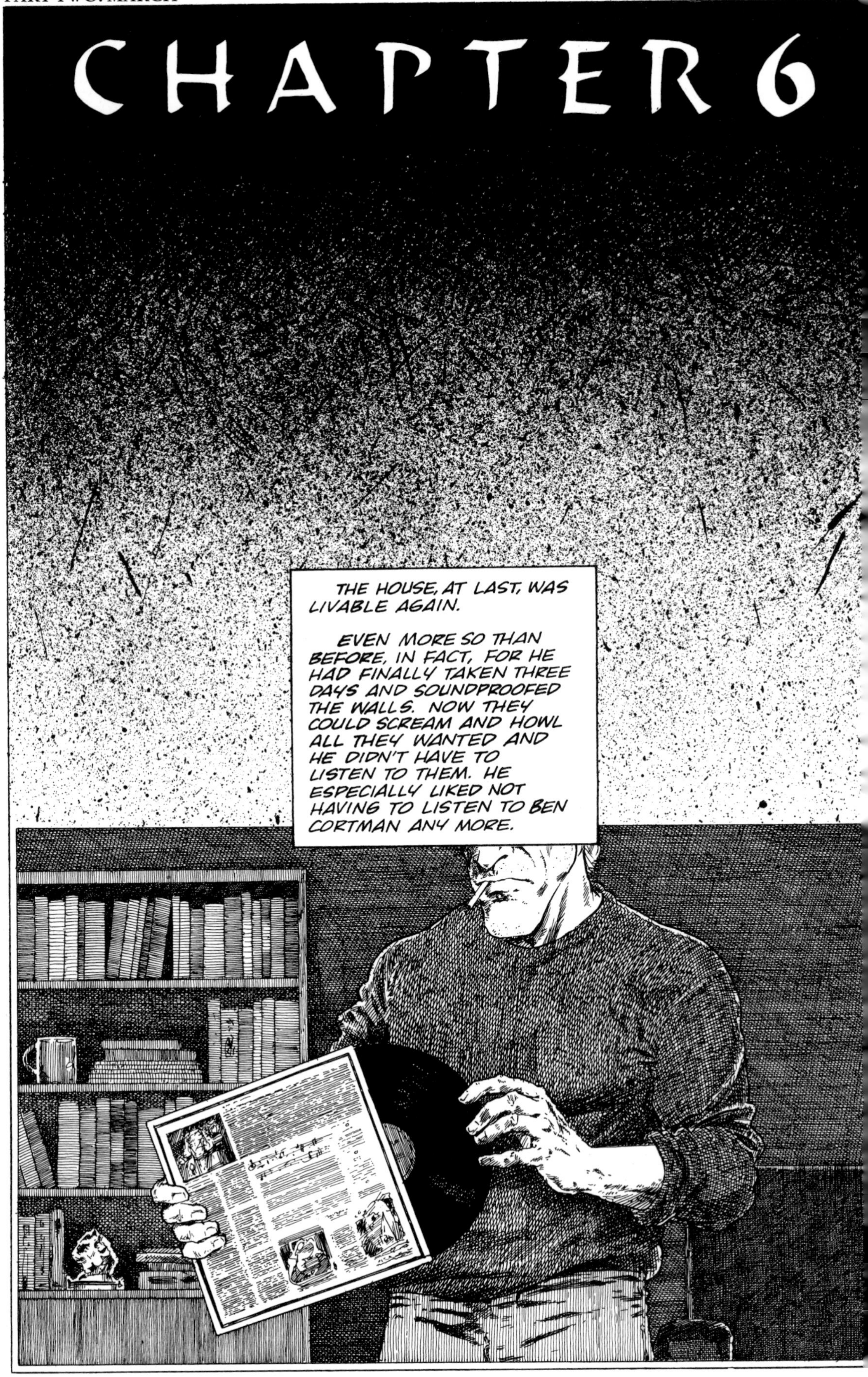
CHAPTER 6
THE HOUSE, AT LAST, WAS LIVABLE AGAIN.
EVEN MORE SO THAN BEFORE, IN FACT, FOR HE HAD FINALLY TAKEN THREE DAYS AND SOUNDPROOFED THE WALLS. NOW THEY COULD SCREAM AND HOWL ALL THEY WANTED AND HE DIDN'T HAVE TO LISTEN TO THEM. HE ESPECIALLY LIKED NOT HAVING TO LISTEN TO BEN CORTMAN ANY MORE.

IT HAD ALL TAKEN TIME AND WORK. FIRST OF ALL WAS THE MATTER OF A NEW CAR TO REPLACE THE ONE THEY'D DESTROYED. THIS HAD BEEN MORE DIFFICULT THAN HE'D IMAGINED.

HE HAD TO GET TO SANTA MONICA TO A DEALERSHIP THAT CARRIED THE SAME MAKE OF STATION WAGON AS HIS OLD ONE. IT WAS THE ONLY ONE HE HAD HAD ANY EXPERIENCE WITH, AND THIS DIDN'T SEEM QUITE THE TIME TO BE EXPERIMENTING.

FINALLY, IN A GARAGE ABOUT A MILE FROM HIS HOUSE, HE FOUND A CAR HE COULD GET STARTED, AND HE DROVE QUICKLY TO SANTA MONICA TO PICK UP ANOTHER STATION WAGON. HE PUT A NEW BATTERY IN IT, FILLED ITS TANK WITH GASOLINE, PUT GASOLINE DRUMS IN THE BACK, AND DROVE HOME. HE GOT BACK TO THE HOUSE AN HOUR BEFORE SUNSET.

HE MADE SURE OF THAT.

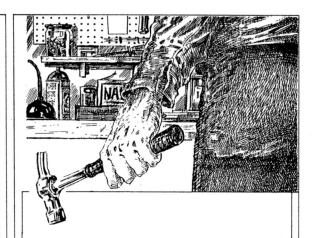

LUCKILY THE GENERATOR HAD NOT BEEN RUINED. THE VAMPIRES APPARENTLY HAD NO IDEA OF ITS IMPORTANCE TO HIM, FOR, EXCEPT FOR A TORN WIRE AND A FEW CUDGEL BLOWS, THEY HAD LEFT IT ALONE. HE'D MANAGED TO FIX IT QUICKLY THE MORNING AFTER THE ATTACK AND KEEP HIS FROZEN FOODS FROM SPOILING. HE WAS GRATEFUL FOR THAT, BECAUSE HE WAS SURE THERE WERE NO PLACES LEFT WHERE HE COULD GET MORE FROZEN FOODS NOW THAT ELECTRICITY WAS GONE FROM THE CITY.

FOR THE REST OF IT, HE HAD TO STRAIGHTEN UP THE GARAGE AND CLEAN OUT THE DEBRIS OF BROKEN BULBS, FUSES, WIRING, PLUGS, SOLDER, SPARE MOTOR PARTS, AND A BOX OF SEEDS HE'D PUT THERE ONCE; HE DIDN'T REMEMBER JUST WHEN.

THE WASHING MACHINE THEY HAD RUINED BEYOND REPAIR, FORCING HIM TO REPLACE IT. BUT THAT WASN'T HARD. THE WORST PART WAS MOPPING UP ALL THE GASOLINE THEY'D SPILLED FROM THE DRUMS. THEY'D REALLY OUTDONE THEMSELVES SPILLING GASOLINE, HE THOUGHT IRRITABLY WHILE HE MOPPED IT UP.

HE'D ALMOST ENJOYED ALL THE WORK ONCE IT WAS STARTED. IT GAVE HIM SOMETHING TO LOSE HIMSELF IN, SOMETHING TO POUR ALL THE ENERGY OF HIS STILL PULSING FURY INTO. IT BROKE THE MONOTONY OF HIS DAILY TASKS: THE CARRYING AWAY OF BODIES, THE REPAIRING OF THE HOUSE'S EXTERIOR, THE HANGING OF GARLIC.

HE DRANK SPARINGLY DURING THOSE DAYS, MANAGING TO PASS ALMOST THE ENTIRE DAY WITHOUT A DRINK, EVEN ALLOWING HIS EVENING DRINKS TO ASSUME THE FUNCTION OF RELAXING NIGHTCAPS RATHER THAN SENSELESS ESCAPE. HIS APPETITE INCREASED AND HE GAINED FOUR POUNDS AND LOST A LITTLE BELLY. HE EVEN SLEPT NIGHTS, A TIRED SLEEP WITHOUT THE DREAMS.

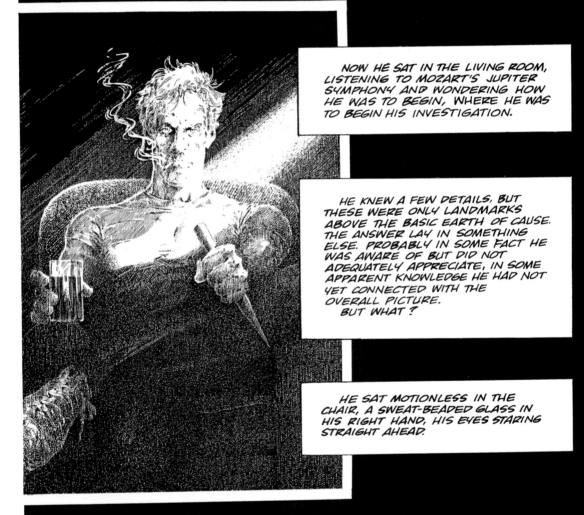

NOW HE SAT IN THE LIVING ROOM, LISTENING TO MOZART'S JUPITER SYMPHONY AND WONDERING HOW HE WAS TO BEGIN, WHERE HE WAS TO BEGIN HIS INVESTIGATION.

HE KNEW A FEW DETAILS, BUT THESE WERE ONLY LANDMARKS ABOVE THE BASIC EARTH OF CAUSE. THE ANSWER LAY IN SOMETHING ELSE. PROBABLY IN SOME FACT HE WAS AWARE OF BUT DID NOT ADEQUATELY APPRECIATE, IN SOME APPARENT KNOWLEDGE HE HAD NOT YET CONNECTED WITH THE OVERALL PICTURE.
BUT WHAT?

HE SAT MOTIONLESS IN THE CHAIR, A SWEAT-BEADED GLASS IN HIS RIGHT HAND, HIS EYES STARING STRAIGHT AHEAD.

MAYBE IF HE WENT BACK. MAYBE THE ANSWER LAY IN THE PAST, IN SOME OBSCURE CREVICE OF MEMORY. GO BACK, THEN, HE TOLD HIS MIND, GO BACK.
IT TORE HIS HEART OUT TO GO BACK.

THERE HAD BEEN ANOTHER DUST STORM DURING THE NIGHT. HIGH, SPINNING WINDS HAD SCOURED THE HOUSE WITH GRIT, DRIVEN IT THROUGH THE CRACKS, SIFTED IT THROUGH PLASTER PORES, AND LEFT A HAIR-THIN LAYER OF DUST ACROSS ALL THE FURNITURE SURFACES. OVER THEIR BED THE DUST FILTERED LIKE FINE POWDER, SETTLING IN THEIR HAIR AND ON THEIR EYELIDS AND UNDER THEIR NAILS, CLOGGING THEIR PORES.

HALF THE NIGHT HE'D LAIN AWAKE TRYING TO SINGLE OUT THE SOUND OF VIRGINIA'S LABORED BREATHING. BUT HE COULDN'T HEAR ANYTHING ABOVE THE SHRIEKING, GRATING SOUND OF THE STORM.

HE NEVER GOT USED TO THE DUST STORMS. WHENEVER THEY CAME, HE SPENT A RESTLESS, TOSSING NIGHT, AND WENT TO THE PLANT THE NEXT DAY WITH JADED MIND AND BODY.

NOW THERE WAS VIRGINIA TO WORRY ABOUT TOO.

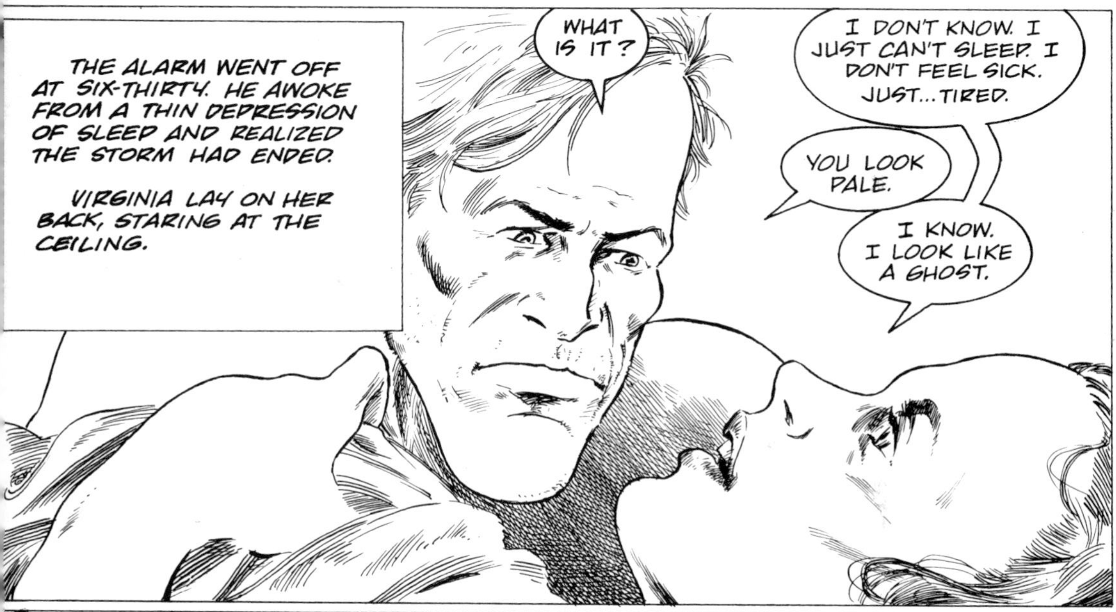
THE ALARM WENT OFF AT SIX-THIRTY. HE AWOKE FROM A THIN DEPRESSION OF SLEEP AND REALIZED THE STORM HAD ENDED.
VIRGINIA LAY ON HER BACK, STARING AT THE CEILING.
WHAT IS IT?
I DON'T KNOW. I JUST CAN'T SLEEP. I DON'T FEEL SICK. JUST...TIRED.
YOU LOOK PALE.
I KNOW. I LOOK LIKE A GHOST.

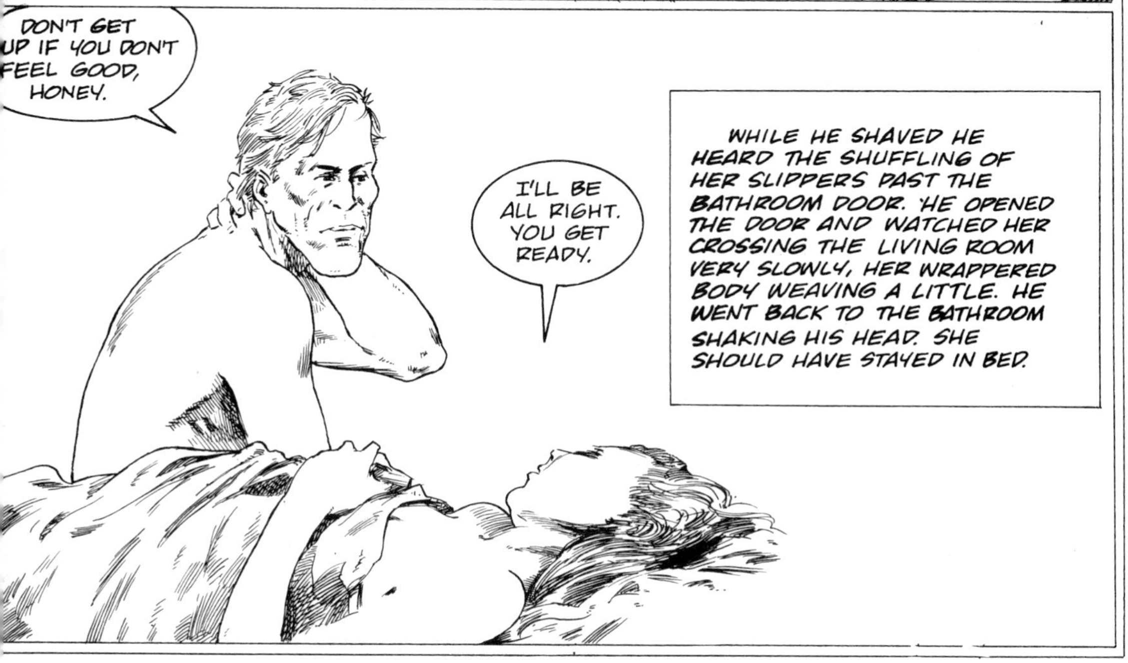
DON'T GET UP IF YOU DON'T FEEL GOOD, HONEY.
I'LL BE ALL RIGHT. YOU GET READY.
WHILE HE SHAVED HE HEARD THE SHUFFLING OF HER SLIPPERS PAST THE BATHROOM DOOR. HE OPENED THE DOOR AND WATCHED HER CROSSING THE LIVING ROOM VERY SLOWLY, HER WRAPPERED BODY WEAVING A LITTLE. HE WENT BACK TO THE BATHROOM SHAKING HIS HEAD. SHE SHOULD HAVE STAYED IN BED.

BEFORE GOING TO THE BEDROOM TO GET DRESSED, HE CHECKED KATHY'S ROOM.

SHE WAS STILL ASLEEP, HER SMALL BLONDE HEAD MOTIONLESS ON THE PILLOW, HER CHEEKS PINK WITH HEAVY SLEEP.

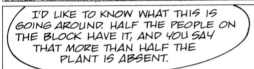

HE ENTERED THE KITCHEN TEN MINUTES LATER. VIRGINIA WAS SITTING AT THE TABLE. ON THE STOVE COFFEE WAS PERCOLATING, BUT NOTHING ELSE WAS COOKING.

SWEETHEART, IF YOU DON'T FEEL WELL, GO BACK TO BED. I'LL FIX BREAKFAST.

I'M ALL RIGHT, BUT NOTHING FOR M BOB. THANKS.

I'D LIKE TO KNOW WHAT THIS IS GOING AROUND. HALF THE PEOPLE ON THE BLOCK HAVE IT, AND YOU SAY THAT MORE THAN HALF THE PLANT IS ABSENT.

MAYBE IT'S SOME KIND OF VIRUS.

BETWEEN THE STORMS AND THE MOSQUITOES AND EVERYONE BEING SICK, LIFE IS RAPIDLY BECOMING A PAIN.

YOU CALL UP DR. BUSCH TODAY.

I WILL. BUT THERE'S NO **REASON** WHY I SHOULD BE LIKE THIS.

YOU'RE **REALLY** GOING TO GET SICK IF YOU DON'T EAT.

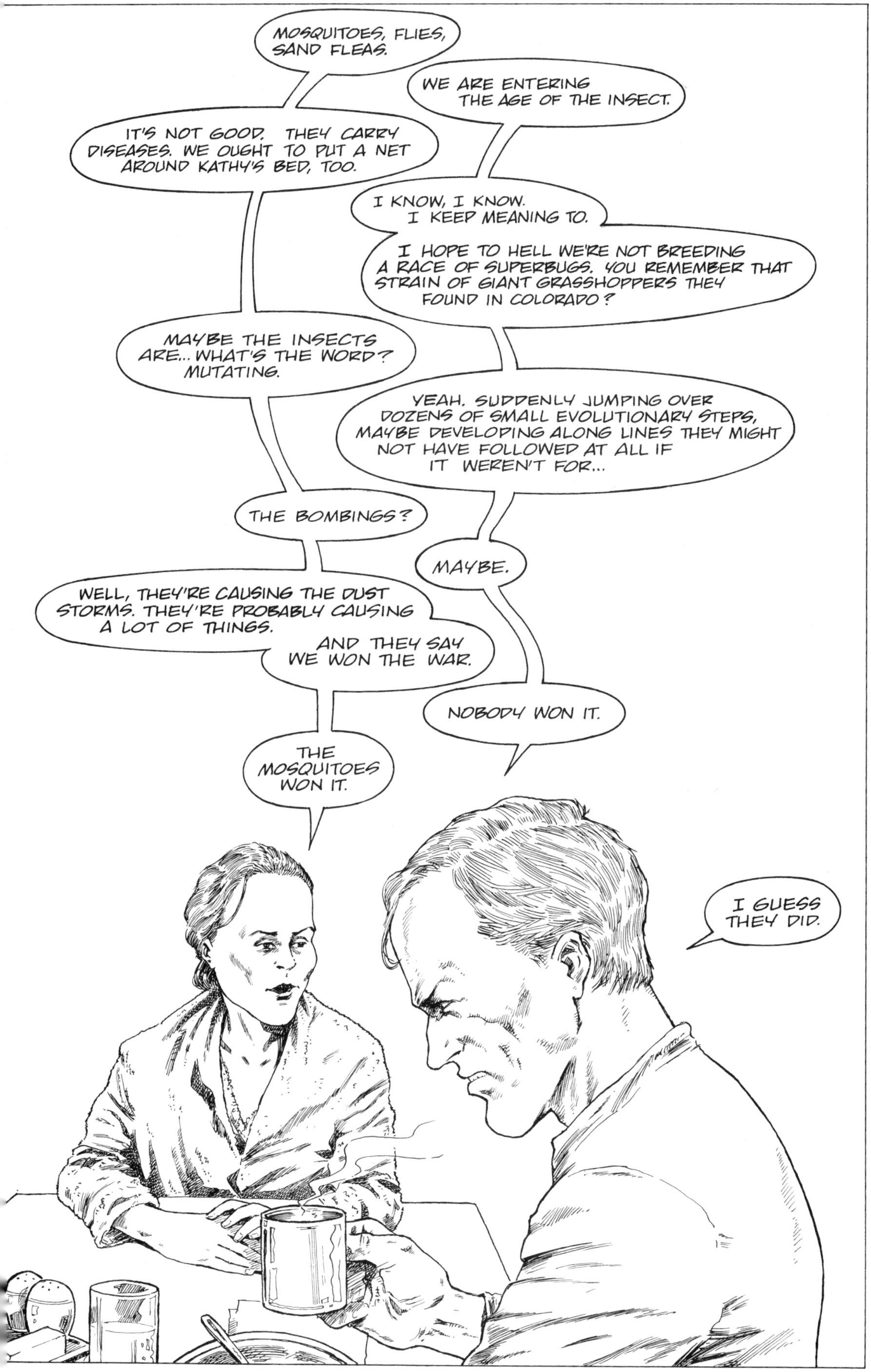
MOSQUITOES, FLIES, SAND FLEAS.
WE ARE ENTERING THE AGE OF THE INSECT.
IT'S NOT GOOD. THEY CARRY DISEASES. WE OUGHT TO PUT A NET AROUND KATHY'S BED, TOO.
I KNOW, I KNOW. I KEEP MEANING TO.
I HOPE TO HELL WE'RE NOT BREEDING A RACE OF SUPERBUGS. YOU REMEMBER THAT STRAIN OF GIANT GRASSHOPPERS THEY FOUND IN COLORADO?
MAYBE THE INSECTS ARE... WHAT'S THE WORD? MUTATING.
YEAH. SUDDENLY JUMPING OVER DOZENS OF SMALL EVOLUTIONARY STEPS, MAYBE DEVELOPING ALONG LINES THEY MIGHT NOT HAVE FOLLOWED AT ALL IF IT WEREN'T FOR...
THE BOMBINGS?
MAYBE.
WELL, THEY'RE CAUSING THE DUST STORMS. THEY'RE PROBABLY CAUSING A LOT OF THINGS.
AND THEY SAY WE WON THE WAR.
NOBODY WON IT.
THE MOSQUITOES WON IT.
I GUESS THEY DID.

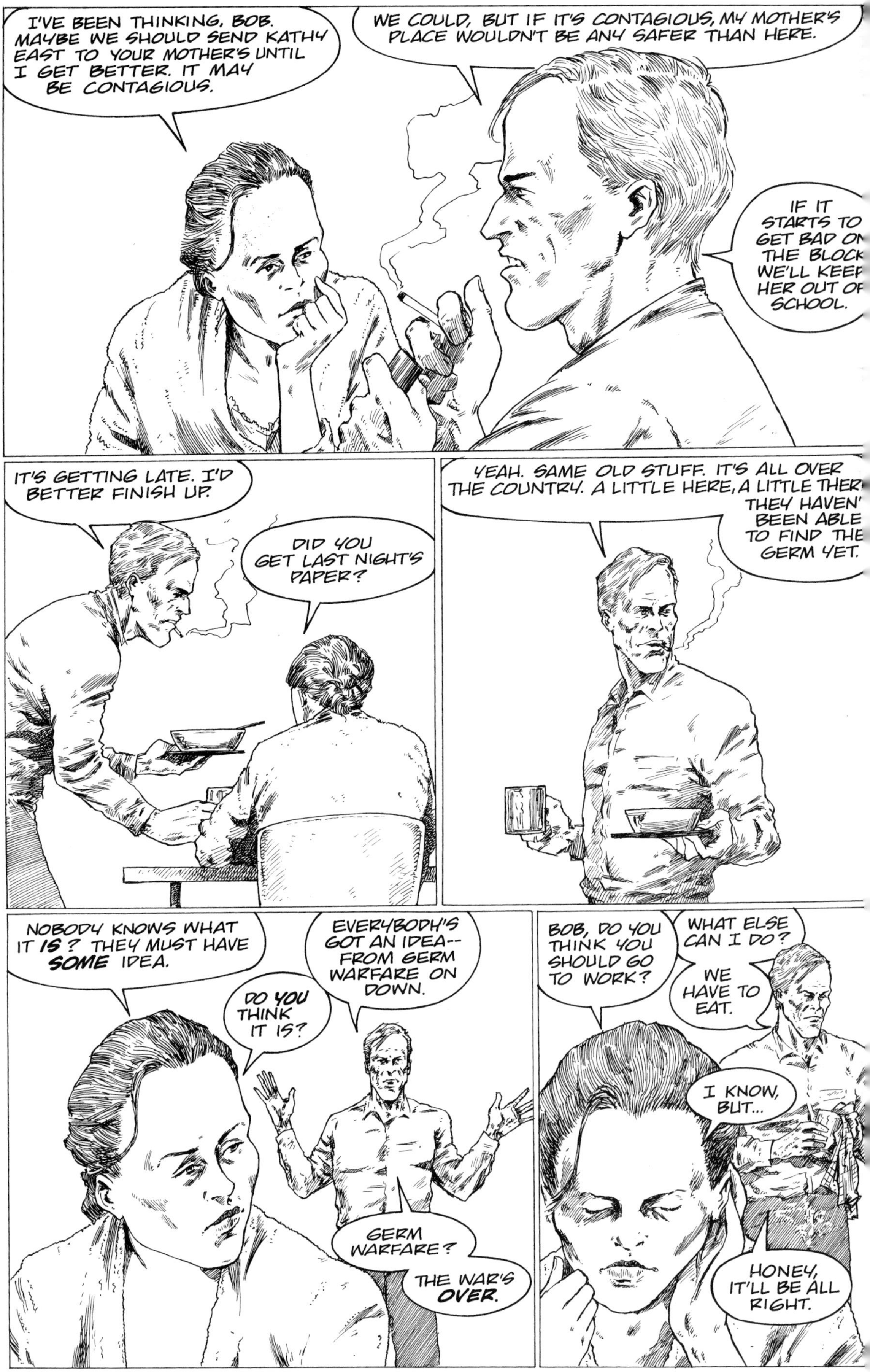

I'VE BEEN THINKING, BOB. MAYBE WE SHOULD SEND KATHY EAST TO YOUR MOTHER'S UNTIL I GET BETTER. IT MAY BE CONTAGIOUS.
WE COULD, BUT IF IT'S CONTAGIOUS, MY MOTHER'S PLACE WOULDN'T BE ANY SAFER THAN HERE.
IF IT STARTS TO GET BAD ON THE BLOCK WE'LL KEEP HER OUT OF SCHOOL.
IT'S GETTING LATE. I'D BETTER FINISH UP.
DID YOU GET LAST NIGHT'S PAPER?
YEAH. SAME OLD STUFF. IT'S ALL OVER THE COUNTRY. A LITTLE HERE, A LITTLE THERE. THEY HAVEN'T BEEN ABLE TO FIND THE GERM YET.
NOBODY KNOWS WHAT IT **IS**? THEY MUST HAVE **SOME** IDEA.
EVERYBODY'S GOT AN IDEA-- FROM GERM WARFARE ON DOWN.
DO **YOU** THINK IT IS?
GERM WARFARE?
THE WAR'S **OVER**.
BOB, DO YOU THINK YOU SHOULD GO TO WORK?
WHAT ELSE CAN I DO?
WE HAVE TO EAT.
I KNOW, BUT...
HONEY, IT'LL BE ALL RIGHT.

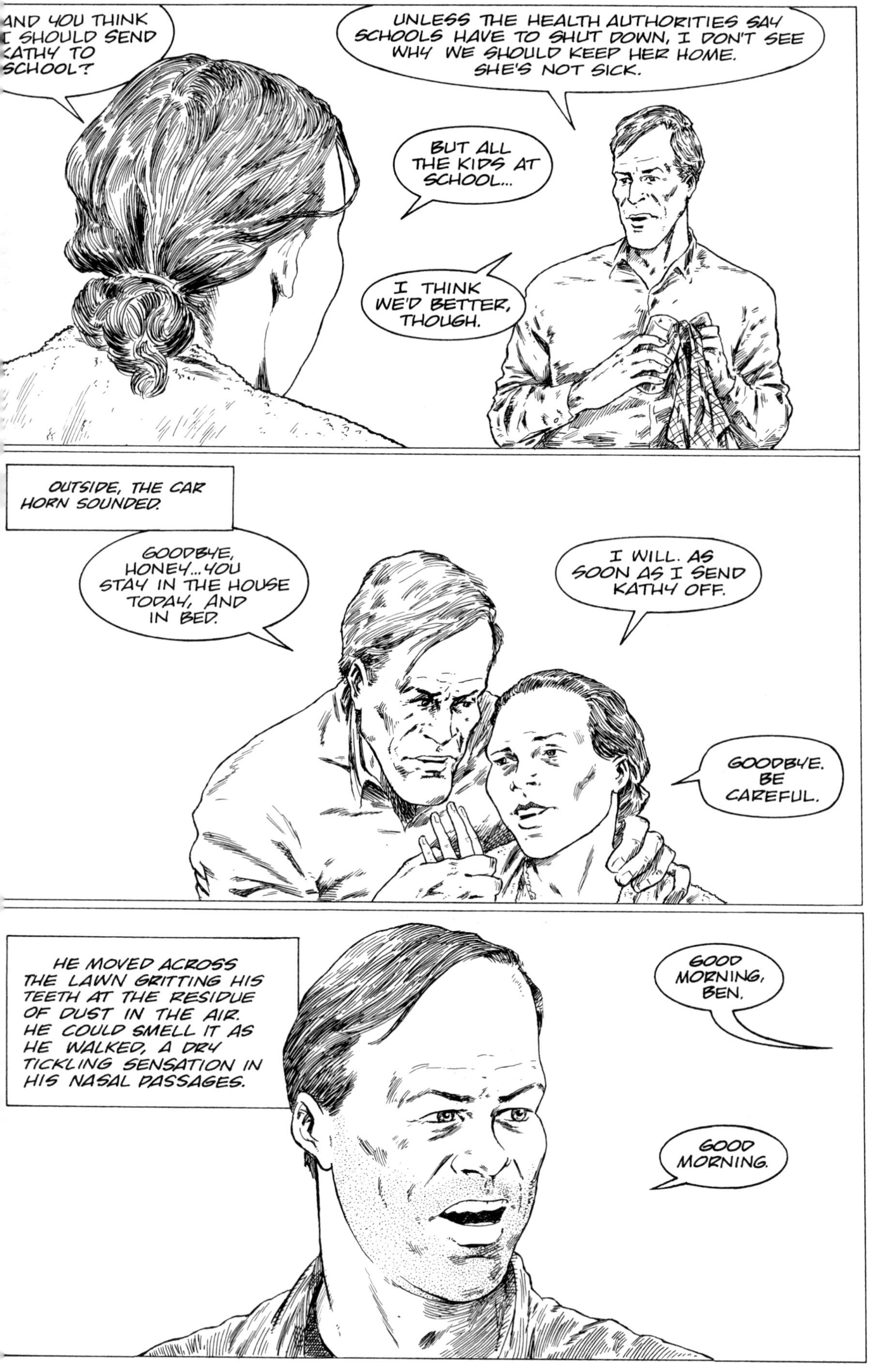
AND YOU THINK I SHOULD SEND KATHY TO SCHOOL?
UNLESS THE HEALTH AUTHORITIES SAY SCHOOLS HAVE TO SHUT DOWN, I DON'T SEE WHY WE SHOULD KEEP HER HOME. SHE'S NOT SICK.
BUT ALL THE KIDS AT SCHOOL...
I THINK WE'D BETTER, THOUGH.
OUTSIDE, THE CAR HORN SOUNDED.
GOODBYE, HONEY...YOU STAY IN THE HOUSE TODAY, AND IN BED.
I WILL. AS SOON AS I SEND KATHY OFF.
GOODBYE. BE CAREFUL.
HE MOVED ACROSS THE LAWN GRITTING HIS TEETH AT THE RESIDUE OF DUST IN THE AIR. HE COULD SMELL IT AS HE WALKED, A DRY TICKLING SENSATION IN HIS NASAL PASSAGES.
GOOD MORNING, BEN.
GOOD MORNING.

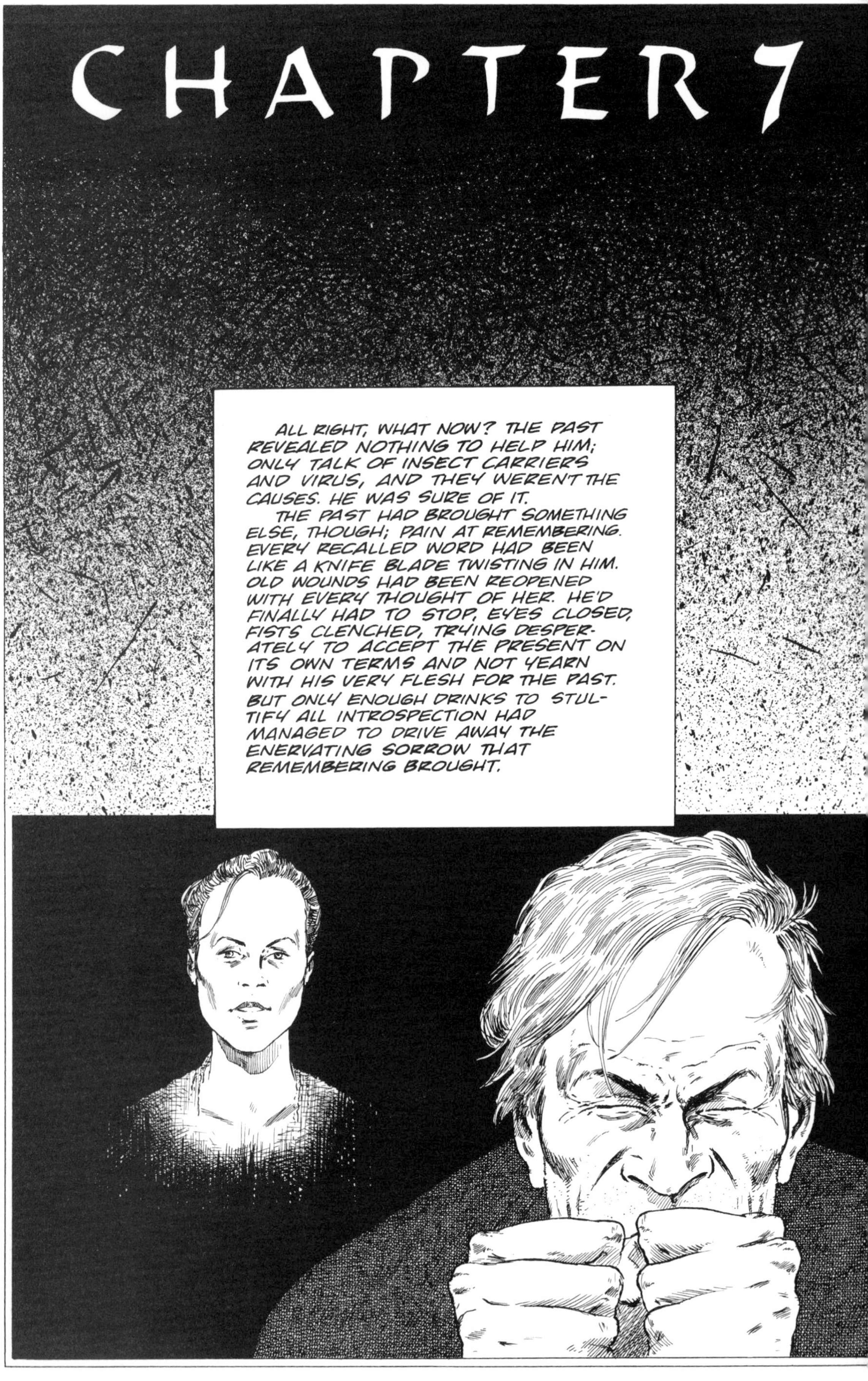
CHAPTER 7
ALL RIGHT, WHAT NOW? THE PAST REVEALED NOTHING TO HELP HIM; ONLY TALK OF INSECT CARRIERS AND VIRUS, AND THEY WEREN'T THE CAUSES. HE WAS SURE OF IT.
THE PAST HAD BROUGHT SOMETHING ELSE, THOUGH; PAIN AT REMEMBERING. EVERY RECALLED WORD HAD BEEN LIKE A KNIFE BLADE TWISTING IN HIM. OLD WOUNDS HAD BEEN REOPENED WITH EVERY THOUGHT OF HER. HE'D FINALLY HAD TO STOP, EYES CLOSED, FISTS CLENCHED, TRYING DESPERATELY TO ACCEPT THE PRESENT ON ITS OWN TERMS AND NOT YEARN WITH HIS VERY FLESH FOR THE PAST. BUT ONLY ENOUGH DRINKS TO STULTIFY ALL INTROSPECTION HAD MANAGED TO DRIVE AWAY THE ENERVATING SORROW THAT REMEMBERING BROUGHT.

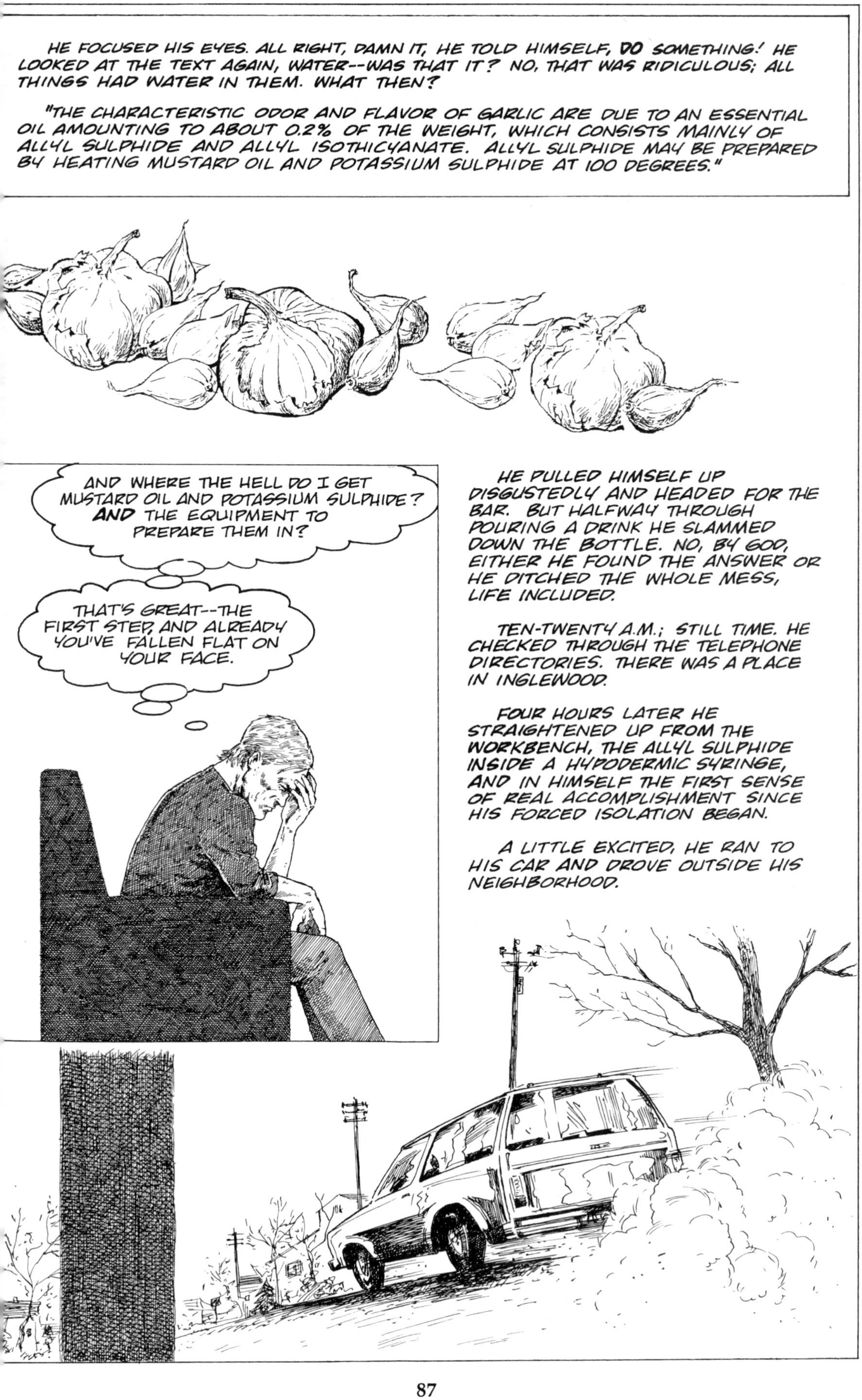
HE FOCUSED HIS EYES. ALL RIGHT, DAMN IT, HE TOLD HIMSELF, **DO** SOMETHING! HE LOOKED AT THE TEXT AGAIN, WATER--WAS THAT IT? NO, THAT WAS RIDICULOUS; ALL THINGS HAD WATER IN THEM. WHAT THEN?
"THE CHARACTERISTIC ODOR AND FLAVOR OF GARLIC ARE DUE TO AN ESSENTIAL OIL AMOUNTING TO ABOUT 0.2% OF THE WEIGHT, WHICH CONSISTS MAINLY OF ALLYL SULPHIDE AND ALLYL ISOTHICYANATE. ALLYL SULPHIDE MAY BE PREPARED BY HEATING MUSTARD OIL AND POTASSIUM SULPHIDE AT 100 DEGREES."
AND WHERE THE HELL DO I GET MUSTARD OIL AND POTASSIUM SULPHIDE? **AND** THE EQUIPMENT TO PREPARE THEM IN?
THAT'S GREAT--THE FIRST STEP, AND ALREADY YOU'VE FALLEN FLAT ON YOUR FACE.
HE PULLED HIMSELF UP DISGUSTEDLY AND HEADED FOR THE BAR. BUT HALFWAY THROUGH POURING A DRINK HE SLAMMED DOWN THE BOTTLE. NO, BY GOD, EITHER HE FOUND THE ANSWER OR HE DITCHED THE WHOLE MESS, LIFE INCLUDED.
TEN-TWENTY A.M.; STILL TIME. HE CHECKED THROUGH THE TELEPHONE DIRECTORIES. THERE WAS A PLACE IN INGLEWOOD.
FOUR HOURS LATER HE STRAIGHTENED UP FROM THE WORKBENCH, THE ALLYL SULPHIDE INSIDE A HYPODERMIC SYRINGE, AND IN HIMSELF THE FIRST SENSE OF REAL ACCOMPLISHMENT SINCE HIS FORCED ISOLATION BEGAN.
A LITTLE EXCITED, HE RAN TO HIS CAR AND DROVE OUTSIDE HIS NEIGHBORHOOD.

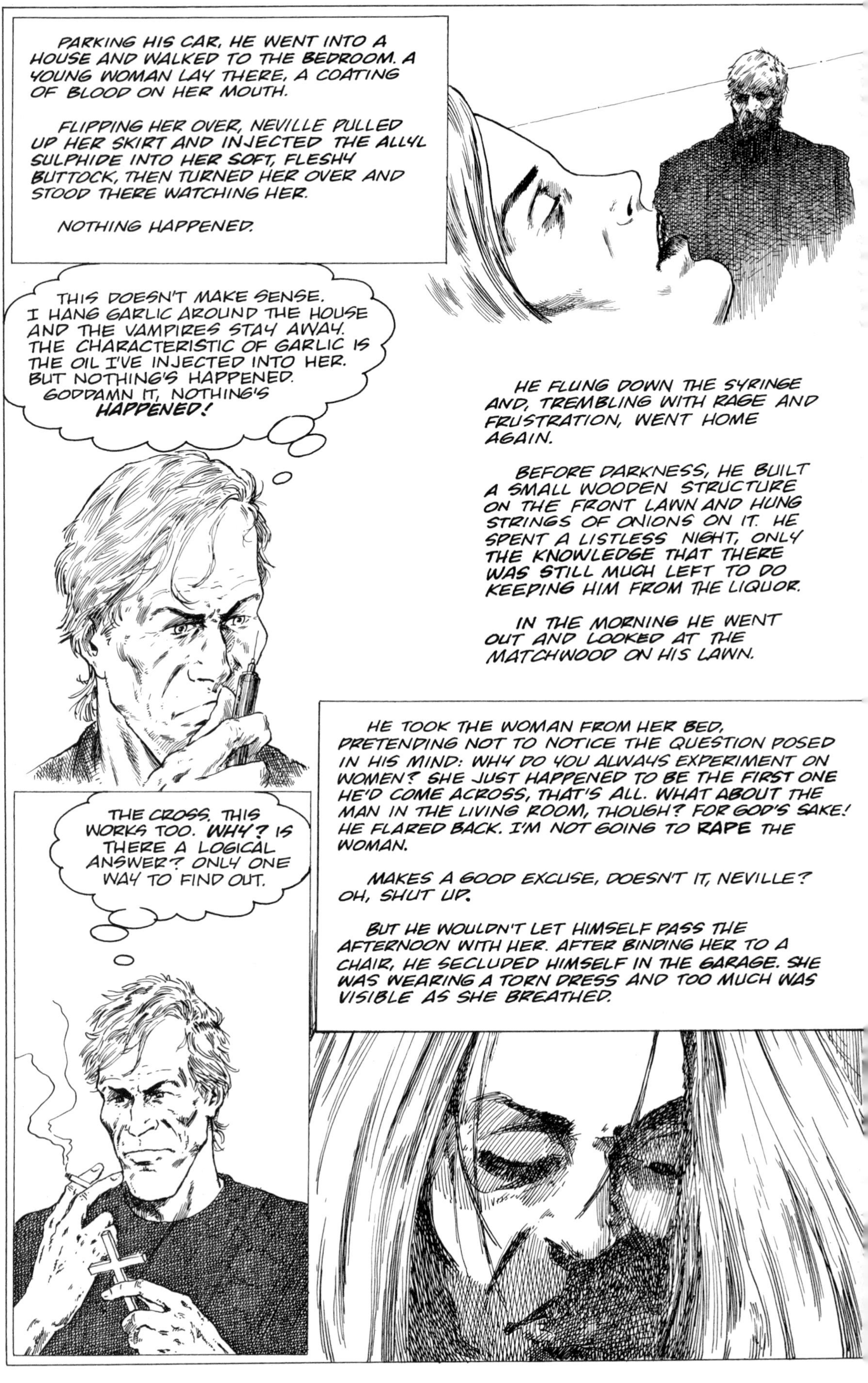
PARKING HIS CAR, HE WENT INTO A HOUSE AND WALKED TO THE BEDROOM. A YOUNG WOMAN LAY THERE, A COATING OF BLOOD ON HER MOUTH.
FLIPPING HER OVER, NEVILLE PULLED UP HER SKIRT AND INJECTED THE ALLYL SULPHIDE INTO HER SOFT, FLESHY BUTTOCK, THEN TURNED HER OVER AND STOOD THERE WATCHING HER.
NOTHING HAPPENED.
THIS DOESN'T MAKE SENSE. I HANG GARLIC AROUND THE HOUSE AND THE VAMPIRES STAY AWAY. THE CHARACTERISTIC OF GARLIC IS THE OIL I'VE INJECTED INTO HER. BUT NOTHING'S HAPPENED. GODDAMN IT, NOTHING'S HAPPENED!
HE FLUNG DOWN THE SYRINGE AND, TREMBLING WITH RAGE AND FRUSTRATION, WENT HOME AGAIN.
BEFORE DARKNESS, HE BUILT A SMALL WOODEN STRUCTURE ON THE FRONT LAWN AND HUNG STRINGS OF ONIONS ON IT. HE SPENT A LISTLESS NIGHT, ONLY THE KNOWLEDGE THAT THERE WAS STILL MUCH LEFT TO DO KEEPING HIM FROM THE LIQUOR.
IN THE MORNING HE WENT OUT AND LOOKED AT THE MATCHWOOD ON HIS LAWN.
THE CROSS. THIS WORKS TOO. WHY? IS THERE A LOGICAL ANSWER? ONLY ONE WAY TO FIND OUT.
HE TOOK THE WOMAN FROM HER BED, PRETENDING NOT TO NOTICE THE QUESTION POSED IN HIS MIND: WHY DO YOU ALWAYS EXPERIMENT ON WOMEN? SHE JUST HAPPENED TO BE THE FIRST ONE HE'D COME ACROSS, THAT'S ALL. WHAT ABOUT THE MAN IN THE LIVING ROOM, THOUGH? FOR GOD'S SAKE! HE FLARED BACK. I'M NOT GOING TO RAPE THE WOMAN.
MAKES A GOOD EXCUSE, DOESN'T IT, NEVILLE? OH, SHUT UP.
BUT HE WOULDN'T LET HIMSELF PASS THE AFTERNOON WITH HER. AFTER BINDING HER TO A CHAIR, HE SECLUDED HIMSELF IN THE GARAGE. SHE WAS WEARING A TORN DRESS AND TOO MUCH WAS VISIBLE AS SHE BREATHED.

AT LAST, MERCIFULLY, NIGHT CAME. HE LOCKED THE GARAGE DOOR, WENT BACK TO THE HOUSE, AND LOCKED THE FRONT DOOR, PUTTING THE HEAVY BAR ACROSS IT. THEN HE MADE A DRINK AND SAT DOWN ON THE COUCH ACROSS FROM THE WOMAN.

FROM THE CEILING, RIGHT BEFORE HER FACE, HUNG THE CROSS.

AT SIX-THIRTY HER EYES OPENED. SUDDENLY, LIKE THE EYES OF A SLEEPER WHO HAS A DEFINITE JOB TO DO UPON AWAKENING; WHO DOES NOT MOVE INTO CONSCIOUSNESS WITH A VAGUE ENTRY, BUT WITH A SINGLE, CLEARCUT MOTION, KNOWING JUST WHAT IS TO BE DONE.

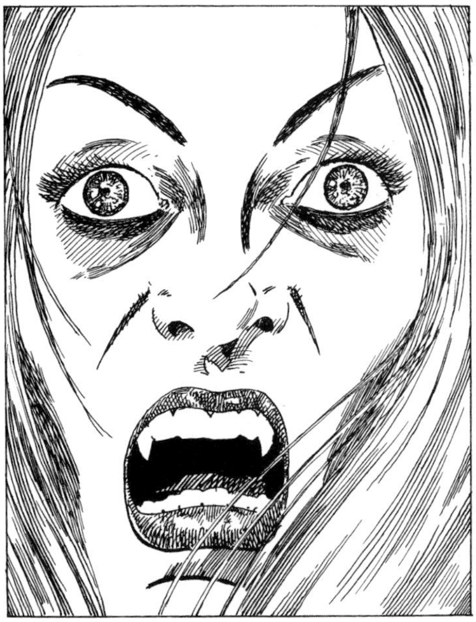

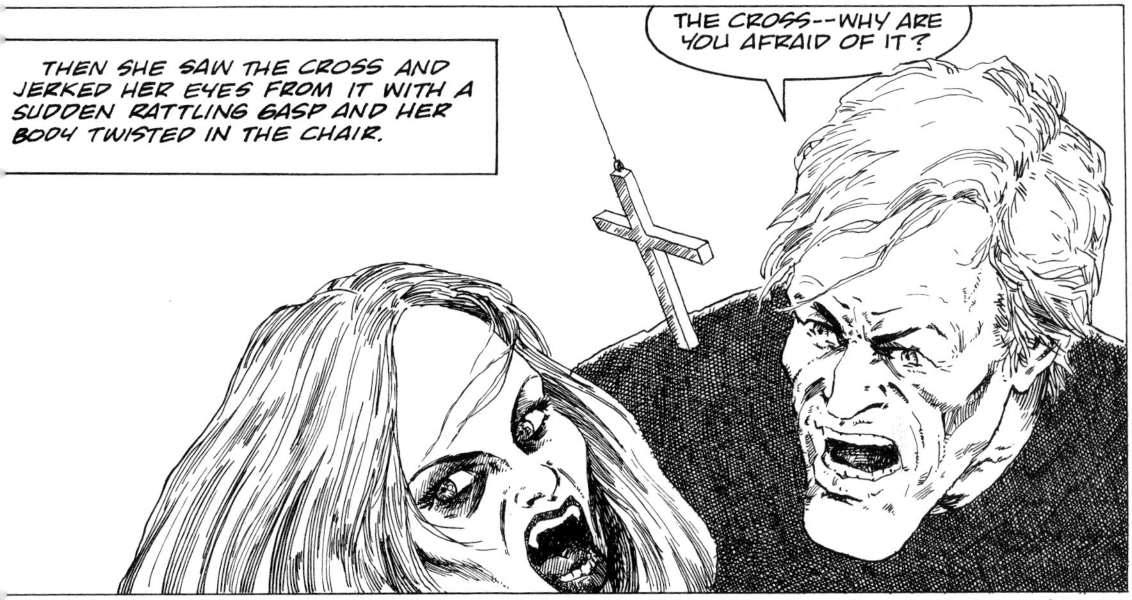
THEN SHE SAW THE CROSS AND JERKED HER EYES FROM IT WITH A SUDDEN RATTLING GASP AND HER BODY TWISTED IN THE CHAIR.
THE CROSS--WHY ARE YOU AFRAID OF IT?

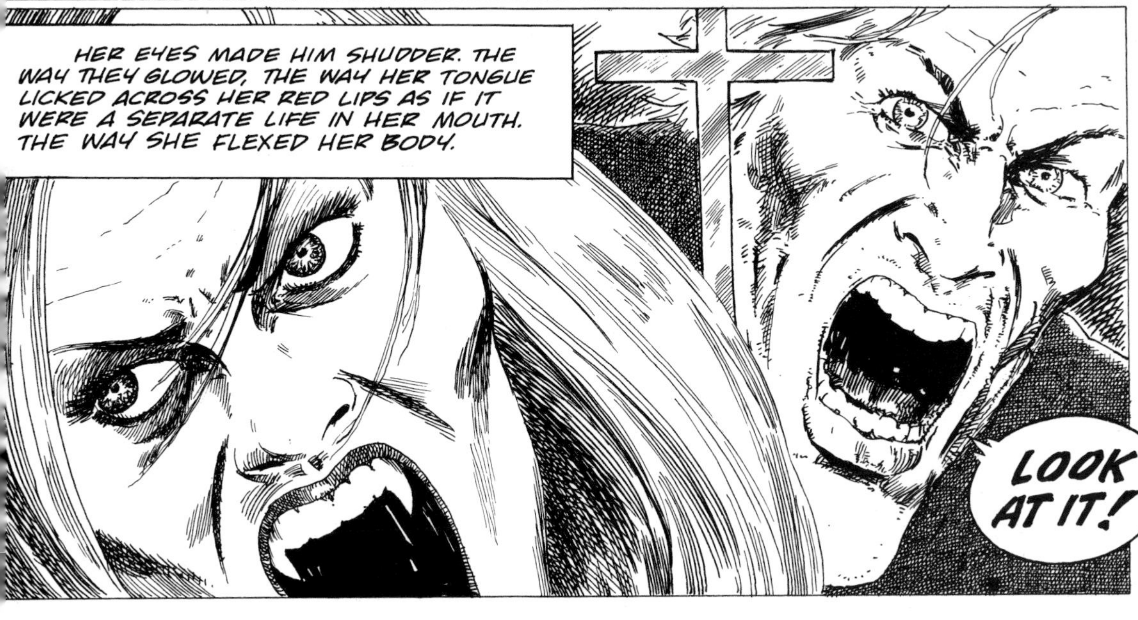
HER EYES MADE HIM SHUDDER. THE WAY THEY GLOWED, THE WAY HER TONGUE LICKED ACROSS HER RED LIPS AS IF IT WERE A SEPARATE LIFE IN HER MOUTH. THE WAY SHE FLEXED HER BODY.
LOOK AT IT!

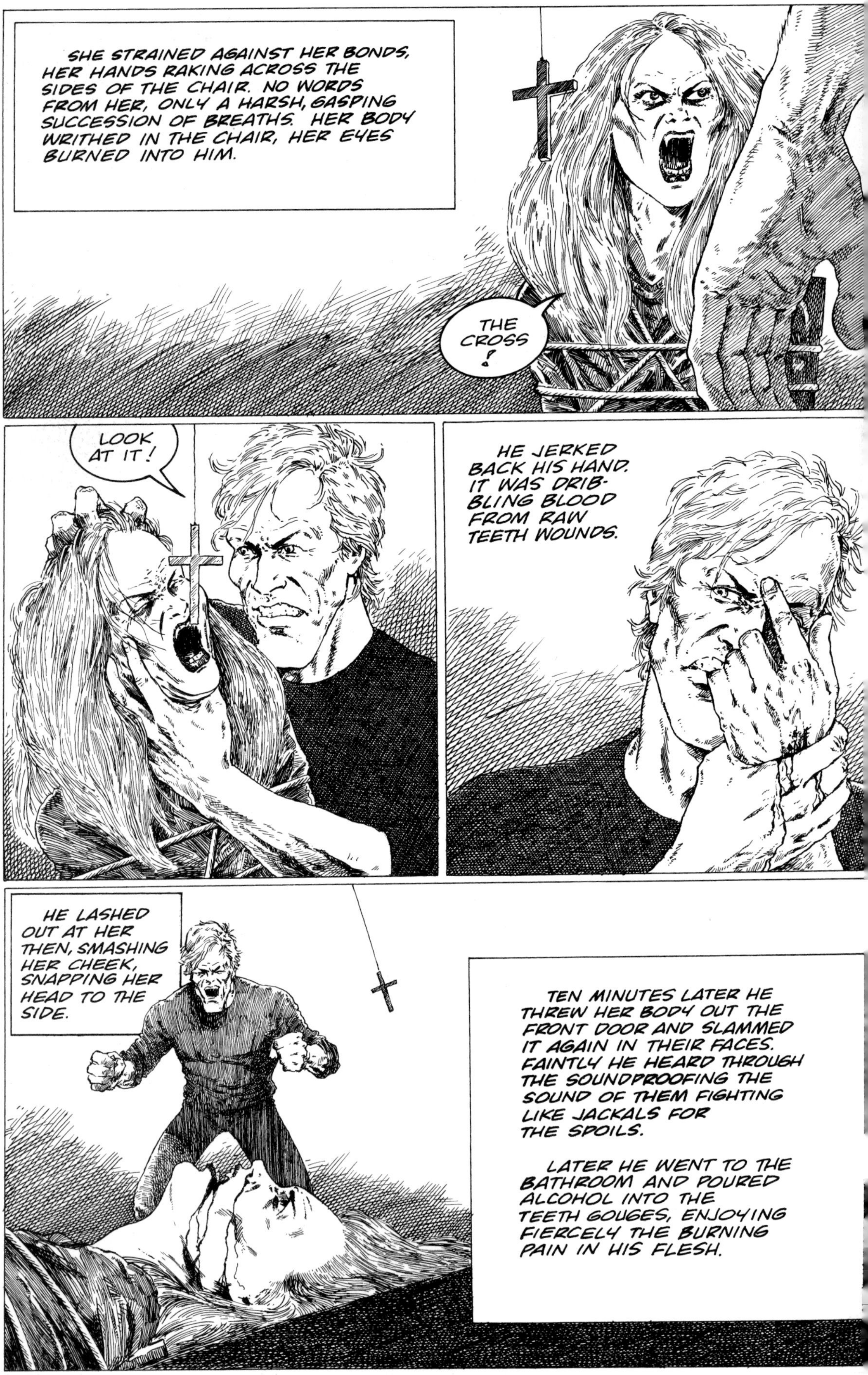
SHE STRAINED AGAINST HER BONDS, HER HANDS RAKING ACROSS THE SIDES OF THE CHAIR. NO WORDS FROM HER, ONLY A HARSH, GASPING SUCCESSION OF BREATHS. HER BODY WRITHED IN THE CHAIR, HER EYES BURNED INTO HIM.
THE CROSS!
LOOK AT IT!
HE JERKED BACK HIS HAND. IT WAS DRIB-BLING BLOOD FROM RAW TEETH WOUNDS.
HE LASHED OUT AT HER THEN, SMASHING HER CHEEK, SNAPPING HER HEAD TO THE SIDE.
TEN MINUTES LATER HE THREW HER BODY OUT THE FRONT DOOR AND SLAMMED IT AGAIN IN THEIR FACES. FAINTLY HE HEARD THROUGH THE SOUNDPROOFING THE SOUND OF THEM FIGHTING LIKE JACKALS FOR THE SPOILS.
LATER HE WENT TO THE BATHROOM AND POURED ALCOHOL INTO THE TEETH GOUGES, ENJOYING FIERCELY THE BURNING PAIN IN HIS FLESH.

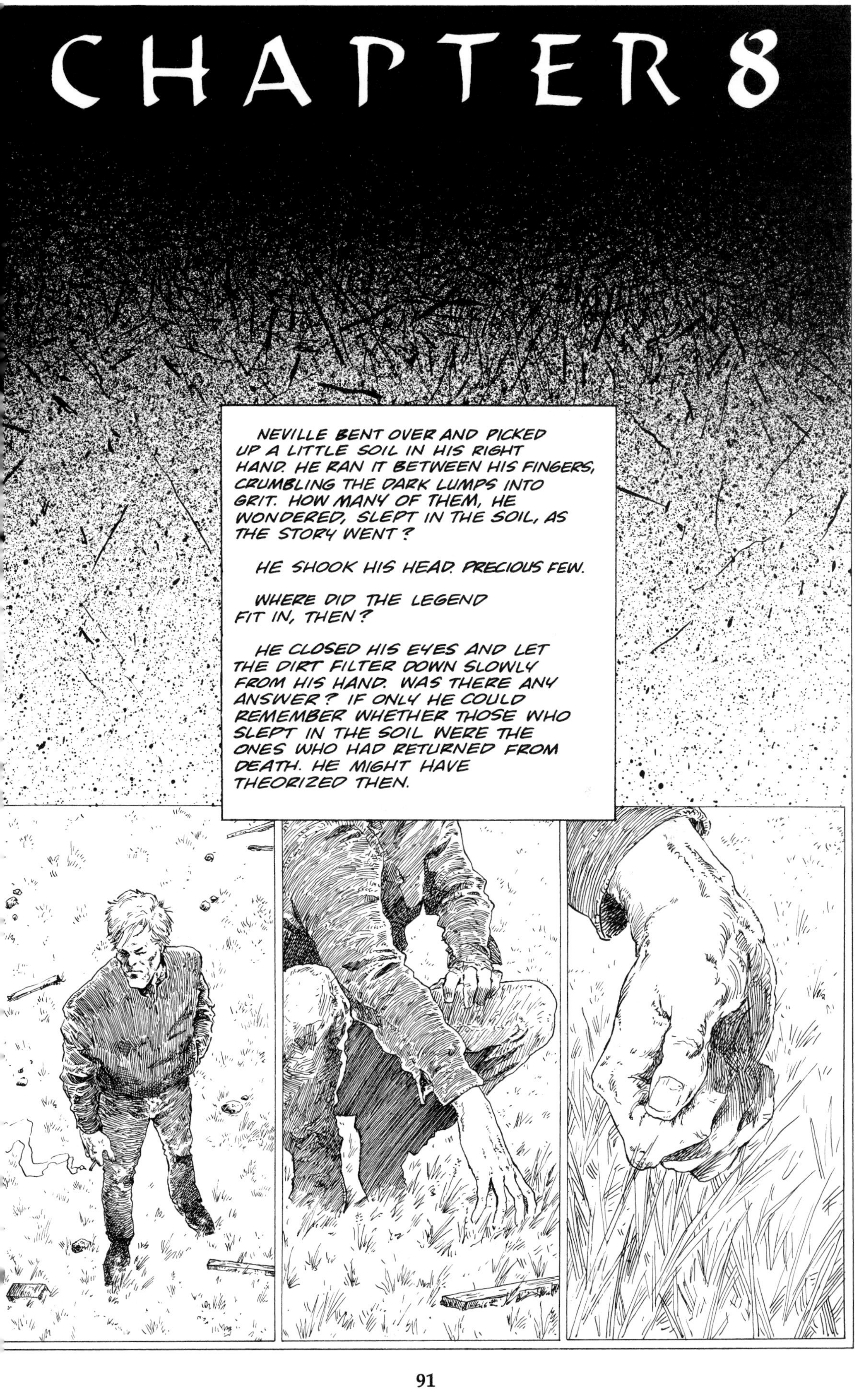
CHAPTER 8
NEVILLE BENT OVER AND PICKED UP A LITTLE SOIL IN HIS RIGHT HAND. HE RAN IT BETWEEN HIS FINGERS, CRUMBLING THE DARK LUMPS INTO GRIT. HOW MANY OF THEM, HE WONDERED, SLEPT IN THE SOIL, AS THE STORY WENT?
HE SHOOK HIS HEAD. PRECIOUS FEW.
WHERE DID THE LEGEND FIT IN, THEN?
HE CLOSED HIS EYES AND LET THE DIRT FILTER DOWN SLOWLY FROM HIS HAND. WAS THERE ANY ANSWER? IF ONLY HE COULD REMEMBER WHETHER THOSE WHO SLEPT IN THE SOIL WERE THE ONES WHO HAD RETURNED FROM DEATH. HE MIGHT HAVE THEORIZED THEN.

BUT HE COULDN'T REMEMBER. ANOTHER UNANSWERABLE QUESTION, THEN. ADD IT TO THE QUESTION THAT HAD OCCURRED TO HIM THE NIGHT BEFORE.

WHAT WOULD A MOHAMMEDAN VAMPIRE DO IF FACED WITH A CROSS?

THE BARKING SOUND OF HIS LAUGH IN THE SILENT MORNING AIR STARTLED HIM. GOOD GOD, HE THOUGHT, IT'S BEEN SO LONG SINCE I'VE LAUGHED, I'VE FORGOTTEN HOW. IT SOUNDED LIKE THE COUGH OF A SICK HOUND. WELL, THAT'S WHAT I AM, AFTER ALL, ISN'T IT? HE DECIDED. A VERY SICK DOG.

THERE HAD BEEN A DUST STORM ABOUT FOUR THAT MORNING. STRANGE HOW IT BROUGHT BACK MEMORIES. VIRGINIA, KATHY, ALL THOSE HORRIBLE DAYS...

HE CAUGHT HIMSELF. NO, NO, THERE WAS DANGER THERE. IT WAS THINKING OF THE PAST THAT DROVE HIM TO THE BOTTLE. HE WAS JUST GOING TO HAVE TO ACCEPT THE PRESENT.

HE FOUND HIMSELF WONDERING AGAIN WHY HE CHOSE TO GO ON LIVING. PROBABLY, HE THOUGHT, THERE'S NO REAL REASON. I'M JUST TOO DUMB TO END IT ALL.

HE LOOKED AROUND AS IF THERE WAS SOMETHING TO SEE ALONG THE STILLNESS OF CIMARRON STREET.

ALL RIGHT, HE DECIDED IMPULSIVELY, LET'S SEE IF THE RUNNING WATER BIT MAKES SENSE.

HE BURIED A HOSE UNDER THE GROUND AND RAN IT INTO A SMALL TROUGH CONSTRUCTED OF WOOD. THE WATER RAN THROUGH THE TROUGH AND OUT ANOTHER HOLE INTO MORE HOSING, WHICH CONDUCTED THE WATER INTO THE EARTH.

WHEN HE'D FINISHED, HE WENT IN AND TOOK A SHOWER, SHAVED, AND TOOK THE BANDAGE OFF HIS HAND. THE WOUND HAD HEALED CLEANLY. BUT THEN, HE HADN'T BEEN OVERLY CONCERNED ABOUT THAT. TIME HAD MORE THAN PROVED TO HIM THAT HE WAS IMMUNE TO THEIR INFECTION.

AT SIX-TWENTY HE WENT INTO THE LIVING ROOM AND LOOKED THROUGH THE PEEPHOLE. IN A WHILE, BEN CORTMAN CAME WALKING ONTO THE LAWN.

"COME OUT, NEVILLE," ROBERT NEVILLE MUTTERED, AND CORTMAN ECHOED THE WORDS IN A LOUD CRY.

MOTIONLESS, NEVILLE WATCHED.

IT WAS STRANGE LOOKING OUT AT BEN CORTMAN; A BEN COMPLETELY ALIEN TO HIM NOW. ONCE HE HAD SPOKEN TO THAT MAN, RIDDEN TO WORK WITH HIM, TALKED ABOUT CARS AND BASEBALL AND POLITICS WITH HIM, LATER ON ABOUT THE DISEASE, ABOUT HOW VIRGINIA AND KATHY WERE GETTING ALONG, ABOUT HOW FREDA CORTMAN WAS, ABOUT...

NEVILLE SHOOK HIS HEAD. THERE WAS NO POINT GOING INTO THAT. THE PAST WAS AS DEAD AS CORTMAN.

COME OUT, NEVILLE!!

THE WORLD'S GONE MAD, HE THOUGHT. THE DEAD WALK ABOUT AND I THINK NOTHING OF IT. HOW QUICKLY ONE ACCEPTS THE INCREDIBLE IF ONLY ONE SEES IT ENOUGH! HE WONDERED WHO IT WAS BEN CORTMAN REMINDED HIM OF... SOMEBODY, BUT FOR THE LIFE OF HIM HE COULDN'T THINK WHO.

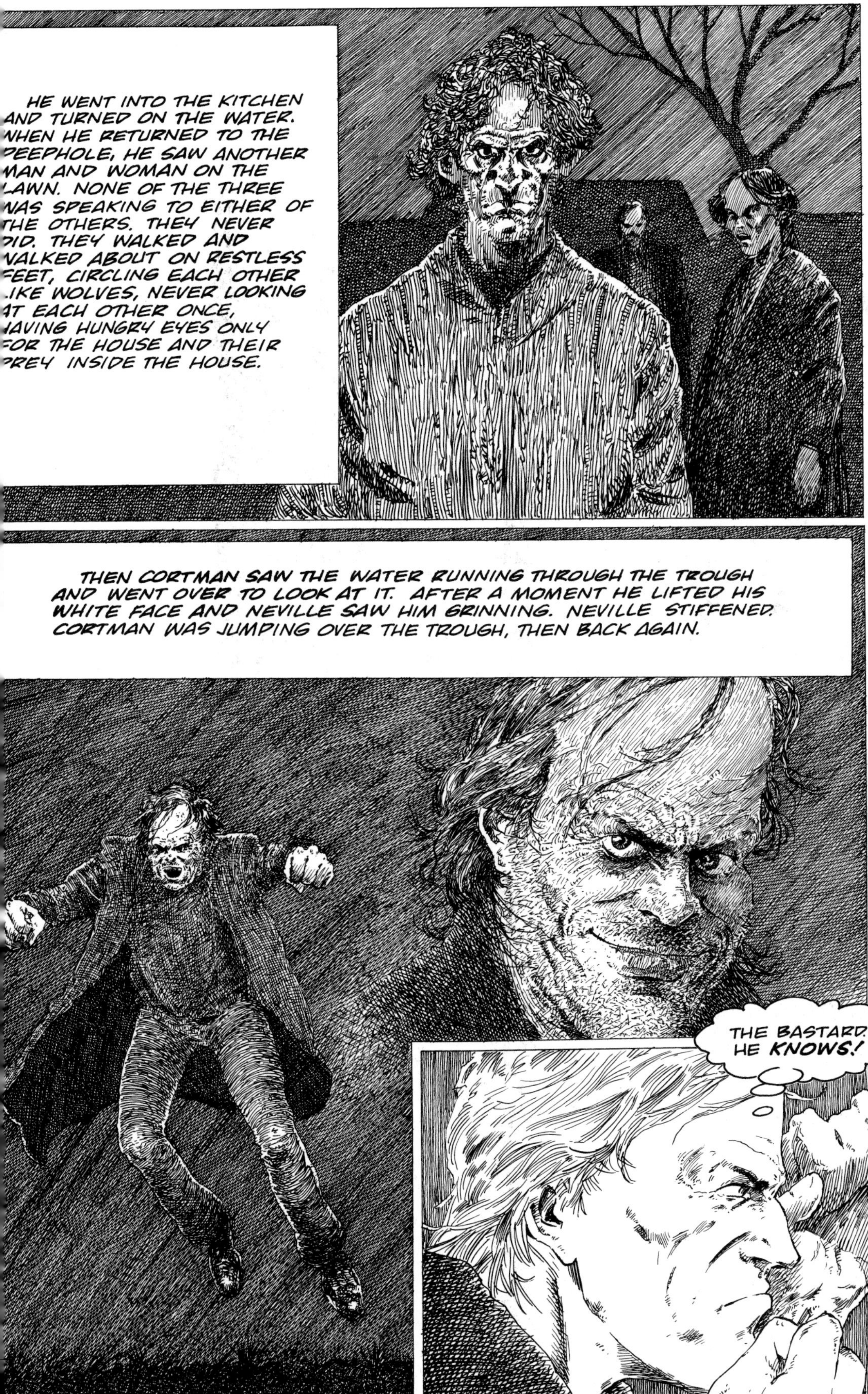
HE WENT INTO THE KITCHEN AND TURNED ON THE WATER. WHEN HE RETURNED TO THE PEEPHOLE, HE SAW ANOTHER MAN AND WOMAN ON THE LAWN. NONE OF THE THREE WAS SPEAKING TO EITHER OF THE OTHERS. THEY NEVER DID. THEY WALKED AND WALKED ABOUT ON RESTLESS FEET, CIRCLING EACH OTHER LIKE WOLVES, NEVER LOOKING AT EACH OTHER ONCE, HAVING HUNGRY EYES ONLY FOR THE HOUSE AND THEIR PREY INSIDE THE HOUSE.
THEN CORTMAN SAW THE WATER RUNNING THROUGH THE TROUGH AND WENT OVER TO LOOK AT IT. AFTER A MOMENT HE LIFTED HIS WHITE FACE AND NEVILLE SAW HIM GRINNING. NEVILLE STIFFENED. CORTMAN WAS JUMPING OVER THE TROUGH, THEN BACK AGAIN.
THE BASTARD. HE *KNOWS!*

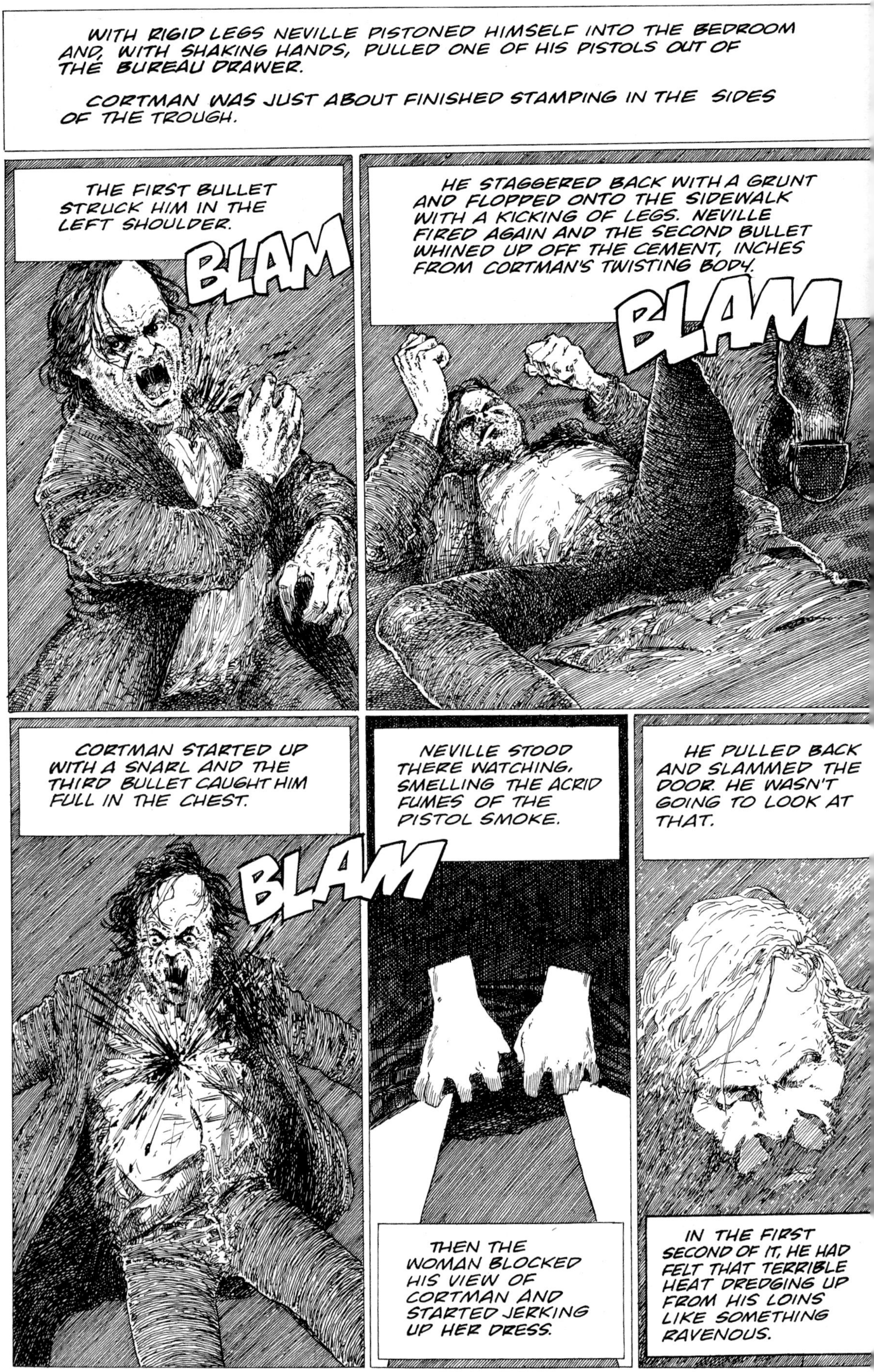
WITH RIGID LEGS NEVILLE PISTONED HIMSELF INTO THE BEDROOM AND, WITH SHAKING HANDS, PULLED ONE OF HIS PISTOLS OUT OF THE BUREAU DRAWER.
CORTMAN WAS JUST ABOUT FINISHED STAMPING IN THE SIDES OF THE TROUGH.
THE FIRST BULLET STRUCK HIM IN THE LEFT SHOULDER.
BLAM
HE STAGGERED BACK WITH A GRUNT AND FLOPPED ONTO THE SIDEWALK WITH A KICKING OF LEGS. NEVILLE FIRED AGAIN AND THE SECOND BULLET WHINED UP OFF THE CEMENT, INCHES FROM CORTMAN'S TWISTING BODY.
BLAM
CORTMAN STARTED UP WITH A SNARL AND THE THIRD BULLET CAUGHT HIM FULL IN THE CHEST.
BLAM
NEVILLE STOOD THERE WATCHING, SMELLING THE ACRID FUMES OF THE PISTOL SMOKE.
THEN THE WOMAN BLOCKED HIS VIEW OF CORTMAN AND STARTED JERKING UP HER DRESS.
HE PULLED BACK AND SLAMMED THE DOOR. HE WASN'T GOING TO LOOK AT THAT.
IN THE FIRST SECOND OF IT, HE HAD FELT THAT TERRIBLE HEAT DREDGING UP FROM HIS LOINS LIKE SOMETHING RAVENOUS.

LATER HE LOOKED OUT AGAIN AND SAW BEN CORTMAN PACING AROUND, CALLING FOR HIM TO COME OUT.

AND, IN THE MOONLIGHT, NEVILLE SUDDENLY REALIZED WHO CORTMAN REMINDED HIM OF. MY GOD--**OLIVER HARDY!** LESS PLUMP, TO BE SURE, THAN THE ROLY-POLY COMEDIAN; NO DEAD RINGER, BUT STILL HE COULDN'T DISPEL THE IMAGE. HIS CHEST SHUDDERED WITH REPRESSED LAUGHTER AND HE TURNED AWAY AS THE SHAKING REACHED HIS SHOULDERS.

OLIVER HARDY FLOPPING ON HIS BACK UNDER THE DRIVING IMPACT OF BULLETS. OLIVER HARDY ALWAYS COMING BACK FOR MORE, NO MATTER WHAT HAPPENED. RIPPED BY BULLETS, PUNCTURED BY KNIVES, FLATTENED BY CARS, SMASHED UNDER COLLAPSING CHIMNEYS AND BOATS, SUBMERGED IN WATER, FLUNG THROUGH PIPES. AND ALWAYS RETURNING, PATIENT AND BRUISED. THAT WAS WHO BEN CORTMAN WAS--A HIDEOUSLY MALIGNANT OLIVER HARDY BUFFETED AND LONG-SUFFERING.

MY GOD, IT WAS HILARIOUS!

HE COULDN'T STOP LAUGHING BECAUSE IT WAS MORE THAN LAUGHTER; IT WAS RELEASE. TEARS FLOODED DOWN HIS CHEEKS. THE GLASS IN HIS HAND SHOOK SO BADLY, THE LIQUOR SPILLED ALL OVER HIM AND MADE HIM **LAUGH HARDER.** THEN THE GLASS FELL THUMPING ON THE RUG AS HIS BODY JERKED WITH SPASMS OF UNCONTROLLABLE AMUSEMENT AND THE ROOM WAS FILLED WITH HIS GASPING, NERVE-SHATTERED LAUGHTER.

LATER, HE CRIED.

THE DAYS PASSED AND ROBERT NEVILLE WENT ABOUT HIS ROUTINE OF SEARCHING FOR VAMPIRES. HE WOULD DRIVE THE STAKE INTO THE STOMACH, INTO THE SHOULDER, INTO THE NECK WITH A SINGLE MALLET BLOW. INTO THE LEGS AND THE ARMS, AND ALWAYS THE SAME RESULT: THE BLOOD PULSING OUT, SLICK AND CRIMSON, OVER THE FLESH.

HE THOUGHT HE'D FOUND THE ANSWER. IT WAS A MATTER OF LOSING THE BLOOD THEY LIVED BY; IT WAS HEMORRHAGE.

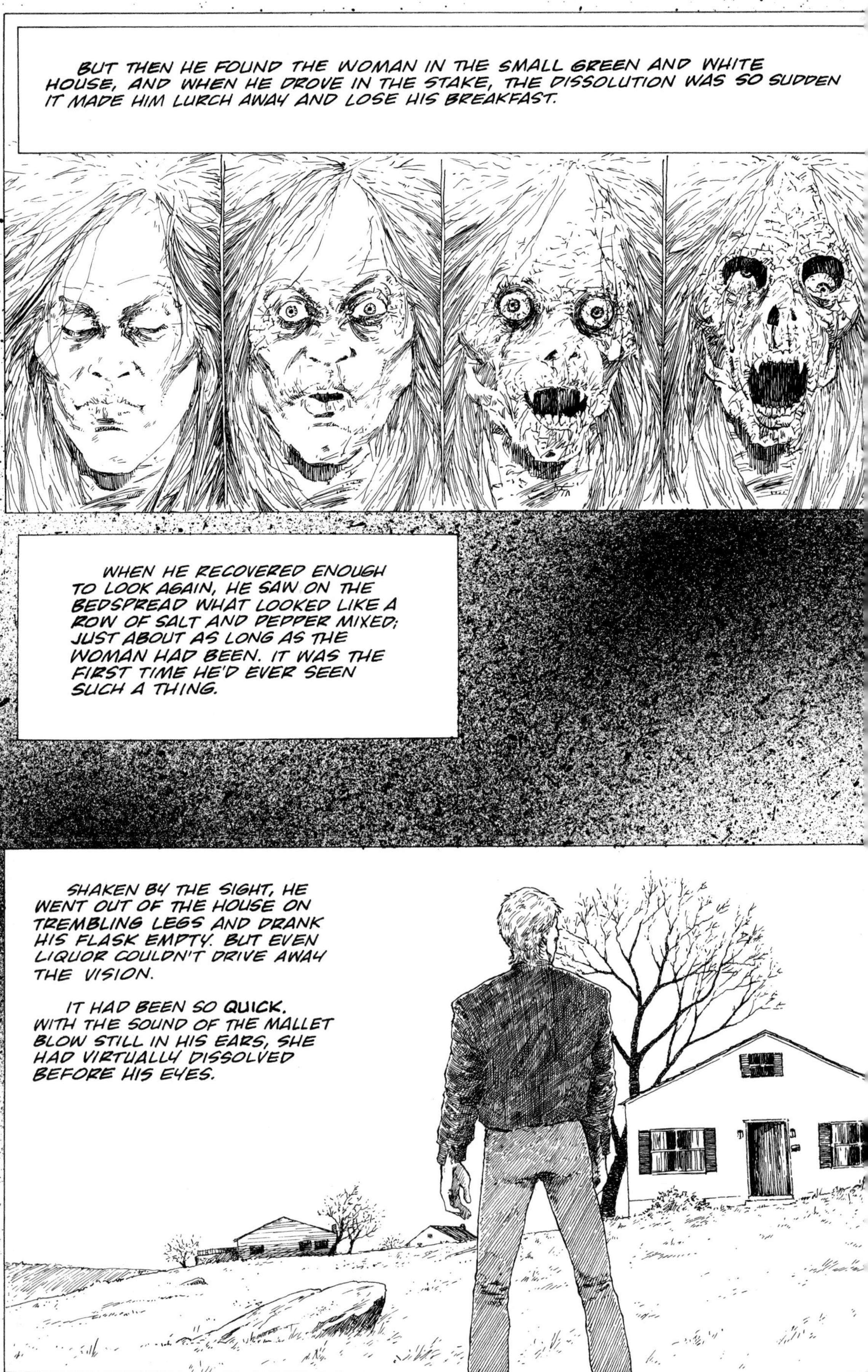
BUT THEN HE FOUND THE WOMAN IN THE SMALL GREEN AND WHITE HOUSE, AND WHEN HE DROVE IN THE STAKE, THE DISSOLUTION WAS SO SUDDEN IT MADE HIM LURCH AWAY AND LOSE HIS BREAKFAST.
WHEN HE RECOVERED ENOUGH TO LOOK AGAIN, HE SAW ON THE BEDSPREAD WHAT LOOKED LIKE A ROW OF SALT AND PEPPER MIXED; JUST ABOUT AS LONG AS THE WOMAN HAD BEEN. IT WAS THE FIRST TIME HE'D EVER SEEN SUCH A THING.
SHAKEN BY THE SIGHT, HE WENT OUT OF THE HOUSE ON TREMBLING LEGS AND DRANK HIS FLASK EMPTY. BUT EVEN LIQUOR COULDN'T DRIVE AWAY THE VISION.
IT HAD BEEN SO **QUICK**. WITH THE SOUND OF THE MALLET BLOW STILL IN HIS EARS, SHE HAD VIRTUALLY DISSOLVED BEFORE HIS EYES.

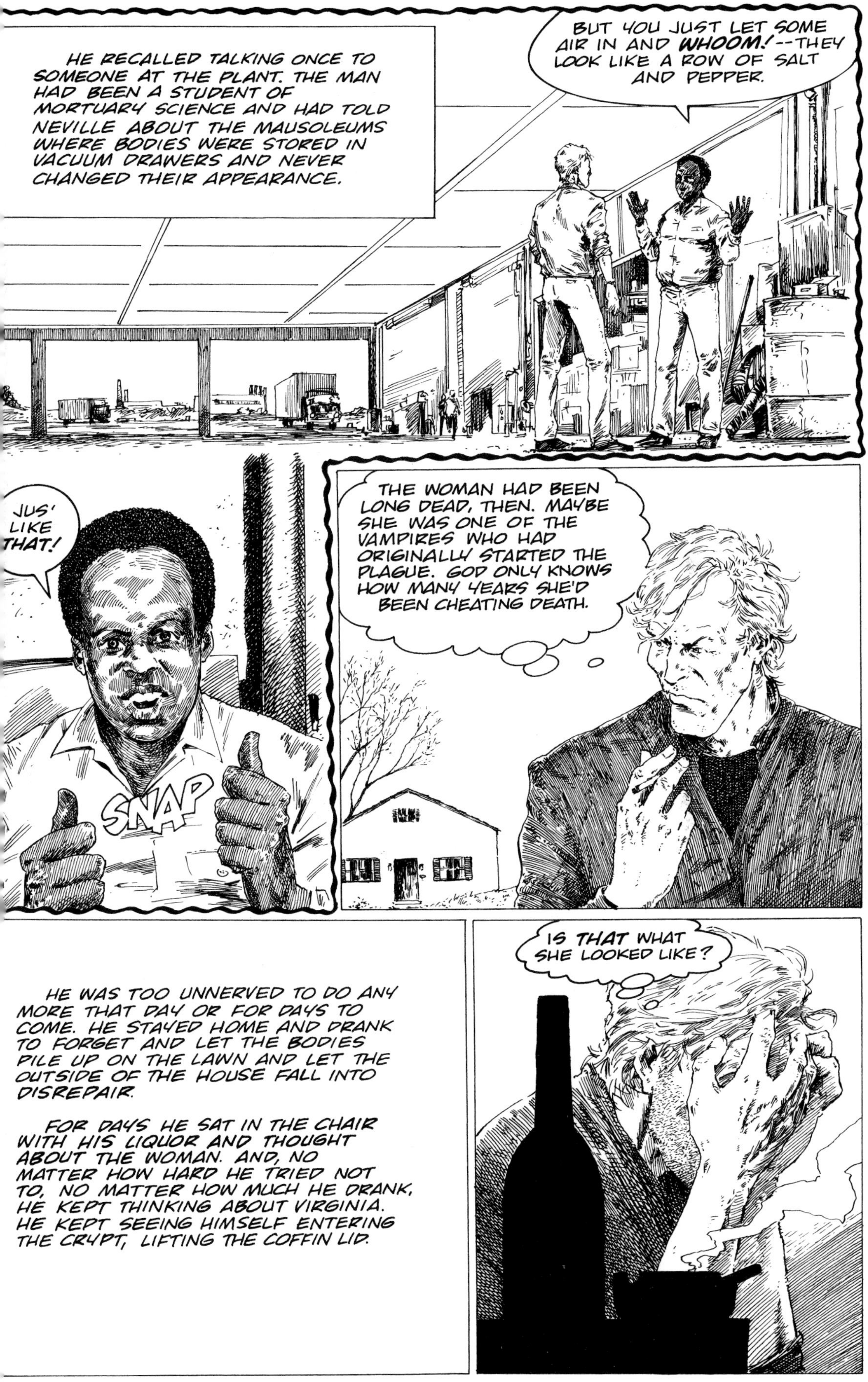
HE RECALLED TALKING ONCE TO SOMEONE AT THE PLANT. THE MAN HAD BEEN A STUDENT OF MORTUARY SCIENCE AND HAD TOLD NEVILLE ABOUT THE MAUSOLEUMS WHERE BODIES WERE STORED IN VACUUM DRAWERS AND NEVER CHANGED THEIR APPEARANCE.
BUT YOU JUST LET SOME AIR IN AND WHOOM! --THEY LOOK LIKE A ROW OF SALT AND PEPPER.
JUS' LIKE THAT!
SNAP
THE WOMAN HAD BEEN LONG DEAD, THEN. MAYBE SHE WAS ONE OF THE VAMPIRES WHO HAD ORIGINALLY STARTED THE PLAGUE. GOD ONLY KNOWS HOW MANY YEARS SHE'D BEEN CHEATING DEATH.
HE WAS TOO UNNERVED TO DO ANY MORE THAT DAY OR FOR DAYS TO COME. HE STAYED HOME AND DRANK TO FORGET AND LET THE BODIES PILE UP ON THE LAWN AND LET THE OUTSIDE OF THE HOUSE FALL INTO DISREPAIR.
FOR DAYS HE SAT IN THE CHAIR WITH HIS LIQUOR AND THOUGHT ABOUT THE WOMAN. AND, NO MATTER HOW HARD HE TRIED NOT TO, NO MATTER HOW MUCH HE DRANK, HE KEPT THINKING ABOUT VIRGINIA. HE KEPT SEEING HIMSELF ENTERING THE CRYPT, LIFTING THE COFFIN LID.
IS THAT WHAT SHE LOOKED LIKE?

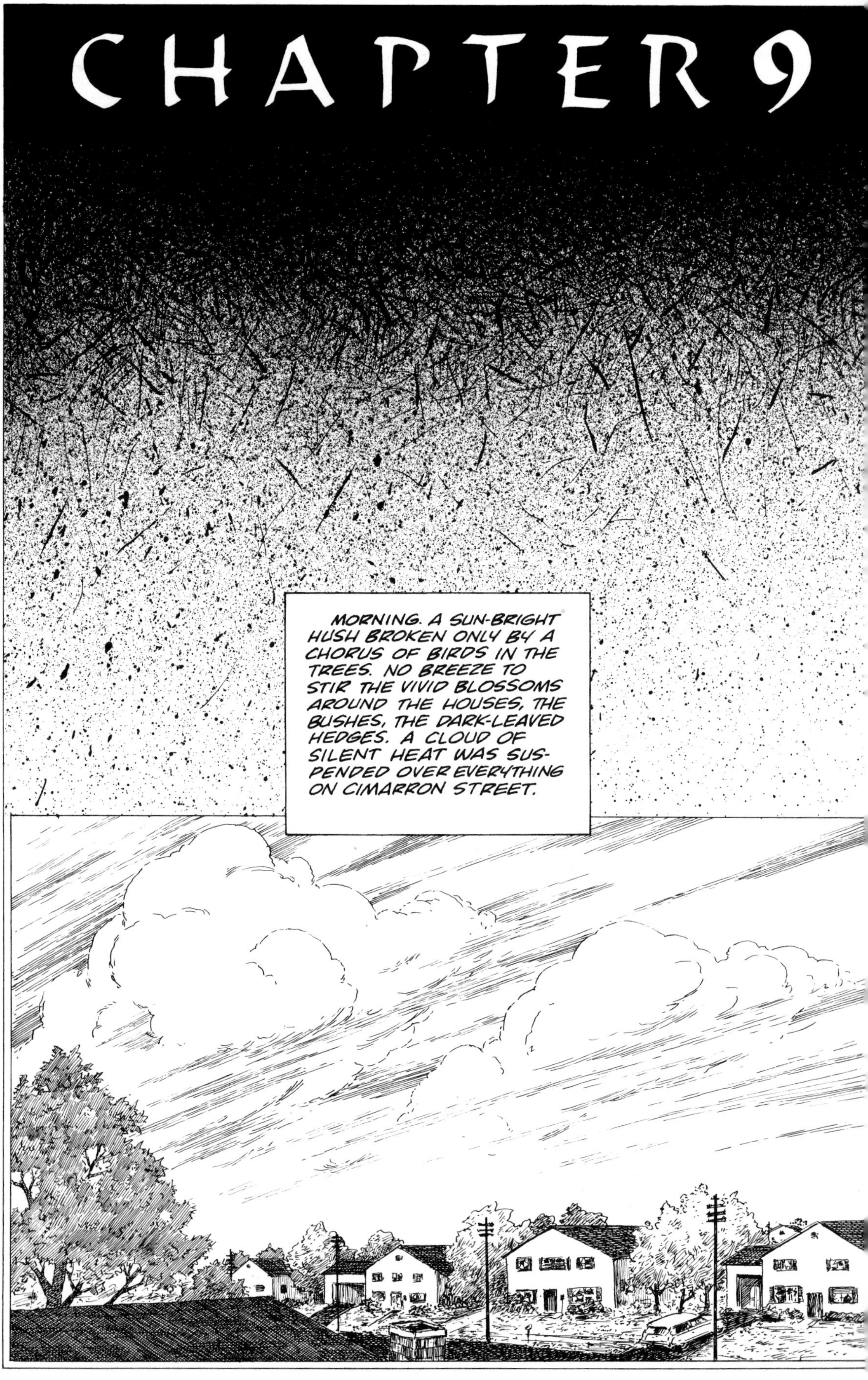
CHAPTER 9
MORNING. A SUN-BRIGHT HUSH BROKEN ONLY BY A CHORUS OF BIRDS IN THE TREES. NO BREEZE TO STIR THE VIVID BLOSSOMS AROUND THE HOUSES, THE BUSHES, THE DARK-LEAVED HEDGES. A CLOUD OF SILENT HEAT WAS SUSPENDED OVER EVERYTHING ON CIMARRON STREET.

VIRGINIA NEVILLE'S HEART HAD STOPPED.

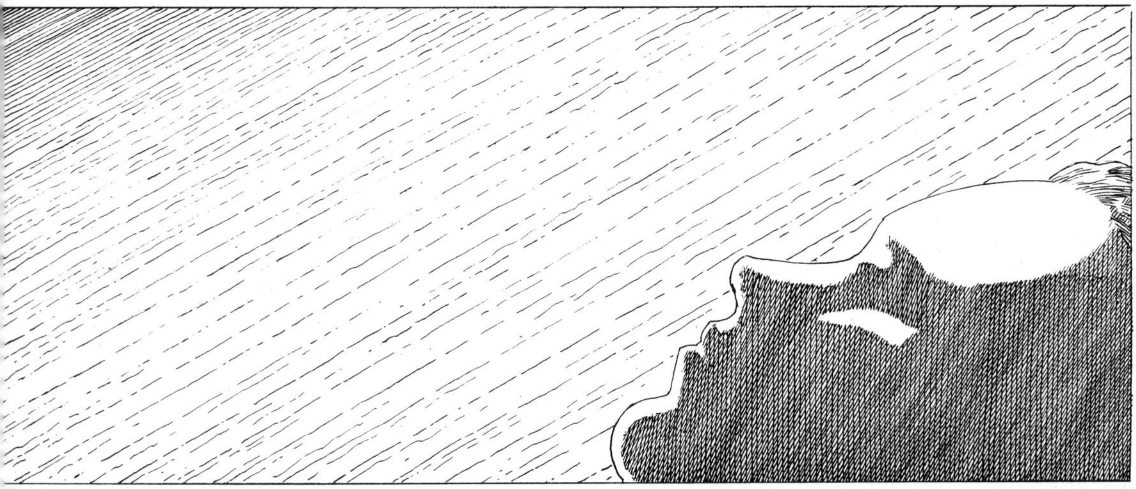

HE SAT BESIDE HER ON THE BED, LOOKING DOWN AT HER WHITE FACE. HE HELD HER FINGERS IN HIS HAND, HIS FINGERTIPS STROKING AND STROKING.

SOMETHING HAD HAPPENED TO HIS BRAIN.

IN THE SECOND HE HAD FELT NO HEARTBEAT BENEATH HIS TREMBLING FINGERS, THE CORE OF HIS BRAIN SEEMED TO HAVE PETRIFIED, SENDING OUT JAGGED LINES OF CALCIFICATION UNTIL HIS HEAD FELT LIKE STONE. TIME WAS CAUGHT ON HOOKS AND COULD NOT PROGRESS. EVERYTHING STOOD FIXED. WITH VIRGINIA, LIFE AND THE WORLD HAD SHUDDERED TO A HALT.

THEN, SLOWLY, HE FOUND HIS BODY TREMBLING, HIS NERVES BEYOND CONTROL, BEREFT OF WILL. FOR MORE THAN AN HOUR HE SAT IN THIS PALSIED STATE, HIS EYES FASTENED DUMBLY TO HER FACE.

THEN, ABRUPTLY, IT ENDED, AND WITH A CHOKED MUTTERING IN HIS THROAT HE LURCHED UP FROM THE BED AND LEFT THE ROOM.

HALF THE WHISKY SPLASHED ON THE SINK TOP AS HE POURED. HE FILLED THE GLASS AND DRANK IT DOWN WITH GREAT CONVULSIVE SWALLOWS.

IT'S A DREAM. IT WAS AS IF A VOICE SPOKE THE WORDS ALOUD IN HIS HEAD.

"VIRGINIA!"

HE TOOK A STEP AND CRIED ALOUD AS THE ROOM FLUNG ITSELF OFF BALANCE. HE PUSHED HIMSELF UP AND STUMBLED TO THE LIVING ROOM. HE STOOD THERE LIKE A STATUE IN AN EARTHQUAKE, HIS MARBLE EYES FROZEN ON THE BEDROOM DOOR.

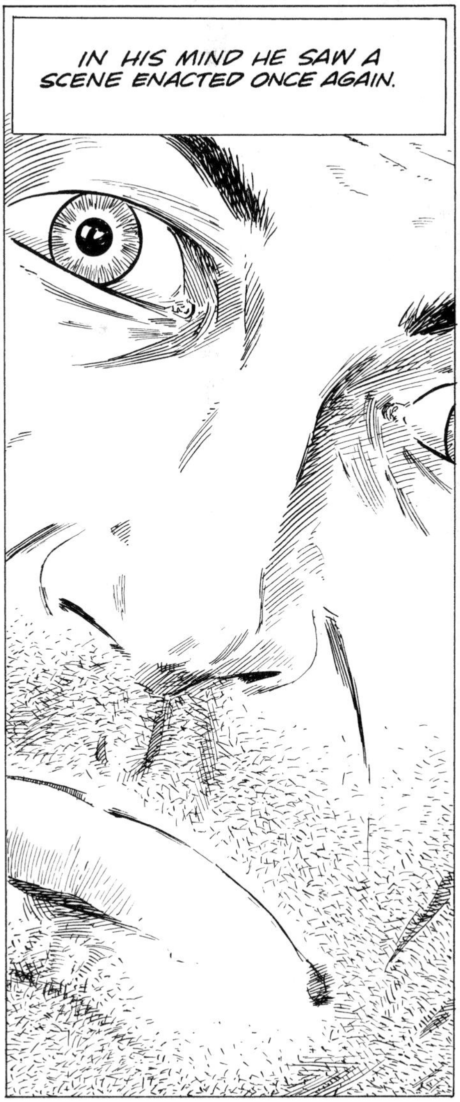
IN HIS MIND HE SAW A SCENE ENACTED ONCE AGAIN.

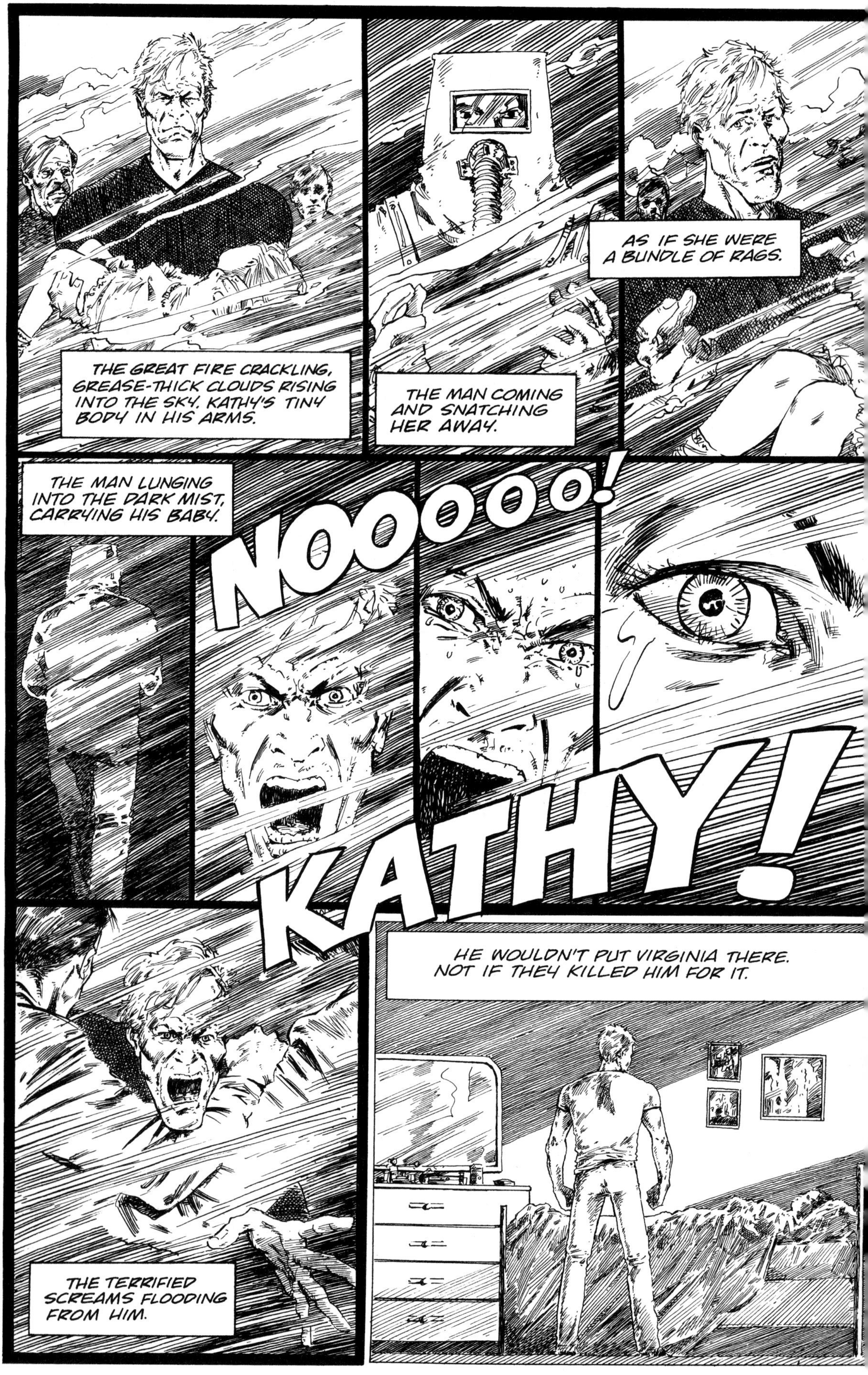
THE GREAT FIRE CRACKLING, GREASE-THICK CLOUDS RISING INTO THE SKY. KATHY'S TINY BODY IN HIS ARMS.
THE MAN COMING AND SNATCHING HER AWAY.
AS IF SHE WERE A BUNDLE OF RAGS.
THE MAN LUNGING INTO THE DARK MIST, CARRYING HIS BABY.
NOOOOOO!
KATHY!
THE TERRIFIED SCREAMS FLOODING FROM HIM.
HE WOULDN'T PUT VIRGINIA THERE. NOT IF THEY KILLED HIM FOR IT.

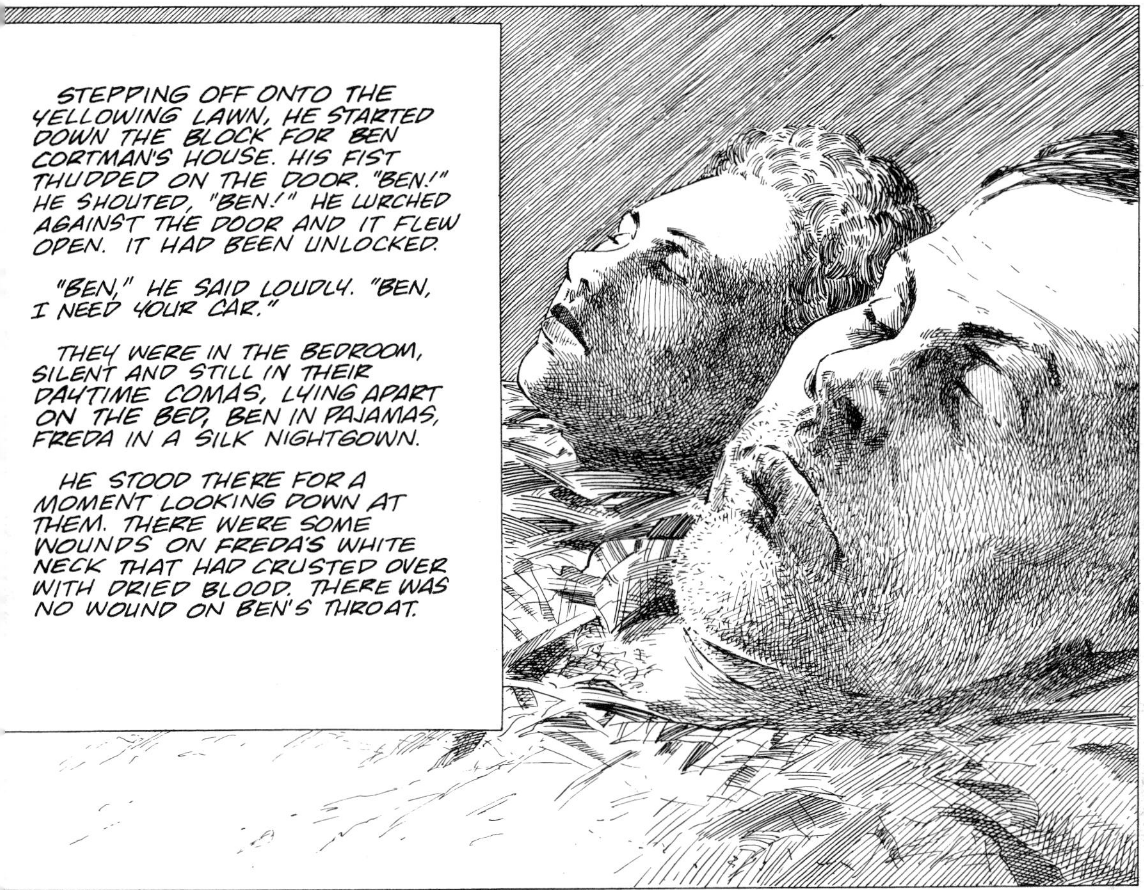
STEPPING OFF ONTO THE YELLOWING LAWN, HE STARTED DOWN THE BLOCK FOR BEN CORTMAN'S HOUSE. HIS FIST THUDDED ON THE DOOR. "BEN!" HE SHOUTED, "BEN!" HE LURCHED AGAINST THE DOOR AND IT FLEW OPEN. IT HAD BEEN UNLOCKED.
"BEN," HE SAID LOUDLY. "BEN, I NEED YOUR CAR."
THEY WERE IN THE BEDROOM, SILENT AND STILL IN THEIR DAYTIME COMAS, LYING APART ON THE BED, BEN IN PAJAMAS, FREDA IN A SILK NIGHTGOWN.
HE STOOD THERE FOR A MOMENT LOOKING DOWN AT THEM. THERE WERE SOME WOUNDS ON FREDA'S WHITE NECK THAT HAD CRUSTED OVER WITH DRIED BLOOD. THERE WAS NO WOUND ON BEN'S THROAT.

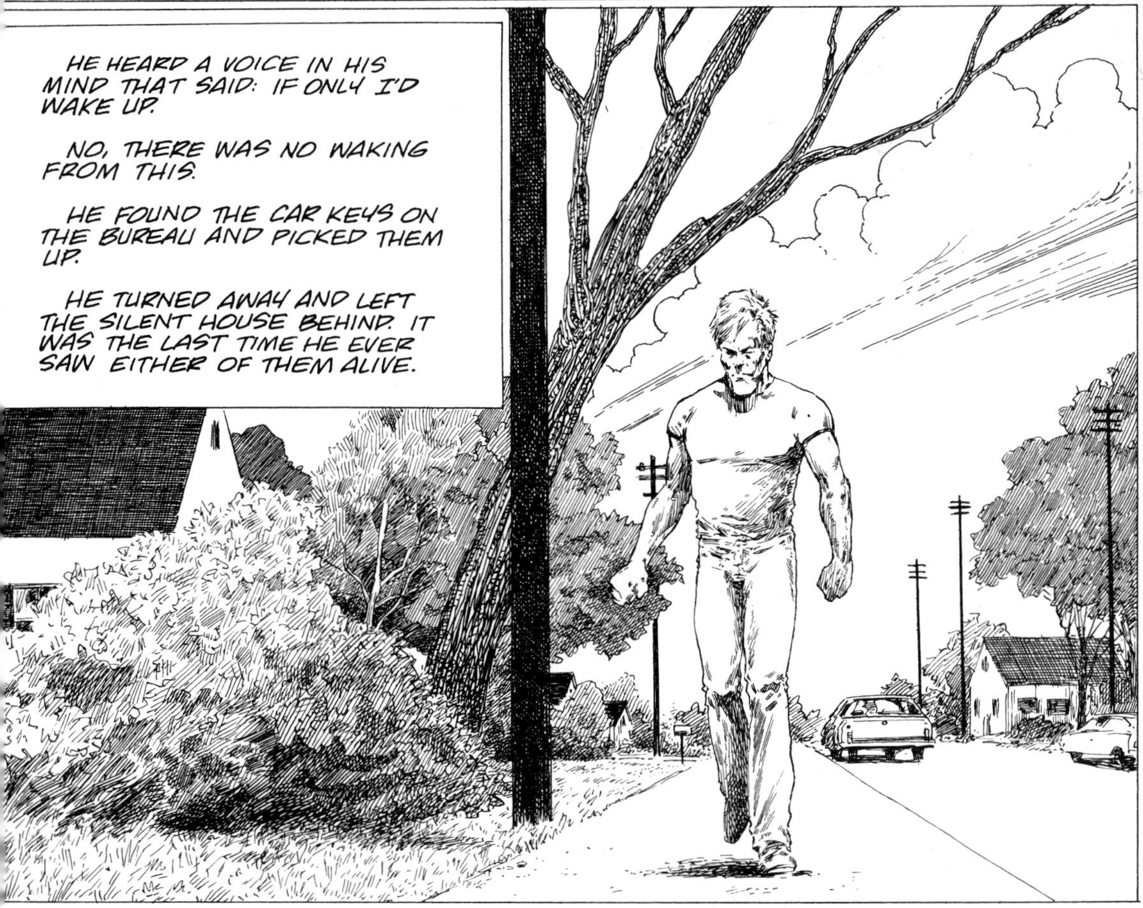
HE HEARD A VOICE IN HIS MIND THAT SAID: IF ONLY I'D WAKE UP.
NO, THERE WAS NO WAKING FROM THIS.
HE FOUND THE CAR KEYS ON THE BUREAU AND PICKED THEM UP.
HE TURNED AWAY AND LEFT THE SILENT HOUSE BEHIND. IT WAS THE LAST TIME HE EVER SAW EITHER OF THEM ALIVE.

WHY DID I GET THE CAR? HE WONDERED. I CAN'T BURN HER. I WON'T. BUT WHAT ELSE WAS THERE? FUNERAL PARLORS WERE CLOSED. WHAT FEW MORTICIANS WERE HEALTHY ENOUGH TO PRACTICE WERE PREVENTED FROM DOING SO BY LAW. EVERYONE WITHOUT EXCEPTION HAD TO BE TRANSPORTED TO THE FIRES IMMEDIATELY, UPON DEATH. IT WAS THE ONLY WAY THEY KNEW NOW TO PREVENT COMMUNICATION. ONLY FLAMES COULD DESTROY THE BACTERIA THAT CAUSED THE PLAGUE.

NO, IF THERE WAS ANYTHING LEFT IN THE WORLD, IT WAS HIS VOW THAT VIRGINIA WOULD NOT BE BURNED IN THE FIRE.

AN HOUR PASSED BEFORE HE FINALLY REACHED A DECISION. THEN HE WENT AND GOT HER NEEDLE AND THREAD. HE KEPT SEWING UNTIL ONLY HER FACE SHOWED. THEN HE SEWED THE BLANKET TOGETHER OVER HER MOUTH, OVER HER NOSE, HER EYES.

HE DRANK ANOTHER GLASS OF WHISKY. IT DIDN'T SEEM TO AFFECT HIM AT ALL.

"COME ON, BABY," HE WHISPERED.

THE WORDS SEEMED TO LOOSEN EVERYTHING. HE FELT HIMSELF SHAKING, FELT THE TEARS RUNNING SLOWLY DOWN HIS CHEEKS AS HE CARRIED HER THROUGH THE LIVING ROOM AND OUTSIDE.

HE PUT HER IN THE BACK SEAT AND GOT THE SHOVEL FROM THE GARAGE.

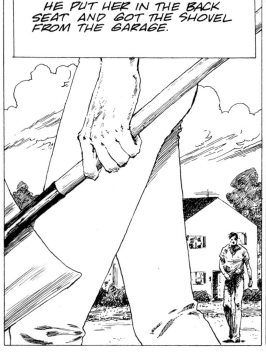

WAIT! PLEASE.

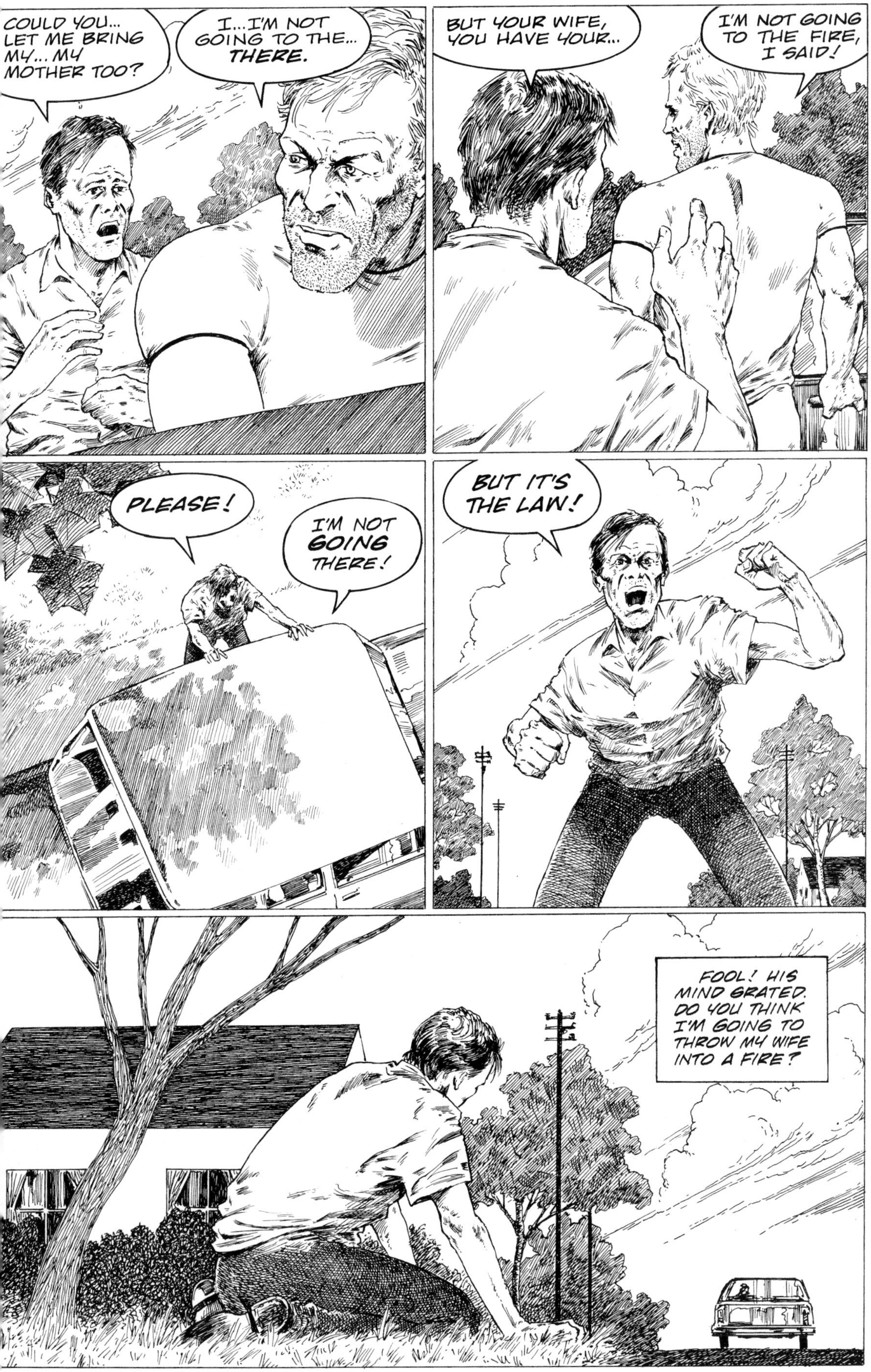
COULD YOU... LET ME BRING MY... MY MOTHER TOO?
I... I'M NOT GOING TO THE... THERE.
BUT YOUR WIFE, YOU HAVE YOUR...
I'M NOT GOING TO THE FIRE, I SAID!
PLEASE!
I'M NOT GOING THERE!
BUT IT'S THE LAW!
FOOL! HIS MIND GRATED. DO YOU THINK I'M GOING TO THROW MY WIFE INTO A FIRE?

HE TURNED LEFT AT COMPTON BOULEVARD AND STARTED WEST. AS HE DROVE HE LOOKED AT THE HUGE LOT ON HIS RIGHT. HE COULDN'T USE ANY OF THE CEMETERIES. THEY WERE LOCKED AND WATCHED. MEN HAD BEEN SHOT TRYING TO BURY THEIR LOVED ONES.

HE TURNED RIGHT AT THE NEXT BLOCK AND RIGHT AGAIN INTO A QUIET STREET THAT ENDED IN THE VACANT LOT.

NO ONE SAW HIM CARRY HER FROM THE CAR AND DEEP INTO THE HIGH-WEEDED LOT. NO ONE SAW HIM PUT HER DOWN ON AN OPEN PATCH OF GROUND AND THEN DISAPPEAR FROM VIEW AS HE KNELT.

SLOWLY HE DUG, PUSHING THE SHOVEL INTO THE SOFT EARTH, THE BRIGHT SUN POURING HEAT INTO THE LITTLE CLEARING LIKE MOLTEN AIR INTO A DISH. SWEAT RAN IN MANY LINES DOWN HIS CHEEKS AND FOREHEAD AS HE DUG, AND THE EARTH SWAM DIZZILY BEFORE HIS EYES. NEWLY THROWN DIRT FILLED HIS NOSTRILS WITH ITS HOT, PUNGENT SMELL.

AT LAST THE HOLE WAS FINISHED. THIS WAS THE PART HE DREADED.

BUT HE KNEW HE COULDN'T WAIT. IF HE WAS SEEN THEY WOULD COME OUT AND GET HIM. BEING SHOT WAS NOTHING. BUT SHE WOULD BE BURNED THEN. HIS LIPS TIGHTENED. NO.

GENTLY, AS CAREFULLY AS HE COULD, HE LOWERED HER INTO THE SHALLOW GRAVE, MAKING SURE THAT HER HEAD DID NOT BUMP.

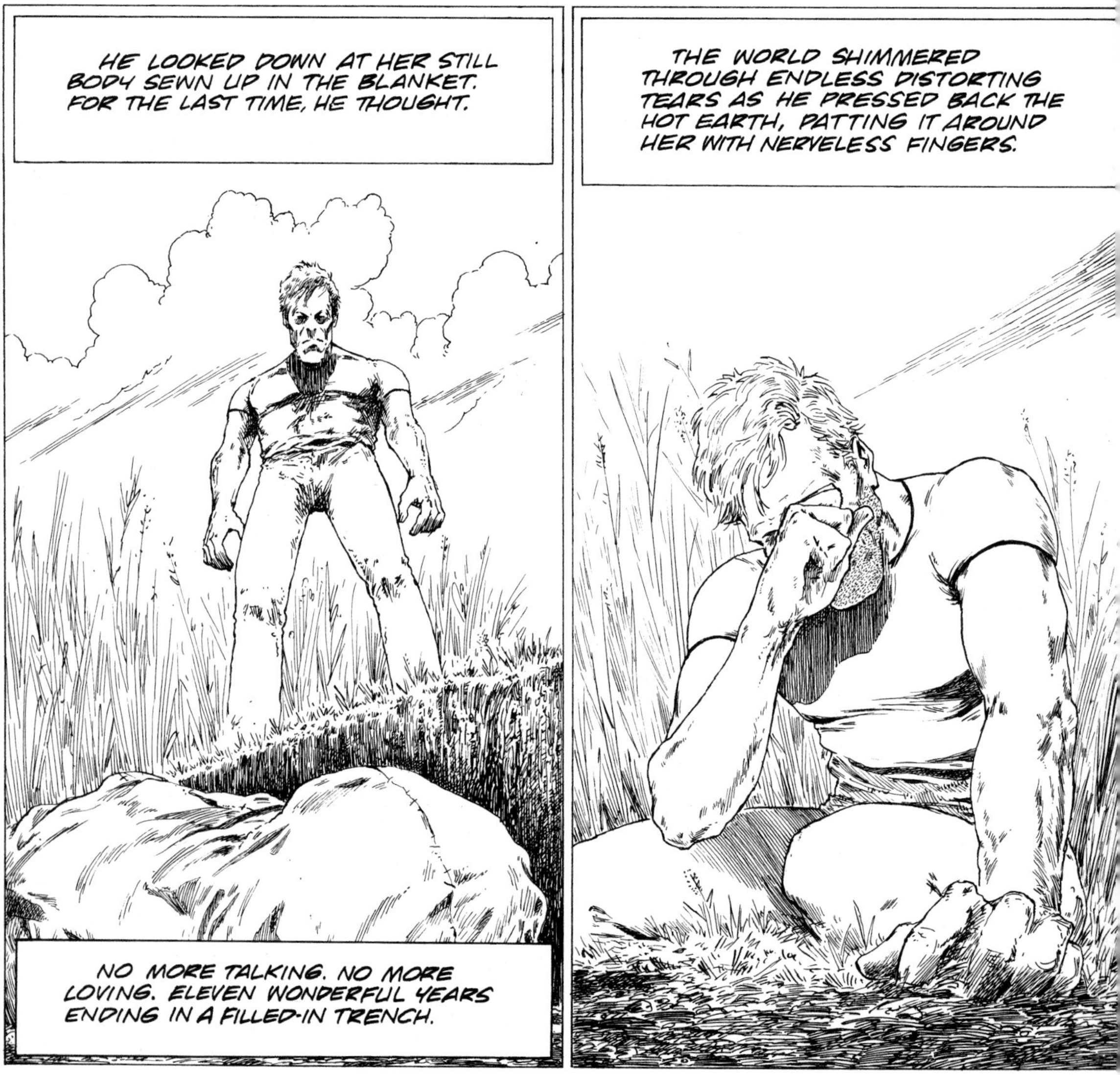
HE LOOKED DOWN AT HER STILL BODY SEWN UP IN THE BLANKET. FOR THE LAST TIME, HE THOUGHT.
NO MORE TALKING. NO MORE LOVING. ELEVEN WONDERFUL YEARS ENDING IN A FILLED-IN TRENCH.
THE WORLD SHIMMERED THROUGH ENDLESS DISTORTING TEARS AS HE PRESSED BACK THE HOT EARTH, PATTING IT AROUND HER WITH NERVELESS FINGERS.

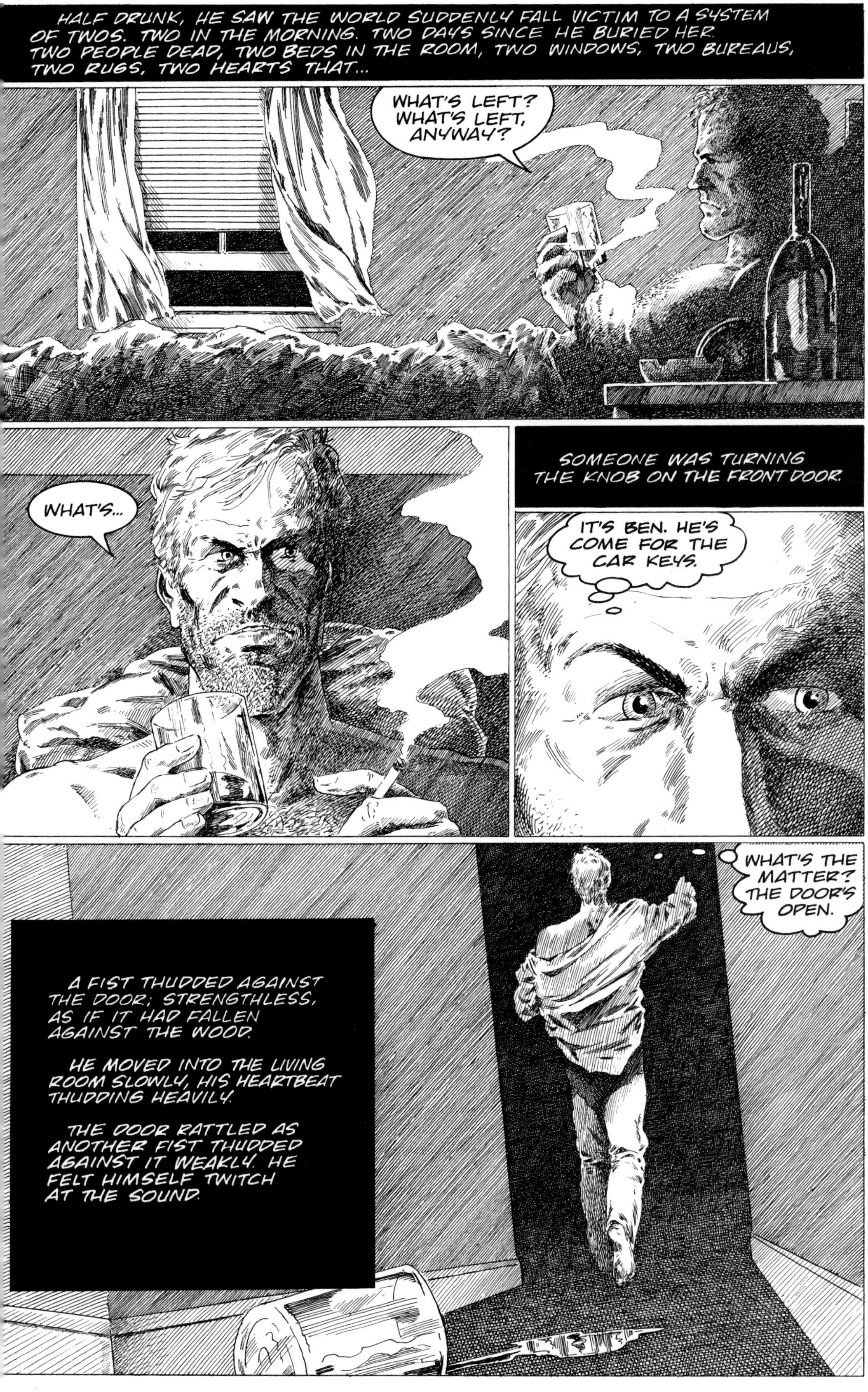
HALF DRUNK, HE SAW THE WORLD SUDDENLY FALL VICTIM TO A SYSTEM OF TWOS. TWO IN THE MORNING. TWO DAYS SINCE HE BURIED HER. TWO PEOPLE DEAD, TWO BEDS IN THE ROOM, TWO WINDOWS, TWO BUREAUS, TWO RUGS, TWO HEARTS THAT...
WHAT'S LEFT? WHAT'S LEFT, ANYWAY?
WHAT'S...
SOMEONE WAS TURNING THE KNOB ON THE FRONT DOOR.
IT'S BEN. HE'S COME FOR THE CAR KEYS.
A FIST THUDDED AGAINST THE DOOR; STRENGTHLESS, AS IF IT HAD FALLEN AGAINST THE WOOD.
HE MOVED INTO THE LIVING ROOM SLOWLY, HIS HEARTBEAT THUDDING HEAVILY.
THE DOOR RATTLED AS ANOTHER FIST THUDDED AGAINST IT WEAKLY. HE FELT HIMSELF TWITCH AT THE SOUND.
WHAT'S THE MATTER? THE DOOR'S OPEN.

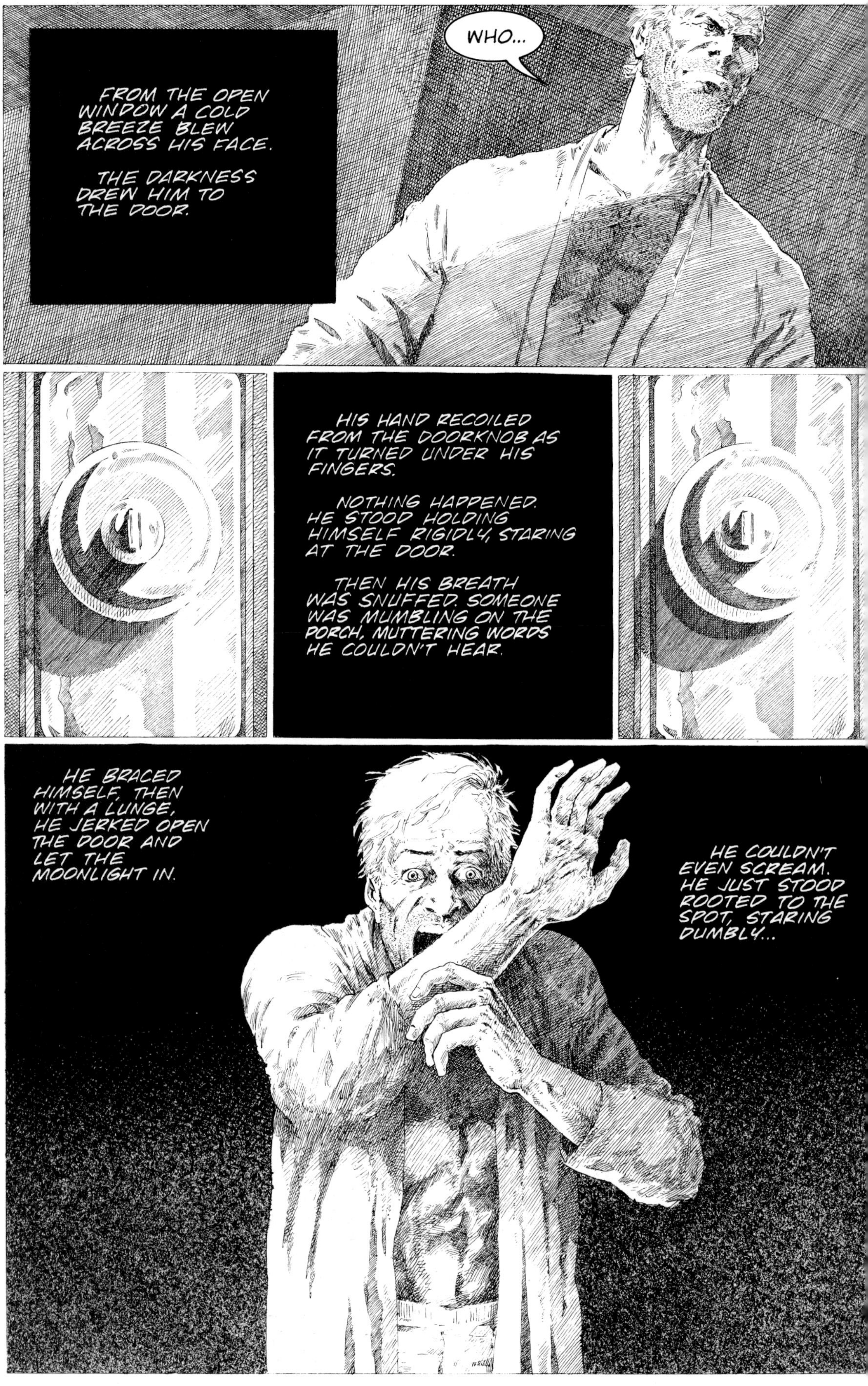
FROM THE OPEN WINDOW A COLD BREEZE BLEW ACROSS HIS FACE.
THE DARKNESS DREW HIM TO THE DOOR.
WHO...
HIS HAND RECOILED FROM THE DOORKNOB AS IT TURNED UNDER HIS FINGERS.
NOTHING HAPPENED. HE STOOD HOLDING HIMSELF RIGIDLY, STARING AT THE DOOR.
THEN HIS BREATH WAS SNUFFED. SOMEONE WAS MUMBLING ON THE PORCH, MUTTERING WORDS HE COULDN'T HEAR.
HE BRACED HIMSELF, THEN WITH A LUNGE, HE JERKED OPEN THE DOOR AND LET THE MOONLIGHT IN.
HE COULDN'T EVEN SCREAM. HE JUST STOOD ROOTED TO THE SPOT, STARING DUMBLY...

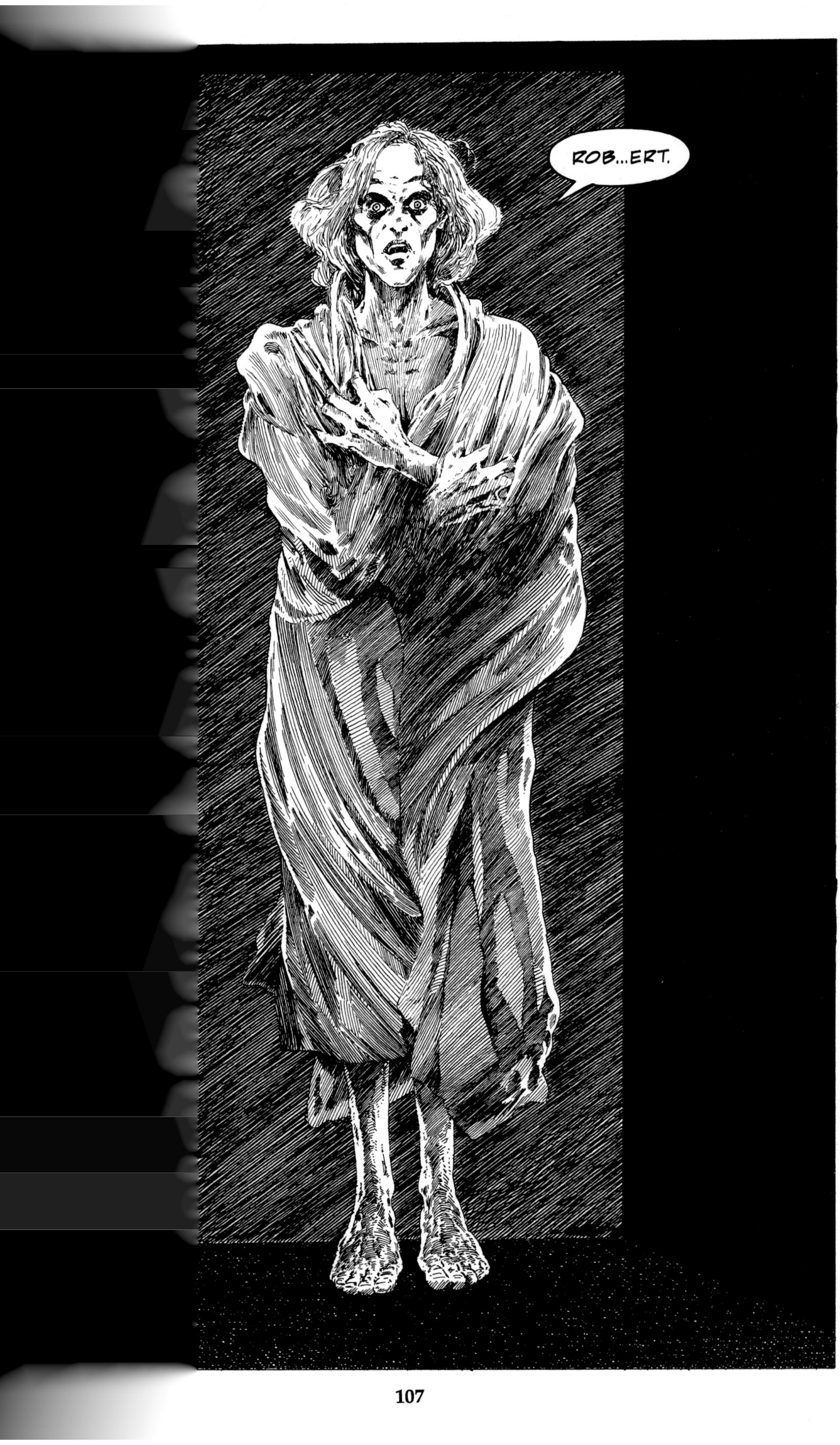
ROB...ERT.

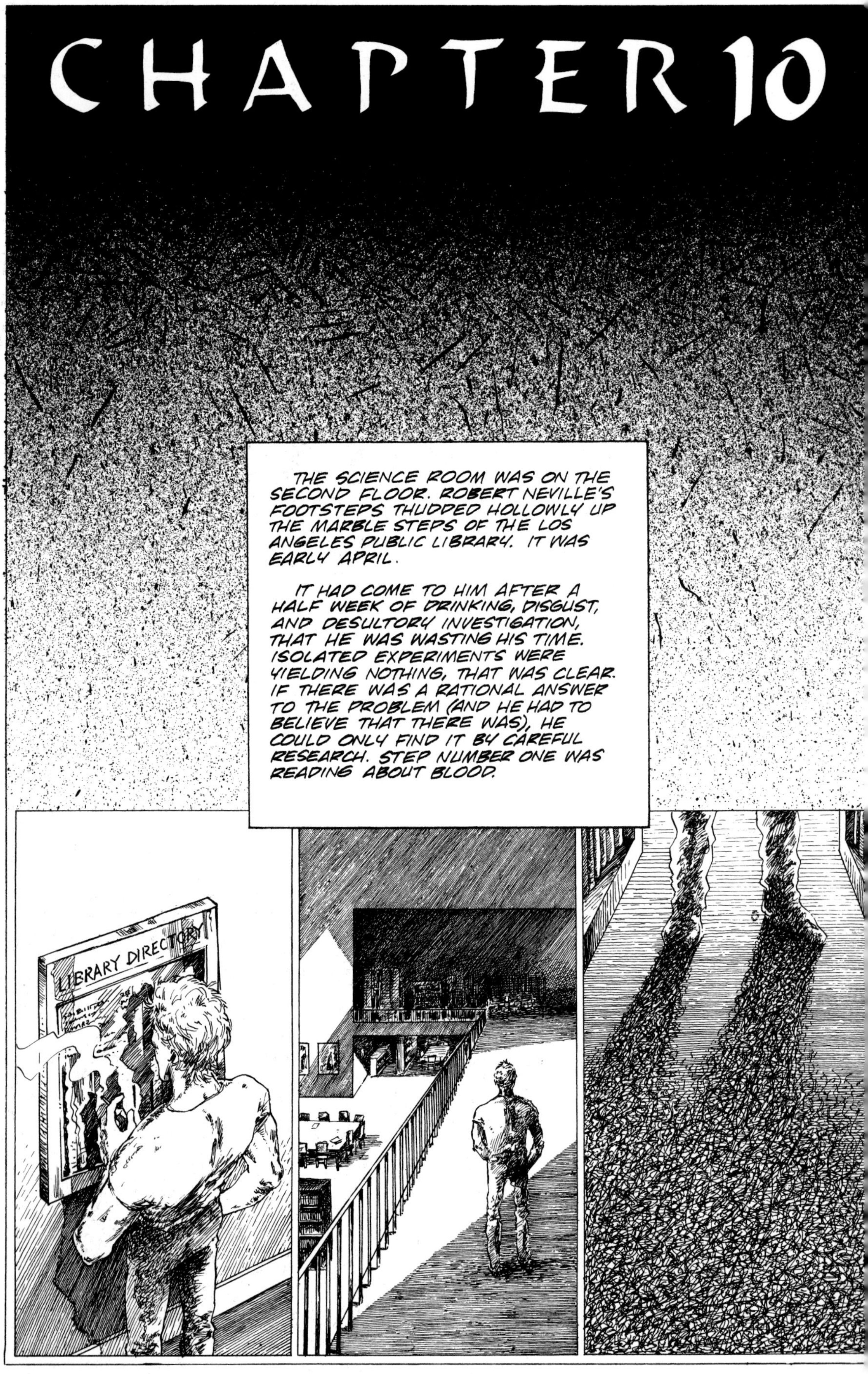
CHAPTER 10
THE SCIENCE ROOM WAS ON THE SECOND FLOOR. ROBERT NEVILLE'S FOOTSTEPS THUDDED HOLLOWLY UP THE MARBLE STEPS OF THE LOS ANGELES PUBLIC LIBRARY. IT WAS EARLY APRIL.
IT HAD COME TO HIM AFTER A HALF WEEK OF DRINKING, DISGUST, AND DESULTORY INVESTIGATION, THAT HE WAS WASTING HIS TIME. ISOLATED EXPERIMENTS WERE YIELDING NOTHING, THAT WAS CLEAR. IF THERE WAS A RATIONAL ANSWER TO THE PROBLEM (AND HE HAD TO BELIEVE THAT THERE WAS), HE COULD ONLY FIND IT BY CAREFUL RESEARCH. STEP NUMBER ONE WAS READING ABOUT BLOOD.
LIBRARY DIRECTORY

ALL THESE BOOKS, HE THOUGHT, THE RESIDUE OF THE PLANET'S INTELLECT, THE SCRAPINGS OF FUTILE MINDS, THE LEFTOVERS, THE POTPOURRI OF ARTIFACTS THAT HAD NO POWER TO SAVE MEN FROM PERISHING.

IN THE MAIN READING SECTION OF THE SCIENCE ROOM HE FOUND THE SHELVES MARKED "MEDICINE." HE LOOKED THROUGH THE TITLES. BOOKS ON HYGIENE, ON ANATOMY, ON PHYSIOLOGY, ON CURATIVE PRACTICES. FARTHER DOWN, ON BACTERIOLOGY.

HE PULLED OUT FIVE BOOKS ON GENERAL PHYSIOLOGY AND SEVERAL WORKS ON BLOOD. THESE HE STACKED ON ONE OF THE DUST-SURFACED TABLES. THEN HE PULLED OUT SEVERAL VOLUMES ON BACTERIOLGY. THAT WAS ENOUGH FOR A START. HE EXPECTED HE'D BE COMING BACK.

LEAVING THE SCIENCE ROOM, HE MADE HIS WAY TO THE HUGE FRONT DOORS. THEY COULDN'T BE OPENED FROM THE INSIDE, EITHER; THEY WERE TOO WELL LOCKED. HE HAD TO GO OUT AS HE HAD ENTERED, THROUGH THE **BROKEN WINDOW**.

AS HE STARTED THE CAR, HE SAW THAT HE WAS PARKED ALONG A RED-PAINTED CURB, FACING IN THE WRONG DIRECTION ON A ONE-WAY STREET. HE STUCK HIS HEAD OUT THE WINDOW AND LOOKED UP AND DOWN THE STREET.

"**POLICEMAN!**" HE FOUND HIMSELF CALLING. "OH, **POLICEMAN!**"

HE LAUGHED FOR A MILE WITHOUT STOPPING, WONDERING JUST WHAT WAS SO FUNNY ABOUT IT.

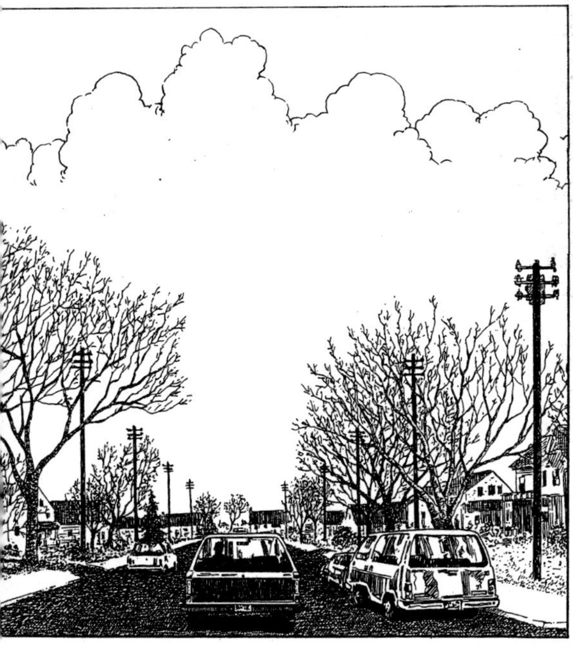

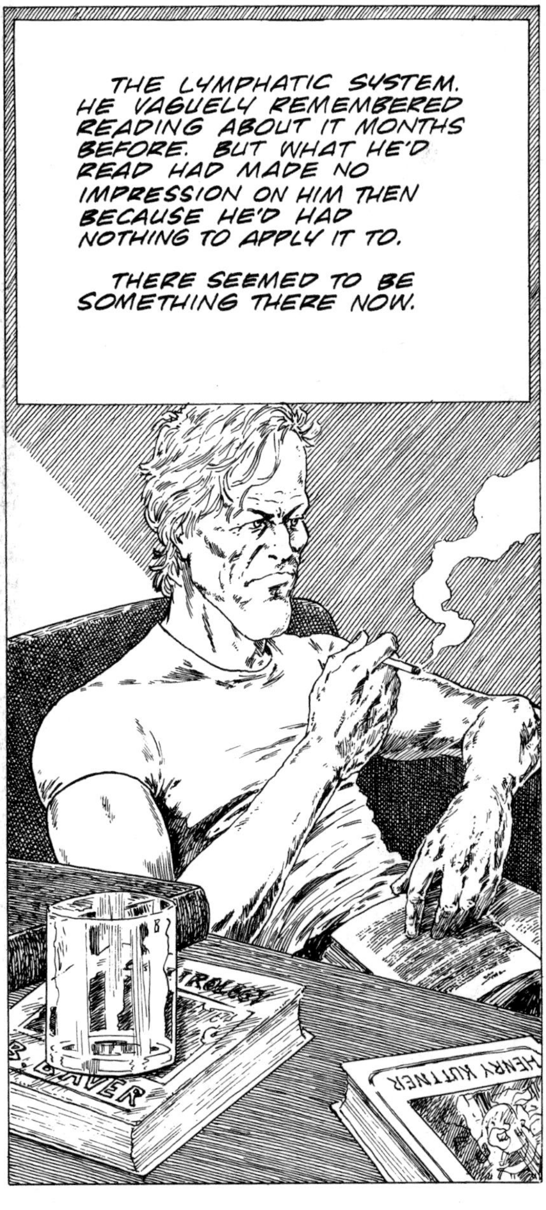
THE LYMPHATIC SYSTEM. HE VAGUELY REMEMBERED READING ABOUT IT MONTHS BEFORE. BUT WHAT HE'D READ HAD MADE NO IMPRESSION ON HIM THEN BECAUSE HE'D HAD NOTHING TO APPLY IT TO.
THERE SEEMED TO BE SOMETHING THERE NOW.
HENRY KUTTNER

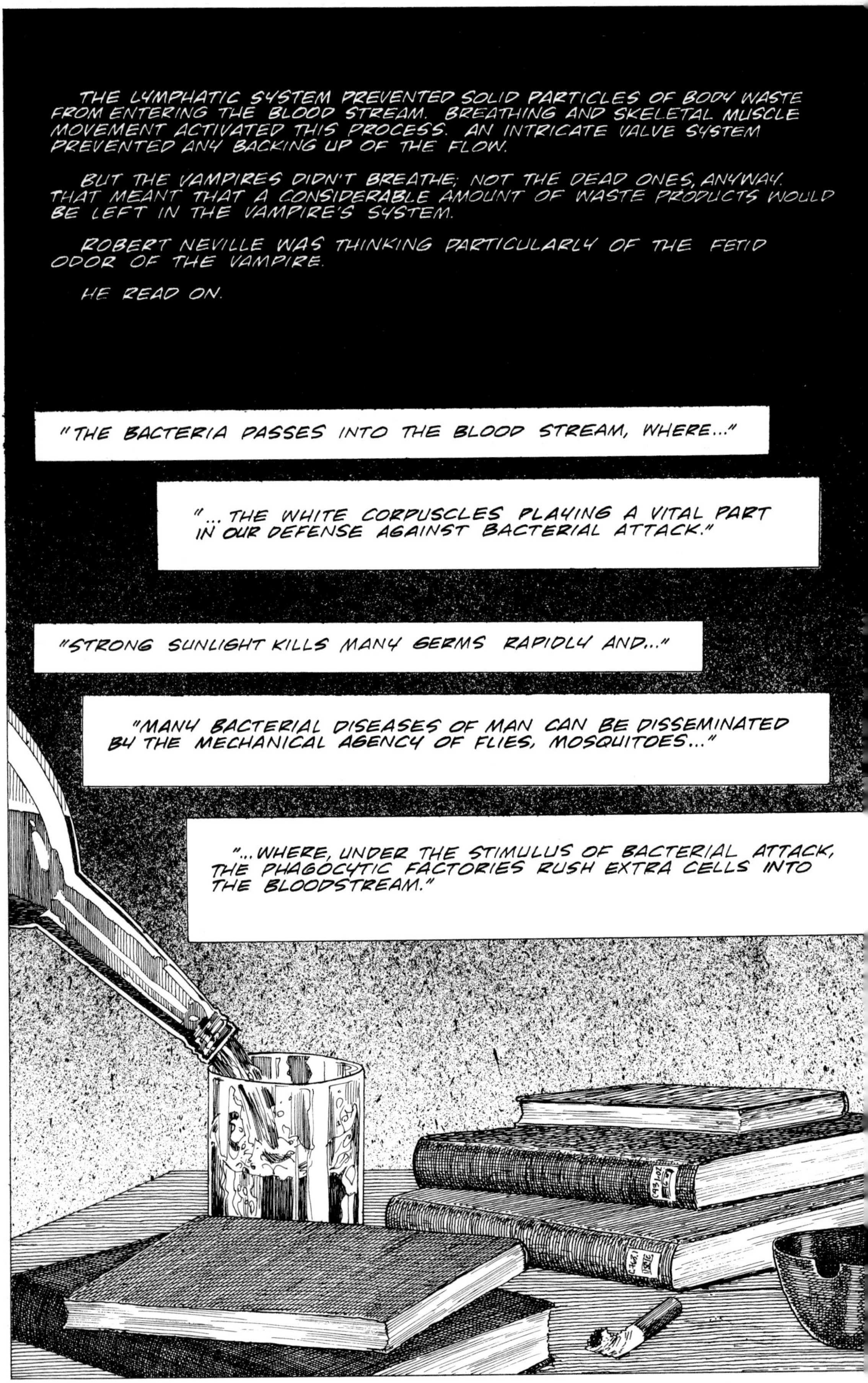
THE LYMPHATIC SYSTEM PREVENTED SOLID PARTICLES OF BODY WASTE FROM ENTERING THE BLOOD STREAM. BREATHING AND SKELETAL MUSCLE MOVEMENT ACTIVATED THIS PROCESS. AN INTRICATE VALVE SYSTEM PREVENTED ANY BACKING UP OF THE FLOW.
BUT THE VAMPIRES DIDN'T BREATHE; NOT THE DEAD ONES, ANYWAY. THAT MEANT THAT A CONSIDERABLE AMOUNT OF WASTE PRODUCTS WOULD BE LEFT IN THE VAMPIRE'S SYSTEM.
ROBERT NEVILLE WAS THINKING PARTICULARLY OF THE FETID ODOR OF THE VAMPIRE.
HE READ ON.
"THE BACTERIA PASSES INTO THE BLOOD STREAM, WHERE..."
"...THE WHITE CORPUSCLES PLAYING A VITAL PART IN OUR DEFENSE AGAINST BACTERIAL ATTACK."
"STRONG SUNLIGHT KILLS MANY GERMS RAPIDLY AND..."
"MANY BACTERIAL DISEASES OF MAN CAN BE DISSEMINATED BY THE MECHANICAL AGENCY OF FLIES, MOSQUITOES..."
"...WHERE, UNDER THE STIMULUS OF BACTERIAL ATTACK, THE PHAGOCYTIC FACTORIES RUSH EXTRA CELLS INTO THE BLOODSTREAM."

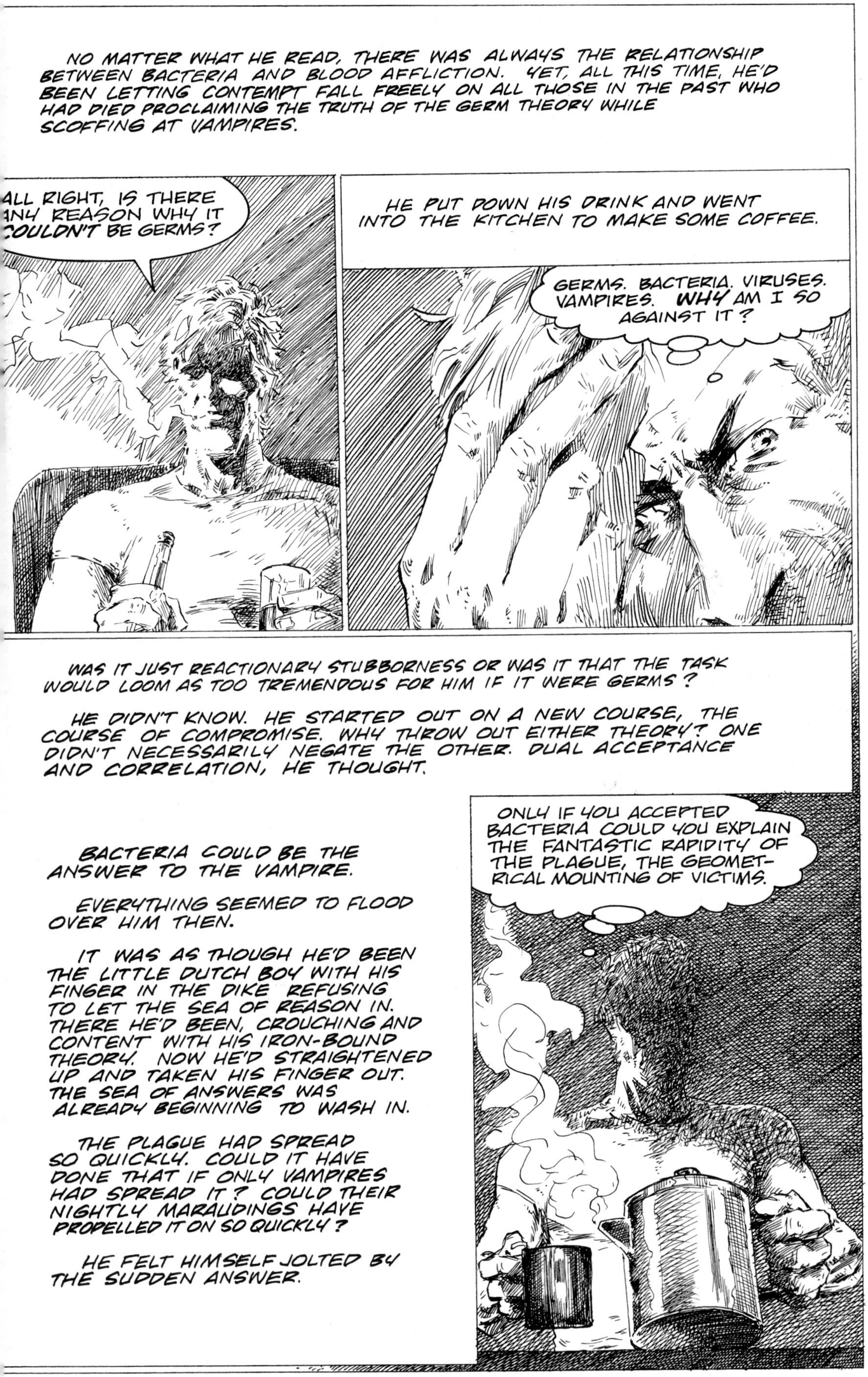
NO MATTER WHAT HE READ, THERE WAS ALWAYS THE RELATIONSHIP BETWEEN BACTERIA AND BLOOD AFFLICTION. YET, ALL THIS TIME, HE'D BEEN LETTING CONTEMPT FALL FREELY ON ALL THOSE IN THE PAST WHO HAD DIED PROCLAIMING THE TRUTH OF THE GERM THEORY WHILE SCOFFING AT VAMPIRES.
ALL RIGHT, IS THERE ANY REASON WHY IT COULDN'T BE GERMS?
HE PUT DOWN HIS DRINK AND WENT INTO THE KITCHEN TO MAKE SOME COFFEE.
GERMS. BACTERIA. VIRUSES. VAMPIRES. WHY AM I SO AGAINST IT?
WAS IT JUST REACTIONARY STUBBORNESS OR WAS IT THAT THE TASK WOULD LOOM AS TOO TREMENDOUS FOR HIM IF IT WERE GERMS?
HE DIDN'T KNOW. HE STARTED OUT ON A NEW COURSE, THE COURSE OF COMPROMISE. WHY THROW OUT EITHER THEORY? ONE DIDN'T NECESSARILY NEGATE THE OTHER. DUAL ACCEPTANCE AND CORRELATION, HE THOUGHT.
BACTERIA COULD BE THE ANSWER TO THE VAMPIRE.
EVERYTHING SEEMED TO FLOOD OVER HIM THEN.
IT WAS AS THOUGH HE'D BEEN THE LITTLE DUTCH BOY WITH HIS FINGER IN THE DIKE REFUSING TO LET THE SEA OF REASON IN. THERE HE'D BEEN, CROUCHING AND CONTENT WITH HIS IRON-BOUND THEORY. NOW HE'D STRAIGHTENED UP AND TAKEN HIS FINGER OUT. THE SEA OF ANSWERS WAS ALREADY BEGINNING TO WASH IN.
THE PLAGUE HAD SPREAD SO QUICKLY. COULD IT HAVE DONE THAT IF ONLY VAMPIRES HAD SPREAD IT? COULD THEIR NIGHTLY MARAUDINGS HAVE PROPELLED IT ON SO QUICKLY?
HE FELT HIMSELF JOLTED BY THE SUDDEN ANSWER.
ONLY IF YOU ACCEPTED BACTERIA COULD YOU EXPLAIN THE FANTASTIC RAPIDITY OF THE PLAGUE, THE GEOMETRICAL MOUNTING OF VICTIMS.

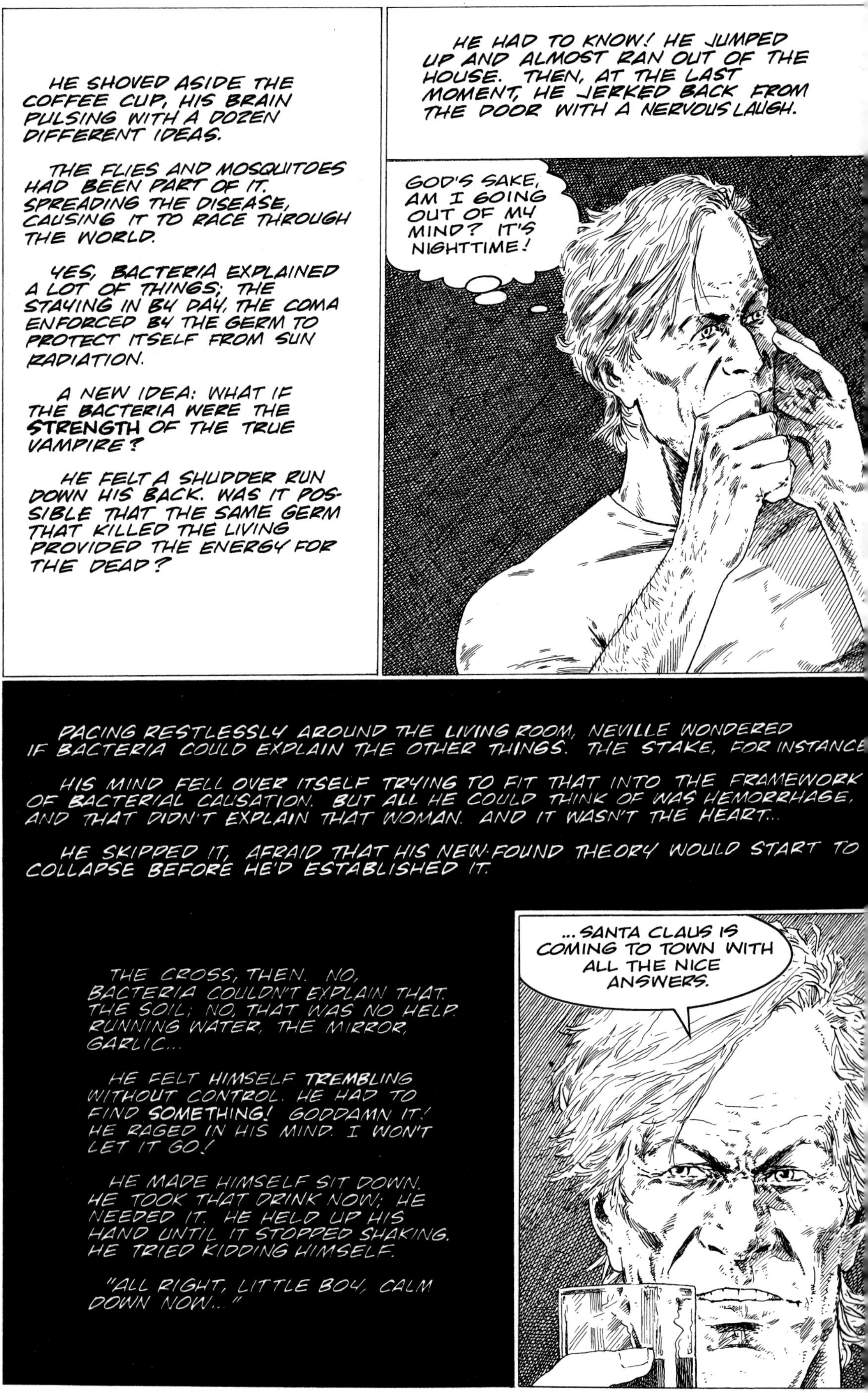
HE SHOVED ASIDE THE COFFEE CUP, HIS BRAIN PULSING WITH A DOZEN DIFFERENT IDEAS.
THE FLIES AND MOSQUITOES HAD BEEN PART OF IT. SPREADING THE DISEASE, CAUSING IT TO RACE THROUGH THE WORLD.
YES, BACTERIA EXPLAINED A LOT OF THINGS; THE STAYING IN BY DAY, THE COMA ENFORCED BY THE GERM TO PROTECT ITSELF FROM SUN RADIATION.
A NEW IDEA: WHAT IF THE BACTERIA WERE THE **STRENGTH** OF THE TRUE VAMPIRE?
HE FELT A SHUDDER RUN DOWN HIS BACK. WAS IT POSSIBLE THAT THE SAME GERM THAT KILLED THE LIVING PROVIDED THE ENERGY FOR THE DEAD?
HE HAD TO KNOW! HE JUMPED UP AND ALMOST RAN OUT OF THE HOUSE. THEN, AT THE LAST MOMENT, HE JERKED BACK FROM THE DOOR WITH A NERVOUS LAUGH.
GOD'S SAKE, AM I GOING OUT OF MY MIND? IT'S NIGHTTIME!
PACING RESTLESSLY AROUND THE LIVING ROOM, NEVILLE WONDERED IF BACTERIA COULD EXPLAIN THE OTHER THINGS. THE STAKE, FOR INSTANCE
HIS MIND FELL OVER ITSELF TRYING TO FIT THAT INTO THE FRAMEWORK OF BACTERIAL CAUSATION. BUT ALL HE COULD THINK OF WAS HEMORRHAGE, AND THAT DIDN'T EXPLAIN THAT WOMAN. AND IT WASN'T THE HEART...
HE SKIPPED IT, AFRAID THAT HIS NEW-FOUND THEORY WOULD START TO COLLAPSE BEFORE HE'D ESTABLISHED IT.
THE CROSS, THEN. NO, BACTERIA COULDN'T EXPLAIN THAT. THE SOIL; NO, THAT WAS NO HELP. RUNNING WATER, THE MIRROR, GARLIC...
HE FELT HIMSELF **TREMBLING** WITHOUT CONTROL. HE HAD TO FIND **SOMETHING!** GODDAMN IT! HE RAGED IN HIS MIND. I WON'T LET IT GO!
HE MADE HIMSELF SIT DOWN. HE TOOK THAT DRINK NOW; HE NEEDED IT. HE HELD UP HIS HAND UNTIL IT STOPPED SHAKING. HE TRIED KIDDING HIMSELF.
"ALL RIGHT, LITTLE BOY, CALM DOWN NOW..."
...SANTA CLAUS IS COMING TO TOWN WITH ALL THE NICE ANSWERS.

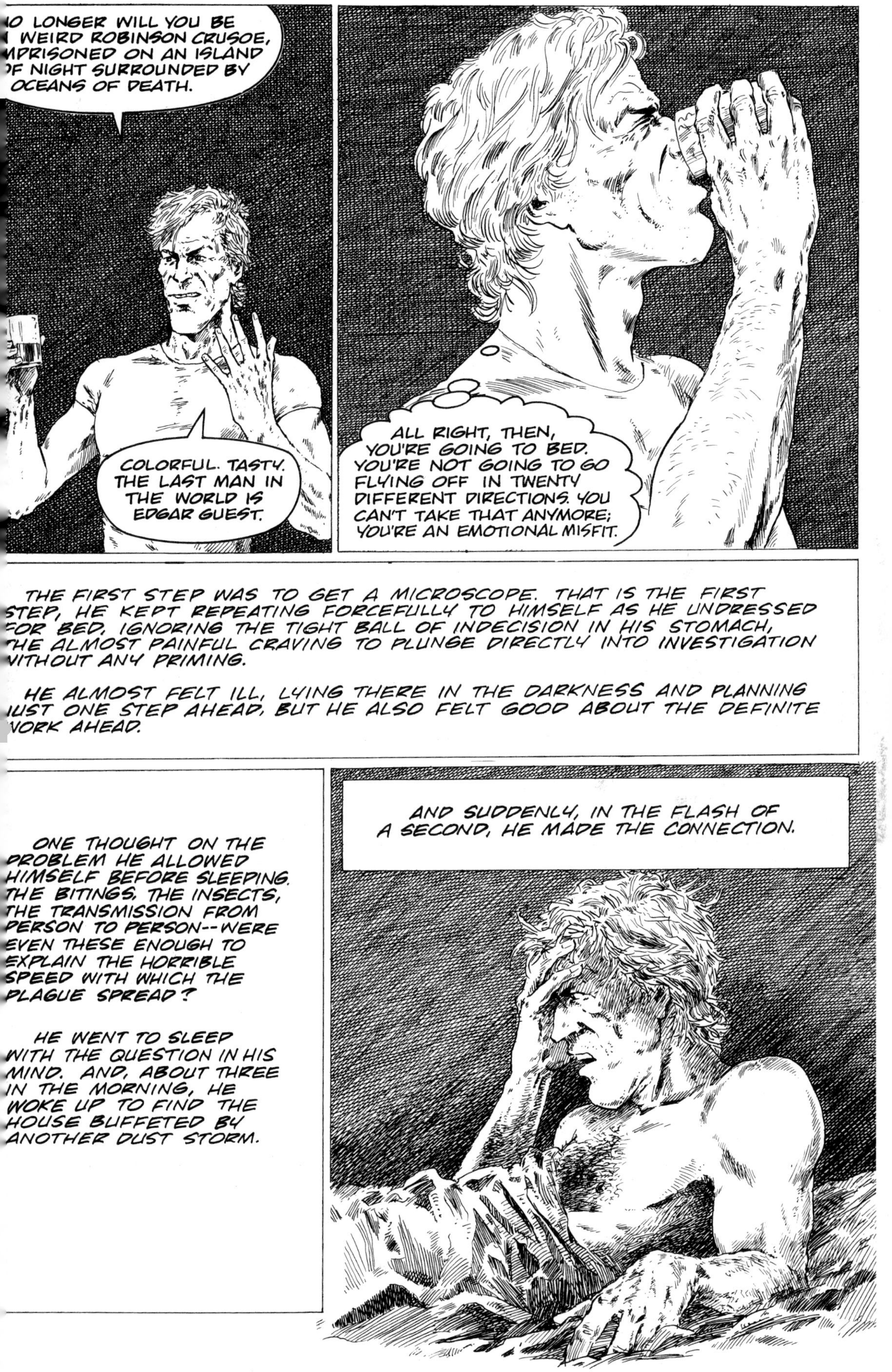
O LONGER WILL YOU BE
WEIRD ROBINSON CRUSOE,
MPRISONED ON AN ISLAND
F NIGHT SURROUNDED BY
OCEANS OF DEATH.
COLORFUL. TASTY. THE LAST MAN IN THE WORLD IS EDGAR GUEST.
ALL RIGHT, THEN, YOU'RE GOING TO BED. YOU'RE NOT GOING TO GO FLYING OFF IN TWENTY DIFFERENT DIRECTIONS. YOU CAN'T TAKE THAT ANYMORE; YOU'RE AN EMOTIONAL MISFIT.
THE FIRST STEP WAS TO GET A MICROSCOPE. THAT IS THE FIRST STEP, HE KEPT REPEATING FORCEFULLY TO HIMSELF AS HE UNDRESSED FOR BED, IGNORING THE TIGHT BALL OF INDECISION IN HIS STOMACH, THE ALMOST PAINFUL CRAVING TO PLUNGE DIRECTLY INTO INVESTIGATION WITHOUT ANY PRIMING.
HE ALMOST FELT ILL, LYING THERE IN THE DARKNESS AND PLANNING JUST ONE STEP AHEAD, BUT HE ALSO FELT GOOD ABOUT THE DEFINITE WORK AHEAD.
ONE THOUGHT ON THE PROBLEM HE ALLOWED HIMSELF BEFORE SLEEPING. THE BITINGS, THE INSECTS, THE TRANSMISSION FROM PERSON TO PERSON--WERE EVEN THESE ENOUGH TO EXPLAIN THE HORRIBLE SPEED WITH WHICH THE PLAGUE SPREAD?
HE WENT TO SLEEP WITH THE QUESTION IN HIS MIND. AND, ABOUT THREE IN THE MORNING, HE WOKE UP TO FIND THE HOUSE BUFFETED BY ANOTHER DUST STORM.
AND SUDDENLY, IN THE FLASH OF A SECOND, HE MADE THE CONNECTION.

CHAPTER 11

THE FIRST ONE HE GOT WAS WORTHLESS. BUT, OF COURSE, HE KNEW NOTHING ABOUT MICROSCOPES, AND HE'D TAKEN THE FIRST ONE HE'D FOUND. THREE DAYS LATER HE HURLED IT AGAINST THE WALL WITH A STRANGLED CURSE AND STAMPED IT INTO PIECES WITH HIS HEELS.

THEN, WHEN HE'D CALMED DOWN, HE WENT TO THE LIBRARY AND GOT A BOOK ON MICROSCOPES.

THE NEXT TIME HE WENT OUT, HE DIDN'T COME BACK UNTIL HE'D FOUND A DECENT INSTRUMENT.

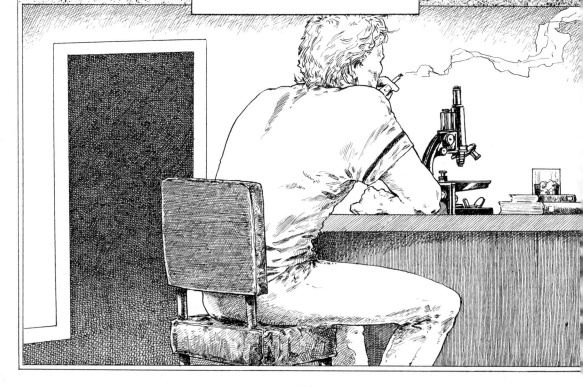

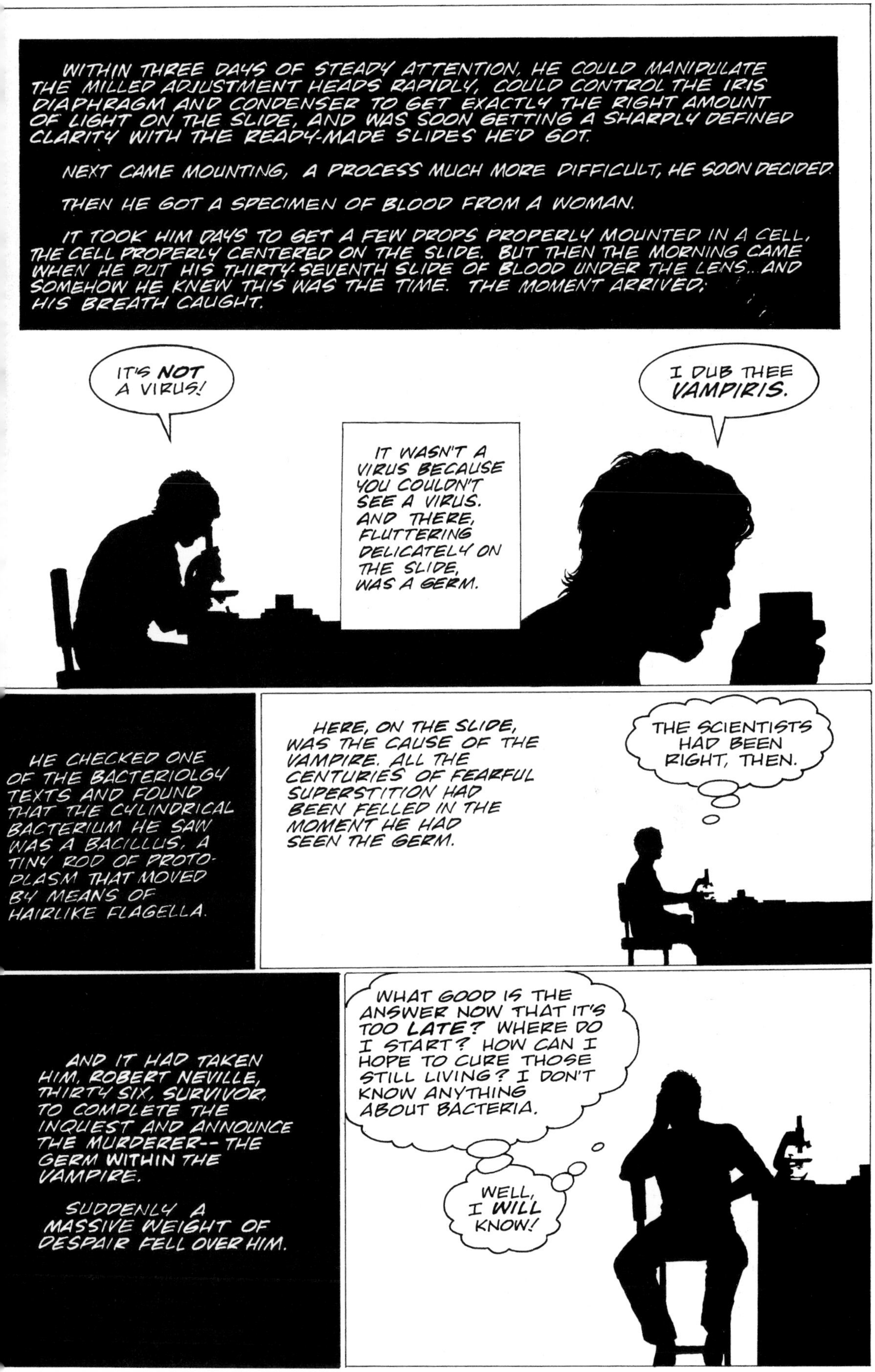
WITHIN THREE DAYS OF STEADY ATTENTION, HE COULD MANIPULATE THE MILLED ADJUSTMENT HEADS RAPIDLY, COULD CONTROL THE IRIS DIAPHRAGM AND CONDENSER TO GET EXACTLY THE RIGHT AMOUNT OF LIGHT ON THE SLIDE, AND WAS SOON GETTING A SHARPLY DEFINED CLARITY WITH THE READY-MADE SLIDES HE'D GOT.
NEXT CAME MOUNTING, A PROCESS MUCH MORE DIFFICULT, HE SOON DECIDED.
THEN HE GOT A SPECIMEN OF BLOOD FROM A WOMAN.
IT TOOK HIM DAYS TO GET A FEW DROPS PROPERLY MOUNTED IN A CELL, THE CELL PROPERLY CENTERED ON THE SLIDE. BUT THEN THE MORNING CAME WHEN HE PUT HIS THIRTY-SEVENTH SLIDE OF BLOOD UNDER THE LENS... AND SOMEHOW HE KNEW THIS WAS THE TIME. THE MOMENT ARRIVED; HIS BREATH CAUGHT.
IT'S NOT A VIRUS!
IT WASN'T A VIRUS BECAUSE YOU COULDN'T SEE A VIRUS. AND THERE, FLUTTERING DELICATELY ON THE SLIDE, WAS A GERM.
I DUB THEE VAMPIRIS.
HE CHECKED ONE OF THE BACTERIOLGY TEXTS AND FOUND THAT THE CYLINDRICAL BACTERIUM HE SAW WAS A BACILLUS, A TINY ROD OF PROTOPLASM THAT MOVED BY MEANS OF HAIRLIKE FLAGELLA.
HERE, ON THE SLIDE, WAS THE CAUSE OF THE VAMPIRE. ALL THE CENTURIES OF FEARFUL SUPERSTITION HAD BEEN FELLED IN THE MOMENT HE HAD SEEN THE GERM.
THE SCIENTISTS HAD BEEN RIGHT, THEN.
AND IT HAD TAKEN HIM, ROBERT NEVILLE, THIRTY SIX, SURVIVOR, TO COMPLETE THE INQUEST AND ANNOUNCE THE MURDERER-- THE GERM WITHIN THE VAMPIRE.
SUDDENLY A MASSIVE WEIGHT OF DESPAIR FELL OVER HIM.
WHAT GOOD IS THE ANSWER NOW THAT IT'S TOO LATE? WHERE DO I START? HOW CAN I HOPE TO CURE THOSE STILL LIVING? I DON'T KNOW ANYTHING ABOUT BACTERIA.
WELL, I WILL KNOW!

CERTAIN KINDS OF BACILLI, WHEN CONDITIONS BECAME UNFAVORABLE, WERE CAPABLE OF CREATING, FROM THEMSELVES, BODIES CALLED SPORES. THEY CONDENSED THEIR CELL CONTENTS INTO THE SPORE, WHICH THEN DETACHED ITSELF FROM THE BACILLUS. THESE FREE SPORES WERE HIGHLY RESISTANT TO PHYSICAL AND CHEMICAL CHANGE.

LATER, WHEN CONDITIONS WERE MORE FAVORABLE FOR SURVIVAL, THE SPORE GERMINATED AGAIN, BRINGING INTO EXISTENCE ALL THE QUALITIES OF THE ORIGINAL BACILLUS.

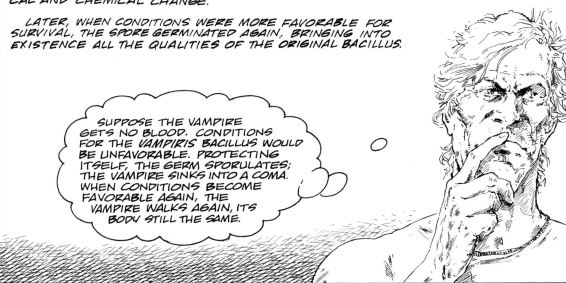

SUPPOSE THE VAMPIRE GETS NO BLOOD. CONDITIONS FOR THE *VAMPIRIS* BACILLUS WOULD BE UNFAVORABLE. PROTECTING ITSELF, THE GERM SPORULATES; THE VAMPIRE SINKS INTO A COMA. WHEN CONDITIONS BECOME FAVORABLE AGAIN, THE VAMPIRE WALKS AGAIN, ITS BODY STILL THE SAME.

BUT HOW WOULD THE GERM KNOW IF BLOOD WERE AVAILABLE?

BACTERIA, WHEN NOT PROPERLY FED, METABOLIZED ABNORMALLY, ABSORBED WATER, AND SWELLED UP, ULTIMATELY TO EXPLODE AND DESTROY ALL CELLS.

SPORULATION AGAIN; IT HAS TO FIT IN.

ALL RIGHT, SUPPOSE THE VAMPIRE DIDN'T GO INTO A COMA. SUPPOSE THE BODY DECOMPOSED WITHOUT BLOOD. THE GERM STILL MIGHT SPORULATE AND--

YES! THE DUST STORMS!

116

THE FREED SPORES WOULD BE BLOWN ABOUT BY THE STORMS. THEY COULD LODGE IN MINUTE SKIN ABRASIONS CAUSED BY THE SCALING DUST. ONCE IN THE SKIN, THE SPORE COULD GERMINATE AND MULTIPLY BY FISSION. AS THIS MULTIPLICATION PROGRESSED, THE SURROUNDING TISSUES WOULD BE DESTROYED, THE CHANNELS PLUGGED WITH BACILLI. DESTRUCTION OF TISSUE WOULD LIBERATE POISONOUS, DECOMPOSED BODIES INTO SURROUNDING HEALTHY TISSUES. EVENTUALLY THE POISONS WOULD REACH THE BLOOD STREAM.

PROCESS COMPLETE.

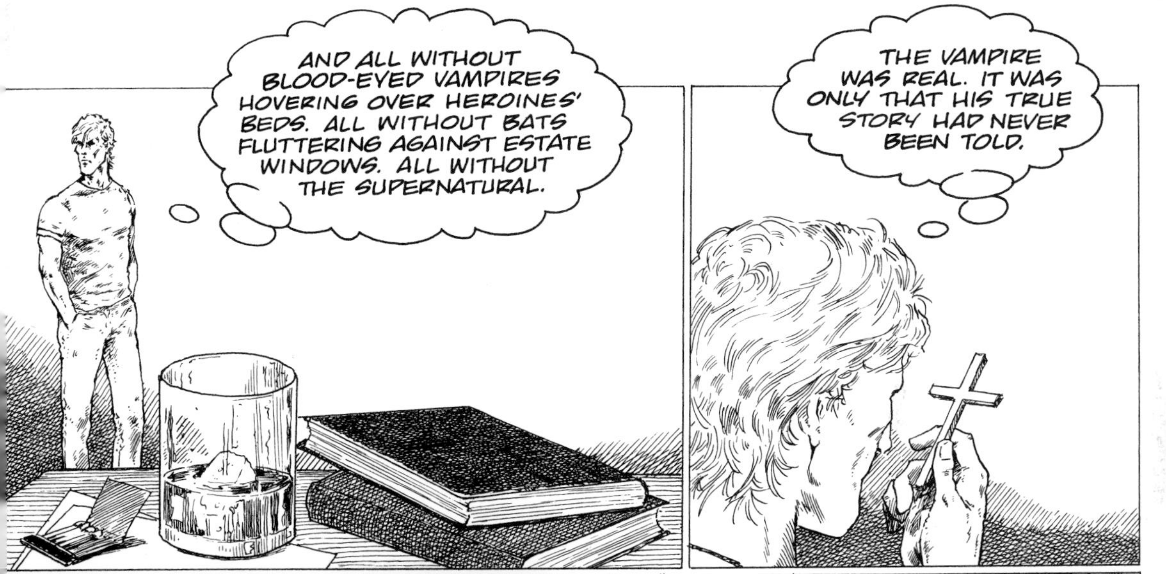
AND ALL WITHOUT BLOOD-EYED VAMPIRES HOVERING OVER HEROINES' BEDS. ALL WITHOUT BATS FLUTTERING AGAINST ESTATE WINDOWS. ALL WITHOUT THE SUPERNATURAL.
THE VAMPIRE WAS REAL. IT WAS ONLY THAT HIS TRUE STORY HAD NEVER BEEN TOLD.

CONSIDERING THAT, NEVILLE RECOUNTED THE HISTORICAL PLAGUES.

THE FALL OF ATHENS. VERY MUCH LIKE THIS PLAGUE. BEFORE ANYTHING COULD BE DONE, THE CITY HAD FALLEN. HISTORIANS WROTE OF BUBONIC PLAGUE. ROBERT NEVILLE WAS INCLINED TO BELIEVE THAT THE VAMPIRE HAD CAUSED IT.

NO, NOT THE VAMPIRE. THAT PROWLING, VULPINE GHOST WAS AS MUCH A TOOL OF THE GERM AS THE LIVING INNOCENTS WHO WERE ORIGINALLY AFFLICTED. IT WAS THE **GERM** THAT WAS THE VILLAIN.

AND WHAT OF THE BLACK PLAGUE, THAT HORRIBLE BLIGHT THAT SWEPT ACROSS EUROPE, LEAVING IN ITS WAKE A TOLL OF THREE FOURTHS OF THE POPULATION?

VAMPIRES?

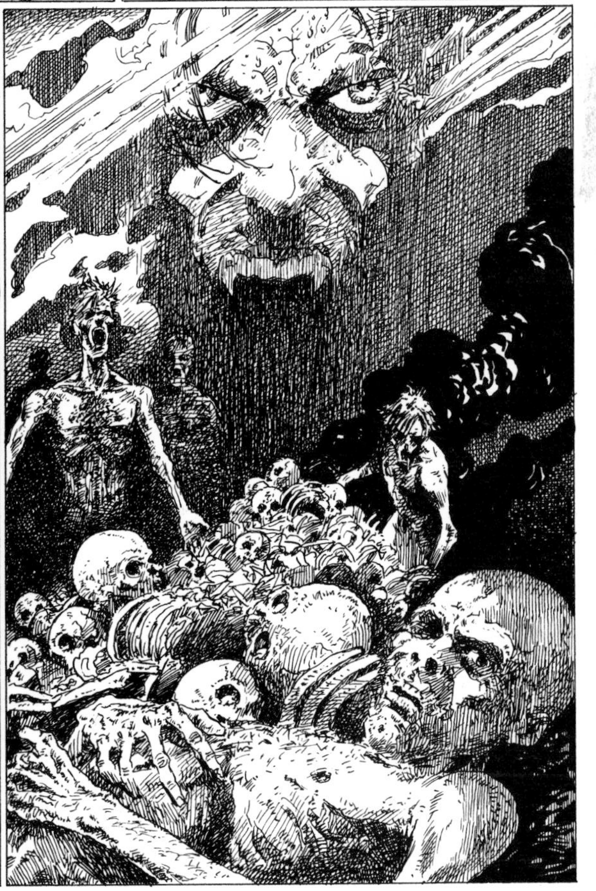

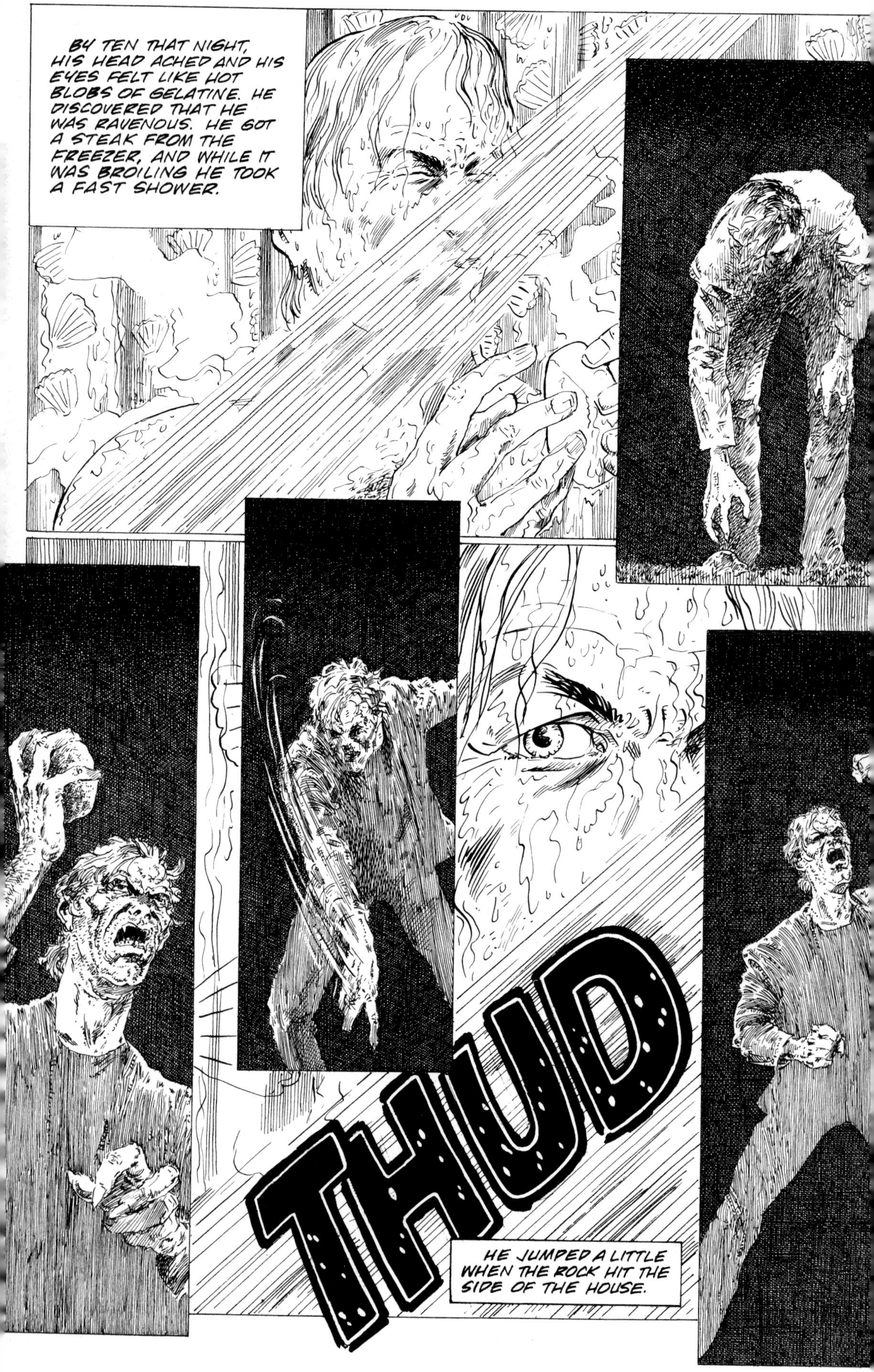
BY TEN THAT NIGHT, HIS HEAD ACHED AND HIS EYES FELT LIKE HOT BLOBS OF GELATINE. HE DISCOVERED THAT HE WAS RAVENOUS. HE GOT A STEAK FROM THE FREEZER, AND WHILE IT WAS BROILING HE TOOK A FAST SHOWER.
THUD
HE JUMPED A LITTLE WHEN THE ROCK HIT THE SIDE OF THE HOUSE.

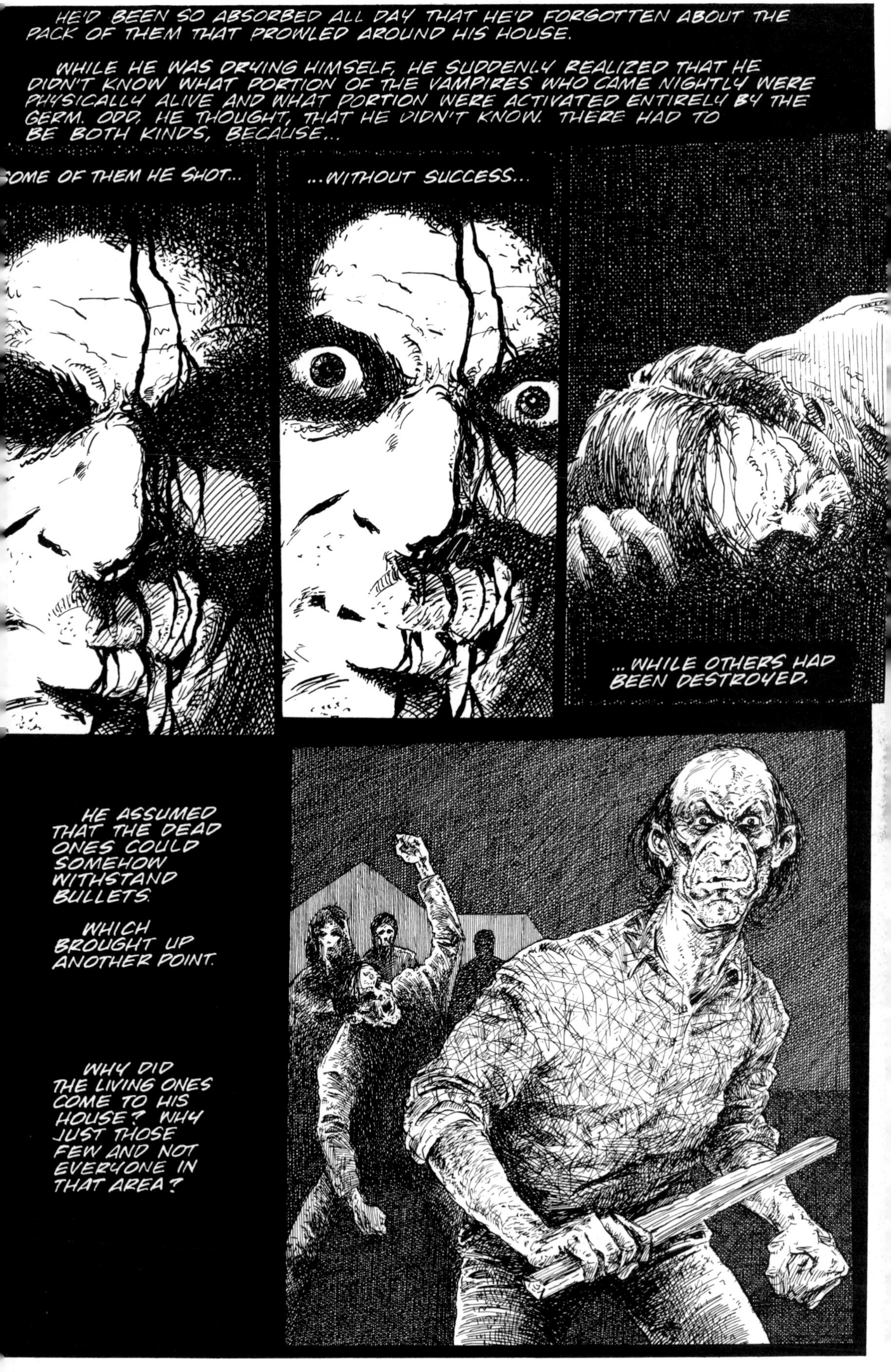
HE'D BEEN SO ABSORBED ALL DAY THAT HE'D FORGOTTEN ABOUT THE PACK OF THEM THAT PROWLED AROUND HIS HOUSE.
WHILE HE WAS DRYING HIMSELF, HE SUDDENLY REALIZED THAT HE DIDN'T KNOW WHAT PORTION OF THE VAMPIRES WHO CAME NIGHTLY WERE PHYSICALLY ALIVE AND WHAT PORTION WERE ACTIVATED ENTIRELY BY THE GERM. ODD, HE THOUGHT, THAT HE DIDN'T KNOW. THERE HAD TO BE BOTH KINDS, BECAUSE...
SOME OF THEM HE SHOT...
...WITHOUT SUCCESS...
...WHILE OTHERS HAD BEEN DESTROYED.
HE ASSUMED THAT THE DEAD ONES COULD SOMEHOW WITHSTAND BULLETS.
WHICH BROUGHT UP ANOTHER POINT.
WHY DID THE LIVING ONES COME TO HIS HOUSE? WHY JUST THOSE FEW AND NOT EVERYONE IN THAT AREA?

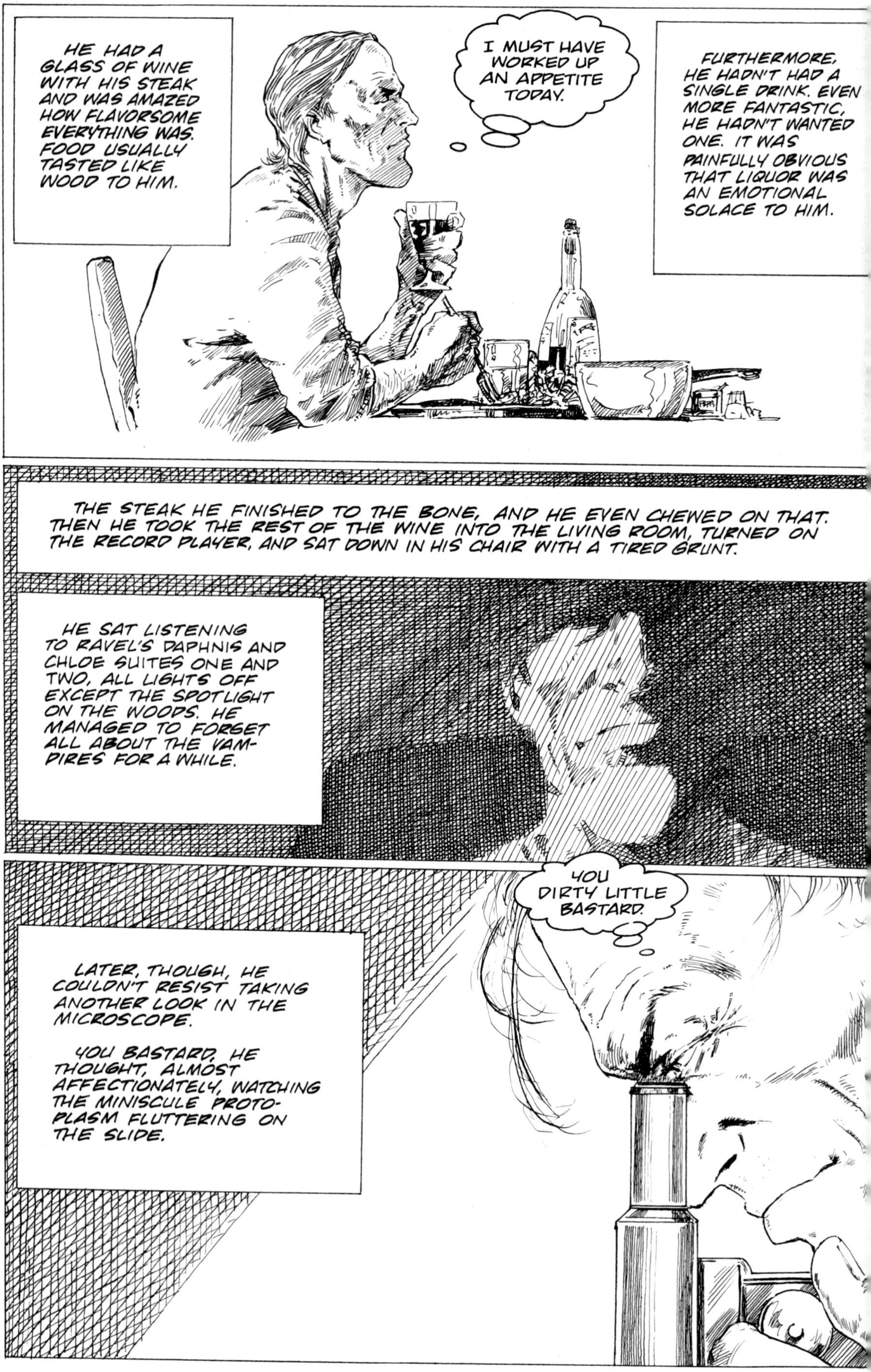
HE HAD A GLASS OF WINE WITH HIS STEAK AND WAS AMAZED HOW FLAVORSOME EVERYTHING WAS. FOOD USUALLY TASTED LIKE WOOD TO HIM.
I MUST HAVE WORKED UP AN APPETITE TODAY.
FURTHERMORE, HE HADN'T HAD A SINGLE DRINK. EVEN MORE FANTASTIC, HE HADN'T WANTED ONE. IT WAS PAINFULLY OBVIOUS THAT LIQUOR WAS AN EMOTIONAL SOLACE TO HIM.
THE STEAK HE FINISHED TO THE BONE, AND HE EVEN CHEWED ON THAT. THEN HE TOOK THE REST OF THE WINE INTO THE LIVING ROOM, TURNED ON THE RECORD PLAYER, AND SAT DOWN IN HIS CHAIR WITH A TIRED GRUNT.
HE SAT LISTENING TO RAVEL'S DAPHNIS AND CHLOE SUITES ONE AND TWO, ALL LIGHTS OFF EXCEPT THE SPOTLIGHT ON THE WOODS. HE MANAGED TO FORGET ALL ABOUT THE VAMPIRES FOR A WHILE.
LATER, THOUGH, HE COULDN'T RESIST TAKING ANOTHER LOOK IN THE MICROSCOPE.
YOU BASTARD, HE THOUGHT, ALMOST AFFECTIONATELY, WATCHING THE MINISCULE PROTOPLASM FLUTTERING ON THE SLIDE.
YOU DIRTY LITTLE BASTARD.

CHAPTER 12

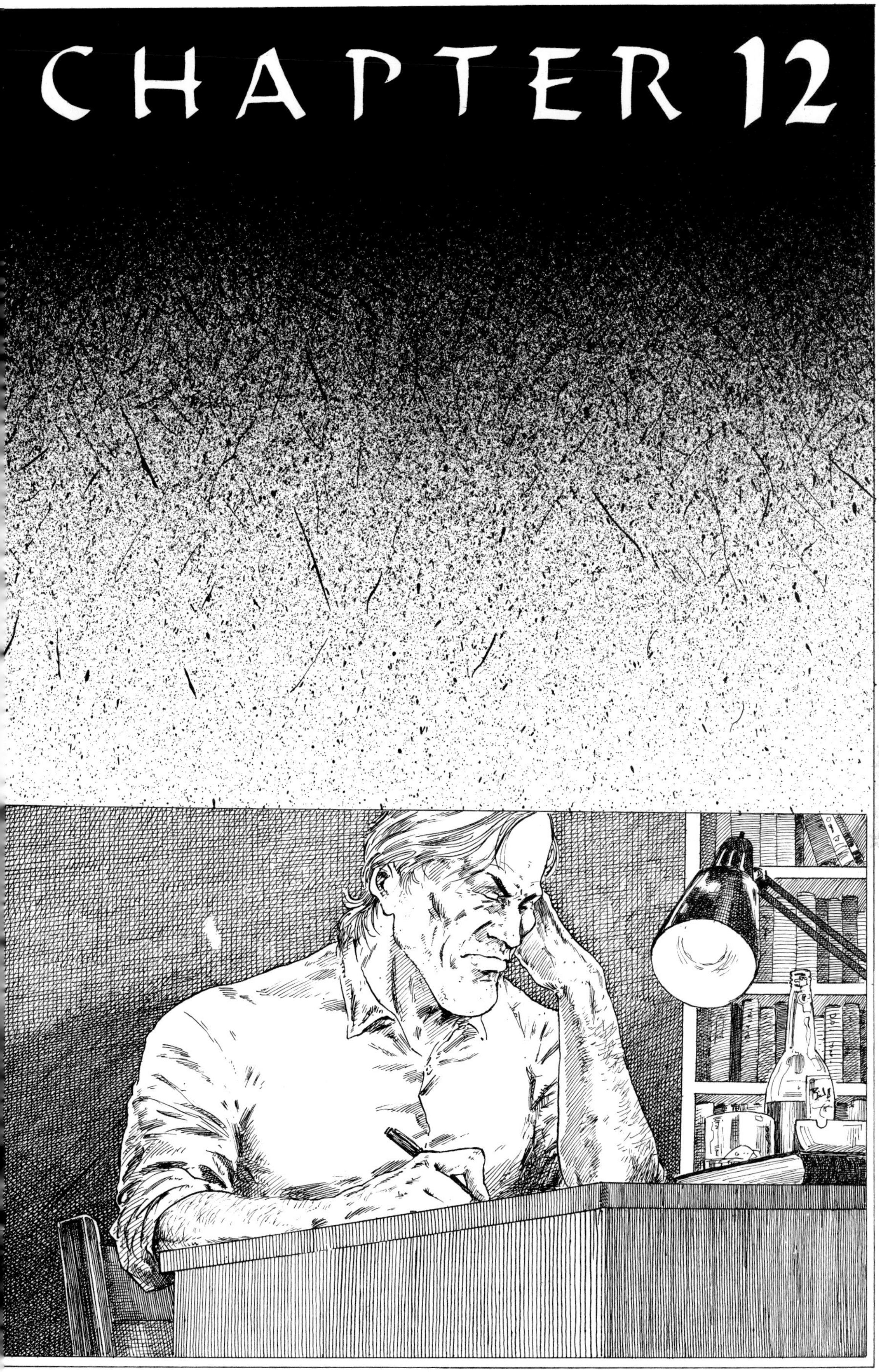

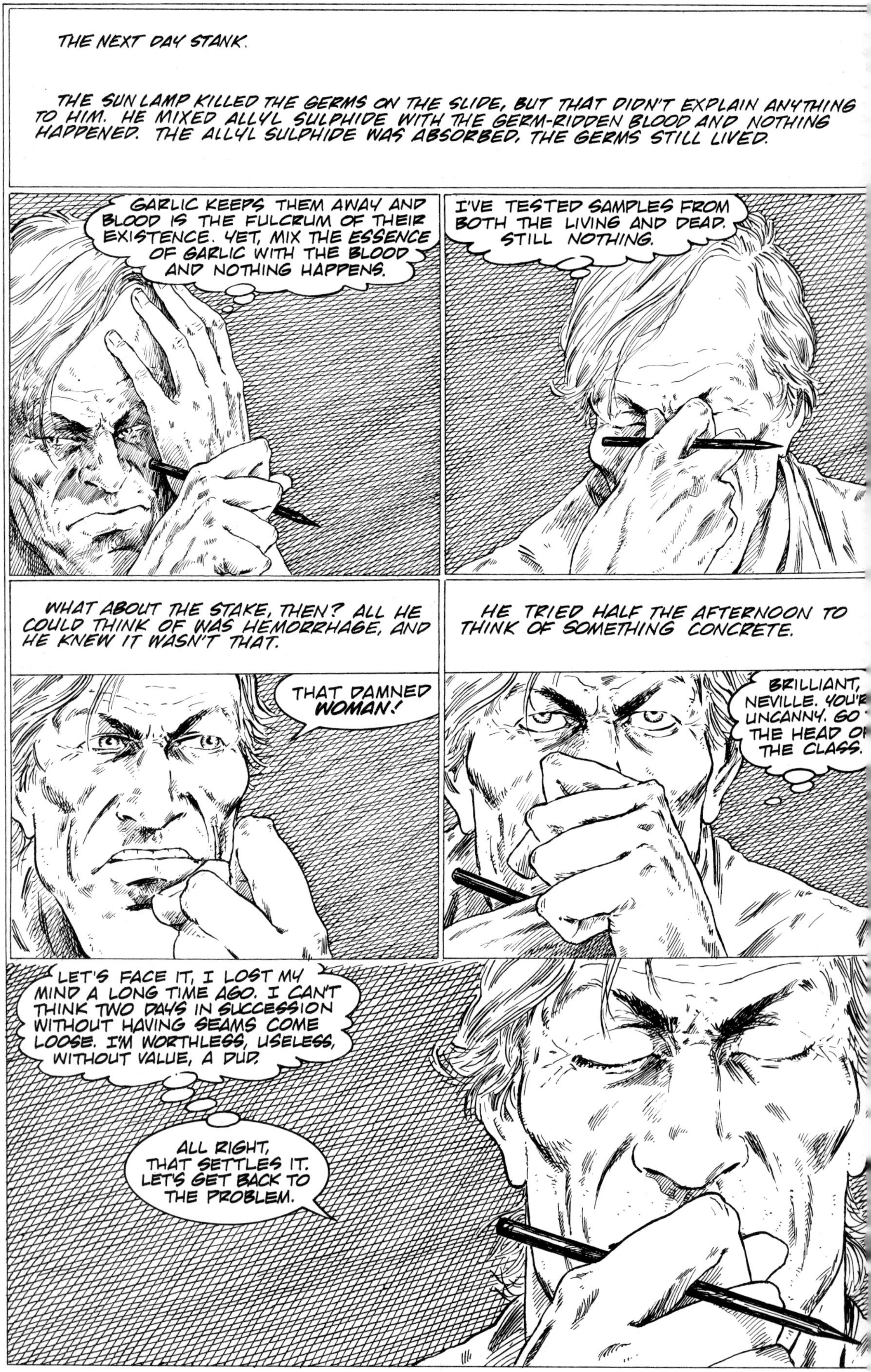
THE NEXT DAY STANK.
THE SUN LAMP KILLED THE GERMS ON THE SLIDE, BUT THAT DIDN'T EXPLAIN ANYTHING TO HIM. HE MIXED ALLYL SULPHIDE WITH THE GERM-RIDDEN BLOOD AND NOTHING HAPPENED. THE ALLYL SULPHIDE WAS ABSORBED, THE GERMS STILL LIVED.
GARLIC KEEPS THEM AWAY AND BLOOD IS THE FULCRUM OF THEIR EXISTENCE. YET, MIX THE ESSENCE OF GARLIC WITH THE BLOOD AND NOTHING HAPPENS.
I'VE TESTED SAMPLES FROM BOTH THE LIVING AND DEAD. STILL NOTHING.
WHAT ABOUT THE STAKE, THEN? ALL HE COULD THINK OF WAS HEMORRHAGE, AND HE KNEW IT WASN'T THAT.
THAT DAMNED WOMAN!
HE TRIED HALF THE AFTERNOON TO THINK OF SOMETHING CONCRETE.
BRILLIANT, NEVILLE. YOU' UNCANNY. GO THE HEAD O THE CLASS.
LET'S FACE IT, I LOST MY MIND A LONG TIME AGO. I CAN'T THINK TWO DAYS IN SUCCESSION WITHOUT HAVING SEAMS COME LOOSE. I'M WORTHLESS, USELESS, WITHOUT VALUE, A DUD.
ALL RIGHT, THAT SETTLES IT. LET'S GET BACK TO THE PROBLEM.

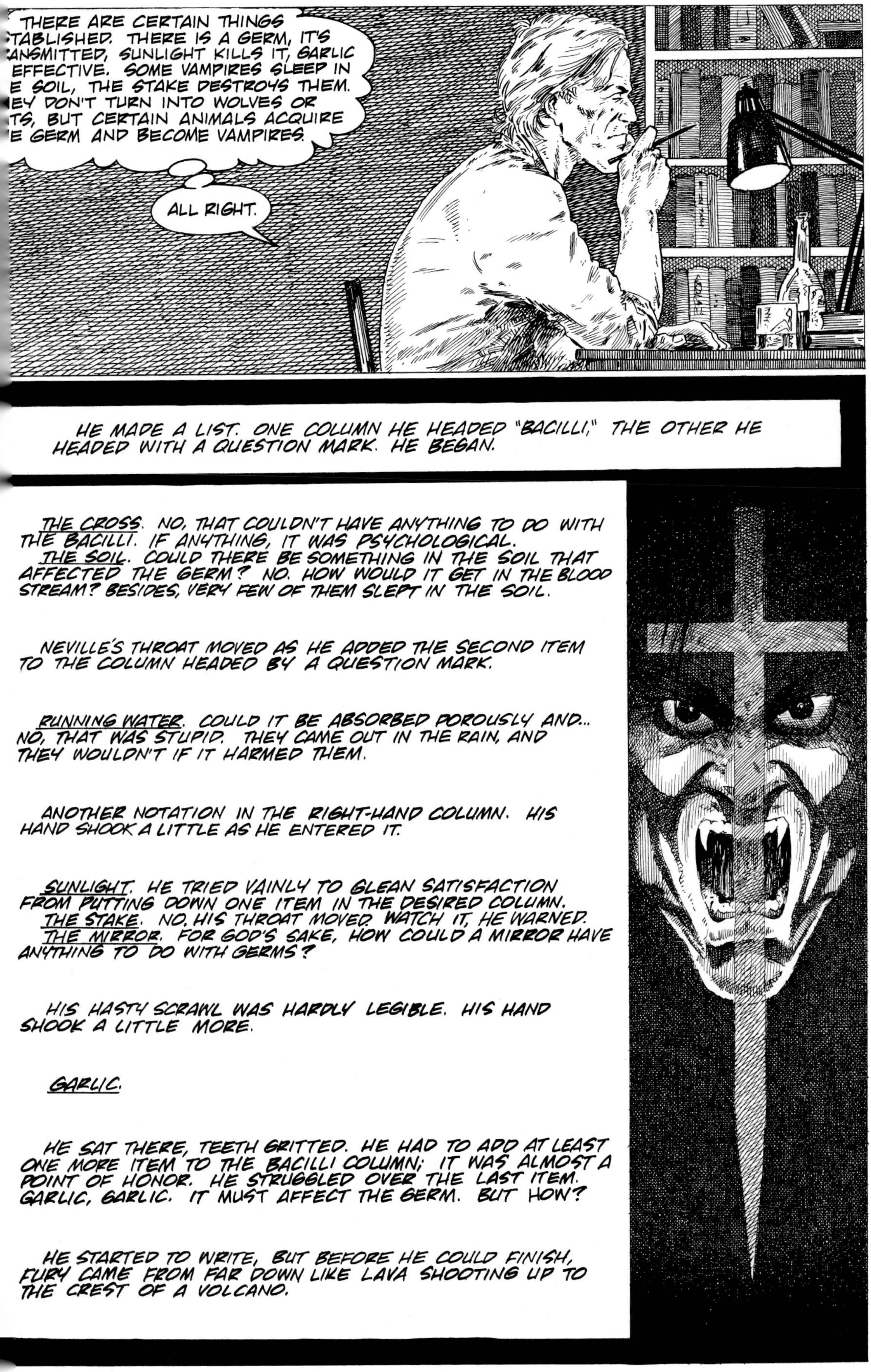
THERE ARE CERTAIN THINGS
TABLISHED. THERE IS A GERM, IT'S
ANSMITTED, SUNLIGHT KILLS IT, GARLIC
EFFECTIVE. SOME VAMPIRES SLEEP IN
E SOIL, THE STAKE DESTROYS THEM.
EY DON'T TURN INTO WOLVES OR
TS, BUT CERTAIN ANIMALS ACQUIRE
E GERM AND BECOME VAMPIRES.
ALL RIGHT.
HE MADE A LIST. ONE COLUMN HE HEADED "BACILLI," THE OTHER HE HEADED WITH A QUESTION MARK. HE BEGAN.
THE CROSS. NO, THAT COULDN'T HAVE ANYTHING TO DO WITH THE BACILLI. IF ANYTHING, IT WAS PSYCHOLOGICAL.
THE SOIL. COULD THERE BE SOMETHING IN THE SOIL THAT AFFECTED THE GERM? NO. HOW WOULD IT GET IN THE BLOOD STREAM? BESIDES, VERY FEW OF THEM SLEPT IN THE SOIL.
NEVILLE'S THROAT MOVED AS HE ADDED THE SECOND ITEM TO THE COLUMN HEADED BY A QUESTION MARK.
RUNNING WATER. COULD IT BE ABSORBED POROUSLY AND... NO, THAT WAS STUPID. THEY CAME OUT IN THE RAIN, AND THEY WOULDN'T IF IT HARMED THEM.
ANOTHER NOTATION IN THE RIGHT-HAND COLUMN. HIS HAND SHOOK A LITTLE AS HE ENTERED IT.
SUNLIGHT. HE TRIED VAINLY TO GLEAN SATISFACTION FROM PUTTING DOWN ONE ITEM IN THE DESIRED COLUMN.
THE STAKE. NO. HIS THROAT MOVED. WATCH IT, HE WARNED.
THE MIRROR. FOR GOD'S SAKE, HOW COULD A MIRROR HAVE ANYTHING TO DO WITH GERMS?
HIS HASTY SCRAWL WAS HARDLY LEGIBLE. HIS HAND SHOOK A LITTLE MORE.
GARLIC.
HE SAT THERE, TEETH GRITTED. HE HAD TO ADD AT LEAST ONE MORE ITEM TO THE BACILLI COLUMN; IT WAS ALMOST A POINT OF HONOR. HE STRUGGLED OVER THE LAST ITEM. GARLIC, GARLIC. IT MUST AFFECT THE GERM. BUT HOW?
HE STARTED TO WRITE, BUT BEFORE HE COULD FINISH, FURY CAME FROM FAR DOWN LIKE LAVA SHOOTING UP TO THE CREST OF A VOLCANO.

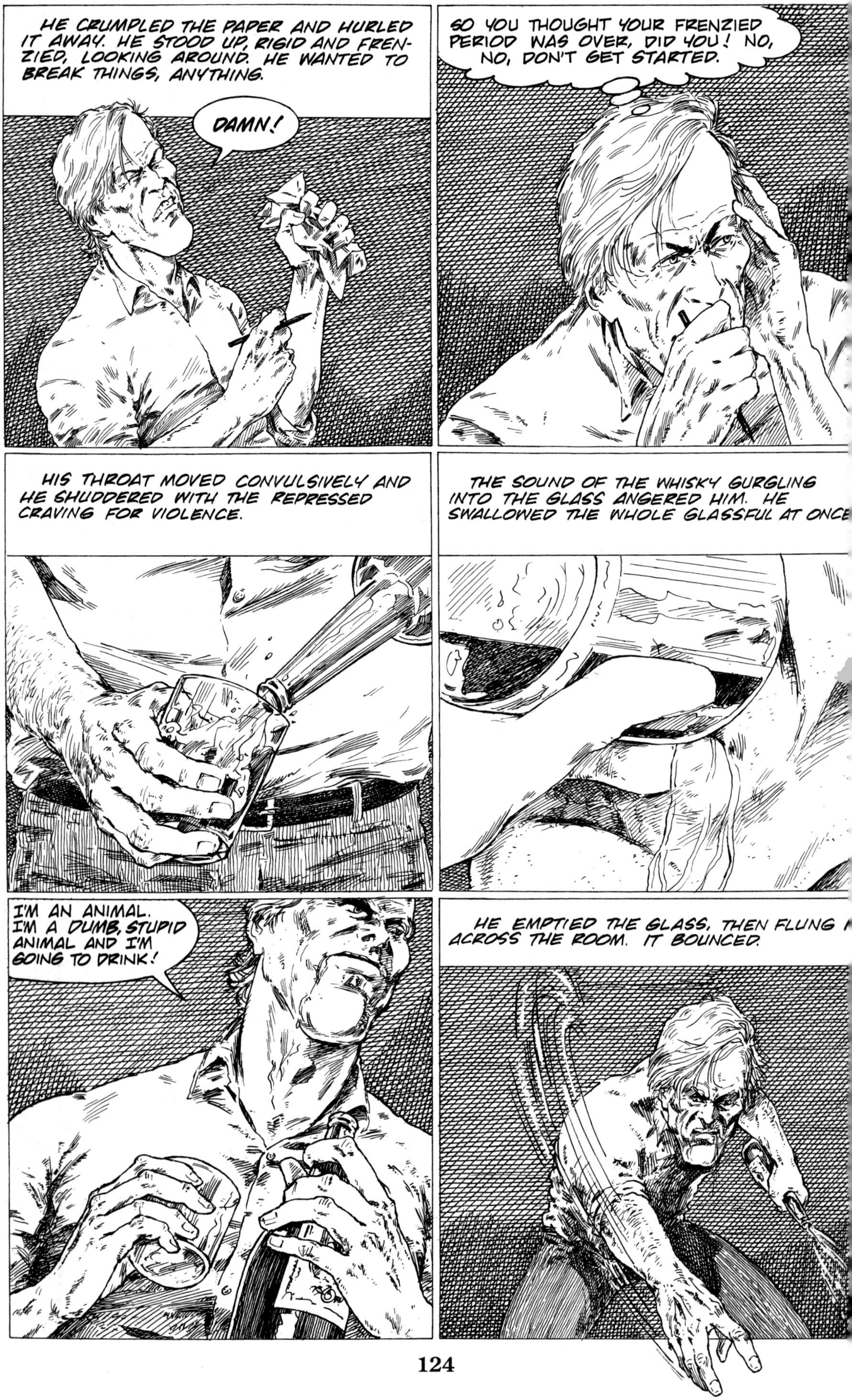
HE CRUMPLED THE PAPER AND HURLED IT AWAY. HE STOOD UP, RIGID AND FRENZIED, LOOKING AROUND. HE WANTED TO BREAK THINGS, ANYTHING.
DAMN!
SO YOU THOUGHT YOUR FRENZIED PERIOD WAS OVER, DID YOU! NO, NO, DON'T GET STARTED.
HIS THROAT MOVED CONVULSIVELY AND HE SHUDDERED WITH THE REPRESSED CRAVING FOR VIOLENCE.
THE SOUND OF THE WHISKY GURGLING INTO THE GLASS ANGERED HIM. HE SWALLOWED THE WHOLE GLASSFUL AT ONCE
I'M AN ANIMAL. I'M A DUMB, STUPID ANIMAL AND I'M GOING TO DRINK!
HE EMPTIED THE GLASS, THEN FLUNG IT ACROSS THE ROOM. IT BOUNCED.

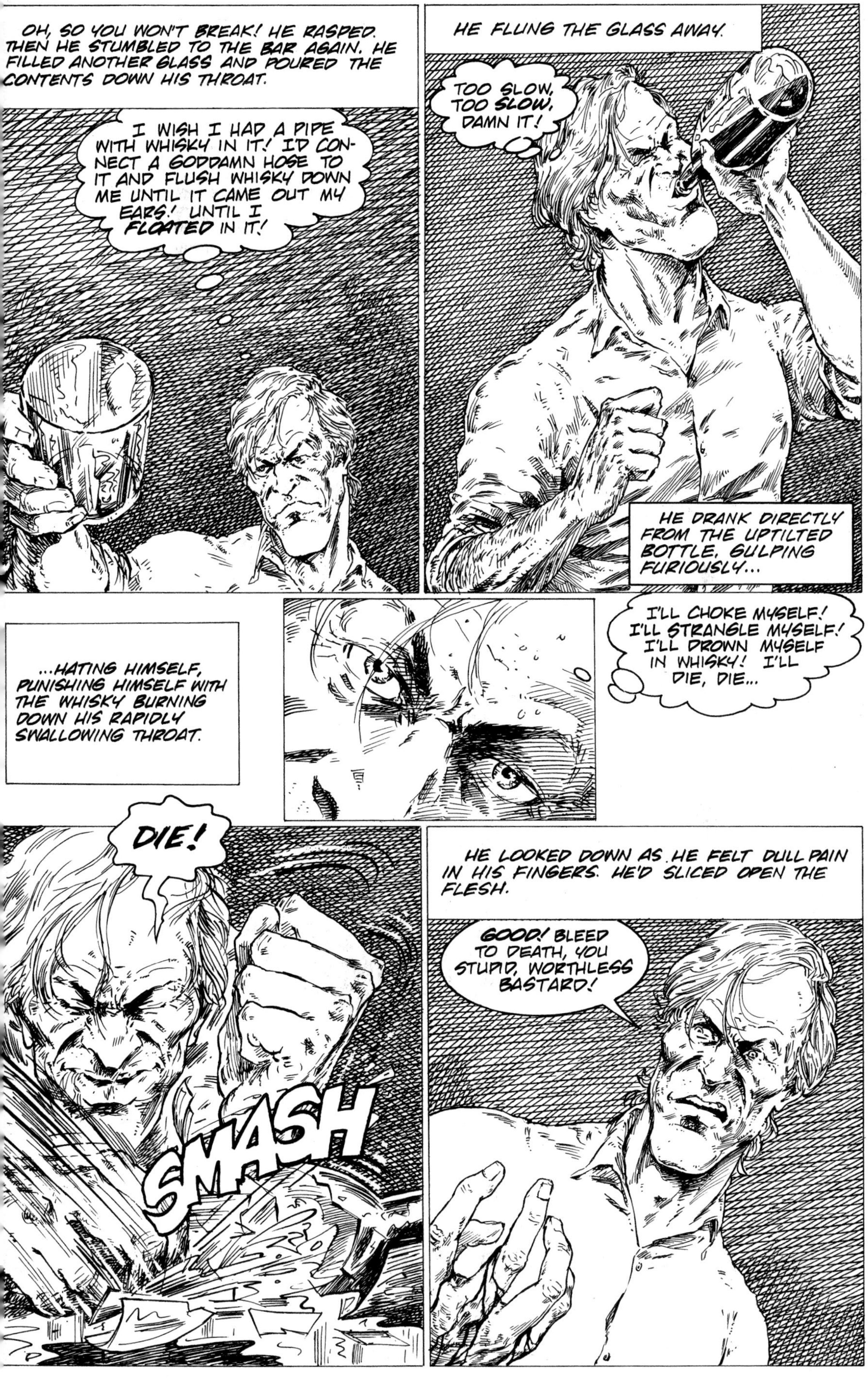
OH, SO YOU WON'T BREAK! HE RASPED. THEN HE STUMBLED TO THE BAR AGAIN. HE FILLED ANOTHER GLASS AND POURED THE CONTENTS DOWN HIS THROAT.
I WISH I HAD A PIPE WITH WHISKY IN IT! I'D CONNECT A GODDAMN HOSE TO IT AND FLUSH WHISKY DOWN ME UNTIL IT CAME OUT MY EARS! UNTIL I FLOATED IN IT!
HE FLUNG THE GLASS AWAY.
TOO SLOW, TOO SLOW, DAMN IT!
HE DRANK DIRECTLY FROM THE UPTILTED BOTTLE, GULPING FURIOUSLY...
...HATING HIMSELF, PUNISHING HIMSELF WITH THE WHISKY BURNING DOWN HIS RAPIDLY SWALLOWING THROAT.
I'LL CHOKE MYSELF! I'LL STRANGLE MYSELF! I'LL DROWN MYSELF IN WHISKY! I'LL DIE, DIE...
DIE!
SMASH
HE LOOKED DOWN AS HE FELT DULL PAIN IN HIS FINGERS. HE'D SLICED OPEN THE FLESH.
GOOD! BLEED TO DEATH, YOU STUPID, WORTHLESS BASTARD!

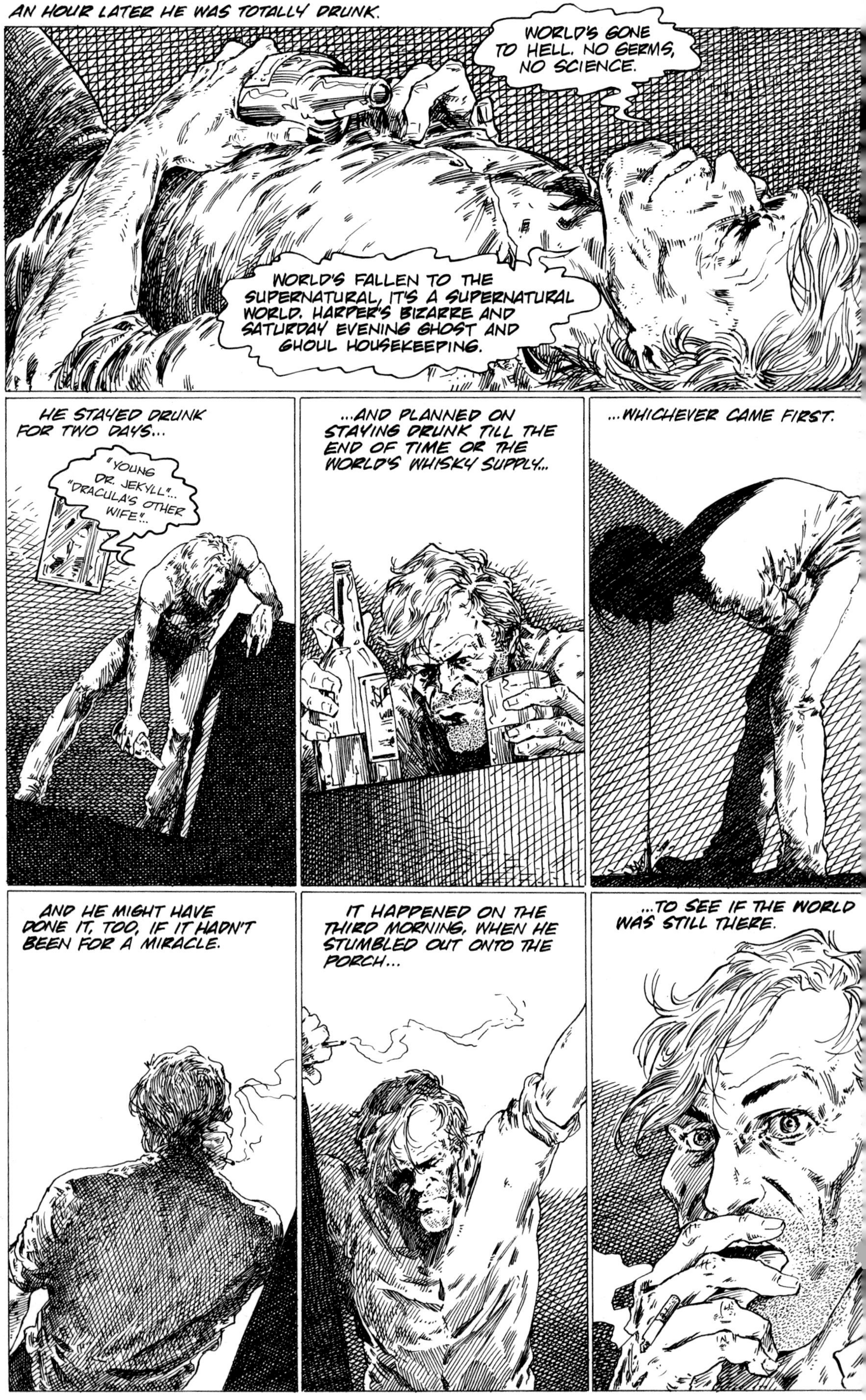
AN HOUR LATER HE WAS TOTALLY DRUNK.
WORLD'S GONE TO HELL. NO GERMS, NO SCIENCE.
WORLD'S FALLEN TO THE SUPERNATURAL, IT'S A SUPERNATURAL WORLD. HARPER'S BIZARRE AND SATURDAY EVENING GHOST AND GHOUL HOUSEKEEPING.
HE STAYED DRUNK FOR TWO DAYS...
"YOUNG DR. JEKYLL"... "DRACULA'S OTHER WIFE"...
...AND PLANNED ON STAYING DRUNK TILL THE END OF TIME OR THE WORLD'S WHISKY SUPPLY...
...WHICHEVER CAME FIRST.
AND HE MIGHT HAVE DONE IT, TOO, IF IT HADN'T BEEN FOR A MIRACLE.
IT HAPPENED ON THE THIRD MORNING, WHEN HE STUMBLED OUT ONTO THE PORCH...
...TO SEE IF THE WORLD WAS STILL THERE.

THERE WAS A DOG ROVING ABOUT ON THE LAWN.

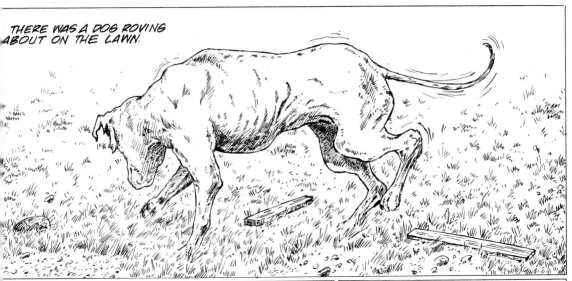

THE SECOND IT HEARD HIM, IT STOPPED SNUFFLING OVER THE GRASS...

...AND IT BOUNDED OFF TO THE SIDE WITH A TWITCH OF SCRAWNY LIMBS.

FOR A MOMENT ROBERT NEVILLE WAS SO SHOCKED HE COULDN'T MOVE. HE STOOD PETRIFIED, STARING AT THE DOG...

...WHICH WAS LIMPING QUICKLY ACROSS THE STREET, ITS ROPELIKE TAIL PULLED BETWEEN ITS LEGS.

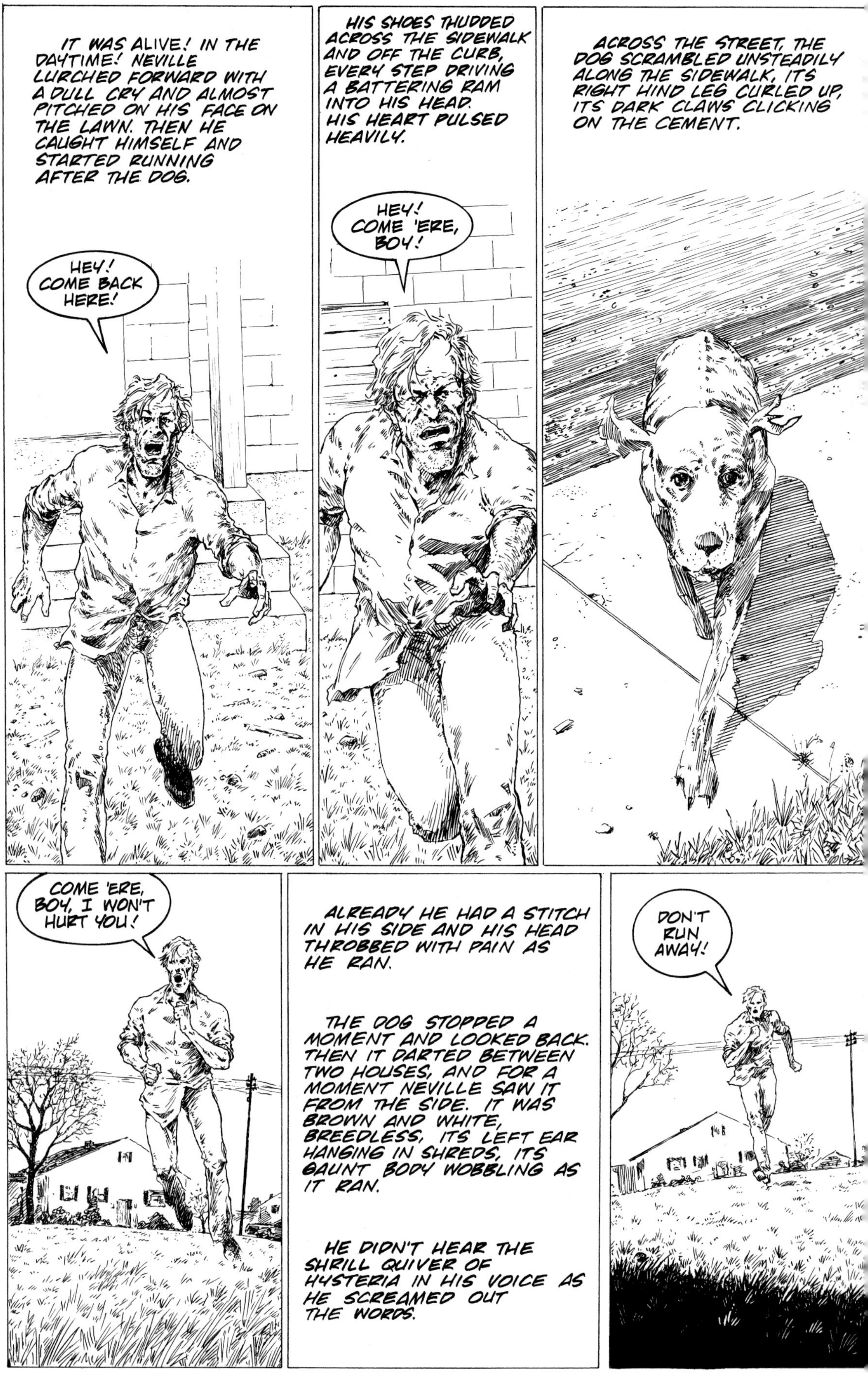
IT WAS ALIVE! IN THE DAYTIME! NEVILLE LURCHED FORWARD WITH A DULL CRY AND ALMOST PITCHED ON HIS FACE ON THE LAWN. THEN HE CAUGHT HIMSELF AND STARTED RUNNING AFTER THE DOG.
HEY! COME BACK HERE!
HIS SHOES THUDDED ACROSS THE SIDEWALK AND OFF THE CURB, EVERY STEP DRIVING A BATTERING RAM INTO HIS HEAD. HIS HEART PULSED HEAVILY.
HEY! COME 'ERE, BOY!
ACROSS THE STREET, THE DOG SCRAMBLED UNSTEADILY ALONG THE SIDEWALK, ITS RIGHT HIND LEG CURLED UP, ITS DARK CLAWS CLICKING ON THE CEMENT.
COME 'ERE, BOY, I WON'T HURT YOU!
ALREADY HE HAD A STITCH IN HIS SIDE AND HIS HEAD THROBBED WITH PAIN AS HE RAN.
THE DOG STOPPED A MOMENT AND LOOKED BACK. THEN IT DARTED BETWEEN TWO HOUSES, AND FOR A MOMENT NEVILLE SAW IT FROM THE SIDE. IT WAS BROWN AND WHITE, BREEDLESS, ITS LEFT EAR HANGING IN SHREDS, ITS GAUNT BODY WOBBLING AS IT RAN.
HE DIDN'T HEAR THE SHRILL QUIVER OF HYSTERIA IN HIS VOICE AS HE SCREAMED OUT THE WORDS.
DON'T RUN AWAY!

HIS THROAT CHOKED UP AS THE DOG DISAPPEARED BETWEEN THE HOUSES. WITH A GRUNT OF FEAR HE HOBBLED ON FASTER, IGNORING THE PAIN OF HANGOVER, EVERYTHING LOST IN THE NEED TO CATCH THAT DOG.

BUT WHEN HE GOT INTO THE BACKYARD THE DOG WAS GONE.

HE RAN TO THE REDWOOD FENCE AND LOOKED OVER.

NOTHING!

HE TWISTED BACK SUDDENLY TO SEE IF THE DOG WERE GOING BACK OUT THE WAY IT HAD ENTERED.

THERE WAS NO DOG.

FOR AN HOUR HE WANDERED AROUND THE NEIGHBORHOOD ON TREMBLING LEGS, SEARCHING VAINLY, CALLING OUT EVERY FEW MOMENTS.

COME 'ERE, BOY, COME 'ERE!

AT LAST HE STUMBLED HOME, HIS FACE A MASK OF HOPELESS DEJECTION. TO COME ACROSS A LIVING BEING, AFTER ALL THIS TIME TO FIND A COMPANION, AND THEN TO LOSE IT. EVEN IF IT WAS ONLY A DOG. ONLY A DOG? TO ROBERT NEVILLE THAT DOG WAS THE PEAK OF A PLANET'S EVOLUTION.

HE COULDN'T EAT OR DRINK ANYTHING. HE FOUND HIMSELF SO ILL AND TREMBLING AT THE SHOCK AND THE LOSS THAT HE HAD TO LIE DOWN. BUT HE COULDN'T SLEEP. HE LAY THERE SHAKING FEVERISHLY, HIS HEAD MOVING FROM SIDE TO SIDE.

COME 'ERE, BOY, COME 'ERE, I WON'T HURT YOU.

IN THE AFTERNOON HE SEARCHED AGAIN. FOR TWO BLOCKS IN EACH DIRECTION FROM HIS HOUSE HE SEARCHED EACH YARD, EACH STREET, EACH INDIVIDUAL HOUSE. BUT HE FOUND NOTHING.

WHEN HE GOT HOME, ABOUT FIVE, HE PUT OUT A BOWL OF MILK, AND A PIECE OF HAMBURGER. HE PUT A RING OF GARLIC BULBS AROUND IT, HOPING THE VAMPIRES WOULDN'T TOUCH IT.

BUT LATER IT CAME TO HIM THAT THE DOG MUST BE AFFLICTED TOO, AND THE GARLIC WOULD KEEP IT AWAY ALSO. HE COULDN'T UNDERSTAND THAT. IF THE DOG HAD THE GERM, HOW COULD IT ROAM OUTDOORS DURING THE DAYLIGHT? UNLESS IT HAD SUCH A SMALL DOSING OF BACILLI IN ITS VEINS THAT IT WASN'T REALLY AFFECTED YET. BUT, IF THAT WERE TRUE, HOW HAD IT SURVIVED THE NIGHTLY ATTACKS?

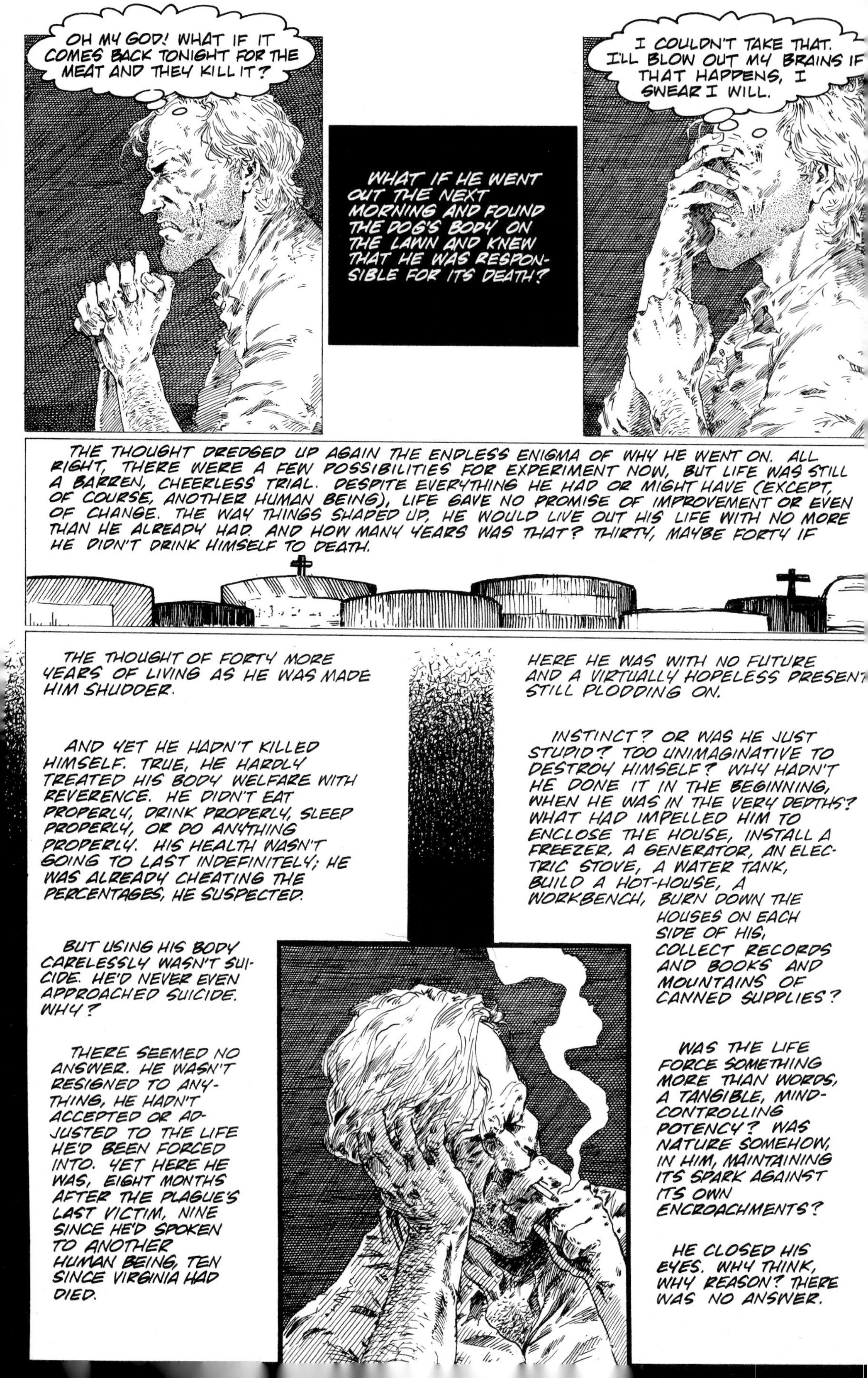
OH MY GOD! WHAT IF IT COMES BACK TONIGHT FOR THE MEAT AND THEY KILL IT?
WHAT IF HE WENT OUT THE NEXT MORNING AND FOUND THE DOG'S BODY ON THE LAWN AND KNEW THAT HE WAS RESPONSIBLE FOR ITS DEATH?
I COULDN'T TAKE THAT. I'LL BLOW OUT MY BRAINS IF THAT HAPPENS, I SWEAR I WILL.
THE THOUGHT DREDGED UP AGAIN THE ENDLESS ENIGMA OF WHY HE WENT ON. ALL RIGHT, THERE WERE A FEW POSSIBILITIES FOR EXPERIMENT NOW, BUT LIFE WAS STILL A BARREN, CHEERLESS TRIAL. DESPITE EVERYTHING HE HAD OR MIGHT HAVE (EXCEPT, OF COURSE, ANOTHER HUMAN BEING), LIFE GAVE NO PROMISE OF IMPROVEMENT OR EVEN OF CHANGE. THE WAY THINGS SHAPED UP, HE WOULD LIVE OUT HIS LIFE WITH NO MORE THAN HE ALREADY HAD. AND HOW MANY YEARS WAS THAT? THIRTY, MAYBE FORTY IF HE DIDN'T DRINK HIMSELF TO DEATH.
THE THOUGHT OF FORTY MORE YEARS OF LIVING AS HE WAS MADE HIM SHUDDER.
AND YET HE HADN'T KILLED HIMSELF. TRUE, HE HARDLY TREATED HIS BODY WELFARE WITH REVERENCE. HE DIDN'T EAT PROPERLY, DRINK PROPERLY, SLEEP PROPERLY, OR DO ANYTHING PROPERLY. HIS HEALTH WASN'T GOING TO LAST INDEFINITELY; HE WAS ALREADY CHEATING THE PERCENTAGES, HE SUSPECTED.
BUT USING HIS BODY CARELESSLY WASN'T SUICIDE. HE'D NEVER EVEN APPROACHED SUICIDE. WHY?
THERE SEEMED NO ANSWER. HE WASN'T RESIGNED TO ANYTHING, HE HADN'T ACCEPTED OR ADJUSTED TO THE LIFE HE'D BEEN FORCED INTO. YET HERE HE WAS, EIGHT MONTHS AFTER THE PLAGUE'S LAST VICTIM, NINE SINCE HE'D SPOKEN TO ANOTHER HUMAN BEING, TEN SINCE VIRGINIA HAD DIED.
HERE HE WAS WITH NO FUTURE AND A VIRTUALLY HOPELESS PRESENT STILL PLODDING ON.
INSTINCT? OR WAS HE JUST STUPID? TOO UNIMAGINATIVE TO DESTROY HIMSELF? WHY HADN'T HE DONE IT IN THE BEGINNING, WHEN HE WAS IN THE VERY DEPTHS? WHAT HAD IMPELLED HIM TO ENCLOSE THE HOUSE, INSTALL A FREEZER, A GENERATOR, AN ELECTRIC STOVE, A WATER TANK, BUILD A HOT-HOUSE, A WORKBENCH, BURN DOWN THE HOUSES ON EACH SIDE OF HIS, COLLECT RECORDS AND BOOKS AND MOUNTAINS OF CANNED SUPPLIES?
WAS THE LIFE FORCE SOMETHING MORE THAN WORDS, A TANGIBLE, MIND-CONTROLLING POTENCY? WAS NATURE SOMEHOW, IN HIM, MAINTAINING ITS SPARK AGAINST ITS OWN ENCROACHMENTS?
HE CLOSED HIS EYES. WHY THINK, WHY REASON? THERE WAS NO ANSWER.

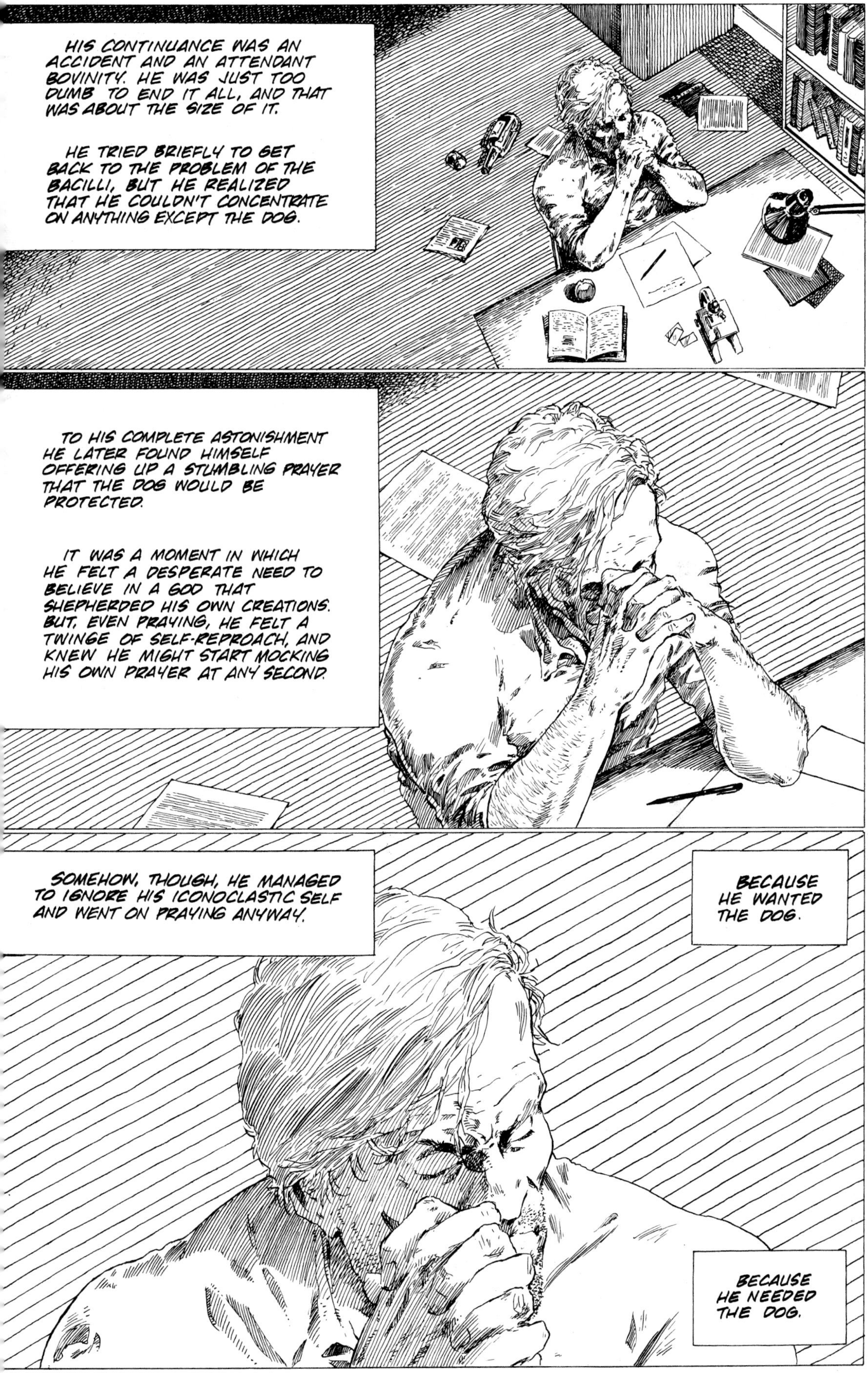
HIS CONTINUANCE WAS AN ACCIDENT AND AN ATTENDANT BOVINITY. HE WAS JUST TOO DUMB TO END IT ALL, AND THAT WAS ABOUT THE SIZE OF IT.
HE TRIED BRIEFLY TO GET BACK TO THE PROBLEM OF THE BACILLI, BUT HE REALIZED THAT HE COULDN'T CONCENTRATE ON ANYTHING EXCEPT THE DOG.
TO HIS COMPLETE ASTONISHMENT HE LATER FOUND HIMSELF OFFERING UP A STUMBLING PRAYER THAT THE DOG WOULD BE PROTECTED.
IT WAS A MOMENT IN WHICH HE FELT A DESPERATE NEED TO BELIEVE IN A GOD THAT SHEPHERDED HIS OWN CREATIONS. BUT, EVEN PRAYING, HE FELT A TWINGE OF SELF-REPROACH, AND KNEW HE MIGHT START MOCKING HIS OWN PRAYER AT ANY SECOND.
SOMEHOW, THOUGH, HE MANAGED TO IGNORE HIS ICONOCLASTIC SELF AND WENT ON PRAYING ANYWAY.
BECAUSE HE WANTED THE DOG.
BECAUSE HE NEEDED THE DOG.

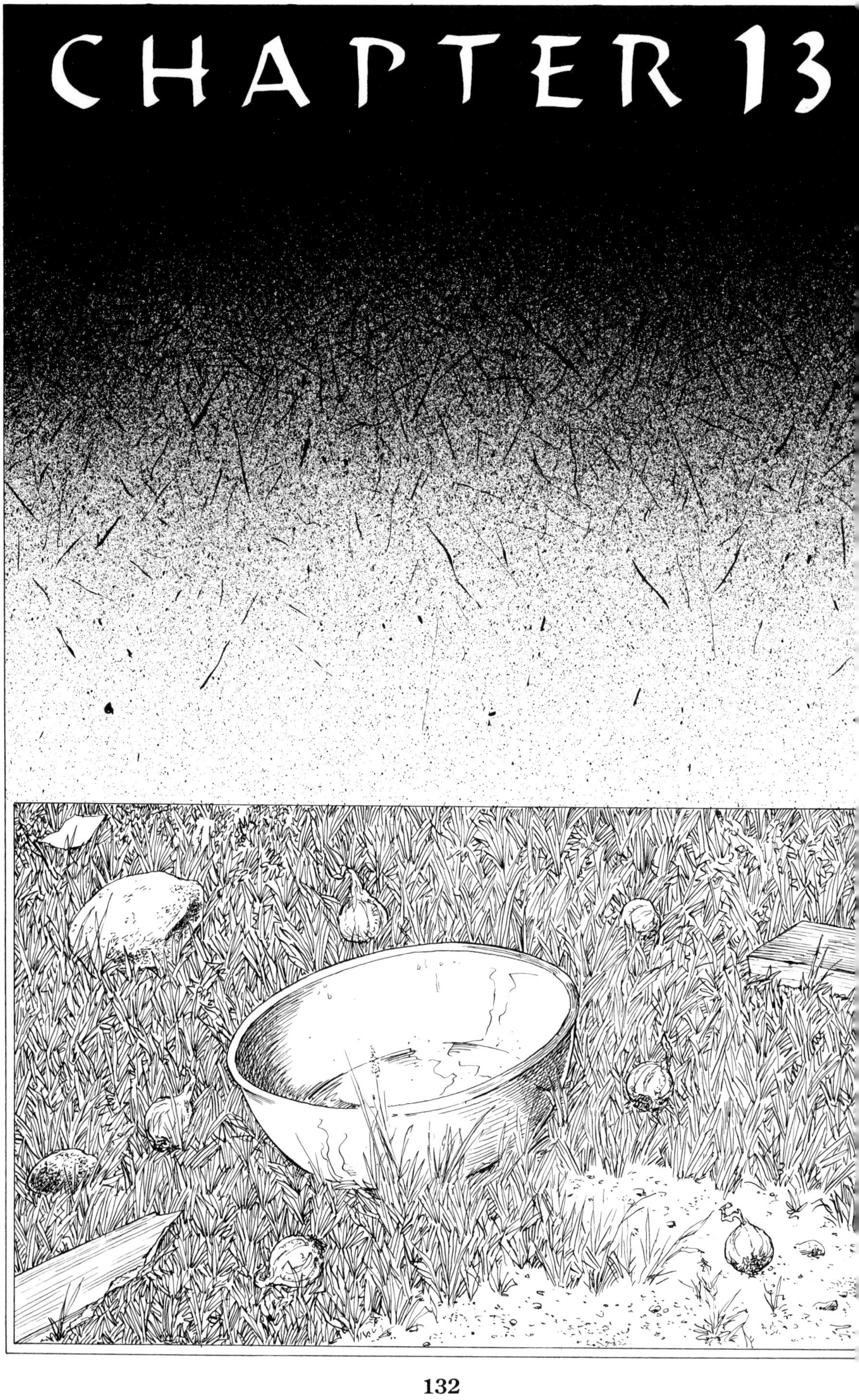
CHAPTER 13

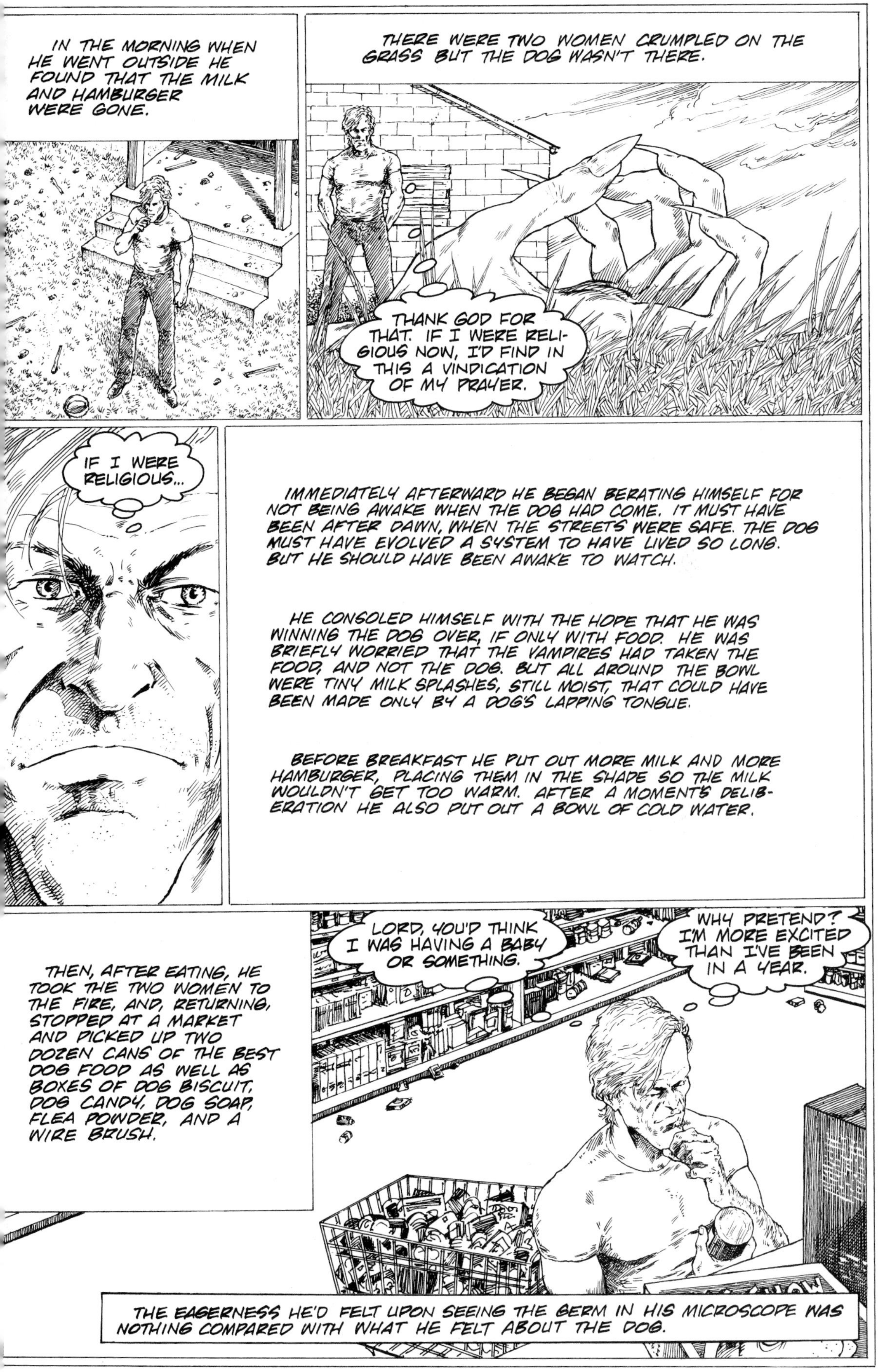
IN THE MORNING WHEN HE WENT OUTSIDE HE FOUND THAT THE MILK AND HAMBURGER WERE GONE.
THERE WERE TWO WOMEN CRUMPLED ON THE GRASS BUT THE DOG WASN'T THERE.
THANK GOD FOR THAT. IF I WERE RELI-GIOUS NOW, I'D FIND IN THIS A VINDICATION OF MY PRAYER.
IF I WERE RELIGIOUS...
IMMEDIATELY AFTERWARD HE BEGAN BERATING HIMSELF FOR NOT BEING AWAKE WHEN THE DOG HAD COME. IT MUST HAVE BEEN AFTER DAWN, WHEN THE STREETS WERE SAFE. THE DOG MUST HAVE EVOLVED A SYSTEM TO HAVE LIVED SO LONG. BUT HE SHOULD HAVE BEEN AWAKE TO WATCH.
HE CONSOLED HIMSELF WITH THE HOPE THAT HE WAS WINNING THE DOG OVER, IF ONLY WITH FOOD. HE WAS BRIEFLY WORRIED THAT THE VAMPIRES HAD TAKEN THE FOOD, AND NOT THE DOG. BUT ALL AROUND THE BOWL WERE TINY MILK SPLASHES, STILL MOIST, THAT COULD HAVE BEEN MADE ONLY BY A DOG'S LAPPING TONGUE.
BEFORE BREAKFAST HE PUT OUT MORE MILK AND MORE HAMBURGER, PLACING THEM IN THE SHADE SO THE MILK WOULDN'T GET TOO WARM. AFTER A MOMENT'S DELIB-ERATION HE ALSO PUT OUT A BOWL OF COLD WATER.
THEN, AFTER EATING, HE TOOK THE TWO WOMEN TO THE FIRE, AND, RETURNING, STOPPED AT A MARKET AND PICKED UP TWO DOZEN CANS OF THE BEST DOG FOOD AS WELL AS BOXES OF DOG BISCUIT, DOG CANDY, DOG SOAP, FLEA POWDER, AND A WIRE BRUSH.
LORD, YOU'D THINK I WAS HAVING A BABY OR SOMETHING.
WHY PRETEND? I'M MORE EXCITED THAN I'VE BEEN IN A YEAR.
THE EAGERNESS HE'D FELT UPON SEEING THE GERM IN HIS MICROSCOPE WAS NOTHING COMPARED WITH WHAT HE FELT ABOUT THE DOG.

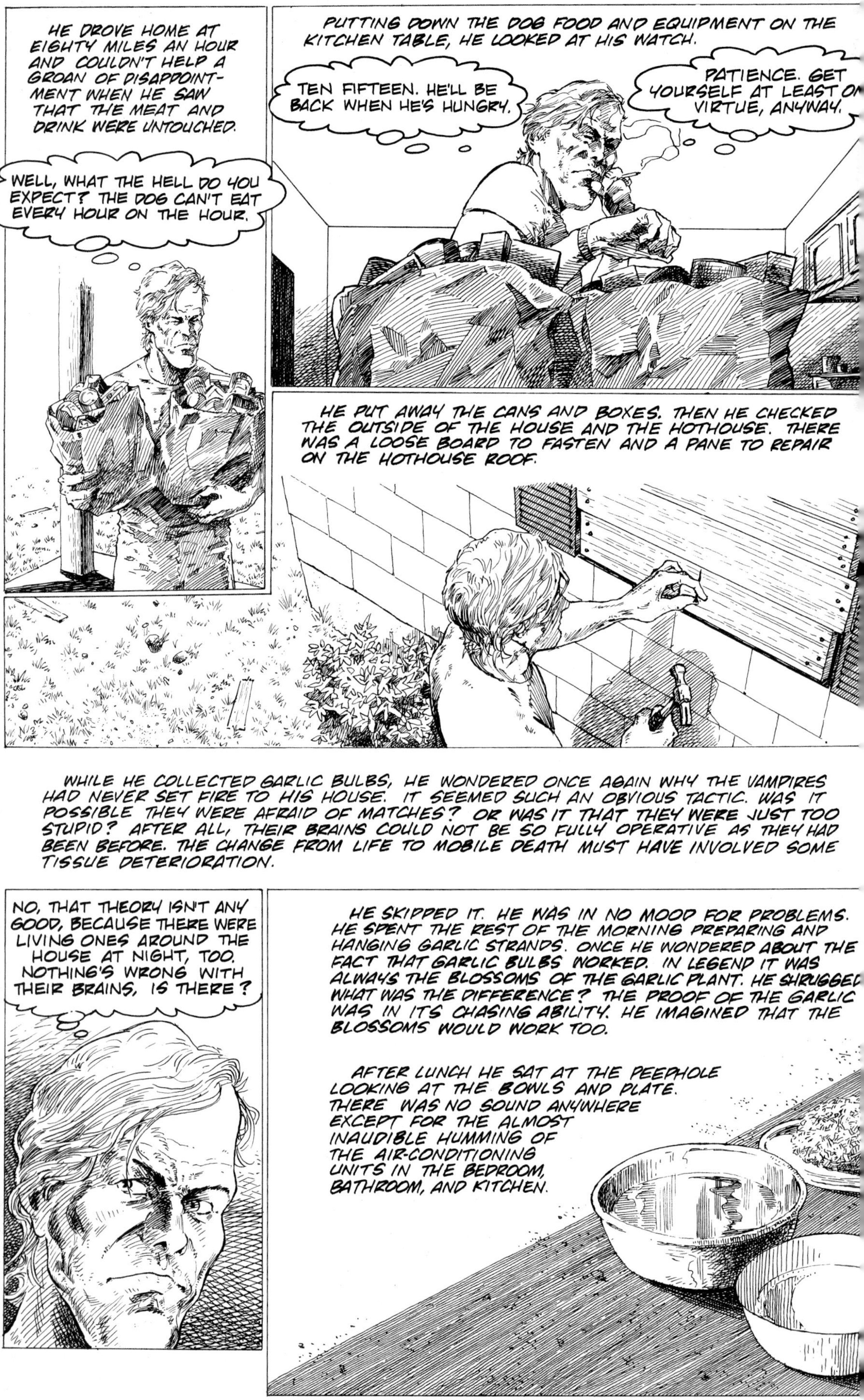
HE DROVE HOME AT EIGHTY MILES AN HOUR AND COULDN'T HELP A GROAN OF DISAPPOINTMENT WHEN HE SAW THAT THE MEAT AND DRINK WERE UNTOUCHED.
WELL, WHAT THE HELL DO YOU EXPECT? THE DOG CAN'T EAT EVERY HOUR ON THE HOUR.
PUTTING DOWN THE DOG FOOD AND EQUIPMENT ON THE KITCHEN TABLE, HE LOOKED AT HIS WATCH.
TEN FIFTEEN. HE'LL BE BACK WHEN HE'S HUNGRY.
PATIENCE. GET YOURSELF AT LEAST ON VIRTUE, ANYWAY.
HE PUT AWAY THE CANS AND BOXES. THEN HE CHECKED THE OUTSIDE OF THE HOUSE AND THE HOTHOUSE. THERE WAS A LOOSE BOARD TO FASTEN AND A PANE TO REPAIR ON THE HOTHOUSE ROOF.
WHILE HE COLLECTED GARLIC BULBS, HE WONDERED ONCE AGAIN WHY THE VAMPIRES HAD NEVER SET FIRE TO HIS HOUSE. IT SEEMED SUCH AN OBVIOUS TACTIC. WAS IT POSSIBLE THEY WERE AFRAID OF MATCHES? OR WAS IT THAT THEY WERE JUST TOO STUPID? AFTER ALL, THEIR BRAINS COULD NOT BE SO FULLY OPERATIVE AS THEY HAD BEEN BEFORE. THE CHANGE FROM LIFE TO MOBILE DEATH MUST HAVE INVOLVED SOME TISSUE DETERIORATION.
NO, THAT THEORY ISN'T ANY GOOD, BECAUSE THERE WERE LIVING ONES AROUND THE HOUSE AT NIGHT, TOO. NOTHING'S WRONG WITH THEIR BRAINS, IS THERE?
HE SKIPPED IT. HE WAS IN NO MOOD FOR PROBLEMS. HE SPENT THE REST OF THE MORNING PREPARING AND HANGING GARLIC STRANDS. ONCE HE WONDERED ABOUT THE FACT THAT GARLIC BULBS WORKED. IN LEGEND IT WAS ALWAYS THE BLOSSOMS OF THE GARLIC PLANT. HE SHRUGGED. WHAT WAS THE DIFFERENCE? THE PROOF OF THE GARLIC WAS IN ITS CHASING ABILITY. HE IMAGINED THAT THE BLOSSOMS WOULD WORK TOO.
AFTER LUNCH HE SAT AT THE PEEPHOLE LOOKING AT THE BOWLS AND PLATE. THERE WAS NO SOUND ANYWHERE EXCEPT FOR THE ALMOST INAUDIBLE HUMMING OF THE AIR-CONDITIONING UNITS IN THE BEDROOM, BATHROOM, AND KITCHEN.

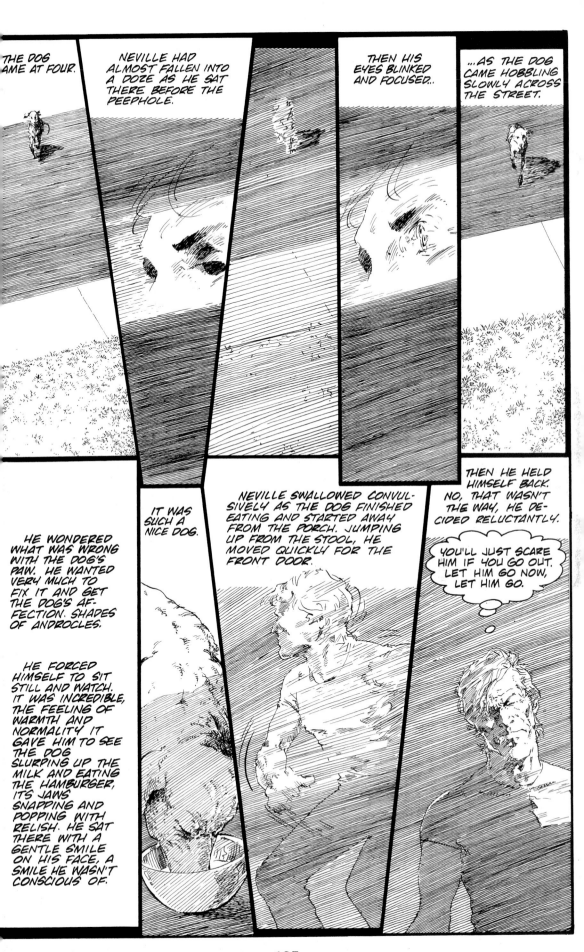

THE DOG CAME AT FOUR.

NEVILLE HAD ALMOST FALLEN INTO A DOZE AS HE SAT THERE BEFORE THE PEEPHOLE.

THEN HIS EYES BLINKED AND FOCUSED...

...AS THE DOG CAME HOBBLING SLOWLY ACROSS THE STREET.

HE WONDERED WHAT WAS WRONG WITH THE DOG'S PAW. HE WANTED VERY MUCH TO FIX IT AND GET THE DOG'S AFFECTION. SHADES OF ANDROCLES.

HE FORCED HIMSELF TO SIT STILL AND WATCH. IT WAS INCREDIBLE, THE FEELING OF WARMTH AND NORMALITY IT GAVE HIM TO SEE THE DOG SLURPING UP THE MILK AND EATING THE HAMBURGER, ITS JAWS SNAPPING AND POPPING WITH RELISH. HE SAT THERE WITH A GENTLE SMILE ON HIS FACE, A SMILE HE WASN'T CONSCIOUS OF.

IT WAS SUCH A NICE DOG.

NEVILLE SWALLOWED CONVULSIVELY AS THE DOG FINISHED EATING AND STARTED AWAY FROM THE PORCH. JUMPING UP FROM THE STOOL, HE MOVED QUICKLY FOR THE FRONT DOOR.

THEN HE HELD HIMSELF BACK. NO, THAT WASN'T THE WAY, HE DECIDED RELUCTANTLY.

YOU'LL JUST SCARE HIM IF YOU GO OUT. LET HIM GO NOW, LET HIM GO.

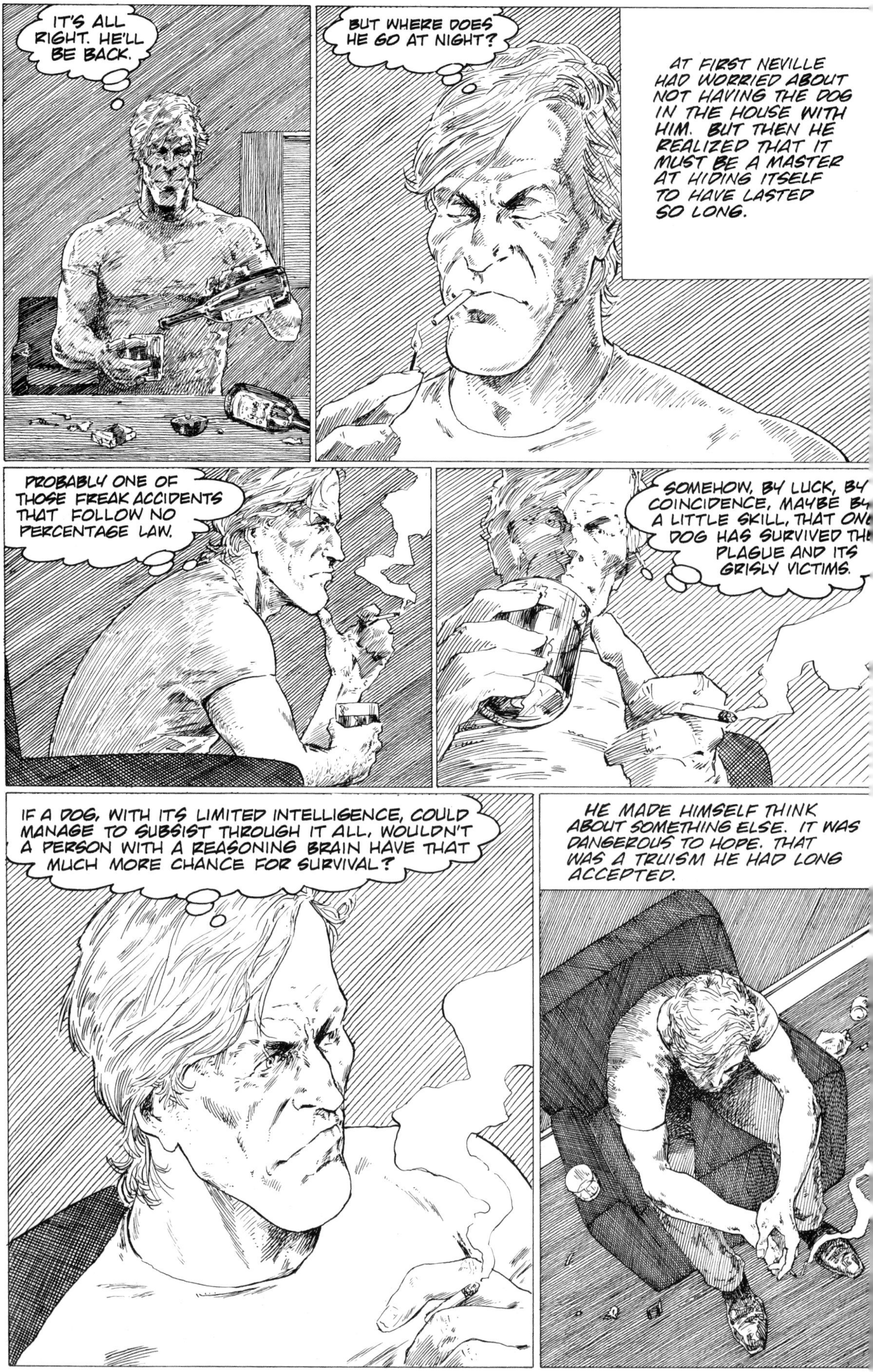
IT'S ALL RIGHT. HE'LL BE BACK.
BUT WHERE DOES HE GO AT NIGHT?
AT FIRST NEVILLE HAD WORRIED ABOUT NOT HAVING THE DOG IN THE HOUSE WITH HIM. BUT THEN HE REALIZED THAT IT MUST BE A MASTER AT HIDING ITSELF TO HAVE LASTED SO LONG.
PROBABLY ONE OF THOSE FREAK ACCIDENTS THAT FOLLOW NO PERCENTAGE LAW.
SOMEHOW, BY LUCK, BY COINCIDENCE, MAYBE BY A LITTLE SKILL, THAT ONE DOG HAS SURVIVED THE PLAGUE AND ITS GRISLY VICTIMS.
IF A DOG, WITH ITS LIMITED INTELLIGENCE, COULD MANAGE TO SUBSIST THROUGH IT ALL, WOULDN'T A PERSON WITH A REASONING BRAIN HAVE THAT MUCH MORE CHANCE FOR SURVIVAL?
HE MADE HIMSELF THINK ABOUT SOMETHING ELSE. IT WAS DANGEROUS TO HOPE. THAT WAS A TRUISM HE HAD LONG ACCEPTED.

THE NEXT MORNING THE DOG CAME AGAIN. THIS TIME ROBERT NEVILLE OPENED THE FRONT DOOR AND WENT OUT. THE DOG IMMEDIATELY BOLTED AWAY, LEGS SCRAMBLING FRANTICALLY ACROSS THE STREET.

NEVILLE TWITCHED WITH THE REPRESSED INSTINCT TO PURSUE. AS CASUALLY AS HE COULD MANAGE, HE SAT DOWN ON EDGE OF THE PORCH.

ACROSS THE STREET THE DOG RAN BETWEEN THE HOUSES AGAIN AND DISAPPEARED.

AFTER FIFTEEN MINUTES OF SITTING, NEVILLE WENT IN AGAIN.

AFTER A SMALL BREAKFAST HE PUT OUT MORE FOOD.

THE DOG CAME AT FOUR AND NEVILLE WENT OUT AGAIN, THIS TIME MAKING SURE THAT THE DOG WAS FINISHED EATING.

ONCE MORE THE DOG FLED. BUT THIS TIME, SEEING THAT IT WAS NOT PURSUED, IT STOPPED ACROSS THE STREET AND LOOKED BACK FOR A MOMENT.

"IT'S ALL RIGHT, BOY," NEVILLE CALLED OUT, BUT AT THE SOUND OF HIS VOICE THE DOG RAN AWAY AGAIN.

NEVILLE SAT ON THE PORCH STIFFLY, TEETH GRITTED WITH IMPATIENCE. GODDAMN IT, WHAT'S THE MATTER WITH HIM? HE THOUGHT, THE DAMN MUTT!

HE FORCED HIMSELF TO THINK OF WHAT THE DOG MUST HAVE GONE THROUGH. THE ENDLESS NIGHTS OF GROVELING IN THE BLACKNESS, HIDDEN GOD KNEW WHERE, ITS GAUNT CHEST LABORING IN THE NIGHT WHILE ALL AROUND ITS SHIVERING FORM THE VAMPIRES WALKED. THE FORAGING FOR FOOD AND WATER, THE STRUGGLE FOR LIFE IN A WORLD WITHOUT MASTERS. HOUSED IN A BODY THAT MAN HAD MADE DEPENDENT ON HIMSELF.

POOR LITTLE FELLA, HE THOUGHT, I'LL BE GOOD TO YOU WHEN YOU COME AND LIVE WITH ME.

MAYBE A DOG HAD MORE CHANCE OF SURVIVAL THAN A HUMAN. DOGS WERE SMALLER, THEY COULD HIDE IN PLACES THE VAMPIRES COULDN'T GO. THEY COULD PROBABLY SENSE THE ALIEN NATURE OF THOSE ABOUT THEM, PROBABLY SMELL IT.

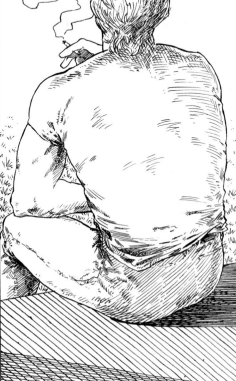

THAT DIDN'T MAKE HIM ANY HAPPIER. FOR ALWAYS, IN SPITE OF REASON, HE HAD CLUNG TO THE HOPE THAT SOMEDAY HE WOULD FIND SOMEONE LIKE HIMSELF--A MAN, A WOMAN, A CHILD, IT DIDN'T MATTER. SEX WAS FAST LOSING ITS MEANING WITHOUT THE ENDLESS PRODDING OF MASS HYPNOSIS. LONELINESS HE STILL FELT.

SOMETIMES HE HAD INDULGED IN DAYDREAMS ABOUT FINDING SOMEONE. MORE OFTEN, THOUGH, HE HAD TRIED TO ADJUST TO WHAT HE SINCERELY BELIEVED WAS THE INEVITABLE--THAT HE WAS ACTUALLY THE ONLY ONE LEFT IN THE WORLD. AT LEAST IN AS MUCH OF THE WORLD AS HE COULD EVER HOPE TO KNOW.

THINKING ABOUT IT, HE ALMOST FORGOT THAT NIGHTFALL WAS APPROACHING.

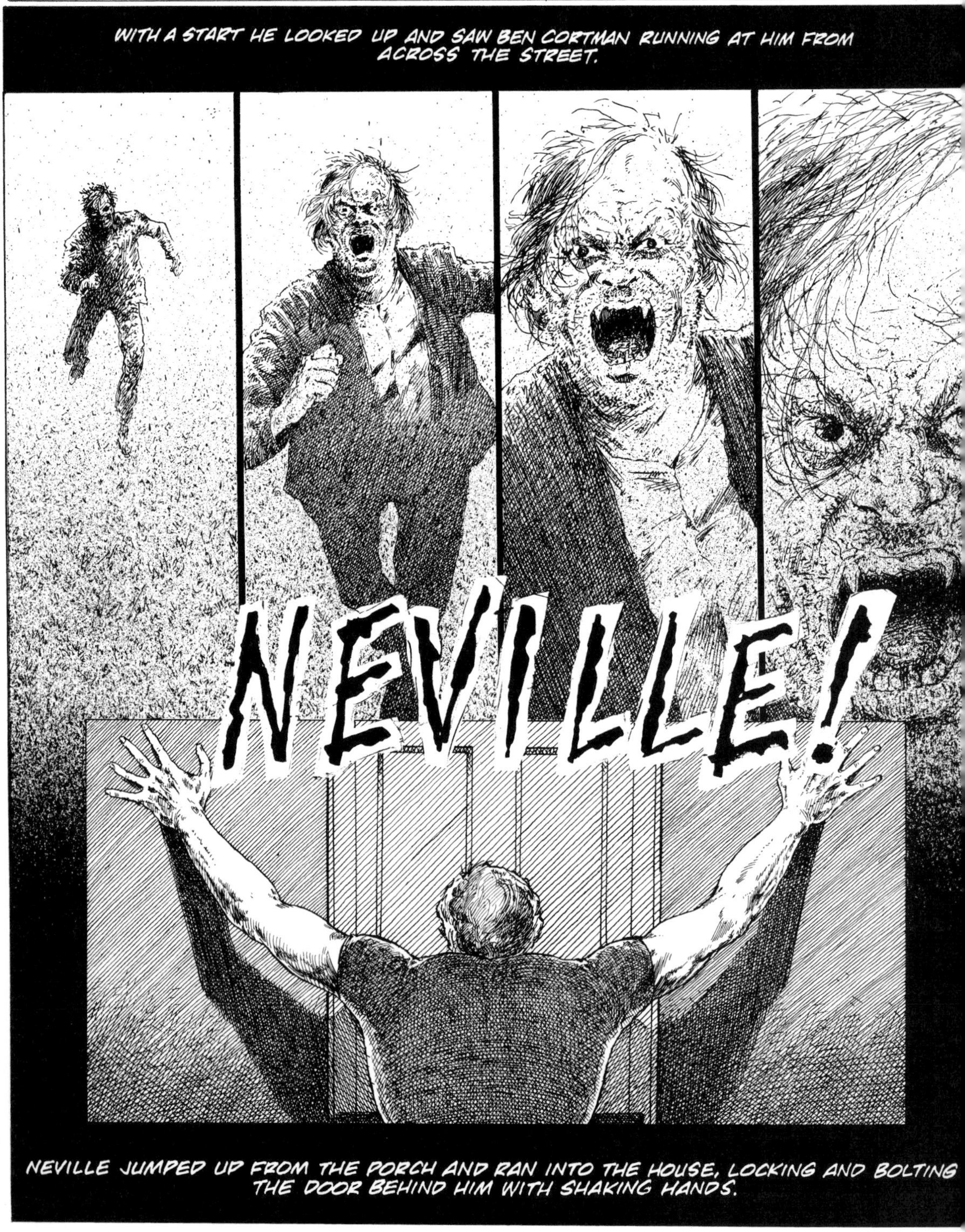
WITH A START HE LOOKED UP AND SAW BEN CORTMAN RUNNING AT HIM FROM ACROSS THE STREET.
NEVILLE!
NEVILLE JUMPED UP FROM THE PORCH AND RAN INTO THE HOUSE, LOCKING AND BOLTING THE DOOR BEHIND HIM WITH SHAKING HANDS.

FOR A CERTAIN PERIOD OF TIME HE WENT OUT ON THE PORCH JUST AS THE DOG HAD FINISHED EATING. EVERY TIME HE WENT OUT THE DOG RAN AWAY. BUT AS THE DAYS PASSED IT RAN WITH DECREASING SPEED, AND SOON IT WAS STOPPING HALFWAY ACROSS THE STREET TO LOOK BACK AND BARK AT HIM. IT WAS A GAME THEY PLAYED.

THEN ONE DAY NEVILLE SAT ON THE PORCH BEFORE THE DOG CAME. AND, WHEN IT APPEARED ACROSS THE STREET, HE REMAINED SEATED.

FOR ABOUT FIFTEEN MINUTES THE DOG HOVERED NEAR THE CURB SUSPICIOUSLY, UNWILLING TO APPROACH THE FOOD.

NEVILLE EDGED AS FAR AWAY FROM THE FOOD AS HE COULD TO ENCOURAGE THE DOG.

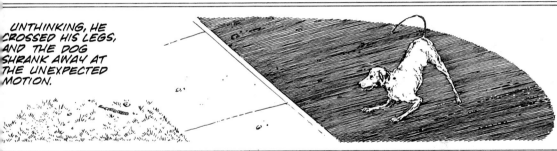

UNTHINKING, HE CROSSED HIS LEGS, AND THE DOG SHRANK AWAY AT THE UNEXPECTED MOTION.

NEVILLE HELD HIMSELF QUIETLY THEN AND THE DOG KEPT MOVING AROUND RESTLESSLY IN THE STREET, ITS EYES MOVING FROM NEVILLE TO THE FOOD AND BACK AGAIN.

COME ON, BOY. EAT YOUR FOOD, THAT'S A GOOD DOG.

ANOTHER TEN MINUTES PASSED. THE DOG WAS NOW ON THE LAWN, MOVING IN CONCENTRIC ARCS THAT BECAME SHORTER AND SHORTER.

THE DOG STOPPED. THEN SLOWLY, VERY SLOWLY, ONE PAW AT A TIME, IT BEGAN MOVING UP ON THE DISH AND BOWLS, ITS EYES NEVER LEAVING NEVILLE FOR A SECOND.

"THAT'S THE BOY," NEVILLE SAID QUIETLY.

THIS TIME THE DOG DIDN'T FLINCH OR BACK AWAY AT THE SOUND OF HIS VOICE. STILL, NEVILLE MADE SURE HE SAT MOTIONLESS SO THAT NO ABRUPT MOVEMENT WOULD STARTLE THE DOG.

THE DOG MOVED YET CLOSER, STALKING THE PLATE, ITS BODY TENSE AND WAITING FOR THE LEAST MOTION FROM NEVILLE.

"THAT'S RIGHT," NEVILLE TOLD THE DOG.

SUDDENLY THE DOG DARTED IN AND GRABBED THE MEAT. NEVILLE'S PLEASED LAUGHTER FOLLOWED ITS FRANTICALLY ERRATIC WOBBLE ACROSS THE STREET.

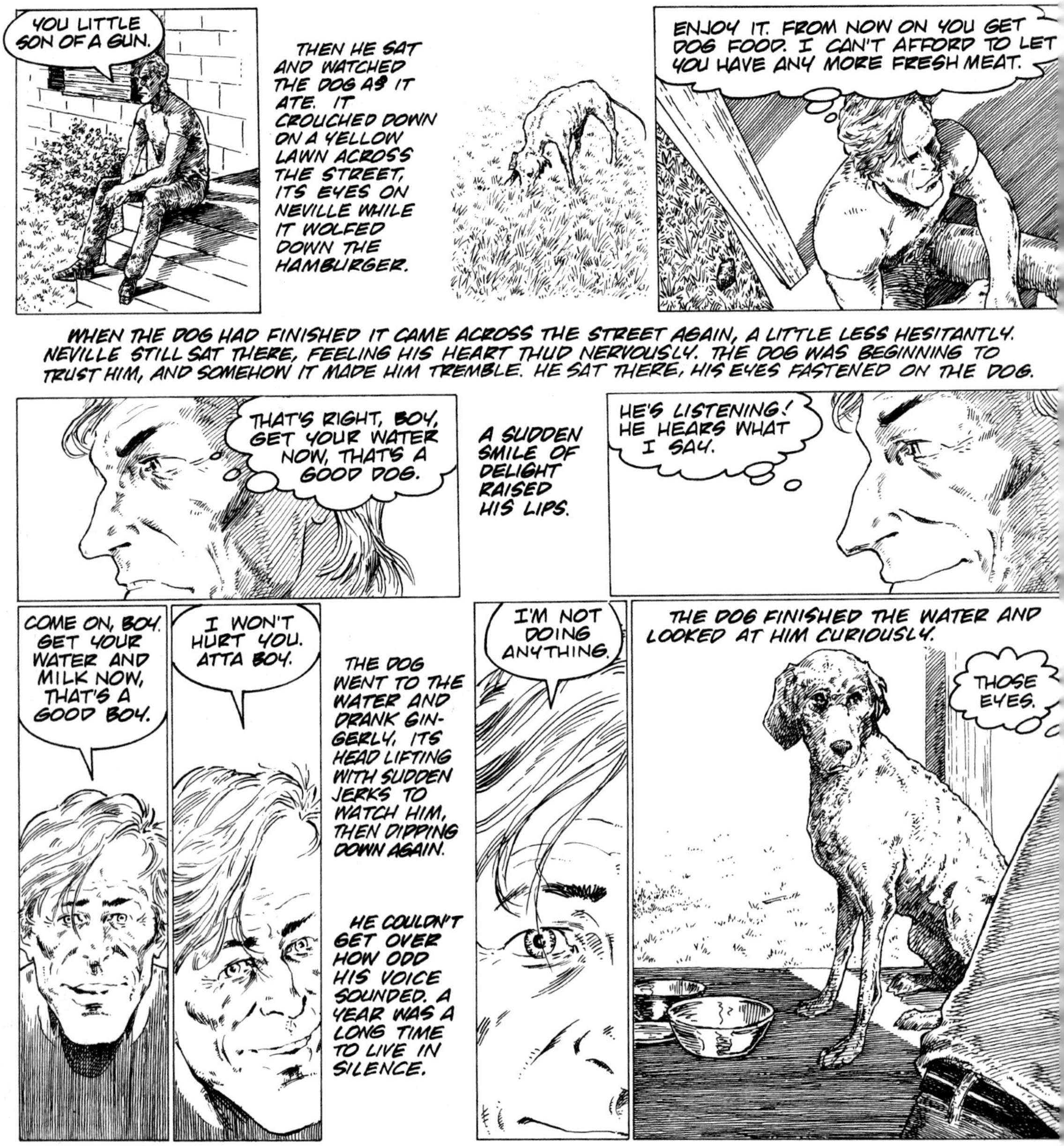

YOU LITTLE SON OF A GUN.
THEN HE SAT AND WATCHED THE DOG AS IT ATE. IT CROUCHED DOWN ON A YELLOW LAWN ACROSS THE STREET, ITS EYES ON NEVILLE WHILE IT WOLFED DOWN THE HAMBURGER.
ENJOY IT. FROM NOW ON YOU GET DOG FOOD. I CAN'T AFFORD TO LET YOU HAVE ANY MORE FRESH MEAT.
WHEN THE DOG HAD FINISHED IT CAME ACROSS THE STREET AGAIN, A LITTLE LESS HESITANTLY. NEVILLE STILL SAT THERE, FEELING HIS HEART THUD NERVOUSLY. THE DOG WAS BEGINNING TO TRUST HIM, AND SOMEHOW IT MADE HIM TREMBLE. HE SAT THERE, HIS EYES FASTENED ON THE DOG.
THAT'S RIGHT, BOY, GET YOUR WATER NOW, THAT'S A GOOD DOG.
A SUDDEN SMILE OF DELIGHT RAISED HIS LIPS.
HE'S LISTENING! HE HEARS WHAT I SAY.
COME ON, BOY, GET YOUR WATER AND MILK NOW, THAT'S A GOOD BOY.
I WON'T HURT YOU. ATTA BOY.
THE DOG WENT TO THE WATER AND DRANK GINGERLY, ITS HEAD LIFTING WITH SUDDEN JERKS TO WATCH HIM, THEN DIPPING DOWN AGAIN.
HE COULDN'T GET OVER HOW ODD HIS VOICE SOUNDED. A YEAR WAS A LONG TIME TO LIVE IN SILENCE.
I'M NOT DOING ANYTHING.
THE DOG FINISHED THE WATER AND LOOKED AT HIM CURIOUSLY.
THOSE EYES.

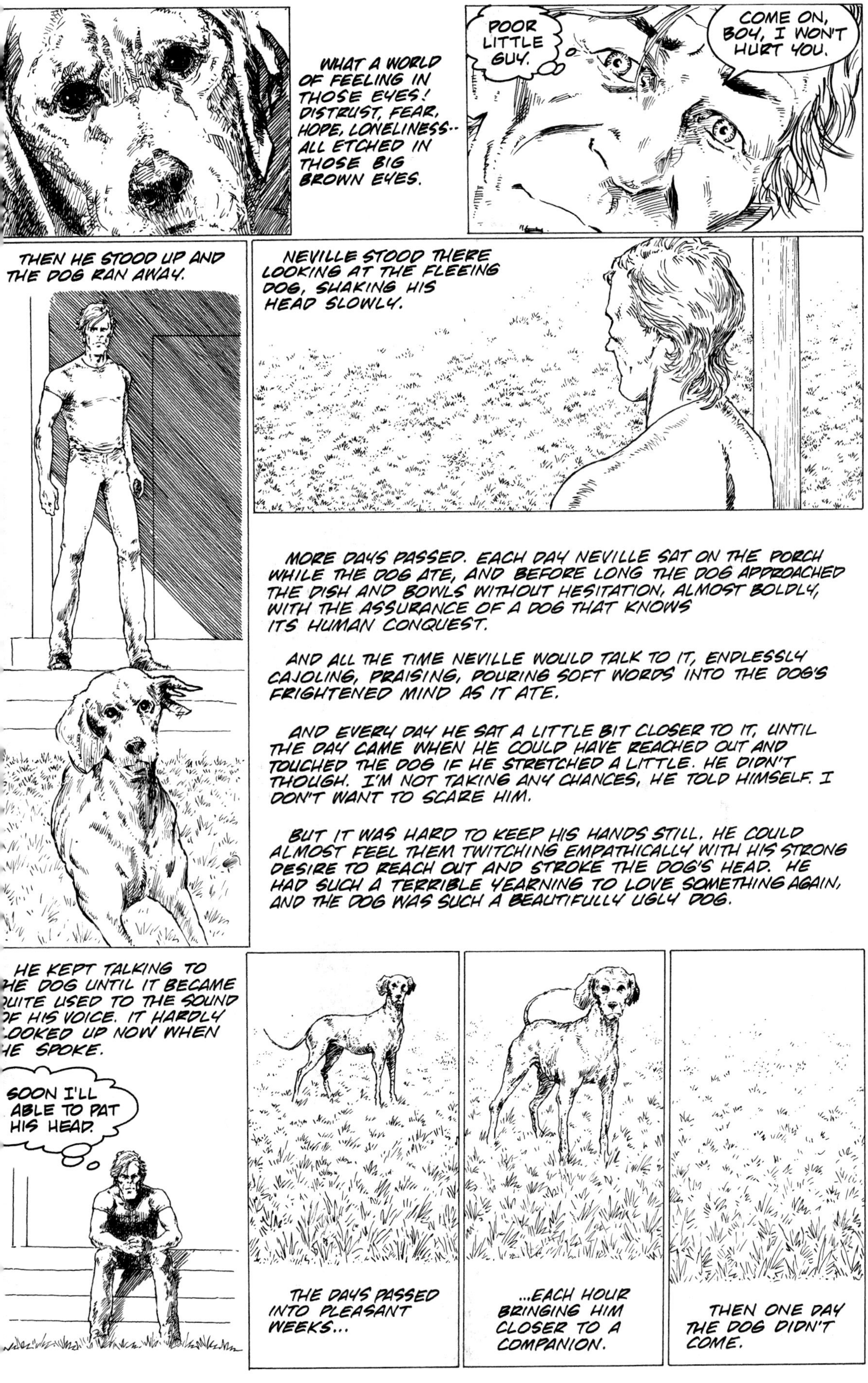

WHAT A WORLD OF FEELING IN THOSE EYES! DISTRUST, FEAR, HOPE, LONELINESS.. ALL ETCHED IN THOSE BIG BROWN EYES.
POOR LITTLE GUY.
COME ON, BOY, I WON'T HURT YOU.
THEN HE STOOD UP AND THE DOG RAN AWAY.
NEVILLE STOOD THERE LOOKING AT THE FLEEING DOG, SHAKING HIS HEAD SLOWLY.
MORE DAYS PASSED. EACH DAY NEVILLE SAT ON THE PORCH WHILE THE DOG ATE, AND BEFORE LONG THE DOG APPROACHED THE DISH AND BOWLS WITHOUT HESITATION, ALMOST BOLDLY, WITH THE ASSURANCE OF A DOG THAT KNOWS ITS HUMAN CONQUEST.
AND ALL THE TIME NEVILLE WOULD TALK TO IT, ENDLESSLY CAJOLING, PRAISING, POURING SOFT WORDS INTO THE DOG'S FRIGHTENED MIND AS IT ATE.
AND EVERY DAY HE SAT A LITTLE BIT CLOSER TO IT, UNTIL THE DAY CAME WHEN HE COULD HAVE REACHED OUT AND TOUCHED THE DOG IF HE STRETCHED A LITTLE. HE DIDN'T THOUGH. I'M NOT TAKING ANY CHANCES, HE TOLD HIMSELF. I DON'T WANT TO SCARE HIM.
BUT IT WAS HARD TO KEEP HIS HANDS STILL. HE COULD ALMOST FEEL THEM TWITCHING EMPATHICALLY WITH HIS STRONG DESIRE TO REACH OUT AND STROKE THE DOG'S HEAD. HE HAD SUCH A TERRIBLE YEARNING TO LOVE SOMETHING AGAIN, AND THE DOG WAS SUCH A BEAUTIFULLY UGLY DOG.
HE KEPT TALKING TO HE DOG UNTIL IT BECAME UITE USED TO THE SOUND OF HIS VOICE. IT HARDLY OOKED UP NOW WHEN HE SPOKE.
SOON I'LL ABLE TO PAT HIS HEAD.
THE DAYS PASSED INTO PLEASANT WEEKS...
...EACH HOUR BRINGING HIM CLOSER TO A COMPANION.
THEN ONE DAY THE DOG DIDN'T COME.

NEVILLE WAS FRANTIC. HE'D GOT SO USED TO THE DOG'S COMING AND GOING THAT IT HAD BECOME THE FULCRUM OF HIS DAILY SCHEDULE, EVERYTHING FITTING AROUND THE DOG'S MEALTIMES, INVESTIGATION FORGOTTEN, EVERYTHING PUSHED ASIDE BUT HIS DESIRE TO HAVE THE DOG IN HIS HOUSE.

HE SPENT A NERVE-RACKED AFTERNOON SEARCHING THE NEIGHBORHOOD, CALLING OUT IN A LOUD VOICE FOR THE DOG. BUT NO AMOUNT OF SEARCHING HELPED, AND HE WENT HOME TO A TASTELESS DINNER. THE DOG DIDN'T COME THAT NIGHT OR THE NEXT MORNING. AGAIN NEVILL SEARCHED, BUT WITH LESS HOPE. THEY'VE GOT HIM, HE KEPT HEARING THE WORDS IN HIS MIND, THE DIRTY BASTARDS HAVE GOT HIM. BUT HE COULDN'T REALLY BELIEVE IT. HE WOULDN'T LET HIMSELF BELIEVE IT.

ON THE AFTERNOON OF THE THIRD DAY HE WAS IN THE GARAGE WHEN HE HEARD THE SOUN OF THE METAL BOWL CLINKING OUTSIDE. WITH A GASP HE RAN OUT INTO THE DAYLIGHT.

NEVILLE'S HEART LEAPED. THE DOG'S EYES WERE GLAZED AND IT WAS PANTING FOR BREATH, ITS DARK TONGUE HANGING OUT.

THE DOG BACKED ACROSS THE LAWN ON TREMBLING STALKS OF LEGS. QUICKLY NEVILLE SAT DOWN ON THE PORCH STEPS AND STAYED THERE TREMBLING. HE SAT THERE WATCHING IT TREMBLE FITFULLY AS IT LAPPED UP THE WATER. THEN, INSTINCTIVELY, HE REACHED OUT HIS HAND.

HE COULDN'T STOP THE DOG FROM LEAVING. HE TRIED TO FOLLOW IT, BUT IT WAS GONE BEFORE HE COULD DISCOVER WHERE IT HID. HE DECIDED IT MUST BE UNDER A HOUSE SOMEWHERE.

HE COULDN'T SLEEP THAT NIGHT. HE PACED RESTLESSLY, DRINKING POTS OF COFFEE AND CURSING THE SLUGGISHNESS OF TIME. HE HAD TO GET HOLD OF THE DOG, HE HAD TO. AND SOON. HE HAD TO CURE IT. BUT HOW? THERE HAD TO BE A WAY. EVEN WITH THE LITTLE HE KNEW THERE MUST BE A WAY.

THE NEXT MORNING HE SAT RIGHT BESIDE THE BOWL AND FELT HIS LIPS SHAKING AS THE DOG CAME LIMPING SLOWLY ACROSS THE STREET. IT DIDN'T EAT ANYTHING. ITS EYES WERE MORE DULL AND LISTLESS THAN THEY'D BEEN THE DAY BEFORE. NEVILLE WANTED TO JUMP AT IT AND TRY TO GRAB HOLD OF IT, TAKE IT IN THE HOUSE, NURSE IT.

BUT HE KNEW THAT IF HE JUMPED AND MISSED HE MIGHT UNDO EVERYTHING. THE DOG MIGHT NEVER RETURN.

142

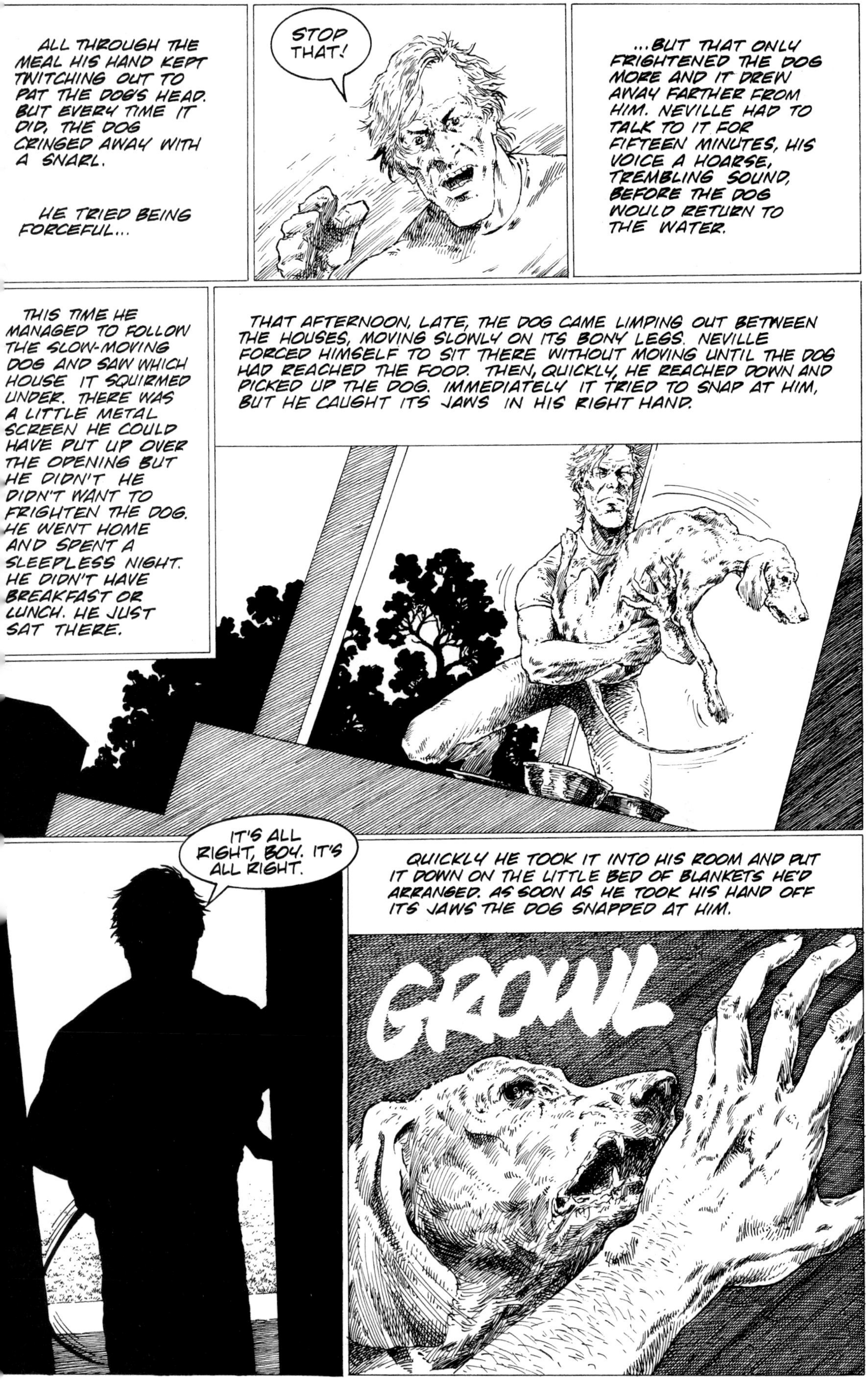
ALL THROUGH THE MEAL HIS HAND KEPT TWITCHING OUT TO PAT THE DOG'S HEAD. BUT EVERY TIME IT DID, THE DOG CRINGED AWAY WITH A SNARL.
HE TRIED BEING FORCEFUL...
STOP THAT!
...BUT THAT ONLY FRIGHTENED THE DOG MORE AND IT DREW AWAY FARTHER FROM HIM. NEVILLE HAD TO TALK TO IT FOR FIFTEEN MINUTES, HIS VOICE A HOARSE, TREMBLING SOUND, BEFORE THE DOG WOULD RETURN TO THE WATER.
THIS TIME HE MANAGED TO FOLLOW THE SLOW-MOVING DOG AND SAW WHICH HOUSE IT SQUIRMED UNDER. THERE WAS A LITTLE METAL SCREEN HE COULD HAVE PUT UP OVER THE OPENING BUT HE DIDN'T HE DIDN'T WANT TO FRIGHTEN THE DOG. HE WENT HOME AND SPENT A SLEEPLESS NIGHT. HE DIDN'T HAVE BREAKFAST OR LUNCH. HE JUST SAT THERE.
THAT AFTERNOON, LATE, THE DOG CAME LIMPING OUT BETWEEN THE HOUSES, MOVING SLOWLY ON ITS BONY LEGS. NEVILLE FORCED HIMSELF TO SIT THERE WITHOUT MOVING UNTIL THE DOG HAD REACHED THE FOOD. THEN, QUICKLY, HE REACHED DOWN AND PICKED UP THE DOG. IMMEDIATELY IT TRIED TO SNAP AT HIM, BUT HE CAUGHT ITS JAWS IN HIS RIGHT HAND.
IT'S ALL RIGHT, BOY. IT'S ALL RIGHT.
QUICKLY HE TOOK IT INTO HIS ROOM AND PUT IT DOWN ON THE LITTLE BED OF BLANKETS HE'D ARRANGED. AS SOON AS HE TOOK HIS HAND OFF ITS JAWS THE DOG SNAPPED AT HIM.
GROWL

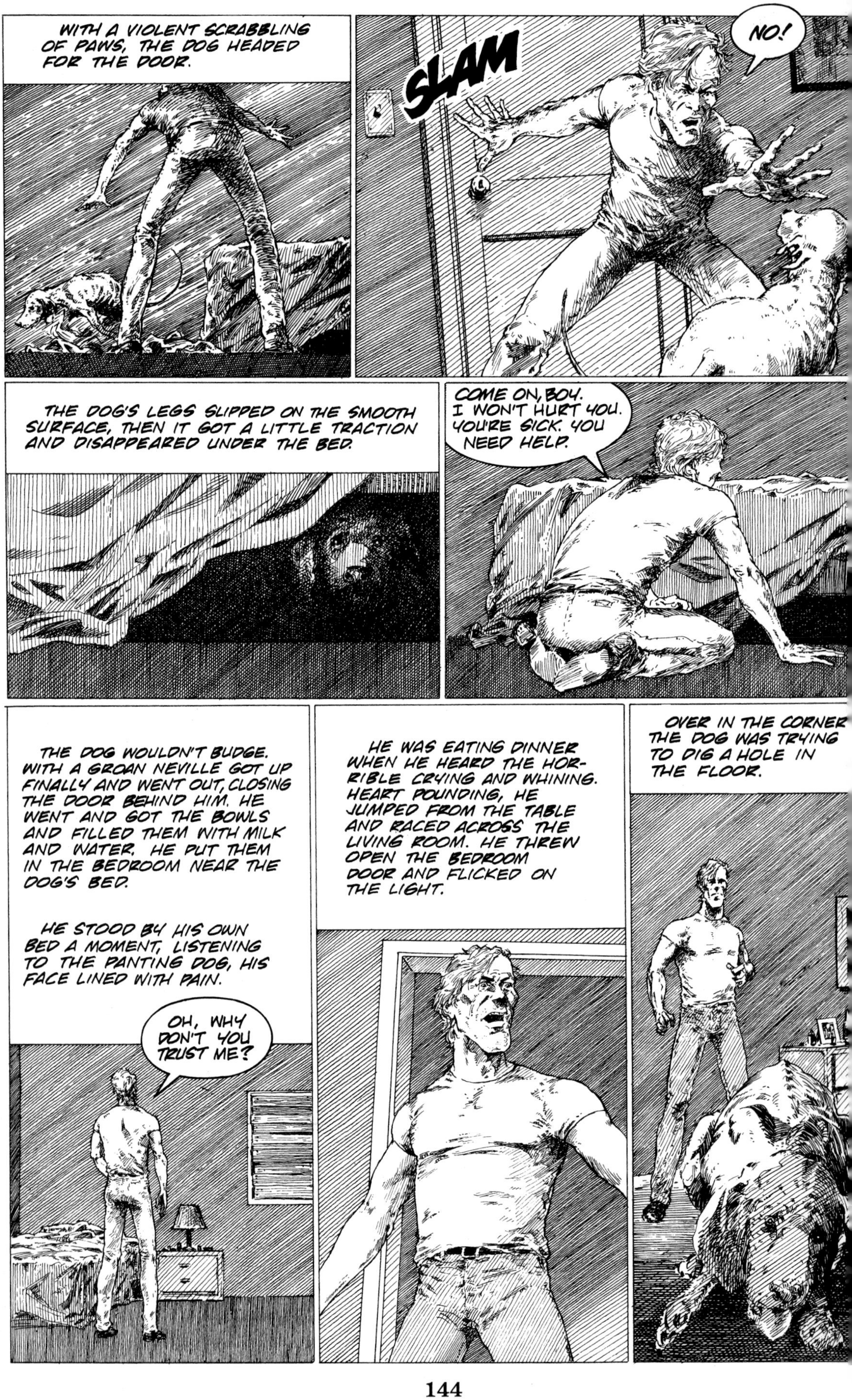
WITH A VIOLENT SCRABBLING OF PAWS, THE DOG HEADED FOR THE DOOR.
SLAM
NO!
THE DOG'S LEGS SLIPPED ON THE SMOOTH SURFACE, THEN IT GOT A LITTLE TRACTION AND DISAPPEARED UNDER THE BED.
COME ON, BOY. I WON'T HURT YOU. YOU'RE SICK. YOU NEED HELP.
THE DOG WOULDN'T BUDGE. WITH A GROAN NEVILLE GOT UP FINALLY AND WENT OUT, CLOSING THE DOOR BEHIND HIM. HE WENT AND GOT THE BOWLS AND FILLED THEM WITH MILK AND WATER. HE PUT THEM IN THE BEDROOM NEAR THE DOG'S BED.
HE STOOD BY HIS OWN BED A MOMENT, LISTENING TO THE PANTING DOG, HIS FACE LINED WITH PAIN.
OH, WHY DON'T YOU TRUST ME?
HE WAS EATING DINNER WHEN HE HEARD THE HORRIBLE CRYING AND WHINING. HEART POUNDING, HE JUMPED FROM THE TABLE AND RACED ACROSS THE LIVING ROOM. HE THREW OPEN THE BEDROOM DOOR AND FLICKED ON THE LIGHT.
OVER IN THE CORNER THE DOG WAS TRYING TO DIG A HOLE IN THE FLOOR.

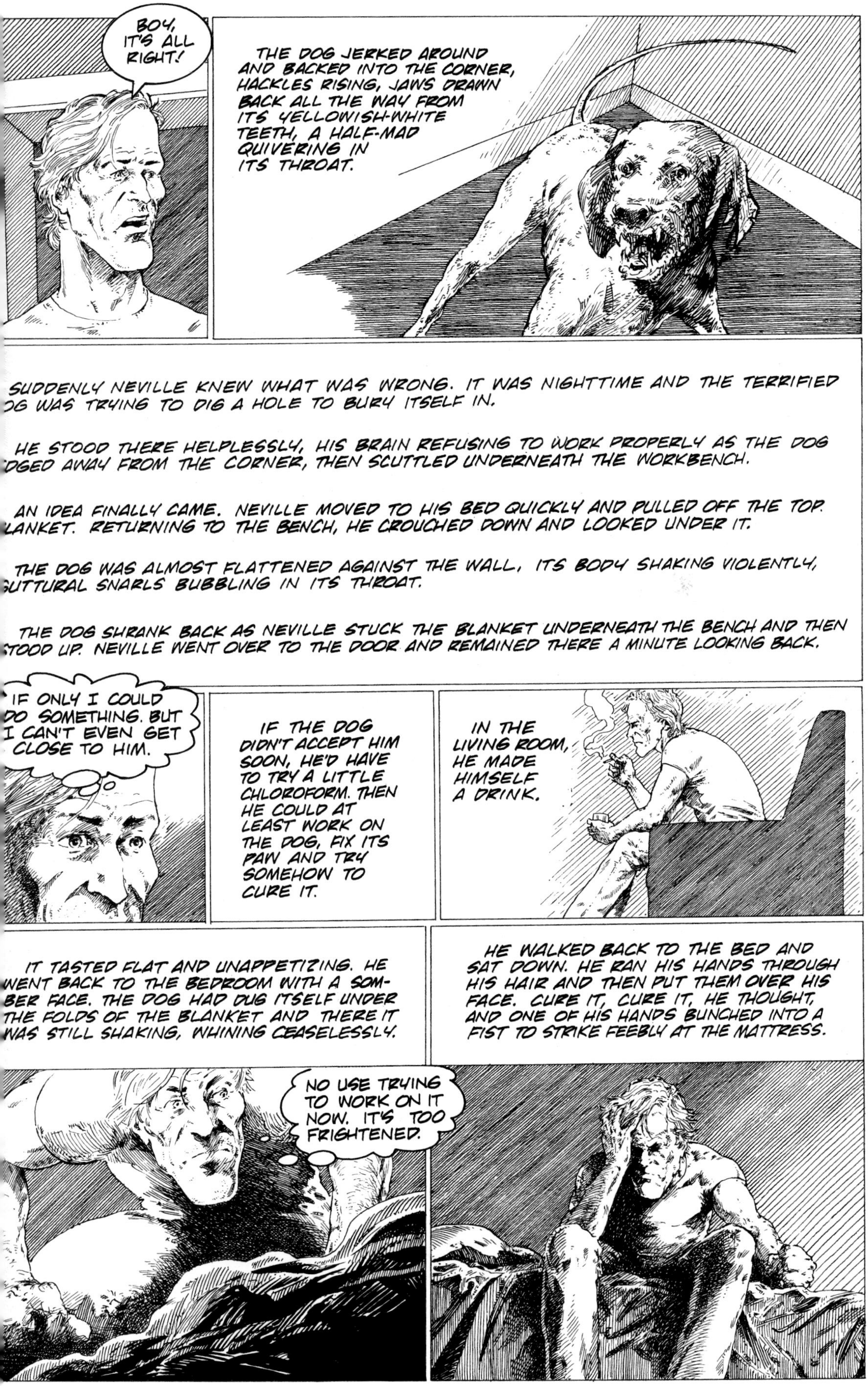
BOY, IT'S ALL RIGHT!
THE DOG JERKED AROUND AND BACKED INTO THE CORNER, HACKLES RISING, JAWS DRAWN BACK ALL THE WAY FROM ITS YELLOWISH-WHITE TEETH, A HALF-MAD QUIVERING IN ITS THROAT.
SUDDENLY NEVILLE KNEW WHAT WAS WRONG. IT WAS NIGHTTIME AND THE TERRIFIED OG WAS TRYING TO DIG A HOLE TO BURY ITSELF IN.
HE STOOD THERE HELPLESSLY, HIS BRAIN REFUSING TO WORK PROPERLY AS THE DOG DGED AWAY FROM THE CORNER, THEN SCUTTLED UNDERNEATH THE WORKBENCH.
AN IDEA FINALLY CAME. NEVILLE MOVED TO HIS BED QUICKLY AND PULLED OFF THE TOP LANKET. RETURNING TO THE BENCH, HE CROUCHED DOWN AND LOOKED UNDER IT.
THE DOG WAS ALMOST FLATTENED AGAINST THE WALL, ITS BODY SHAKING VIOLENTLY, UTTURAL SNARLS BUBBLING IN ITS THROAT.
THE DOG SHRANK BACK AS NEVILLE STUCK THE BLANKET UNDERNEATH THE BENCH AND THEN TOOD UP. NEVILLE WENT OVER TO THE DOOR AND REMAINED THERE A MINUTE LOOKING BACK.
IF ONLY I COULD DO SOMETHING. BUT I CAN'T EVEN GET CLOSE TO HIM.
IF THE DOG DIDN'T ACCEPT HIM SOON, HE'D HAVE TO TRY A LITTLE CHLOROFORM. THEN HE COULD AT LEAST WORK ON THE DOG, FIX ITS PAW AND TRY SOMEHOW TO CURE IT.
IN THE LIVING ROOM, HE MADE HIMSELF A DRINK.
IT TASTED FLAT AND UNAPPETIZING. HE WENT BACK TO THE BEDROOM WITH A SOMBER FACE. THE DOG HAD DUG ITSELF UNDER THE FOLDS OF THE BLANKET AND THERE IT WAS STILL SHAKING, WHINING CEASELESSLY.
HE WALKED BACK TO THE BED AND SAT DOWN. HE RAN HIS HANDS THROUGH HIS HAIR AND THEN PUT THEM OVER HIS FACE. CURE IT, CURE IT, HE THOUGHT, AND ONE OF HIS HANDS BUNCHED INTO A FIST TO STRIKE FEEBLY AT THE MATTRESS.
NO USE TRYING TO WORK ON IT NOW. IT'S TOO FRIGHTENED.

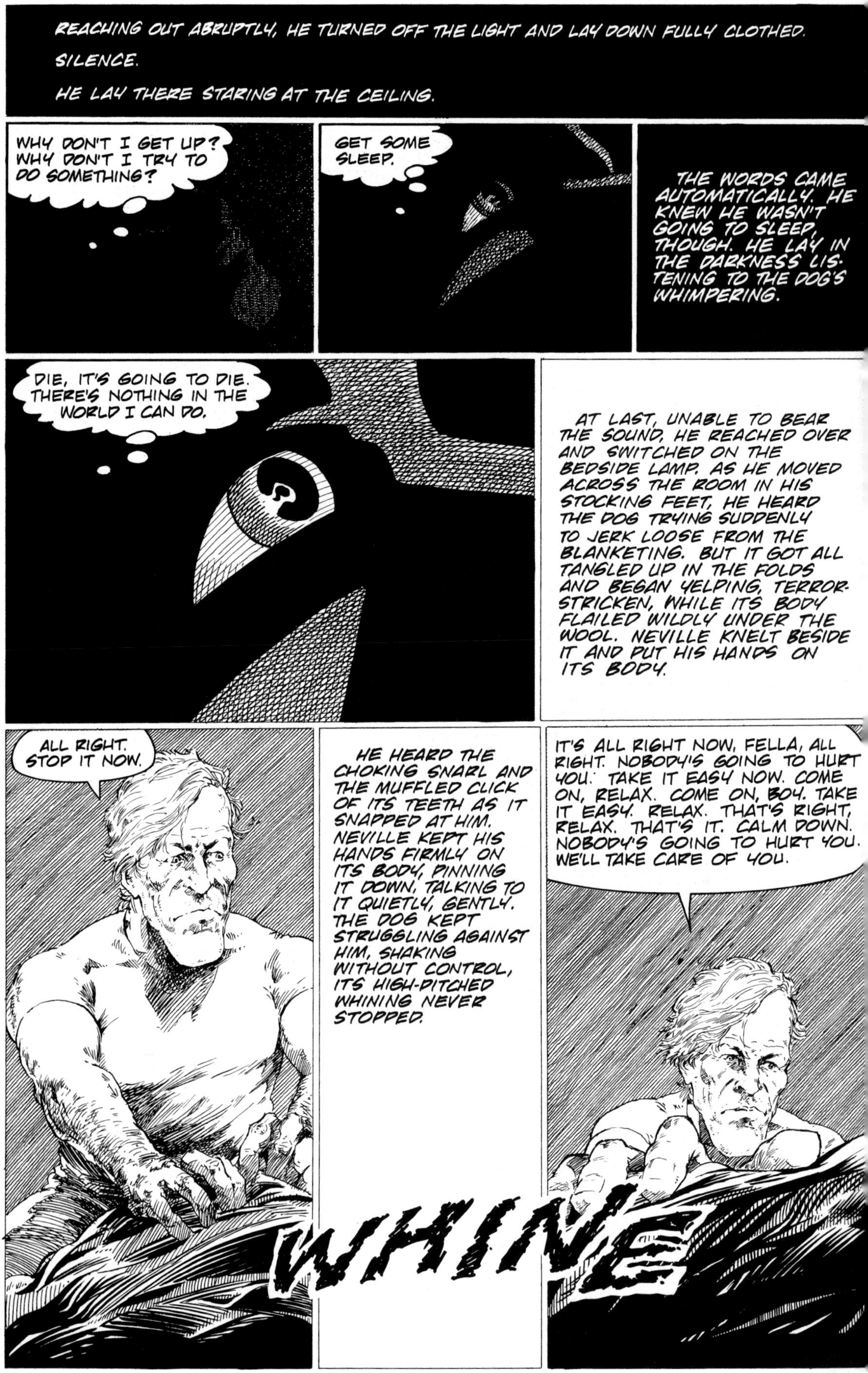
REACHING OUT ABRUPTLY, HE TURNED OFF THE LIGHT AND LAY DOWN FULLY CLOTHED.
SILENCE.
HE LAY THERE STARING AT THE CEILING.
WHY DON'T I GET UP? WHY DON'T I TRY TO DO SOMETHING?
GET SOME SLEEP.
THE WORDS CAME AUTOMATICALLY. HE KNEW HE WASN'T GOING TO SLEEP, THOUGH. HE LAY IN THE DARKNESS LISTENING TO THE DOG'S WHIMPERING.
DIE, IT'S GOING TO DIE. THERE'S NOTHING IN THE WORLD I CAN DO.
AT LAST, UNABLE TO BEAR THE SOUND, HE REACHED OVER AND SWITCHED ON THE BEDSIDE LAMP. AS HE MOVED ACROSS THE ROOM IN HIS STOCKING FEET, HE HEARD THE DOG TRYING SUDDENLY TO JERK LOOSE FROM THE BLANKETING. BUT IT GOT ALL TANGLED UP IN THE FOLDS AND BEGAN YELPING, TERROR-STRICKEN, WHILE ITS BODY FLAILED WILDLY UNDER THE WOOL. NEVILLE KNELT BESIDE IT AND PUT HIS HANDS ON ITS BODY.
ALL RIGHT. STOP IT NOW.
HE HEARD THE CHOKING SNARL AND THE MUFFLED CLICK OF ITS TEETH AS IT SNAPPED AT HIM. NEVILLE KEPT HIS HANDS FIRMLY ON ITS BODY, PINNING IT DOWN, TALKING TO IT QUIETLY, GENTLY. THE DOG KEPT STRUGGLING AGAINST HIM, SHAKING WITHOUT CONTROL, ITS HIGH-PITCHED WHINING NEVER STOPPED.
IT'S ALL RIGHT NOW, FELLA, ALL RIGHT. NOBODY'S GOING TO HURT YOU. TAKE IT EASY NOW. COME ON, RELAX. COME ON, BOY. TAKE IT EASY. RELAX. THAT'S RIGHT, RELAX. THAT'S IT. CALM DOWN. NOBODY'S GOING TO HURT YOU. WE'LL TAKE CARE OF YOU.
WHINE

HE WENT ON TALKING INTERMITTENTLY FOR ALMOST AN HOUR, HIS VOICE A LOW, HYPNOTIC MURMURING IN THE SILENCE OF THE ROOM. AND SLOWLY, HESITANTLY, THE DOG'S TREMBLING EASED OFF. A SMILE FALTERED ON NEVILLE'S LIPS AS HE WENT ON TALKING, TALKING.

"THAT'S RIGHT. TAKE IT EASY, NOW. WE'LL TAKE CARE OF YOU."

SOON THE DOG LAY STILL BENEATH HIS STRONG HANDS, THE ONLY MOVEMENT ITS HARSH BREATHING. NEVILLE BEGAN PATTING ITS HEAD, BEGAN RUNNING HIS RIGHT HAND OVER ITS BODY, STROKING AND SOOTHING. CAREFULLY HE SAT DOWN ON THE COOL LINOLEUM STILL PATTING THE DOG.

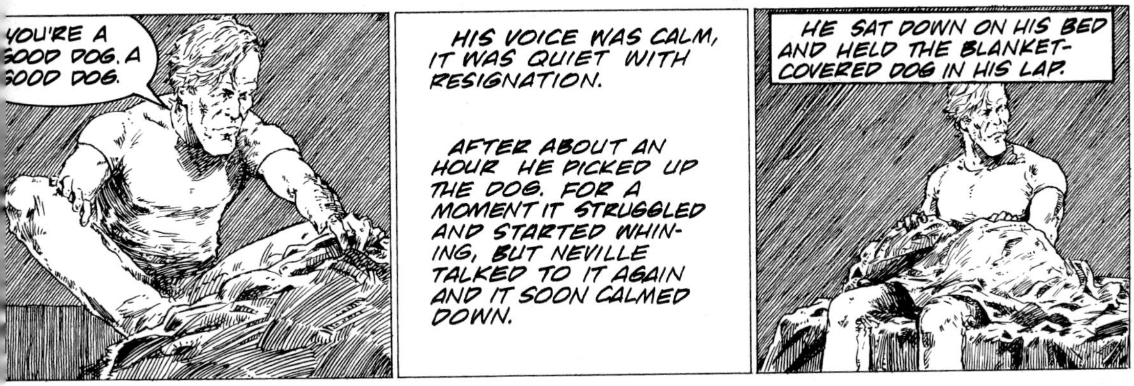
YOU'RE A GOOD DOG. A GOOD DOG.
HIS VOICE WAS CALM, IT WAS QUIET WITH RESIGNATION.
AFTER ABOUT AN HOUR HE PICKED UP THE DOG. FOR A MOMENT IT STRUGGLED AND STARTED WHINING, BUT NEVILLE TALKED TO IT AGAIN AND IT SOON CALMED DOWN.
HE SAT DOWN ON HIS BED AND HELD THE BLANKET-COVERED DOG IN HIS LAP.

FOR HOURS HE HELD THE DOG, PATTING AND STROKING AND TALKING. THE DOG LAY IMMOBILE IN HIS LAP, BREATHING EASIER. IT WAS ABOUT ELEVEN THAT NIGHT WHEN NEVILLE SLOWLY UNDID THE BLANKET FOLDS AND EXPOSED THE DOG'S HEAD.

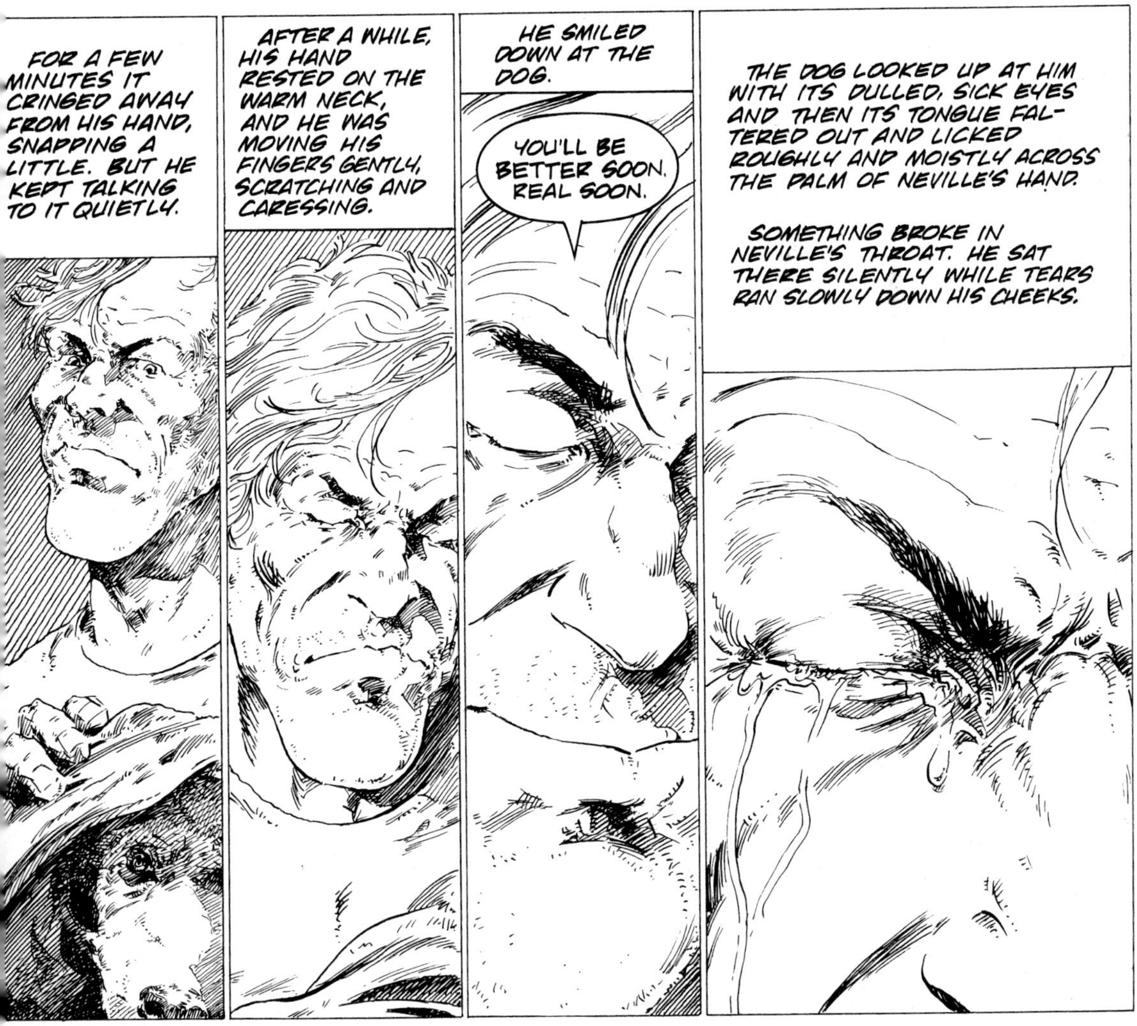
FOR A FEW MINUTES IT CRINGED AWAY FROM HIS HAND, SNAPPING A LITTLE. BUT HE KEPT TALKING TO IT QUIETLY.
AFTER A WHILE, HIS HAND RESTED ON THE WARM NECK, AND HE WAS MOVING HIS FINGERS GENTLY, SCRATCHING AND CARESSING.
HE SMILED DOWN AT THE DOG.
YOU'LL BE BETTER SOON. REAL SOON.
THE DOG LOOKED UP AT HIM WITH ITS DULLED, SICK EYES AND THEN ITS TONGUE FALTERED OUT AND LICKED ROUGHLY AND MOISTLY ACROSS THE PALM OF NEVILLE'S HAND.
SOMETHING BROKE IN NEVILLE'S THROAT. HE SAT THERE SILENTLY WHILE TEARS RAN SLOWLY DOWN HIS CHEEKS.

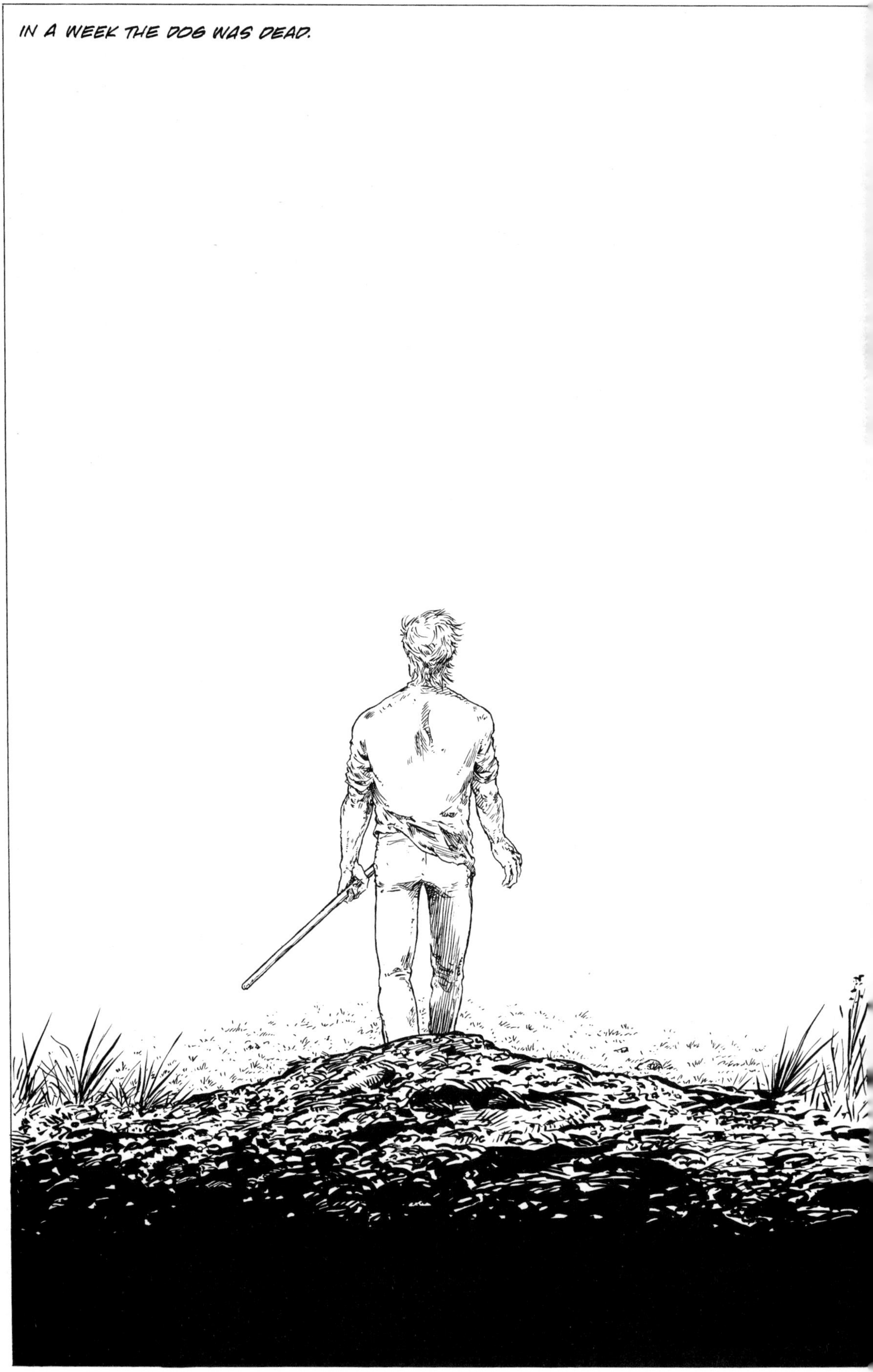
IN A WEEK THE DOG WAS DEAD.

CHAPTER 14

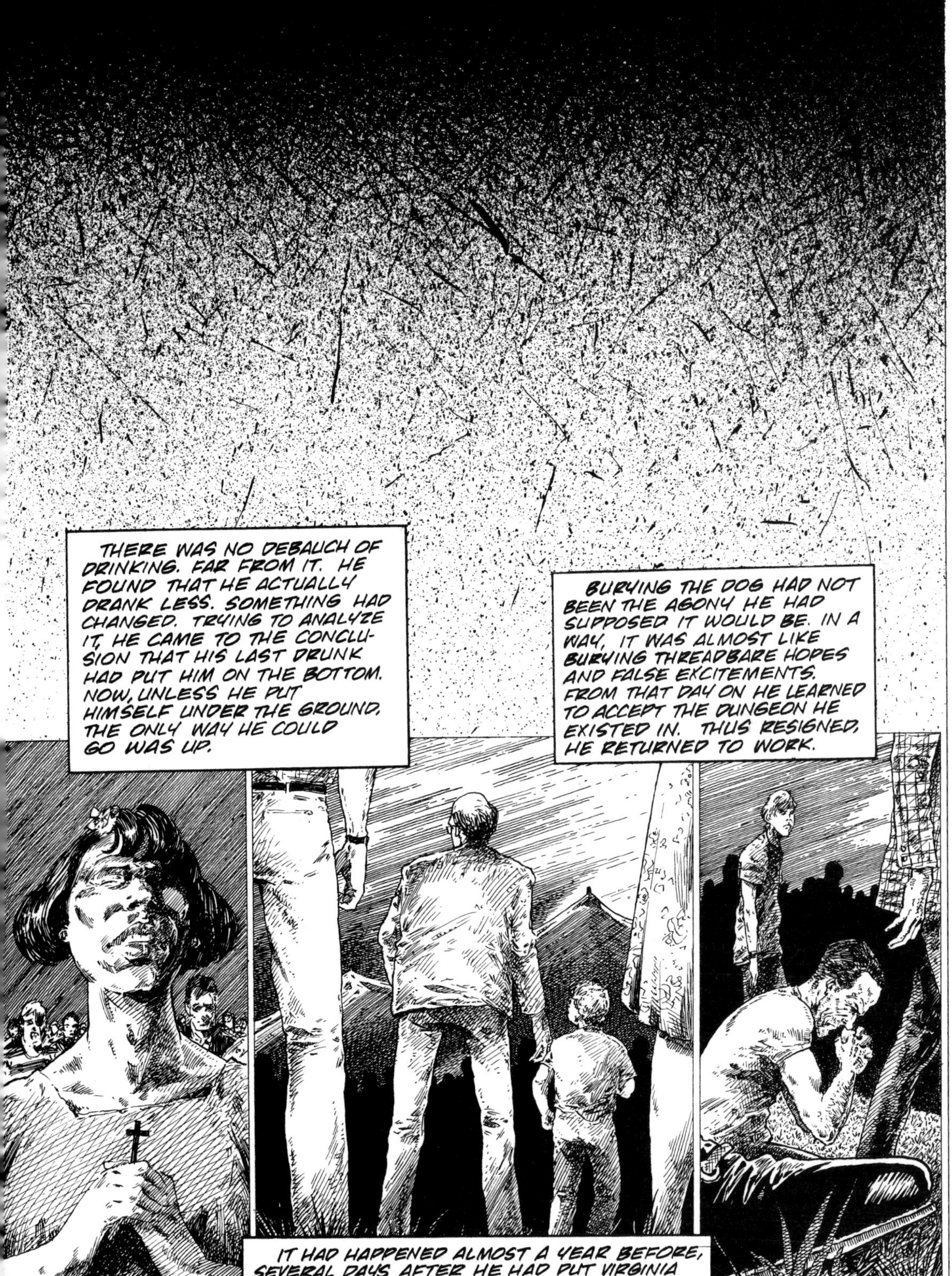

THERE WAS NO DEBAUCH OF DRINKING. FAR FROM IT. HE FOUND THAT HE ACTUALLY DRANK LESS. SOMETHING HAD CHANGED. TRYING TO ANALYZE IT, HE CAME TO THE CONCLUSION THAT HIS LAST DRUNK HAD PUT HIM ON THE BOTTOM. NOW, UNLESS HE PUT HIMSELF UNDER THE GROUND, THE ONLY WAY HE COULD GO WAS UP.
BURYING THE DOG HAD NOT BEEN THE AGONY HE HAD SUPPOSED IT WOULD BE. IN A WAY, IT WAS ALMOST LIKE BURYING THREADBARE HOPES AND FALSE EXCITEMENTS. FROM THAT DAY ON HE LEARNED TO ACCEPT THE DUNGEON HE EXISTED IN. THUS RESIGNED, HE RETURNED TO WORK.
IT HAD HAPPENED ALMOST A YEAR BEFORE, SEVERAL DAYS AFTER HE HAD PUT VIRGINIA TO HER SECOND AND FINAL REST.

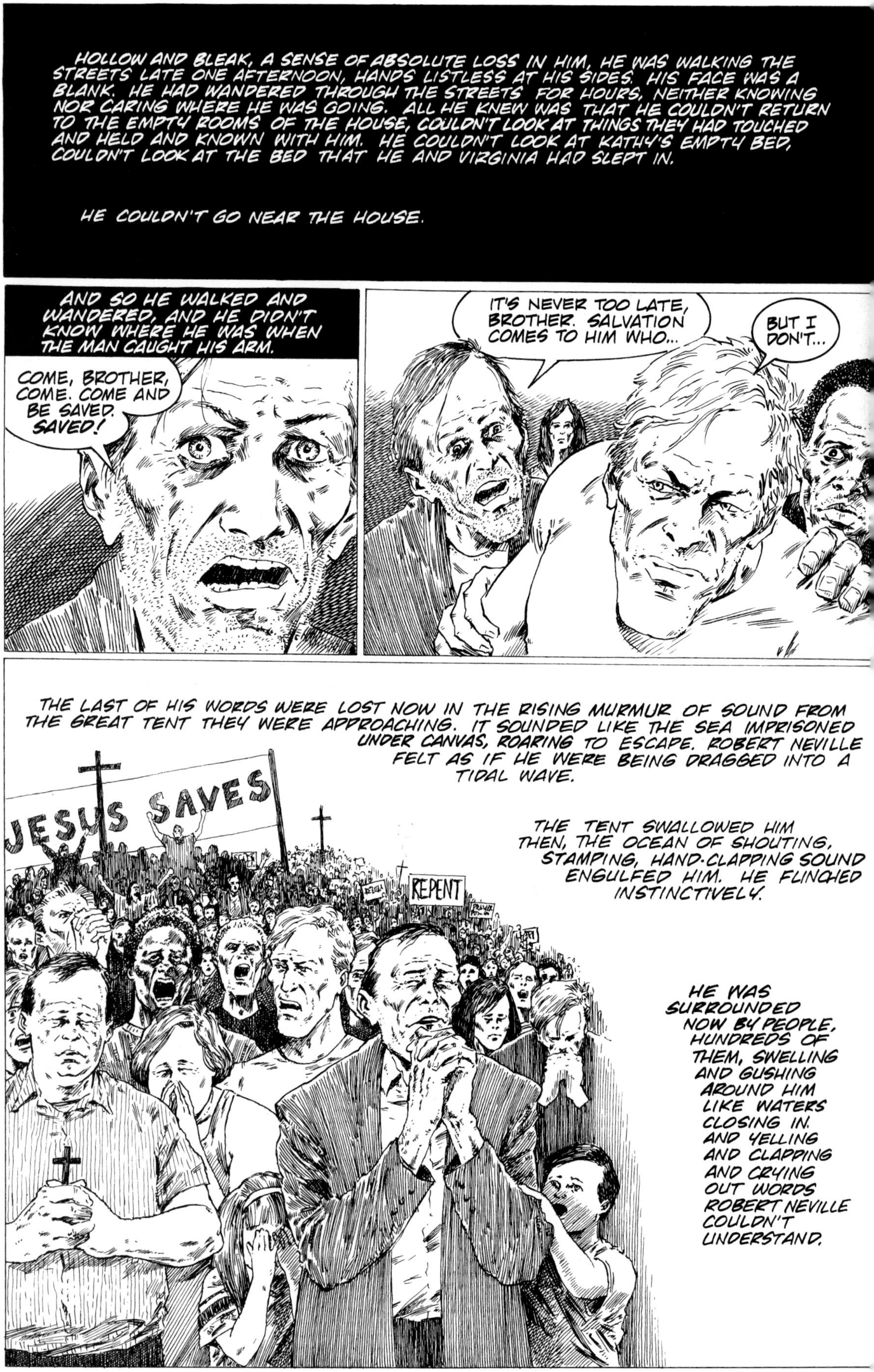
HOLLOW AND BLEAK, A SENSE OF ABSOLUTE LOSS IN HIM, HE WAS WALKING THE STREETS LATE ONE AFTERNOON, HANDS LISTLESS AT HIS SIDES. HIS FACE WAS A BLANK. HE HAD WANDERED THROUGH THE STREETS FOR HOURS, NEITHER KNOWING NOR CARING WHERE HE WAS GOING. ALL HE KNEW WAS THAT HE COULDN'T RETURN TO THE EMPTY ROOMS OF THE HOUSE, COULDN'T LOOK AT THINGS THEY HAD TOUCHED AND HELD AND KNOWN WITH HIM. HE COULDN'T LOOK AT KATHY'S EMPTY BED, COULDN'T LOOK AT THE BED THAT HE AND VIRGINIA HAD SLEPT IN.
HE COULDN'T GO NEAR THE HOUSE.
AND SO HE WALKED AND WANDERED, AND HE DIDN'T KNOW WHERE HE WAS WHEN THE MAN CAUGHT HIS ARM.
COME, BROTHER, COME. COME AND BE SAVED. SAVED!
IT'S NEVER TOO LATE, BROTHER. SALVATION COMES TO HIM WHO...
BUT I DON'T...
THE LAST OF HIS WORDS WERE LOST NOW IN THE RISING MURMUR OF SOUND FROM THE GREAT TENT THEY WERE APPROACHING. IT SOUNDED LIKE THE SEA IMPRISONED UNDER CANVAS, ROARING TO ESCAPE. ROBERT NEVILLE FELT AS IF HE WERE BEING DRAGGED INTO A TIDAL WAVE.
JESUS SAVES
REPENT
THE TENT SWALLOWED HIM THEN, THE OCEAN OF SHOUTING, STAMPING, HAND-CLAPPING SOUND ENGULFED HIM. HE FLINCHED INSTINCTIVELY.
HE WAS SURROUNDED NOW BY PEOPLE, HUNDREDS OF THEM, SWELLING AND GUSHING AROUND HIM LIKE WATERS CLOSING IN. AND YELLING AND CLAPPING AND CRYING OUT WORDS ROBERT NEVILLE COULDN'T UNDERSTAND.

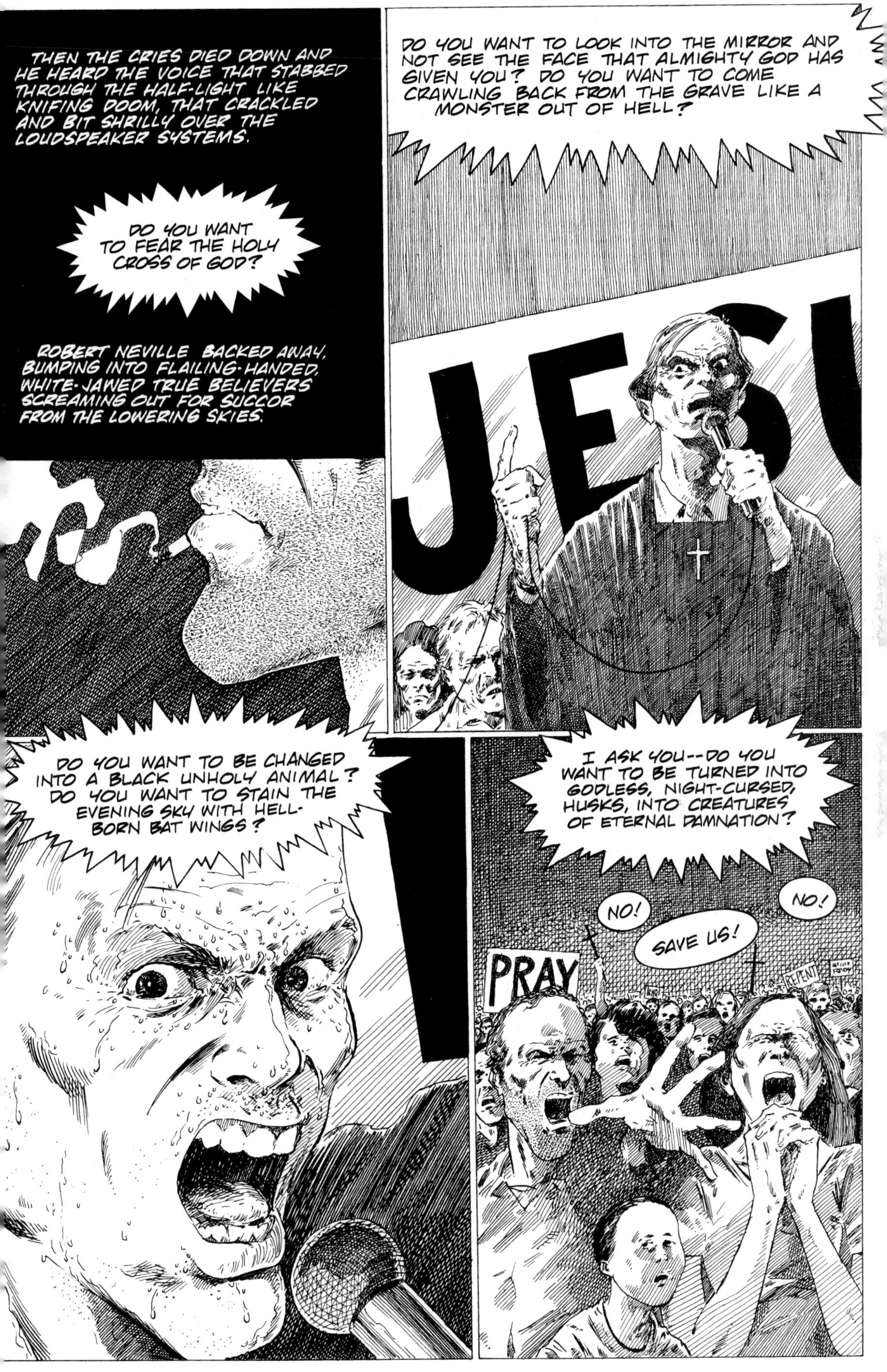
THEN THE CRIES DIED DOWN AND HE HEARD THE VOICE THAT STABBED THROUGH THE HALF-LIGHT LIKE KNIFING DOOM, THAT CRACKLED AND BIT SHRILLY OVER THE LOUDSPEAKER SYSTEMS.
DO YOU WANT TO FEAR THE HOLY CROSS OF GOD?
ROBERT NEVILLE BACKED AWAY, BUMPING INTO FLAILING-HANDED, WHITE-JAWED TRUE BELIEVERS SCREAMING OUT FOR SUCCOR FROM THE LOWERING SKIES.
DO YOU WANT TO LOOK INTO THE MIRROR AND NOT SEE THE FACE THAT ALMIGHTY GOD HAS GIVEN YOU? DO YOU WANT TO COME CRAWLING BACK FROM THE GRAVE LIKE A MONSTER OUT OF HELL?
JESU
DO YOU WANT TO BE CHANGED INTO A BLACK UNHOLY ANIMAL? DO YOU WANT TO STAIN THE EVENING SKY WITH HELL-BORN BAT WINGS?
I ASK YOU--DO YOU WANT TO BE TURNED INTO GODLESS, NIGHT-CURSED, HUSKS, INTO CREATURES OF ETERNAL DAMNATION?
NO!
NO!
SAVE US!
PRAY
REPENT

WELL, I'M TELLING YOU! I'M TELLING YOU, SO LISTEN TO THE WORD OF GOD! BEHOLD, EVIL SHALL GO FORTH FROM NATION TO NATION AND THE SLAIN OF THE LORD SHALL BE AT THAT DAY FROM ONE END OF THE EARTH EVEN UNTO THE OTHER END OF THE EARTH! I TELL YOU THAT UNLESS WE BECOME AS LITTLE CHILDREN-- UNLESS WE BEG FOR FORGIVENESS FOR OUR GRIEVOUS OFFENSES-- WE ARE DAMNED!

THE PEOPLE TWISTED AND MOANED AND SMOTE THEIR BROWS AND SHRIEKED IN MORTAL TERROR AND SCREAMED OUT TERRIBLE HALLELUJAHS. ROBERT NEVILLE WAS SHOVED ABOUT, STUMBLING AND LOST IN A TREADMILL OF HOPES, IN A CROSSFIRE OF FRENZIED WORSHIP.

HE ESCAPED, WEAK AND TREMBLING, STUMBLING AWAY FROM THEM.

HE THOUGHT ABOUT THAT NOW AS HE SAT IN HIS LIVING ROOM, A PSYCHOLOGY TEXT RESTING ON HIS LAP. A QUOTATION HAD STARTED THE TRAIN OF THOUGHT, SENDING HIM BACK TO THAT EVENING TEN MONTHS BEFORE, WHEN HE'D BEEN PULLED INTO THE WILD REVIVAL MEETING.

"THIS CONDITION, KNOWN AS HYSTERICAL BLINDNESS, MAY BE PARTIAL OR COMPLETE."

THAT WAS THE QUOTATION HE'D READ.

WE ARE DAMNED!

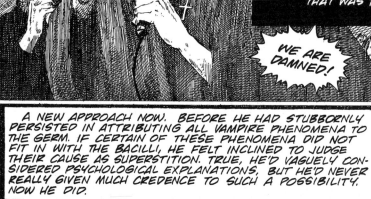

A NEW APPROACH NOW. BEFORE HE HAD STUBBORNLY PERSISTED IN ATTRIBUTING ALL VAMPIRE PHENOMENA TO THE GERM. IF CERTAIN OF THESE PHENOMENA DID NOT FIT IN WITH THE BACILLI, HE FELT INCLINED TO JUDGE THEIR CAUSE AS SUPERSTITION. TRUE, HE'D VAGUELY CONSIDERED PSYCHOLOGICAL EXPLANATIONS, BUT HE'D NEVER REALLY GIVEN MUCH CREDENCE TO SUCH A POSSIBILITY. NOW HE DID.

CONSIDER THE SHOCK UNDERGONE BY A VICTIM OF THE PLAGUE.

YELLOW JOURNALISM HAD BEEN RAMPANT IN THE FINAL DAYS. AND, IN ADDITION, A GREAT UPSURGE IN REVIVALISM HAD OCCURRED.

AND THEN TO REGAIN CONSCIOUSNESS BENEATH HOT, HEAVY SOIL AND KNOW THAT DEATH HAD NOT BROUGHT REST.

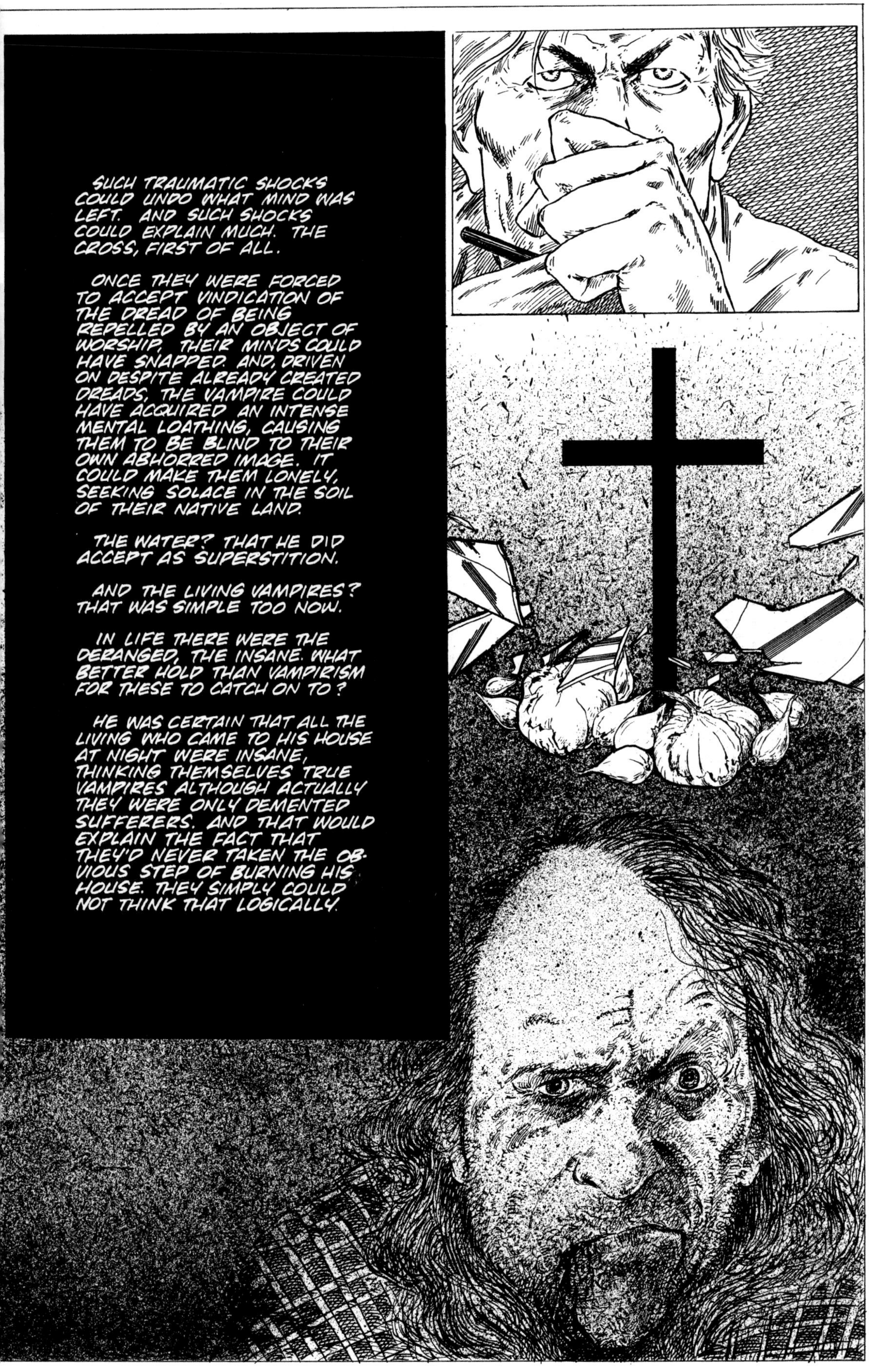
SUCH TRAUMATIC SHOCKS COULD UNDO WHAT MIND WAS LEFT. AND SUCH SHOCKS COULD EXPLAIN MUCH. THE CROSS, FIRST OF ALL.
ONCE THEY WERE FORCED TO ACCEPT VINDICATION OF THE DREAD OF BEING REPELLED BY AN OBJECT OF WORSHIP, THEIR MINDS COULD HAVE SNAPPED. AND, DRIVEN ON DESPITE ALREADY CREATED DREADS, THE VAMPIRE COULD HAVE ACQUIRED AN INTENSE MENTAL LOATHING, CAUSING THEM TO BE BLIND TO THEIR OWN ABHORRED IMAGE. IT COULD MAKE THEM LONELY, SEEKING SOLACE IN THE SOIL OF THEIR NATIVE LAND.
THE WATER? THAT HE DID ACCEPT AS SUPERSTITION.
AND THE LIVING VAMPIRES? THAT WAS SIMPLE TOO NOW.
IN LIFE THERE WERE THE DERANGED, THE INSANE. WHAT BETTER HOLD THAN VAMPIRISM FOR THESE TO CATCH ON TO?
HE WAS CERTAIN THAT ALL THE LIVING WHO CAME TO HIS HOUSE AT NIGHT WERE INSANE, THINKING THEMSELVES TRUE VAMPIRES ALTHOUGH ACTUALLY THEY WERE ONLY DEMENTED SUFFERERS. AND THAT WOULD EXPLAIN THE FACT THAT THEY'D NEVER TAKEN THE OBVIOUS STEP OF BURNING HIS HOUSE. THEY SIMPLY COULD NOT THINK THAT LOGICALLY.

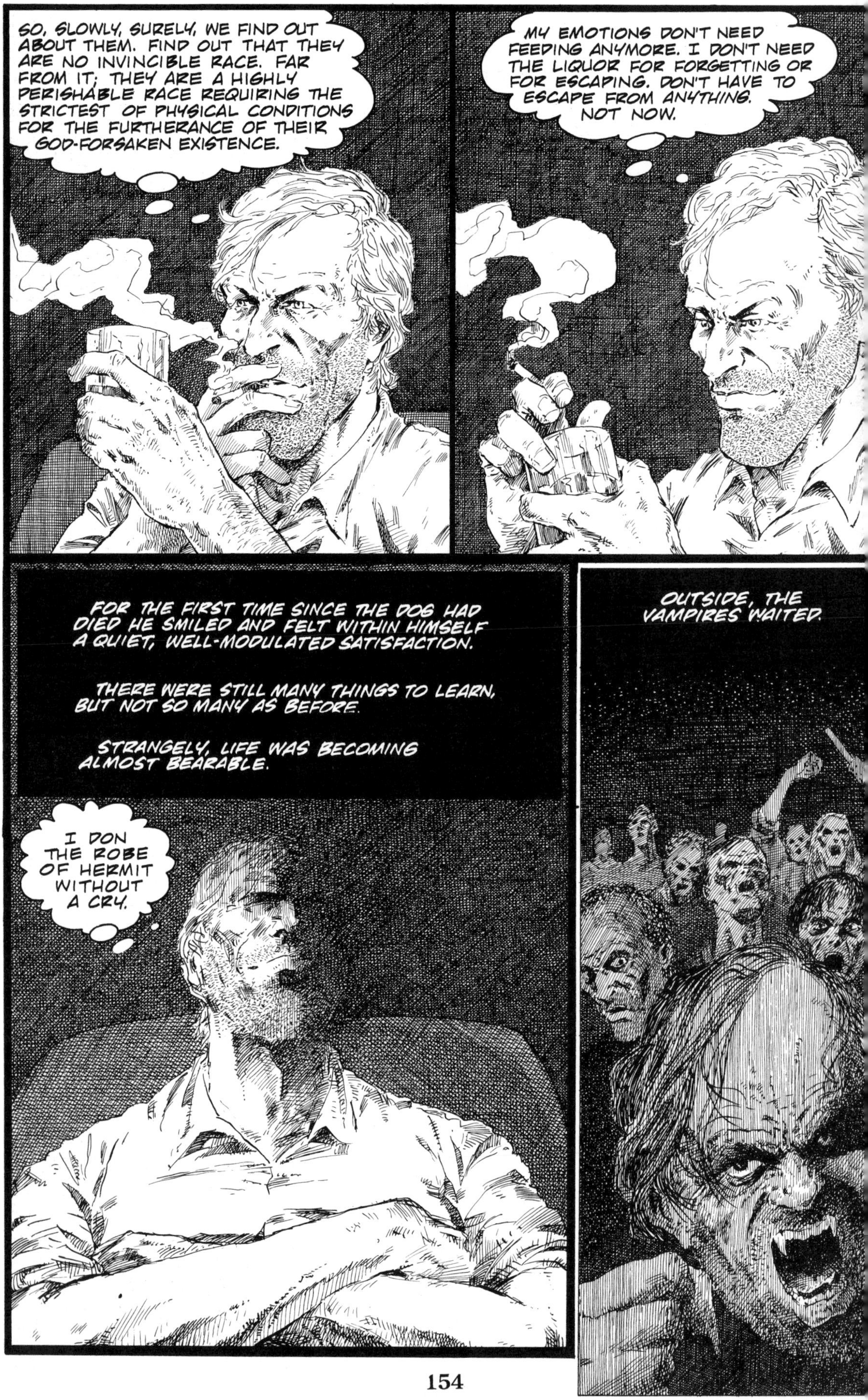
SO, SLOWLY, SURELY, WE FIND OUT ABOUT THEM. FIND OUT THAT THEY ARE NO INVINCIBLE RACE. FAR FROM IT; THEY ARE A HIGHLY PERISHABLE RACE REQUIRING THE STRICTEST OF PHYSICAL CONDITIONS FOR THE FURTHERANCE OF THEIR GOD-FORSAKEN EXISTENCE.
MY EMOTIONS DON'T NEED FEEDING ANYMORE. I DON'T NEED THE LIQUOR FOR FORGETTING OR FOR ESCAPING. DON'T HAVE TO ESCAPE FROM ANYTHING. NOT NOW.
FOR THE FIRST TIME SINCE THE DOG HAD DIED HE SMILED AND FELT WITHIN HIMSELF A QUIET, WELL-MODULATED SATISFACTION.
THERE WERE STILL MANY THINGS TO LEARN, BUT NOT SO MANY AS BEFORE.
STRANGELY, LIFE WAS BECOMING ALMOST BEARABLE.
I DON THE ROBE OF HERMIT WITHOUT A CRY.
OUTSIDE, THE VAMPIRES WAITED.

CHAPTER 15

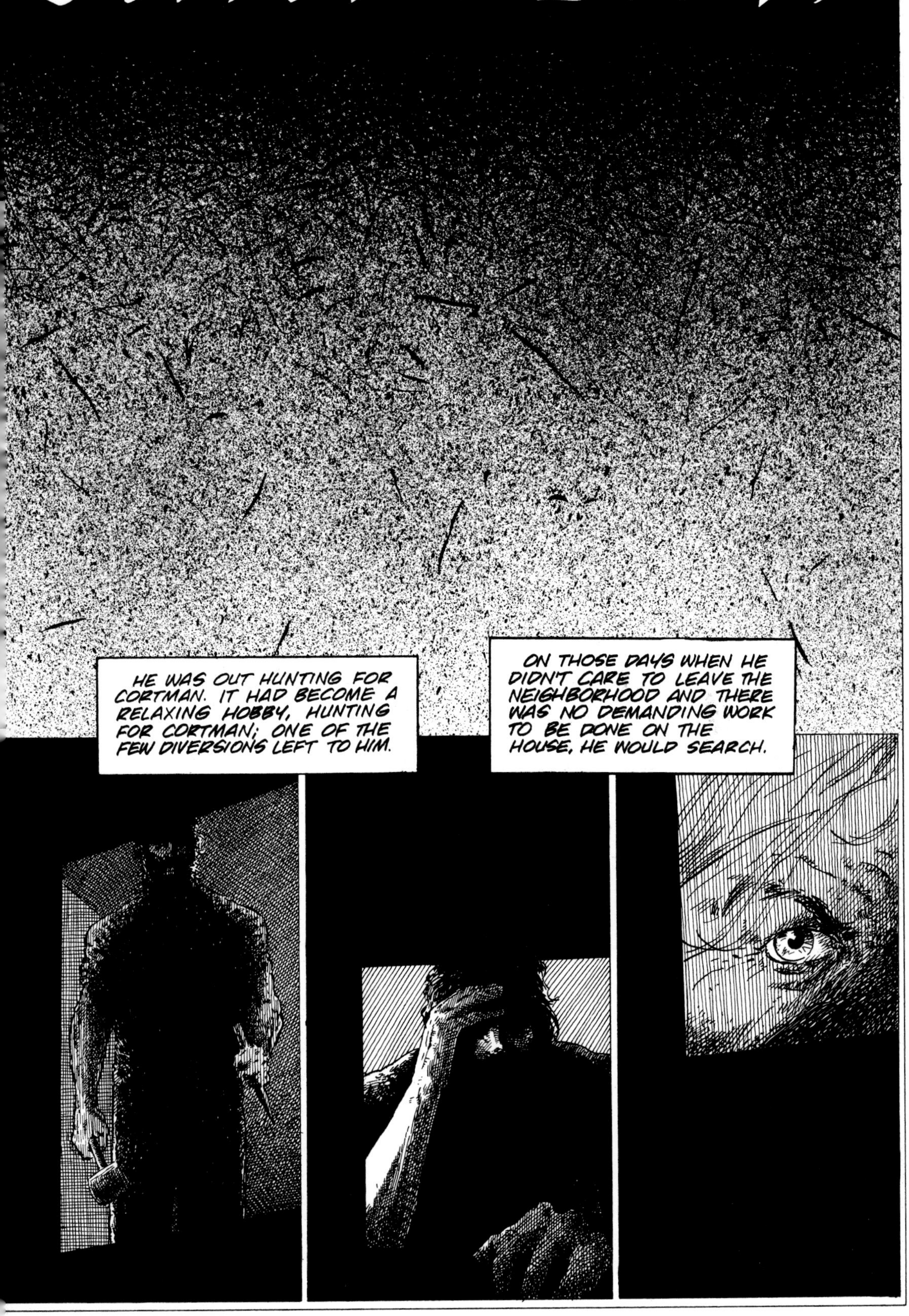
HE WAS OUT HUNTING FOR CORTMAN. IT HAD BECOME A RELAXING HOBBY, HUNTING FOR CORTMAN; ONE OF THE FEW DIVERSIONS LEFT TO HIM.
ON THOSE DAYS WHEN HE DIDN'T CARE TO LEAVE THE NEIGHBORHOOD AND THERE WAS NO DEMANDING WORK TO BE DONE ON THE HOUSE, HE WOULD SEARCH.

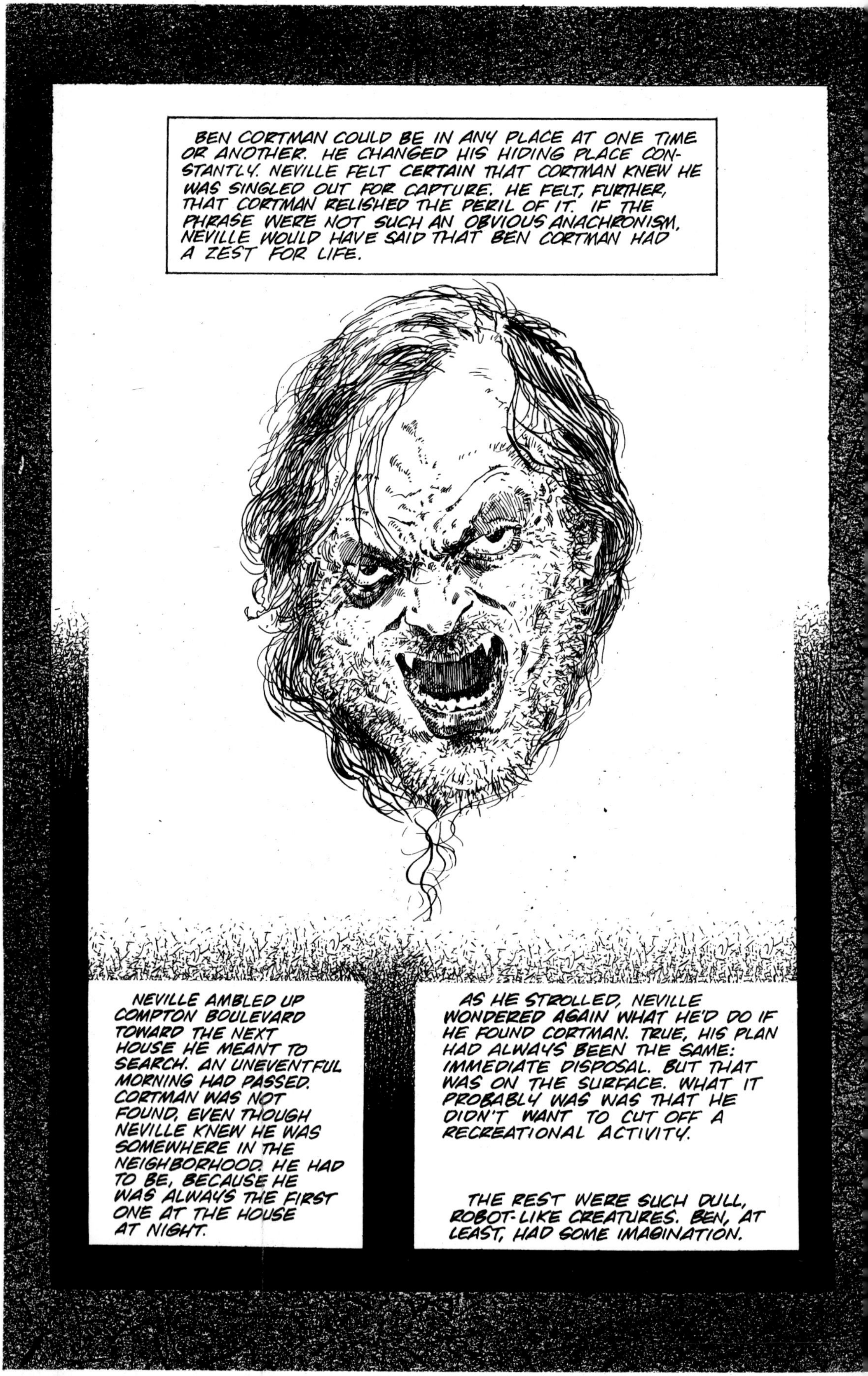
BEN CORTMAN COULD BE IN ANY PLACE AT ONE TIME OR ANOTHER. HE CHANGED HIS HIDING PLACE CONSTANTLY. NEVILLE FELT CERTAIN THAT CORTMAN KNEW HE WAS SINGLED OUT FOR CAPTURE. HE FELT, FURTHER, THAT CORTMAN RELISHED THE PERIL OF IT. IF THE PHRASE WERE NOT SUCH AN OBVIOUS ANACHRONISM, NEVILLE WOULD HAVE SAID THAT BEN CORTMAN HAD A ZEST FOR LIFE.
NEVILLE AMBLED UP COMPTON BOULEVARD TOWARD THE NEXT HOUSE HE MEANT TO SEARCH. AN UNEVENTFUL MORNING HAD PASSED. CORTMAN WAS NOT FOUND, EVEN THOUGH NEVILLE KNEW HE WAS SOMEWHERE IN THE NEIGHBORHOOD. HE HAD TO BE, BECAUSE HE WAS ALWAYS THE FIRST ONE AT THE HOUSE AT NIGHT.
AS HE STROLLED, NEVILLE WONDERED AGAIN WHAT HE'D DO IF HE FOUND CORTMAN. TRUE, HIS PLAN HAD ALWAYS BEEN THE SAME: IMMEDIATE DISPOSAL. BUT THAT WAS ON THE SURFACE. WHAT IT PROBABLY WAS WAS THAT HE DIDN'T WANT TO CUT OFF A RECREATIONAL ACTIVITY.
THE REST WERE SUCH DULL, ROBOT-LIKE CREATURES. BEN, AT LEAST, HAD SOME IMAGINATION.

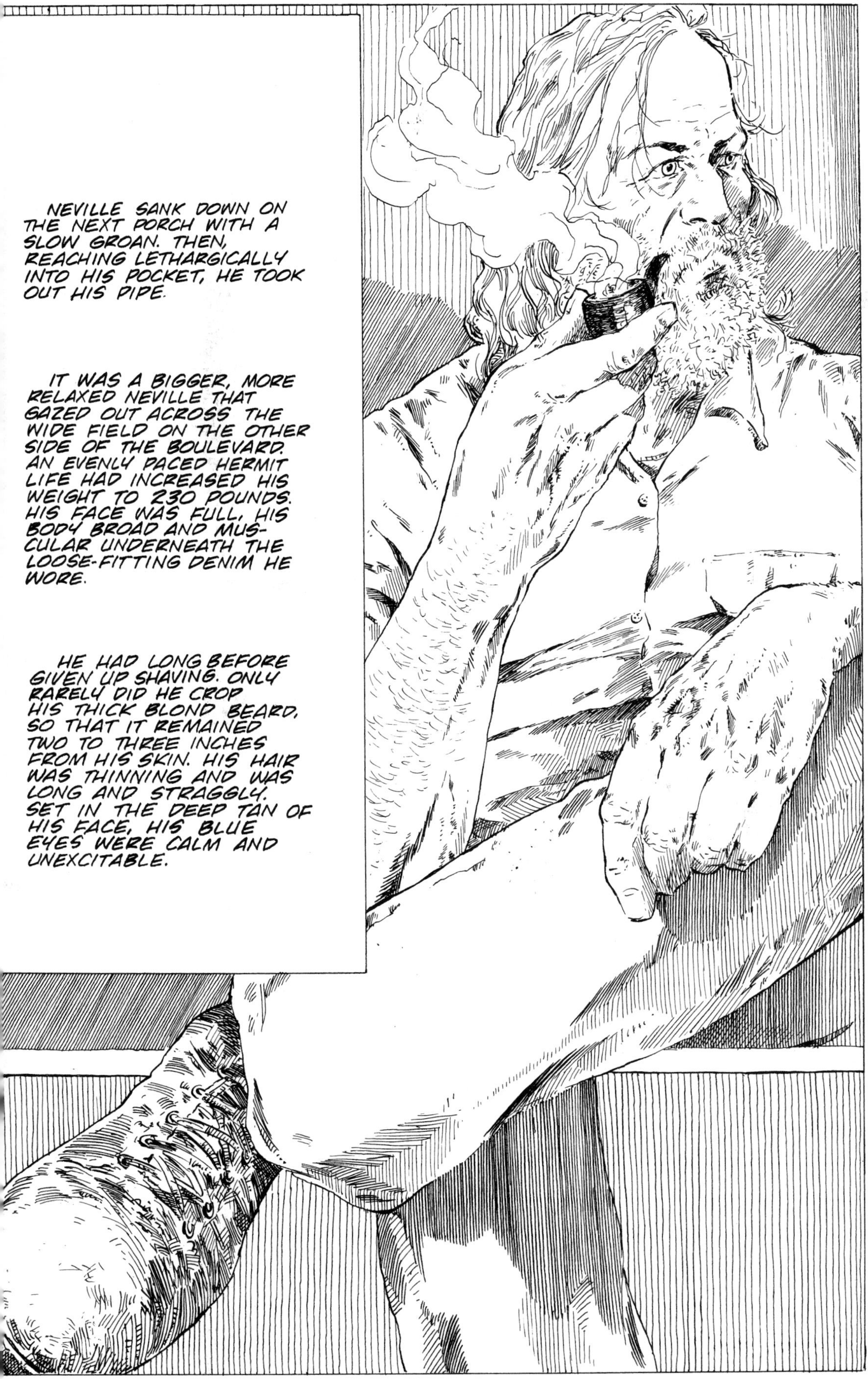
NEVILLE SANK DOWN ON THE NEXT PORCH WITH A SLOW GROAN. THEN, REACHING LETHARGICALLY INTO HIS POCKET, HE TOOK OUT HIS PIPE.
IT WAS A BIGGER, MORE RELAXED NEVILLE THAT GAZED OUT ACROSS THE WIDE FIELD ON THE OTHER SIDE OF THE BOULEVARD. AN EVENLY PACED HERMIT LIFE HAD INCREASED HIS WEIGHT TO 230 POUNDS. HIS FACE WAS FULL, HIS BODY BROAD AND MUSCULAR UNDERNEATH THE LOOSE-FITTING DENIM HE WORE.
HE HAD LONG BEFORE GIVEN UP SHAVING. ONLY RARELY DID HE CROP HIS THICK BLOND BEARD, SO THAT IT REMAINED TWO TO THREE INCHES FROM HIS SKIN. HIS HAIR WAS THINNING AND WAS LONG AND STRAGGLY. SET IN THE DEEP TAN OF HIS FACE, HIS BLUE EYES WERE CALM AND UNEXCITABLE.

FAR OUT ACROSS THAT FIELD HE KNEW THERE WAS STILL A DEPRESSION IN THE GROUND WHERE HE HAD BURIED VIRGINIA, WHERE SHE HAD UNBURIED HERSELF. BUT KNOWING IT BROUGHT NO GLIMMER OF REFLECTIVE SORROW TO HIS EYES. RATHER THAN GO ON SUFFERING, HE HAD LEARNED TO STULTIFY HIMSELF TO INTROSPECTION. TIME HAD LOST ITS MULTI-DIMENSIONAL SCOPE.

THERE WAS ONLY THE PRESENT FOR ROBERT NEVILLE; A PRESENT BASED ON DAY-TO-DAY SURVIVAL MARKED BY NEITHER HEIGHTS OF JOY NOR DEPTHS OF DESPAIR. I AM PREDOMINANTLY VEGETABLE, HE OFTEN THOUGHT TO HIMSELF. THAT WAS THE WAY HE WANTED IT.

ROBERT NEVILLE SAT GAZING AT THE WHITE SPOT OUT IN THE FIELD FOR SEVERAL MINUTES BEFORE HE REALIZED IT WAS MOVING.

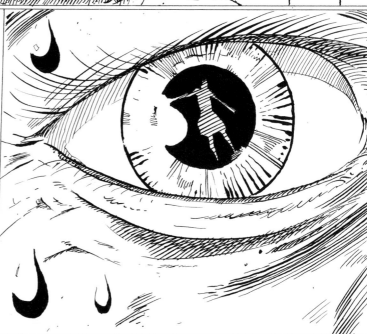

HIS EYES BLINKED ONCE AND THE SKIN TIGHTENED OVER HIS FACE. HE MADE A SLIGHT SOUND IN HIS THROAT, A SOUND OF DOUBTING QUESTION. THEN, STANDING UP, HE RAISED HIS LEFT HAND TO SHADE THE SUNLIGHT FROM HIS EYES.

HIS TEETH BIT CONVULSIVELY INTO THE PIPESTEM.

A WOMAN.

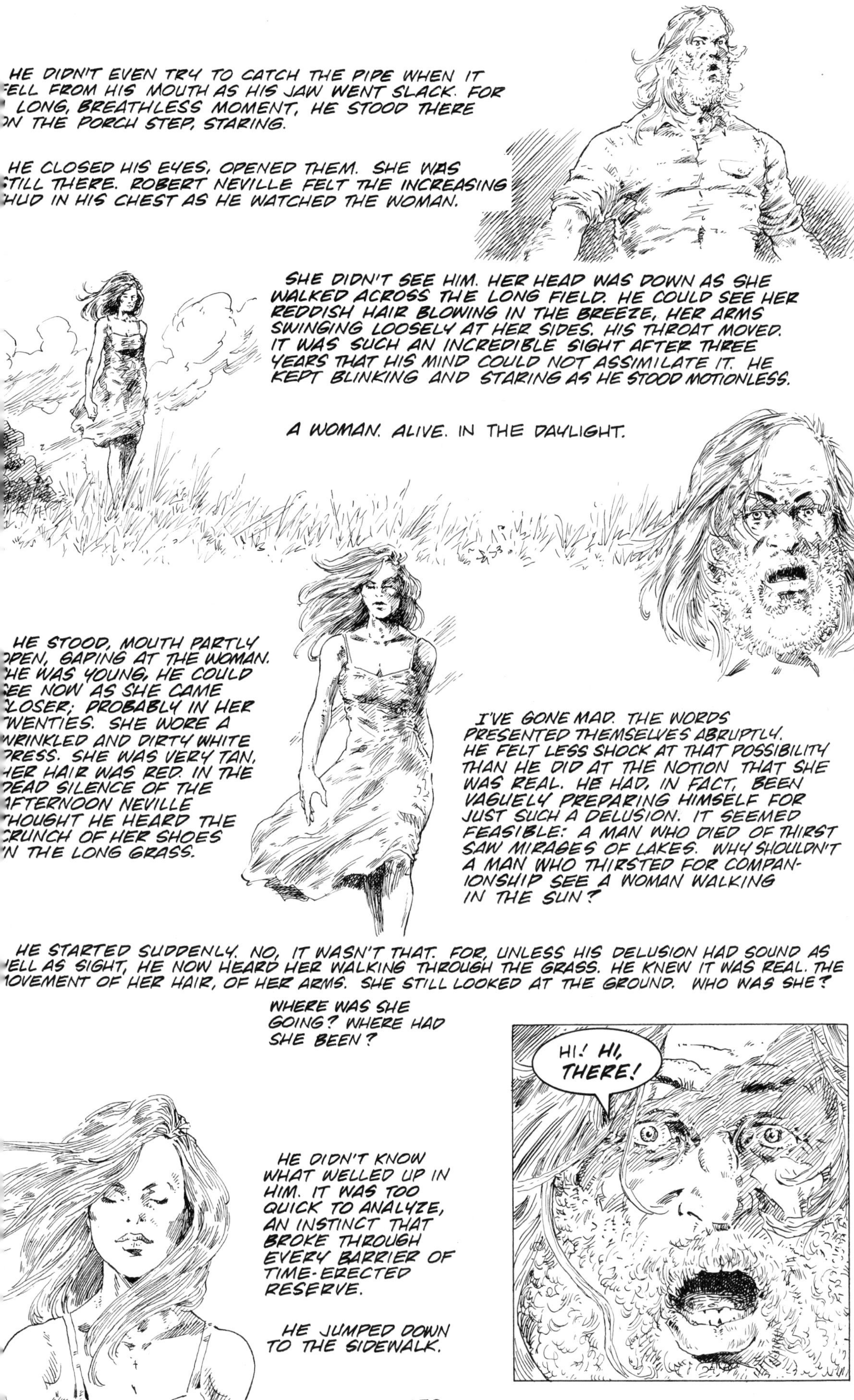
HE DIDN'T EVEN TRY TO CATCH THE PIPE WHEN IT
FELL FROM HIS MOUTH AS HIS JAW WENT SLACK. FOR
LONG, BREATHLESS MOMENT, HE STOOD THERE
ON THE PORCH STEP, STARING.
HE CLOSED HIS EYES, OPENED THEM. SHE WAS
STILL THERE. ROBERT NEVILLE FELT THE INCREASING
HUD IN HIS CHEST AS HE WATCHED THE WOMAN.
SHE DIDN'T SEE HIM. HER HEAD WAS DOWN AS SHE
WALKED ACROSS THE LONG FIELD. HE COULD SEE HER
REDDISH HAIR BLOWING IN THE BREEZE, HER ARMS
SWINGING LOOSELY AT HER SIDES. HIS THROAT MOVED.
IT WAS SUCH AN INCREDIBLE SIGHT AFTER THREE
YEARS THAT HIS MIND COULD NOT ASSIMILATE IT. HE
KEPT BLINKING AND STARING AS HE STOOD MOTIONLESS.
A WOMAN. ALIVE. IN THE DAYLIGHT.
HE STOOD, MOUTH PARTLY
OPEN, GAPING AT THE WOMAN.
HE WAS YOUNG, HE COULD
EE NOW AS SHE CAME
CLOSER; PROBABLY IN HER
TWENTIES. SHE WORE A
WRINKLED AND DIRTY WHITE
DRESS. SHE WAS VERY TAN,
HER HAIR WAS RED. IN THE
DEAD SILENCE OF THE
AFTERNOON NEVILLE
THOUGHT HE HEARD THE
CRUNCH OF HER SHOES
N THE LONG GRASS.
I'VE GONE MAD. THE WORDS
PRESENTED THEMSELVES ABRUPTLY.
HE FELT LESS SHOCK AT THAT POSSIBILITY
THAN HE DID AT THE NOTION THAT SHE
WAS REAL. HE HAD, IN FACT, BEEN
VAGUELY PREPARING HIMSELF FOR
JUST SUCH A DELUSION. IT SEEMED
FEASIBLE: A MAN WHO DIED OF THIRST
SAW MIRAGES OF LAKES. WHY SHOULDN'T
A MAN WHO THIRSTED FOR COMPAN-
IONSHIP SEE A WOMAN WALKING
IN THE SUN?
HE STARTED SUDDENLY. NO, IT WASN'T THAT. FOR, UNLESS HIS DELUSION HAD SOUND AS
WELL AS SIGHT, HE NOW HEARD HER WALKING THROUGH THE GRASS. HE KNEW IT WAS REAL. THE
MOVEMENT OF HER HAIR, OF HER ARMS. SHE STILL LOOKED AT THE GROUND. WHO WAS SHE?
WHERE WAS SHE
GOING? WHERE HAD
SHE BEEN?
HI! HI, THERE!
HE DIDN'T KNOW
WHAT WELLED UP IN
HIM. IT WAS TOO
QUICK TO ANALYZE,
AN INSTINCT THAT
BROKE THROUGH
EVERY BARRIER OF
TIME-ERECTED
RESERVE.
HE JUMPED DOWN
TO THE SIDEWALK.

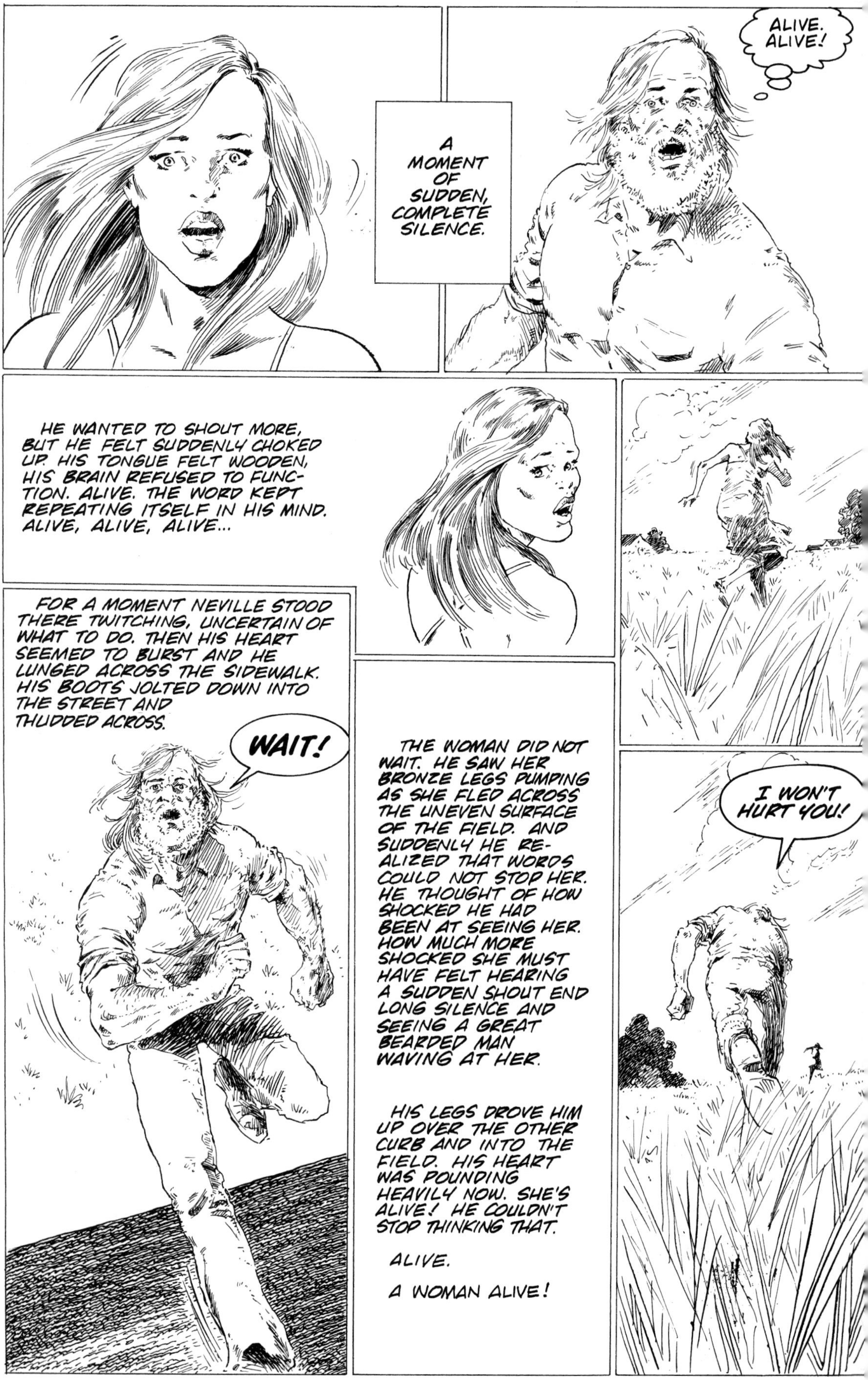
A MOMENT OF SUDDEN, COMPLETE SILENCE.
ALIVE. ALIVE!
HE WANTED TO SHOUT MORE, BUT HE FELT SUDDENLY CHOKED UP. HIS TONGUE FELT WOODEN, HIS BRAIN REFUSED TO FUNCTION. ALIVE. THE WORD KEPT REPEATING ITSELF IN HIS MIND. ALIVE, ALIVE, ALIVE...
FOR A MOMENT NEVILLE STOOD THERE TWITCHING, UNCERTAIN OF WHAT TO DO. THEN HIS HEART SEEMED TO BURST AND HE LUNGED ACROSS THE SIDEWALK. HIS BOOTS JOLTED DOWN INTO THE STREET AND THUDDED ACROSS.
WAIT!
THE WOMAN DID NOT WAIT. HE SAW HER BRONZE LEGS PUMPING AS SHE FLED ACROSS THE UNEVEN SURFACE OF THE FIELD. AND SUDDENLY HE REALIZED THAT WORDS COULD NOT STOP HER. HE THOUGHT OF HOW SHOCKED HE HAD BEEN AT SEEING HER. HOW MUCH MORE SHOCKED SHE MUST HAVE FELT HEARING A SUDDEN SHOUT END LONG SILENCE AND SEEING A GREAT BEARDED MAN WAVING AT HER.
HIS LEGS DROVE HIM UP OVER THE OTHER CURB AND INTO THE FIELD. HIS HEART WAS POUNDING HEAVILY NOW. SHE'S ALIVE! HE COULDN'T STOP THINKING THAT.
ALIVE.
A WOMAN ALIVE!
I WON'T HURT YOU!

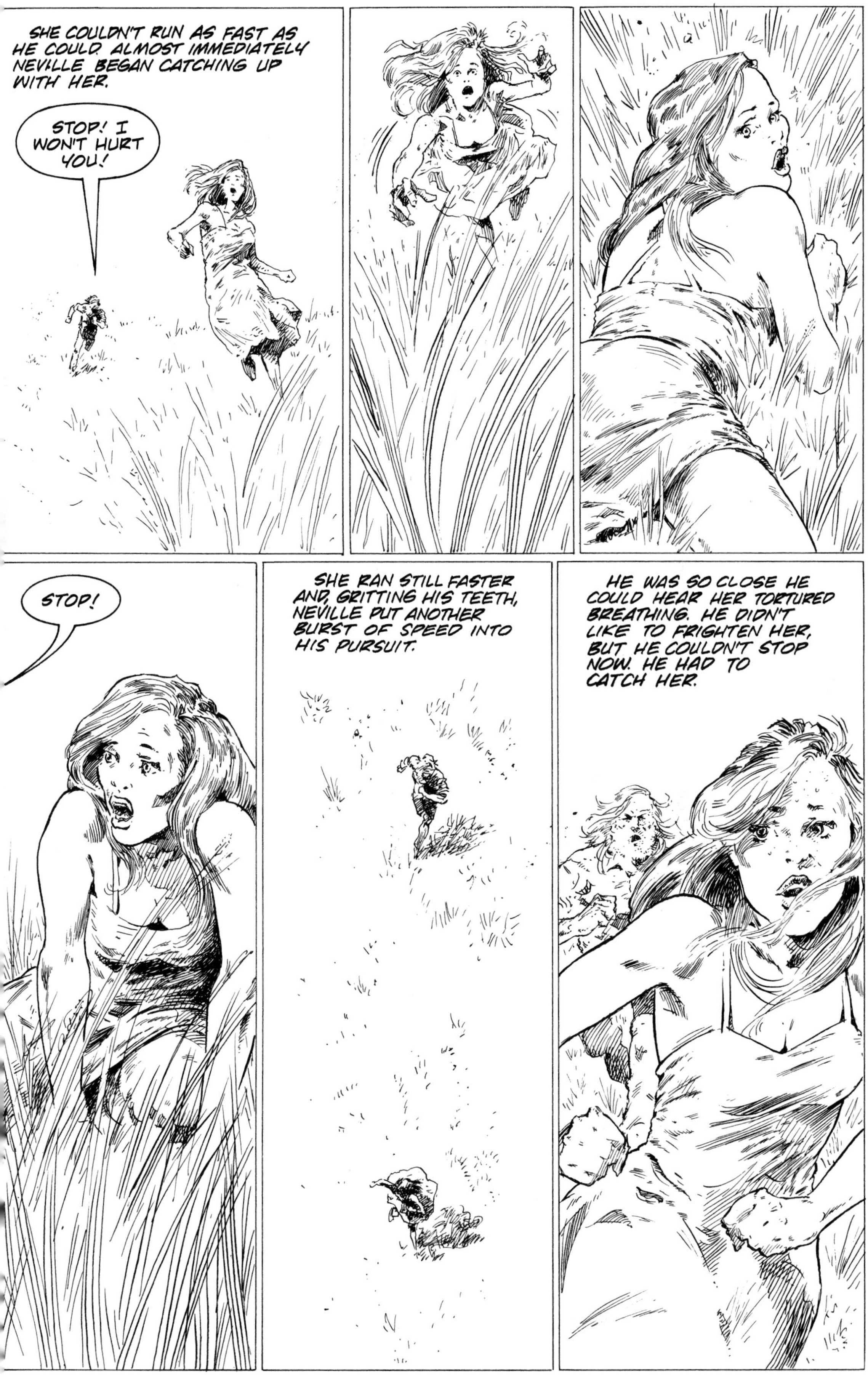
SHE COULDN'T RUN AS FAST AS HE COULD. ALMOST IMMEDIATELY NEVILLE BEGAN CATCHING UP WITH HER.
STOP! I WON'T HURT YOU!
STOP!
SHE RAN STILL FASTER AND, GRITTING HIS TEETH, NEVILLE PUT ANOTHER BURST OF SPEED INTO HIS PURSUIT.
HE WAS SO CLOSE HE COULD HEAR HER TORTURED BREATHING. HE DIDN'T LIKE TO FRIGHTEN HER, BUT HE COULDN'T STOP NOW. HE HAD TO CATCH HER.

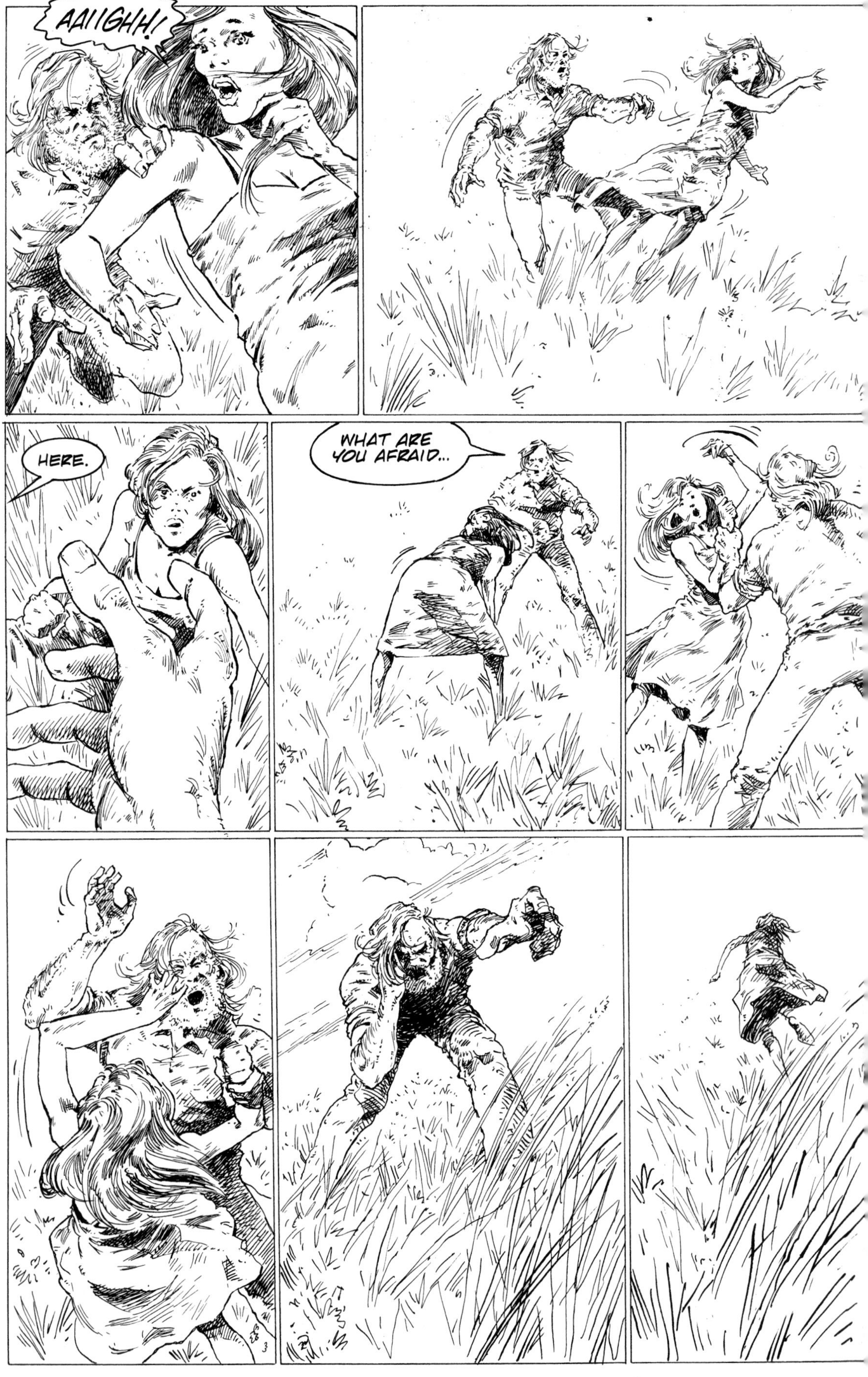
AAIIGHH!
HERE.
WHAT ARE YOU AFRAID...

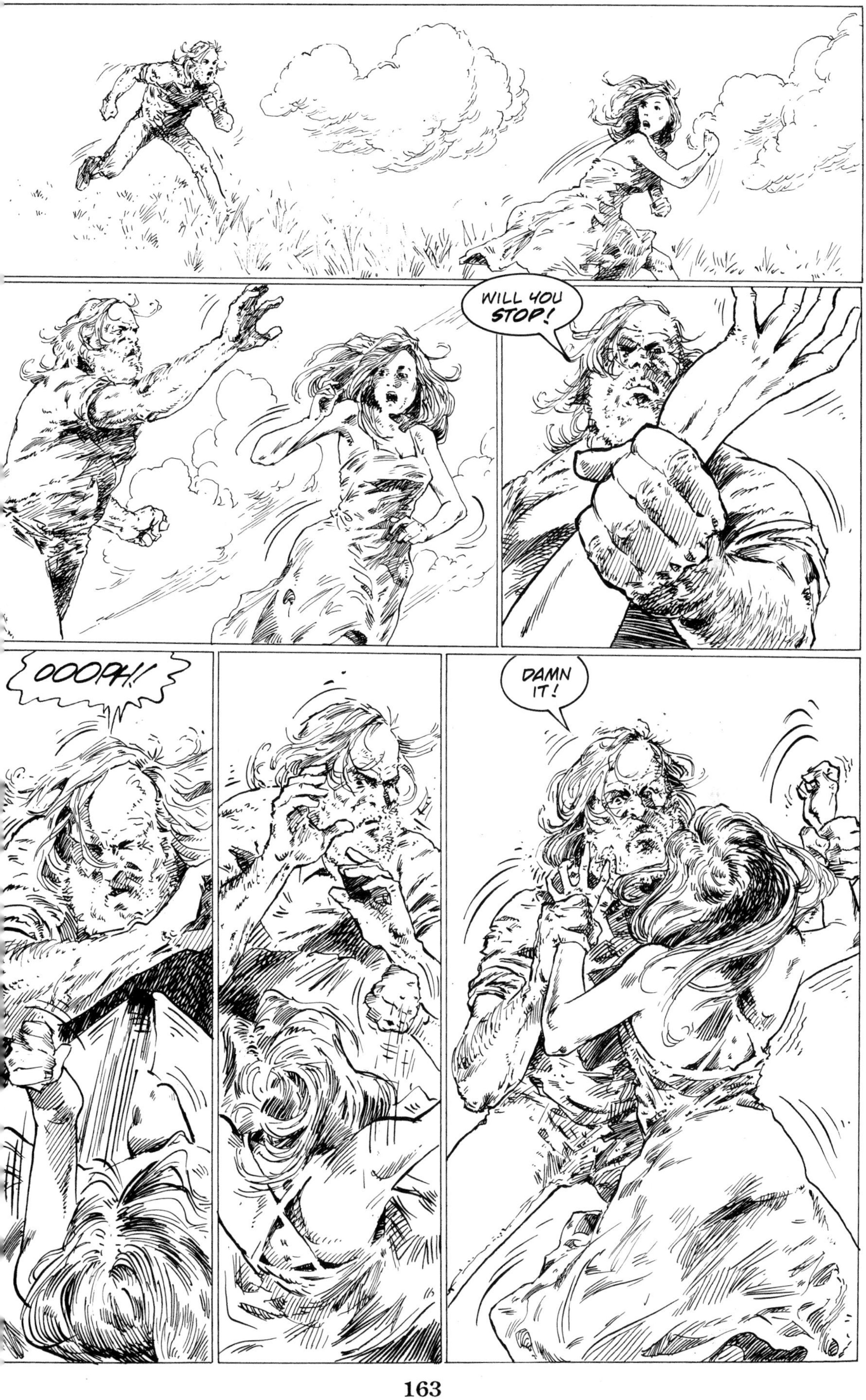
WILL YOU STOP!
OOOPH!!
DAMN IT!

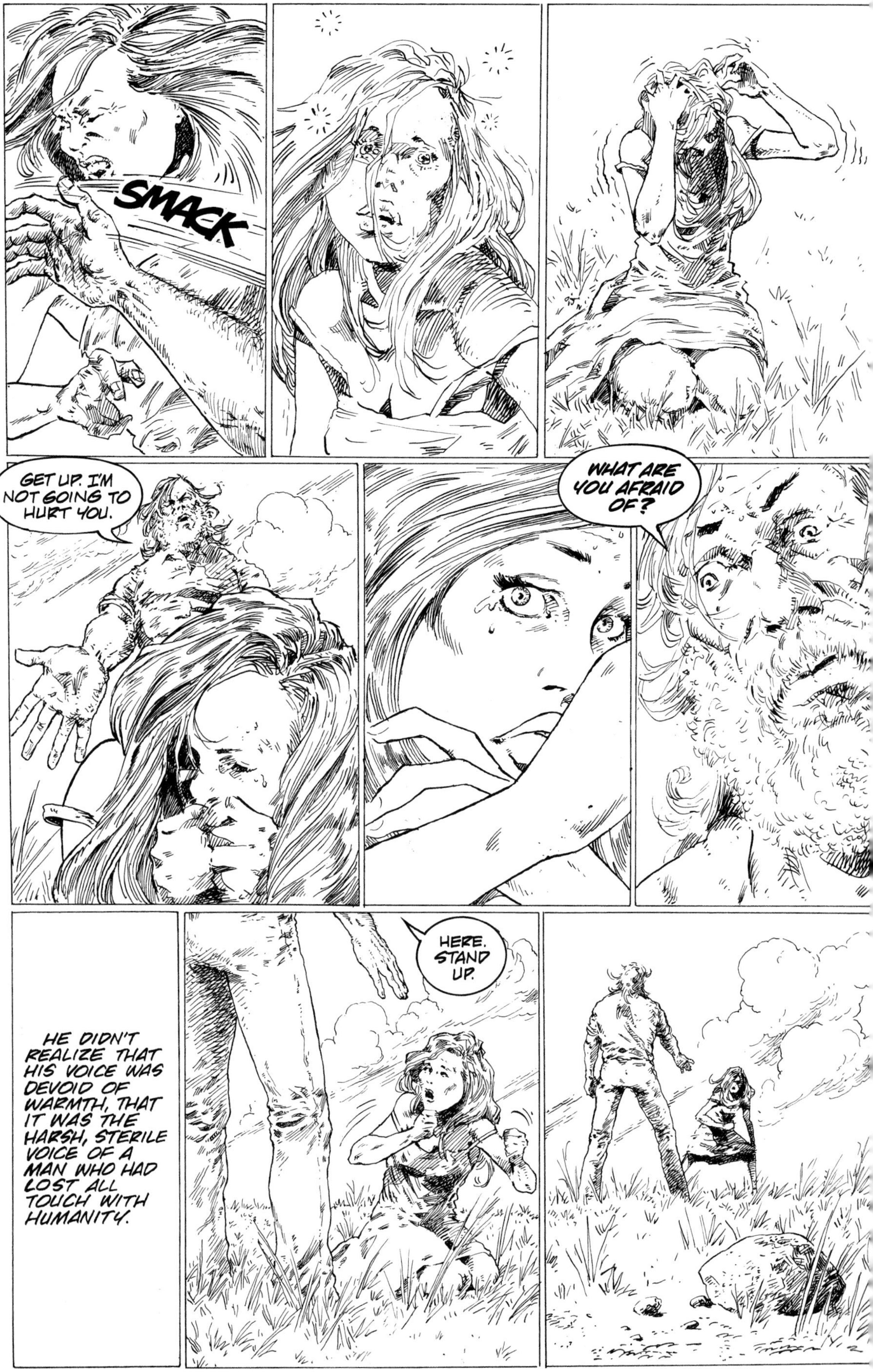
SMACK
GET UP. I'M NOT GOING TO HURT YOU.
WHAT ARE YOU AFRAID OF?
HE DIDN'T REALIZE THAT HIS VOICE WAS DEVOID OF WARMTH, THAT IT WAS THE HARSH, STERILE VOICE OF A MAN WHO HAD LOST ALL TOUCH WITH HUMANITY.
HERE. STAND UP.

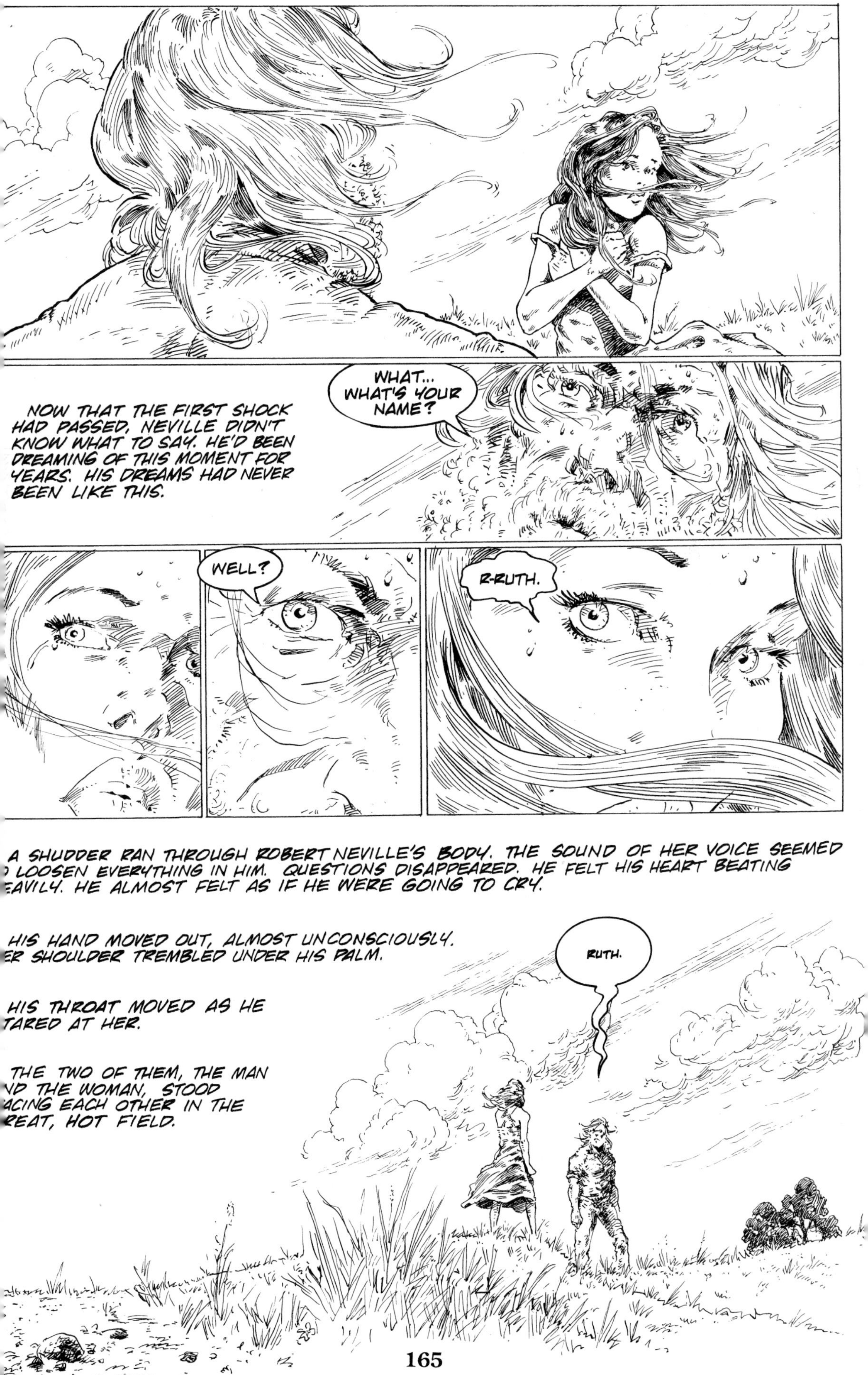

NOW THAT THE FIRST SHOCK HAD PASSED, NEVILLE DIDN'T KNOW WHAT TO SAY. HE'D BEEN DREAMING OF THIS MOMENT FOR YEARS. HIS DREAMS HAD NEVER BEEN LIKE THIS.
WHAT... WHAT'S YOUR NAME?
WELL?
R-RUTH.
A SHUDDER RAN THROUGH ROBERT NEVILLE'S BODY. THE SOUND OF HER VOICE SEEMED
LOOSEN EVERYTHING IN HIM. QUESTIONS DISAPPEARED. HE FELT HIS HEART BEATING
EAVILY. HE ALMOST FELT AS IF HE WERE GOING TO CRY.
HIS HAND MOVED OUT, ALMOST UNCONSCIOUSLY.
ER SHOULDER TREMBLED UNDER HIS PALM.
HIS THROAT MOVED AS HE
TARED AT HER.
RUTH.
THE TWO OF THEM, THE MAN
D THE WOMAN, STOOD
ACING EACH OTHER IN THE
REAT, HOT FIELD.

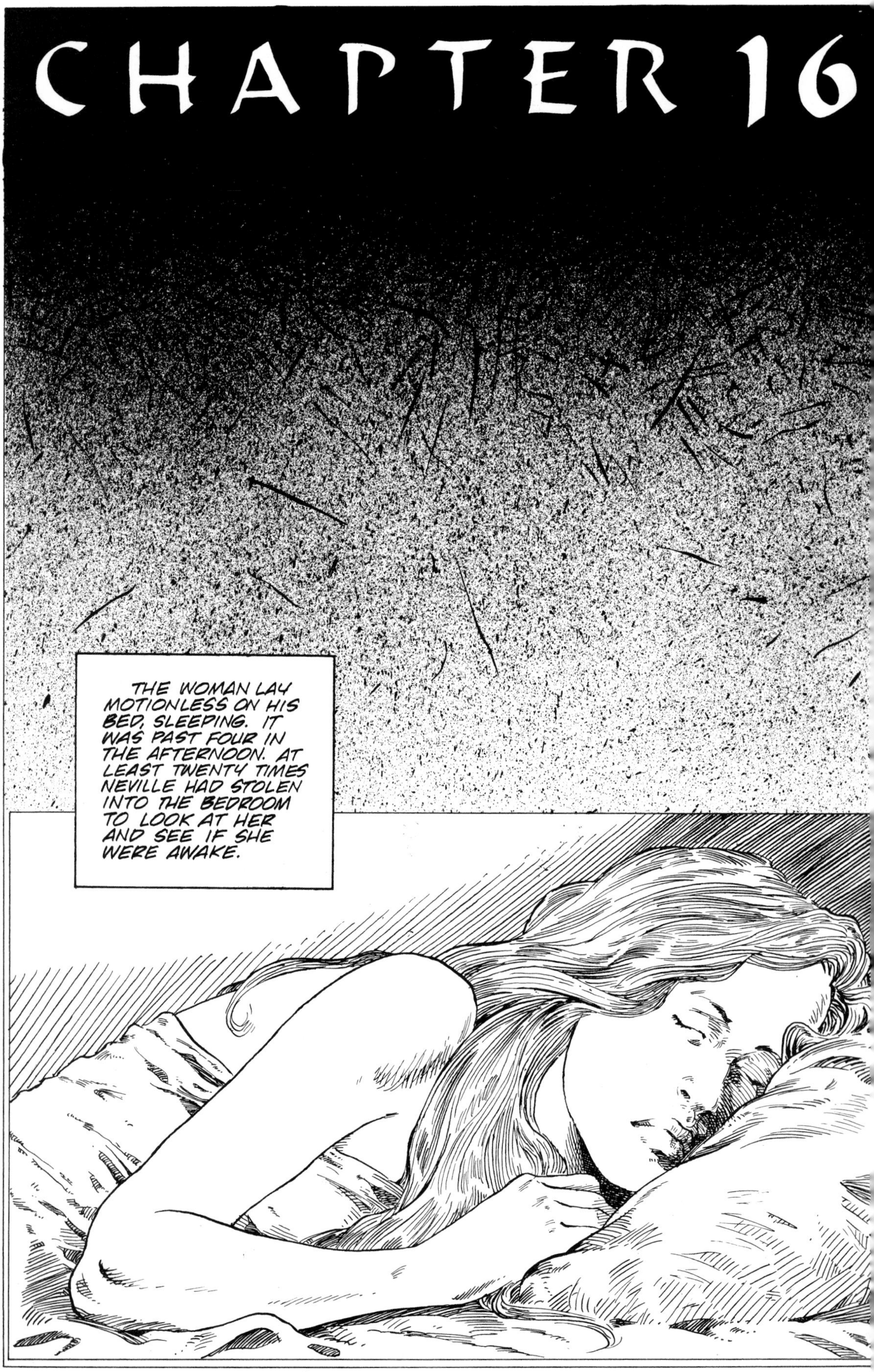
CHAPTER 16
THE WOMAN LAY MOTIONLESS ON HIS BED, SLEEPING. IT WAS PAST FOUR IN THE AFTERNOON. AT LEAST TWENTY TIMES NEVILLE HAD STOLEN INTO THE BEDROOM TO LOOK AT HER AND SEE IF SHE WERE AWAKE.

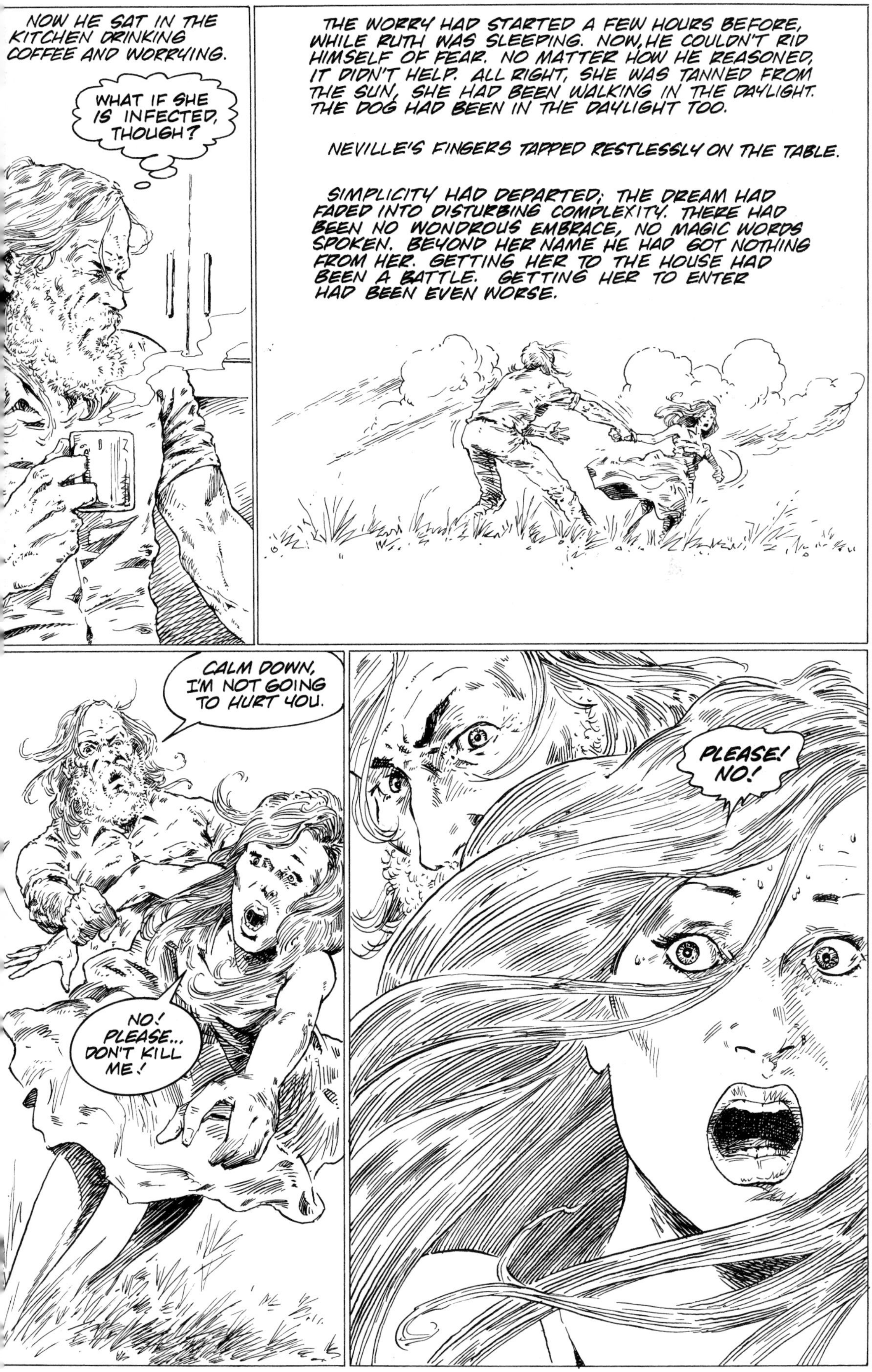
NOW HE SAT IN THE KITCHEN DRINKING COFFEE AND WORRYING.
WHAT IF SHE IS INFECTED, THOUGH?
THE WORRY HAD STARTED A FEW HOURS BEFORE, WHILE RUTH WAS SLEEPING. NOW, HE COULDN'T RID HIMSELF OF FEAR. NO MATTER HOW HE REASONED, IT DIDN'T HELP. ALL RIGHT, SHE WAS TANNED FROM THE SUN, SHE HAD BEEN WALKING IN THE DAYLIGHT. THE DOG HAD BEEN IN THE DAYLIGHT TOO.
NEVILLE'S FINGERS TAPPED RESTLESSLY ON THE TABLE.
SIMPLICITY HAD DEPARTED; THE DREAM HAD FADED INTO DISTURBING COMPLEXITY. THERE HAD BEEN NO WONDROUS EMBRACE, NO MAGIC WORDS SPOKEN. BEYOND HER NAME HE HAD GOT NOTHING FROM HER. GETTING HER TO THE HOUSE HAD BEEN A BATTLE. GETTING HER TO ENTER HAD BEEN EVEN WORSE.
CALM DOWN, I'M NOT GOING TO HURT YOU.
NO! PLEASE... DON'T KILL ME!
PLEASE! NO!

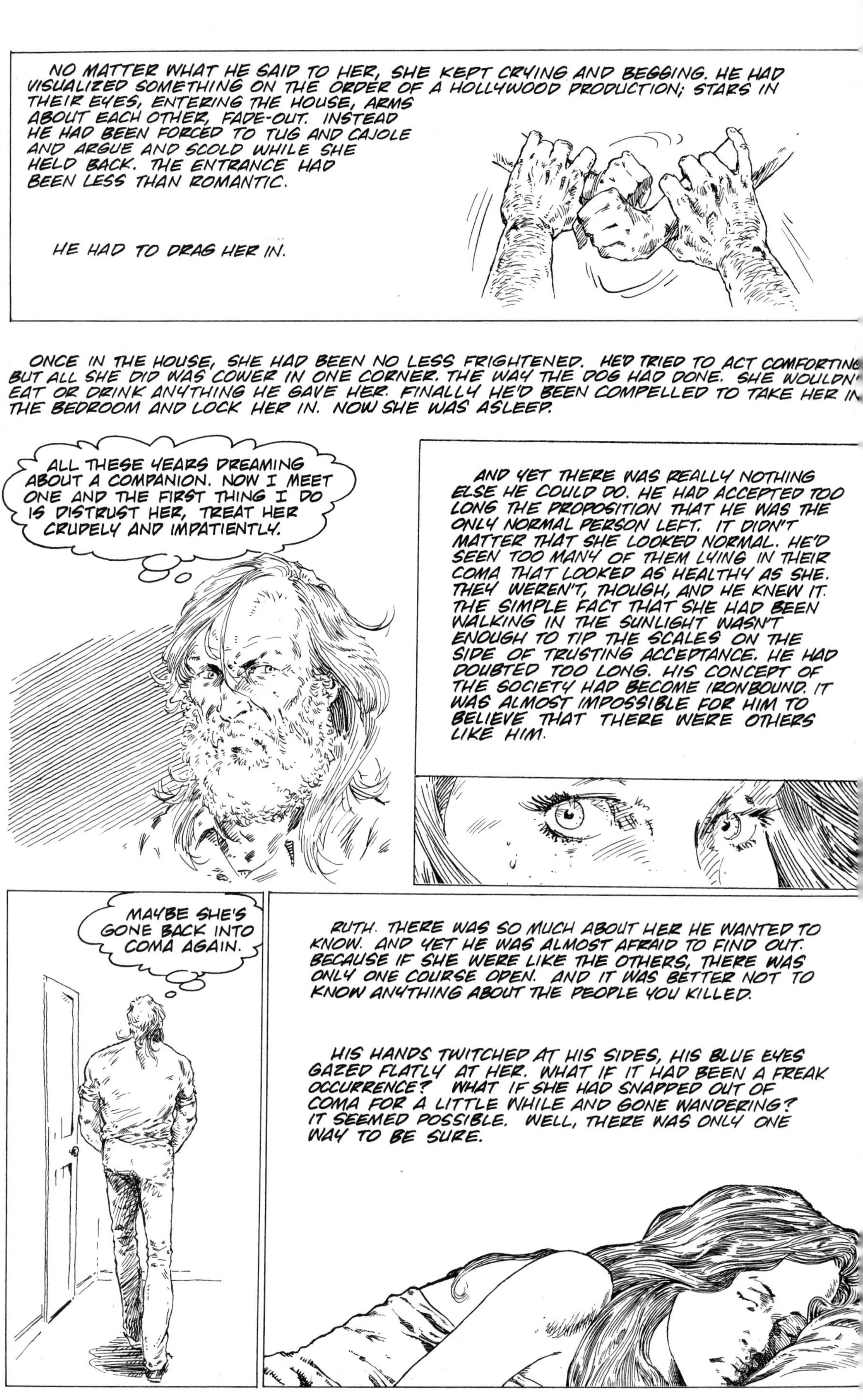
NO MATTER WHAT HE SAID TO HER, SHE KEPT CRYING AND BEGGING. HE HAD VISUALIZED SOMETHING ON THE ORDER OF A HOLLYWOOD PRODUCTION; STARS IN THEIR EYES, ENTERING THE HOUSE, ARMS ABOUT EACH OTHER, FADE-OUT. INSTEAD HE HAD BEEN FORCED TO TUG AND CAJOLE AND ARGUE AND SCOLD WHILE SHE HELD BACK. THE ENTRANCE HAD BEEN LESS THAN ROMANTIC.
HE HAD TO DRAG HER IN.
ONCE IN THE HOUSE, SHE HAD BEEN NO LESS FRIGHTENED. HE'D TRIED TO ACT COMFORTIN BUT ALL SHE DID WAS COWER IN ONE CORNER. THE WAY THE DOG HAD DONE. SHE WOULDN' EAT OR DRINK ANYTHING HE GAVE HER. FINALLY HE'D BEEN COMPELLED TO TAKE HER IN THE BEDROOM AND LOCK HER IN. NOW SHE WAS ASLEEP.
ALL THESE YEARS DREAMING ABOUT A COMPANION. NOW I MEET ONE AND THE FIRST THING I DO IS DISTRUST HER, TREAT HER CRUDELY AND IMPATIENTLY.
AND YET THERE WAS REALLY NOTHING ELSE HE COULD DO. HE HAD ACCEPTED TOO LONG THE PROPOSITION THAT HE WAS THE ONLY NORMAL PERSON LEFT. IT DIDN'T MATTER THAT SHE LOOKED NORMAL. HE'D SEEN TOO MANY OF THEM LYING IN THEIR COMA THAT LOOKED AS HEALTHY AS SHE. THEY WEREN'T, THOUGH, AND HE KNEW IT. THE SIMPLE FACT THAT SHE HAD BEEN WALKING IN THE SUNLIGHT WASN'T ENOUGH TO TIP THE SCALES ON THE SIDE OF TRUSTING ACCEPTANCE. HE HAD DOUBTED TOO LONG. HIS CONCEPT OF THE SOCIETY HAD BECOME IRONBOUND. IT WAS ALMOST IMPOSSIBLE FOR HIM TO BELIEVE THAT THERE WERE OTHERS LIKE HIM.
MAYBE SHE'S GONE BACK INTO COMA AGAIN.
RUTH. THERE WAS SO MUCH ABOUT HER HE WANTED TO KNOW. AND YET HE WAS ALMOST AFRAID TO FIND OUT. BECAUSE IF SHE WERE LIKE THE OTHERS, THERE WAS ONLY ONE COURSE OPEN. AND IT WAS BETTER NOT TO KNOW ANYTHING ABOUT THE PEOPLE YOU KILLED.
HIS HANDS TWITCHED AT HIS SIDES, HIS BLUE EYES GAZED FLATLY AT HER. WHAT IF IT HAD BEEN A FREAK OCCURRENCE? WHAT IF SHE HAD SNAPPED OUT OF COMA FOR A LITTLE WHILE AND GONE WANDERING? IT SEEMED POSSIBLE. WELL, THERE WAS ONLY ONE WAY TO BE SURE.

STARING DOWN AT HER, HE NOTICED THE THIN GOLD CHAIN AROUND HER THROAT. THE TINY GOLD CROSS.

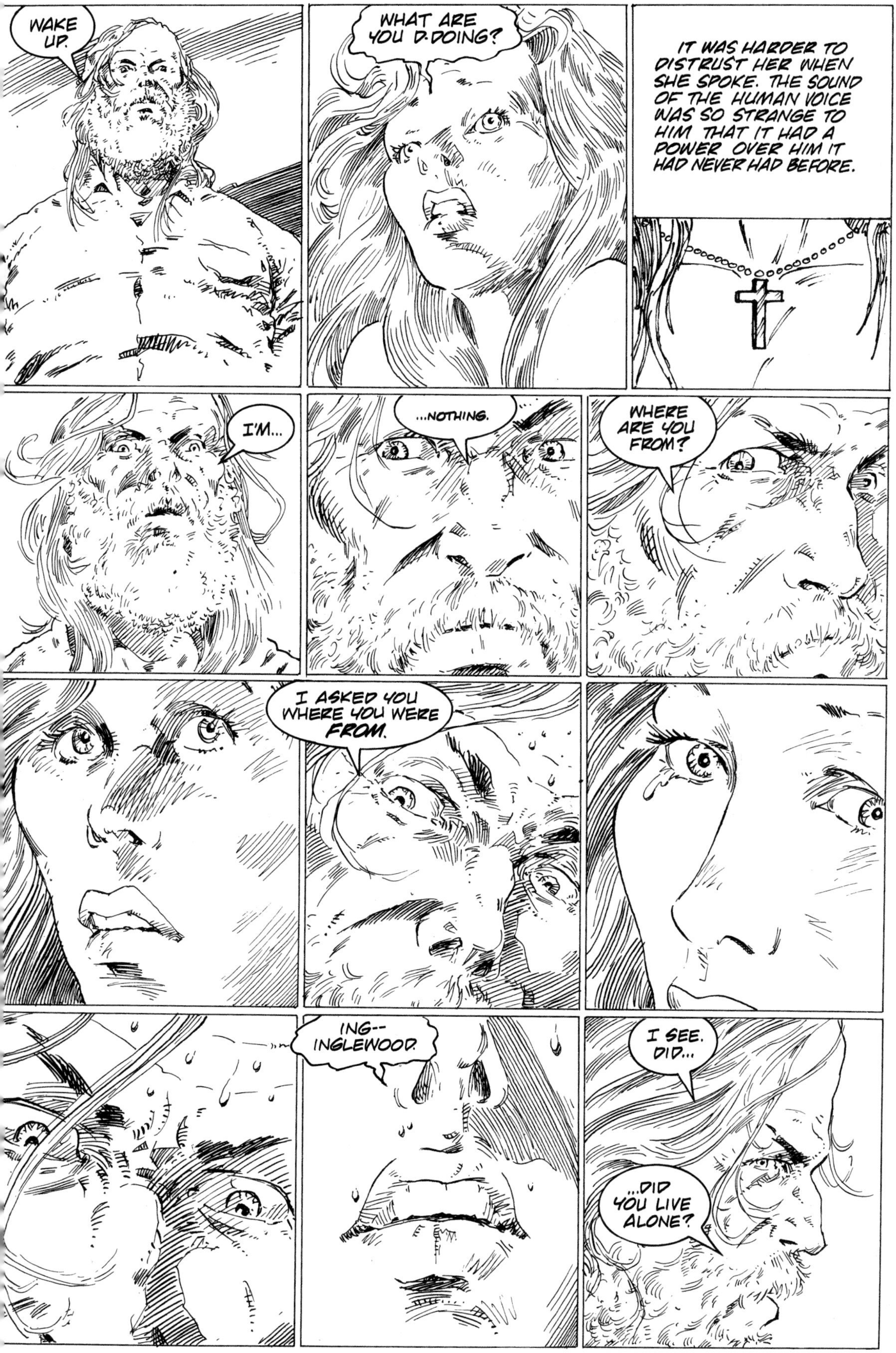
WAKE UP.
WHAT ARE YOU D-DOING?
IT WAS HARDER TO DISTRUST HER WHEN SHE SPOKE. THE SOUND OF THE HUMAN VOICE WAS SO STRANGE TO HIM THAT IT HAD A POWER OVER HIM IT HAD NEVER HAD BEFORE.
I'M...
...NOTHING.
WHERE ARE YOU FROM?
I ASKED YOU WHERE YOU WERE FROM.
ING-- INGLEWOOD.
I SEE. DID...
...DID YOU LIVE ALONE?

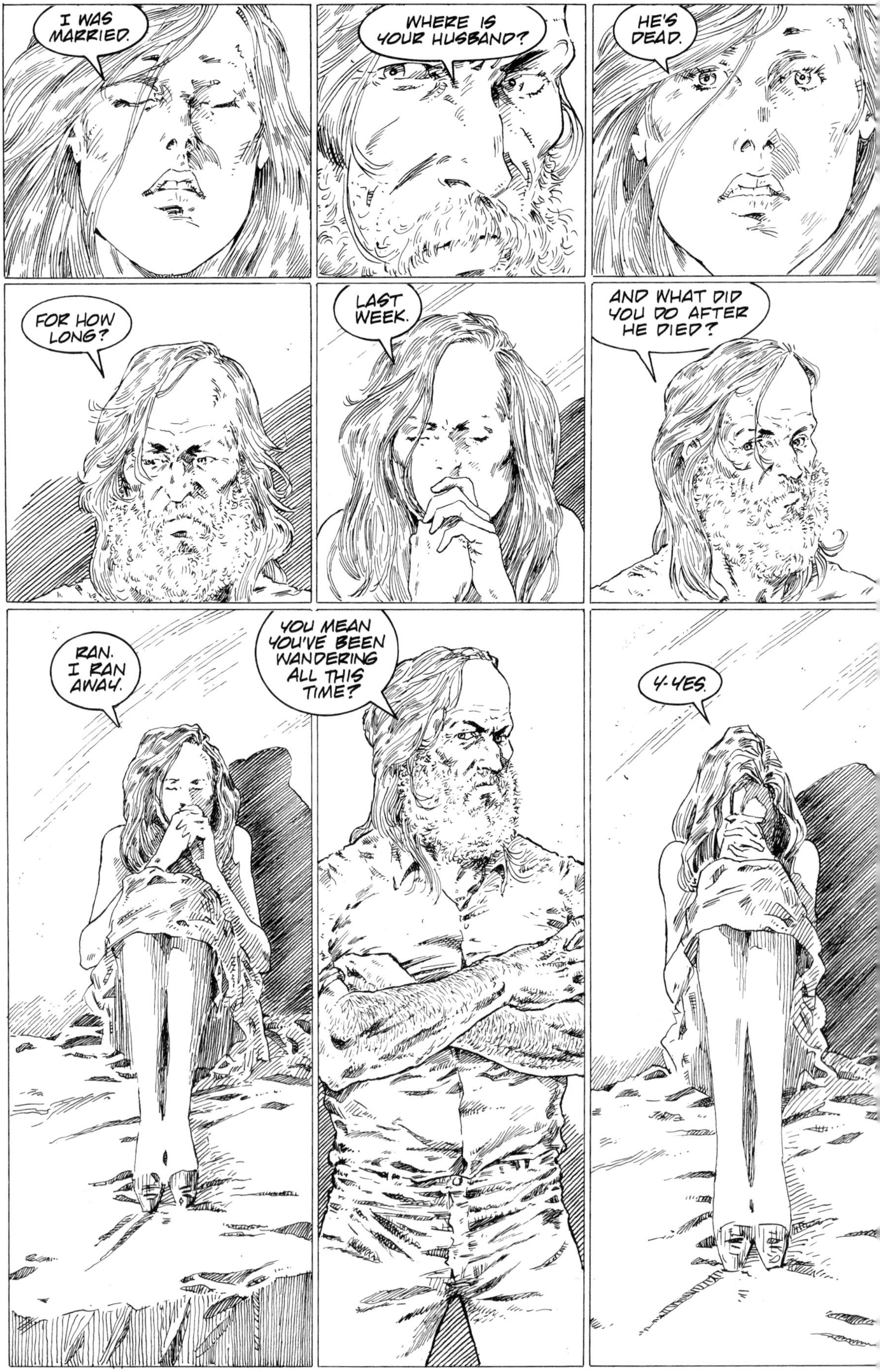
I WAS MARRIED.
WHERE IS YOUR HUSBAND?
HE'S DEAD.
FOR HOW LONG?
LAST WEEK.
AND WHAT DID YOU DO AFTER HE DIED?
RAN. I RAN AWAY.
YOU MEAN YOU'VE BEEN WANDERING ALL THIS TIME?
Y-YES.

HE LOOKED AT HER WITHOUT A WORD. THEN ABRUPTLY HE TURNED AND HIS BOOTS HUMPED LOUDLY AS HE WALKED INTO THE KITCHEN. PULLING OPEN A CABINET DOOR, HE REW DOWN A HANDFUL OF GARLIC CLOVES. HE PUT THEM ON A DISH, TORE THEM INTO IECES, AND MASHED THEM TO A PULP. THE ACRID FUMES ASSAILED HIS NOSTRILS.

SHE WAS PROPPED UP ON ONE ELBOW WHEN HE CAME BACK. WITHOUT HESITATION HE USHED THE DISH ALMOST TO HER FACE.

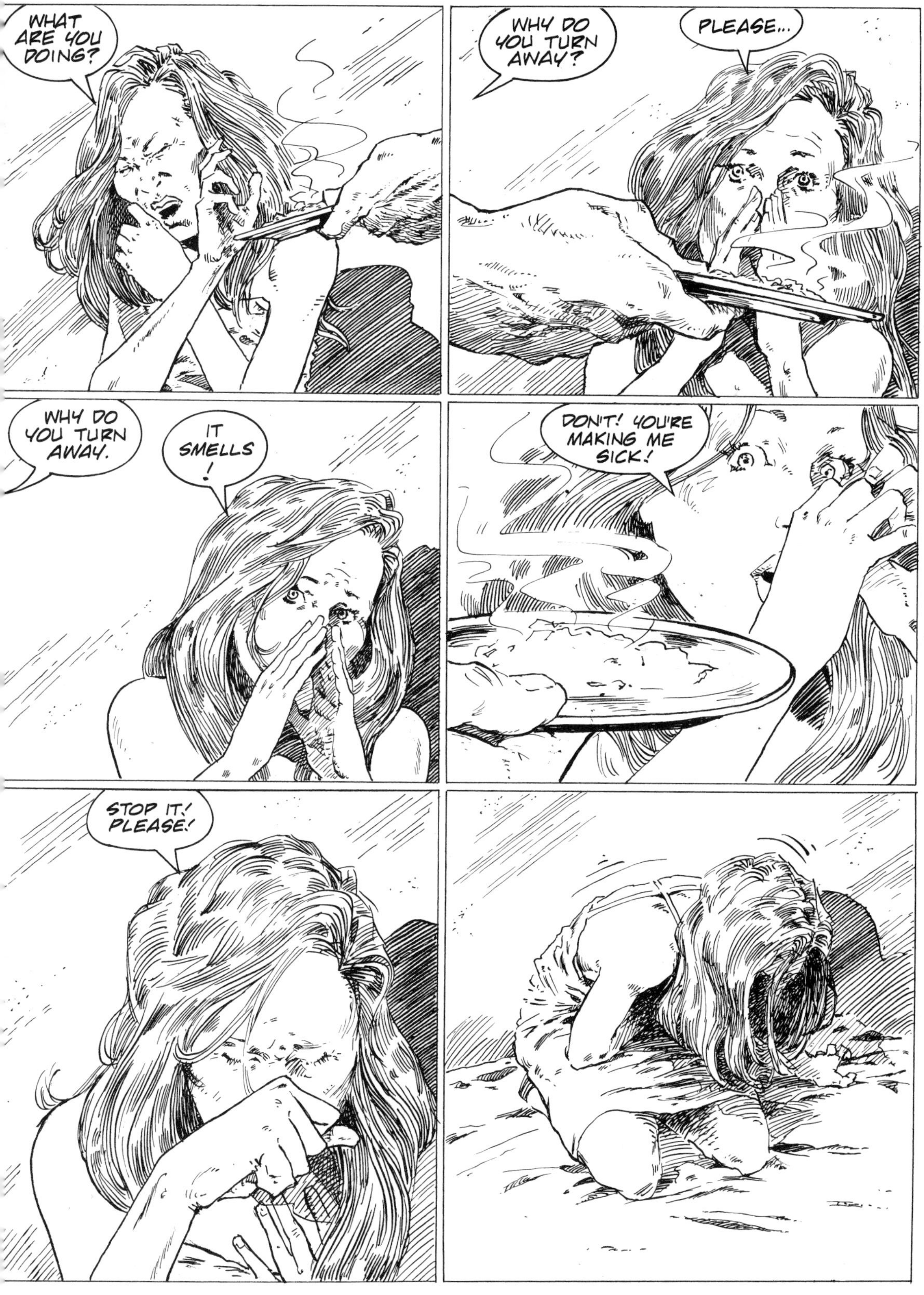

WHAT ARE YOU DOING?
WHY DO YOU TURN AWAY?
PLEASE...
WHY DO YOU TURN AWAY.
IT SMELLS!
DON'T! YOU'RE MAKING ME SICK!
STOP IT! PLEASE!

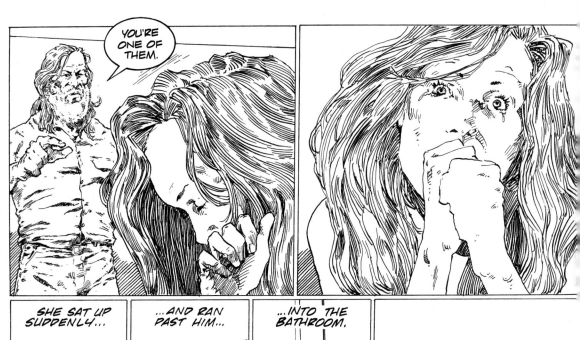

YOU'RE ONE OF THEM.

SHE SAT UP SUDDENLY...

...AND RAN PAST HIM...

...INTO THE BATHROOM.

SLAM

HE COULD HEAR THE SOUND OF HER TERRIBLE RETCHING.

THIN-LIPPED, HE PUT THE DISH DOWN ON THE BEDSIDE TABLE. HIS THROAT MOVED AS HE SWALLOWED.

INFECTED. IT HAD BEEN A CLEAR SIGN. HE HAD LEARNED OVER A YEAR BEFORE THAT GARLIC WAS AN ALLERGEN TO ANY SYSTEM INFECTED WITH THE VAMPIRIS BACILLUS. WHEN THE SYSTEM WAS EXPOSED TO GARLIC, THE STIMULATED TISSUES SENSITIZED THE CELLS, CAUSING AN ABNORMAL REACTION TO ANY FURTHER CONTACT WITH GARLIC. THAT WAS WHY PUTTING IT INTO THEIR VEINS HAD ACCOMPLISHED LITTLE. THEY HAD TO BE EXPOSED TO THE ODOR.

AND THE WOMAN HAD REACTED IN THE WRONG WAY.

BUT...
IF WHAT SHE HAD SAID WAS TRUE, SHE'D BEEN WANDERING AROUND FOR A WEEK. SHE WOULD NATURALLY BE EXHAUSTED AND WEAK, AND UNDER THOSE CONDITIONS THE SMELL OF SO MUCH GARLIC COULD HAVE MADE HER RETCH.

HIS FISTS THUDDED DOWN ONTO THE MATTRESS. HE STILL DIDN'T KNOW, THEN, NOT FOR
RTAIN. AND, OBJECTIVELY, HE KNEW HE HAD NO RIGHT TO DECIDE ON INADEQUATE EVIDENCE. IT
S SOMETHING HE'D LEARNED THE HARD WAY, SOMETHING HE KNEW AND BELIEVED ABSOLUTELY.

HE WAS STILL SITTING THERE WHEN SHE UNLOCKED THE BATHROOM DOOR AND CAME OUT.

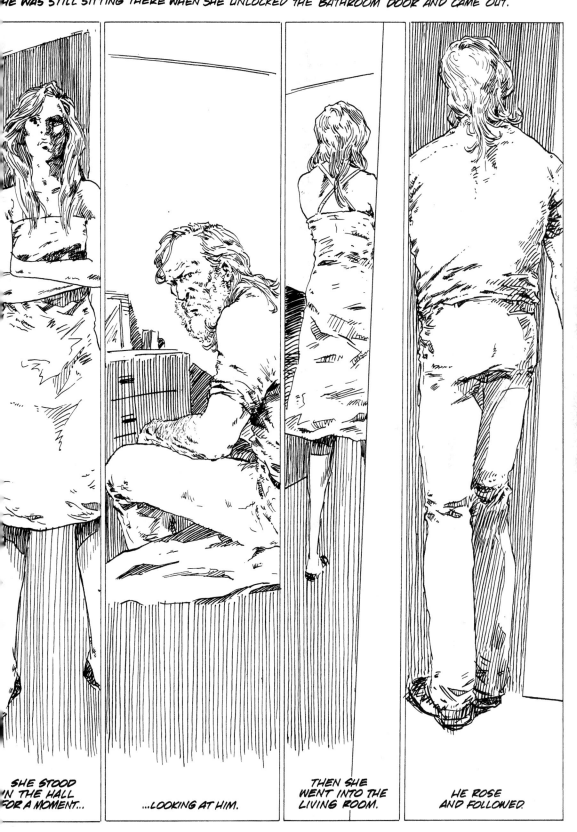

SHE STOOD
'N THE HALL
FOR A MOMENT...

...LOOKING AT HIM.

THEN SHE
WENT INTO THE
LIVING ROOM.

HE ROSE
AND FOLLOWED.

173

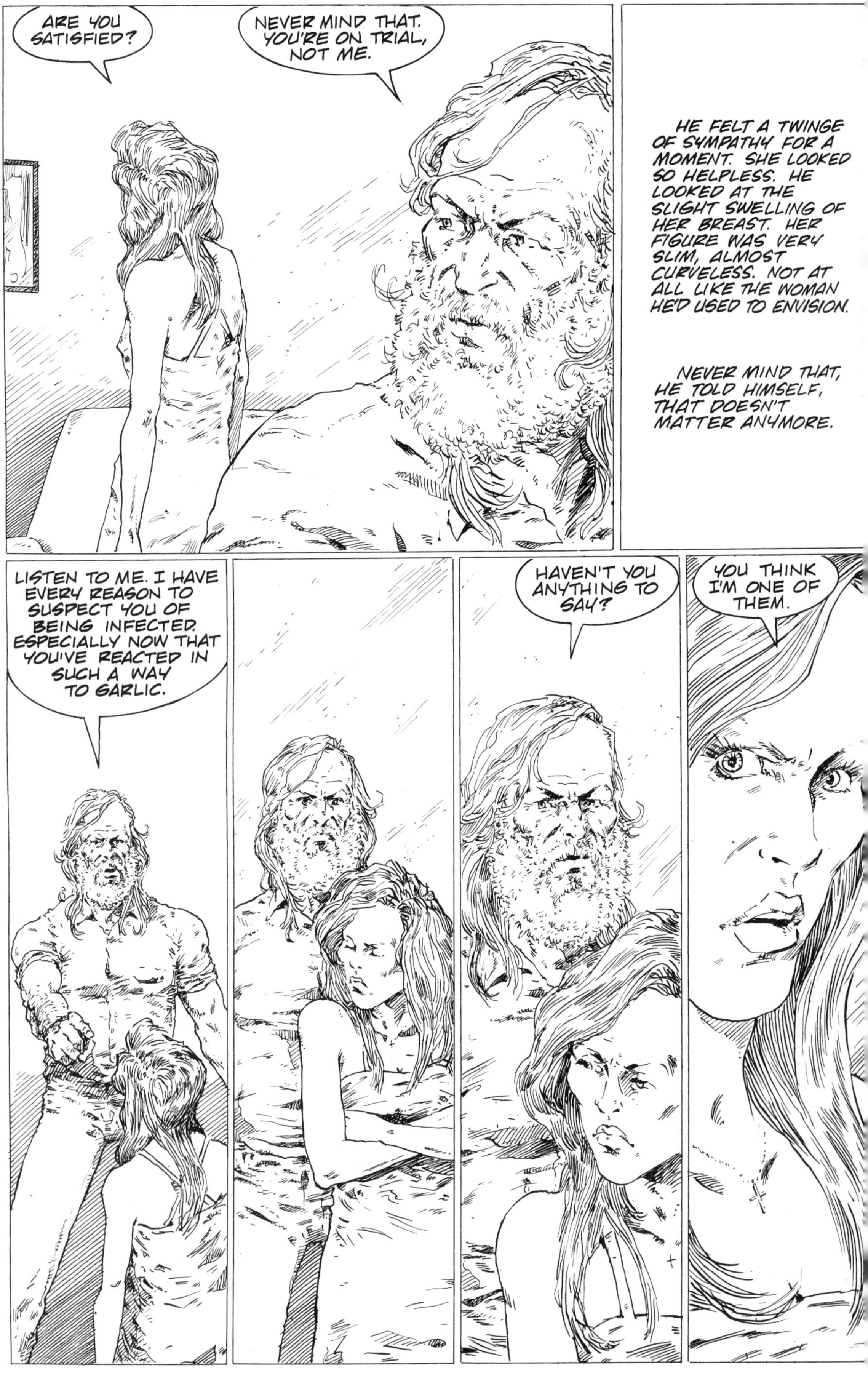
ARE YOU SATISFIED?
NEVER MIND THAT. YOU'RE ON TRIAL, NOT ME.
HE FELT A TWINGE OF SYMPATHY FOR A MOMENT. SHE LOOKED SO HELPLESS. HE LOOKED AT THE SLIGHT SWELLING OF HER BREAST. HER FIGURE WAS VERY SLIM, ALMOST CURVELESS. NOT AT ALL LIKE THE WOMAN HE'D USED TO ENVISION.
NEVER MIND THAT, HE TOLD HIMSELF, THAT DOESN'T MATTER ANYMORE.
LISTEN TO ME. I HAVE EVERY REASON TO SUSPECT YOU OF BEING INFECTED. ESPECIALLY NOW THAT YOU'VE REACTED IN SUCH A WAY TO GARLIC.
HAVEN'T YOU ANYTHING TO SAY?
YOU THINK I'M ONE OF THEM.

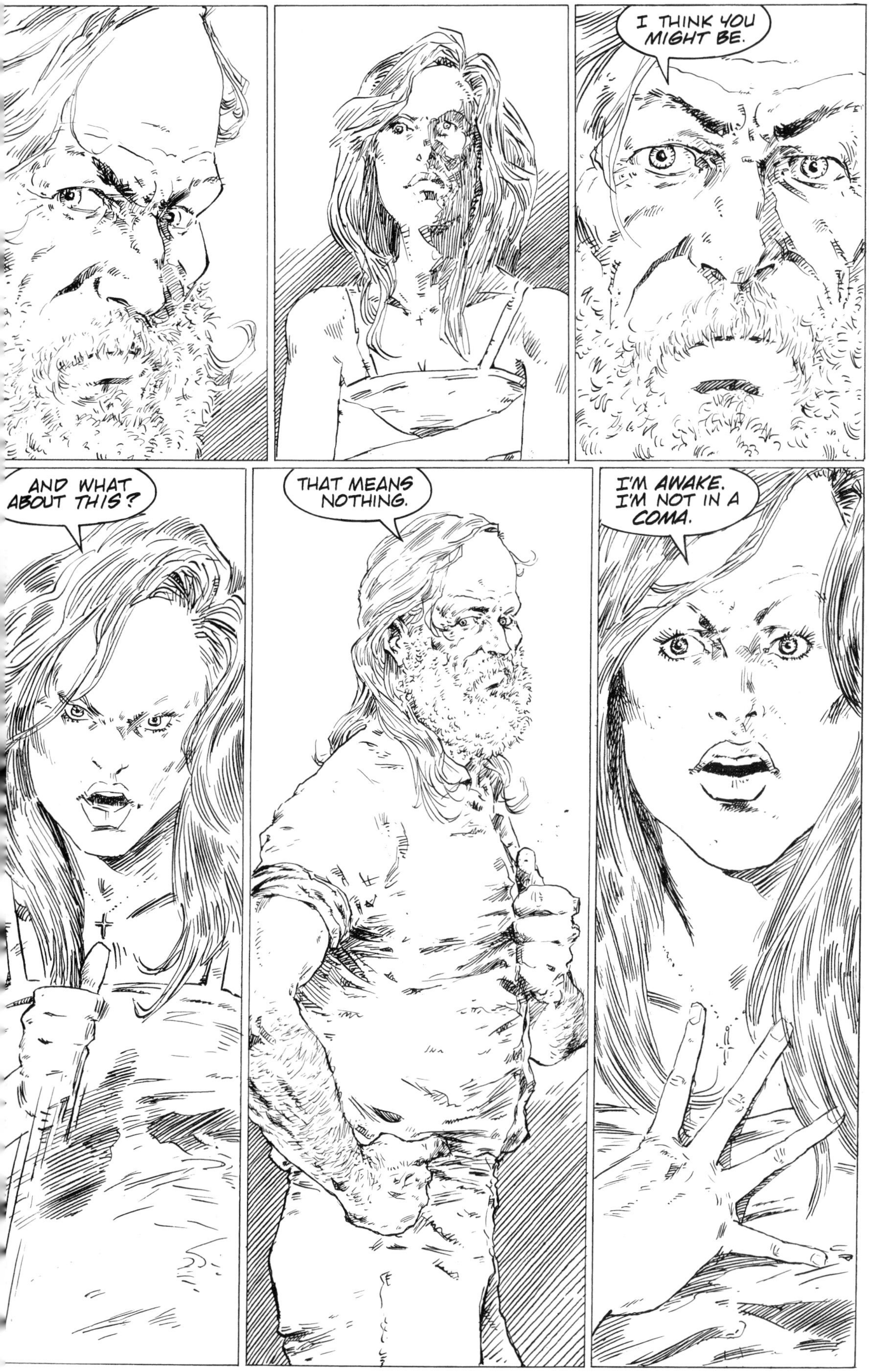
I THINK YOU MIGHT BE.
AND WHAT ABOUT THIS?
THAT MEANS NOTHING.
I'M AWAKE. I'M NOT IN A COMA.

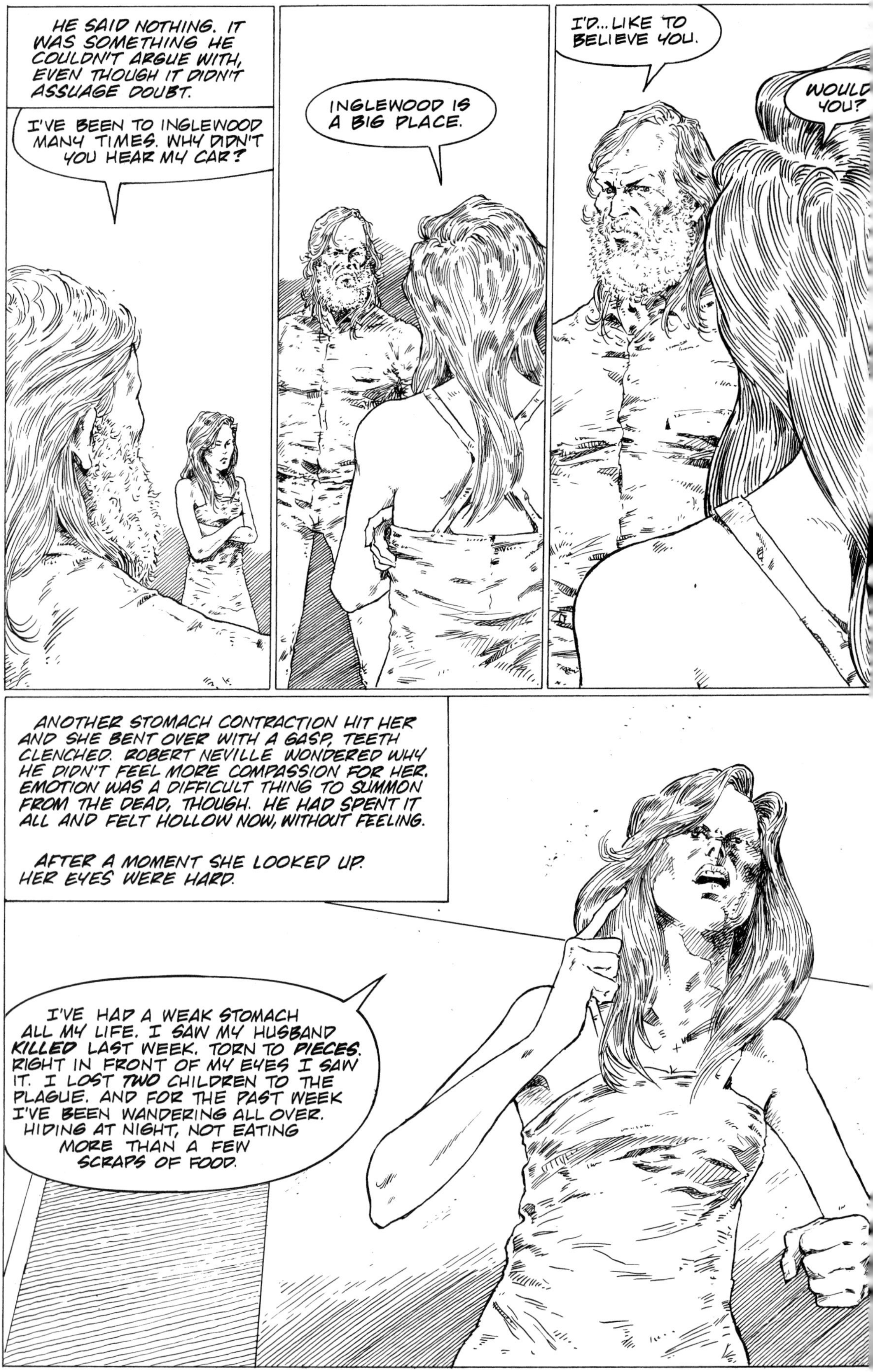
HE SAID NOTHING. IT WAS SOMETHING HE COULDN'T ARGUE WITH, EVEN THOUGH IT DIDN'T ASSUAGE DOUBT.
I'VE BEEN TO INGLEWOOD MANY TIMES. WHY DIDN'T YOU HEAR MY CAR?
INGLEWOOD IS A BIG PLACE.
I'D... LIKE TO BELIEVE YOU.
WOULD YOU?
ANOTHER STOMACH CONTRACTION HIT HER AND SHE BENT OVER WITH A GASP, TEETH CLENCHED. ROBERT NEVILLE WONDERED WHY HE DIDN'T FEEL MORE COMPASSION FOR HER. EMOTION WAS A DIFFICULT THING TO SUMMON FROM THE DEAD, THOUGH. HE HAD SPENT IT ALL AND FELT HOLLOW NOW, WITHOUT FEELING.
AFTER A MOMENT SHE LOOKED UP. HER EYES WERE HARD.
I'VE HAD A WEAK STOMACH ALL MY LIFE. I SAW MY HUSBAND **KILLED** LAST WEEK. TORN TO **PIECES**. RIGHT IN FRONT OF MY EYES I SAW IT. I LOST **TWO** CHILDREN TO THE PLAGUE. AND FOR THE PAST WEEK I'VE BEEN WANDERING ALL OVER. HIDING AT NIGHT, NOT EATING MORE THAN A FEW SCRAPS OF FOOD.

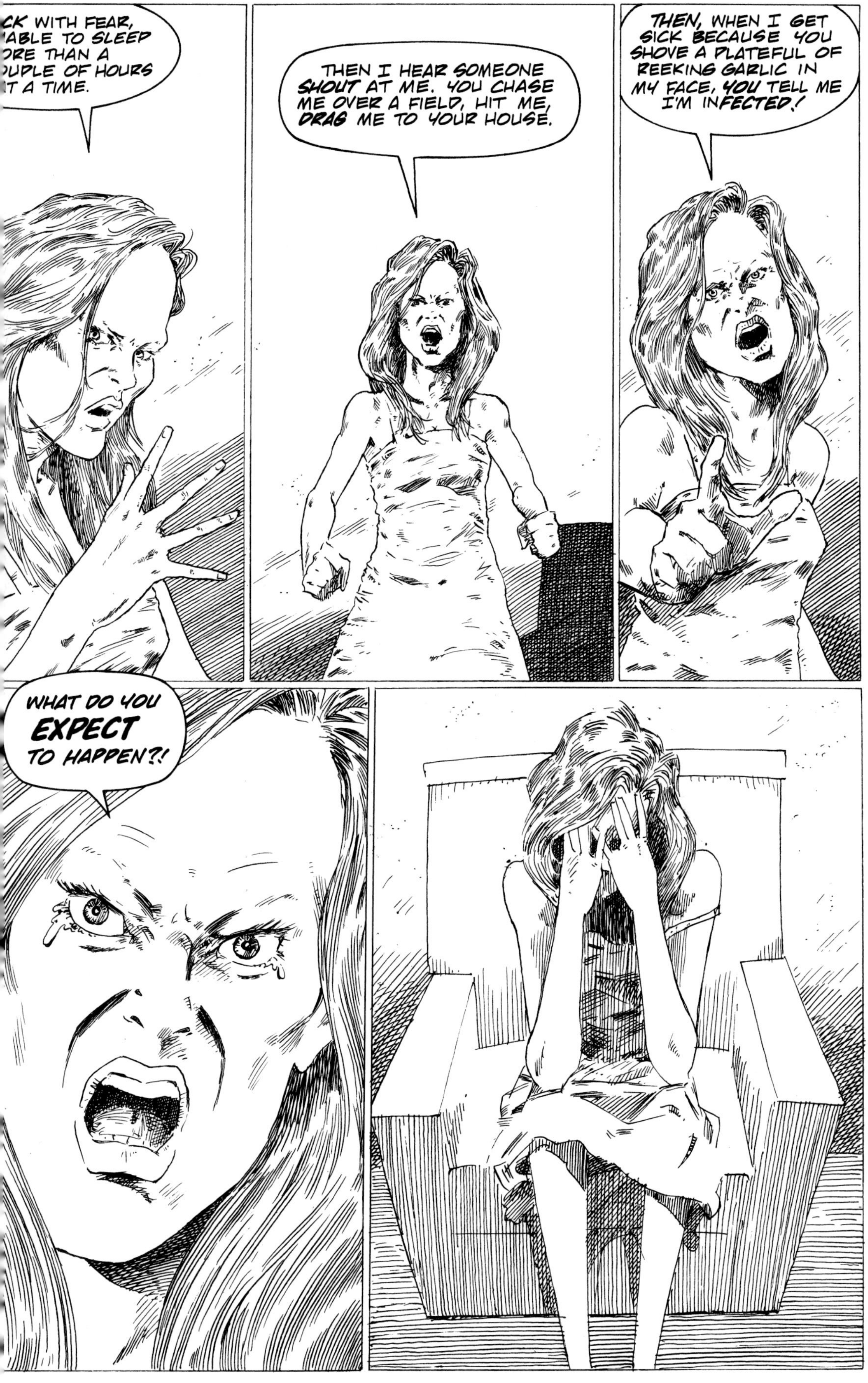

CK WITH FEAR, ABLE TO SLEEP ORE THAN A OUPLE OF HOURS T A TIME.
THEN I HEAR SOMEONE SHOUT AT ME. YOU CHASE ME OVER A FIELD, HIT ME, DRAG ME TO YOUR HOUSE.
THEN, WHEN I GET SICK BECAUSE YOU SHOVE A PLATEFUL OF REEKING GARLIC IN MY FACE, YOU TELL ME I'M INFECTED!
WHAT DO YOU EXPECT TO HAPPEN?!

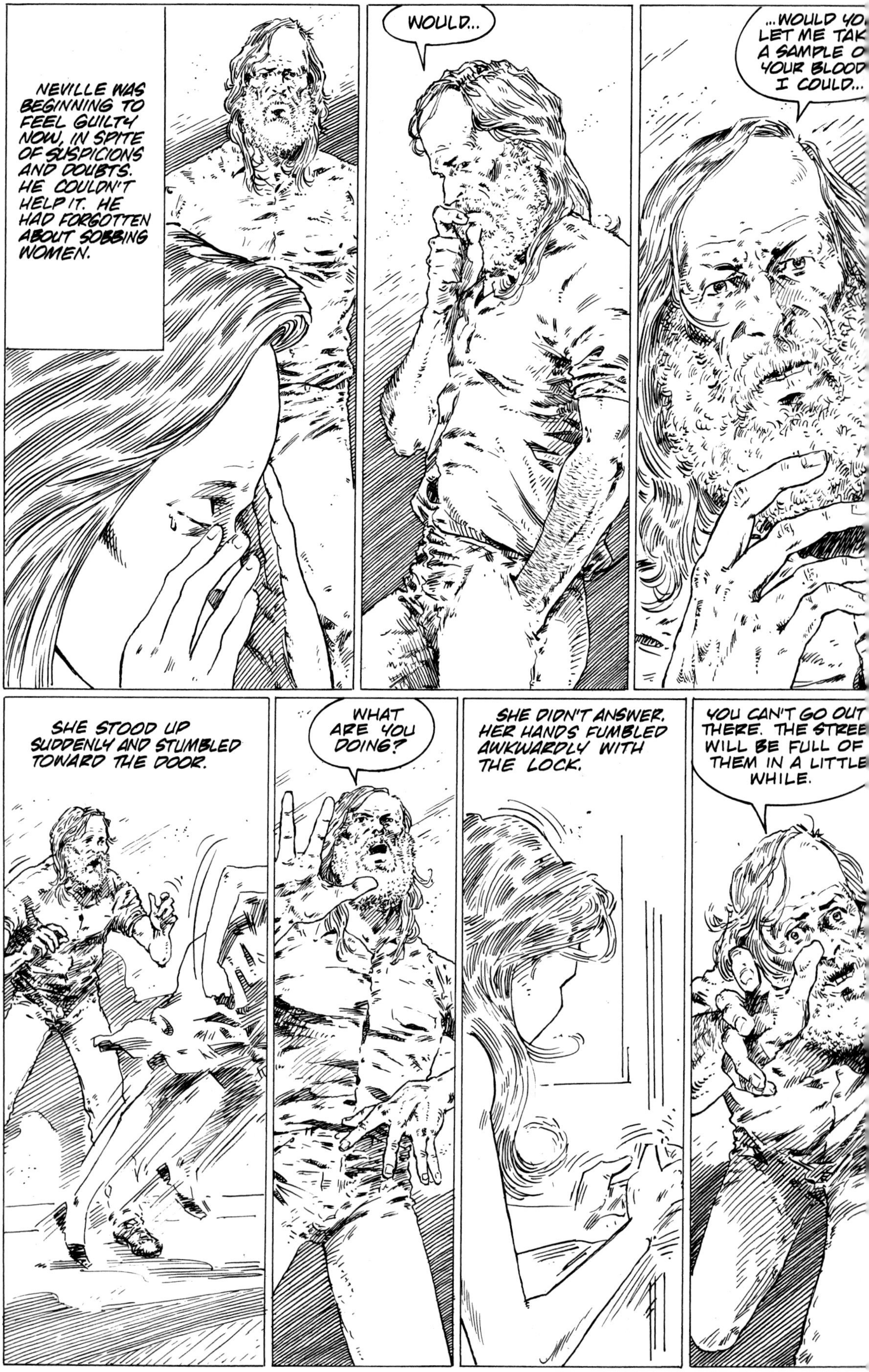

NEVILLE WAS BEGINNING TO FEEL GUILTY NOW, IN SPITE OF SUSPICIONS AND DOUBTS. HE COULDN'T HELP IT. HE HAD FORGOTTEN ABOUT SOBBING WOMEN.
WOULD...
...WOULD YO LET ME TAK A SAMPLE O YOUR BLOOD I COULD...
SHE STOOD UP SUDDENLY AND STUMBLED TOWARD THE DOOR.
WHAT ARE YOU DOING?
SHE DIDN'T ANSWER. HER HANDS FUMBLED AWKWARDLY WITH THE LOCK.
YOU CAN'T GO OUT THERE. THE STREE WILL BE FULL OF THEM IN A LITTLE WHILE.

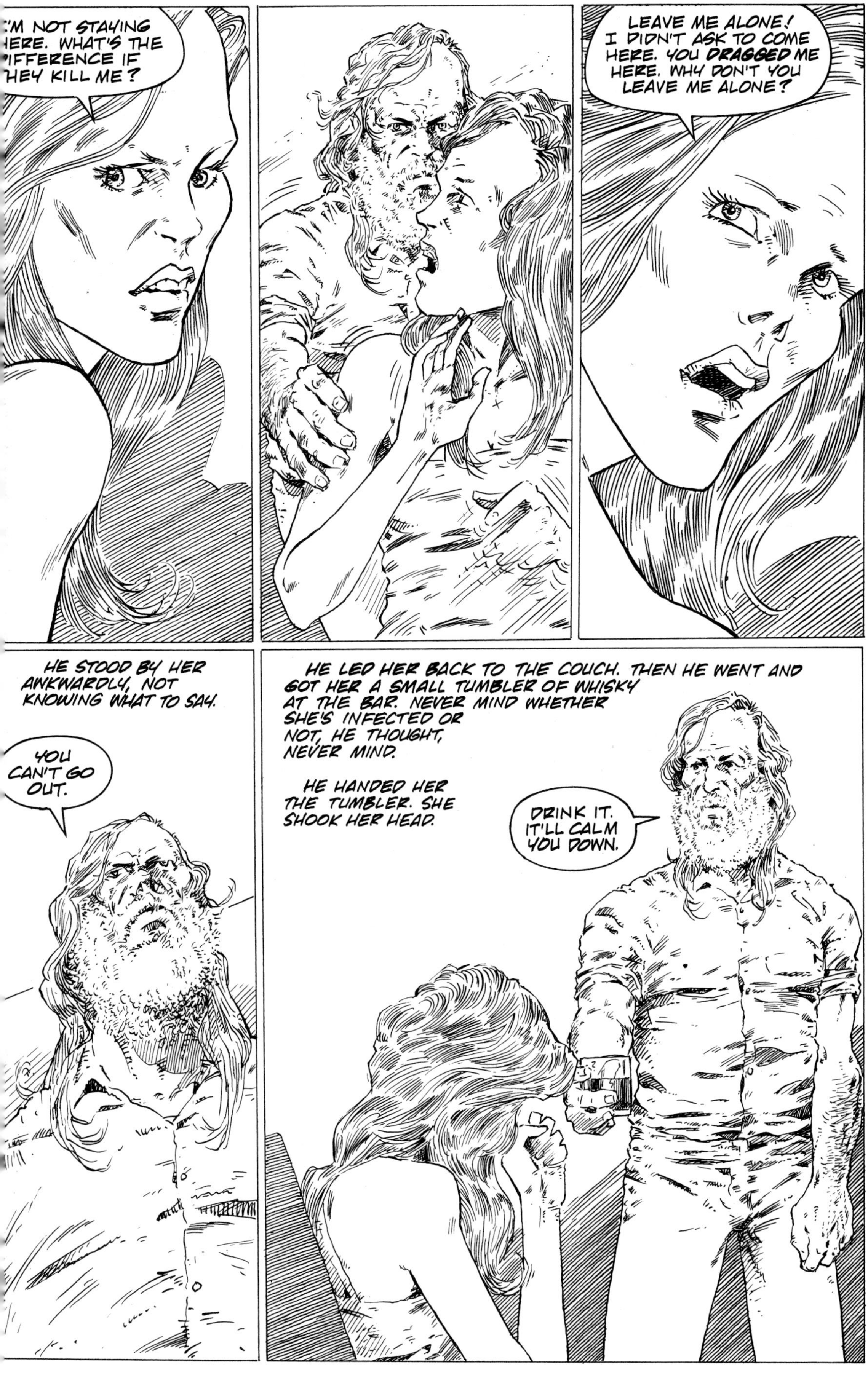
I'M NOT STAYING HERE. WHAT'S THE DIFFERENCE IF THEY KILL ME?
LEAVE ME ALONE! I DIDN'T ASK TO COME HERE. YOU DRAGGED ME HERE. WHY DON'T YOU LEAVE ME ALONE?
HE STOOD BY HER AWKWARDLY, NOT KNOWING WHAT TO SAY.
YOU CAN'T GO OUT.
HE LED HER BACK TO THE COUCH. THEN HE WENT AND GOT HER A SMALL TUMBLER OF WHISKY AT THE BAR. NEVER MIND WHETHER SHE'S INFECTED OR NOT, HE THOUGHT, NEVER MIND.
HE HANDED HER THE TUMBLER. SHE SHOOK HER HEAD.
DRINK IT. IT'LL CALM YOU DOWN.

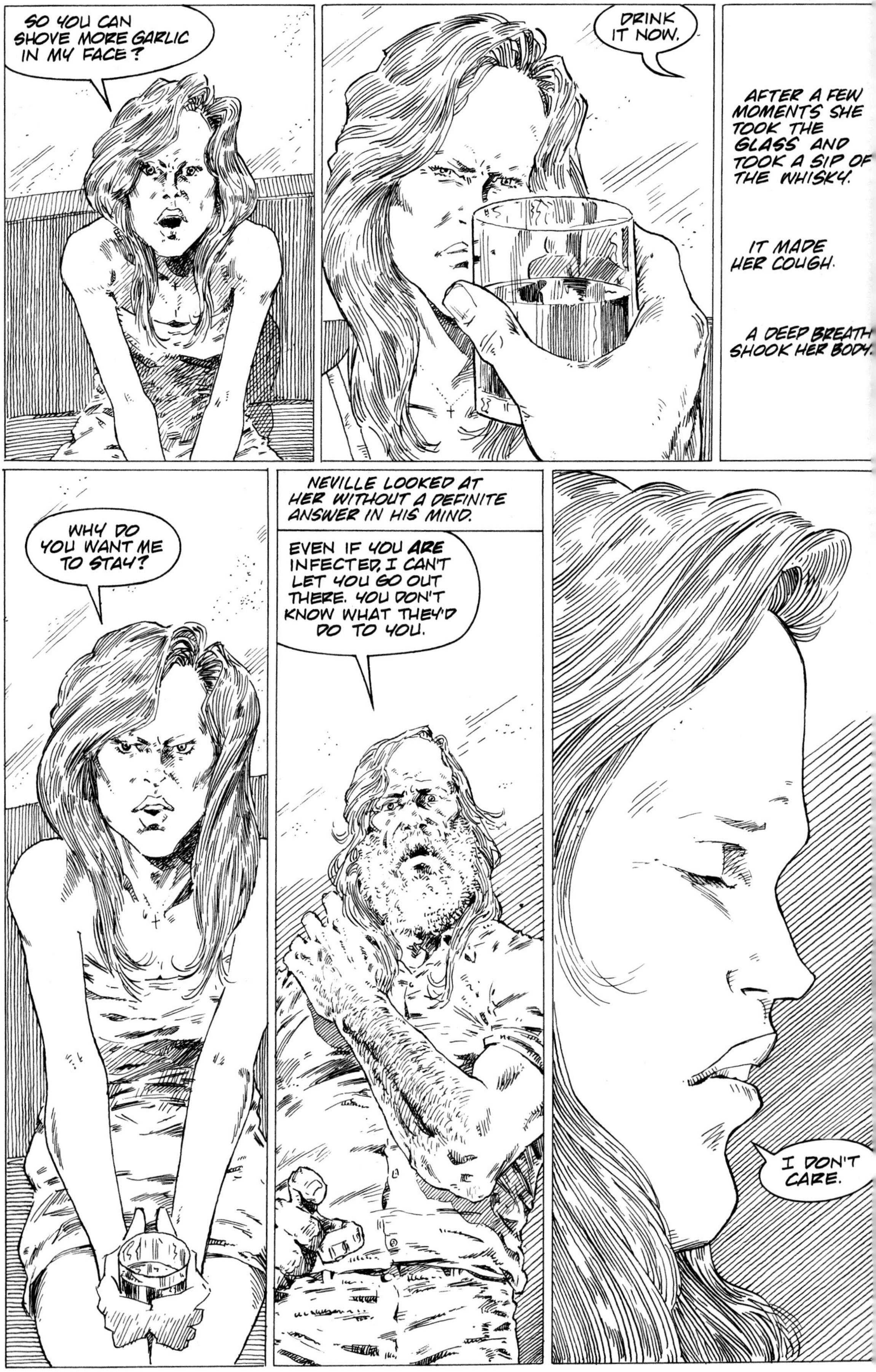
SO YOU CAN SHOVE MORE GARLIC IN MY FACE?
DRINK IT NOW.
AFTER A FEW MOMENTS SHE TOOK THE GLASS AND TOOK A SIP OF THE WHISKY.
IT MADE HER COUGH.
A DEEP BREATH SHOOK HER BODY.
WHY DO YOU WANT ME TO STAY?
NEVILLE LOOKED AT HER WITHOUT A DEFINITE ANSWER IN HIS MIND.
EVEN IF YOU ARE INFECTED, I CAN'T LET YOU GO OUT THERE. YOU DON'T KNOW WHAT THEY'D DO TO YOU.
I DON'T CARE.

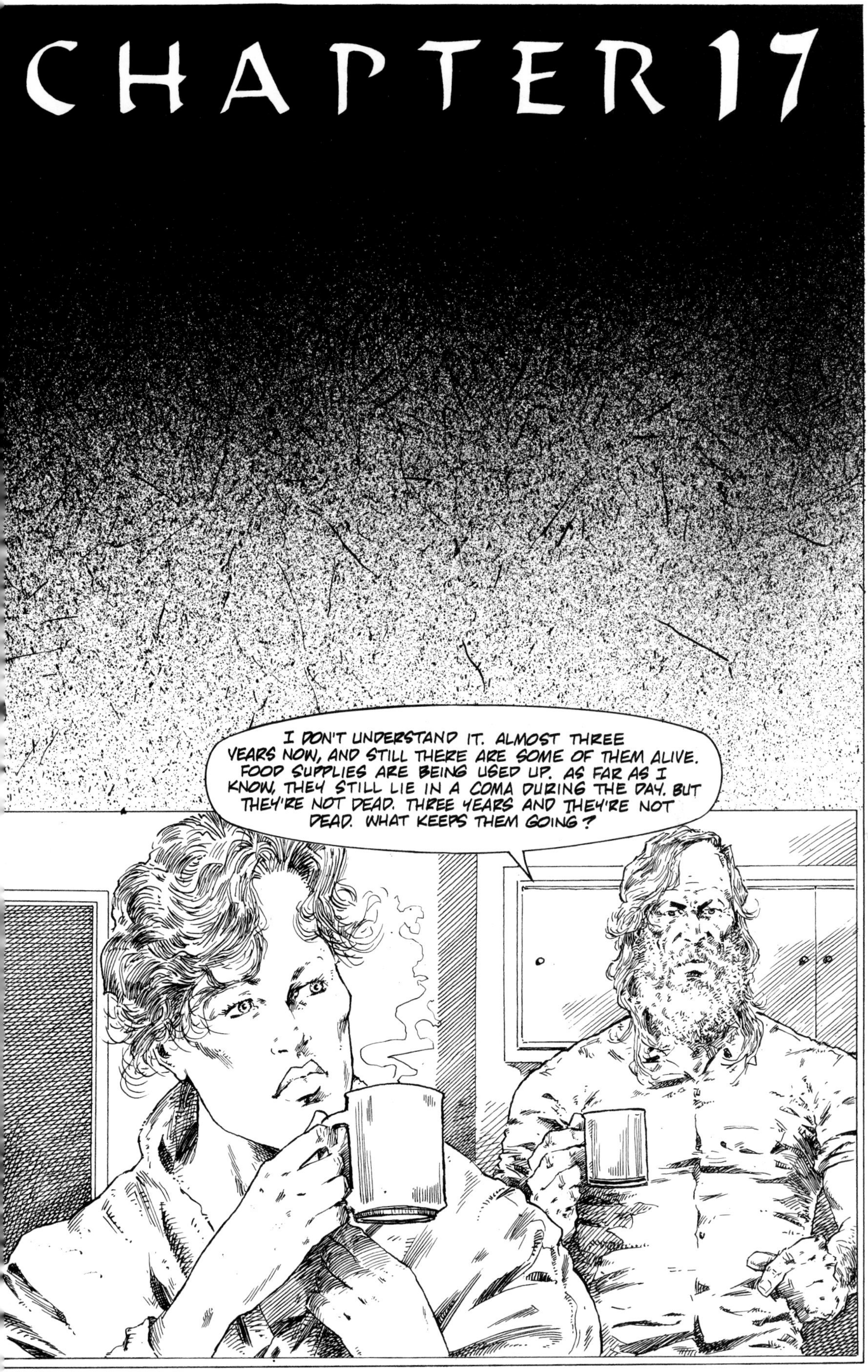
CHAPTER 17
I DON'T UNDERSTAND IT. ALMOST THREE YEARS NOW, AND STILL THERE ARE SOME OF THEM ALIVE. FOOD SUPPLIES ARE BEING USED UP. AS FAR AS I KNOW, THEY STILL LIE IN A COMA DURING THE DAY. BUT THEY'RE NOT DEAD. THREE YEARS AND THEY'RE NOT DEAD. WHAT KEEPS THEM GOING?

ROBERT NEVILLE AND RUTH HAD FINISHED SUPPER AND WERE DRINKING COFFEE. SHE WAS WEARING HIS BATHROBE. ABOUT FIVE O'CLOCK SHE HAD RELENTED, TAKEN A BATH, AND CHANGED. HER SLENDER BODY WAS SHAPELESS IN THE VOLUMINOUS FOLDS. SHE'D BORROWED HIS COMB AND DRAWN HER HAIR BACK INTO A PONY TAIL FASTENED WITH A PIECE OF TWINE.

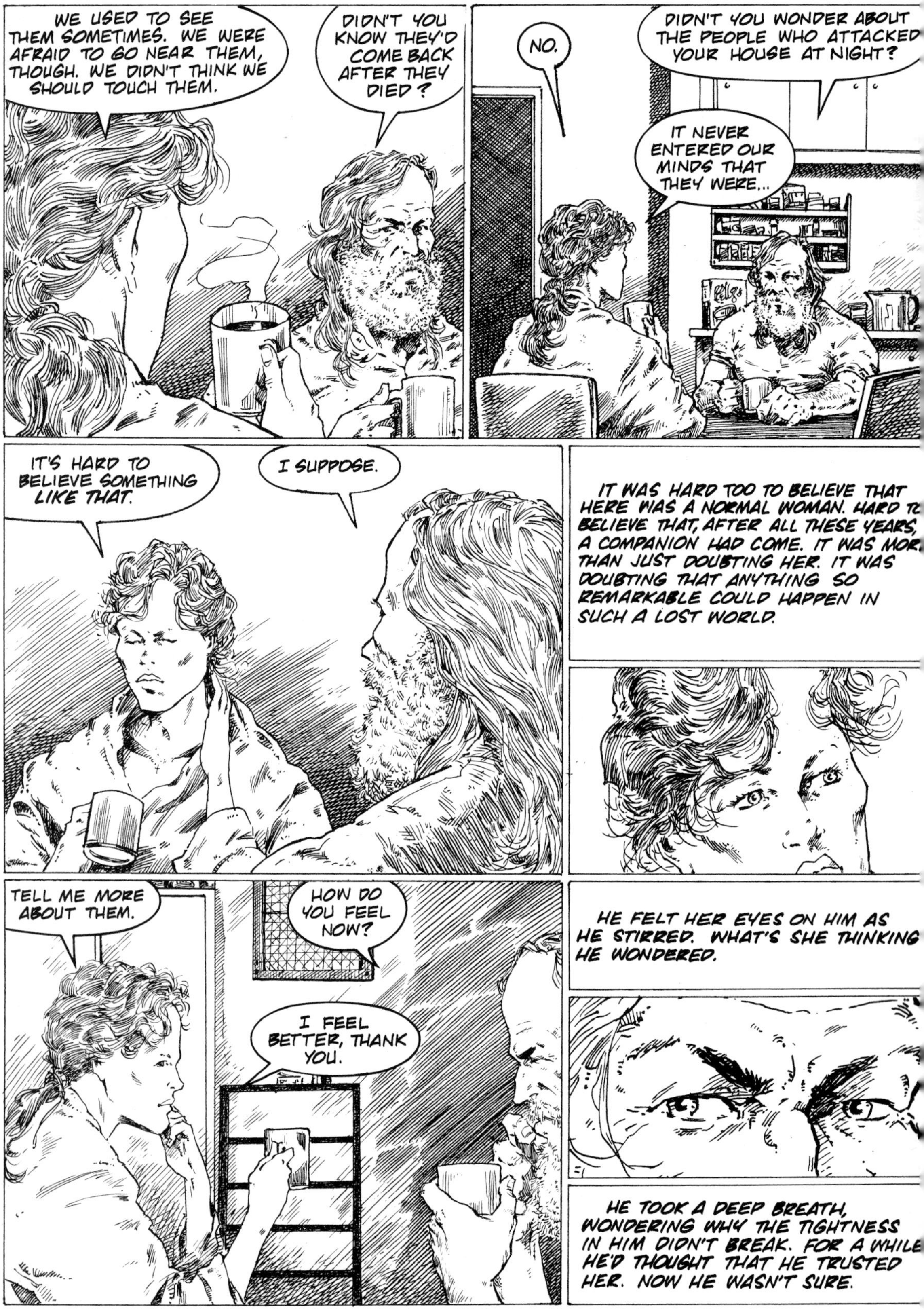

WE USED TO SEE THEM SOMETIMES. WE WERE AFRAID TO GO NEAR THEM, THOUGH. WE DIDN'T THINK WE SHOULD TOUCH THEM.
DIDN'T YOU KNOW THEY'D COME BACK AFTER THEY DIED?
NO.
DIDN'T YOU WONDER ABOUT THE PEOPLE WHO ATTACKED YOUR HOUSE AT NIGHT?
IT NEVER ENTERED OUR MINDS THAT THEY WERE...
IT'S HARD TO BELIEVE SOMETHING LIKE THAT.
I SUPPOSE.
IT WAS HARD TOO TO BELIEVE THAT HERE WAS A NORMAL WOMAN. HARD T BELIEVE THAT, AFTER ALL THESE YEARS, A COMPANION HAD COME. IT WAS MOR THAN JUST DOUBTING HER. IT WAS DOUBTING THAT ANYTHING SO REMARKABLE COULD HAPPEN IN SUCH A LOST WORLD.
TELL ME MORE ABOUT THEM.
HOW DO YOU FEEL NOW?
I FEEL BETTER, THANK YOU.
HE FELT HER EYES ON HIM AS HE STIRRED. WHAT'S SHE THINKING HE WONDERED.
HE TOOK A DEEP BREATH, WONDERING WHY THE TIGHTNESS IN HIM DIDN'T BREAK. FOR A WHILE HE'D THOUGHT THAT HE TRUSTED HER. NOW HE WASN'T SURE.

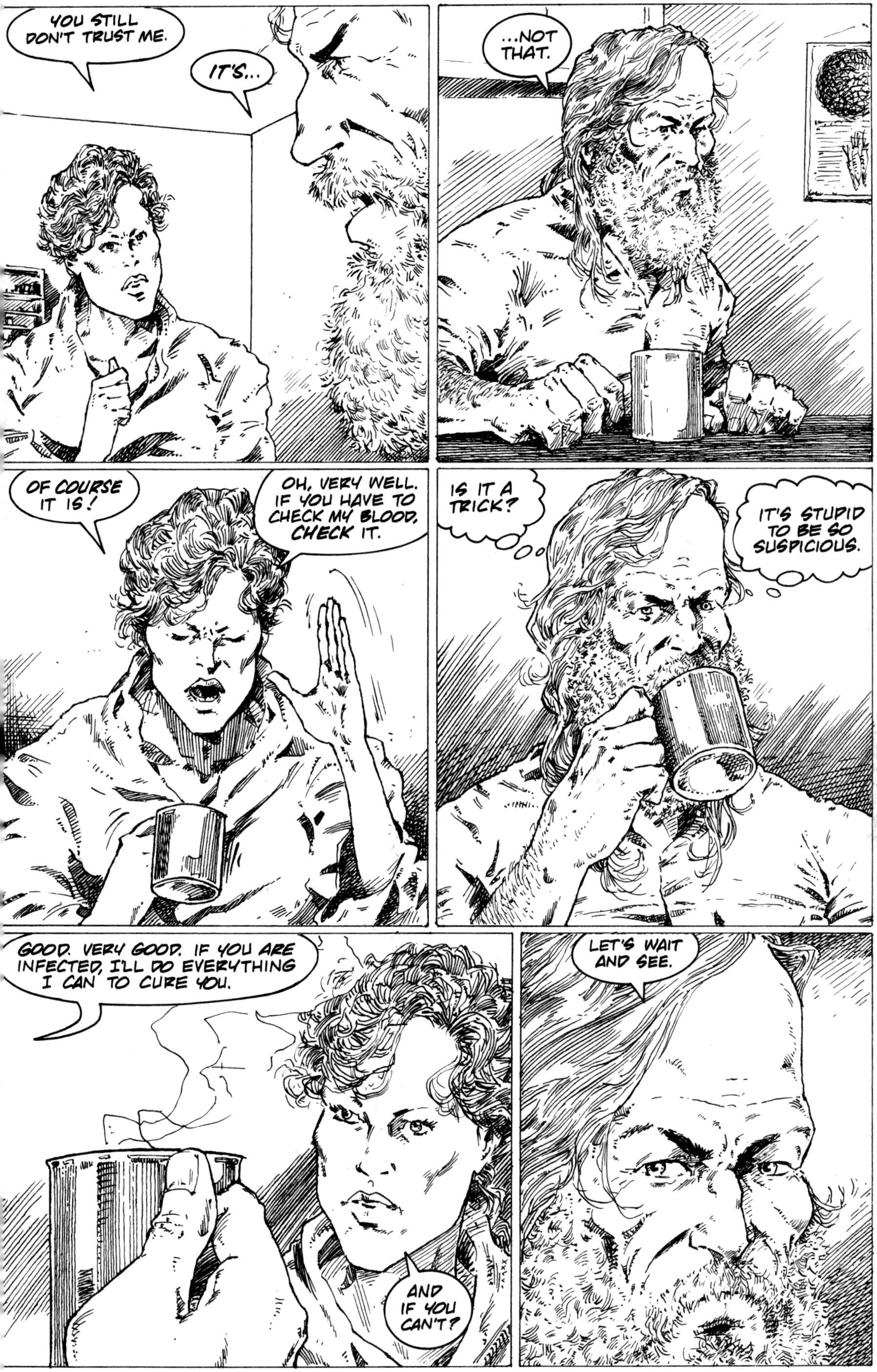
YOU STILL DON'T TRUST ME.
IT'S...
...NOT THAT.
OF COURSE IT IS!
OH, VERY WELL. IF YOU HAVE TO CHECK MY BLOOD, CHECK IT.
IS IT A TRICK?
IT'S STUPID TO BE SO SUSPICIOUS.
GOOD. VERY GOOD. IF YOU ARE INFECTED, I'LL DO EVERYTHING I CAN TO CURE YOU.
AND IF YOU CAN'T?
LET'S WAIT AND SEE.

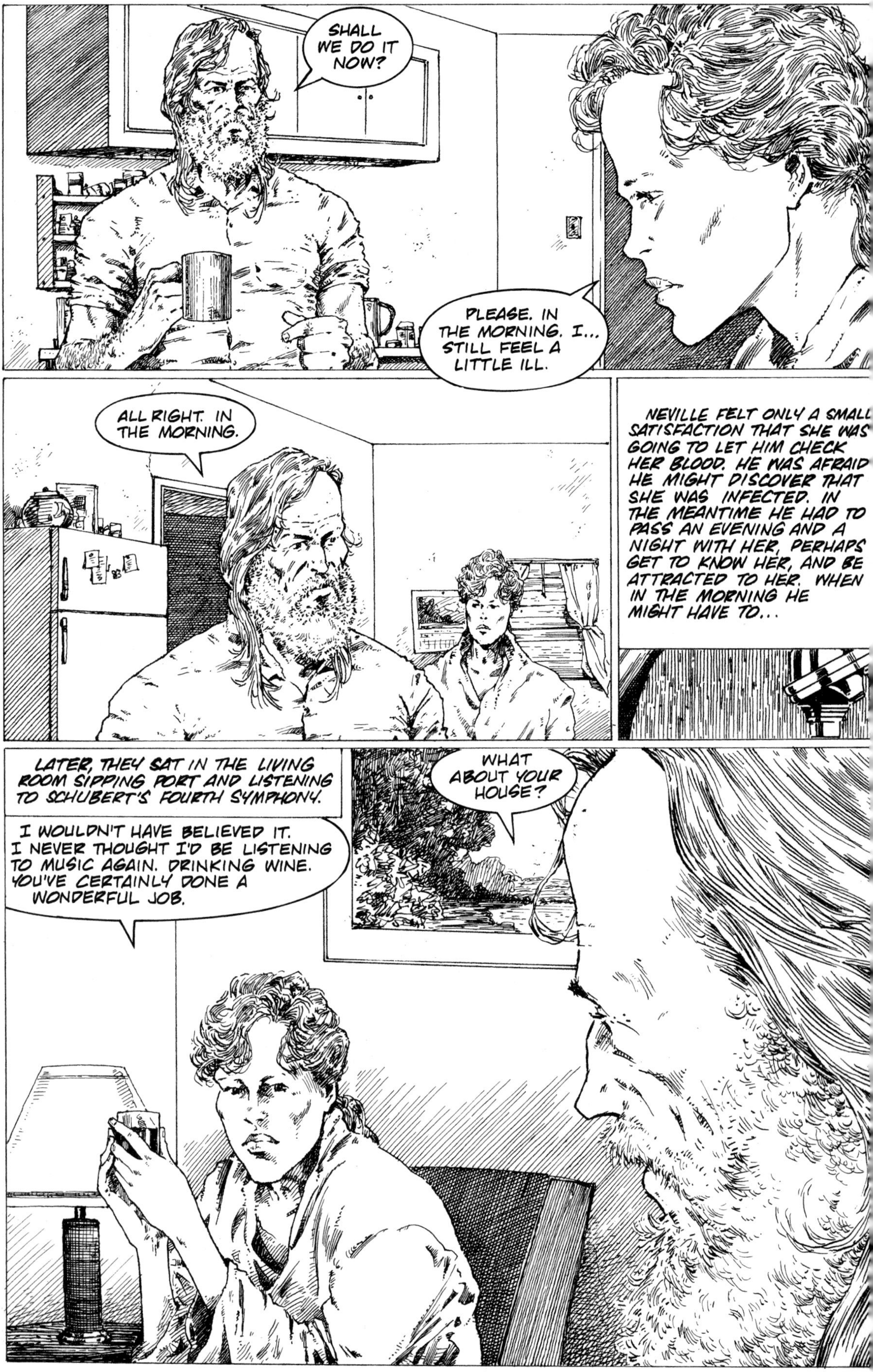
SHALL WE DO IT NOW?
PLEASE. IN THE MORNING. I... STILL FEEL A LITTLE ILL.
ALL RIGHT. IN THE MORNING.
NEVILLE FELT ONLY A SMALL SATISFACTION THAT SHE WAS GOING TO LET HIM CHECK HER BLOOD. HE WAS AFRAID HE MIGHT DISCOVER THAT SHE WAS INFECTED. IN THE MEANTIME HE HAD TO PASS AN EVENING AND A NIGHT WITH HER, PERHAPS GET TO KNOW HER, AND BE ATTRACTED TO HER. WHEN IN THE MORNING HE MIGHT HAVE TO...
LATER, THEY SAT IN THE LIVING ROOM SIPPING PORT AND LISTENING TO SCHUBERT'S FOURTH SYMPHONY.
I WOULDN'T HAVE BELIEVED IT. I NEVER THOUGHT I'D BE LISTENING TO MUSIC AGAIN. DRINKING WINE. YOU'VE CERTAINLY DONE A WONDERFUL JOB.
WHAT ABOUT YOUR HOUSE?

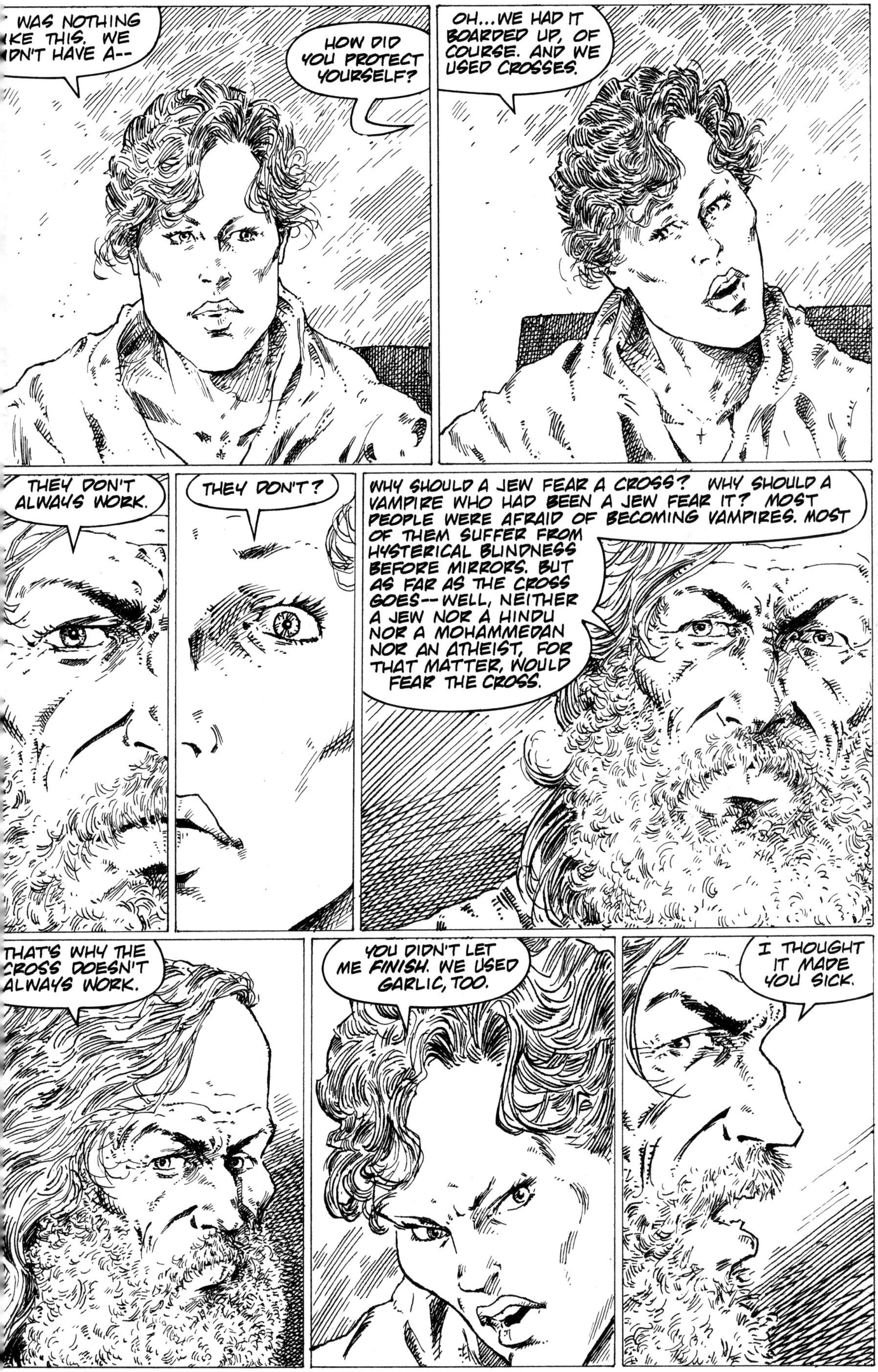
WAS NOTHING
KE THIS. WE
DN'T HAVE A--
HOW DID YOU PROTECT YOURSELF?
OH...WE HAD IT BOARDED UP, OF COURSE. AND WE USED CROSSES.
THEY DON'T ALWAYS WORK.
THEY DON'T?
WHY SHOULD A JEW FEAR A CROSS? WHY SHOULD A VAMPIRE WHO HAD BEEN A JEW FEAR IT? MOST PEOPLE WERE AFRAID OF BECOMING VAMPIRES. MOST OF THEM SUFFER FROM HYSTERICAL BLINDNESS BEFORE MIRRORS. BUT AS FAR AS THE CROSS GOES--WELL, NEITHER A JEW NOR A HINDU NOR A MOHAMMEDAN NOR AN ATHEIST, FOR THAT MATTER, WOULD FEAR THE CROSS.
THAT'S WHY THE CROSS DOESN'T ALWAYS WORK.
YOU DIDN'T LET ME FINISH. WE USED GARLIC, TOO.
I THOUGHT IT MADE YOU SICK.

I WAS ALREADY SICK. I USED TO WEIGH A HUNDRED AND TWENTY. I WEIGH NINETY-EIGHT POUNDS NOW.

HE NODDED. BUT AS HE WENT INTO THE KITCHEN TO GET ANOTHER BOTTLE OF WINE, HE THOUGHT...

SHE WOULD HAVE ADJUSTED TO IT BY NOW. AFTER THREE YEARS. THEN AGAIN, SHE MIGHT NOT HAVE. WHAT'S THE POINT IN DOUBTING HER NOW? SHE'S GOING TO LET ME CHECK HER BLOOD. WHAT ELSE CAN SHE DO?

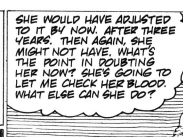

IT'S ME. I'VE BEEN BY MYSELF TOO LONG. I WON'T BELIEVE ANYTHING UNLESS I SEE IT IN A MICROSCOPE. HEREDITY TRIUMPHS AGAIN. I'M MY FATHER'S SON, DAMN HIS MOLDERING BONES.

STANDING IN THE DARK KITCHEN, DIGGING HIS BLUNT NAIL UNDER THE WRAPPING AROUND THE NECK OF THE BOTTLE, ROBERT NEVILLE LOOKED INTO THE LIVING ROOM AT RUTH.

HIS EYES RAN OVER THE ROBE, RESTING A MOMENT ON THE SLIGHT PROMINENCE OF HER BREASTS, DROPPING THEN TO THE BRONZED CALVES AND ANKLES, UP TO THE SMOOTH KNEECAPS. SHE HAD A BODY LIKE A YOUNG GIRL'S. SHE CERTAINLY DIDN'T LOOK LIKE THE MOTHER OF TWO.

THE MOST UNUSUAL FEATURE OF THE ENTIRE AFFAIR, HE THOUGHT, WAS THAT HE FELT NO PHYSICAL DESIRE FOR HER.

IF SHE HAD COME TWO YEARS BEFORE, MAYBE EVEN LATER, HE MIGHT HAVE VIOLATED HER.

THERE HAD BEEN SOME TERRIBLE MOMENTS IN THOSE DAYS, MOMENTS WHEN THE MOST TERRIBLE SOLUTIONS TO HIS NEED WERE CONSIDERED, WERE OFTEN DWELT UPON UNTIL THEY DROVE HIM HALF MAD.

BUT THEN THE EXPERIMENTS HAD BEGUN. SMOKING HAD TAPERED OFF, DRINKING LOST ITS COMPULSIVE NATURE. DELIBERATELY AND WITH SURPRISING SUCCESS, HE HAD SUBMERGED HIMSELF IN INVESTIGATION.

HIS SEX DRIVE HAD DIMINISHED, HAD VIRTUALLY DISAPPEARED. SALVATION OF THE MONK, HE THOUGHT. THE DRIVE HAD TO GO SOONER OR LATER, OR NO NORMAL MAN COULD DEDICATE HIMSELF TO ANY LIFE THAT EXCLUDED SEX.

NOW, HAPPILY, HE FELT ALMOST NOTHING; PERHAPS A HARDLY DISCERNIBLE STIRRING FAR BENEATH THE ROCKY STRATA OF ABSTINENCE. HE WAS CONTENT TO LEAVE IT AT THAT. ESPECIALLY SINCE THERE WAS NO CERTAINTY THAT RUTH WAS THE COMPANION HE HAD WAITED FOR. OR EVEN THE CERTAINTY THAT HE COULD ALLOW HER TO LIVE BEYOND TOMORROW.

CURE HER?

CURING WAS UNLIKELY.

HE WENT BACK INTO THE LIVING ROOM WITH THE OPENED BOTTLE. SHE SMILED AT HIM BRIEFLY AS HE POURED MORE WINE FOR HER.

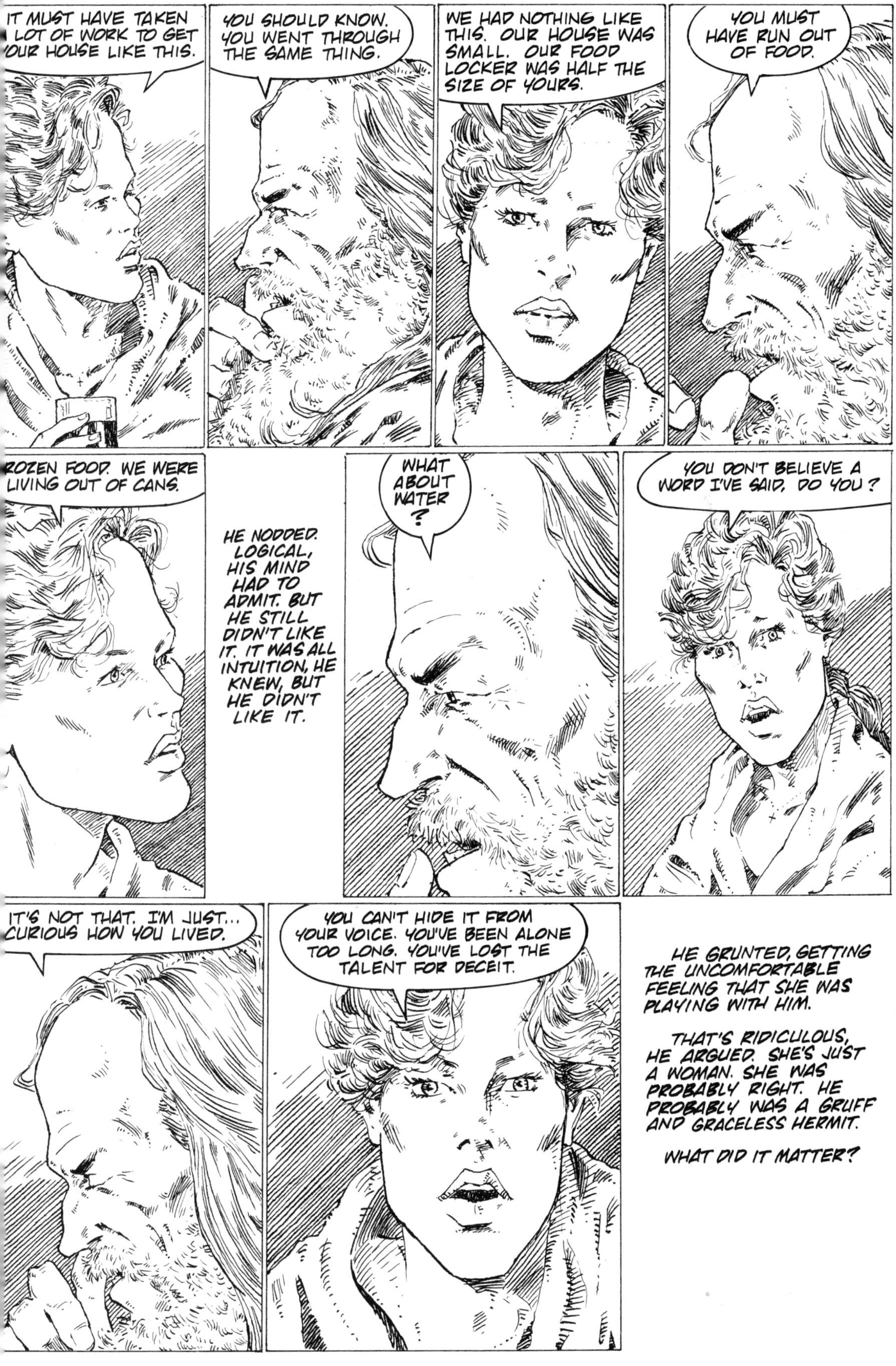

IT MUST HAVE TAKEN LOT OF WORK TO GET OUR HOUSE LIKE THIS.
YOU SHOULD KNOW. YOU WENT THROUGH THE SAME THING.
WE HAD NOTHING LIKE THIS. OUR HOUSE WAS SMALL. OUR FOOD LOCKER WAS HALF THE SIZE OF YOURS.
YOU MUST HAVE RUN OUT OF FOOD.
ROZEN FOOD. WE WERE LIVING OUT OF CANS.
HE NODDED. LOGICAL, HIS MIND HAD TO ADMIT. BUT HE STILL DIDN'T LIKE IT. IT WAS ALL INTUITION, HE KNEW, BUT HE DIDN'T LIKE IT.
WHAT ABOUT WATER ?
YOU DON'T BELIEVE A WORD I'VE SAID, DO YOU ?
IT'S NOT THAT. I'M JUST... CURIOUS HOW YOU LIVED.
YOU CAN'T HIDE IT FROM YOUR VOICE. YOU'VE BEEN ALONE TOO LONG. YOU'VE LOST THE TALENT FOR DECEIT.
HE GRUNTED, GETTING THE UNCOMFORTABLE FEELING THAT SHE WAS PLAYING WITH HIM.
THAT'S RIDICULOUS, HE ARGUED. SHE'S JUST A WOMAN. SHE WAS PROBABLY RIGHT. HE PROBABLY WAS A GRUFF AND GRACELESS HERMIT.
WHAT DID IT MATTER?

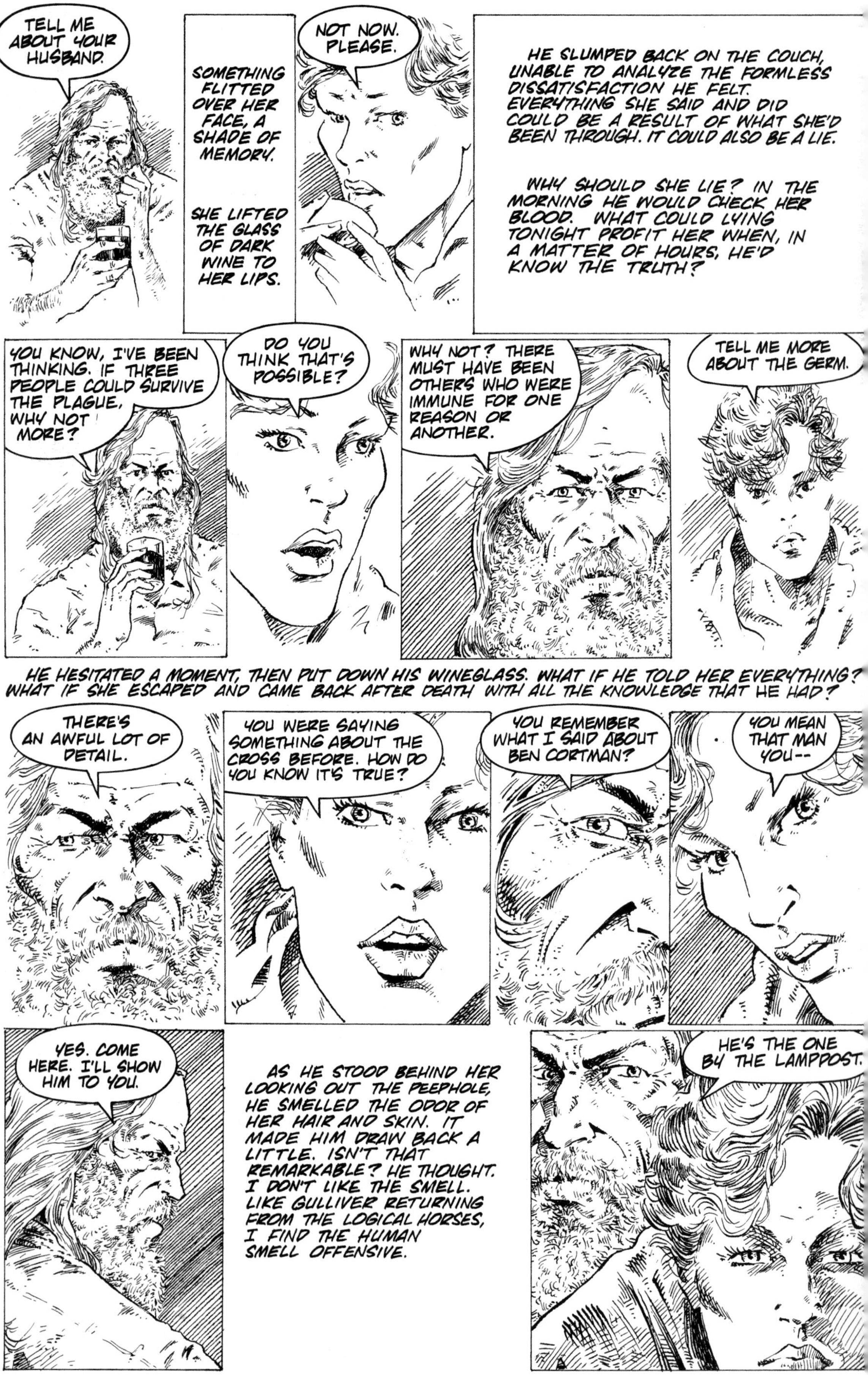
TELL ME ABOUT YOUR HUSBAND.
SOMETHING FLITTED OVER HER FACE, A SHADE OF MEMORY.
SHE LIFTED THE GLASS OF DARK WINE TO HER LIPS.
NOT NOW. PLEASE.
HE SLUMPED BACK ON THE COUCH, UNABLE TO ANALYZE THE FORMLESS DISSATISFACTION HE FELT. EVERYTHING SHE SAID AND DID COULD BE A RESULT OF WHAT SHE'D BEEN THROUGH. IT COULD ALSO BE A LIE.
WHY SHOULD SHE LIE? IN THE MORNING HE WOULD CHECK HER BLOOD. WHAT COULD LYING TONIGHT PROFIT HER WHEN, IN A MATTER OF HOURS, HE'D KNOW THE TRUTH?
YOU KNOW, I'VE BEEN THINKING. IF THREE PEOPLE COULD SURVIVE THE PLAGUE, WHY NOT MORE?
DO YOU THINK THAT'S POSSIBLE?
WHY NOT? THERE MUST HAVE BEEN OTHERS WHO WERE IMMUNE FOR ONE REASON OR ANOTHER.
TELL ME MORE ABOUT THE GERM.
HE HESITATED A MOMENT, THEN PUT DOWN HIS WINEGLASS. WHAT IF HE TOLD HER EVERYTHING? WHAT IF SHE ESCAPED AND CAME BACK AFTER DEATH WITH ALL THE KNOWLEDGE THAT HE HAD?
THERE'S AN AWFUL LOT OF DETAIL.
YOU WERE SAYING SOMETHING ABOUT THE CROSS BEFORE. HOW DO YOU KNOW IT'S TRUE?
YOU REMEMBER WHAT I SAID ABOUT BEN CORTMAN?
YOU MEAN THAT MAN YOU--
YES. COME HERE. I'LL SHOW HIM TO YOU.
AS HE STOOD BEHIND HER LOOKING OUT THE PEEPHOLE, HE SMELLED THE ODOR OF HER HAIR AND SKIN. IT MADE HIM DRAW BACK A LITTLE. ISN'T THAT REMARKABLE? HE THOUGHT. I DON'T LIKE THE SMELL. LIKE GULLIVER RETURNING FROM THE LOGICAL HORSES, I FIND THE HUMAN SMELL OFFENSIVE.
HE'S THE ONE BY THE LAMPPOST.

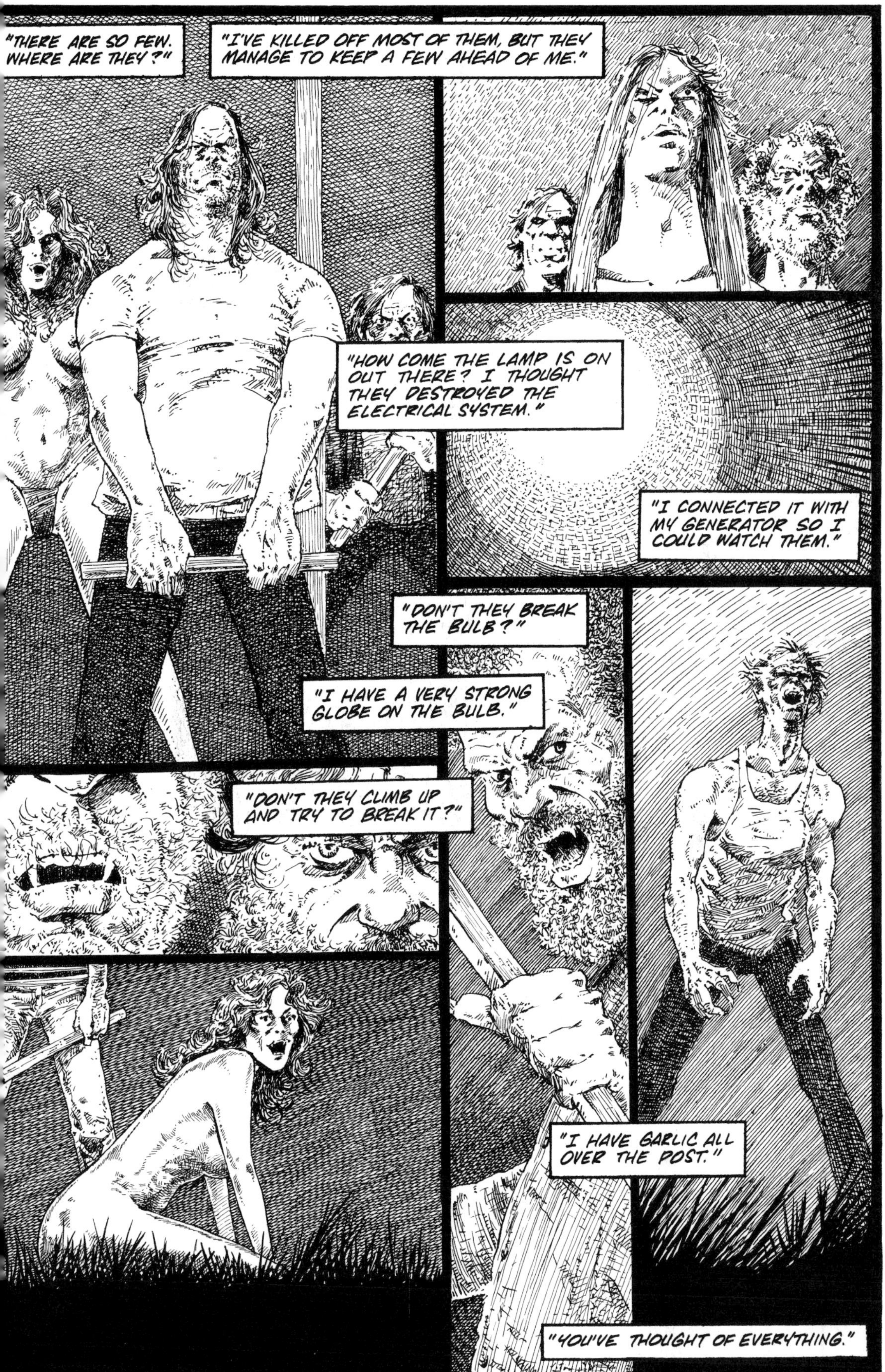
"THERE ARE SO FEW. WHERE ARE THEY?"
"I'VE KILLED OFF MOST OF THEM, BUT THEY MANAGE TO KEEP A FEW AHEAD OF ME."
"HOW COME THE LAMP IS ON OUT THERE? I THOUGHT THEY DESTROYED THE ELECTRICAL SYSTEM."
"I CONNECTED IT WITH MY GENERATOR SO I COULD WATCH THEM."
"DON'T THEY BREAK THE BULB?"
"I HAVE A VERY STRONG GLOBE ON THE BULB."
"DON'T THEY CLIMB UP AND TRY TO BREAK IT?"
"I HAVE GARLIC ALL OVER THE POST."
"YOU'VE THOUGHT OF EVERYTHING."

STEPPING BACK, HE LOOKED AT HER A MOMENT. HOW CAN SHE LOOK AT THEM SO CALMLY, HE WONDERED. ASK ME QUESTIONS, MAKE COMMENTS, WHEN ONLY A WEEK AGO SHE SAW THEIR KIND TEAR HER HUSBAND TO PIECES? DOUBTS AGAIN, HE THOUGHT. WON'T THEY EVER STOP?

HE KNEW THEY WOULDN'T UNTIL HE KNEW ABOUT HER FOR SURE.

SHE TURNED AWAY FROM THE WINDOW THEN.

WILL YOU EXCUSE ME A MOMENT?

HE WATCHED HER WALK INTO THE BATHROOM AND HEARD HER LOCK THE DOOR BEHIND HER. THEN HE WENT BACK TO THE COUCH AFTER CLOSING THE PEEPHOLE DOOR. A WRY SMILE PLAYED ON HIS LIPS. HE LOOKED DOWN INTO THE TAWNY WINE DEPTHS AND TUGGED ABSTRACTEDLY AT HIS BEARD.

"WILL YOU EXCUSE ME A MOMENT?"

FOR SOME REASON THE WORDS SEEMED GROTESQUELY AMUSING, THE CARRY-OVER FROM A LOST AGE. EMILY POST MINCING THROUGH THE GRAVEYARD. ETIQUETTE FOR YOUNG VAMPIRES.

THE SMILE WAS GONE.

AND WHAT NOW? WHAT DID THE FUTURE HOLD FOR HIM? IN A WEEK WOULD SHE STILL BE HERE WITH HIM, OR CRUMPLED IN THE NEVER COOLING FIRE?

HE KNEW THAT IF SHE WERE INFECTED, HE'D HAVE TO TRY TO CURE HER WHETHER IT WORKED OR NOT. BUT WHAT IF SHE WERE FREE OF THE BACILLUS? IN A WAY, THAT WAS A MORE NERVE-RACKING POSSIBILITY. THE OTHER WAY HE WOULD MERELY GO ON AS BEFORE, BREAKING NEITHER SCHEDULE NOR STANDARDS. BUT IF SHE STAYED, IF THEY HAD TO ESTABLISH A RELATIONSHIP, PERHAPS BECOME HUSBAND AND WIFE, HAVE CHILDREN...

YES, THAT WAS MORE TERRIFYING.

HE SUDDENLY REALIZED THAT HE HAD BECOME AN ILL-TEMPERED AND INVETERATE BACHELOR AGAIN. HE NO LONGER THOUGHT ABOUT HIS WIFE, HIS CHILD, HIS PAST LIFE. THE PRESENT WAS ENOUGH. AND HE WAS AFRAID OF THE POSSIBLE DEMAND THAT HE MAKE SACRIFICES AND ACCEPT RESPONSIBILITY AGAIN. HE WAS AFRAID OF GIVING OUT HIS HEART, OF REMOVING THE CHAINS HE HAD FORGED AROUND IT TO KEEP EMOTION PRISONER. HE WAS AFRAID OF LOVING AGAIN.

WHEN SHE CAME OUT OF THE BATHROOM HE WAS STILL SITTING THERE, THINKING. THE RECORD PLAYER, UNNOTICED BY HIM, LET OUT ONLY A THIN SCRATCHING SOUND.

RUTH LIFTED THE RECORD FROM THE TURNTABLE AND TURNED IT. THE THIRD MOVEMENT OF THE SYMPHONY BEGAN.

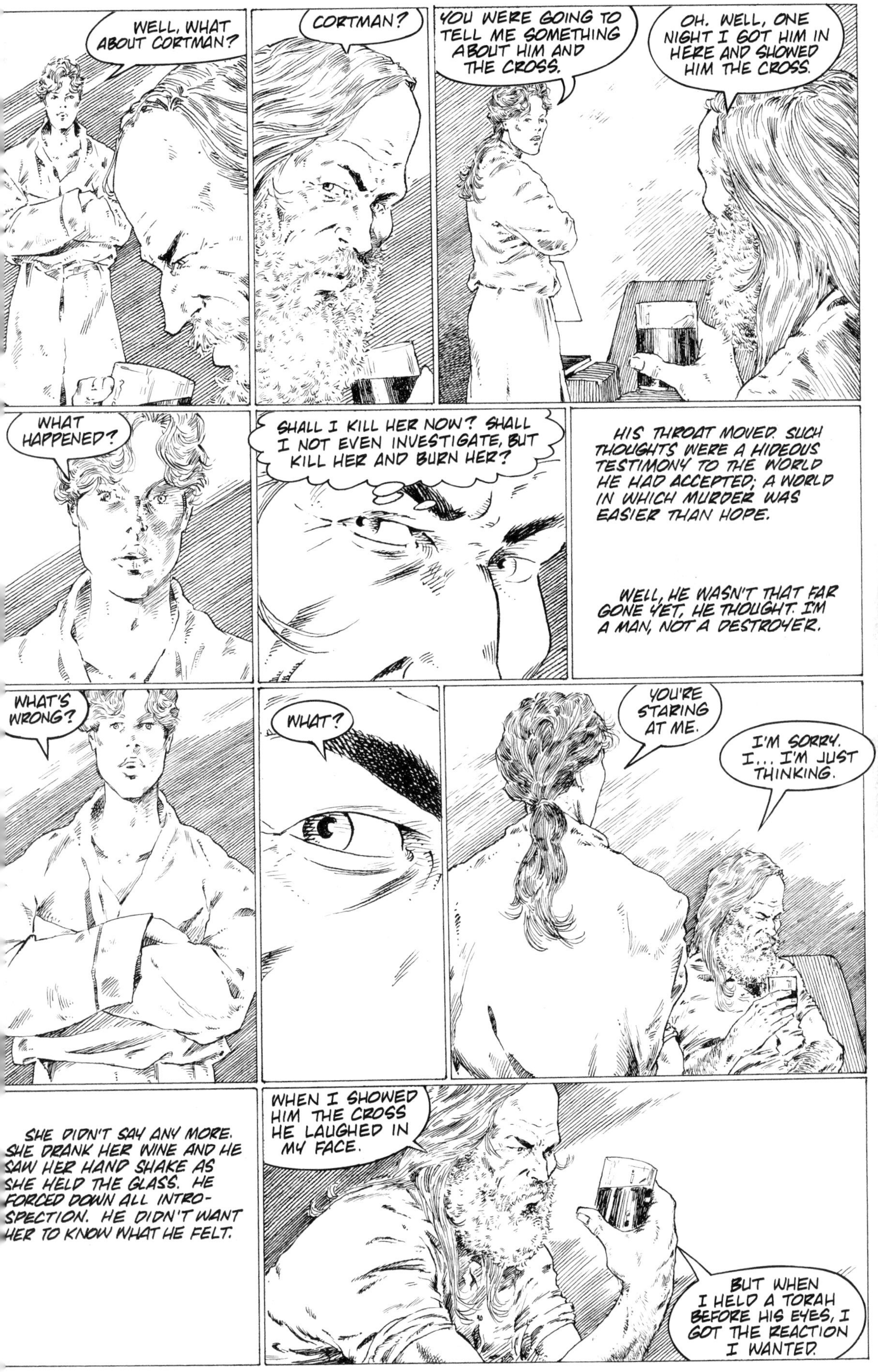
WELL, WHAT ABOUT CORTMAN?
CORTMAN?
YOU WERE GOING TO TELL ME SOMETHING ABOUT HIM AND THE CROSS.
OH. WELL, ONE NIGHT I GOT HIM IN HERE AND SHOWED HIM THE CROSS.
WHAT HAPPENED?
SHALL I KILL HER NOW? SHALL I NOT EVEN INVESTIGATE, BUT KILL HER AND BURN HER?
HIS THROAT MOVED. SUCH THOUGHTS WERE A HIDEOUS TESTIMONY TO THE WORLD HE HAD ACCEPTED; A WORLD IN WHICH MURDER WAS EASIER THAN HOPE.
WELL, HE WASN'T THAT FAR GONE YET, HE THOUGHT. I'M A MAN, NOT A DESTROYER.
WHAT'S WRONG?
WHAT?
YOU'RE STARING AT ME.
I'M SORRY. I... I'M JUST THINKING.
SHE DIDN'T SAY ANY MORE. SHE DRANK HER WINE AND HE SAW HER HAND SHAKE AS SHE HELD THE GLASS. HE FORCED DOWN ALL INTRO-SPECTION. HE DIDN'T WANT HER TO KNOW WHAT HE FELT.
WHEN I SHOWED HIM THE CROSS HE LAUGHED IN MY FACE.
BUT WHEN I HELD A TORAH BEFORE HIS EYES, I GOT THE REACTION I WANTED.

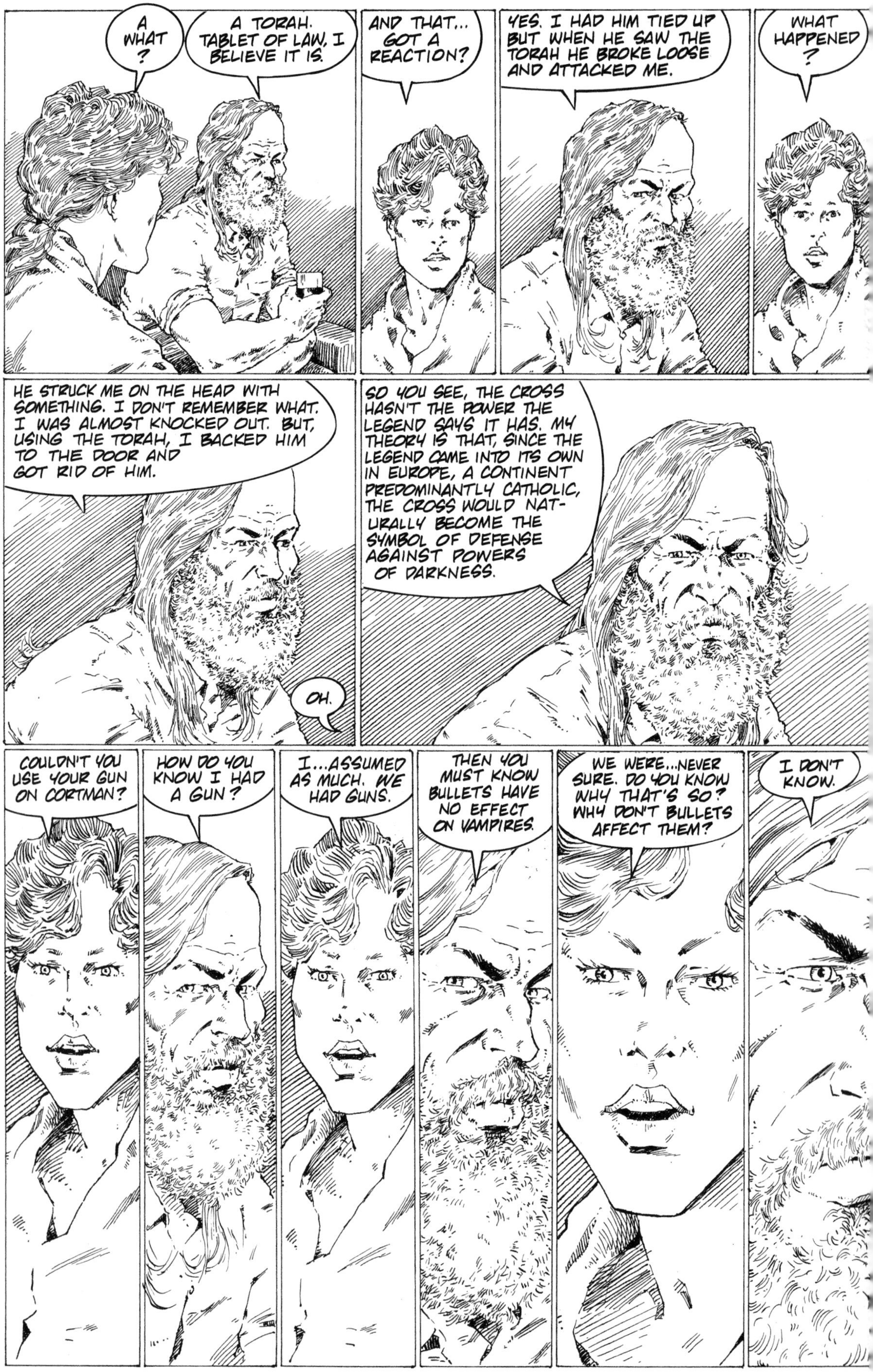
A WHAT ?
A TORAH. TABLET OF LAW, I BELIEVE IT IS.
AND THAT... GOT A REACTION?
YES. I HAD HIM TIED UP BUT WHEN HE SAW THE TORAH HE BROKE LOOSE AND ATTACKED ME.
WHAT HAPPENED ?
HE STRUCK ME ON THE HEAD WITH SOMETHING. I DON'T REMEMBER WHAT. I WAS ALMOST KNOCKED OUT. BUT, USING THE TORAH, I BACKED HIM TO THE DOOR AND GOT RID OF HIM.
OH.
SO YOU SEE, THE CROSS HASN'T THE POWER THE LEGEND SAYS IT HAS. MY THEORY IS THAT, SINCE THE LEGEND CAME INTO ITS OWN IN EUROPE, A CONTINENT PREDOMINANTLY CATHOLIC, THE CROSS WOULD NATURALLY BECOME THE SYMBOL OF DEFENSE AGAINST POWERS OF DARKNESS.
COULDN'T YOU USE YOUR GUN ON CORTMAN?
HOW DO YOU KNOW I HAD A GUN?
I...ASSUMED AS MUCH. WE HAD GUNS.
THEN YOU MUST KNOW BULLETS HAVE NO EFFECT ON VAMPIRES.
WE WERE...NEVER SURE. DO YOU KNOW WHY THAT'S SO? WHY DON'T BULLETS AFFECT THEM?
I DON'T KNOW.

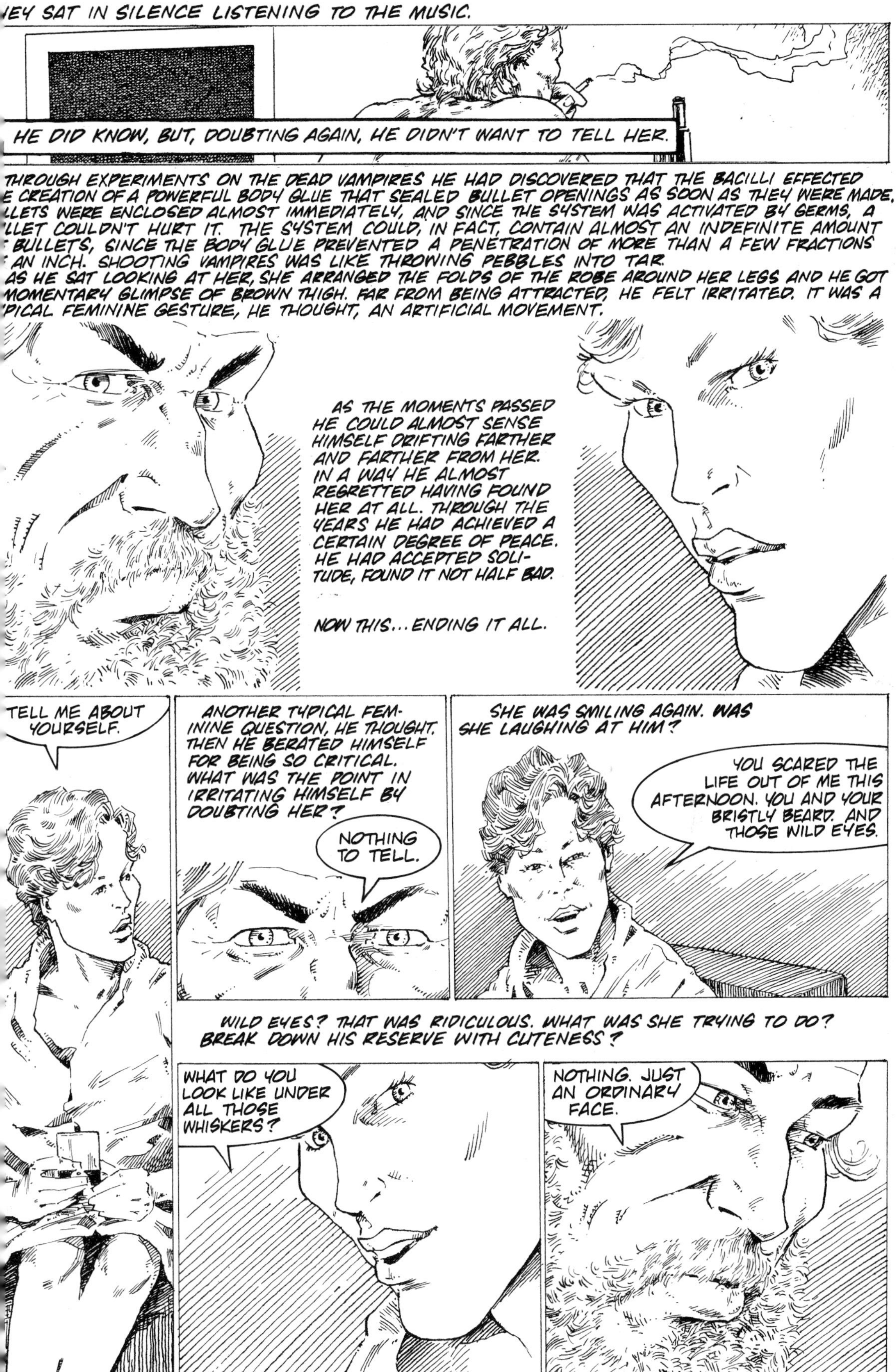

IEY SAT IN SILENCE LISTENING TO THE MUSIC.
HE DID KNOW, BUT, DOUBTING AGAIN, HE DIDN'T WANT TO TELL HER.
THROUGH EXPERIMENTS ON THE DEAD VAMPIRES HE HAD DISCOVERED THAT THE BACILLI EFFECTED
E CREATION OF A POWERFUL BODY GLUE THAT SEALED BULLET OPENINGS AS SOON AS THEY WERE MADE.
LLETS WERE ENCLOSED ALMOST IMMEDIATELY, AND SINCE THE SYSTEM WAS ACTIVATED BY GERMS, A
LLET COULDN'T HURT IT. THE SYSTEM COULD, IN FACT, CONTAIN ALMOST AN INDEFINITE AMOUNT
BULLETS, SINCE THE BODY GLUE PREVENTED A PENETRATION OF MORE THAN A FEW FRACTIONS
AN INCH. SHOOTING VAMPIRES WAS LIKE THROWING PEBBLES INTO TAR.
AS HE SAT LOOKING AT HER, SHE ARRANGED THE FOLDS OF THE ROBE AROUND HER LEGS AND HE GOT
MOMENTARY GLIMPSE OF BROWN THIGH. FAR FROM BEING ATTRACTED, HE FELT IRRITATED. IT WAS A
PICAL FEMININE GESTURE, HE THOUGHT, AN ARTIFICIAL MOVEMENT.
AS THE MOMENTS PASSED HE COULD ALMOST SENSE HIMSELF DRIFTING FARTHER AND FARTHER FROM HER. IN A WAY HE ALMOST REGRETTED HAVING FOUND HER AT ALL. THROUGH THE YEARS HE HAD ACHIEVED A CERTAIN DEGREE OF PEACE. HE HAD ACCEPTED SOLITUDE, FOUND IT NOT HALF BAD.
NOW THIS... ENDING IT ALL.
TELL ME ABOUT YOURSELF.
ANOTHER TYPICAL FEMININE QUESTION, HE THOUGHT. THEN HE BERATED HIMSELF FOR BEING SO CRITICAL. WHAT WAS THE POINT IN IRRITATING HIMSELF BY DOUBTING HER?
NOTHING TO TELL.
SHE WAS SMILING AGAIN. WAS SHE LAUGHING AT HIM?
YOU SCARED THE LIFE OUT OF ME THIS AFTERNOON. YOU AND YOUR BRISTLY BEARD. AND THOSE WILD EYES.
WILD EYES? THAT WAS RIDICULOUS. WHAT WAS SHE TRYING TO DO? BREAK DOWN HIS RESERVE WITH CUTENESS?
WHAT DO YOU LOOK LIKE UNDER ALL THOSE WHISKERS?
NOTHING. JUST AN ORDINARY FACE.

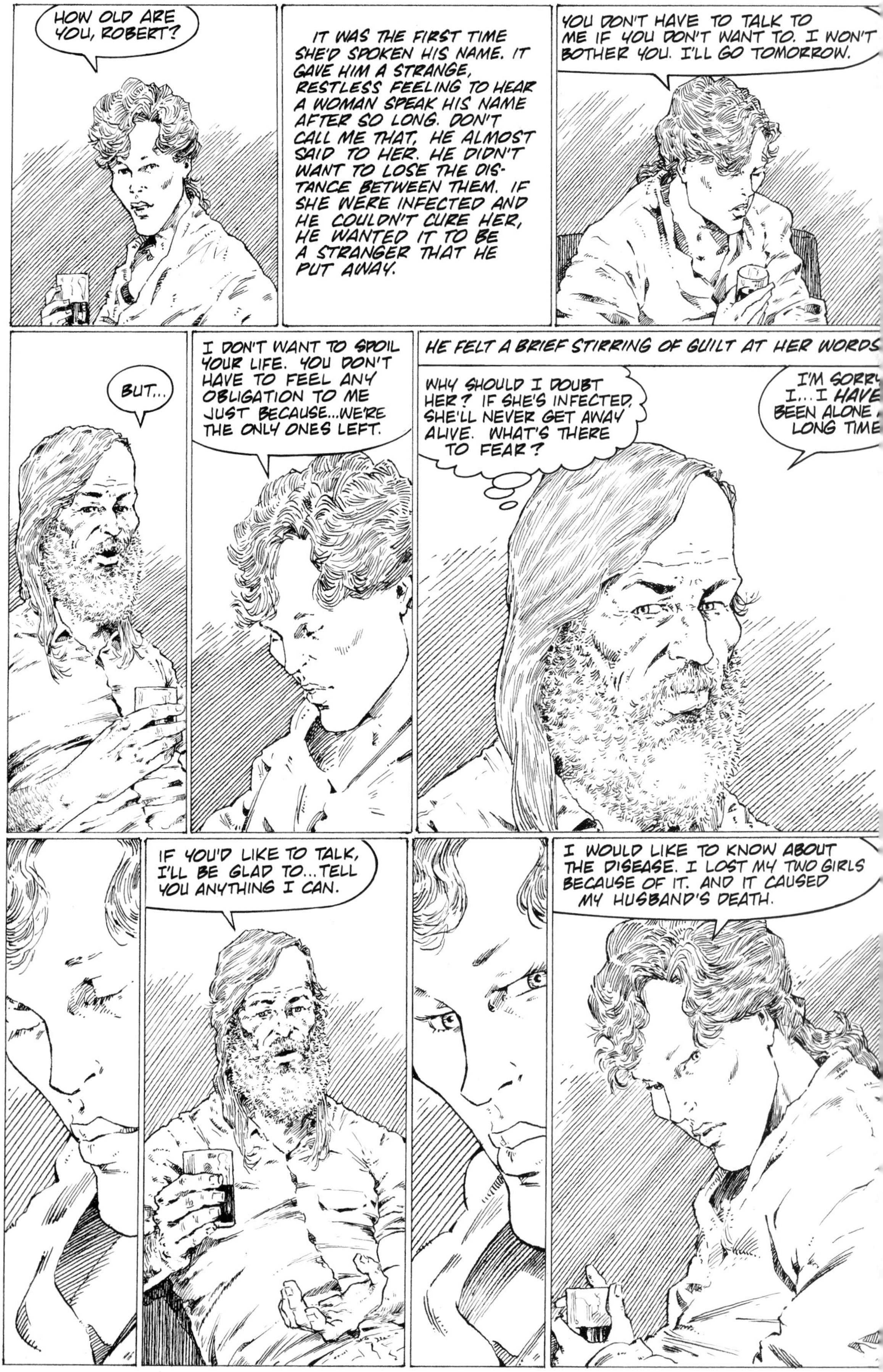
HOW OLD ARE YOU, ROBERT?
IT WAS THE FIRST TIME SHE'D SPOKEN HIS NAME. IT GAVE HIM A STRANGE, RESTLESS FEELING TO HEAR A WOMAN SPEAK HIS NAME AFTER SO LONG. DON'T CALL ME THAT, HE ALMOST SAID TO HER. HE DIDN'T WANT TO LOSE THE DISTANCE BETWEEN THEM. IF SHE WERE INFECTED AND HE COULDN'T CURE HER, HE WANTED IT TO BE A STRANGER THAT HE PUT AWAY.
YOU DON'T HAVE TO TALK TO ME IF YOU DON'T WANT TO. I WON'T BOTHER YOU. I'LL GO TOMORROW.
BUT...
I DON'T WANT TO SPOIL YOUR LIFE. YOU DON'T HAVE TO FEEL ANY OBLIGATION TO ME JUST BECAUSE...WE'RE THE ONLY ONES LEFT.
HE FELT A BRIEF STIRRING OF GUILT AT HER WORDS
WHY SHOULD I DOUBT HER? IF SHE'S INFECTED, SHE'LL NEVER GET AWAY ALIVE. WHAT'S THERE TO FEAR?
I'M SORRY I... I HAVE BEEN ALONE LONG TIME
IF YOU'D LIKE TO TALK, I'LL BE GLAD TO...TELL YOU ANYTHING I CAN.
I WOULD LIKE TO KNOW ABOUT THE DISEASE. I LOST MY TWO GIRLS BECAUSE OF IT. AND IT CAUSED MY HUSBAND'S DEATH.

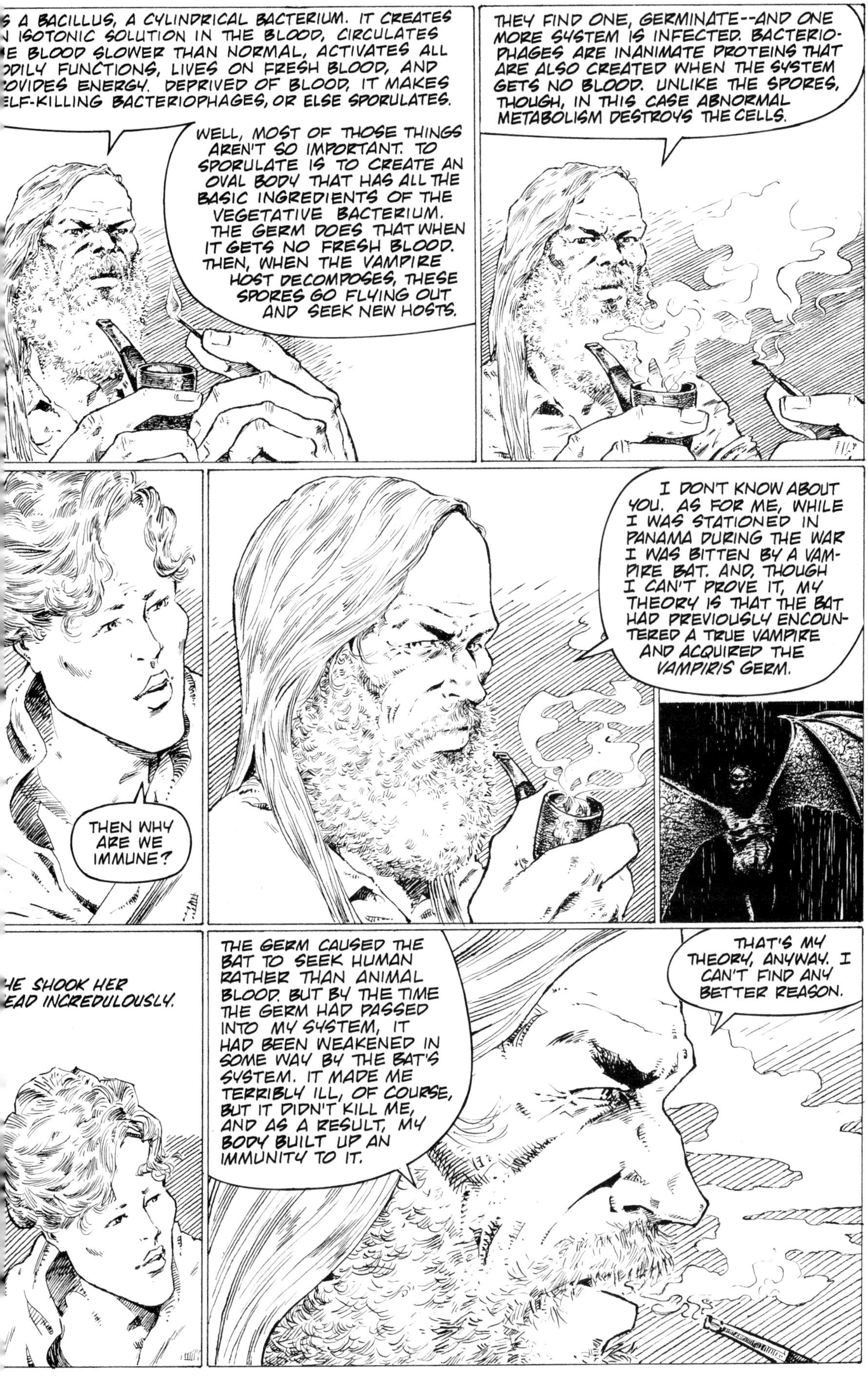
S A BACILLUS, A CYLINDRICAL BACTERIUM. IT CREATES N ISOTONIC SOLUTION IN THE BLOOD, CIRCULATES E BLOOD SLOWER THAN NORMAL, ACTIVATES ALL ODILY FUNCTIONS, LIVES ON FRESH BLOOD, AND OVIDES ENERGY. DEPRIVED OF BLOOD, IT MAKES ELF-KILLING BACTERIOPHAGES, OR ELSE SPORULATES.
WELL, MOST OF THOSE THINGS AREN'T SO IMPORTANT. TO SPORULATE IS TO CREATE AN OVAL BODY THAT HAS ALL THE BASIC INGREDIENTS OF THE VEGETATIVE BACTERIUM. THE GERM DOES THAT WHEN IT GETS NO FRESH BLOOD. THEN, WHEN THE VAMPIRE HOST DECOMPOSES, THESE SPORES GO FLYING OUT AND SEEK NEW HOSTS.
THEY FIND ONE, GERMINATE--AND ONE MORE SYSTEM IS INFECTED. BACTERIOPHAGES ARE INANIMATE PROTEINS THAT ARE ALSO CREATED WHEN THE SYSTEM GETS NO BLOOD. UNLIKE THE SPORES, THOUGH, IN THIS CASE ABNORMAL METABOLISM DESTROYS THE CELLS.
THEN WHY ARE WE IMMUNE?
I DON'T KNOW ABOUT YOU. AS FOR ME, WHILE I WAS STATIONED IN PANAMA DURING THE WAR I WAS BITTEN BY A VAMPIRE BAT. AND, THOUGH I CAN'T PROVE IT, MY THEORY IS THAT THE BAT HAD PREVIOUSLY ENCOUNTERED A TRUE VAMPIRE AND ACQUIRED THE VAMPIRIS GERM.
HE SHOOK HER EAD INCREDULOUSLY.
THE GERM CAUSED THE BAT TO SEEK HUMAN RATHER THAN ANIMAL BLOOD. BUT BY THE TIME THE GERM HAD PASSED INTO MY SYSTEM, IT HAD BEEN WEAKENED IN SOME WAY BY THE BAT'S SYSTEM. IT MADE ME TERRIBLY ILL, OF COURSE, BUT IT DIDN'T KILL ME, AND AS A RESULT, MY BODY BUILT UP AN IMMUNITY TO IT.
THAT'S MY THEORY, ANYWAY. I CAN'T FIND ANY BETTER REASON.

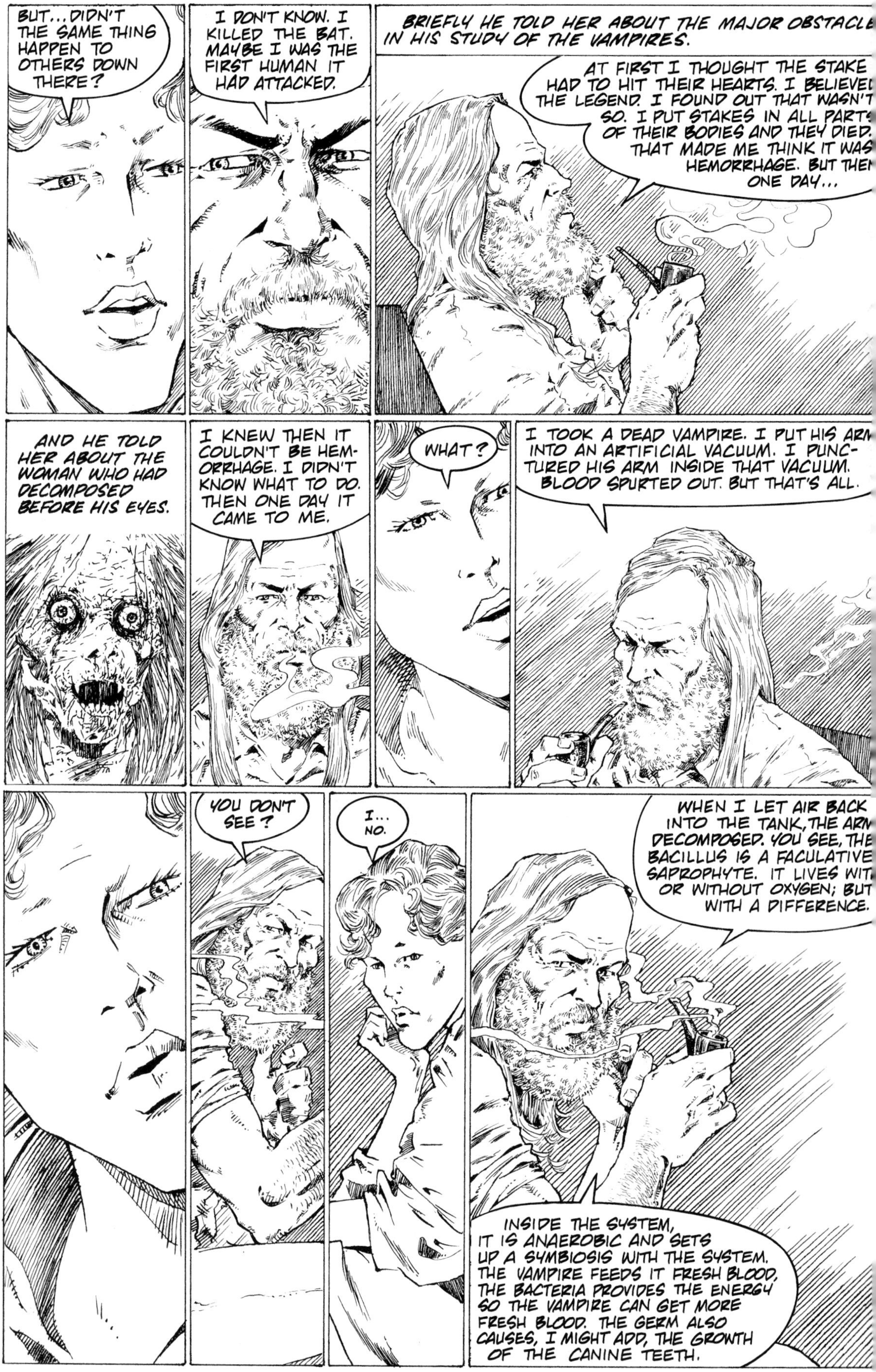

BUT... DIDN'T THE SAME THING HAPPEN TO OTHERS DOWN THERE?
I DON'T KNOW. I KILLED THE BAT. MAYBE I WAS THE FIRST HUMAN IT HAD ATTACKED.
BRIEFLY HE TOLD HER ABOUT THE MAJOR OBSTACLE IN HIS STUDY OF THE VAMPIRES.
AT FIRST I THOUGHT THE STAKE HAD TO HIT THEIR HEARTS. I BELIEVED THE LEGEND. I FOUND OUT THAT WASN'T SO. I PUT STAKES IN ALL PARTS OF THEIR BODIES AND THEY DIED. THAT MADE ME THINK IT WAS HEMORRHAGE. BUT THEN ONE DAY...
AND HE TOLD HER ABOUT THE WOMAN WHO HAD DECOMPOSED BEFORE HIS EYES.
I KNEW THEN IT COULDN'T BE HEM-ORRHAGE. I DIDN'T KNOW WHAT TO DO. THEN ONE DAY IT CAME TO ME.
WHAT?
I TOOK A DEAD VAMPIRE. I PUT HIS ARM INTO AN ARTIFICIAL VACUUM. I PUNC-TURED HIS ARM INSIDE THAT VACUUM. BLOOD SPURTED OUT. BUT THAT'S ALL.
YOU DON'T SEE?
I... NO.
WHEN I LET AIR BACK INTO THE TANK, THE ARM DECOMPOSED. YOU SEE, THE BACILLUS IS A FACULATIVE SAPROPHYTE. IT LIVES WITH OR WITHOUT OXYGEN; BUT WITH A DIFFERENCE.
INSIDE THE SYSTEM, IT IS ANAEROBIC AND SETS UP A SYMBIOSIS WITH THE SYSTEM. THE VAMPIRE FEEDS IT FRESH BLOOD, THE BACTERIA PROVIDES THE ENERGY SO THE VAMPIRE CAN GET MORE FRESH BLOOD. THE GERM ALSO CAUSES, I MIGHT ADD, THE GROWTH OF THE CANINE TEETH.

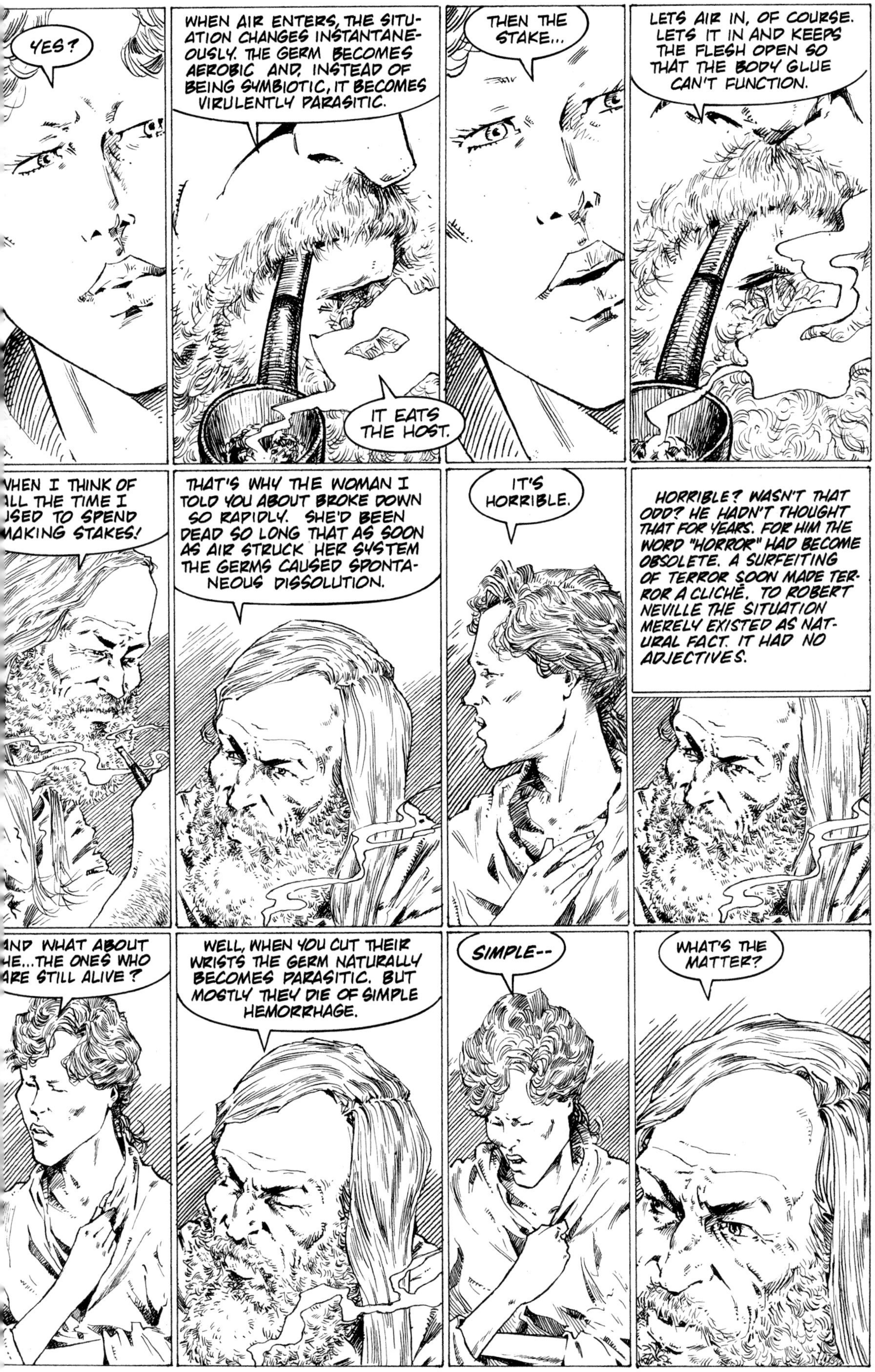
YES?
WHEN AIR ENTERS, THE SITUATION CHANGES INSTANTANEOUSLY. THE GERM BECOMES AEROBIC AND, INSTEAD OF BEING SYMBIOTIC, IT BECOMES VIRULENTLY PARASITIC.
IT EATS THE HOST.
THEN THE STAKE...
LETS AIR IN, OF COURSE. LETS IT IN AND KEEPS THE FLESH OPEN SO THAT THE BODY GLUE CAN'T FUNCTION.
WHEN I THINK OF ALL THE TIME I USED TO SPEND MAKING STAKES!
THAT'S WHY THE WOMAN I TOLD YOU ABOUT BROKE DOWN SO RAPIDLY. SHE'D BEEN DEAD SO LONG THAT AS SOON AS AIR STRUCK HER SYSTEM THE GERMS CAUSED SPONTANEOUS DISSOLUTION.
IT'S HORRIBLE.
HORRIBLE? WASN'T THAT ODD? HE HADN'T THOUGHT THAT FOR YEARS. FOR HIM THE WORD "HORROR" HAD BECOME OBSOLETE. A SURFEITING OF TERROR SOON MADE TERROR A CLICHÉ. TO ROBERT NEVILLE THE SITUATION MERELY EXISTED AS NATURAL FACT. IT HAD NO ADJECTIVES.
AND WHAT ABOUT THE...THE ONES WHO ARE STILL ALIVE?
WELL, WHEN YOU CUT THEIR WRISTS THE GERM NATURALLY BECOMES PARASITIC. BUT MOSTLY THEY DIE OF SIMPLE HEMORRHAGE.
SIMPLE--
WHAT'S THE MATTER?

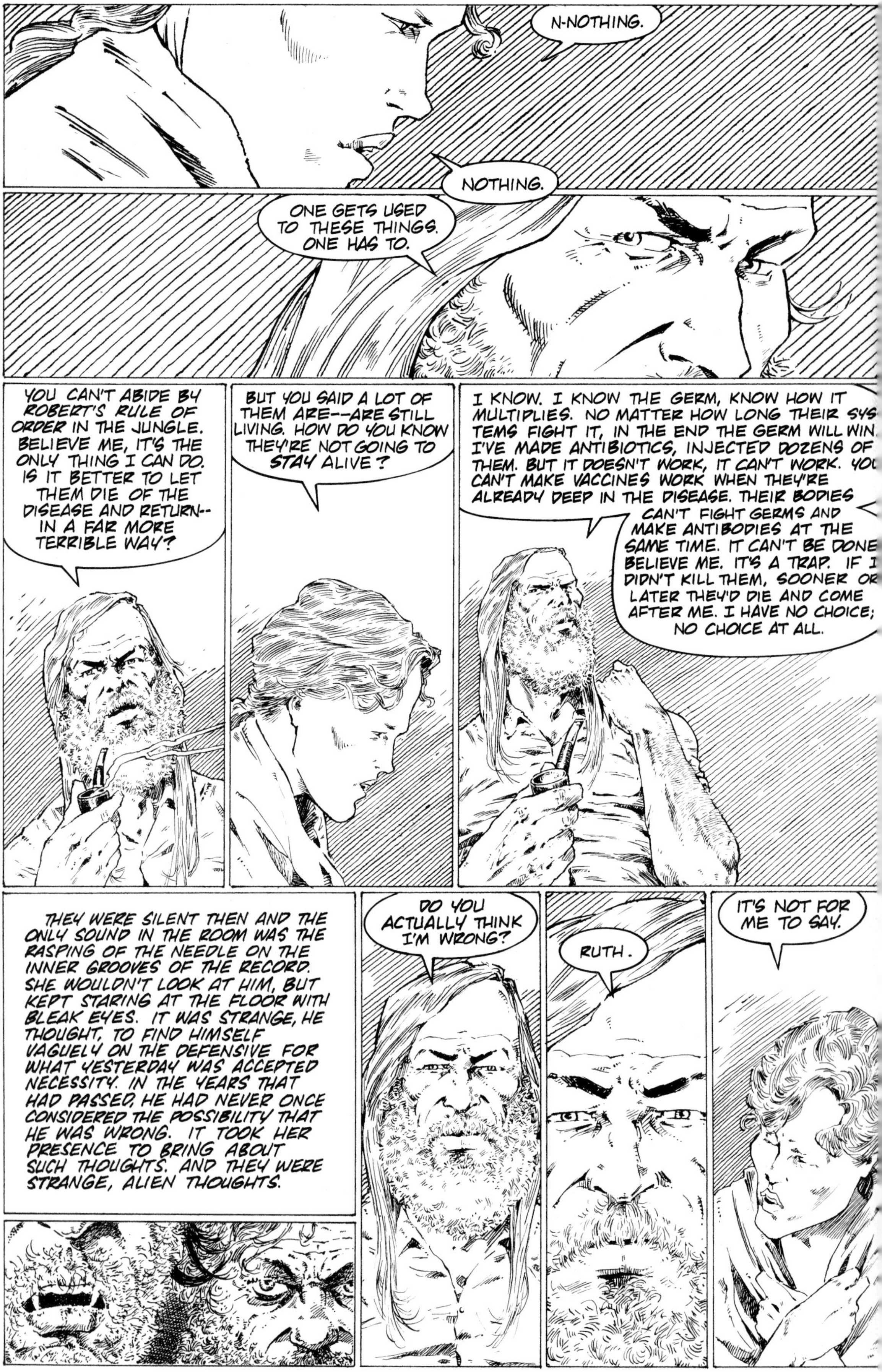
N-NOTHING.
NOTHING.
ONE GETS USED TO THESE THINGS. ONE HAS TO.
YOU CAN'T ABIDE BY ROBERT'S RULE OF ORDER IN THE JUNGLE. BELIEVE ME, IT'S THE ONLY THING I CAN DO. IS IT BETTER TO LET THEM DIE OF THE DISEASE AND RETURN-- IN A FAR MORE TERRIBLE WAY?
BUT YOU SAID A LOT OF THEM ARE--ARE STILL LIVING. HOW DO YOU KNOW THEY'RE NOT GOING TO STAY ALIVE?
I KNOW. I KNOW THE GERM, KNOW HOW IT MULTIPLIES. NO MATTER HOW LONG THEIR SYS TEMS FIGHT IT, IN THE END THE GERM WILL WIN. I'VE MADE ANTIBIOTICS, INJECTED DOZENS OF THEM. BUT IT DOESN'T WORK, IT CAN'T WORK. YOU CAN'T MAKE VACCINES WORK WHEN THEY'RE ALREADY DEEP IN THE DISEASE. THEIR BODIES CAN'T FIGHT GERMS AND MAKE ANTIBODIES AT THE SAME TIME. IT CAN'T BE DONE. BELIEVE ME. IT'S A TRAP. IF I DIDN'T KILL THEM, SOONER OR LATER THEY'D DIE AND COME AFTER ME. I HAVE NO CHOICE; NO CHOICE AT ALL.
THEY WERE SILENT THEN AND THE ONLY SOUND IN THE ROOM WAS THE RASPING OF THE NEEDLE ON THE INNER GROOVES OF THE RECORD. SHE WOULDN'T LOOK AT HIM, BUT KEPT STARING AT THE FLOOR WITH BLEAK EYES. IT WAS STRANGE, HE THOUGHT, TO FIND HIMSELF VAGUELY ON THE DEFENSIVE FOR WHAT YESTERDAY WAS ACCEPTED NECESSITY. IN THE YEARS THAT HAD PASSED, HE HAD NEVER ONCE CONSIDERED THE POSSIBILITY THAT HE WAS WRONG. IT TOOK HER PRESENCE TO BRING ABOUT SUCH THOUGHTS. AND THEY WERE STRANGE, ALIEN THOUGHTS.
DO YOU ACTUALLY THINK I'M WRONG?
RUTH.
IT'S NOT FOR ME TO SAY.

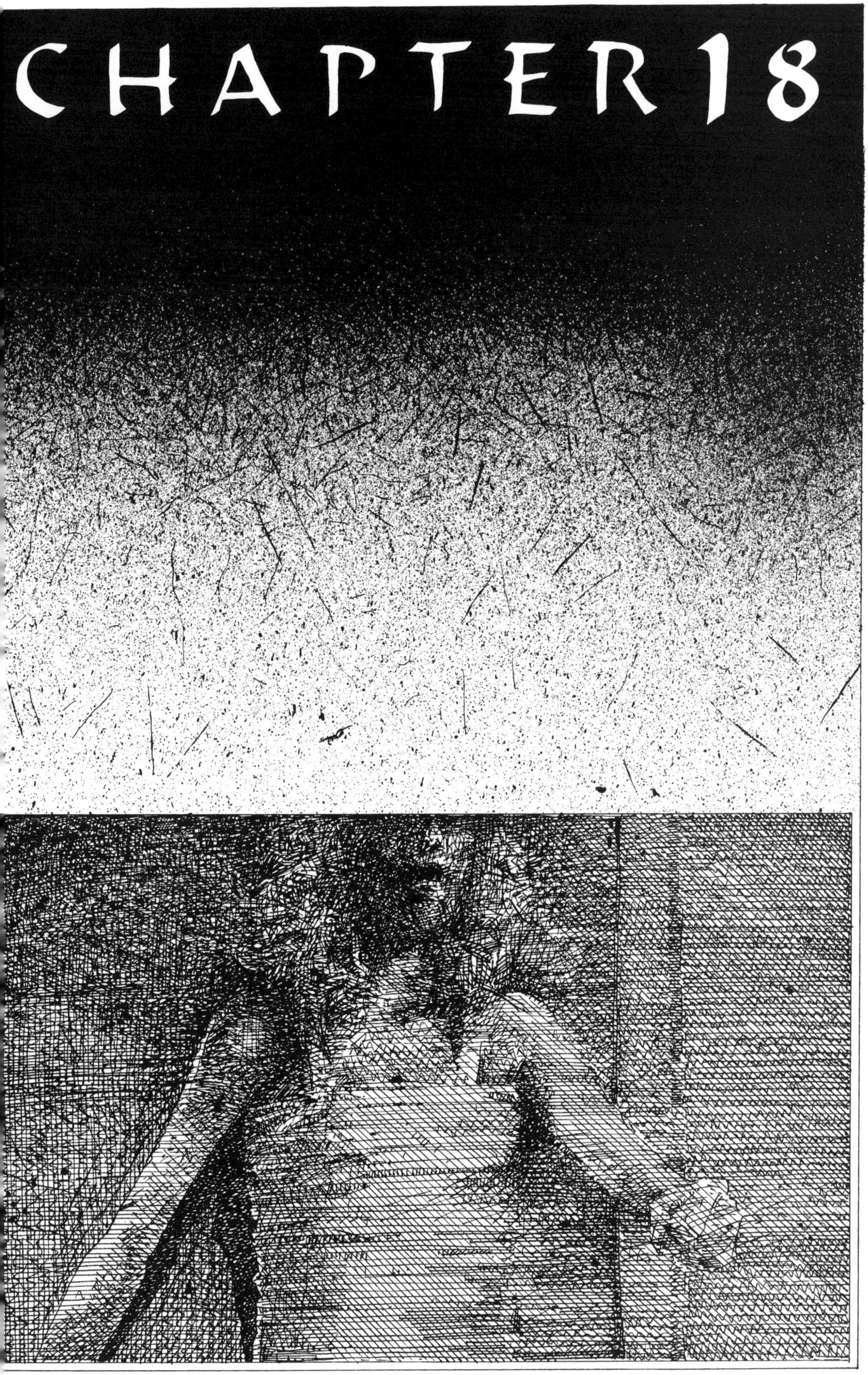
CHAPTER 18

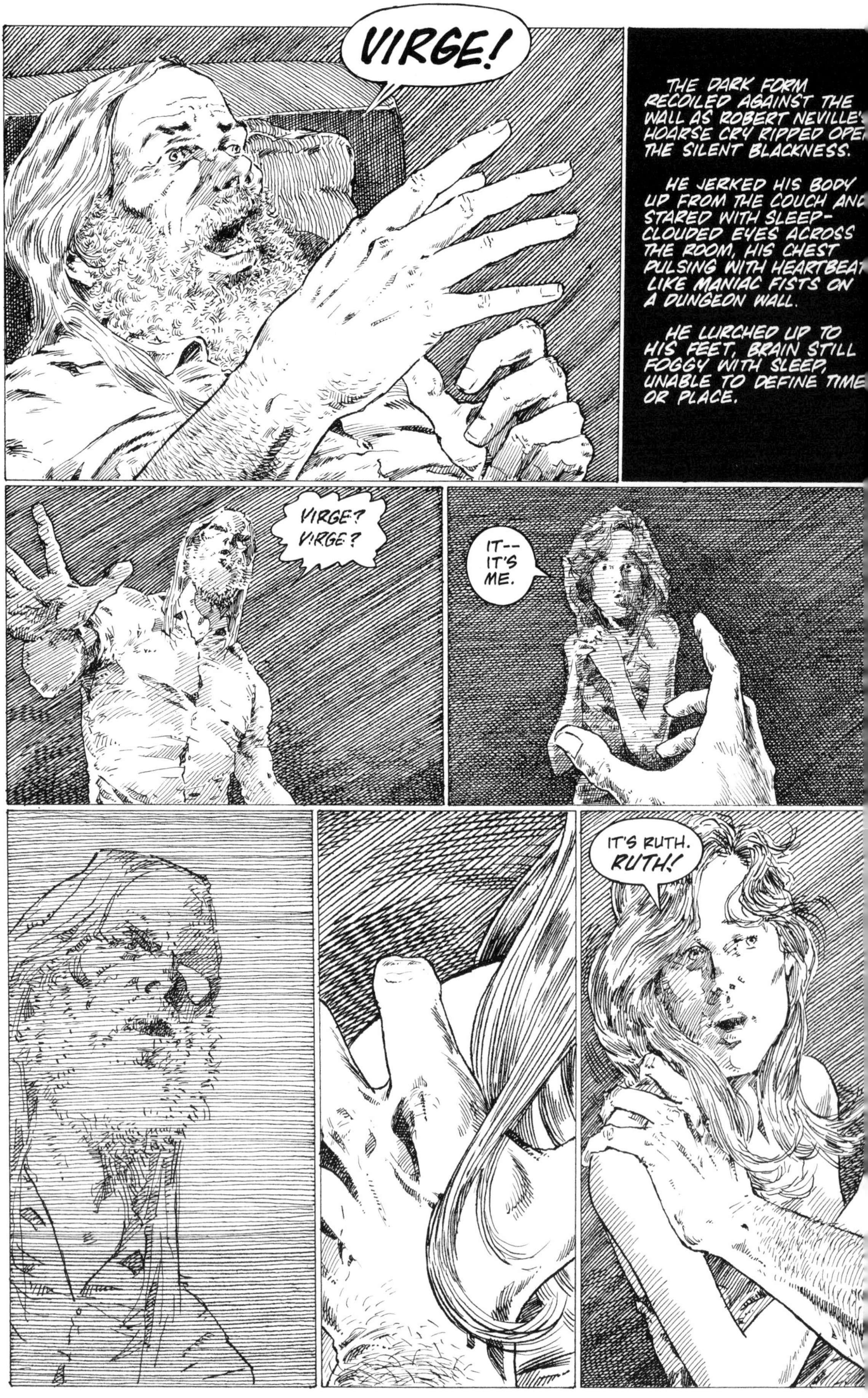
VIRGE!
THE DARK FORM RECOILED AGAINST THE WALL AS ROBERT NEVILLE'S HOARSE CRY RIPPED OPEN THE SILENT BLACKNESS.
HE JERKED HIS BODY UP FROM THE COUCH AND STARED WITH SLEEP-CLOUDED EYES ACROSS THE ROOM, HIS CHEST PULSING WITH HEARTBEATS LIKE MANIAC FISTS ON A DUNGEON WALL.
HE LURCHED UP TO HIS FEET, BRAIN STILL FOGGY WITH SLEEP, UNABLE TO DEFINE TIME OR PLACE.
VIRGE? VIRGE?
IT-- IT'S ME.
IT'S RUTH. RUTH!

HE STOOD THERE ROCKING SLOWLY IN THE DARKNESS, EYES GAZING WITHOUT COMPREHENSION AT THE DARK FORM BEFORE HIM.

IT'S RUTH!

WAKING CAME LIKE A HOSE BLAST OF NUMBING SHOCK. SOMETHING TWISTED COLD KNOTS INTO HIS CHEST AND STOMACH. IT WASN'T VIRGE. HE SHOOK HIS HEAD SUDDENLY, RUBBED SHAKING FINGERS ACROSS HIS EYES.
THEN HE STOOD STARING, WEIGHTED BENEATH A SUDDEN DEPRESSION.

OH. OH, I...

WHAT ARE YOU DOING?

NOTHING. I...COULDN'T SLEEP.

CLICK

WHY ARE YOU DRESSED?

I WAS... JUST LOOKING OUT.

201

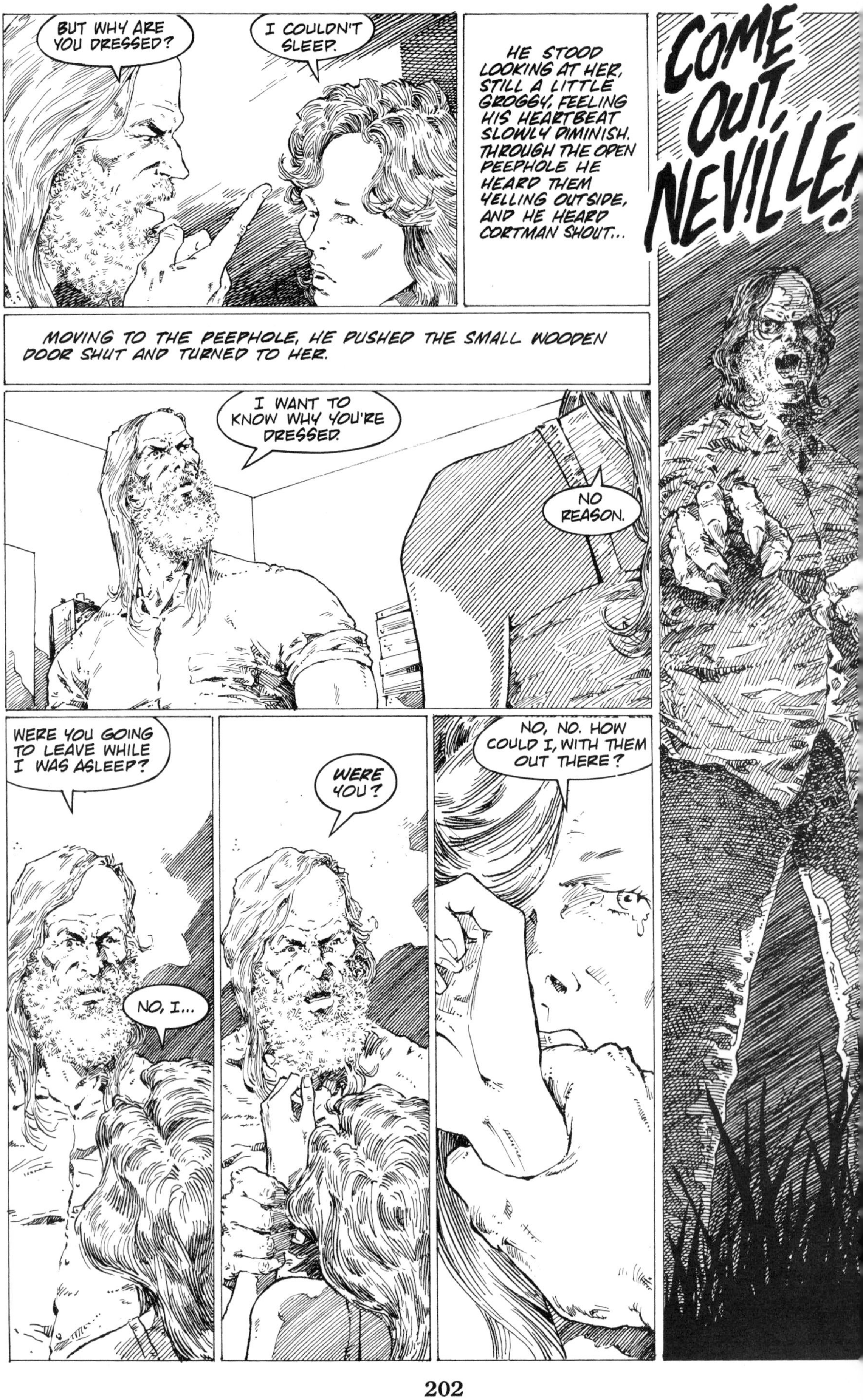
BUT WHY ARE YOU DRESSED?
I COULDN'T SLEEP.
HE STOOD LOOKING AT HER, STILL A LITTLE GROGGY, FEELING HIS HEARTBEAT SLOWLY DIMINISH. THROUGH THE OPEN PEEPHOLE HE HEARD THEM YELLING OUTSIDE, AND HE HEARD CORTMAN SHOUT...
COME OUT, NEVILLE!
MOVING TO THE PEEPHOLE, HE PUSHED THE SMALL WOODEN DOOR SHUT AND TURNED TO HER.
I WANT TO KNOW WHY YOU'RE DRESSED.
NO REASON.
WERE YOU GOING TO LEAVE WHILE I WAS ASLEEP?
NO, I...
WERE YOU?
NO, NO. HOW COULD I, WITH THEM OUT THERE?

HIS THROAT MOVED SLOWLY AS [H]E REMEMBERED THE SHOCK OF [W]AKING UP AND THINKING THAT [H]E WAS VIRGE.

AND HE'D THOUGHT THE PAST WAS DEAD. HOW LONG DID IT TAKE FOR A PAST TO DIE?

VIRGE... VIRGE... STILL WITH ME...

WAS THAT HER NAME?

IT'S ALL RIGHT. GO TO BED.

I'M SORRY. I DIDN'T MEAN...

SUDDENLY HE KNEW HE DIDN'T WANT HER TO GO TO BED. HE WANTED HER TO STAY WITH HIM. HE DIDN'T KNOW WHY, HE JUST DIDN'T WANT TO BE ALONE.

I THOUGHT YOU WERE MY WIFE. I WOKE UP AND I THOUGHT--

SHE CAME BACK, YOU SEE. I BURIED HER, BUT ONE NIGHT SHE CAME BACK. SHE LOOKED LIKE--LIKE YOU DID. AN OUTLINE, A SHADOW. DEAD. BUT SHE CAME BACK. I TRIED TO KEEP HER WITH ME. I TRIED, BUT SHE WASN'T THE SAME ANYMORE...YOU SEE. ALL SHE WANTED WAS--

203

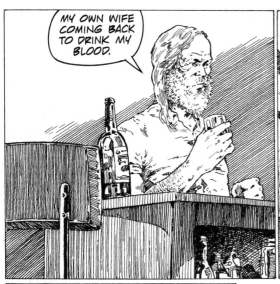

MY OWN WIFE COMING BACK TO DRINK MY BLOOD.

TURNING AWAY, HE PACE RESTLESSLY T. THE PEEPHOLE TURNED, AND WENT AND STOOD AGAIN BEFORE THE BAR.

RUTH SAID NOTHING; SHE JUST STOOD IN THE DARKNESS, LISTENING.

CLANK

I PUT HER AWAY AGAIN. I HAD TO DO THE SAME THING TO HER I'D DONE TO THE OTHERS. MY OWN WIFE. A STAKE. I HAD TO PUT A STAKE IN HER. IT WAS THE ONLY THING I KNEW TO DO. I--

HE COULDN'T FINISH. HE STOOD THERE A LONG TIME, SHIVERING HELPLESSLY, HIS EYES TIGHTLY SHUT.

THEN HE SPOKE AGAIN.

ALMOST THREE YEARS AGO I DID THAT. AND I STILL REMEMBER IT, IT'S STILL WITH ME. WHAT CAN YOU DO WHAT CAN YOU DO?

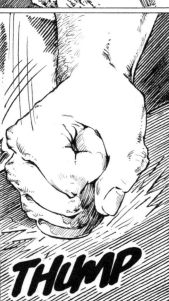

THUMP

NO MATTER HOW YOU TRY, YOU CAN'T FORGET OR--ADJUST, OR-- EVER GET AWAY FROM IT!

I KNOW WHAT YOU FEEL, I KNOW. DIDN'T AT FIRST, I DIDN'T TRUST YO I WAS SAFE, SECURE IN MY LITTL SHELL. NOW...IN A SECOND, IT'S AL GONE. ADJUSTMENT, SECURITY, PEACE--ALL GONE.

ROBERT.

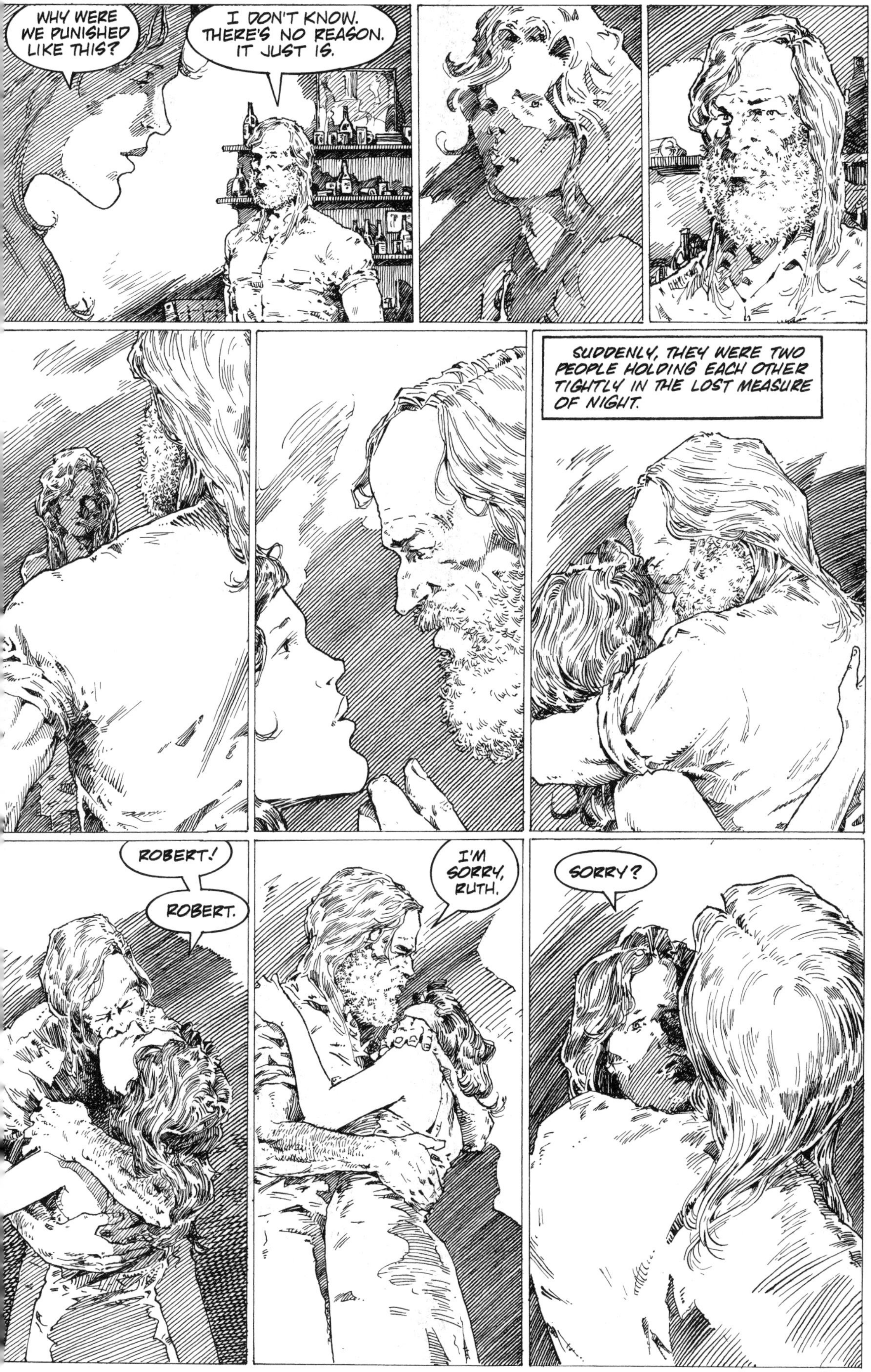
WHY WERE WE PUNISHED LIKE THIS?
I DON'T KNOW. THERE'S NO REASON. IT JUST IS.
SUDDENLY, THEY WERE TWO PEOPLE HOLDING EACH OTHER TIGHTLY IN THE LOST MEASURE OF NIGHT.
ROBERT!
ROBERT.
I'M SORRY, RUTH.
SORRY?

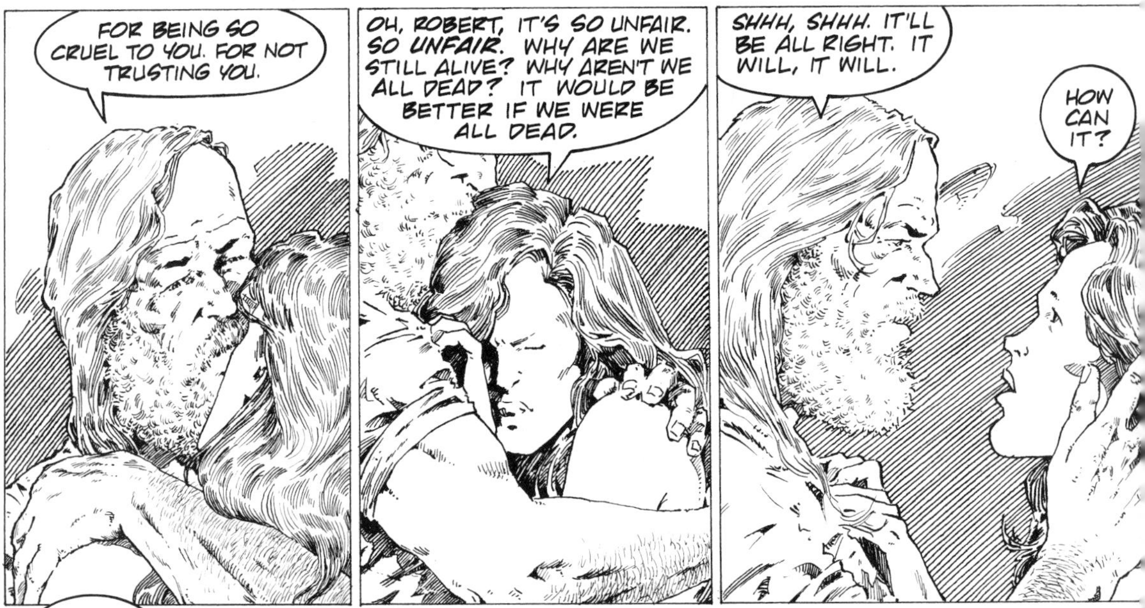
FOR BEING SO CRUEL TO YOU. FOR NOT TRUSTING YOU.
OH, ROBERT, IT'S SO UNFAIR. SO *UNFAIR*. WHY ARE WE STILL ALIVE? WHY AREN'T WE ALL DEAD? IT WOULD BE BETTER IF WE WERE ALL DEAD.
SHHH, SHHH. IT'LL BE ALL RIGHT. IT WILL, IT WILL.
HOW CAN IT?

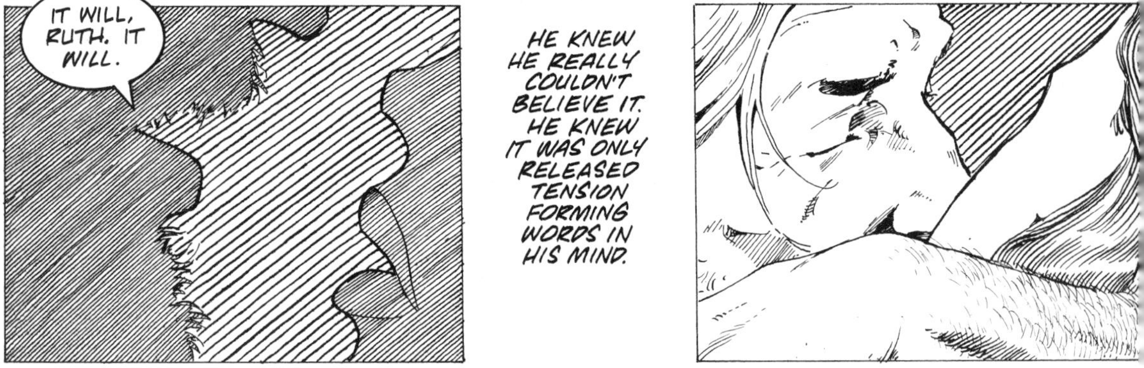
IT WILL, RUTH. IT WILL.
HE KNEW HE REALLY COULDN'T BELIEVE IT. HE KNEW IT WAS ONLY RELEASED TENSION FORMING WORDS IN HIS MIND.

HE DIDN'T KNOW HOW LONG THEY HELD EACH OTHER CLOSE. HE FORGOT EVERYTHING, TIME AND PLACE; IT WAS JUST THE TWO OF THEM TOGETHER, NEEDING EACH OTHER, SURVIVORS OF A BLACK TERROR EMBRACING BECAUSE THEY HAD FOUND EACH OTHER.

BUT THEN HE WANTED TO DO SOMETHING FOR HER, TO HELP HER.

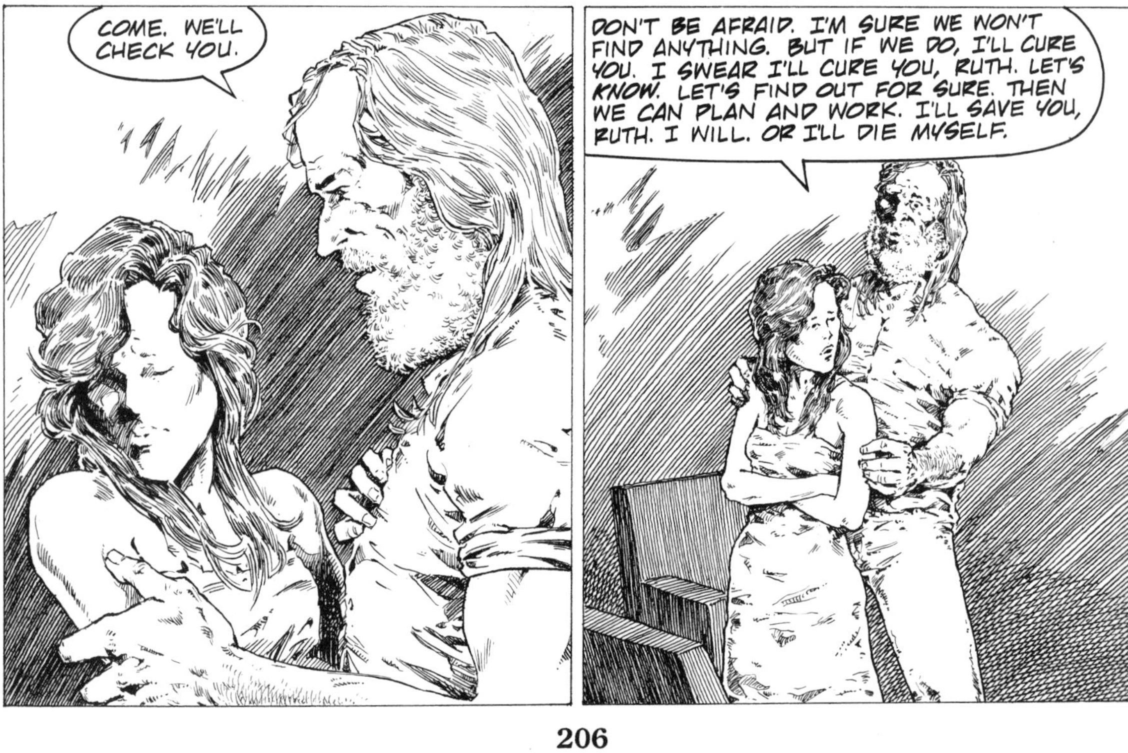
COME. WE'LL CHECK YOU.
DON'T BE AFRAID. I'M SURE WE WON'T FIND ANYTHING. BUT IF WE DO, I'LL CURE YOU. I SWEAR I'LL CURE YOU, RUTH. LET'S *KNOW*. LET'S FIND OUT FOR SURE. THEN WE CAN PLAN AND WORK. I'LL SAVE YOU, RUTH. I WILL. OR I'LL DIE MYSELF.

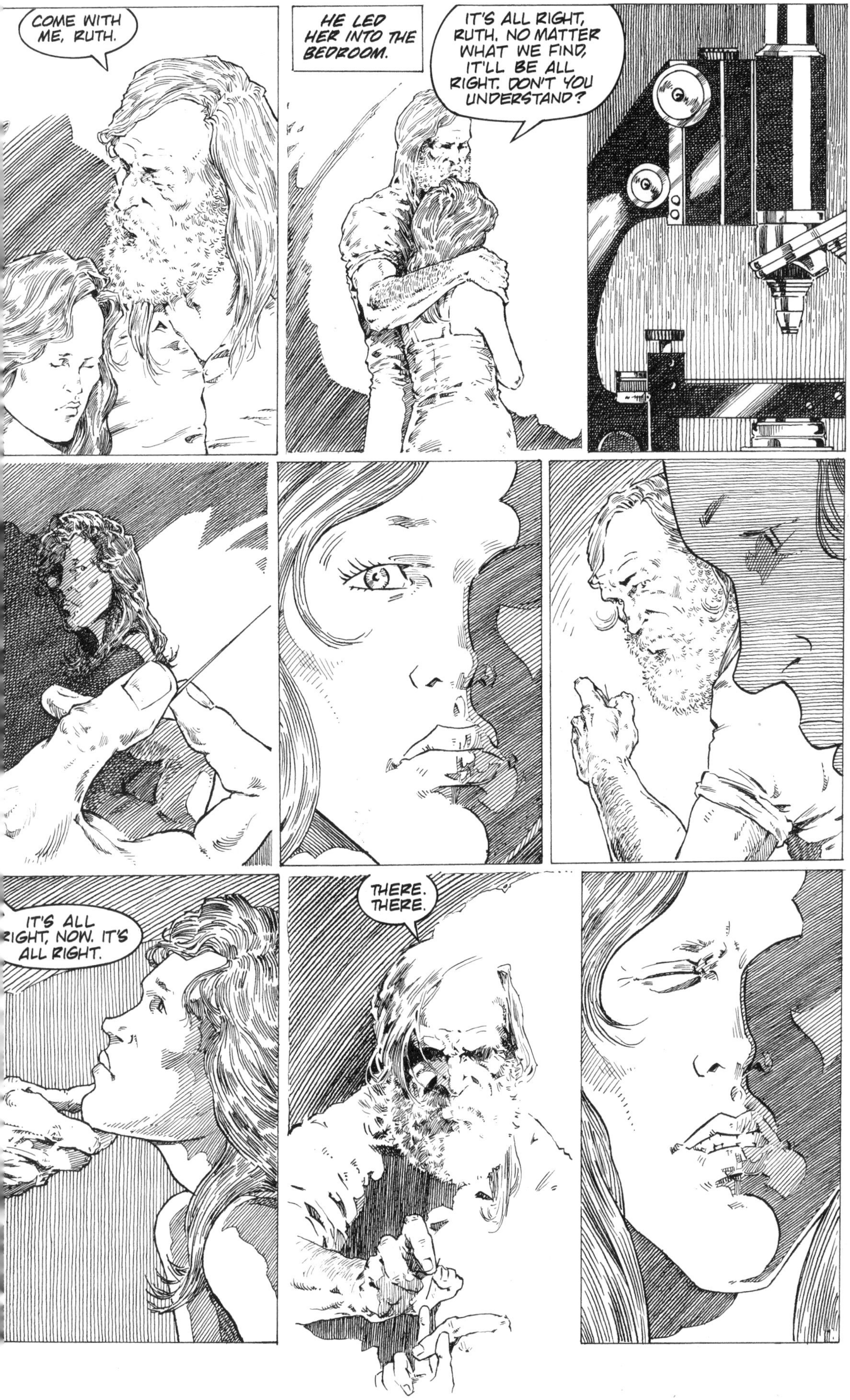
COME WITH ME, RUTH.
HE LED HER INTO THE BEDROOM.
IT'S ALL RIGHT, RUTH. NO MATTER WHAT WE FIND, IT'LL BE ALL RIGHT. DON'T YOU UNDERSTAND?
IT'S ALL RIGHT, NOW. IT'S ALL RIGHT.
THERE. THERE.

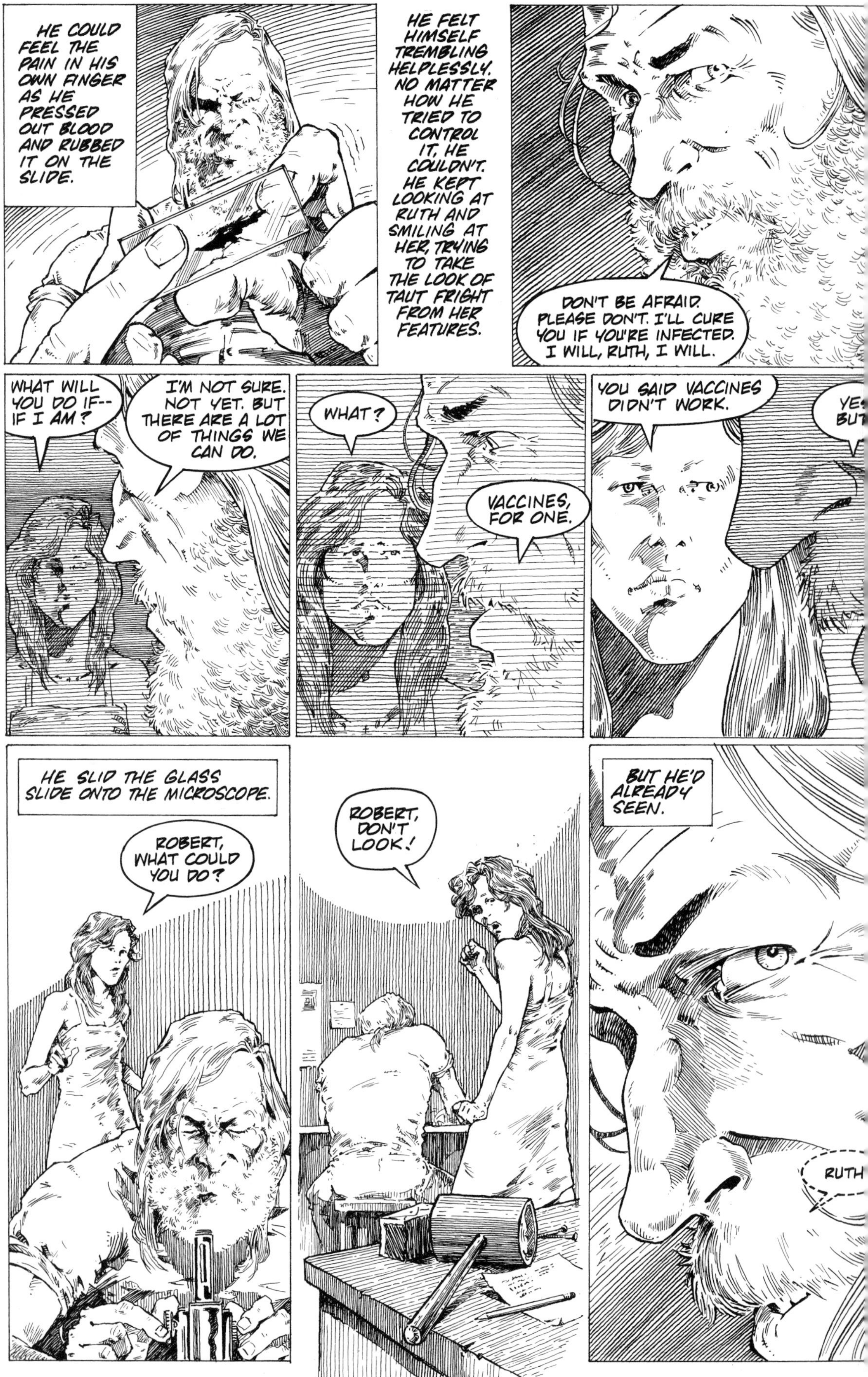
HE COULD FEEL THE PAIN IN HIS OWN FINGER AS HE PRESSED OUT BLOOD AND RUBBED IT ON THE SLIDE.
HE FELT HIMSELF TREMBLING HELPLESSLY. NO MATTER HOW HE TRIED TO CONTROL IT, HE COULDN'T. HE KEPT LOOKING AT RUTH AND SMILING AT HER, TRYING TO TAKE THE LOOK OF TAUT FRIGHT FROM HER FEATURES.
DON'T BE AFRAID. PLEASE DON'T. I'LL CURE YOU IF YOU'RE INFECTED. I WILL, RUTH, I WILL.
WHAT WILL YOU DO IF-- IF I AM?
I'M NOT SURE. NOT YET. BUT THERE ARE A LOT OF THINGS WE CAN DO.
WHAT?
VACCINES, FOR ONE.
YOU SAID VACCINES DIDN'T WORK.
HE SLID THE GLASS SLIDE ONTO THE MICROSCOPE.
ROBERT, WHAT COULD YOU DO?
ROBERT, DON'T LOOK!
BUT HE'D ALREADY SEEN.
RUTH

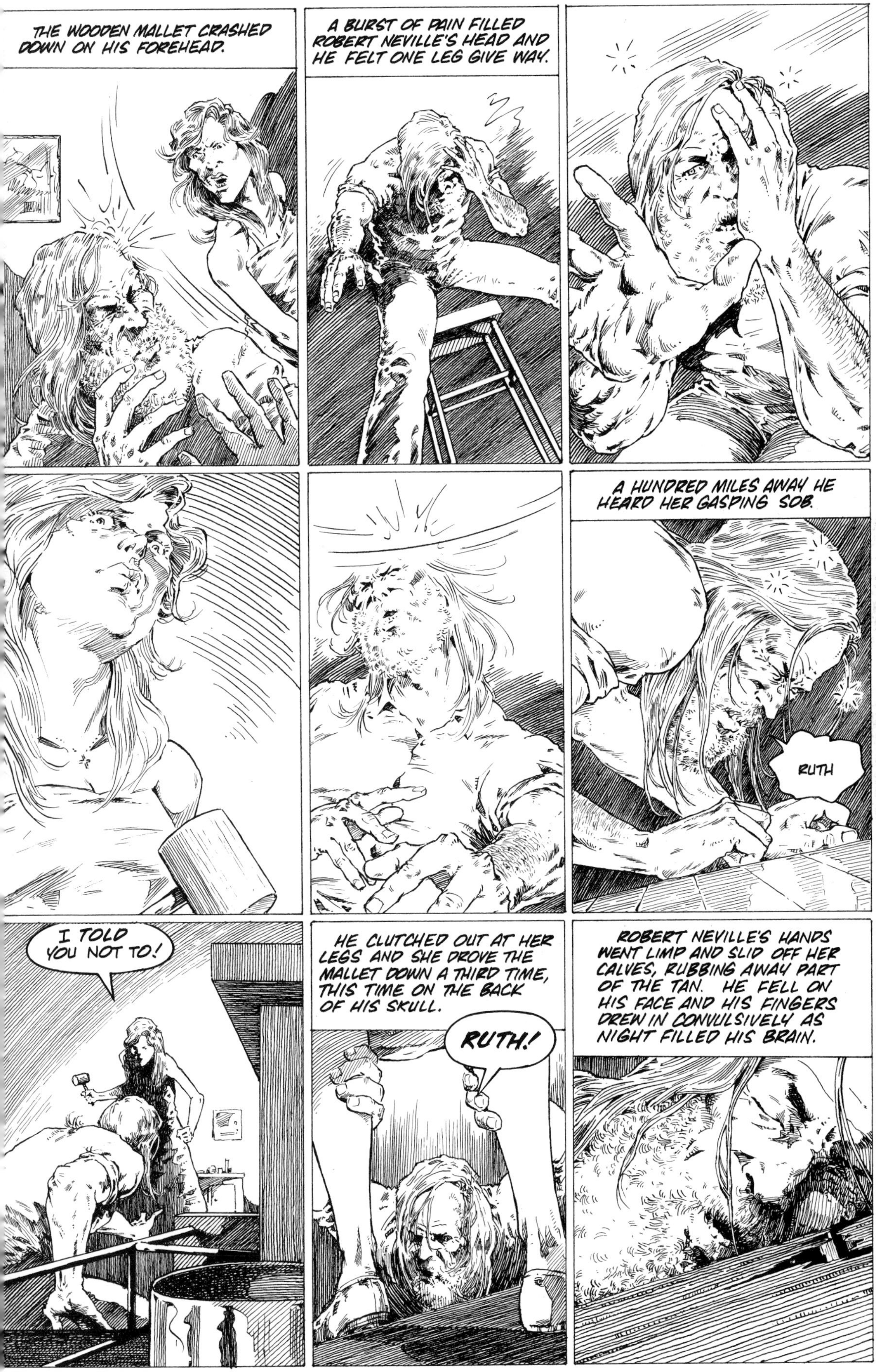

THE WOODEN MALLET CRASHED DOWN ON HIS FOREHEAD.
A BURST OF PAIN FILLED ROBERT NEVILLE'S HEAD AND HE FELT ONE LEG GIVE WAY.
A HUNDRED MILES AWAY HE HEARD HER GASPING SOB.
RUTH
I TOLD YOU NOT TO!
HE CLUTCHED OUT AT HER LEGS AND SHE DROVE THE MALLET DOWN A THIRD TIME, THIS TIME ON THE BACK OF HIS SKULL.
RUTH!
ROBERT NEVILLE'S HANDS WENT LIMP AND SLID OFF HER CALVES, RUBBING AWAY PART OF THE TAN. HE FELL ON HIS FACE AND HIS FINGERS DREW IN CONVULSIVELY AS NIGHT FILLED HIS BRAIN.

CHAPTER 19

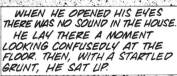

WHEN HE OPENED HIS EYES THERE WAS NO SOUND IN THE HOUSE. HE LAY THERE A MOMENT LOOKING CONFUSEDLY AT THE FLOOR. THEN, WITH A STARTLED GRUNT, HE SAT UP.

A PACKAGE OF NEEDLES EXPLODED IN HIS HEAD AND HE SLUMPED DOWN ON THE COLD FLOOR, HANDS PRESSED TO HIS THROBBING SKULL.

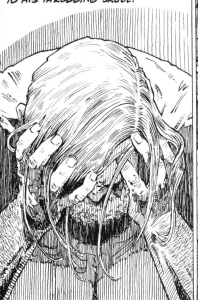

AFTER A FEW MINUTES HE PULLED HIMSELF UP SLOWLY BY GRIPPING THE EDGE OF THE BENCH.

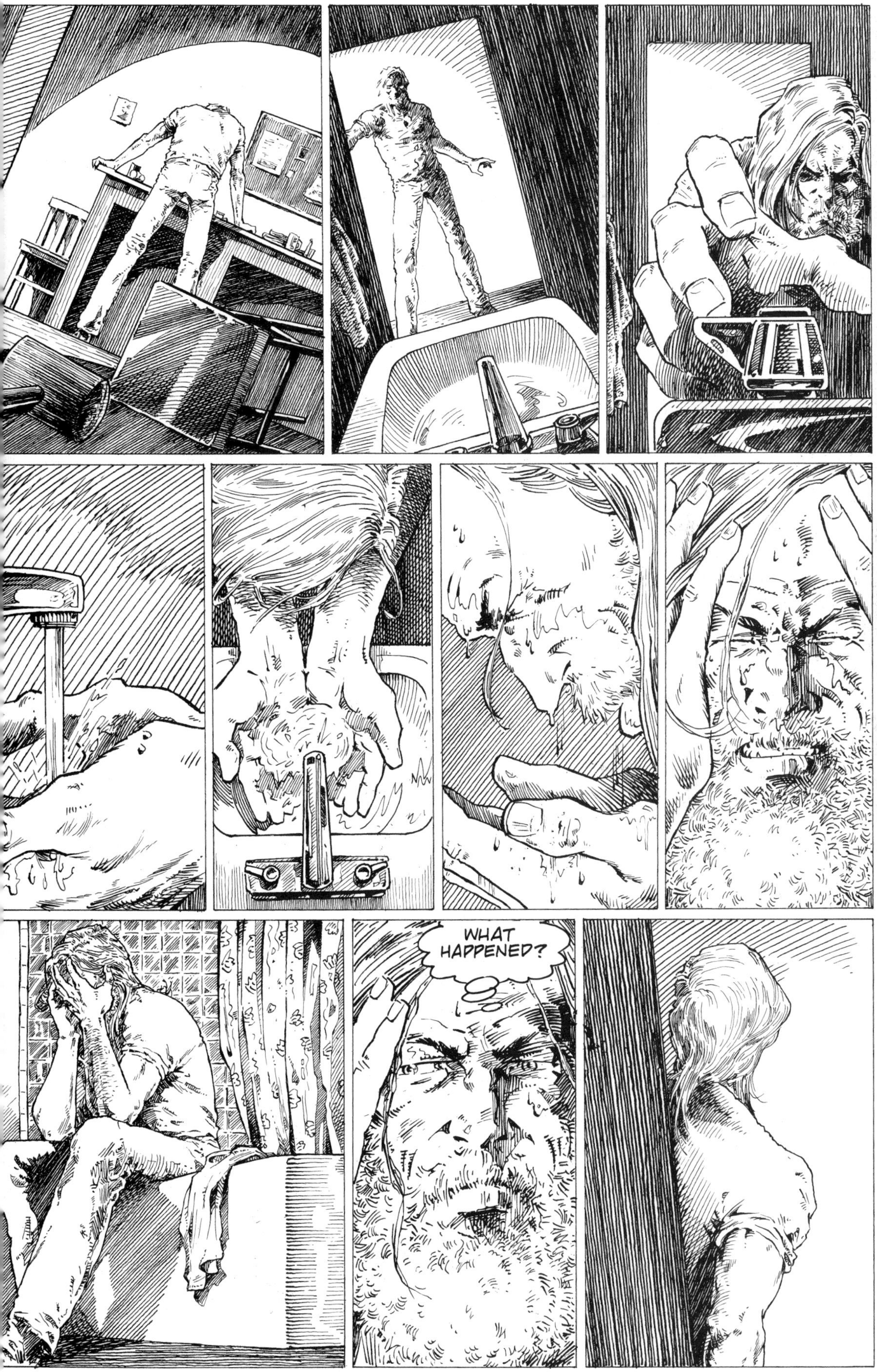
WHAT HAPPENED?

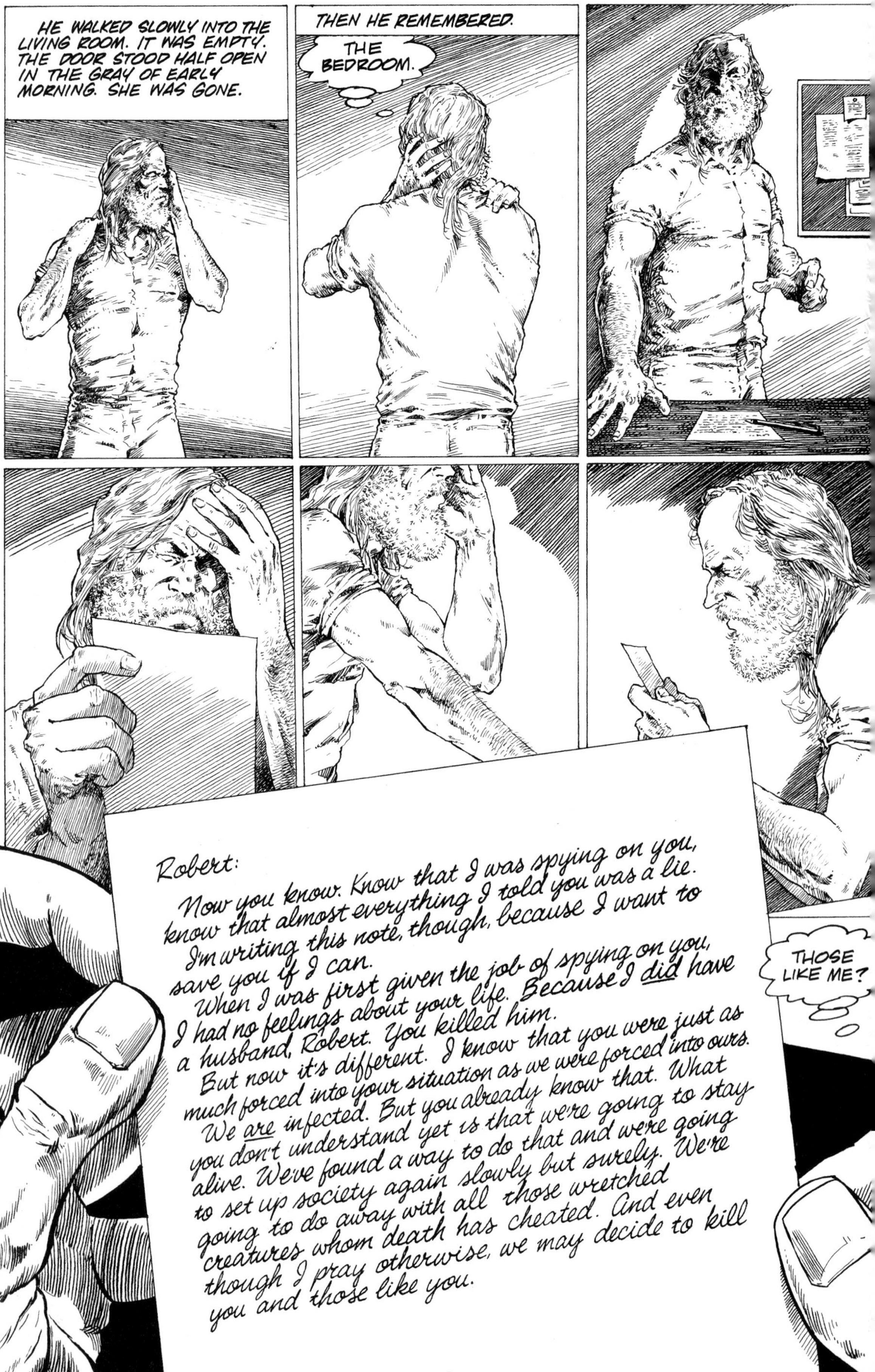
HE WALKED SLOWLY INTO THE LIVING ROOM. IT WAS EMPTY. THE DOOR STOOD HALF OPEN IN THE GRAY OF EARLY MORNING. SHE WAS GONE.
THEN HE REMEMBERED.
THE BEDROOM.
Robert:
Now you know. Know that I was spying on you, know that almost everything I told you was a lie.
I'm writing this note, though, because I want to save you if I can.
When I was first given the job of spying on you, I had no feelings about your life. Because I did have a husband, Robert. You killed him.
But now it's different. I know that you were just as much forced into your situation as we were forced into ours.
We are infected. But you already know that. What you don't understand yet is that we're going to stay alive. We've found a way to do that and we're going to set up society again slowly but surely. We're going to do away with all those wretched creatures whom death has cheated. And even though I pray otherwise, we may decide to kill you and those like you.
THOSE LIKE ME?

I'LL TRY TO SAVE YOU. I'LL TELL THEM YOU'RE TOO WELL ARMED FOR US TO ATTACK NOW. USE THE
ME I'M GIVING YOU, ROBERT! GET AWAY FROM YOUR HOUSE, GO INTO THE MOUNTAINS AND SAVE
OURSELF. THERE ARE ONLY A HANDFUL OF US NOW. BUT SOONER OR LATER WE'LL BE TOO WELL ORGANIZED,
ND NOTHING I SAY WILL STOP THE REST FROM DESTROYING YOU. FOR GOD'S SAKE, ROBERT, GO
OW, WHILE YOU CAN!

I KNOW YOU MAY NOT BELIEVE THIS. YOU MAY NOT BELIEVE THAT WE CAN LIVE IN THE SUN FOR
HORT PERIODS NOW. YOU MAY NOT BELIEVE THAT MY TAN WAS ONLY MAKE-UP. YOU MAY NOT BELIEVE
HAT WE CAN LIVE WITH THE GERM NOW.

THAT'S WHY I'M LEAVING ONE OF MY PILLS.

I TOOK THEM ALL THE TIME I WAS HERE. I
EPT THEM IN A BELT AROUND MY WAIST. YOU'LL
ISCOVER THAT THEY'RE A COMBINATION OF
EFEBRINATED BLOOD AND A DRUG. I DON'T
NOW MYSELF JUST WHAT IT IS. THE BLOOD
EEDS THE GERMS, THE DRUG PREVENTS ITS
ULTIPLICATION. IT WAS THE DISCOVERY OF THIS
LL THAT SAVED US FROM DYING, THAT IS
ELPING TO SET UP SOCIETY AGAIN SLOWLY.

BELIEVE ME, IT'S TRUE. AND ESCAPE!

FORGIVE ME, TOO. I DIDN'T MEAN TO HIT
OU, IT NEARLY KILLED ME TO DO IT. BUT I
AS SO TERRIBLY FRIGHTENED OF WHAT YOU'D
O WHEN YOU FOUND OUT.

FORGIVE ME FOR HAVING TO LIE TO YOU
BOUT SO MANY THINGS. BUT PLEASE BELIEVE
HIS: WHEN WE WERE TOGETHER IN THE
ARKNESS, CLOSE TO EACH OTHER, I WASN'T
YING ON YOU. I WAS LOVING YOU.

RUTH

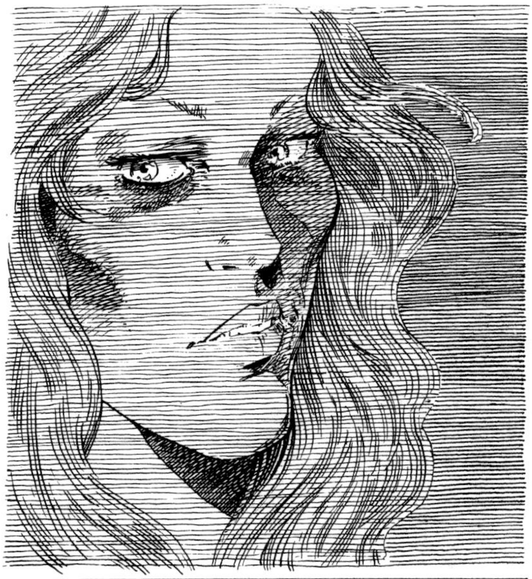

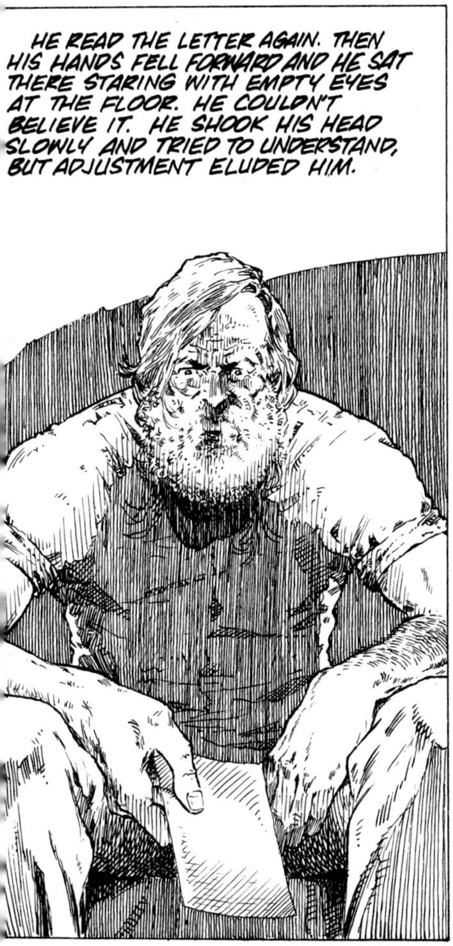
HE READ THE LETTER AGAIN. THEN HIS HANDS FELL FORWARD AND HE SAT THERE STARING WITH EMPTY EYES AT THE FLOOR. HE COULDN'T BELIEVE IT. HE SHOOK HIS HEAD SLOWLY AND TRIED TO UNDERSTAND, BUT ADJUSTMENT ELUDED HIM.

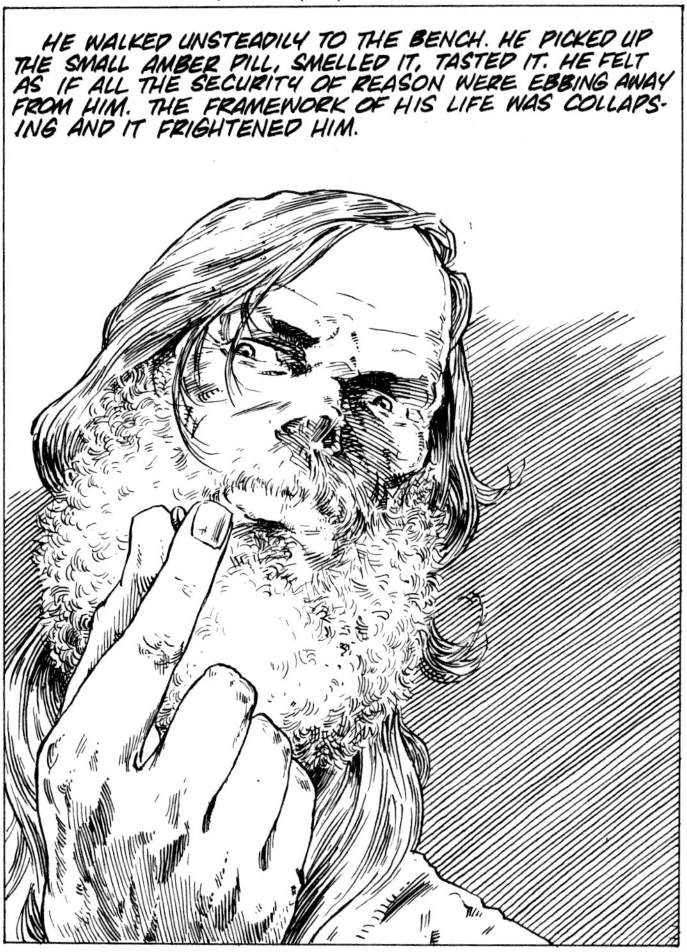
HE WALKED UNSTEADILY TO THE BENCH. HE PICKED UP THE SMALL AMBER PILL, SMELLED IT, TASTED IT. HE FELT AS IF ALL THE SECURITY OF REASON WERE EBBING AWAY FROM HIM. THE FRAMEWORK OF HIS LIFE WAS COLLAPS-ING AND IT FRIGHTENED HIM.

YET HOW COULD HE REFUTE THE EVIDENCE. THE PILL, THE TAN COMING OFF HER LEG, HER WALKING IN THE SUN, HER REACTION TO GARLIC.

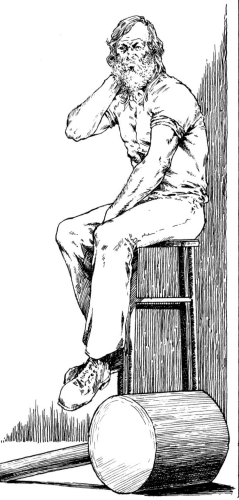

SLOWLY, PLODDINGLY, HIS MIND WENT OVER THE EVIDENCE.

WHEN HE'D FIRST SEEN HER SHE'D RUN FROM HIM. HAD IT BEEN A RUSE? NO, SHE'D BEEN GENUINELY FRIGHTENED. SHE MUST HAVE BEEN STARTLED BY HIS CRY, THEN, EVEN THOUGH SHE'D BEEN EXPECTING IT, AND FORGOTTEN ALL ABOUT HER JOB. THEN LATER, WHEN SHE'D CALMED DOWN, SHE'D TALKED HIM INTO THINKING THAT HER REACTION TO GARLIC WAS THE REACTION OF A SICK STOMACH.

AND SHE HAD LIED AND SMILED AND FEIGNED HOPELESS ACCEPTANCE AND CAREFULLY GOT ALL THE INFORMATION SHE'D BEEN SENT AFTER. AND, WHEN SHE'D WANTED TO LEAVE, SHE COULDN'T BECAUSE OF CORTMAN AND THE OTHERS. HE HAD AWAKENED THEN. THEY HAD EMBRACED, THEY HAD...

I wasn't spying on you. I was loving you.

Ruth

"I WAS LOVING YOU."

LIE. LIE!

GROAN

214

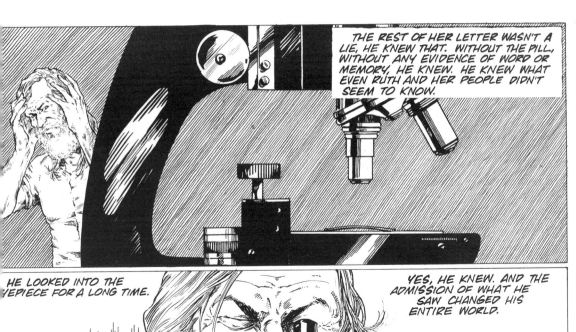

THE REST OF HER LETTER WASN'T A LIE, HE KNEW THAT. WITHOUT THE PILL, WITHOUT ANY EVIDENCE OF WORD OR MEMORY, HE KNEW. HE KNEW WHAT EVEN *RUTH* AND HER PEOPLE DIDN'T SEEM TO KNOW.

HE LOOKED INTO THE EYEPIECE FOR A LONG TIME.

YES, HE KNEW. AND THE ADMISSION OF WHAT HE SAW CHANGED HIS ENTIRE WORLD.

HOW STUPID AND INEFFECTIVE HE FELT FOR NEVER HAVING FORESEEN IT! ESPECIALLY AFTER READING THE PHRASE A HUNDRED, A THOUSAND TIMES:

BUT THEN HE'D NEVER REALLY APPRECIATED IT. SUCH A SHORT PHRASE IT WAS, BUT MEANING SO MUCH:

BACTERIA CAN MUTATE.

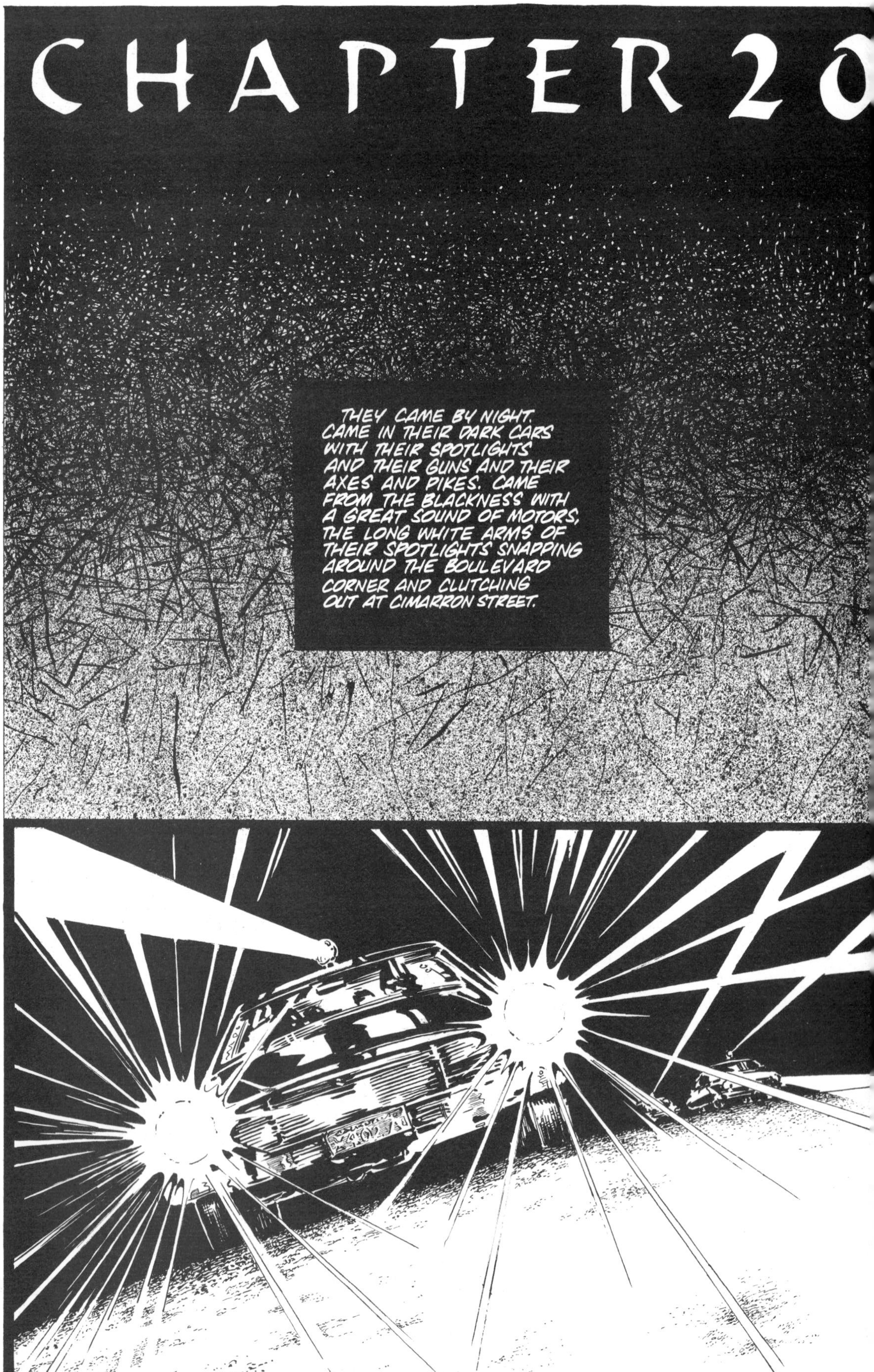
CHAPTER 20
THEY CAME BY NIGHT. CAME IN THEIR DARK CARS WITH THEIR SPOTLIGHTS AND THEIR GUNS AND THEIR AXES AND PIKES. CAME FROM THE BLACKNESS WITH A GREAT SOUND OF MOTORS, THE LONG WHITE ARMS OF THEIR SPOTLIGHTS SNAPPING AROUND THE BOULEVARD CORNER AND CLUTCHING OUT AT CIMARRON STREET.

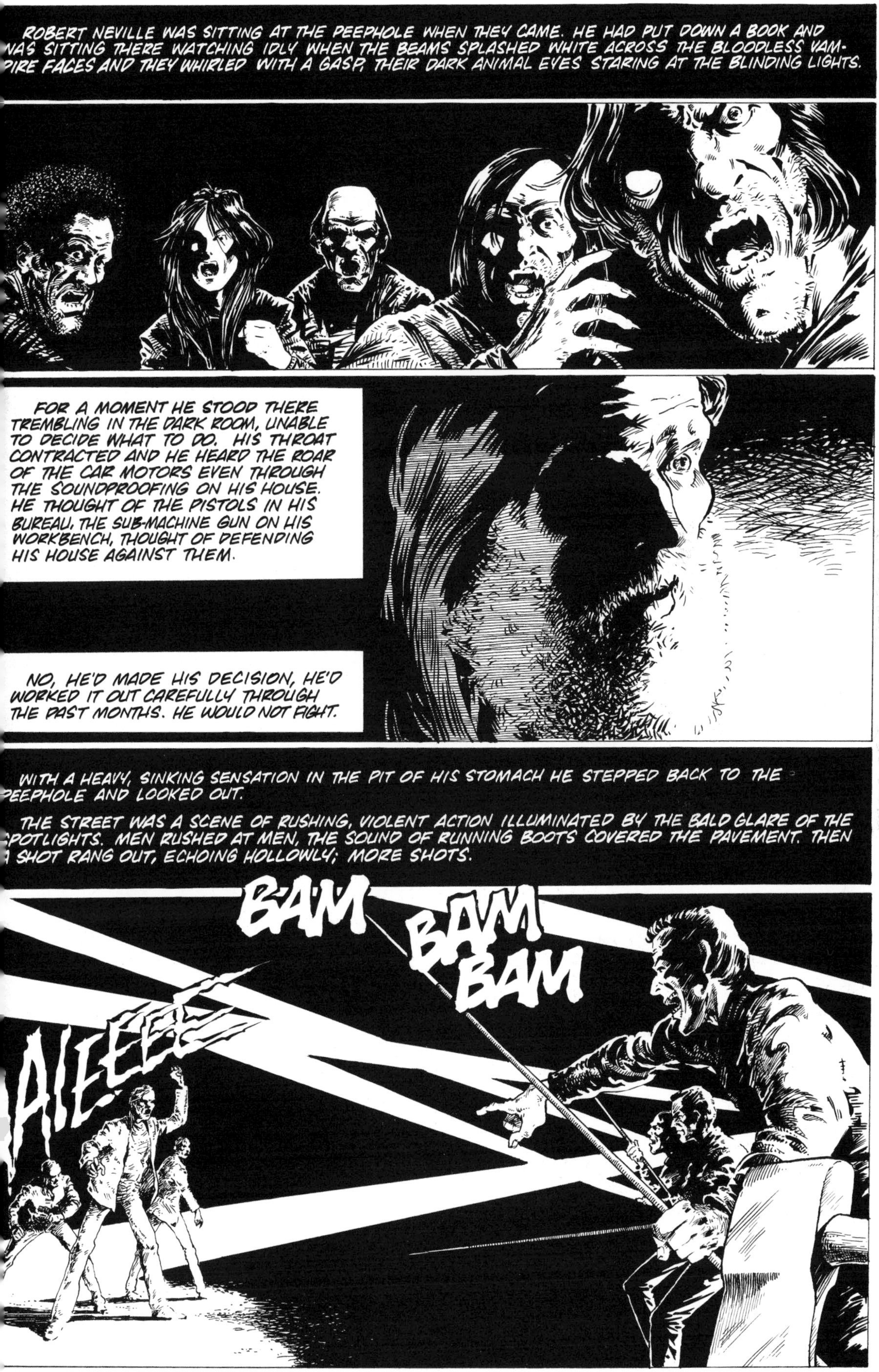
ROBERT NEVILLE WAS SITTING AT THE PEEPHOLE WHEN THEY CAME. HE HAD PUT DOWN A BOOK AND NAS SITTING THERE WATCHING IDLY WHEN THE BEAMS SPLASHED WHITE ACROSS THE BLOODLESS VAM-PIRE FACES AND THEY WHIRLED WITH A GASP, THEIR DARK ANIMAL EYES STARING AT THE BLINDING LIGHTS.
FOR A MOMENT HE STOOD THERE TREMBLING IN THE DARK ROOM, UNABLE TO DECIDE WHAT TO DO. HIS THROAT CONTRACTED AND HE HEARD THE ROAR OF THE CAR MOTORS EVEN THROUGH THE SOUNDPROOFING ON HIS HOUSE. HE THOUGHT OF THE PISTOLS IN HIS BUREAU, THE SUB-MACHINE GUN ON HIS WORKBENCH, THOUGHT OF DEFENDING HIS HOUSE AGAINST THEM.
NO, HE'D MADE HIS DECISION, HE'D WORKED IT OUT CAREFULLY THROUGH THE PAST MONTHS. HE WOULD NOT FIGHT.
WITH A HEAVY, SINKING SENSATION IN THE PIT OF HIS STOMACH HE STEPPED BACK TO THE EEPHOLE AND LOOKED OUT.
THE STREET WAS A SCENE OF RUSHING, VIOLENT ACTION ILLUMINATED BY THE BALD GLARE OF THE POTLIGHTS. MEN RUSHED AT MEN, THE SOUND OF RUNNING BOOTS COVERED THE PAVEMENT. THEN SHOT RANG OUT, ECHOING HOLLOWLY; MORE SHOTS.
BAM
BAM BAM
AIEEEE

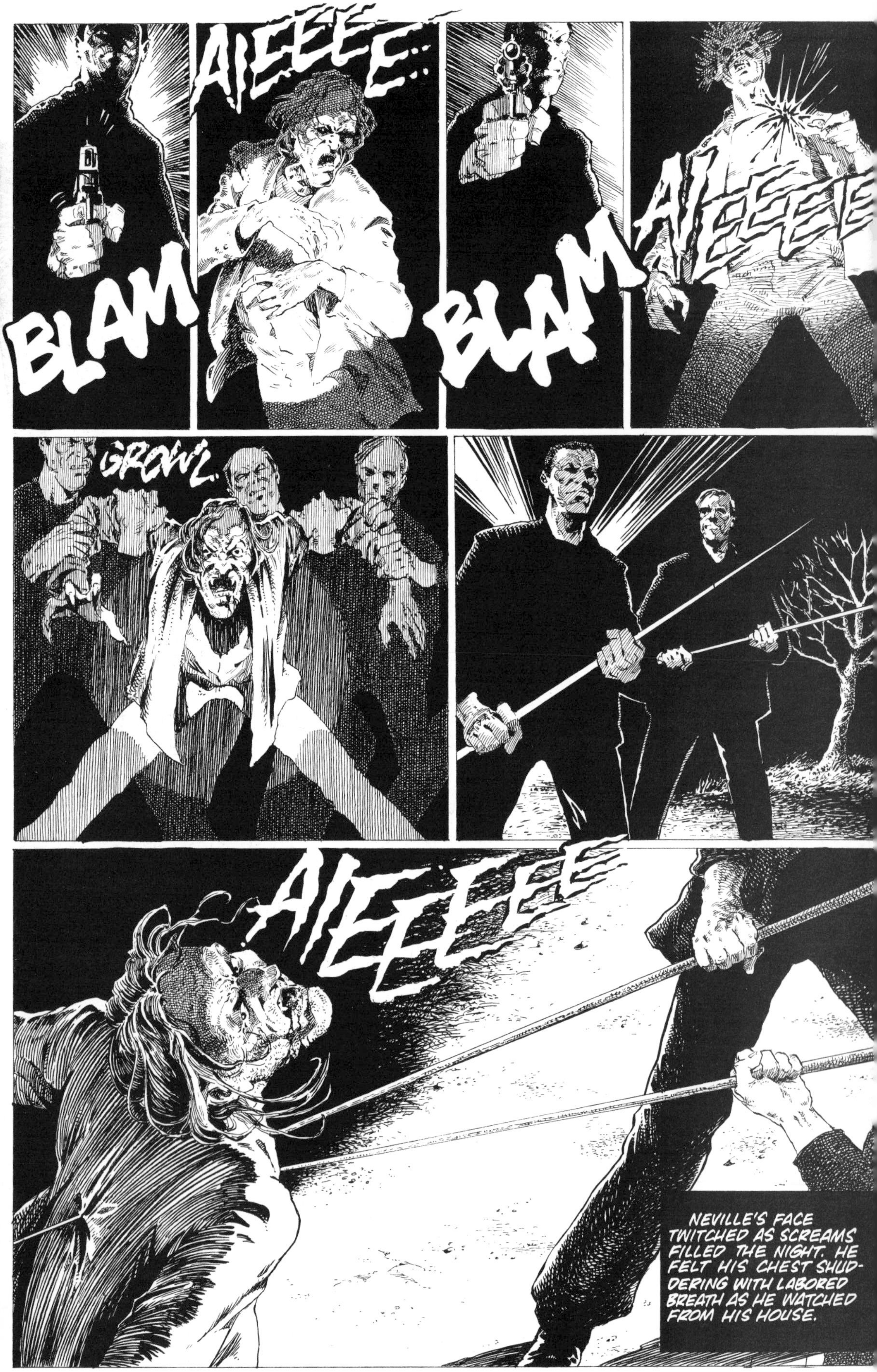

BLAM
AIEEEE...
BLAM
AIEEEE
GROWL
AIEEEEEE
NEVILLE'S FACE TWITCHED AS SCREAMS FILLED THE NIGHT. HE FELT HIS CHEST SHUDDERING WITH LABORED BREATH AS HE WATCHED FROM HIS HOUSE.

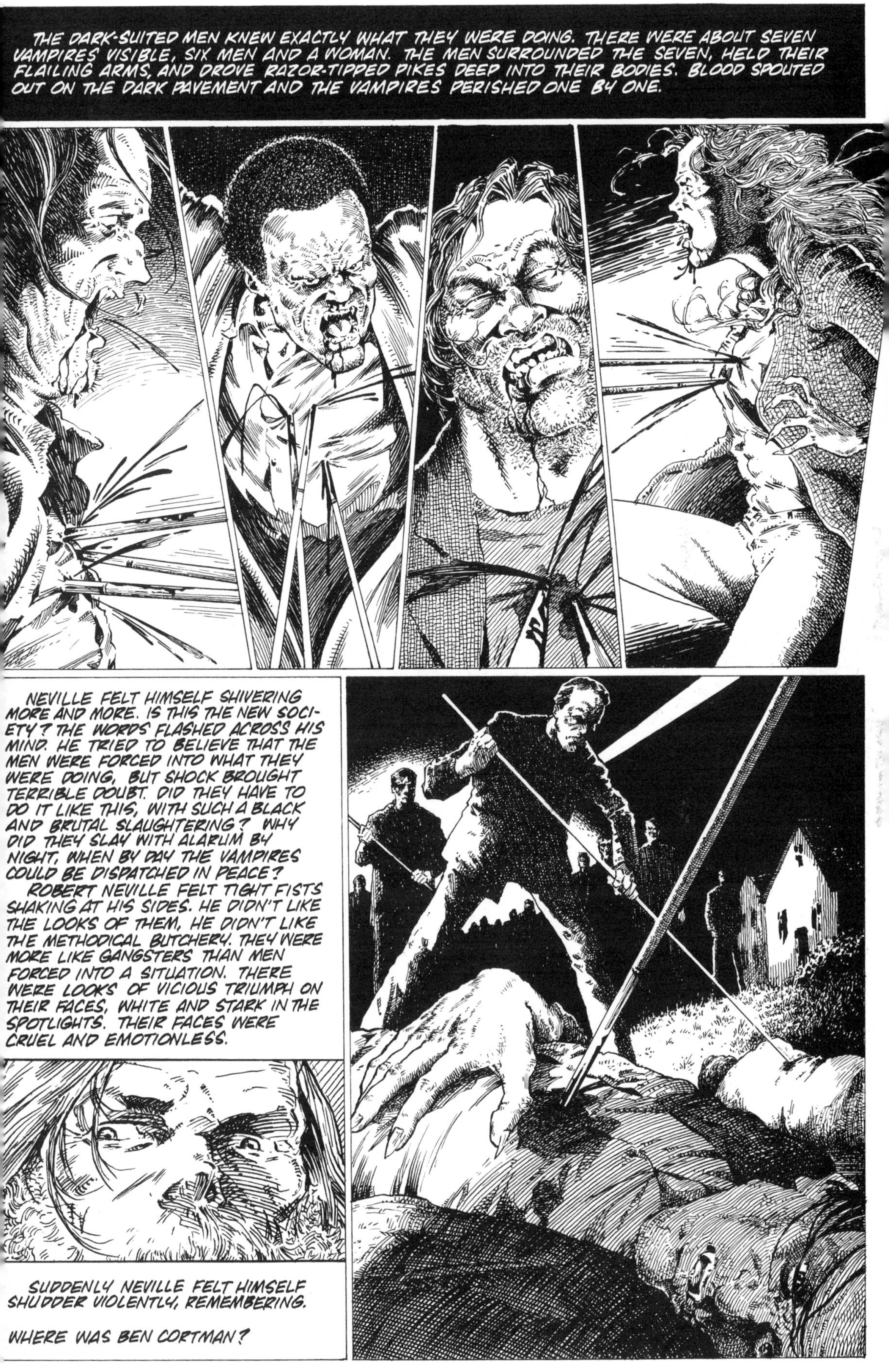
THE DARK-SUITED MEN KNEW EXACTLY WHAT THEY WERE DOING. THERE WERE ABOUT SEVEN VAMPIRES VISIBLE, SIX MEN AND A WOMAN. THE MEN SURROUNDED THE SEVEN, HELD THEIR FLAILING ARMS, AND DROVE RAZOR-TIPPED PIKES DEEP INTO THEIR BODIES. BLOOD SPOUTED OUT ON THE DARK PAVEMENT AND THE VAMPIRES PERISHED ONE BY ONE.
NEVILLE FELT HIMSELF SHIVERING MORE AND MORE. IS THIS THE NEW SOCIETY? THE WORDS FLASHED ACROSS HIS MIND. HE TRIED TO BELIEVE THAT THE MEN WERE FORCED INTO WHAT THEY WERE DOING, BUT SHOCK BROUGHT TERRIBLE DOUBT. DID THEY HAVE TO DO IT LIKE THIS, WITH SUCH A BLACK AND BRUTAL SLAUGHTERING? WHY DID THEY SLAY WITH ALARUM BY NIGHT, WHEN BY DAY THE VAMPIRES COULD BE DISPATCHED IN PEACE?
ROBERT NEVILLE FELT TIGHT FISTS SHAKING AT HIS SIDES. HE DIDN'T LIKE THE LOOKS OF THEM, HE DIDN'T LIKE THE METHODICAL BUTCHERY. THEY WERE MORE LIKE GANGSTERS THAN MEN FORCED INTO A SITUATION. THERE WERE LOOKS OF VICIOUS TRIUMPH ON THEIR FACES, WHITE AND STARK IN THE SPOTLIGHTS. THEIR FACES WERE CRUEL AND EMOTIONLESS.
SUDDENLY NEVILLE FELT HIMSELF SHUDDER VIOLENTLY, REMEMBERING.
WHERE WAS BEN CORTMAN?

HIS EYES FLED OVER THE STREET BUT HE COULDN'T SEE CORTMAN. HE DIDN'T WANT THEM TO GET CORTMAN, HE REALIZED, DIDN'T WANT THEM TO DESTROY CORTMAN LIKE THAT. WITH A SENSE OF INWARD SHOCK HE COULD NOT ANALYZE IN THE RUSH OF THE MOMENT, HE REALIZED THAT HE FELT MORE DEEPLY TOWARD THE VAMPIRES THAN HE DID TOWARD THEIR EXECUTIONERS.

A SHOUT. NEVILLE'S EYES JUMPED TOWARD THE FOCUS OF THE SPOTLIGHTS. HE STIFFENED.

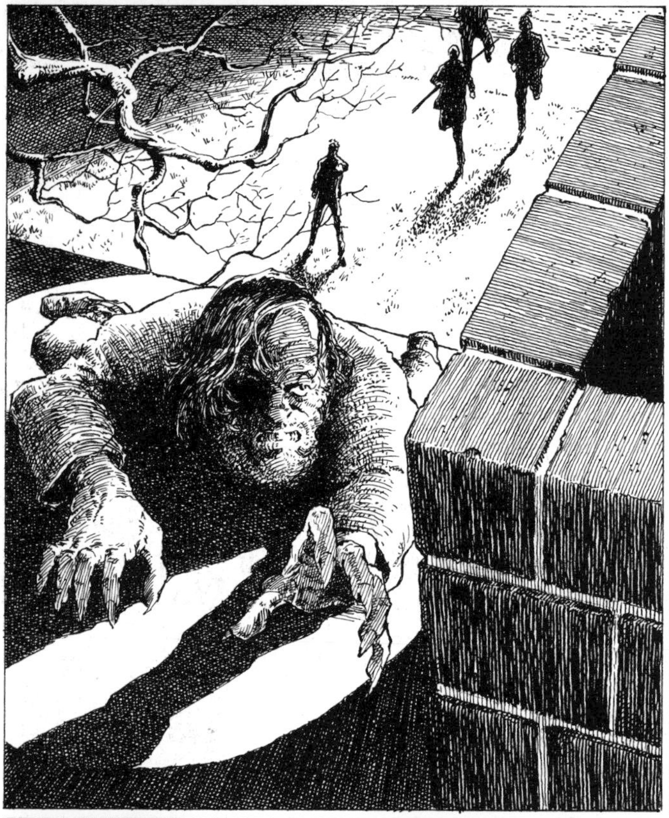

CORTMAN WAS ON THE ROOF OF THE HOUSE ACROSS THE STREET. HE WAS PULLING HIMSELF UP TOWARD THE CHIMNEY, BODY FLATTENED ON THE SHINGLES.

ABRUPTLY IT CAME TO NEVILLE THAT IT WAS IN THAT CHIMNEY THAT BEN CORTMAN HAD HIDDEN MOST OF THE TIME AND HE FELT A WRENCH OF DESPAIR AT THE KNOWLEDGE. WHY HADN'T HE LOOKED MORE CAREFULLY? HE COULDN'T FIGHT THE SICK APPREHENSION HE FELT AT THE THOUGHT OF CORTMAN'S BEING KILLED BY THESE BRUTAL STRANGERS. OBJECTIVELY, IT WAS POINTLESS, BUT HE COULD NOT REPRESS THE FEELING. CORTMAN WAS NOT THEIRS TO PUT TO REST.

BUT THERE WAS NOTHING HE COULD DO.

WITH BLEAK, TORTURED EYES HE WATCHED THE SPOTLIGHTS CLUSTER ON CORTMAN'S WRIGGLING BODY. HE WATCHE THE WHITE HANDS REACHING OUT SLOWL FOR HANDHOLDS ON THE ROOF. SLOWLY, SLOWLY, AS IF CORTMAN HAD ALL THE TIME IN THE WORLD. HE FELT HIMSELF STRAINING WITH CORTMAN'S AGONIZINGLY SLOW MOVEMENTS.

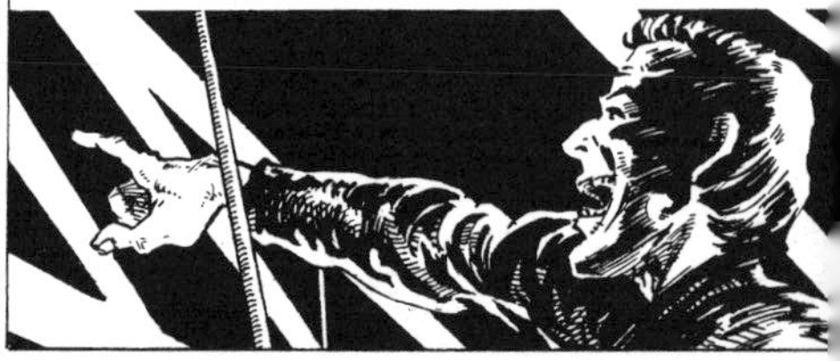

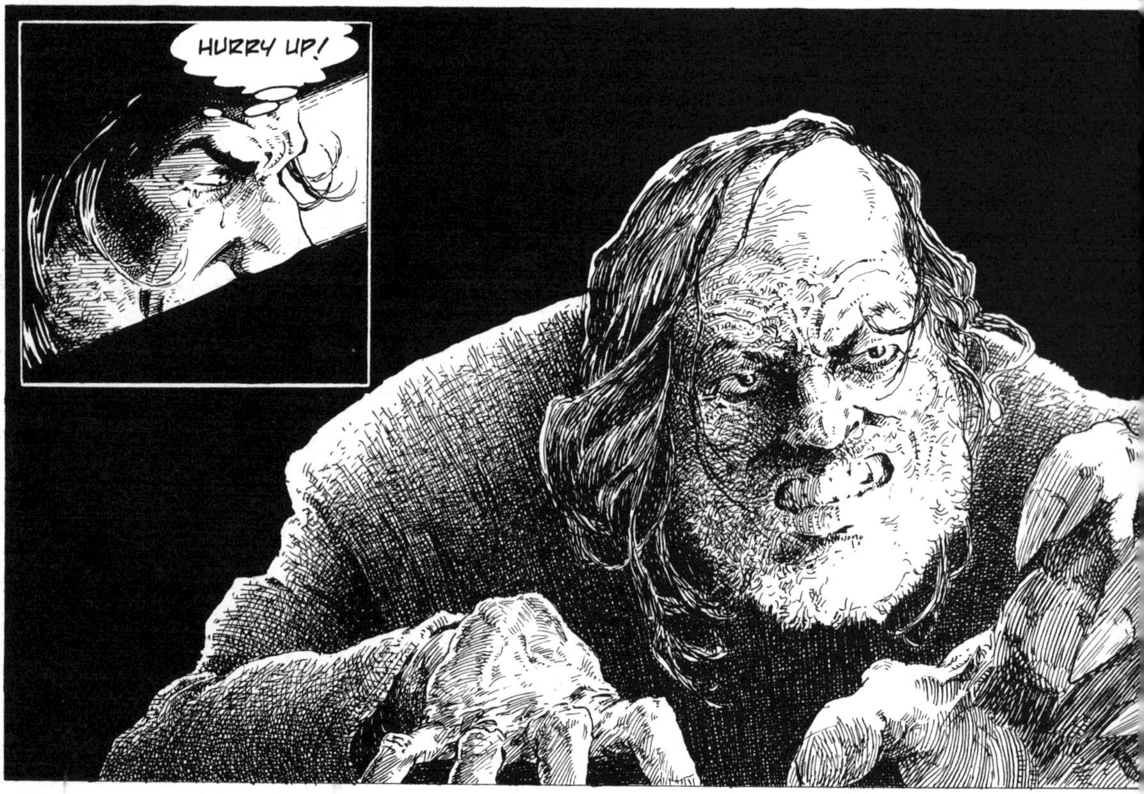
HURRY UP!

CLICK

BLAM
BLAM
BLAM
BLAM
Ping
BLAM
Ping

THE MEN DID NOT SHOUT, THEY DID NOT COMMAND. THE NIGHT WAS TORN OPEN AGAIN WITH THEIR EXPLODING FIRE. NEVILLE ALMOST FELT THE BULLETS IN HIS OWN FLESH. HIS BODY JERKED WITH CONVULSIVE SHUDDERS AS HE WATCHED CORTMAN'S BODY JERK UNDER THE IMPACT OF THE BULLETS. STILL CORTMAN KEPT CRAWLING, AND NEVILLE SAW HIS WHITE FACE, HIS TEETH GRITTED TOGETHER.

BLAM BLAM BLAM
BLAM
BLAM

THE END OF OLIVER HARDY, NEVILLE THOUGHT, THE DEATH OF ALL COMEDY AND ALL LAUGHTER. HE DIDN'T HEAR THE CONTINUOUS FUSILLADE OF SHOTS. HE DIDN'T EVEN FEEL THE TEARS RUNNING DOWN HIS CHEEKS. HIS EYES WERE RIVETED ON THE UNGAINLY FORM OF HIS OLD FRIEND INCHING UP THE BRIGHTLY LIT ROOF.

BLAM
AM BLAM

BLAM BLAM
Ping
BLAM
BLAM

BLAM
BLAM

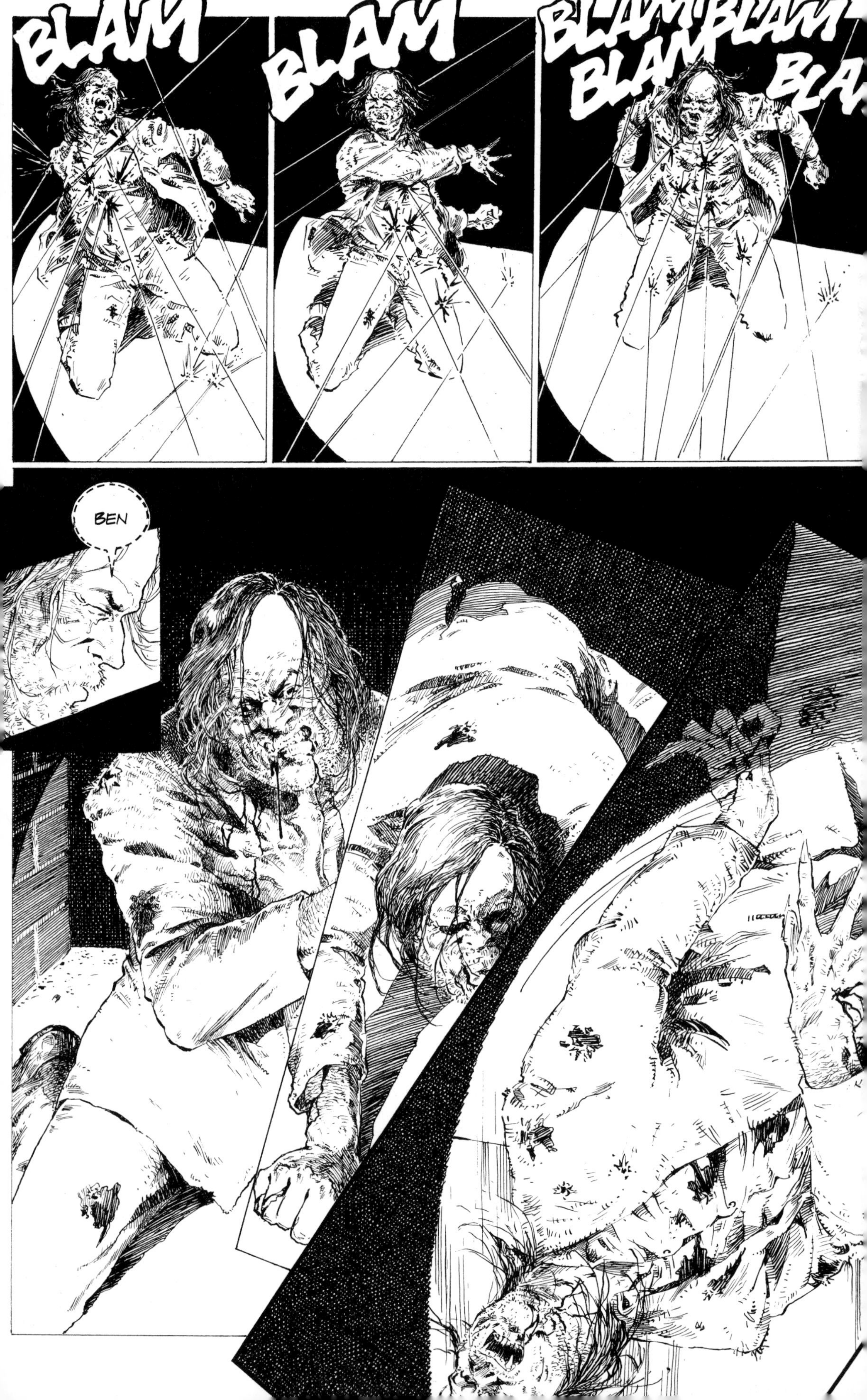
BLAM
BLAM
BLAM BLAM
BLAM
BLA
BEN

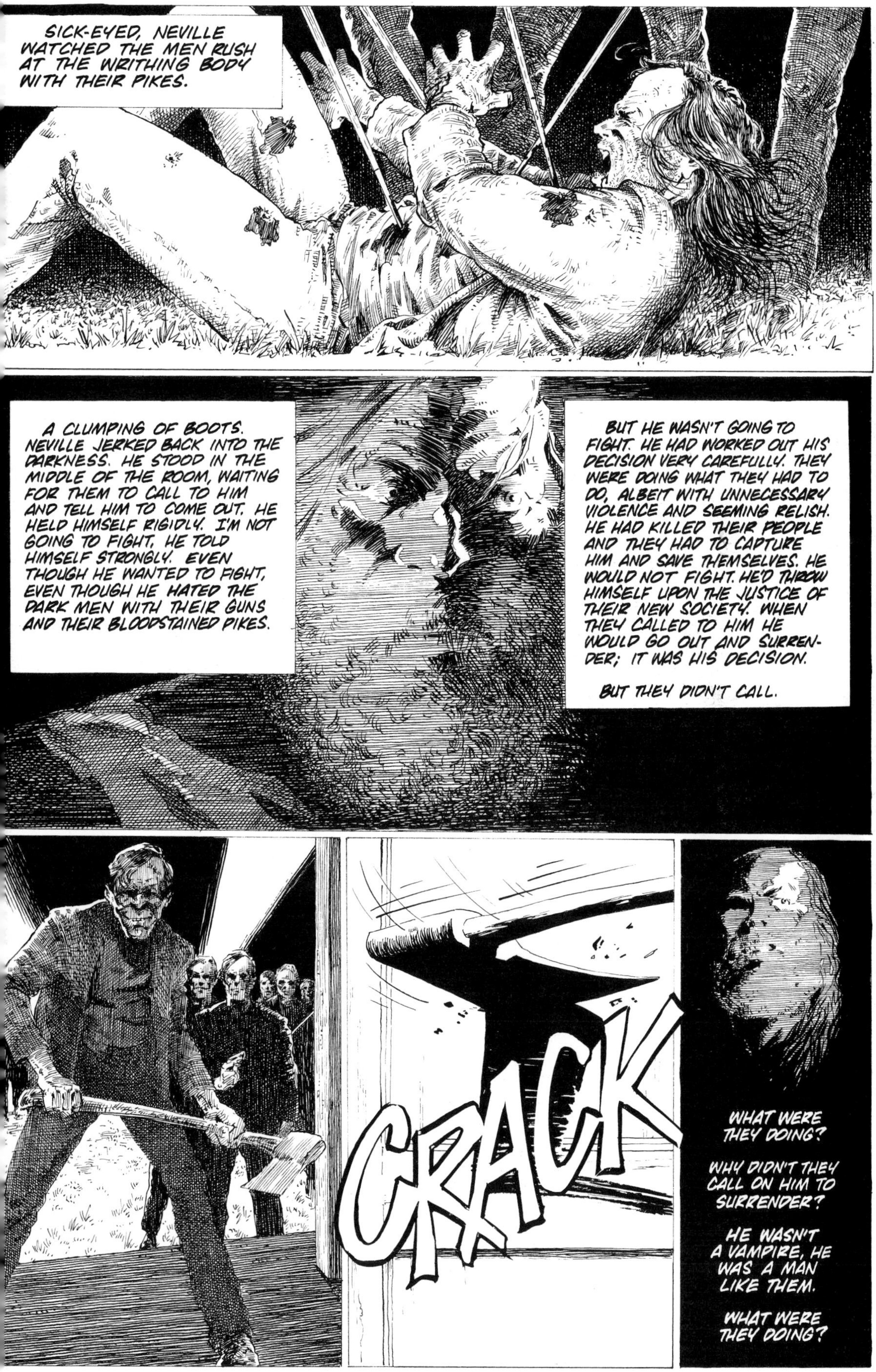
SICK-EYED, NEVILLE WATCHED THE MEN RUSH AT THE WRITHING BODY WITH THEIR PIKES.
A CLUMPING OF BOOTS. NEVILLE JERKED BACK INTO THE DARKNESS. HE STOOD IN THE MIDDLE OF THE ROOM, WAITING FOR THEM TO CALL TO HIM AND TELL HIM TO COME OUT. HE HELD HIMSELF RIGIDLY. I'M NOT GOING TO FIGHT, HE TOLD HIMSELF STRONGLY. EVEN THOUGH HE WANTED TO FIGHT, EVEN THOUGH HE HATED THE DARK MEN WITH THEIR GUNS AND THEIR BLOODSTAINED PIKES.
BUT HE WASN'T GOING TO FIGHT. HE HAD WORKED OUT HIS DECISION VERY CAREFULLY. THEY WERE DOING WHAT THEY HAD TO DO, ALBEIT WITH UNNECESSARY VIOLENCE AND SEEMING RELISH. HE HAD KILLED THEIR PEOPLE AND THEY HAD TO CAPTURE HIM AND SAVE THEMSELVES. HE WOULD NOT FIGHT. HE'D THROW HIMSELF UPON THE JUSTICE OF THEIR NEW SOCIETY. WHEN THEY CALLED TO HIM HE WOULD GO OUT AND SURRENDER; IT WAS HIS DECISION.
BUT THEY DIDN'T CALL.
CRACK
WHAT WERE THEY DOING?
WHY DIDN'T THEY CALL ON HIM TO SURRENDER?
HE WASN'T A VAMPIRE, HE WAS A MAN LIKE THEM.
WHAT WERE THEY DOING?

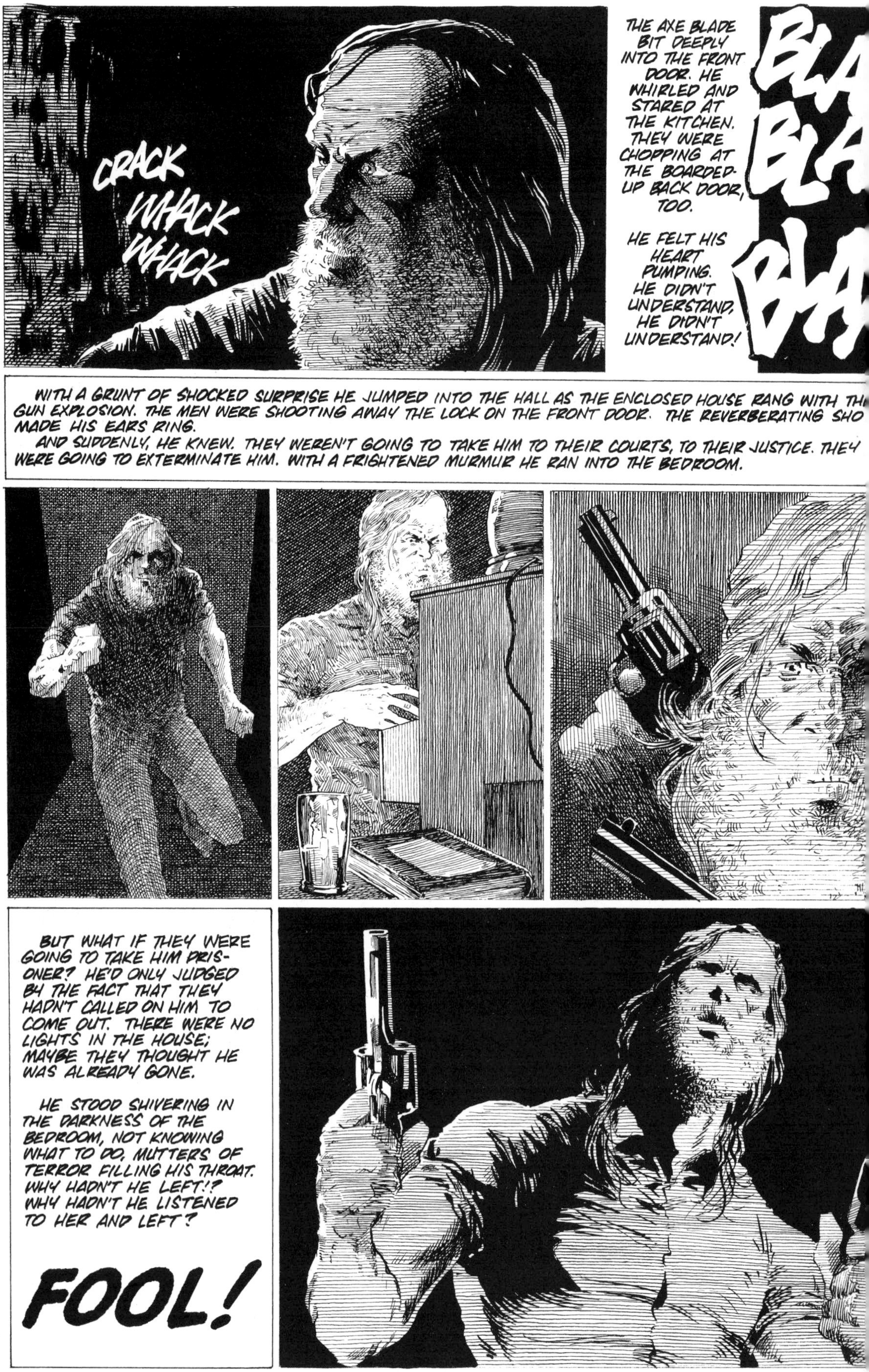
CRACK
WHACK
WHACK
THE AXE BLADE BIT DEEPLY INTO THE FRONT DOOR. HE WHIRLED AND STARED AT THE KITCHEN. THEY WERE CHOPPING AT THE BOARDED-UP BACK DOOR, TOO.
HE FELT HIS HEART PUMPING. HE DIDN'T UNDERSTAND, HE DIDN'T UNDERSTAND!
WITH A GRUNT OF SHOCKED SURPRISE HE JUMPED INTO THE HALL AS THE ENCLOSED HOUSE RANG WITH TH
GUN EXPLOSION. THE MEN WERE SHOOTING AWAY THE LOCK ON THE FRONT DOOR. THE REVERBERATING SHO
MADE HIS EARS RING.
AND SUDDENLY, HE KNEW. THEY WEREN'T GOING TO TAKE HIM TO THEIR COURTS, TO THEIR JUSTICE. THEY WERE GOING TO EXTERMINATE HIM. WITH A FRIGHTENED MURMUR HE RAN INTO THE BEDROOM.
BUT WHAT IF THEY WERE GOING TO TAKE HIM PRISONER? HE'D ONLY JUDGED BY THE FACT THAT THEY HADN'T CALLED ON HIM TO COME OUT. THERE WERE NO LIGHTS IN THE HOUSE; MAYBE THEY THOUGHT HE WAS ALREADY GONE.
HE STOOD SHIVERING IN THE DARKNESS OF THE BEDROOM, NOT KNOWING WHAT TO DO, MUTTERS OF TERROR FILLING HIS THROAT. WHY HADN'T HE LEFT!? WHY HADN'T HE LISTENED TO HER AND LEFT?
FOOL!

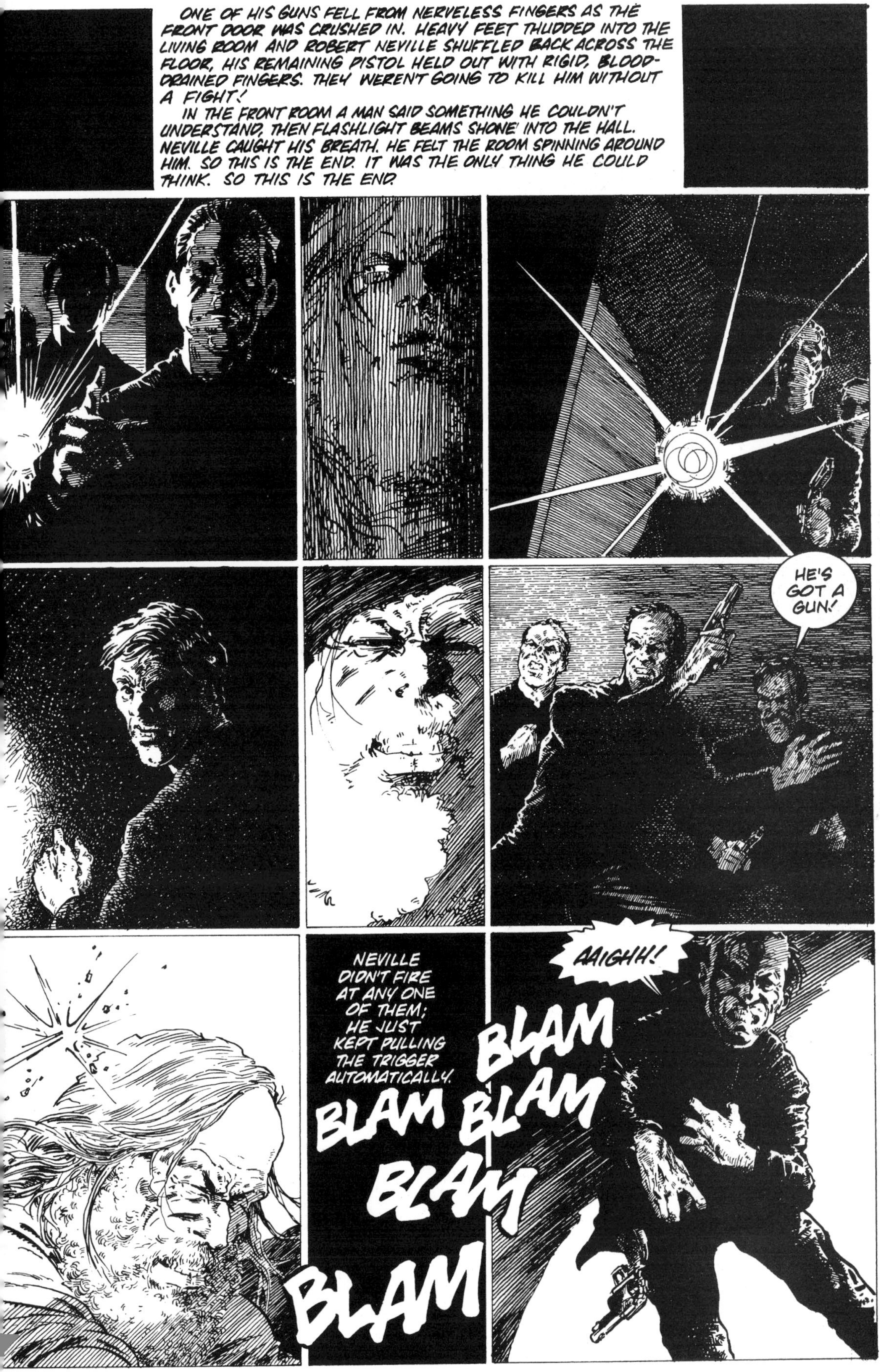
ONE OF HIS GUNS FELL FROM NERVELESS FINGERS AS THE FRONT DOOR WAS CRUSHED IN. HEAVY FEET THUDDED INTO THE LIVING ROOM AND ROBERT NEVILLE SHUFFLED BACK ACROSS THE FLOOR, HIS REMAINING PISTOL HELD OUT WITH RIGID, BLOOD-DRAINED FINGERS. THEY WEREN'T GOING TO KILL HIM WITHOUT A FIGHT!
IN THE FRONT ROOM A MAN SAID SOMETHING HE COULDN'T UNDERSTAND, THEN FLASHLIGHT BEAMS SHONE INTO THE HALL. NEVILLE CAUGHT HIS BREATH. HE FELT THE ROOM SPINNING AROUND HIM. SO THIS IS THE END. IT WAS THE ONLY THING HE COULD THINK. SO THIS IS THE END.
HE'S GOT A GUN!
NEVILLE DIDN'T FIRE AT ANY ONE OF THEM; HE JUST KEPT PULLING THE TRIGGER AUTOMATICALLY.
AAIGHH!
BLAM
BLAM BLAM
BLAM
BLAM

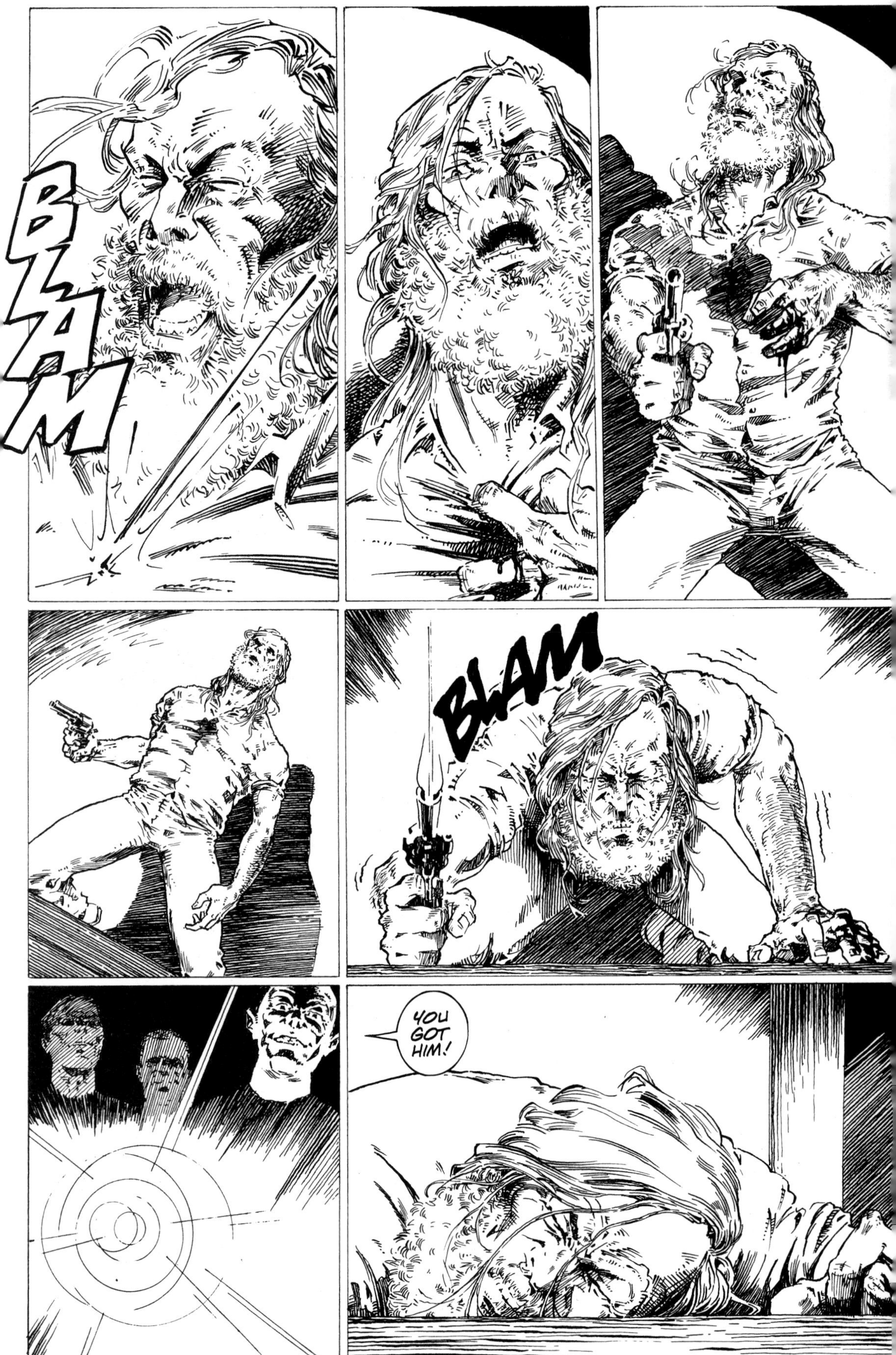
BLAM
BLAM
YOU GOT HIM!

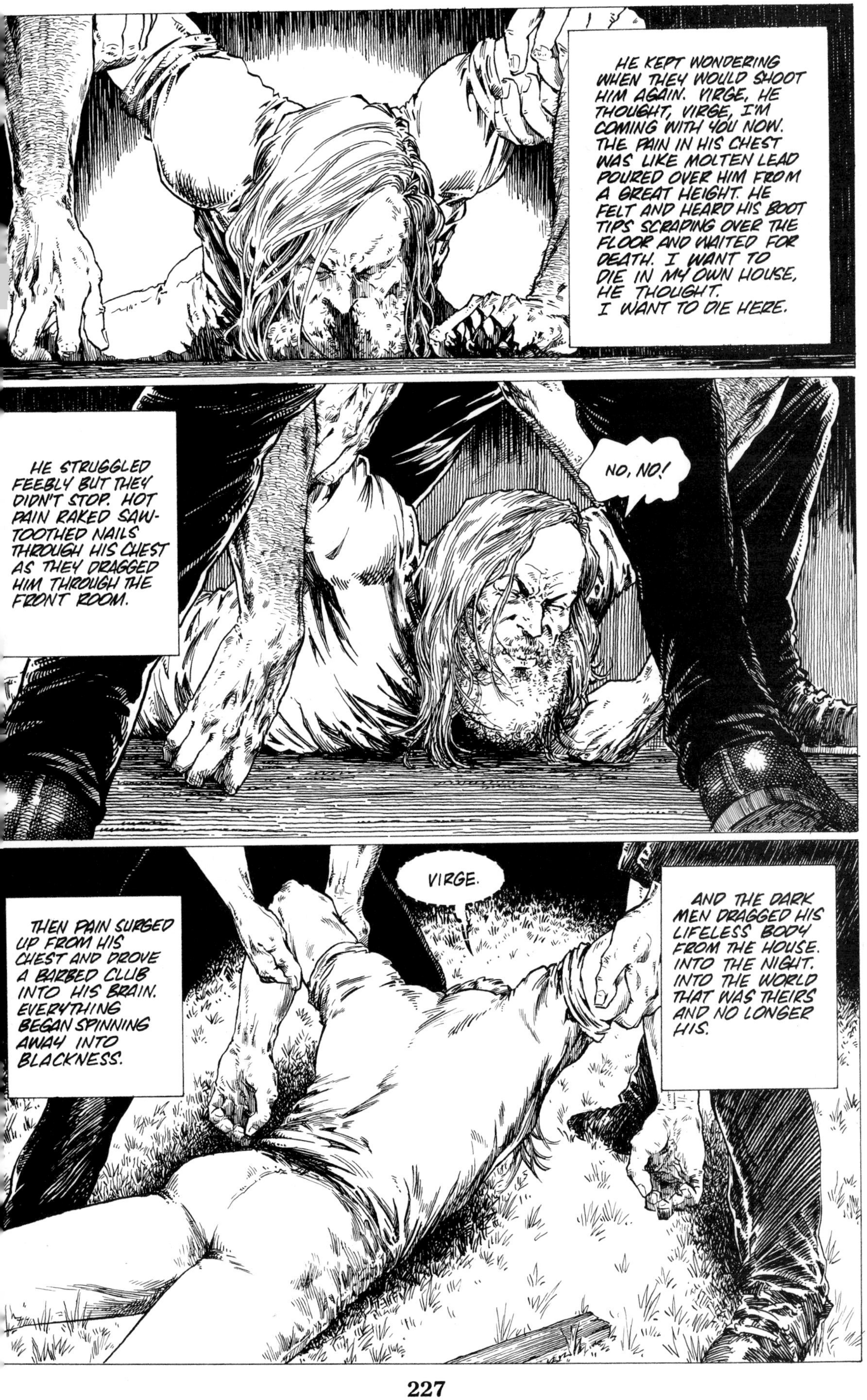

HE KEPT WONDERING WHEN THEY WOULD SHOOT HIM AGAIN. VIRGE, HE THOUGHT, VIRGE, I'M COMING WITH YOU NOW. THE PAIN IN HIS CHEST WAS LIKE MOLTEN LEAD POURED OVER HIM FROM A GREAT HEIGHT. HE FELT AND HEARD HIS BOOT TIPS SCRAPING OVER THE FLOOR AND WAITED FOR DEATH. I WANT TO DIE IN MY OWN HOUSE, HE THOUGHT. I WANT TO DIE HERE.
HE STRUGGLED FEEBLY BUT THEY DIDN'T STOP. HOT PAIN RAKED SAW-TOOTHED NAILS THROUGH HIS CHEST AS THEY DRAGGED HIM THROUGH THE FRONT ROOM.
NO, NO!
THEN PAIN SURGED UP FROM HIS CHEST AND DROVE A BARBED CLUB INTO HIS BRAIN. EVERYTHING BEGAN SPINNING AWAY INTO BLACKNESS.
VIRGE.
AND THE DARK MEN DRAGGED HIS LIFELESS BODY FROM THE HOUSE. INTO THE NIGHT. INTO THE WORLD THAT WAS THEIRS AND NO LONGER HIS.

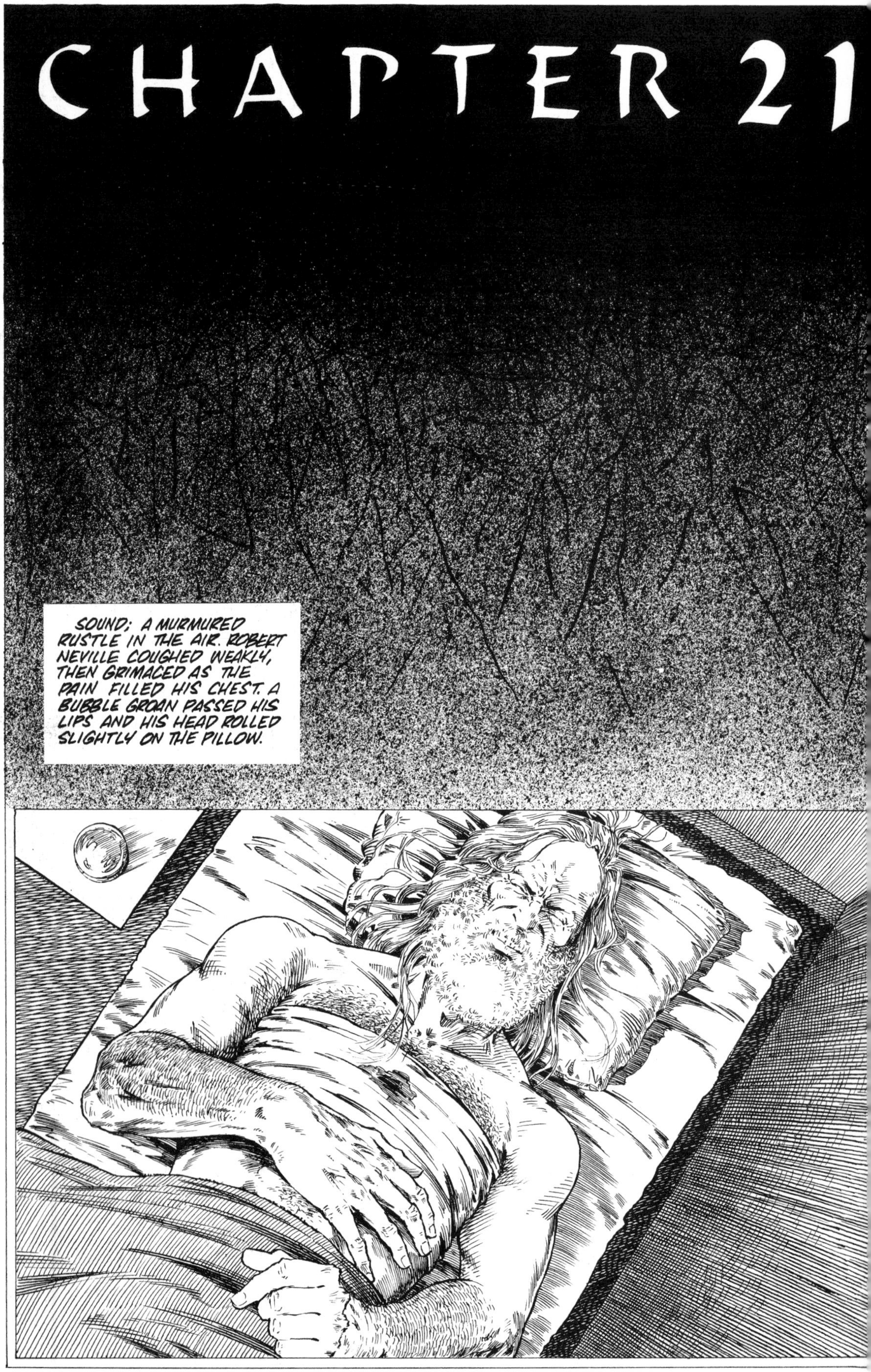
CHAPTER 21
SOUND; A MURMURED RUSTLE IN THE AIR. ROBERT NEVILLE COUGHED WEAKLY, THEN GRIMACED AS THE PAIN FILLED HIS CHEST. A BUBBLE GROAN PASSED HIS LIPS AND HIS HEAD ROLLED SLIGHTLY ON THE PILLOW.

THE SOUND GREW STRONGER, IT BECAME A RUMBLING MIXTURE OF NOISES. HIS HANDS DREW IN SLOWLY AT HIS SIDES. WHY DIDN'T THEY TAKE THE FIRE OFF HIS CHEST? HE COULD FEEL HOT COALS DROPPING THROUGH OPENINGS IN HIS FLESH. ANOTHER GROAN, AGONIZED AND BREATHLESS, TWITCHED HIS GRAYING LIPS. THEN HIS EYES FLUTTERED OPEN.

HE STARED AT THE ROUGH PLASTER CEILING FOR A FULL MINUTE WITHOUT BLINKING. PAIN EBBED AND SWELLED IN HIS CHEST WITH AN ENDLESS, NERVE-CLUTCHING THROB. HIS FACE REMAINED A TAUT, LINED MASK OF RESISTANCE TO THE PAIN. IF HE RELAXED FOR A SECOND, IT ENVELOPED HIM COMPLETELY; HE HAD TO FIGHT IT. FOR THE FIRST FEW MINUTES HE COULD ONLY STRUGGLE WITH THE PAIN, SUFFERING BENEATH ITS HOT STABBING. THEN, AFTER A WHILE, HIS BRAIN BEGAN TO FUNCTION; SLOWLY, LIKE A MACHINE FALTERING, STARTING AND STOPPING, TURNING AND JAMMING GEARS.

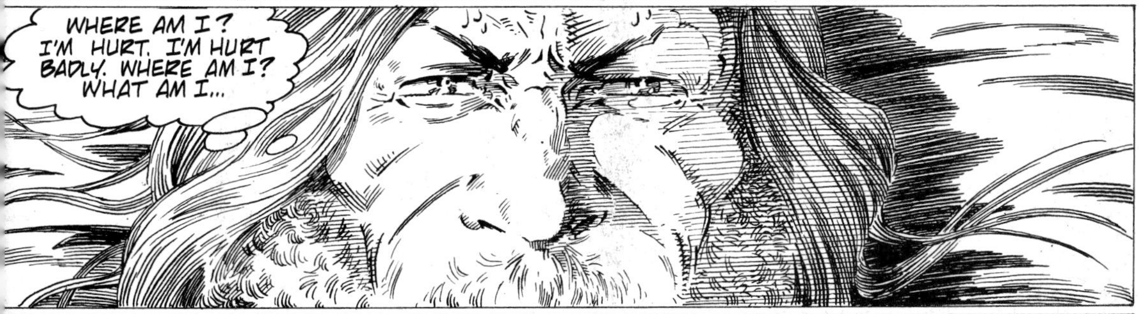
WHERE AM I? I'M HURT. I'M HURT BADLY. WHERE AM I? WHAT AM I...

THEN HE REMEMBERED; THE DARK MEN AND THE ATTACK ON HIS HOUSE. AND HE KNEW WHERE HE AS EVEN BEFORE HE TURNED HIS HEAD SLOWLY, ACHINGLY, AND SAW THE BARRED WINDOWS ACROSS THE NY CUBICLE. HE LOOKED AT THE WINDOWS FOR A LONG TIME, FACE TIGHT, TEETH CLENCHED OGETHER. THE SOUND WAS OUTSIDE; THE RUSHING, CONFUSED SOUND.

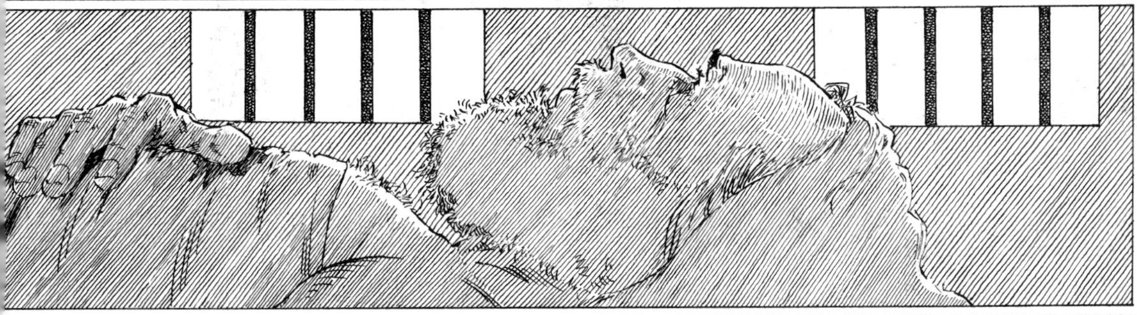

HE LET HIS HEAD ROLL BACK ON THE PILLOW, AND LAY STARING AT THE CEILING. IT WAS ARD TO UNDERSTAND THE MOMENT ON ITS OWN TERMS. HARD TO BELIEVE IT WASN'T LL A NIGHTMARE. OVER THREE YEARS ALONE IN HIS HOUSE. NOW THIS.
BUT HE COULDN'T DOUBT THE SHARP, SHIFTING PAIN IN HIS CHEST AND HE COULDN'T OUBT THE WAY THE MOIST, RED SPOT KEPT GETTING BIGGER AND BIGGER.

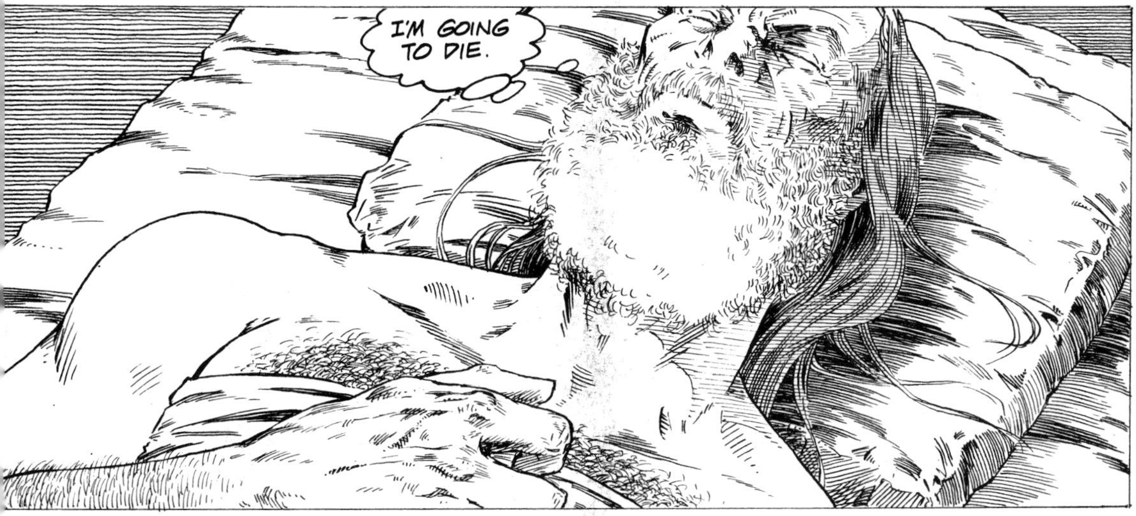
I'M GOING TO DIE.

HE TRIED TO UNDERSTAND THAT. BUT THAT DIDN'T WORK EITHER. IN SPITE OF HAVING LIVED WITH DEATH ALL THESE YEARS, IN SPITE OF HAVING WALKED A TIGHTROPE OF BARE EXISTENCE ACROSS AN ENDLESS MAW OF DEATH-- IN SPITE OF THAT, HE COULDN'T UNDERSTAND IT. PERSONAL DEATH STILL WAS A THING BEYOND COMPREHENSION.

HE WAS STILL ON HIS BACK WHEN THE DOOR BEHIND HIM OPENED.

HE COULDN'T TURN; IT HURT TOO MUCH. HE LAY THERE AND LISTENED TO FOOTSTEPS APPROACH THE BED, THEN STOP. MY EXECUTIONER, HE THOUGHT, THE JUSTICE OF THIS NEW SOCIETY. HE CLOSED HIS EYES AND WAITED.

THE SHOES MOVED AGAIN UNTIL HE KNEW THE PERSON WAS BY THE COT. HE TRIED TO SWALLOW BUT HIS THROAT WAS TOO DRY. HE RAN HIS TONGUE OVER HIS LIPS.

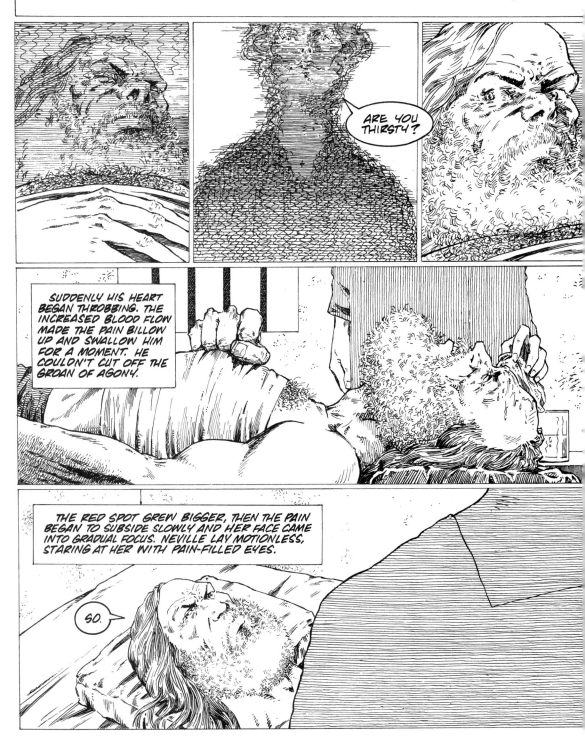

ARE YOU THIRSTY?

SUDDENLY HIS HEART BEGAN THROBBING. THE INCREASED BLOOD FLOW MADE THE PAIN BILLOW UP AND SWALLOW HIM FOR A MOMENT. HE COULDN'T CUT OFF THE GROAN OF AGONY.

THE RED SPOT GREW BIGGER, THEN THE PAIN BEGAN TO SUBSIDE SLOWLY AND HER FACE CAME INTO GRADUAL FOCUS. NEVILLE LAY MOTIONLESS, STARING AT HER WITH PAIN-FILLED EYES.

SO.

SHE DIDN'T ANSWER. SHE SAT ON THE EDGE OF THE BED. SHE PATTED HIS BROW AGAIN. HEN HE HEARD HER POURING WATER INTO A GLASS.

THE PAIN DUG RAZORS INTO HIM AS SHE LIFTED HIS HEAD A LITTLE SO HE COULD RINK. THIS IS WHAT THEY MUST HAVE FELT WHEN THE PIKES WENT INTO THEM, HE HOUGHT. THIS CUTTING, BITING AGONY, THE ESCAPE OF LIFE'S BLOOD.

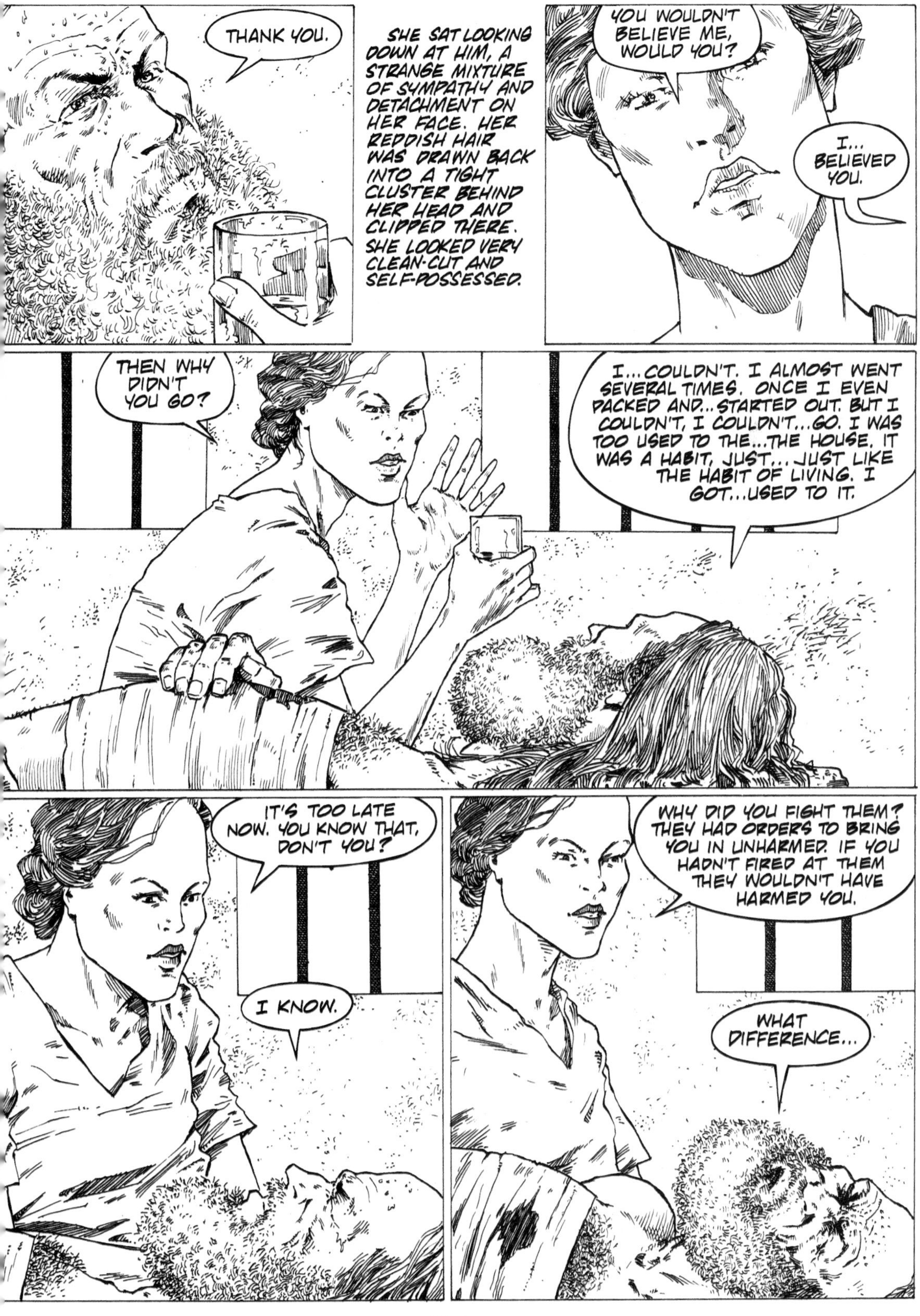

THANK YOU.
SHE SAT LOOKING DOWN AT HIM, A STRANGE MIXTURE OF SYMPATHY AND DETACHMENT ON HER FACE. HER REDDISH HAIR WAS DRAWN BACK INTO A TIGHT CLUSTER BEHIND HER HEAD AND CLIPPED THERE. SHE LOOKED VERY CLEAN-CUT AND SELF-POSSESSED.
YOU WOULDN'T BELIEVE ME, WOULD YOU?
I... BELIEVED YOU.
THEN WHY DIDN'T YOU GO?
I...COULDN'T. I ALMOST WENT SEVERAL TIMES. ONCE I EVEN PACKED AND...STARTED OUT. BUT I COULDN'T, I COULDN'T...GO. I WAS TOO USED TO THE...THE HOUSE. IT WAS A HABIT, JUST... JUST LIKE THE HABIT OF LIVING. I GOT...USED TO IT.
IT'S TOO LATE NOW. YOU KNOW THAT, DON'T YOU?
I KNOW.
WHY DID YOU FIGHT THEM? THEY HAD ORDERS TO BRING YOU IN UNHARMED. IF YOU HADN'T FIRED AT THEM THEY WOULDN'T HAVE HARMED YOU.
WHAT DIFFERENCE...

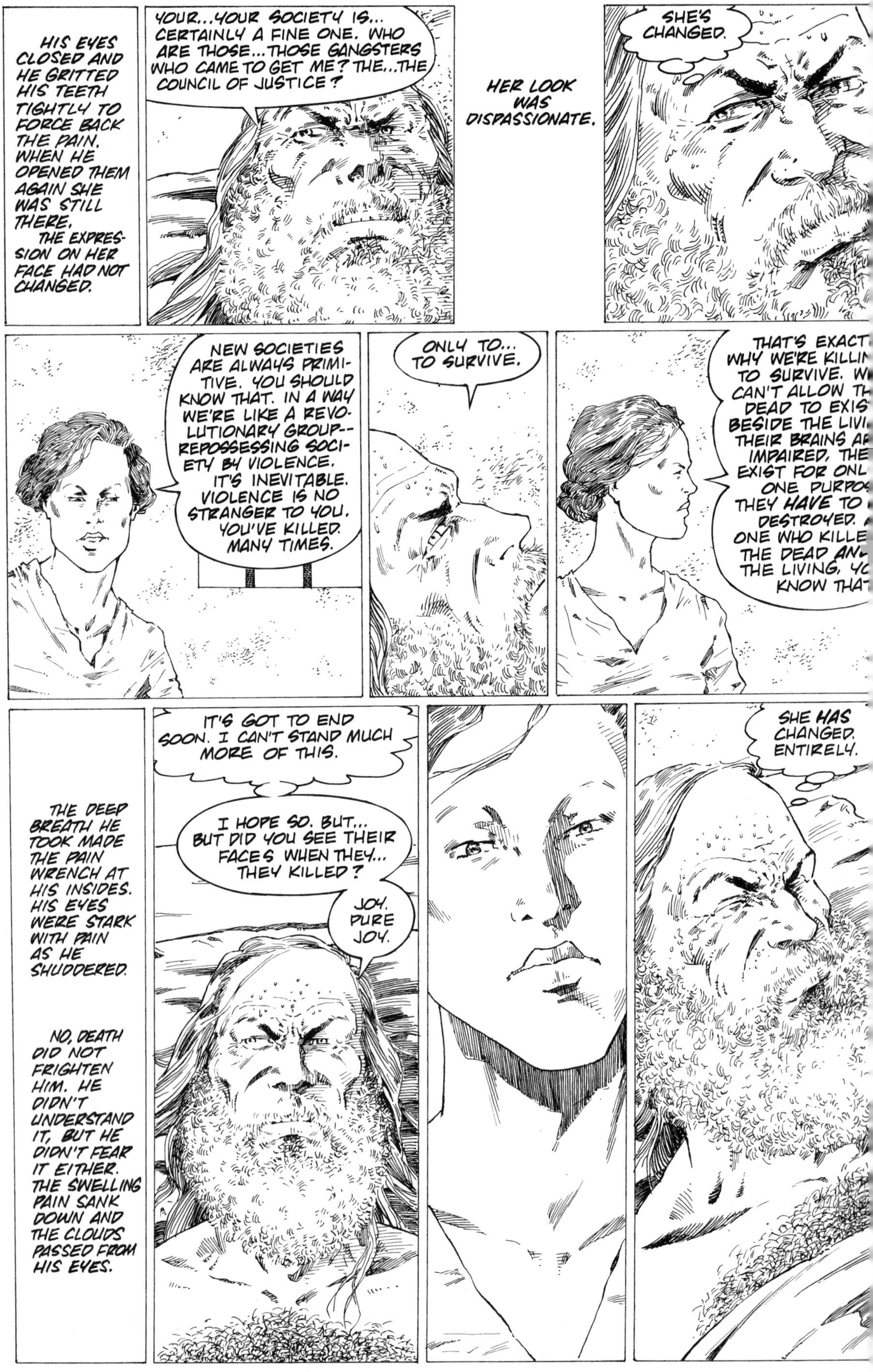
HIS EYES CLOSED AND HE GRITTED HIS TEETH TIGHTLY TO FORCE BACK THE PAIN. WHEN HE OPENED THEM AGAIN SHE WAS STILL THERE.
THE EXPRESSION ON HER FACE HAD NOT CHANGED.
YOUR...YOUR SOCIETY IS... CERTAINLY A FINE ONE. WHO ARE THOSE...THOSE GANGSTERS WHO CAME TO GET ME? THE...THE COUNCIL OF JUSTICE?
HER LOOK WAS DISPASSIONATE.
SHE'S CHANGED.
NEW SOCIETIES ARE ALWAYS PRIMITIVE. YOU SHOULD KNOW THAT. IN A WAY WE'RE LIKE A REVOLUTIONARY GROUP-- REPOSSESSING SOCIETY BY VIOLENCE. IT'S INEVITABLE. VIOLENCE IS NO STRANGER TO YOU. YOU'VE KILLED. MANY TIMES.
ONLY TO... TO SURVIVE.
THAT'S EXACT
WHY WE'RE KILLIN
TO SURVIVE. W
CAN'T ALLOW TH
DEAD TO EXIS
BESIDE THE LIVI
THEIR BRAINS AR
IMPAIRED, THE
EXIST FOR ONL
ONE PURPO
THEY HAVE TO
DESTROYED.
ONE WHO KILLE
THE DEAD AN
THE LIVING, YO
KNOW THA
THE DEEP BREATH HE TOOK MADE THE PAIN WRENCH AT HIS INSIDES. HIS EYES WERE STARK WITH PAIN AS HE SHUDDERED.
NO, DEATH DID NOT FRIGHTEN HIM. HE DIDN'T UNDERSTAND IT, BUT HE DIDN'T FEAR IT EITHER. THE SWELLING PAIN SANK DOWN AND THE CLOUDS PASSED FROM HIS EYES.
IT'S GOT TO END SOON. I CAN'T STAND MUCH MORE OF THIS.
I HOPE SO. BUT... BUT DID YOU SEE THEIR FACES WHEN THEY... THEY KILLED?
JOY. PURE JOY.
SHE HAS CHANGED. ENTIRELY.

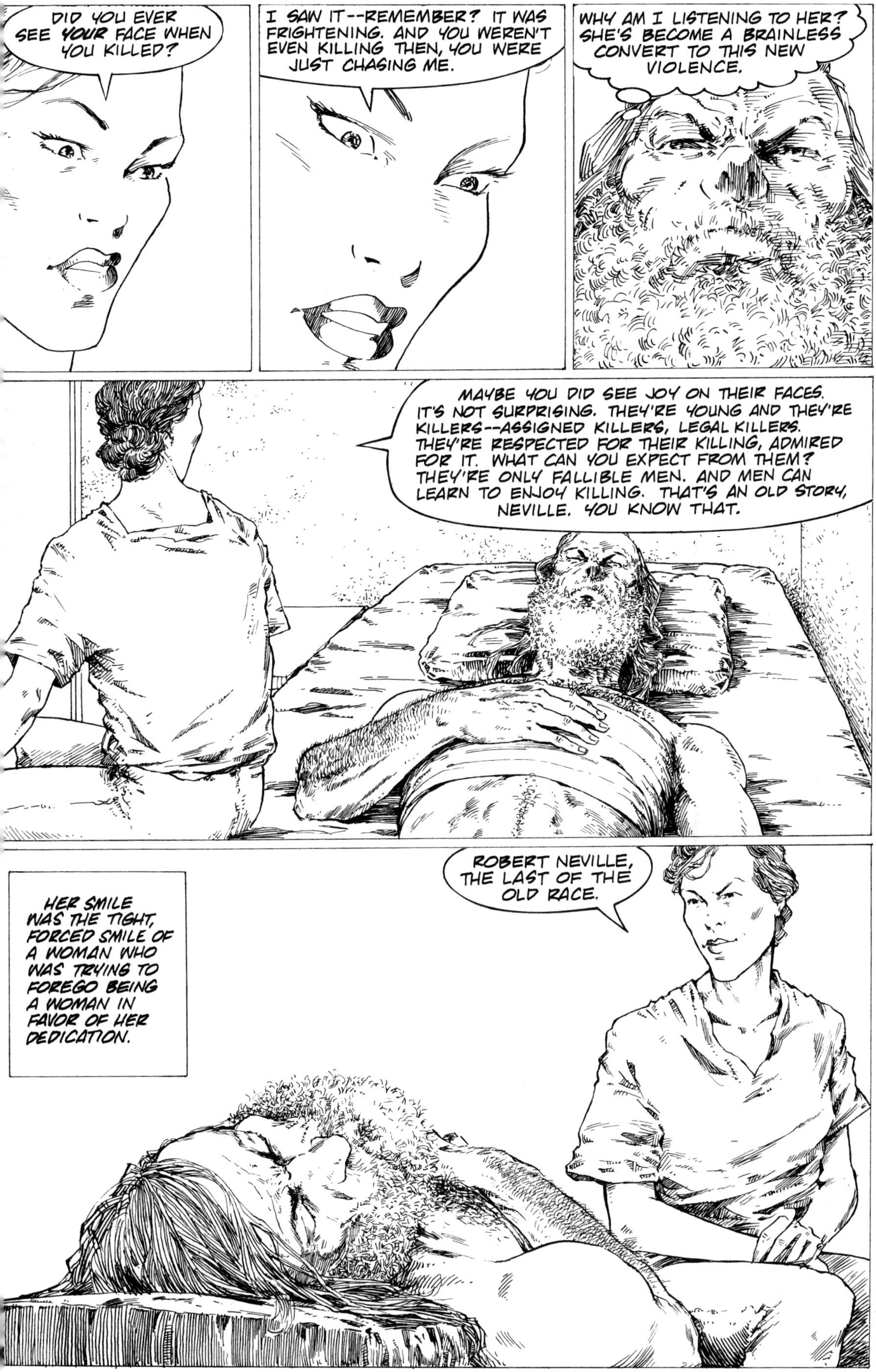
DID YOU EVER SEE YOUR FACE WHEN YOU KILLED?
I SAW IT--REMEMBER? IT WAS FRIGHTENING. AND YOU WEREN'T EVEN KILLING THEN, YOU WERE JUST CHASING ME.
WHY AM I LISTENING TO HER? SHE'S BECOME A BRAINLESS CONVERT TO THIS NEW VIOLENCE.
MAYBE YOU DID SEE JOY ON THEIR FACES. IT'S NOT SURPRISING. THEY'RE YOUNG AND THEY'RE KILLERS--ASSIGNED KILLERS, LEGAL KILLERS. THEY'RE RESPECTED FOR THEIR KILLING, ADMIRED FOR IT. WHAT CAN YOU EXPECT FROM THEM? THEY'RE ONLY FALLIBLE MEN. AND MEN CAN LEARN TO ENJOY KILLING. THAT'S AN OLD STORY, NEVILLE. YOU KNOW THAT.
HER SMILE WAS THE TIGHT, FORCED SMILE OF A WOMAN WHO WAS TRYING TO FOREGO BEING A WOMAN IN FAVOR OF HER DEDICATION.
ROBERT NEVILLE, THE LAST OF THE OLD RACE.

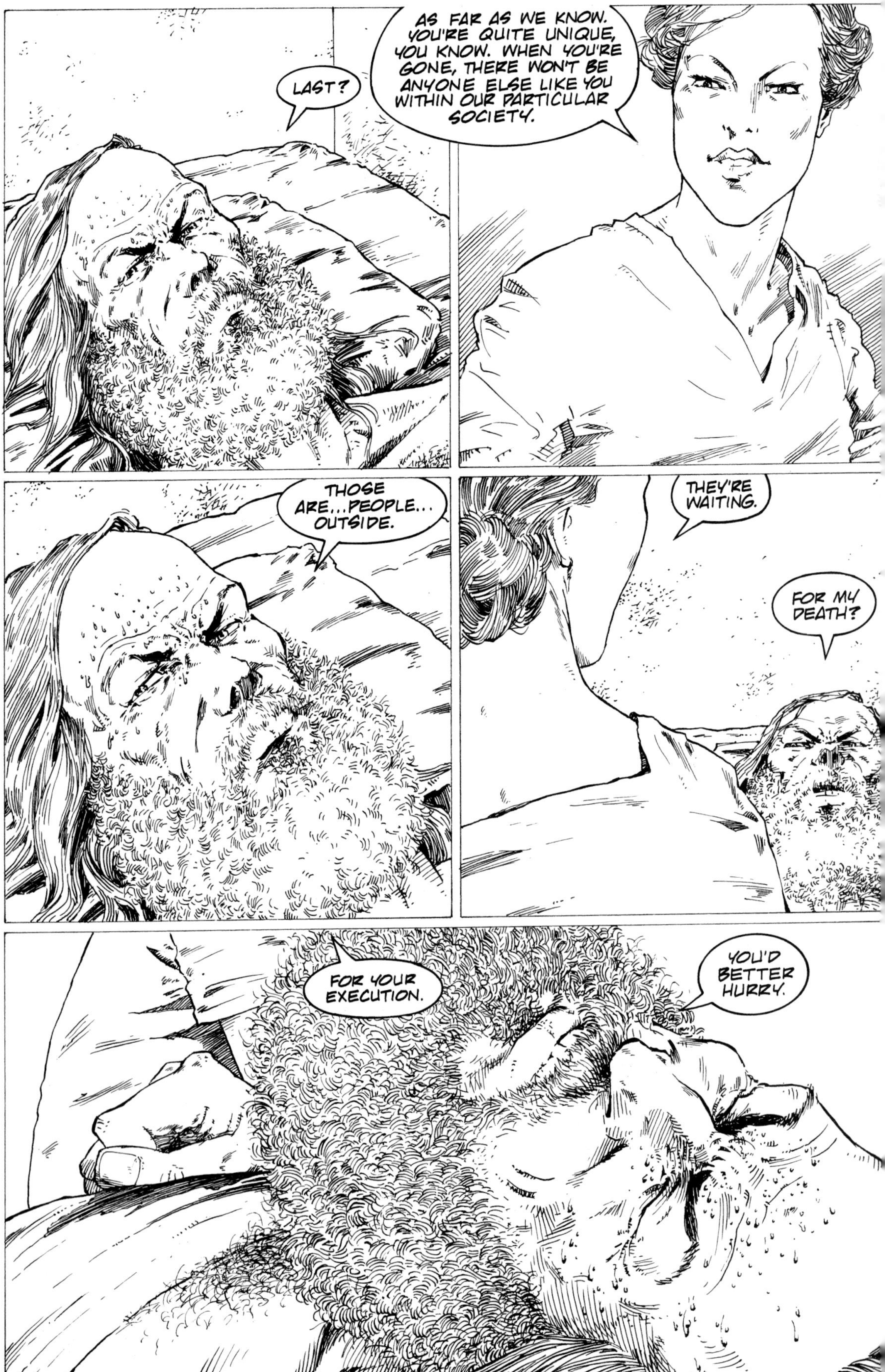
LAST?
AS FAR AS WE KNOW. YOU'RE QUITE UNIQUE, YOU KNOW. WHEN YOU'RE GONE, THERE WON'T BE ANYONE ELSE LIKE YOU WITHIN OUR PARTICULAR SOCIETY.
THOSE ARE...PEOPLE... OUTSIDE.
THEY'RE WAITING.
FOR MY DEATH?
FOR YOUR EXECUTION.
YOU'D BETTER HURRY.

THEY LOOKED AT EACH OTHER FOR A LONG MOMENT. THEN SOMETHING SEEMED TO GIVE IN HER. HER FACE GREW BLANK.

I KNEW IT. I KNEW YOU WOULDN'T BE AFRAID.

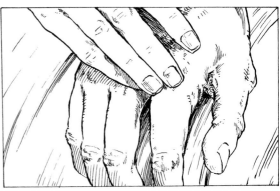

WHEN I FIRST HEARD THAT THEY WERE ORDERED TO YOUR HOUSE, I WAS GOING TO GO THERE AND WARN YOU. BUT THEN I KNEW THAT IF YOU WERE STILL THERE, NOTHING WOULD MAKE YOU GO. THEN I WAS GOING TO TRY TO HELP YOU ESCAPE AFTER THEY BROUGHT YOU IN. BUT THEY TOLD ME YOU'D BEEN SHOT AND I KNEW THAT ESCAPE WAS IMPOSSIBLE TOO.

I'M GLAD YOU'RE NOT AFRAID. YOU'RE VERY BRAVE.

ROBERT.

THEY WERE SILENT AND HE FELT HER HAND TIGHTEN ON HIS.

HOW IS IT YOU CAN...COME IN HERE?

I'M A RANKING OFFICER IN THE NEW SOCIETY.

DON'T... LET IT GET...

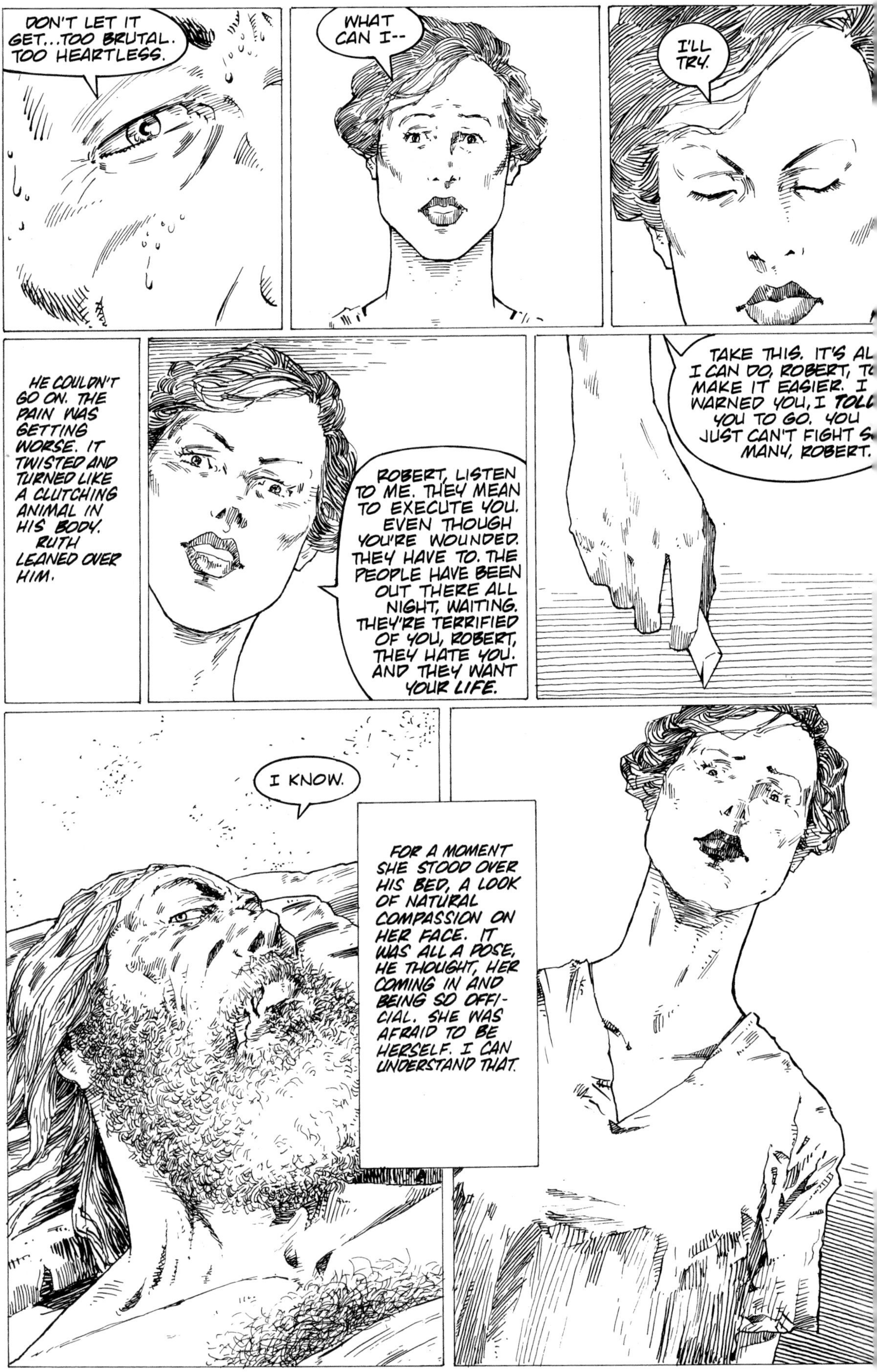

DON'T LET IT GET...TOO BRUTAL. TOO HEARTLESS.
WHAT CAN I--
I'LL TRY.
HE COULDN'T GO ON. THE PAIN WAS GETTING WORSE. IT TWISTED AND TURNED LIKE A CLUTCHING ANIMAL IN HIS BODY. RUTH LEANED OVER HIM.
ROBERT, LISTEN TO ME. THEY MEAN TO EXECUTE YOU. EVEN THOUGH YOU'RE WOUNDED. THEY HAVE TO. THE PEOPLE HAVE BEEN OUT THERE ALL NIGHT, WAITING. THEY'RE TERRIFIED OF YOU, ROBERT, THEY HATE YOU. AND THEY WANT YOUR LIFE.
TAKE THIS. IT'S AL I CAN DO, ROBERT, T MAKE IT EASIER. I WARNED YOU, I TOL YOU TO GO. YOU JUST CAN'T FIGHT S MANY, ROBERT.
I KNOW.
FOR A MOMENT SHE STOOD OVER HIS BED, A LOOK OF NATURAL COMPASSION ON HER FACE. IT WAS ALL A POSE, HE THOUGHT, HER COMING IN AND BEING SO OFFI-CIAL. SHE WAS AFRAID TO BE HERSELF. I CAN UNDERSTAND THAT.

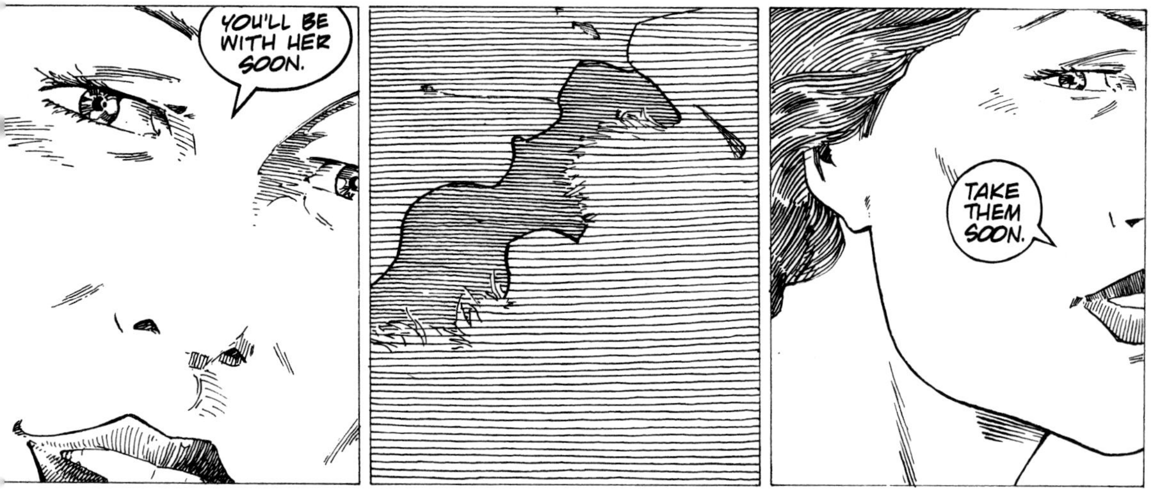
YOU'LL BE WITH HER SOON.
TAKE THEM SOON.

HE HEARD HER FOOTSTEPS MOVING ACROSS THE FLOOR. THEN THE DOOR WAS SHUTTING AND HE HEARD THE SOUND OF IT BEING LOCKED. HE CLOSED HIS EYES AND FELT WARM TEARS PUSHING OUT FROM BENEATH THE LIDS. GOOD-BYE, RUTH.

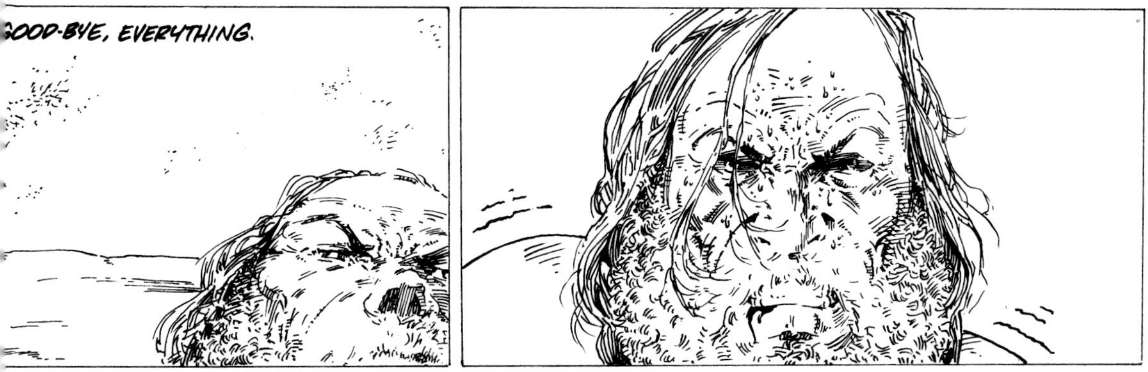
GOOD-BYE, EVERYTHING.

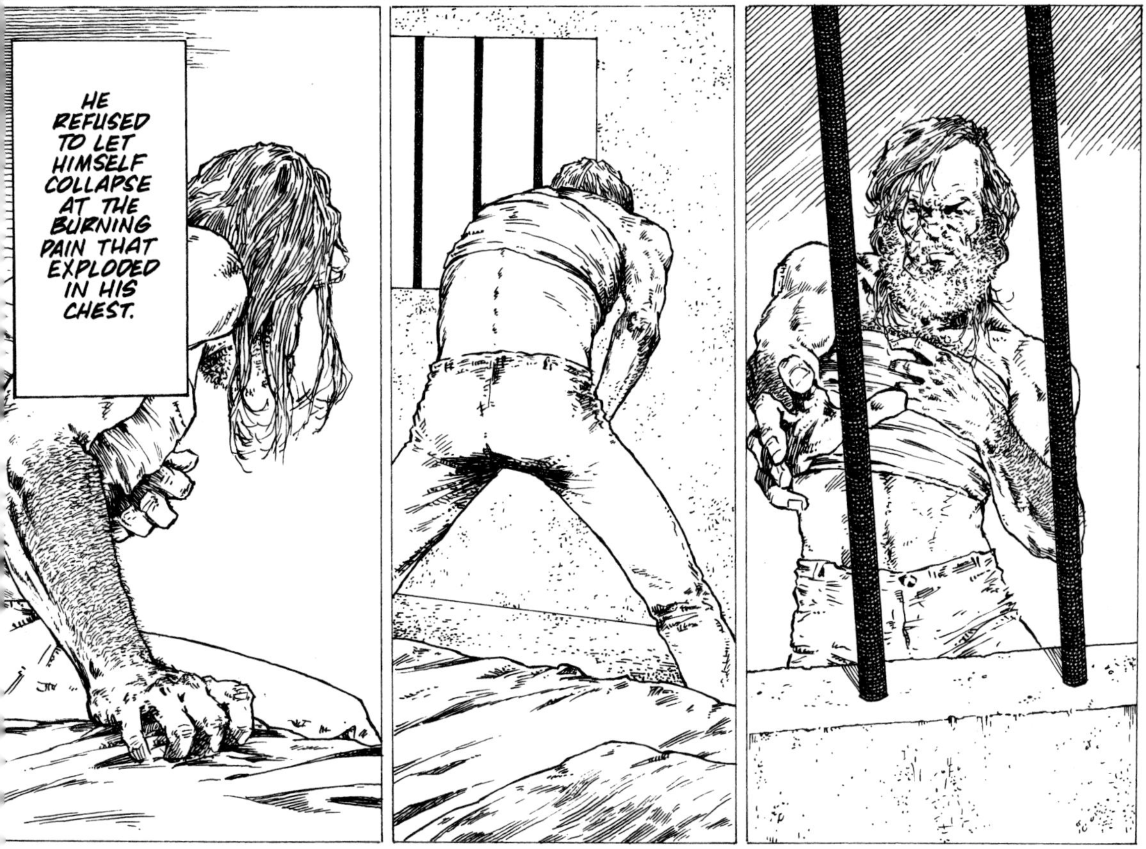
HE REFUSED TO LET HIMSELF COLLAPSE AT THE BURNING PAIN THAT EXPLODED IN HIS CHEST.

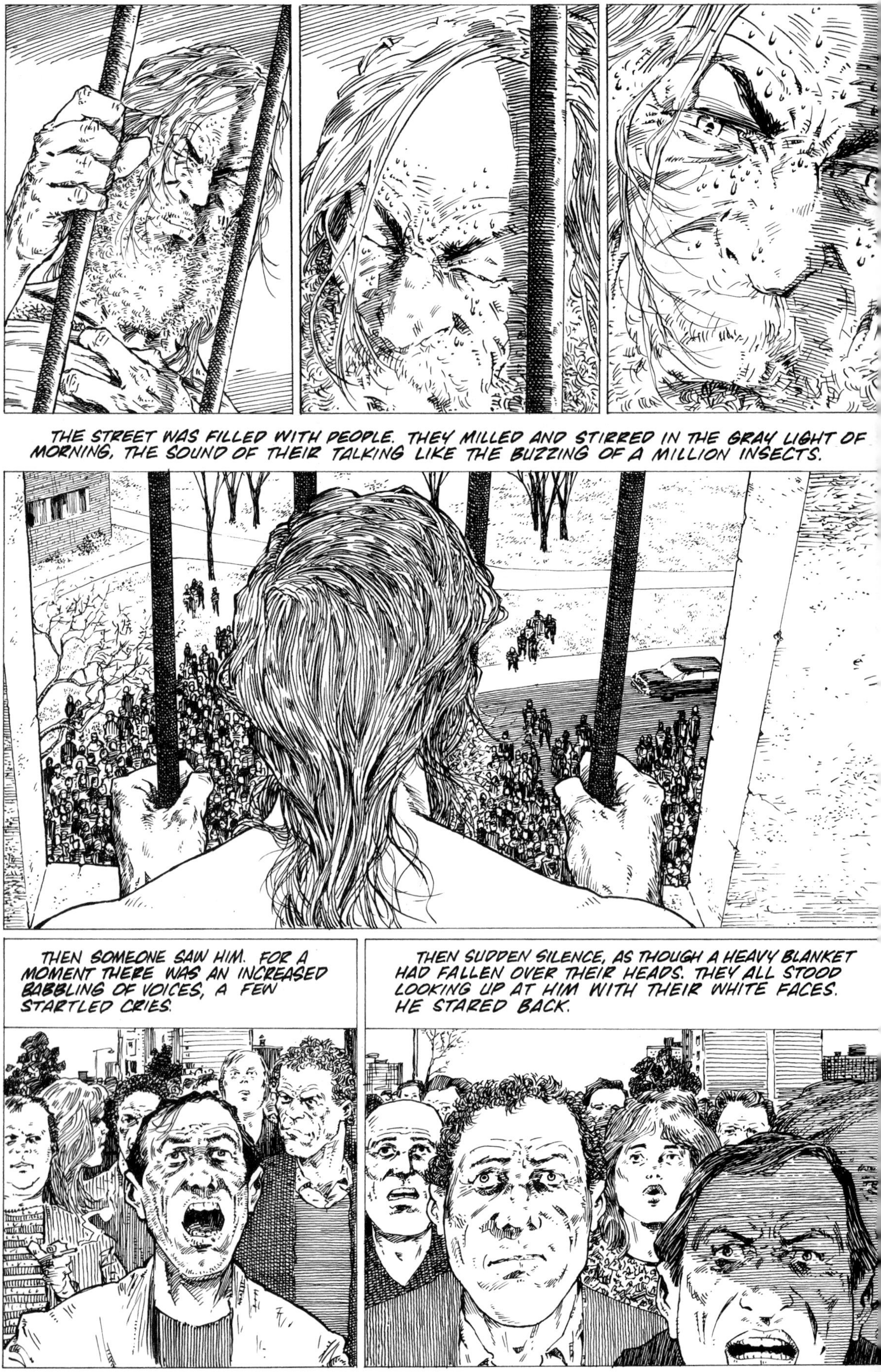
THE STREET WAS FILLED WITH PEOPLE. THEY MILLED AND STIRRED IN THE GRAY LIGHT OF MORNING, THE SOUND OF THEIR TALKING LIKE THE BUZZING OF A MILLION INSECTS.
THEN SOMEONE SAW HIM. FOR A MOMENT THERE WAS AN INCREASED BABBLING OF VOICES, A FEW STARTLED CRIES.
THEN SUDDEN SILENCE, AS THOUGH A HEAVY BLANKET HAD FALLEN OVER THEIR HEADS. THEY ALL STOOD LOOKING UP AT HIM WITH THEIR WHITE FACES. HE STARED BACK.

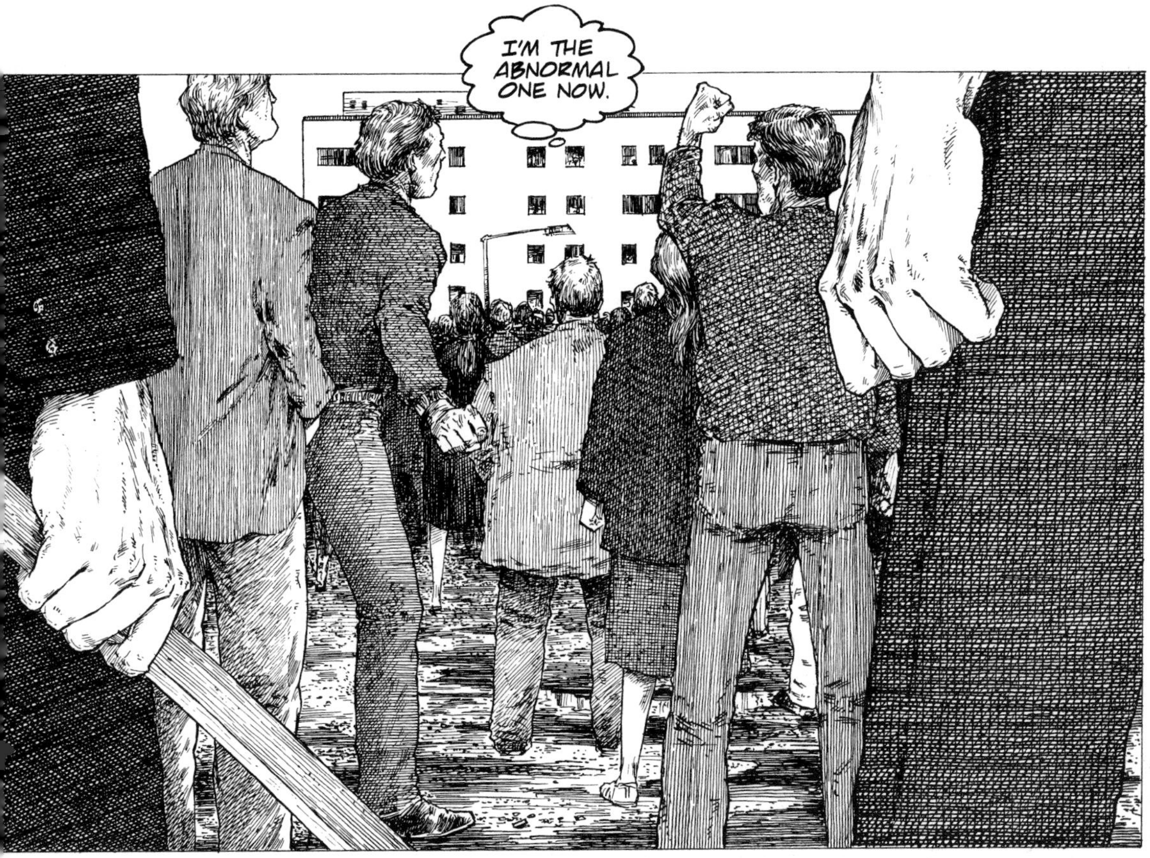
I'M THE ABNORMAL ONE NOW.

ORMALCY WAS A MAJORITY CONCEPT, THE STANDARD OF MANY AND NOT THE STANDAND OF JUST ONE MAN.

ABRUPTLY THAT REALIZATION JOINED WITH WHAT HE SAW ON THEIR FACES--AWE, FEAR, SHRINKING HORROR--AND HE KNEW THAT THEY WERE AFRAID OF HIM. TO THEM HE WAS SOME TERRIBLE SCOURGE THEY HAD NEVER SEEN, A SCOURGE EVEN WORSE THAN THE DISEASE THEY HAD COME TO LIVE WITH. HE WAS AN INVISIBLE SPECTER WHO HAD LEFT FOR EVIDENCE OF HIS EXISTENCE THE BLOODLESS BODIES OF THEIR LOVED ONES. AND HE UNDERSTOOD WHAT THEY FELT AND DID NOT HATE THEM. HIS RIGHT HAND TIGHTENED ON THE TINY ENVELOPE OF PILLS. SO LONG AS THE END DID NOT COME WITH VIOLENCE, SO LONG AS IT DID NOT HAVE TO BE A BUTCHERY BEFORE THEIR EYES.

ROBERT NEVILLE LOOKED OUT OVER THE NEW PEOPLE OF THE EARTH. HE KNEW HE DID NOT BELONG TO THEM; HE KNEW THAT, LIKE THE VAMPIRES, HE WAS ANATHEMA AND BLACK TERROR TO BE DESTROYED. AND, ABRUPTLY, THE CONCEPT CAME, AMUSING TO HIM EVEN IN HIS PAIN.

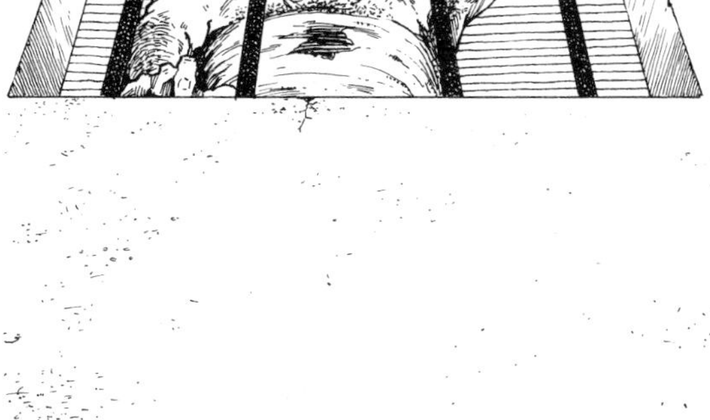

A COUGHING CHUCKLE FILLED HIS THROAT.

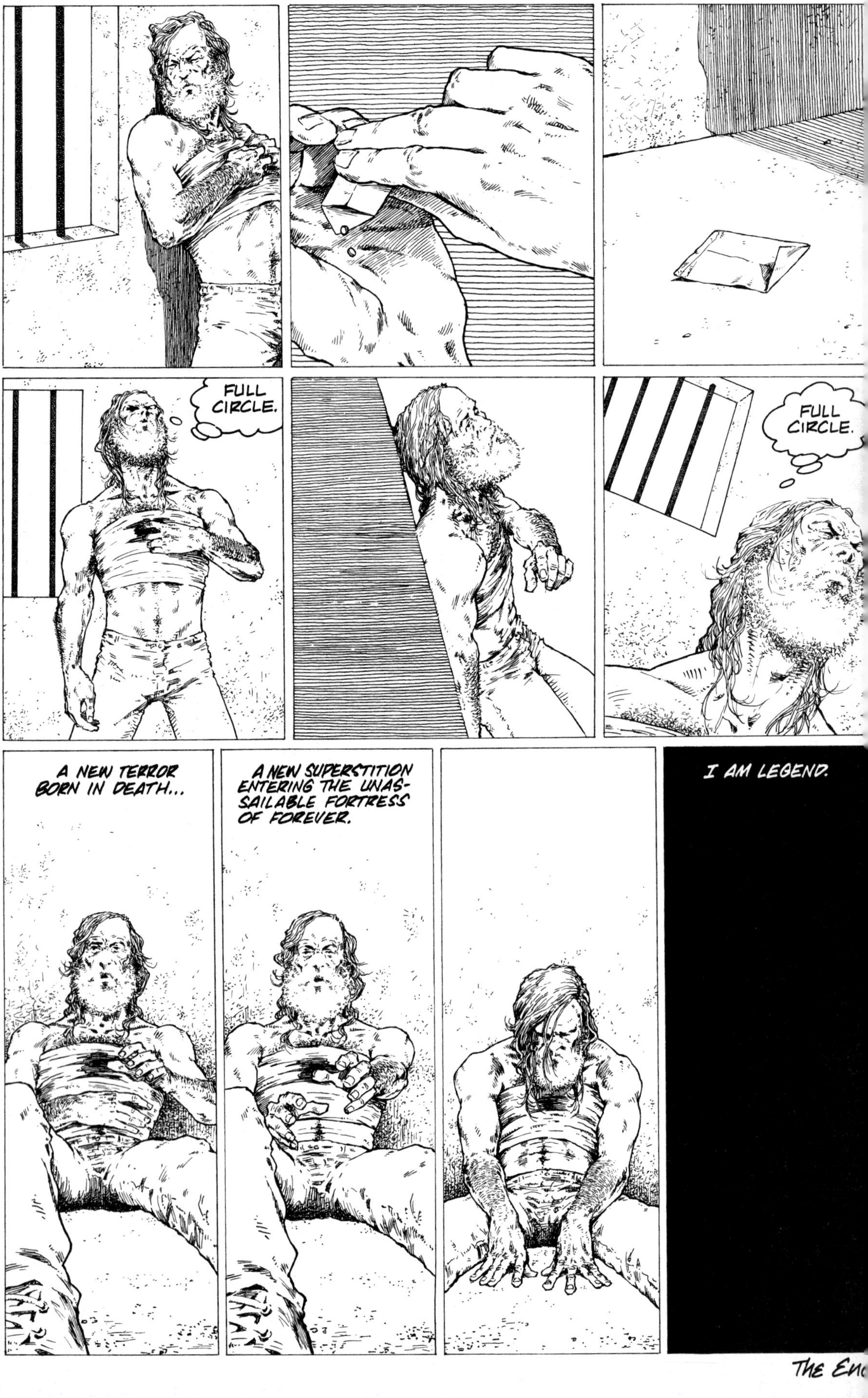

FULL CIRCLE.
FULL CIRCLE.
A NEW TERROR BORN IN DEATH...
A NEW SUPERSTITION ENTERING THE UNAS-SAILABLE FORTRESS OF FOREVER.
I AM LEGEND.

THE End

RICHARD **MATHESON**

is the author of numerous novels and short stories, including such classics as *I AM LEGEND, THE INCREDIBLE SHRINKING MAN, SOMEWHERE IN TIME, WHAT DREAMS MAY COME, DUEL,* and *HELL HOUSE.* He has written in a wide range of genres, from science fiction and fantasy to horror, suspense, and western. Nineteen of his screenplays have been produced as motion pictures, and he has had more than 55 television scripts filmed, including 14 episodes from the classic TV series *The Twilight Zone.* A Grand Master of Horror and past winner of the Bram Stoker Award for Lifetime Achievement, Matheson also won the Edgar, the Spur, and the Writers Guild Award.

He lives in Calabasas, California.

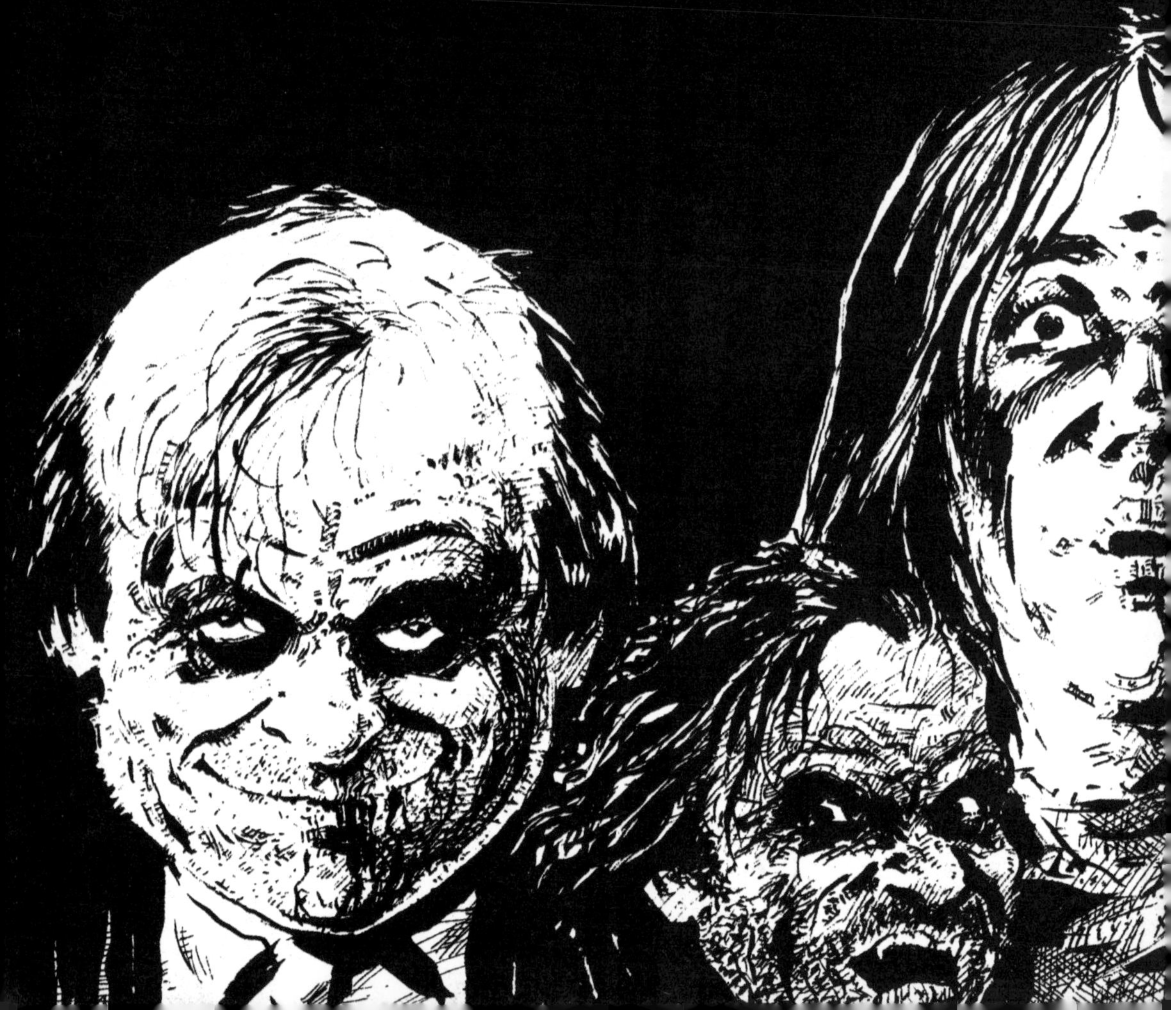

STEVE NILES

is one of the writers responsible for bringing horror comics back to prominence, and was recently named by *Fangoria* magazine as one of its "13 rising talents who promise to keep us terrified for the next 25 years."

Niles got his start in comics when he formed his own publishing company called Arcane Comix, where he published, edited and adapted several comics and anthologies for Eclipse Comics. His adaptations include works by Clive Barker, Richard Matheson, and Harlan Ellison.

He later formed Creep Entertainment with Rob Zombie, as well as the film production company Raw Entertainment with Tom Jane.

Niles resides in Los Angeles. Visit his official site at www.steveniles.com

ELMAN BROWN

currently resides in Pennsylvania horse and buggy country where he is at work creating fantasy art for your future entertainment. His greatest desire is that someday we all live happily ever after.

OTHER IDW PUBLISHING TITLES BY STEVE NILES

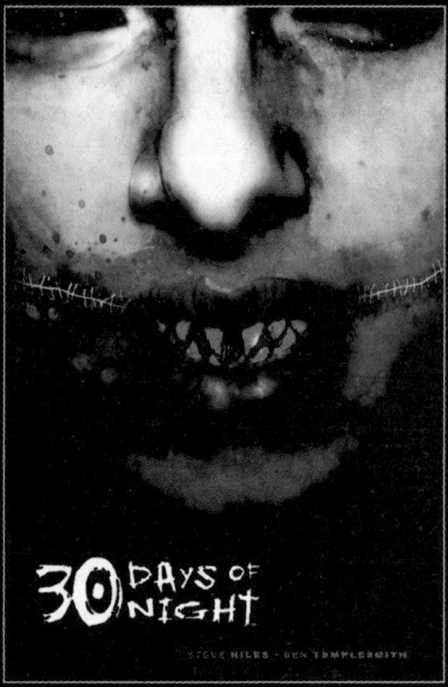
30 DAYS OF NIGHT

30 Days of Night
ISBN: 978-0-971977-55-6

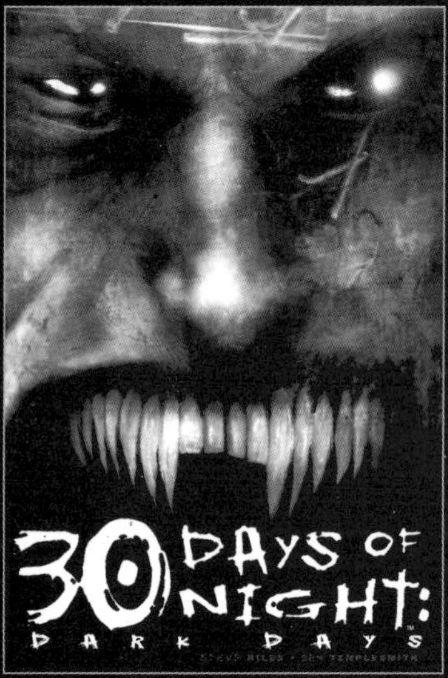
30 DAYS OF NIGHT:
DARK DAYS

30 Days of Night:
Dark Days
ISBN: 978-1-932382-16-7

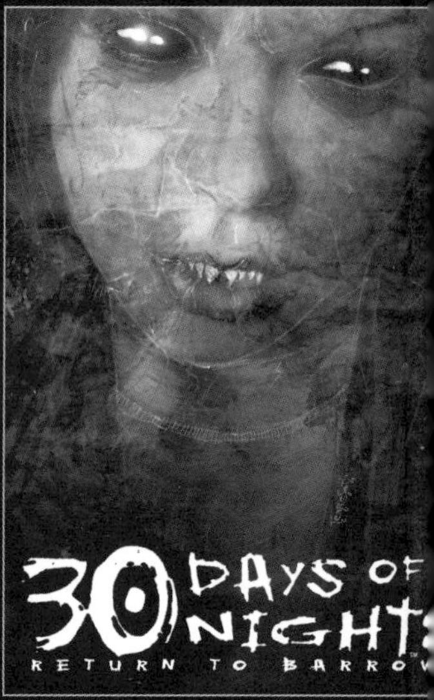
30 DAYS OF NIGHT:
RETURN TO BARRO

30 Days of Night:
Return To Barrow
ISBN: 978-1-932382-36-5

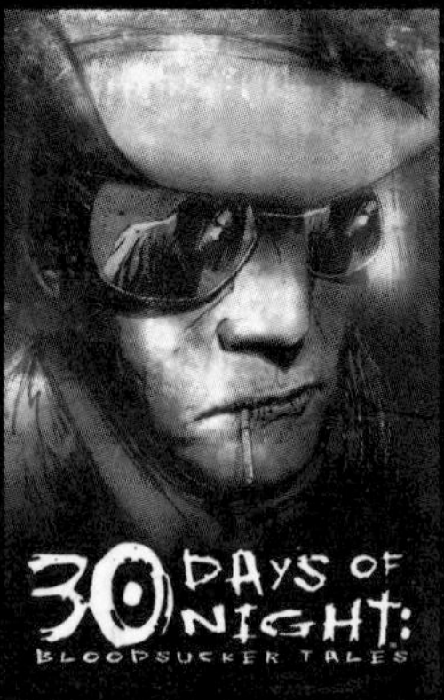
30 DAYS OF NIGHT:
BLOODSUCKER TALES

30 DAYS OF NIGHT BLOODSUCKER TALES
978-1-932382-78-5

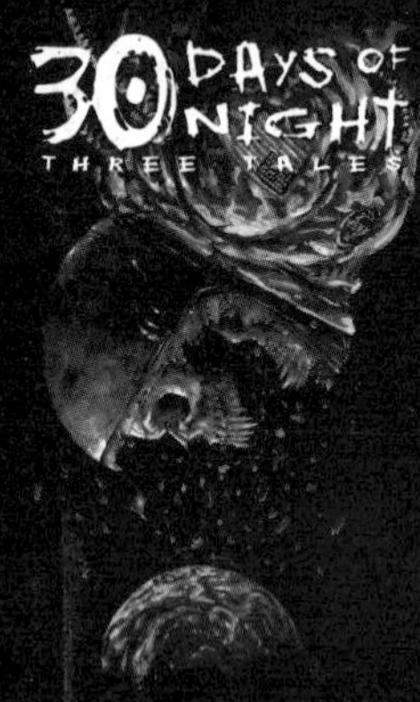
30 DAYS OF NIGHT
THREE TALES

30 DAYS OF NIGHT THREE TALES
978-1-933239-92-7

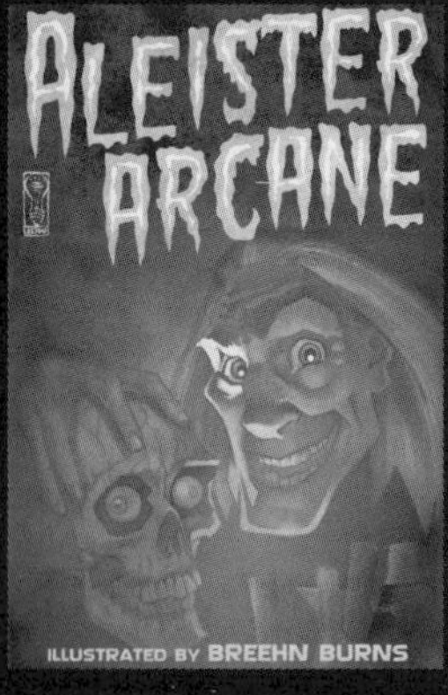
ALEISTER ARCANE
ILLUSTRATED BY BREEHN BURNS

ALEISTER ARCANE
978-1-932382-33-4

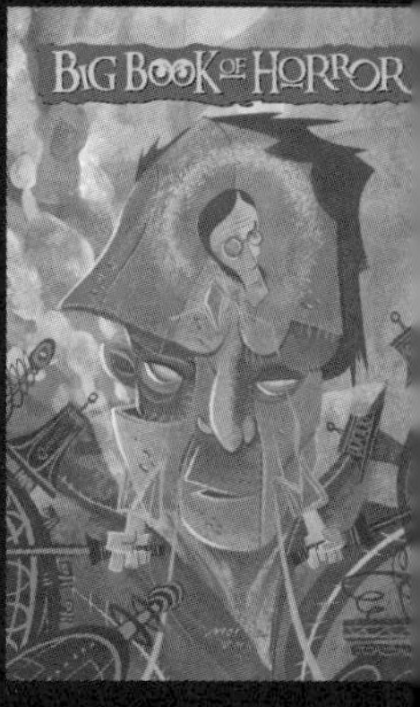
BIG BOOK OF HORROR

BIG BOOK OF HORRO
978-1-600100-014-7

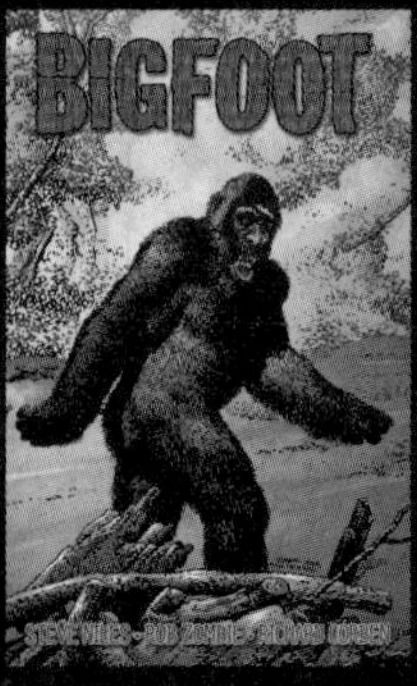
BIGFOOT

BIGFOOT
978-1-933239-13-2

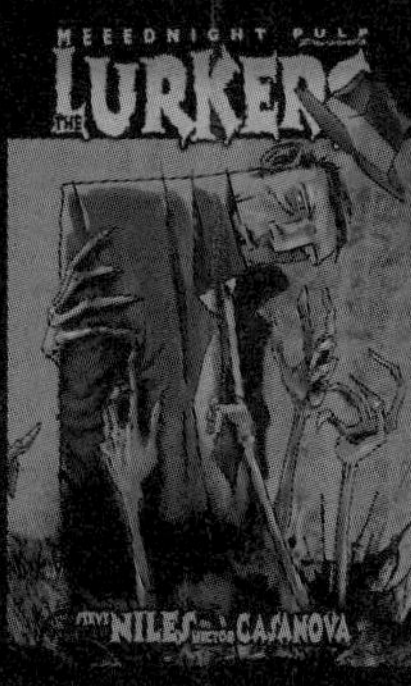
THE LURKERS
STEVE NILES
CASANOVA

THE LURKERS
978-1-932382-80-8

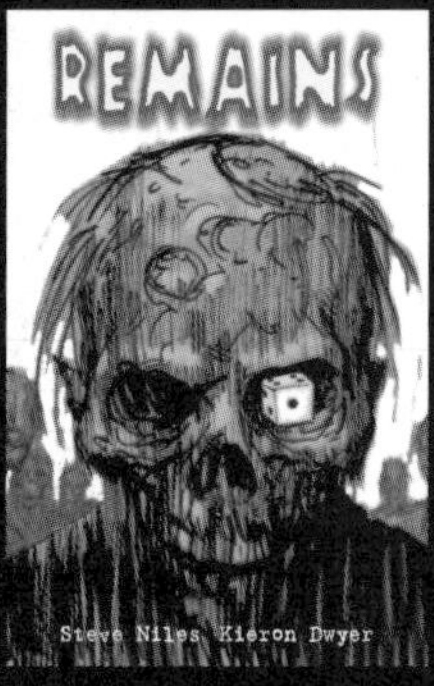
REMAINS
Steve Niles Kieron Dwyer

REMAINS
978-1-932382-38-9

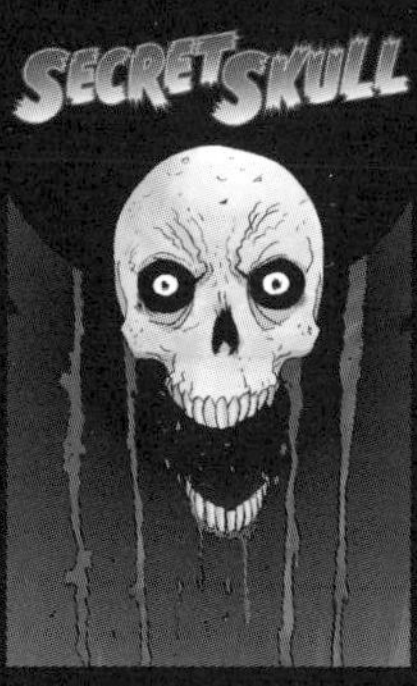
SECRET SKULL

SECRET SKULL
978-1-932382-57-0

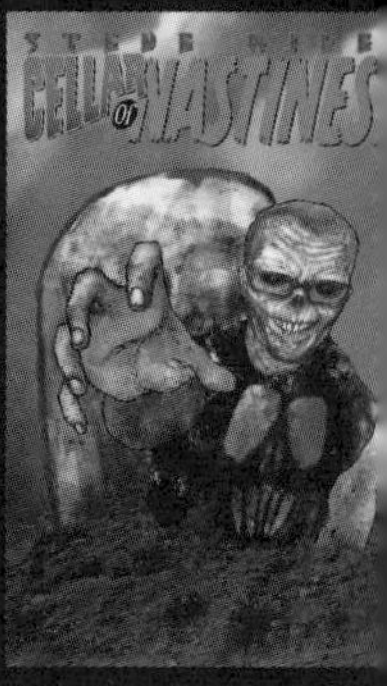

STEVE NILES' CEL
OF NASTINESS
978-1-932382-95-